Practical
Ext JS Projects
with Gears

Frank W. Zammetti

Apress®

Practical Ext JS Projects with Gears

Copyright © 2009 by Frank W. Zammetti

ISBN-13 (pbk): 978-1-4302-1924-8

ISBN-13 (electronic): 978-1-4302-1925-5

Printed and bound in the United States of America 9 8 7 6 5 4 3 2 1

Trademarked names may appear in this book. Rather than use a trademark symbol with every occurrence of a trademarked name, we use the names only in an editorial fashion and to the benefit of the trademark owner, with no intention of infringement of the trademark.

Java™ and all Java-based marks are trademarks or registered trademarks of Sun Microsystems, Inc., in the US and other countries. Apress, Inc., is not affiliated with Sun Microsystems, Inc., and this book was written without endorsement from Sun Microsystems, Inc.

Lead Editor: Steve Anglin
Development Editor: Douglas Pundick
Technical Reviewer: Herman van Rosmalen
Editorial Board: Clay Andres, Steve Anglin, Mark Beckner, Ewan Buckingham, Tony Campbell,
    Gary Cornell, Jonathan Gennick, Michelle Lowman, Matthew Moodie, Jeffrey Pepper, Frank Pohlmann,
    Ben Renow-Clarke, Dominic Shakeshaft, Matt Wade, Tom Welsh
Project Manager: Richard Dal Porto
Copy Editor: Liz Welch
Associate Production Director: Kari Brooks-Copony
Production Editor: Katie Stence
Compositor: Linda Weidemann, Wolf Creek Publishing Services
Proofreader: Kim Burton
Indexer: Brenda Miller
Artist: Anthony Volpe
Cover Designer: Kurt Krames
Manufacturing Director: Tom Debolski

Distributed to the book trade worldwide by Springer-Verlag New York, Inc., 233 Spring Street, 6th Floor, New York, NY 10013. Phone 1-800-SPRINGER, fax 201-348-4505, e-mail orders-ny@springer-sbm.com, or visit http://www.springeronline.com.

For information on translations, please contact Apress directly at 2855 Telegraph Avenue, Suite 600, Berkeley, CA 94705. Phone 510-549-5930, fax 510-549-5939, e-mail info@apress.com, or visit http://www.apress.com.

Apress and friends of ED books may be purchased in bulk for academic, corporate, or promotional use. eBook versions and licenses are also available for most titles. For more information, reference our Special Bulk Sales–eBook Licensing web page at http://www.apress.com/info/bulksales.

The source code for this book is available to readers at http://www.apress.com. You may need to answer questions pertaining to this book in order to successfully download the code.

I'm going to do something unusual for me here and write a serious dedication. This book is dedicated to the memory of Michael A. Baker. Mike, the lead singer for a band named Shadow Gallery, passed away in October 2008 at the far-too-young age of 45. The music of Shadow Gallery has always been a huge inspiration for me, as a musician myself, as a writer, and simply as a human being who appreciates art that touches you. Mike's voice was the emotional anchor of the group's music, an integral part of the experience. I never had the privilege of meeting Mike in person, but through his work I feel like I knew him extremely well, and I don't think I could come up with a greater compliment for any artist. Rest in peace, Mike, and I think I can safely say, on behalf of all Shadow Gallery fans, thank you.

Contents at a Glance

PART 1 ■■■ The Preliminaries

PART 2 ■■■ The Projects

Contents

PART 1 ■■■ The Preliminaries

PART 2 ■■■ The Projects

About the Author

FRANK W. ZAMMETTI is a five-time Oscar nominee, a two-time daytime Emmy winner, and a Grammy finalist three years running. He was also one of the top 36 in last years' *American Idol* competition, hikes in the Andes with Sir Richard Branson twice a year, and is scheduled to fly aboard the next space shuttle flight this summer.

Okay, it's possible that not *all* of that is true.

Frank, however, is in fact an author of a number of web development books with just a <sarcasm>slight</sarcasm> slant toward Ajax development. He is a lead developer/architect/ whatever-his-title-says-this-week for one of the largest financial institutions in the United States, leading development of next-generation web applications.

Frank also contributes to a number of open source projects, leads a couple of them, and has even founded a few. His inane ramblings can be found in the archives of many projects' mailing lists!

Frank has done a few public-speaking engagements over the past two or three years and is most likely the reason scientists are currently developing time travel so that a sort of seven-second delay can be applied to live speakers, as is frequently done with "live" television programs to avoid FCC fines.

Frank has achieved a number of things of note in his life, but without question his crowning achievement has been getting his band Cydonia into the top 250 in the video game Rock Band. This even beats the time he spent in an *actual* rock band!

Frank lives in Pennsylvania with his longtime wife Traci and is a proud parent (on most days anyway) of his two children, Andrew and Ashley. Oh yes, and lest his family have further reason to yell at him, there's also the pets: Belle (dog), and Pandora the guinea pig (R.I.P. Flower, Pandora's long-time cage mate who passed away shortly before this book was completed…how's that for ending on a downer?!?).

About the Technical Reviewer

■**HERMAN VAN ROSMALEN** works as a developer/software architect for De Nederlandsche Bank N.V., the central bank of the Netherlands. He has more than 20 years of experience in developing software applications in a variety of programming languages. Herman has been involved in building mainframe, PC, and client-server applications. Since 2000, however, he has been involved mainly in building all sorts of JEE web-based applications. After working with Struts for years (pre-1.0), he got interested in Ajax and joined the Java Web Parts open source project in 2005; he is now one of the project's administrators. In addition to this book, Herman has served as technical editor for other Apress titles in the *Practical* series. Herman lives in a small town, Pijnacker, in the Netherlands with his wife Liesbeth and their children, Barbara, Leonie, and Ramon. You can reach him via e-mail at herros@gmail.com.

About the Illustrator

■**ANTHONY VOLPE.** What can be said about Anthony? He draws. He draws *really* well. He drew the illustrations for this book. His artistic ability is to Frank's as Albert Einstein's intelligence is to…well, anyone else really! That's why Anthony's illustrations have appeared in all of Frank's books so far. Besides, they are far better than Frank's stick figures that would otherwise be in their place!

Not only that, but he happens to be a longtime friend of Frank to boot.

Anthony has worked with Frank to produce a number of video games for several platforms, a few of which have been recognized with awards (too bad they weren't recognized with actual sales!), and they've even got an Internet cartoon under their belts based on some of the characters from the games.

Anthony is a prolific creative force, with a ton of comics to his credit, fiction writing, and a few video games, and he's produced several albums over the years (some of which you can pick up at finer Internet music retail sites (go, run, buy, *now*!). If you dare, check out his site: http://planetvolpe.com/.

Acknowledgments

I'd like to acknowledge all the fine folks who made this book possible. Al Gore, inventor of the Internet. Bill Gates, inventor of the top seven tax brackets in the United States. Billy Mays, inventor of TALKING WAY TOO LOUDLY ON TELEVISION. Professor Hubert Farnsworth, inventor of the "What-If Machine." Conan O'Brien, inventor of television. Montgomery Scott, inventor of transparent aluminum.

Of course, aside from those luminaries, plenty of other people helped make this book a reality, and I'd like to acknowledge them: Richard Dal Porto, Steve Anglin, Douglas Pundick, Liz Welch, Katie Stence, and everyone else at Apress who I inadvertently left out who continue to make writing these books less like work and more like…well, still work, but it's work that I don't mind doing!

I'd like to acknowledge Herman von Rosmalen and Anthony Volpe, the two names that will forever be linked with mine in literary history (my heart goes out to them on that one!)

A special acknowledgment has to go to whatever alien species originally seeded our world with life that eventually evolved from the primordial ooze into modern-day humans. I just wonder, if when they return to check on their experiment, they'll consider it a success or an abject failure?

Introduction

The Web. A wise man once said: "The Web is like a box of chocolates."

Well, sure, if you can find a box of chocolates that constantly jumps up in your face when you try to open it and is filled with, shall we say, *adult* chocolates?

It used to be that you could slap some HTML up on a server and call it a web page, and people would love you for it. Not anymore! Now, we've moved into the realm of web *applications*, where some useful function has to be performed. More than that, though, it's got to look cool and work in a slick, "modern" way.

That's where the term RIA, or rich Internet application, comes from. People now expect a certain degree of "coolness" when they hit a website. They expect the experience to be more like the native applications they use on a daily basis. They want things to fly into view, they want windows, and they want grids they can sort in place and they want… well, they want a bunch of stuff that historically hasn't been easy to deliver on the Web!

That is, until the modern JavaScript libraries hit the scene. There are lots of great libraries out there today, from jQuery to Dojo, from YUI to script.aculo.us. All of them help you achieve the goal of wicked-cool web applications.

One of them, though, in my opinion, stands above the rest, and that's what we're here to look at: Ext JS.

Ext JS allows you to create applications with a richness that historically has only been seen in native applications. From a top-notch windowing system to a data subsystem, various effects, and drag-and-drop, everything you need to create modern web applications is here. Ext JS isn't limited to the user interface, though; it also contains tons of utility functions that make the core of your application easier and cleaner. What's more, it does all of this in a highly logical, coherent manner that is, in my opinion, unrivaled on the current RIA landscape.

What's even better than Ext JS alone is when you team it with Gears, a product of those uber-geniuses at Google. Now, not only can you create the user interface goodness your employer desires but you can also do things like have a true relational database on the client and even have multithreading capabilities in JavaScript! You can create "sovereign" webapps, that special class of webapp where everything is on a single page and runs entirely in the browser.

While the Ext JS and Gears documentation is excellent, with lots of examples and tutorials to learn from, it's often not enough. Nothing beats having a real application in front of you, one that has been commented and structured well and, better still, that you have the original coder of sitting beside you explaining it all, not just the how's, but the why's behind the code. That's precisely what this book is all about! Contained within it you won't find a bunch of simplistic, contrived examples; you'll instead find seven complete, real-world applications that will be dissected and explained. You'll have the opportunity to hack the code yourself to make changes and enhancements, further providing you with a learn-by-doing experience.

In the end you'll have a solid grounding in what Ext JS and Gears are about, what they offer, and how to use them effectively. You will also have a good time in the process because I have what most people would describe as a unique tone about my writing. I believe that life is tough enough when you're serious every minute of every day, so I try to interject humor and a carefree attitude whenever I can. Humor is highly subjective, but I feel confident in saying you won't find this book boring or stuffy.

An Overview of This Book

Since my editor balked at the idea of one big chapter with a single run-on sentence as I suggested (darn his sense of proper writing style and grammar!), I've instead broken this book down into eight chapters as follows:

- Chapter 1 is the obligatory introductory chapter. We'll take a quick look at web application development, Ajax, and choices in libraries. In no time we'll get into Ext JS itself, including its history, licensing concerns, and the first actual code! We'll then begin looking through Ext JS to start seeing in detail what it offers.

- Chapter 2 covers more "advanced" topics, which just means we'll get into much more of what Ext JS has to offer: things like drag-and-drop, data, and the UI widgets. We'll also take our first look at Gears to see what it offers us.

- Chapter 3 is where we begin our project chapters, beginning with OrganizerExt, a PIM (personal information management) application that lets us store and organize things like contacts, appointments, and notes. We'll see all sorts of cool widgets and utility functions along the way.

- Chapter 4 presents the TimekeeperExt project, which is all about managing projects. Time tracking of resources can be done against the project, and various views of the data are offered. More widgets will present themselves, as well as a new way to architect our Ext JS applications.

- Chapter 5 is when we look at the Code Cabinet Ext project, a handy little utility for code monkey types where we can stash snippets of code and search for them later. We'll further evolve the architecture seen previously, and introduce examples of more Ext JS capabilities.

- Chapter 6 gives us the opportunity to see Local Business Search, which is a *mashup*, or an application that uses some publicly available web services to create an application. We'll create an application that lets us search for businesses in a given area and see information about it, including a map of the area. This is where we'll look at some Ajax, more specifically, JSON-P.

- Chapter 7 provides us with another useful utility application, SQL Workbench. This gives us a way to look at and manipulate the databases that Gears gives us access to. We'll get lots of experience with the Gears database component, and see some new ways of working with Ext JS.

- Chapter 8 is where we break the trend of "serious" applications and create Dueling Cards, a web-based game. We'll see things like drag-and-drop, effects, and even some game theory, not to mention the multithreading capabilities that Gears provides us.

- Chapter 9 finishes things up by looking at an application for tracking your finances that shows off some more cool features of Ext JS, including its charting capabilities.

There's quite a lot of territory to cover, and each chapter will build upon what you learned in the previous chapters. Along the way you'll see multiple ways of doing things so you can decide for yourself which you feel is the best approach.

Obtaining This Book's Source Code

If you're anything like me, you'll agree that work sucks. What I mean is, effort that isn't actually necessary tends to not be something I enjoy. Or, to put it more succinctly: I'm lazy!

However, I generally try to get as much code printed in my books as possible, so that they pass the Bathroom Test™, that is, you can read them during your… how shall I say it… private time and basically be able to follow everything along.

That being said, this isn't the mid-1980s where you'd happily open up your copy of *RUN* (an old Commodore 64-focused magazine) and type in the 20 pages of machine language code for the parachuting game they published. No, we're better than that now (read: lazier), and typing in all the code yourself would be a monumental waste of your valuable time. So all the source code for this book is available for download at the Apress website. Simply go to apress.com, click the Source Code link, and then find this book in the list. Click it and you'll find a download link lurking somewhere on the next page.

Obtaining Updates for this Book

There are *zero* mistakes in this book. Not a single one.

Now, repeat that a bazillion times and the universe might oblige and make it true.

In reality, writing a technical book of virtually any length is an exercise in getting things as right as possible but knowing you've almost certainly borked something, somewhere. You can be sure that every possible effort was made to ensure everything is accurate, from me as the author checking facts to the technical reviewer hammering me over every relatively minor typo in the code to the editor, copy editor, layout editor, and others going over it with a fine-toothed comb multiple times.

Still, if there really *are* no mistakes then I suspect that would be a first in the publishing industry! In light of this, you can always find the current errata list on this book's home page on the Apress website. You can also submit errata of your own, and this is input I very much welcome. In fact, you can feel free to call me if you ever need blood or a kidney (just please ask first… I don't want to wake up in a hotel bathtub filled with ice). Consider it my way of saying thanks for pointing out my ineptness!

Contacting the Author

I have been called bad before. Many have said I do things that are not correct to do. I don't believe in talk such as this. I am nice man, with happy feelings, all of the time![1] If you feel the need or, dare I say, desire, to contact me, please also feel perfectly free to do so! I'm available via email at fzammetti@omnytex.com, and you can catch me online to chat on AOL IM

---

[1] This is a quote from the great movie *Kung Pow: Enter the Fist*. If you haven't seen it, stop reading and go do so now. If you have seen it but don't like it, well, let's just say my editor wouldn't let me print what I suggest you do! In either case, how many times have you seen a footnote in a book's introduction?

(fzammetti), Yahoo! Instant Messenger (fzammetti), or MSN (fzammetti@hotmail.com). I have a bad habit of leaving my IM client open even when I'm not home, so if I don't answer right away don't take it personally! You could also send a carrier pigeon over the northeastern United States and tell them to look for the house with the horribly maintained front lawn (which reminds me: buy another ten copies of this book so I can afford to hire a landscaper!).

I'll also point out that, like every other loser on the planet, I have a blog. I don't update it often, and the topics I cover can absolutely be anything (some not suitable for all audiences, so I wouldn't visit it at work if I were you). If you've really got nothing better to do on a rainy Saturday, feel free to visit and even leave a comment or two: http://www.zammetti.com.

PART 1
■ ■ ■
The Preliminaries

A Netscape engineer who shan't be named once passed a pointer to JavaScript, stored it as a string and later passed it back to C, killing 30.

—Blake Ross

Debugging is twice as hard as writing the code in the first place. Therefore, If you write the code as cleverly as possible, you are, by definition, not smart enough to debug it.

—Brian W. Kernighan

Einstein argued that there must be simplified explanations of nature, because God is not capricious or arbitrary. No such faith comforts the software engineer.

—Fred Brooks

A word to the wise ain't necessary—it's the stupid ones that need the advice.

—Bill Cosby

All sorts of computer errors are now turning up. You'd be surprised to know the number of doctors who claim they are treating pregnant men.

—Isaac Asimov

In ancient times they had no statistics so they had to fall back on lies.

—Stephen Leacock

If you love your job, you haven't worked a day in your life.

—Tommy Lasorda

Oh, so they have internet on computers now!

—Homer Simpson

CHAPTER 1

Introducing Web Development with Ext JS

In this chapter, we'll begin our journey into the world of Ext JS by taking a step back and looking at the evolution of web application development. In fact, we'll take a step even *further* back than that and look at what the term "web application" means in the first place (hint: it may not be quite as obvious as it first seems!). We'll deal with what the term "rich Internet application" (RIA) is all about, and we'll talk briefly about Ajax (what it used to mean and what it means now) and why it's such an important development. We'll even look at some options for developing RIAs other than Ext JS, but before long we'll dive right into the real red meat,[1] as the political pundits say: Ext JS itself! We'll see what it has to offer and how it's structured, learn a bit about its history and philosophy, and then get started with the basics of using it.

Strap yourself in because it's going to be a wild (but exciting) ride!

The Evolution of the Web: Web *Sites* vs. Web *Applications*

If you've been doing web development for more than a few minutes—or so it seems sometimes given the rapid rate of technological development in this area—then you are well aware of the fantastic evolution of the Web. It's like a child growing up right before your eyes in many ways, and we've had our share of teething pains to be sure!

Today we have all sorts of web sites. More than that, we have web *applications*. What's the difference, you ask? A web *site*'s primary purpose is to disseminate information. There tends to be little user interaction beyond some simple forms, and little opportunity for the user to perform an actual function (other than researching the data available on the site). There is a general flow through the site, and while the user can branch off into other flows at various points via hyperlinks, these paths are essentially predetermined. In other words, navigation through the site is hardwired into a limited set of possible paths. Also, web sites, because of

1 At least in American politics, the phrase "red meat" refers to rhetoric during a speech that is brash and "in your face" with the purpose of getting the crowd energized and emotionally behind the speaker.

their focus on delivering information, tend to be a bit simplistic so that they are accessible to the largest possible audience.[2] In Figure 1-1 you can see an example of a simple web site.

Figure 1-1. *An example of a web site*

A web *application*, or web app for short, is an inherently dynamic beast where the user is interested in performing some operation(s) in a (frequently, but not always) indeterminate way. The user can move about a web app in a nonlinear fashion and in ways that the developers may not have expected. The user is usually manipulating data in some fashion, and typically in a persistent manner (i.e., interacting with a server-based data store of some sort[3]). Web apps tend to be more complex from a coding standpoint and often require more of the

---

2   This has been becoming less and less true in recent years. The multimedia nature of the Web as a whole means that web sites no longer are necessarily coded to the lowest common denominator in terms of browser capabilities. Perhaps it's more correct to say that the lowest common denominator is simply rising!

3   In this book we'll in fact be building only applications that interact with a *local* data store. This doesn't mean they aren't web apps, but a web app that doesn't interact with a back-end data store is only in recent years started to become a viable model.

client in terms of technology and pure horsepower to execute them. In Figure 1-2 you can see an example of a web app.

Figure 1-2. *An example of a web app*

This web app has some richer and fancier functionality than is apparent on the printed page.[4] For example, the filmstrip on the left scrolls to show images, and when you click one it "flies" onto the main viewing area. Many of the buttons on the bottom allow you to manipulate the image in various ways, and some lead to pop-up dialogs, which represent alternate "flows," if you will, through the application. In other words, the purpose here is for users to actually *do* something—they aren't simply viewing a predefined set of images as would be the case with a web *site*. This is also an example of an RIA, but based on the definition of RIA (the "I" is for Internet after all), it's a web app too. We'll get to RIAs in particular shortly though.

Web sites and web apps are both of course 100 percent relevant today and probably will be for a very long time (until some fundamental shift in technology changes everything). In fact, the line between the two isn't a hard-and-fast thing. Frequently there is room for debate whether something is a web site or a web app. Take something like Digg (www.digg.com) for example, which is a news site that is driven by input from the community of users who visit it to determine what headlines are seen, which are seen most prominently, and so on. It has

---

4 <shamelessSelfPromotion>If you'd like to see this in action, then purchase my book *Practical Ajax Projects with Java Technology* (Apress, 2006).</shamelessSelfPromotion>

many of the characteristic of both: its primary job is to disseminate information (new items), yet there is plenty of opportunity for users to interact with it (by submitting and rating articles and even posting comments to one another about the news items). It uses a fair amount of client-side coding, which makes it more like a web app, but it's also coded to be accessible to as many people as possible, like a web site.

The point is that we're still in the midst of the evolution I'm talking about, and we'll likely be involved in the evolution for some time to come.

The Rise of the Cool: Rich Internet Applications

The point we find ourselves at now is that we're developing rather complex web apps these days—so complex, in fact, that we probably need a new name for them. If nothing else, we all know that the IT industry loves to invent new terms for things!

We're trying to recapture some of what we lost when we moved to the Web: the power of the native application. Take a look at Figure 1-3, where you can see a fairly typical native application.[5]

These so-called native applications are applications coded for a specific operating system and that run more or less entirely locally on an individual workstation. These types of applications have the benefit of access to the full power of the underlying operating system and the hardware of the computer, so they tend to look better and, most importantly, are more functional and full-featured. Things you take for granted in such an environment (such as local disk storage; multimedia capabilities—video/audio playback, for example; access to I/O devices like disk drives, mice, and printers; more advanced UI metaphors like grids, trees, and drag and drop) all are harder to come by in the web environment than they are in native applications. There is a richer set of user interface (UI) components, sometimes called widgets, from which to build the application: grids that can do all sorts of sorting and splitting and other advanced features; tree lists that can organize data and allow the user to expand and contract groupings as they see fit; toolbars with all kinds of button features; menus and spinners and tabs and fancy check boxes and sliders and so on and so forth! All of these are things available in virtually any graphical user interface (GUI) environment like Windows or Mac OS. On the Web, however, much of that sort of interface richness is harder to come by.

---

5   Note that I'm not holding this up as an example of a *great* native application! This is an old application I had written at work over ten years ago now. It's not stunningly beautiful or anything like that, but it makes the point well enough.

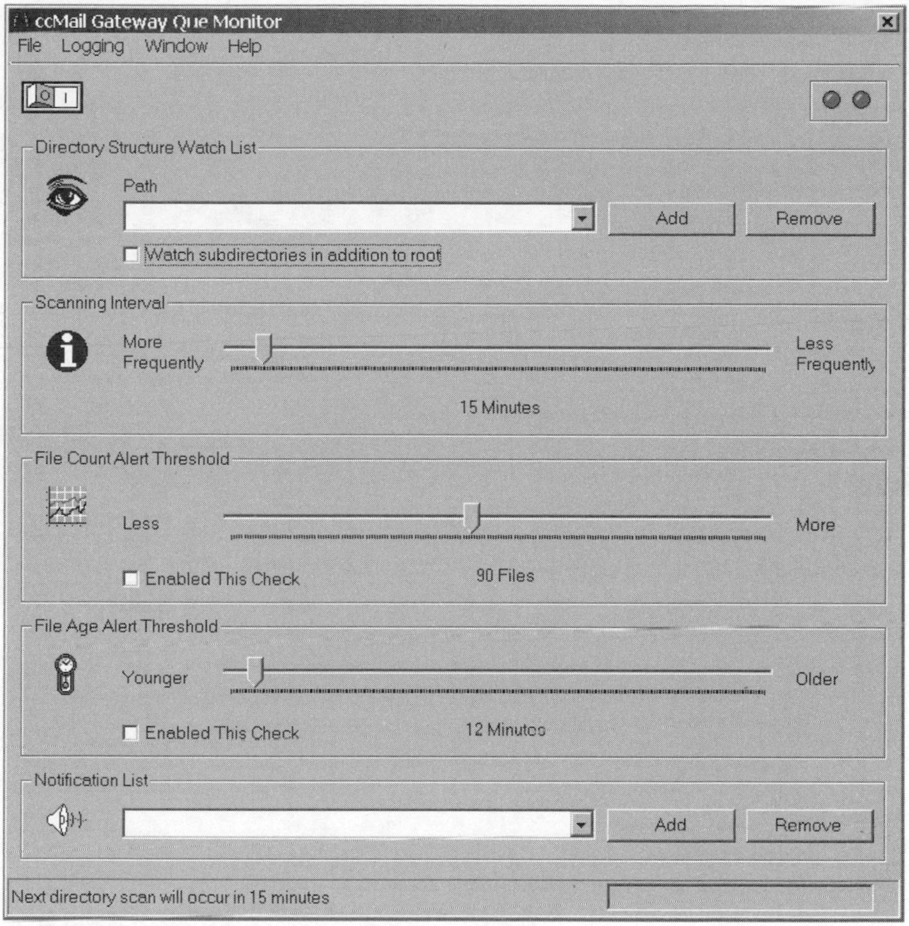

Figure 1-3. *An example of a "rich-client" application*

That's where the RIAs come in. An RIA isn't a single specific thing; it's more of a paradigm, almost an approach to web app development. RIAs are characterized by appearing in many ways to look, feel, and function just like those native applications we left behind.[6] We develop them using more advanced techniques, a much heavier dependency on the clients' capabilities, and with an eye toward building a much more powerful application for the end user. In Figure 1-4 you can see an example of such an application.

---

6   To be clear, native applications are of course still in use today and are still being developed anew. However, it's probably fair to say that more development effort these days goes into web-based applications, so in that sense we've "left native applications" behind, for the most part anyway.

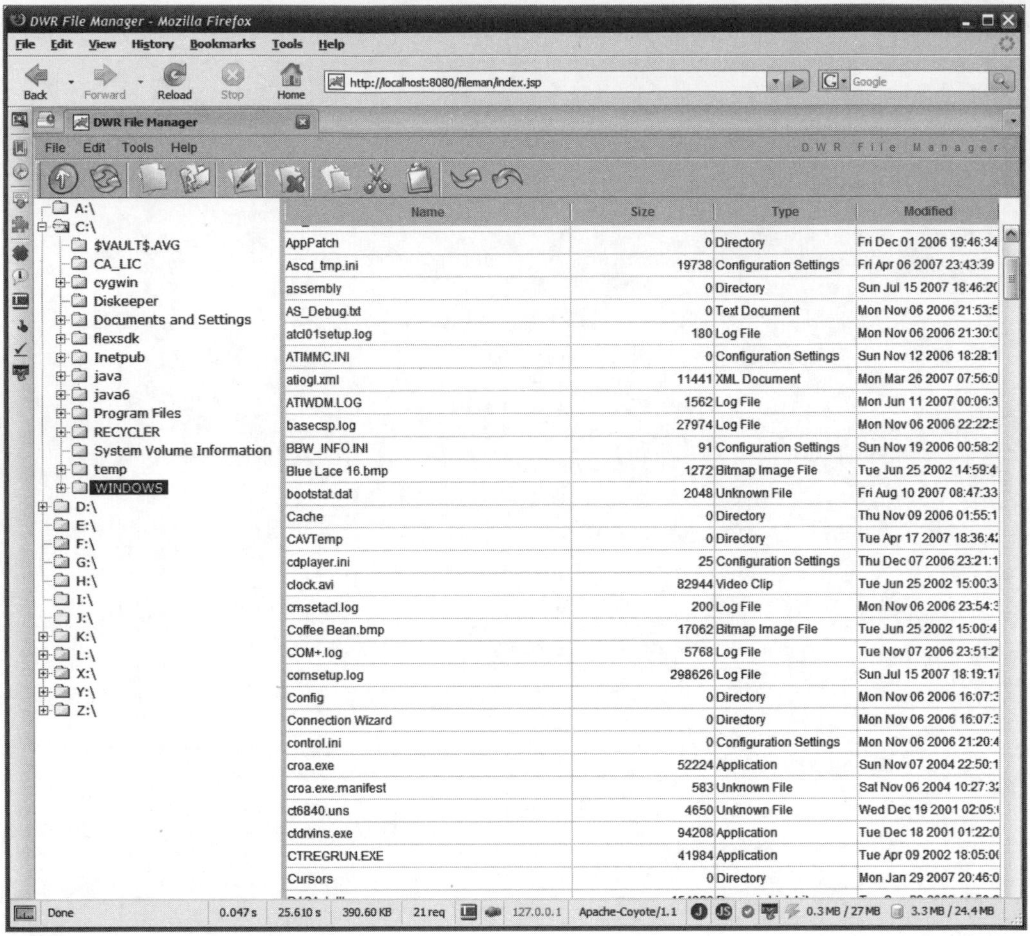

Figure 1-4. *An example of an RIA*

Let's compare and contrast the previous four screenshots, primarily comparing each to the native application example on the basis that it is the ideal we're striving for.

First, the web site, while hopefully (since it's mine!) fairly pleasing visually, doesn't really look like any of the applications, least of all the native application example. The photo-sharing web app looks more like the native application in the sense that it's clear you are supposed to perform some functions with it rather than just more passively obtain information from it, but it still doesn't look a whole lot like the native application; it looks like a hybrid, somewhere between the web site and the native application.

Now, comparing the RIA to the native application, the RIA looks a lot more like the native application. It has menus, toolbars, trees, grids, and just generally looks more robust. It's clear that its focus is in giving the user the ability to manipulate data, files, and directories in this case. It's clearly more focused on the idea of *doing* something than the web site example was.

RIAs, and perhaps more precisely the idea of bringing native applications to the Web, is where we are today, although interestingly we're also taking some of the "coolness" the Web brought about—things like multimedia, animations, and effects—and rolling them into our applications. We've evolved beyond simply bringing native application-like capabilities to the Web; we're now trying to evolve that concept to make applications that are actually cool! This combination of native application-like functionality and web coolness are what modern RIA development is all about (and what Ext JS is all about too!).

Enter Ajax: The Driving Force behind RIAs

There isn't any one thing that ushered in the age of the RIA. Many people were going down that path long before we all even recognized the path! Still, there is something probably *more* responsible for it than any other single thing, and that's Ajax (see Figure 1-5... now you'll always know what code and architectures would look like personified as a plucky super hero!).

Ajax came to life, so to speak, at the hands of one Jesse James Garrett of Adaptive Path (www.adaptivepath.com). Mr. Garrett wrote an essay in February 2005 (you can see it here: www.adaptivepath.com/publications/essays/archives/000385.php) in which he coined the term Ajax.

Figure 1-5. *Ajax personified*

Ajax (for Those Living under a Rock the Past 2–3 Years)

Ajax, as I'd be willing to bet my dog you know already (well, not really, my wife and kids will kill me if I gave away the family dog, although my wallet would thank me), stands for Asynchronous JavaScript and XML. The interesting thing about Ajax, though, is that it doesn't have to be asynchronous (but virtually always is), doesn't have to involve JavaScript (but virtually always does), and doesn't need to use XML at all (and more and more frequently doesn't). In fact, one of the most famous Ajax examples, Google Suggest, doesn't pass back XML at all! The fact is that it doesn't even pass back data per se; it passes back JavaScript that contains data! (The data is essentially "wrapped" in JavaScript, which is then interpreted and executed upon return to the browser. It then writes out the list of drop-down results you see as you type.)

Ajax is, at its core, an exceedingly simple, and by no stretch of the imagination original, concept: it is not necessary to refresh the entire contents of a web page for each user interaction, or each event, if you will. When the user clicks a button, it is no longer necessary to ask the server to render an entirely new page, as is the case with the "classic" Web, which is the term I like to use to describe this model of back-and-forth with the server where each user interaction results in a new page in the browser. Instead, you can define regions on the page to be updated and have much more fine-grained control over user events as well. No longer are you limited to simply submitting a form or navigating to a new page when a link is clicked. You can now do something in direct response to a non-submit button being clicked, a key being pressed in a text box—in fact, to any event happening! The server is no longer completely responsible for rendering what the user sees; some of this logic is now performed in the user's browser. In fact, in a great many cases it is considerably better to simply return a set of data and not a bunch of markup for the browser to display. As we traced along our admittedly rough history of application development, we saw that the classic model of web development is in a sense an aberration to the extent that we actually had it right before then!

Ajax is a return to that thinking. Notice I said "thinking." That should be a very big clue to you about what Ajax really is. It is not a specific technology, and it is not the myriad toolkits available for doing Ajax. In fact, while Ajax originally was a term to describe a technique for communicating with a server in an asynchronous fashion, what it means today is pretty different, but let's come back to that a little later.

The interesting thing about Ajax is that it is in no way, shape, or form new; only the term used to describe it is. I was reminded of this fact a while ago at the Philadelphia Java Users Group. A speaker by the name of Steve Banfield was talking about Ajax, and he said (paraphrasing from memory), "You can always tell someone who has actually done Ajax because they are pissed that it is all of a sudden popular." This could not be truer! I was one of those people doing Ajax years and years ago; I just never thought what I was doing was anything special and hence did not give it a "proper" name. Mr. Garrett holds that distinction.

I mentioned that I personally have been doing Ajax for a number of years, and that is true. What I did not say, however, is that I have been using XML or that I have been using the `XMLHttpRequest` object, which usually powers Ajax applications, or any of the Ajax toolkits out there. I've written a number of applications in the past that pulled tricks with hidden frames and returned data to them, then used that data to populate existing portions of the screen. This data was sometimes in the form of XML, but other times not. The important point here is that the approach that is at the heart of Ajax is nothing new as it does not, contrary to its very own name, require any specific technologies (aside from client-side scripting, which is, with few exceptions, required of an Ajax or Ajax-like solution).

When you get into the Ajax frame of mind—which is what we are really talking about—you are no longer bound by the rules of the classic Web. You can now take back at least some of the power the native applications offer, while still keeping the benefits of the Web in place. Those benefits begin, most importantly perhaps, with the ubiquity of the web browser.

■Note Nowadays, Ajax sometimes has a wider meaning than simply a communication mechanism as described here. In fact, to many people now, an "Ajax application" really means an RIA. I prefer to use the term RIA and continue to use the term Ajax as described here so as to keep the two concepts separate. RIAs nearly always involve Ajax, so in object-oriented programming (OOP) terminology, I prefer a "has a" relationship to an "is a" relationship. But regardless, you should be aware that in conversation, to some, Ajax == RIA.

The Benefits of Ajax (and by Extension, RIAs)

Have you ever been at work and had to give a demo of some new native application, such as a Visual Basic app, that you ran on a machine you have never touched before? Ever have to do it in the boardroom in front of top company executives? Ever had that demo fail miserably because of some DLL conflict you couldn't possibly anticipate (see Figure 1-6)? You are a developer, so the answer to all of those questions is likely yes[7]. If you have never done Windows development, you may not have had these experiences (yeah, right…if you believe it only happens on Windows, then I've got a big hunk of cheese to sell you…it's on display every evening, just look up in the sky and check it out). You will have to take my word for it when I say that such situations were, for a long time, much more common than any of us would have liked. With a web-based application, this is generally not a concern. Ensure the PC has the correct browser and version, and off you go 98 percent of the time.

Figure 1-6. *We've all been there: live demos and engineers do not mix!*

The other major benefit of a web app is distribution. No longer do you need a three-month shakedown period to ensure your new application does not conflict with the existing suite of corporate applications. An app running in a web browser, security issues aside, will not affect, or be affected by, any other application on the PC (and I am sure we all have war stories about exceptions to that, but they are just that: exceptions!).

Of course, you probably knew those benefits already, or you wouldn't be interested in web development in the first place. So we won't spend any more time on this.

Ajax represents a paradigm shift for some people (even most people, given what most web apps are today) because it can fundamentally change the way you develop a web app. More important, perhaps, is that it represents a paradigm shift for the user, and in fact it is the user who will drive the adoption of Ajax. Believe me, you can no longer ignore Ajax as a tool in your toolbox. Ajax is one of the primary enablers of the RIA movement, and that's what we're really talking about here.

Put a non-Ajax web app, or a non-RIA web app in other words, in front of users, and then put that same app using Ajax techniques in front of them, and guess which one they are going to want to use all day nine times out of ten? The Ajax-ified version! They will immediately see

---

7   Unless you work in the public sector, and then it probably was not corporate executives but rather generals or folks of that ilk, which I suppose means you may have run the risk of being lined up against a wall and shot for your "crimes," but either way, you get the point!

the increased responsiveness of the application and will notice that they no longer need to wait for a response from the server while they stare at a spinning browser logo wondering if anything is actually happening. They will see that the application alerts them on the fly of error conditions they would have to wait for the server to tell them about in the non-Ajax web app. They will see functionality like type-ahead suggestions and instantly sortable tables and master-detail displays that update in real time—things that they would not see in a non-Ajax web app. They will see maps that they can drag around the same way they can in the full-blown mapping applications they spent $80 on. All of these things will be obvious advantages to the user. Users have become accustomed to the classic web app model, but when confronted with something that harkens back to those native application days in terms of user-friendliness and responsiveness, there is almost an instantaneous realization that the Web as they knew it is dead, or at least should be!

If you think about many of the big technologies to come down the pike in recent years, it should occur to you that we technology folks rather than the users were driving many of them. Do you think a user ever asked for an Enterprise JavaBean (EJB)–based application? No, we just all thought it was a good idea (how wrong we were!). What about web services? Remember when they were going to fundamentally change the way the world of application construction worked? Sure, we are using them today, but are they, by and large, much more than an interface between cooperating systems? Not usually. Whatever happened to Universal Description, Discovery, and Integration (UDDI) directories and giving an application the ability to find, dynamically link to, and use a registered service on the fly? How good did that sound? To us geeks it was the next coming, but it didn't even register with users.

Ajax is different, though. Users can see the benefits because RIAs nearly always stand out from their less rich predecessors. The differences and the benefits are very real and very tangible to them. In fact, we as technology people, especially those of us doing Java web development, may even recoil at Ajax at first because more is being done on the client, which is contrary to what we have been drilling into our brains all these years. After all, we all believe scriptlets in JavaServer Pages (JSPs) are bad, eschewing them in favor of custom tags. Users do not care about elegant architectures and separation of concerns and abstractions allowing for code reuse. Users just want to be able to drag the map around in Google Maps (see Figure 1-11) and have it happen in real time without waiting for the whole page to refresh like they do (or did anyway) when using Yahoo!'s mapping solution.

The difference is clear. They want it, and they want it now (stop snickering in your head, we're all adults here!).

Now we can come back to what I mentioned earlier: Ajax now means something different than what it originally did. Ajax now means, if you'll pardon my French, web apps that don't suck! The way we approach application design has fundamentally changed, thanks to the Ajax revolution. We now recognize that the classic model of web development—when you fetch a page from a server, the user enters some data, submits that data, and a new page is rendered— is less than optimal. We also now recognize that adding some "cool" to a web app can do wonders for it. Things like animations, multimedia feedback, and real-time graphics are no longer just flashy tricks to attract attention but are core parts of what we do. That's what Ajax has come to mean.

SOVEREIGN WEB APPS

Another term that has fairly recently come into vogue is "sovereign web app." This refers to a web app that runs in a browser independent of any server (except perhaps a server that initially serves it). This is yet another result of the Ajax revolution, and in fact is what we'll be dealing with in this book. Nowhere will I discuss server-side technologies, except perhaps in passing here and there. We are dealing strictly with sovereign web apps, and that means "no server required."

This inherently means that we're going to be doing things in an Ajax-y way, if you will. Since there's no server to render pages, it's quite natural to wind up with a single-page design, which is another popular term employed today. It turns out a single page is all you need in most cases to create a sovereign web app, as you'll see.

The Evolution of Web Development

Now that we've seen the evolution of web sites, to web apps, to RIAs, what about evolution in terms of development? Has there been a parallel evolution there as well, an evolution of techniques, tools, and knowledge? You'd certainly hope, I think, that the answer is yes, and in fact it is.

Early on, way back in the distant year 1995 or so, when most "longtime" web developers (relatively speaking) began, you would frequently see someone with Notepad open if they used Windows, or maybe emacs or vi if they were *nix users. In either case, they were happily hacking away at code right there in their simple text editors, saving the file as an HTML file and loading it up in their browser right there, no server or anything like that. For a while this was quite sufficient because we weren't ready to develop web apps just yet—we were just getting our heads around web sites![8]

Nowadays, there exists full-blown integrated development environments (IDEs) that provide all the tools developers tend to need: debuggers, code completion, code generators, profilers, and so on. Even without a full IDE, we have options like Firebug (www.getfirebug.com), which is an extension to the Firefox (www.firefox.com) browser. In fact, many developers find that Firebug is all they need these days, and I count myself among them.

So, there has clearly been an evolution in terms of tooling for client-side development. What about the code itself, though? Early on, people wrote a whole lot of JavaScript themselves because there wasn't much in the way of options. The best you could hope for was to find some useful code snippets out on the Web that you could… AHEM… borrow. You wound up typically taking that code, hacking it to death, and massaging it to fit your needs. If the code was good to begin with, which was always a questionable thing, the result wouldn't be too bad.

Using code snippets is part and parcel of developing software. We all do it, and the best among us probably do it more than others! But just grabbing snippets here and there isn't

---

8 That's not to say some people don't still work this way—many do. In fact, I myself typically work at a level just above that: while it's not Notepad, I use a text editor called UltraEdit (www.ultraedit.com). It's a pretty advanced editor with lots of features that make life easier, but it's still a text editor in the end, not a full-blown IDE like many people prefer. To each his own!

usually optimal, and also isn't typical in most programming environment where full-blown libraries are king. It took a while to get there, but client-side JavaScript development is now no different.

Choice Is Good: Toolkits Make It a Breeze

After a while, the evolution from simple code snippets to full-blown libraries began to take shape. Libraries of JavaScript emerged that you could use without hacking to fit your needs (well, *mostly* without hacking). The early libraries weren't terribly good—they were just loose collections of snippets—but the underlying idea was solid, which meant that slowly but surely the quality improved.

Today, we have literally thousands of JavaScript libraries to choose from, and many of them are rather good (others, not so much). The following eight are considered by most to be at the top of the heap and get the most usage:

- Dojo (www.dojotoolkit.org) is a general-purpose library that tries to be everything to everyone. It provides all sorts of JavaScript language extensions, utilities, and one of the more advanced widget frameworks out there. In Figure 1-7 you can see an example of an application built with Dojo.

- Prototype (www.prototypejs.org) is a very widely used library that is famous for having a small code footprint and for extending the JavaScript language itself (via extending intrinsic JavaScript objects, such as adding methods to the String object). Prototype is an enabler in that a number of other popular libraries are built on top of it, such as the next list item, script.aculo.us.

- script.aculo.us (http://script.aculo.us) is a library built on top of Prototype that specializes in effects. All the fancy fades, dissolves, compressions, and those sorts of things that are popular in the Web 2.0 world are provided by this library and in a simple-to-use way.

- jQuery (www.jquery.com) is another extremely lightweight JavaScript library that, as the authors themselves put it, is meant to change the way you write JavaScript. Its main focus is on making HTML document traversal, event handling, and animating drop-dead simple. jQuery has become extremely popular in a short period of time in large part to all the neat extensions that are built on top of it, such as lots of very good GUI widgets.

- Rico (http://openrico.org) is a library that provides full Ajax support, drag-and-drop management, and an entire cinematic effects module.

- MochiKit (http://mochikit.com) has perhaps the best tagline going: "MochiKit makes JavaScript suck less." Indeed, many believe it does! MochiKit provides a good variety of tools, including drag and drop, visual effects (including a really good rounded-corner implementation for spicing up tables and <div>s), and DOM functions.

- MooTools (www.mootools.net) is another wide-ranging library like Dojo that seeks to provide virtually everything the modern JavaScript developer would need. Language extensions, general utilities, widgets, animations, and all that kind of stuff is covered. MooTools lets you create a custom version of the library right there on the MooTools web site that suits your needs perfectly. For a long time, this feature was unique to MooTools, but others have copied the idea.

- YUI (http://developer.yahoo.com/yui) is an acronym for Yahoo! User Interface. YUI is popular because it is extremely simple, easy to understand, and exceptionally well documented, with lots of examples to look at. Coming from Yahoo! doesn't hurt in many people's minds. YUI is mostly interested in providing GUI widgets that are relatively simple but cross-browser. There are general-purpose parts to YUI as well, such as Ajax functionality.

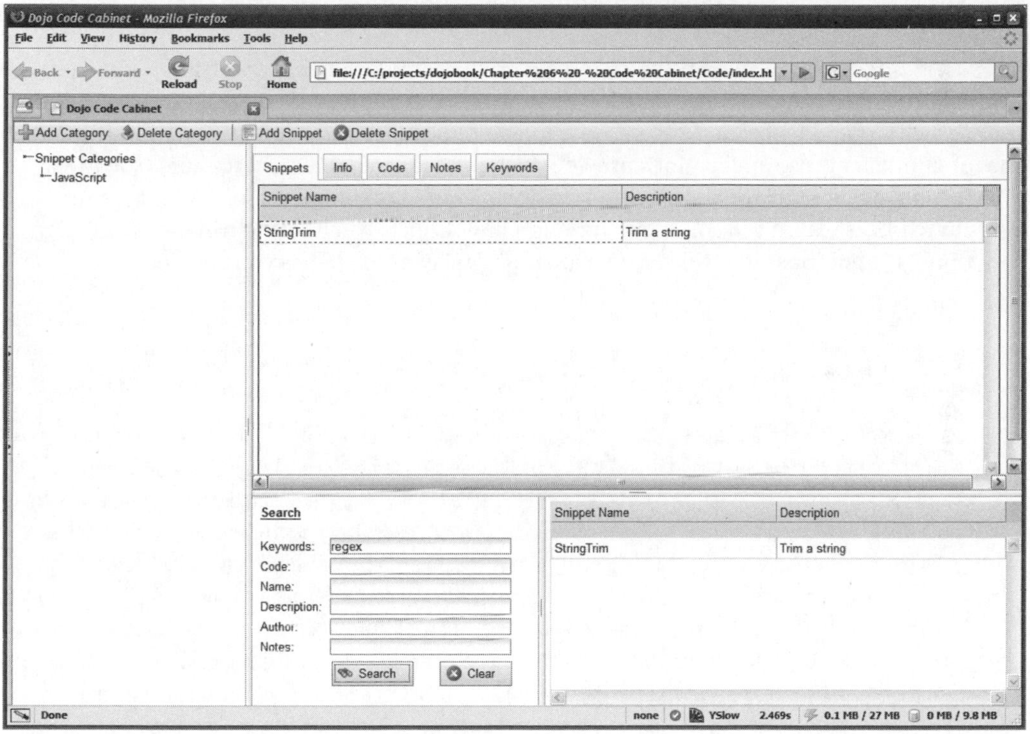

Figure 1-7. *An application built with Dojo*

This is in not an exhaustive list, but as you can clearly see, there are quite a few to choose from. This list barely scratches the surface of what's available today. Of course, while all of these are fine toolkits, we're here to talk about one that's not in that list, one that I feel is quite possibly the best available today: Ext JS.

Enter Ext JS: The Best of the Bunch

A long time ago in a galaxy far, far away (more precisely, early 2006, the planet Earth), a gentleman by the name of Jack Slocum developed a set of extension utilities to the YUI library. These utilities rapidly gained popularity within the YUI community and were quickly organized into an independent library called YUI-Ext. In fall 2006, Jack released the .33 version of this new library under the terms of the Berkeley Software Distribution (BSD) license.

After a while, before 2006 was over in fact, the name of the library was changed to Ext, because it was starting to develop independently of YUI at that point. In fact, support for other libraries was beginning to be developed within Ext.

In 2007, Jack formed a company to further advance the development of Ext, which at some point thereafter began to be known as Ext JS. On April 1, 2007, Ext JS 1.0 was released.

In a short period of time, Ext JS evolved from a handy set of extensions to a popular library into what many people, including yours truly, feel is the most mature JavaScript UI development library available today.

Ext JS is focused on allowing you to create great user interfaces in a web app. In fact, it is best known for its top-notch collection of UI widgets. It allows you to create web apps that mimic the look and feel of desktop native applications, and it also allows you to mimic most of the functionality those applications provide. In short, Ext JS enables you to build true RIAs.

It's not all about widgets, though, as we'll see. There are a lot of useful utility-type functions in Ext JS as well. Need some Ajax functionality? Check. Need some string manipulation functions? It's got those too. Need a data abstraction layer? Ext JS has you covered.

LICENSING QUESTIONS

Ext JS has undergone some licensing changes throughout its lifetime, and some of them have been tumultuous in terms of Ext JS users having issues with the changes for one reason or another. I am in no way, shape, or form a lawyer, and frankly, software licensing can be tricky. Therefore, I urge you to do independent research in this area before using Ext JS to ensure it meets your needs. I won't go anywhere near the debate about whether or not things were done "properly." I leave that to each person to decide. I'll stick to the facts here as best I can (one of the few times I shy away from giving my personal opinion on something!).

At the time of this writing, Ext JS is under a dual-license model. There is a commercial option, which you have to pay for. Under this option, you do not have any obligation to release the source code for your application. You get enhanced support from Ext, LLC (the company Jack Slocum started) for your money.

An open source option is available that allows you to use Ext JS for free, under the terms of the GNU General Public License (GPL) 3.0. In addition, there is a mechanism allowing exceptions for open source projects that don't fall under the terms of the GPL 3.0.

As you can see, licensing isn't a simple matter at all! However, I think the Ext JS team has tried their best to meet the needs of both commercial entities and those folks developing free/open source software alike. Remember that Jack and Co. are trying to feed their families from their efforts, so the fact that they offer a free alternative at all is a Good Thing™ to be sure!

In the end, though, I suggest reading the licensing terms and determining the right option for your project before you get too far into it. Although you can download Ext JS at any time and begin developing right away, it would probably be advisable to sort out the licensing issues sooner than later.

Note too that the story is a little different for something called Ext Core, but that topic is discussed a few pages from now, so keep reading!

Let's take a look at some examples of Ext JS in action. In Figure 1-8 you can see one such example: an RSS feed reader. This is one of the many examples available on the Ext JS web site itself.

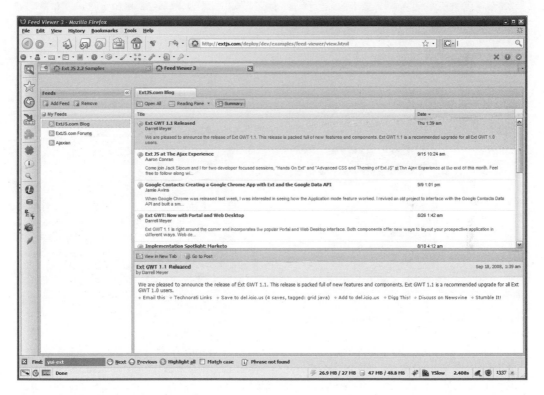

Figure 1-8. *RSS feed reader example*

As you can see, the user interface here is quite nice-looking. Not only that, it's very functional. For example, the left-hand side, which contains the list of feeds, can be expanded or contracted by dragging the divider line left or right. Likewise, the area at the bottom where a selected article is read can similarly be resized by dragging the line above the View in New Tab button. You can also collapse the list of feeds entirely by clicking the double arrow icon in the upper-right corner, and this happens with a nice animation effect. Another feature is that the list of articles on the top right are sortable by clicking the column headings. You can put the list of articles and the reading pane (where you read an article) next to each by clicking the Reading Pane button. Most of this functionality comes with the widgets used to build the UI automatically without you as a developer having to do any real work (other than setting some flags to indicate which capabilities you want).

Next, in Figure 1-9, you can see one of the examples that many people would simply refer to as "wicked cool," and I wouldn't disagree one bit.

Figure 1-9. *Web desktop example*

This is the web desktop example. Yes, what you are looking at is a JavaScript-based web application! As you can see, Ext JS is extremely powerful, giving you windows (which can be dragged around, resized, maximized, and minimized) as well as tabbed interfaces, accordion widgets, grids, and much more. I would say that if that example doesn't impress you, then there's probably something wrong with your brain!

■**Note** Both of these examples, along with tons more, are available directly on the Ext JS web site for you to play with. Especially for the web desktop example, I suggest you take a few minutes to peruse the site. It's fun to play with them for real rather than just seeing them statically on the page.

Fisher Price™ My First Ext JS Application

Before we start looking in detail at Ext JS's overall structure and API, let's talk about what it takes to get a simple Ext JS application off the ground. As it happens, it isn't much at all!

You'll obviously need to download Ext JS from the Ext JS web site (www.extjs.com). There's only a single download, and that's the Ext JS SDK, which is pretty much everything, including source code, examples, documentation, and examples. Once you have that downloaded and unzipped, using Ext JS is as simple as a few imports in an HTML document.

■**Note** There is also a "build your own" option in the download section of the web site. This allows you to build a custom version of Ext JS that only includes those parts you want. This is a great way to optimize the performance of your site, and I encourage you to play with that online tool as time allows.

The imports you'll need are very simple and depend on what parts of Ext JS you wish to use. First, if you intend to use any of the UI widgets, you'll need a style sheet:

```
<link rel="stylesheet" type="text/css" href="extjs/resources/css/ext-all.css" />
```

If, as in the case of all the example code in this chapter, you aren't using widgets, then this style sheet isn't needed. Naturally, you'll need to adjust that path to point to where Ext JS is located.

Once that's done, it's on to JavaScript imports, and here you have some choices. You see, Ext JS can integrate with many of today's most popular libraries. Ext JS will in fact borrow some "plumbing" code from these libraries, things like Ajax functions, animation, events, and so on. Not too long ago, Ext JS actually *required* one of those libraries to work. That is no longer the case; Ext JS can now run quite happily on its own (that is how all the applications in this book are written). However, if you're already using one of these other libraries you may want to use what Ext JS terms "adapters" to integrate with those libraries. So, the JavaScript imports you specify can vary based on what library, if any, you want to use along with Ext JS. Table 1-1 summarizes the required JavaScript imports; it also tells you in what order they are required to appear because ordering is very important for everything to work as expected.

Table 1-1. *JavaScript Imports, and Their Order, Required to Get Ext JS Working*

Configuration	Imports
Ext JS by itself	ext-base.js, then ext-all.js (or ext-all-debug.js for a debug version, or you can specify source files instead)
Yahoo!'s YUI (v. 12 or higher)	yui-utilies.js, then ext-yui-adapter.js, then ext-all.js (or ext-all-debug.js for a debug version, or you can specify source files instead)
jQuery (v. 1.1 or higher)	jquery.js, then jquery-plugin.js, then ext-jquery-adapter.js, then ext-all.js (or ext-all-debug.js for a debug version, or you can specify source files instead)
Prototype (v. 1.5 or higher) and Script.aculo.us (v 1.7 or higher)	prototype.js, then scriptaculous.js, then ext-prototype-adapter.js, then ext-all.js (or ext-all-debug.js for a debug version, or you can specify source files instead)

Figure 1-10 summarizes the relationships between these various files.

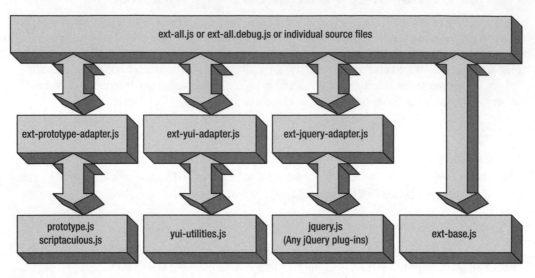

Figure 1-10. *Ext JS JavaScript files and their (optional) dependencies*

All of the files mentioned here (except for ext-all.js and ext-all-debug.js) are adapters and are located in the /adapters directory of your Ext JS directory. So, for example, let's assume we're using Ext JS all by its lonesome, which is how all the applications in this book are presented. Let's further assume we're not using the debug version, in which case we have only these two imports to add to our page:

```
<script type="text/javascript" src="extjs/adapter/ext/ext-base.js"></script>
<script type="text/javascript" src="extjs/ext-all.js"></script>
```

Once you have those files imported into your HTML document, you are ready to rock and roll! Virtually all Ext JS has to offer is immediately available, right at your fingertips.

Now, let's get to some learnin', shall we? We begin by taking a look at Ext JS's overall structure, and we'll then quickly dive into some real code.

Ext JS's High-Level Organizational Structure

One of the things that sets Ext JS apart from most other libraries is the clean structure of its API. You can tell that Jack and Co. believe in the object-oriented paradigm quite strongly because Ext JS follows a highly object-oriented design. Almost everything is within a class (and they even differentiate between regular classes and singletons!). Classes are within namespaces (analogous to packages in languages like Java), and classes extend other classes to form logical hierarchies.

For example, take a CheckBox widget. It extends from the Field class, which extends from the BoxComponent class, which extends from the Component class, which extends from the Observable class, which is the base of the inheritance tree (technically, Observable extends from the basic JavaScript Object class, but that's true of any class in JavaScript and therefore generally isn't something to be concerned with). As is the case in object-oriented design, the final CheckBox class takes behavior and characteristics from each of its ancestors. This allows a CheckBox to be treated like a Component, for instance, because it too is a Component by virtue of its inheritance, which means it has all the methods and fields that any Component has. This all means that (a) there's a logical structure to the entire Ext JS API, and (b) learning about something usually helps you learn about something else because that new knowledge will apply to it as well (or stated another way, once you learn what you can do with a Component, for example, you'll know at least some of what a CheckBox can do automatically).

At the highest level, there are a number of classes in the global scope, and then there is the Ext namespace. The contents of these classes and this namespace form the core of Ext JS, and provide many of the utility-type functionality you'd want from a good JavaScript library.

■**Note** The following section is not meant to be an exhaustive look at everything in Ext JS. It isn't my intent to duplicate the Ext JS API documentation, which is rather good. Instead, I will touch on the things that I see as most useful and of special interest in the context of the projects to come. The bottom line is Ext JS already has great reference documentation, and I'm not trying to re-create that merely to highlight cool stuff!

Global-Scope Classes

As of Ext JS version 2.2, there are six classes in global scope, one of which is a singleton.

■**Note** The code snippets shown next are each part of an HTML file that you can load and see in action. An HTML file is available for each of these classes.

Array

This class extends the built-in Array class, adding some new methods to it. One such method is indexOf():

```
var a = [ "Frank", "Bill", "Mike", "Peter" ];
alert(a.indexOf("Mike"));
```

This will display an alert message with the text "2" because that's the index where Mike is found.

The remove() method is also added, so you can do this:

```
a.remove("Bill");
alert(a);
```

You can see the alert() message in Figure 1-11. Note that Bill was removed, which is reflected in the alert() message.

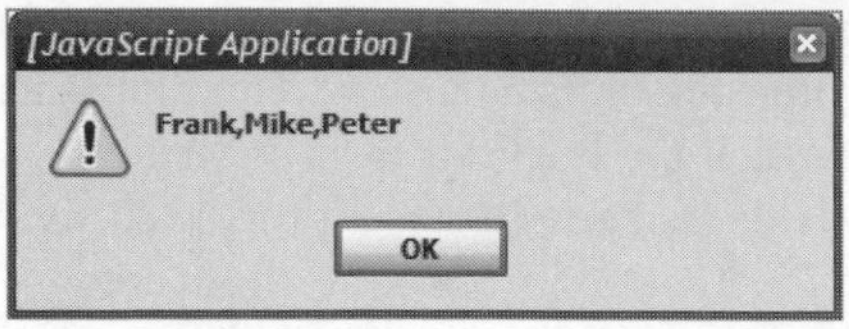

Figure 1-11. *Contents of the array after Bill is removed*

Date

The Date class both extends the JavaScript intrinsic Date class and provides some static utility methods itself. To begin, let's take a look at a couple of methods that allow us to get values from a Date object:

```
var d = new Date("02/17/1973");
var sOut = "";
sOut += "Starting date: " +
  Date.getShortDayName(d.getDay()) + " " +
  Date.getShortMonthName(d.getMonth()) + " " +
  d.getDate() + ", " + d.getFullYear() + "<br>";
Ext.getDom("divOutput").innerHTML = sOut;
```

Here you can see the getShortDayName() and getShortMonthName() methods. The former will return "Sat" for this Date, and the later returns "Feb". getDate() and getFullYear() are methods of the standard Date class. This generates some HTML and writes to a <div> with the ID divOutput.

The format() method is another handy method. It uses a subset of PHP's date() function, which is helpful only if you know PHP! For the rest of us, the Ext JS docs detail the format specification very well. Here's an example of it in action:

```
var dFormatted = d.format("D M j, Y");
```

This results in the Date object seen previously being formatted into a string "Sat Feb 17, 1973" (which just so happens to be the output of the code seen earlier, which was constructed manually).

Next up is a handy function for doing basic date math. For example, let's say we want to add four days to the Date object we've been looking at so far. Here's all you need to do:

```
var d1 = d.add(Date.DAY, 4);
```

Note that calling the add() method doesn't alter the Date object pointed to by the variable d here; it returns a new instance, in this case Wednesday February 21, 1973. You can use negative numbers as well to effectively subtract from a date. In addition, here you can see one of a number of properties present on the Date class. This one is a simple constant that specifies what we're adding to the Date object, the day in this case, so Date.DAY. If you wanted to add four years to the date instead, you could use Date.YEAR. In addition to the rest that you'd expect, like `Date.MONTH` and `Date.MINUTE` and so on, there are a couple of arrays that provide useful information, such as `Date.dayNames` and `Date.monthNames`, which I suspect are self-explanatory.

You can determine whether the year of a given `Date` object is a leap year by calling the `isLeapYear()` method on it, which returns `true` or `false`. You can determine what day of the year the `Date` represents by calling `getDayOfYear()`, which returns a number between 1 and 365 (or 366 in a leap year). The `getWeekOfYear()` method tells you what week of the year the `Date` object falls in. The `getDaysInMonth()` method tells you how many days are in the month of the `Date` object. You can even get the suffix (like "th," "nd," "rd," or "st" for a day. So, you can do this:

```
sOut += "The day of " + d.format("D M j, Y") + " is the " +
  d.getDate() + d.getSuffix() + " (used getSuffix() to get th)<br>";
```

This will result in the text "The day of Sat Feb 17, 1973 is the 17th (used `getSuffix()` to get *th*)". If you've ever written the typical `if` block of code to do this yourself, you'll very much appreciate this method!

Another handy edition to the `Date` class is the `between()` method. This lets you determine if the `Date` object you call `between()` on falls between two specified `Date` objects. Here's an example:

```
var d3 = new Date("02/19/1973");
sOut += d3.format("D M j, Y") + ".between(" +
  d.format("D M j, Y") + ", " + d1.format("D M j, Y") + "): " +
  d3.between(d, d1) + "<br>";
```

This will result in the text "Mon Feb 19, 1973.between(Sat Feb 17, 1973, Wed Feb 21, 1973): true." As you can see, `between()` returns a simple `true` or `false`.

Along the same lines is `getElapsed()`, which tells you how much time, in milliseconds, has elapsed between the `Date` object you call it on and a given `Date` object.

Finally we have the `parseDate()` method, which parses a string into a `Date` object using a format specifier. Here it is in action:

```
sOut += "Date.parseDate('1973-02-17 12:14:06AM', 'Y-m-d h:i:sA')" +
  ": " + Date.parseDate("1973-02-17 12:14:06AM", "Y-m-d h:i:sA");
```

This results in the text "Date.parseDate('1973-02-17 12:14:06AM', 'Y-m-d h:i:sA'): Sat Feb 17 1973 00:14:06 GMT-0500 (Eastern Standard Time)." As you can see, the string has been properly parsed and the standard `toString()` of the `Date` class is the proof of that.

The result of the execution of all these functions is shown in Figure 1-12.

Note The last line may look different depending on the browser you run it in because JavaScript implementations can implement `toString()` of the `Date` class as they see fit (the screenshot is running in Firefox). You *should*, however, see the same date represented.

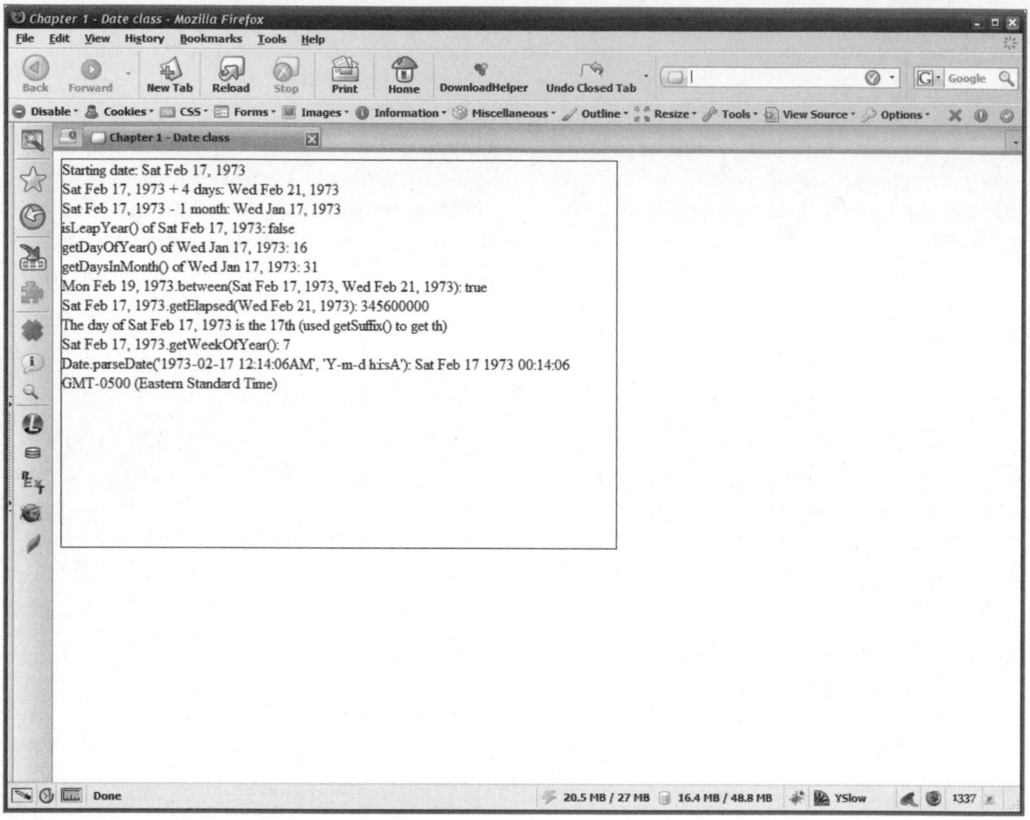

Figure 1-12. *Output of the Date class examples*

Ext

The Ext class is that one singleton I mentioned earlier. You are not meant to instantiate this class. More to the point, you *cannot* instantiate it—you'll see "Ext is not a constructor error" (in Firefox, at least) if you try.

The Ext class has a number of useful members, starting with a batch of public properties. These are summarized in Table 1-2 (which I copied directly from the Ext JS documentation on the grounds that I'm lazy!).

Table 1-2. *Public Properties of the Ext Class*

Property Name	Description
BLANK_IMAGE_URL	Contains a URL to a 1×1 transparent GIF image used by Ext to create inline icons with CSS background images. (Defaults to http://extjs.com/s.gif; you should change this to a URL on your server.)
SSL_SECURE_URL	Contains a URL to a blank file used by Ext when in secure mode for iframe src and onReady src to prevent the Internet Explorer insecure content warning (defaults to javascript:false).
emptyFn	A reusable empty function.

Property Name	Description
enableGarbageCollector	Set to true to automatically uncache orphaned Ext.Elements periodically (defaults to true).
enableListenerCollection	Set to true to automatically purge event listeners after uncaching an element (defaults to false). Note: This only happens if enableGarbageCollector is true.
isAir	Contains true if the detected platform is Adobe AIR.
isBorderBox	Contains true if the detected browser is Internet Explorer running in nonstrict mode.
isChrome	Contains true if the detected browser is Google's Chrome.
isGecko	Contains true if the detected browser uses the Gecko layout engine (e.g., Mozilla or Firefox).
isGecko2	Contains true if the detected browser uses a pre–Gecko 1.9 layout engine (e.g., Firefox 2.x).
isGecko3	Contains true if the detected browser uses a Gecko 1.9+ layout engine (e.g., Firefox 3.x).
isIE	Contains true if the detected browser is Internet Explorer.
isIE6	Contains true if the detected browser is Internet Explorer 6.x.
isIE7	Contains true if the detected browser is Internet Explorer 7.x.
isIE8	Contains true if the detected browser is Internet Explorer 8.x.
isLinux	Contains true if the detected platform is Linux.
isMac	Contains true if the detected platform is Mac OS.
isOpera	Contains true if the detected browser is Opera.
isReady	Contains true when the document is fully initialized and ready for action.
isSafari	Contains true if the detected browser is Safari.
isSafari2	Contains true if the detected browser is Safari 2.x.
isSafari3	Contains true if the detected browser is Safari 3.x.
isSecure	Contains true if the page is running over SSL.
isStrict	True if the browser is in strict (standards-compliant) mode, as opposed to quirks mode.
isWindows	Contains true if the detected platform is Windows.
useShims	By default, Ext intelligently decides whether floating elements should be shimmed. Shimming is a trick used specifically to deal with an Internet Explorer issue where <select> elements will "poke through" elements placed over them with z-index style settings. So, let's say you have a <div> that you want to float over a <select>. By default, the <select> will be seen through the <div>, or at least some portion of the <div>. Shimming means that you place an iFrame, which *can* float over a <select>, behind the <div> and adjust the z-index values of the iFrame and <div> in such a way that the iFrame blocks the <select>, and then the <div>, which can float on top of the iFrame, is positioned in exactly the same location. So, the iFrame blocks the <select>, but the <div> displays on top of the iFrame, so the user sees the <div> floating over the <select> as expected and nothing more. Thankfully, this Ext JS setting allows you to not have to know any of that and simply let Ext JS deal with it! If you are using Flash, or Java applets, you may want to set this to true.

Here's an example of these properties in action:

```
var sOut = "";
sOut += "isAir: " + Ext.isAir + "<br>";
sOut += "isBorderBox: " + Ext.isBorderBox + "<br>";
sOut += "isStrict: " + Ext.isStrict + "<br>";
sOut += "isGecko: " + Ext.isGecko + "<br>";
sOut += "isGecko2: " + Ext.isGecko2 + "<br>";
sOut += "isGecko3: " + Ext.isGecko3 + "<br>";
sOut += "isIE: " + Ext.isIE + "<br>";
sOut += "isIE6: " + Ext.isIE6 + "<br>";
sOut += "isIE7: " + Ext.isIE7 + "<br>";
sOut += "isLinux: " + Ext.isLinux + "<br>";
sOut += "isWindows: " + Ext.isWindows + "<br>";
sOut += "isMac: " + Ext.isMac + "<br>";
sOut += "isOpera: " + Ext.isOpera + "<br>";
sOut += "isSafari: " + Ext.isSafari + "<br>";
sOut += "isSafari2: " + Ext.isSafari2 + "<br>";
sOut += "isSafari3: " + Ext.isSafari3 + "<br>";
sOut += "isReady: " + Ext.isReady + "<br>";
sOut += "isSecure: " + Ext.isSecure + "<br>";
Ext.getDom("divOutput").innerHTML = sOut;
```

Assuming you ran this code in Firefox on Windows, and further assuming that there is a
<div> with the ID divOutput on the page, you'd see the output in Figure 1-13.

There are also a number of methods available via the Ext class. First up is addBehaviors():

```
Ext.addBehaviors({
  "div@click" : function(e, t) {
    alert("You clicked a div");
  }
});
```

This method basically allows you to add event handlers to elements. You call it and pass
to it an object that contains a number of key/value pairs. The key portion is a CSS selector. Any
element on the page with that selector will have applied to it the function defined as the value
of the key/value pair. The name of the event follows the at sign (@)in the key supplied. So here,
any <div> on the page will react to click events by executing the inline function. If you've run
the example from the source bundle that shows everything that is being discussed now (and if
you haven't yet, now would be a real good time!), you can click on the <div> where the text is
located to see the alert() appear. Note that the function arguments e and t are browser Event
objects that describe the event and a reference to the DOM node, respectively.

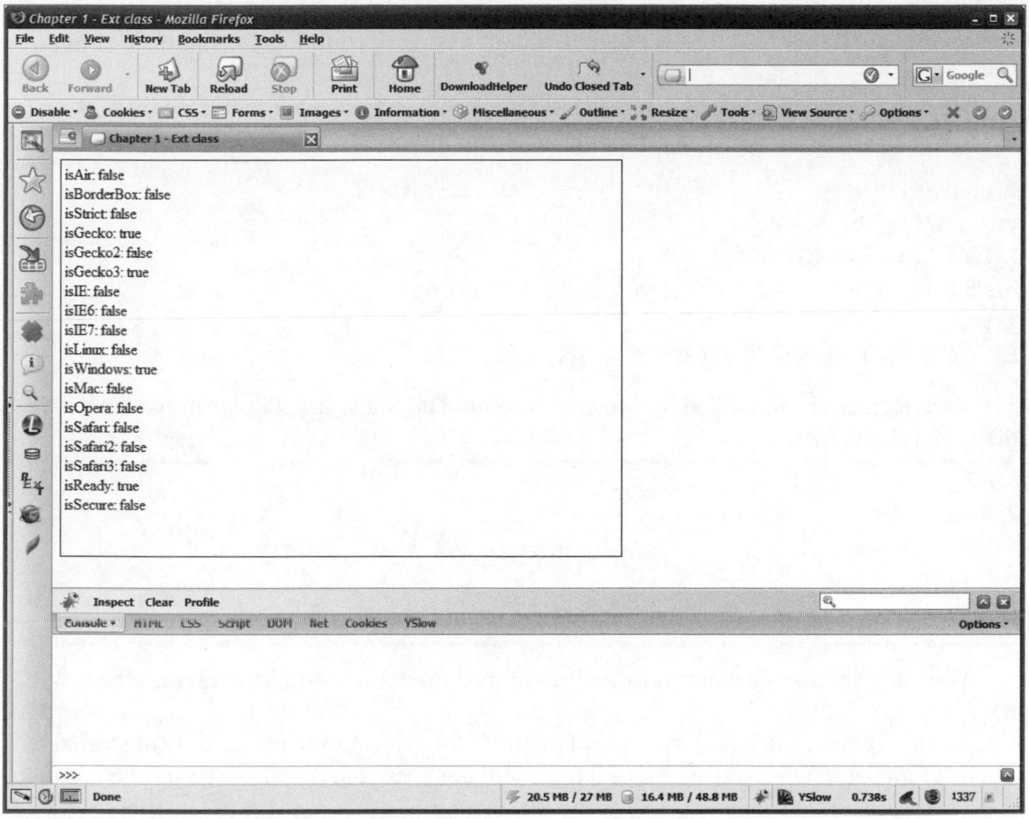

Figure 1-13. *Values of Ext class public properties*

The apply() method is next, and this allows you to apply properties from one object to another:

```
var sOut = "";
function Class1() {
  this.field1 = "liberate me";
}
function Class2() {
  this.field2 = "liberate tutame ex inferis";
}
var obj1 = new Class1();
var obj2 = new Class2();
Ext.apply(obj1, obj2);
sOut += "obj1.field1: " + obj1.field1 + "<br>";
sOut += "obj1.field2: " + obj1.field2 + "<br>";
Ext.getDom("divOutput").innerHTML = sOut;
```

The output to divOutput will be "liberate me," which is defined in Class1, and then you will see "liberate tutame ex inferis,"[9] which is defined in Class2, but which has been applied to obj1 (an instance of Class1).

Having an array and needing to do something with each member of it is a common enough requirement, and Ext JS is there to help with the Ext.each() method:

```
var sOut = "";
var a = [ 2, 4, 6, 8];
Ext.each(a, function(elem) {
  sOut += elem + " * 2: " + elem * 2 + "<br>";
});
Ext.getDom("divOutput").innerHTML = sOut;
```

Each element is multiplied by two and the output added to the sOut string, which when displayed shows this:

```
2 * 2: 4
4 * 2: 8
6 * 2: 12
8 * 2: 16
```

You can of course do whatever you want in the function, as simple or as complex as you need.

In the Ext class you'll find a couple of methods for determining the identity of a variable. There's isArray(), which returns true if the argument passed to it is an array and false otherwise. Likewise, isDate() returns true if the argument is a Date and false if not. There is also isEmpty(), which returns true if the argument is null, undefined, or an empty string.

The num() method is next, and it is used to validate that a given value is numeric. Further, if it isn't, a default value can be returned. For example:

```
var sOut = "";
sOut += "Ext.num(12, 5): " + Ext.num(12) + "<br>";
sOut += "Ext.num(\"Frank\", 123): " + Ext.num("Frank", 123) + "<br>";
Ext.getDom("divOutput").innerHTML = sOut;
```

This results in the following output:

```
Ext.num(12, 5): 12
Ext.num("Frank", 123): 123
```

---

9   SPOILER ALERT... The phrase "liberate me" is Latin for "save me" (maybe... keep reading!). This was the message received from the long-lost ship *Event Horizon* in the movie of the same name. Unfortunately for the rescue crew that found the *Event Horizon*, the message was misheard and was not "liberate me" but was actually "liberate tutame ex inferis," which translated means "save yourself from hell." It doesn't get much more ominous than that! My technical reviewer pointed out that "liberate me" should actually have been translated as "free me," and therefore "liberate tutame ex inferis" would be "free me from hell." Now, I'm no Latin expert, and even though I found some possibly contradictory information on the Web, I tend to trust my tech reviewer here! Either way, that's one scary phrase in the context of the movie's story!

The first call returns 12 because 12 is obviously a numeric value. The second parameter, 5, would have been returned if it wasn't, as is seen in the second call, where Frank isn't numeric and so 123 is returned.

The Ext.getDom() method is one of the methods you'll probably wind up using most. It's a shorthand version of the ubiquitous document.getElementById() method. Simply pass it an ID and you'll get back a reference to the node, or null if it isn't found.

Say you have a reference to a node, and you want to remove it. Ext JS has you covered with the Ext.removeNode() method:

```
Ext.removeNode(Ext.getDom("removeMe"));
```

The Ext.type() method is another general-purpose function that is extremely useful. Pass it basically anything you want and it'll return its type. For example:

```
var sOut = "";
sOut += "Ext.type(new Function()): " +
  Ext.type(new Function()) + "<br>";
sOut += "Ext.type(123): " + Ext.type(123) + "<br>";
sOut += "Ext.type(\"test\"): " + Ext.type("test") + "<br>";
Ext.getDom("divOutput").innerHTML = sOut;
```

When you run this code, you'll see this output:

```
Ext.type(new Function()): function
Ext.type(123): number
Ext.type("test"): string
```

The next two methods I want to discuss go hand in hand: Ext.urlEncode() and Ext.urlDecode(). The Ext.urlEncode() method takes in an object and creates a URL-encoded string (what you'd append to a URL for a GET request that accepts parameters). With it you can do this:

```
var s = Ext.urlEncode({first:"Archie",last:"Bunker"}) ;
```

Now you have a string "first=Archie&last=Bunker" sitting in the variable s. Now, if you want to take that string and get an object out of it, you use Ext.urlDecode():

```
var o = Ext.urlDecode(s);
```

With that you could use alert(o.first); to get an alert() message with the text "Archie" in it.

The final method to discuss is Ext.onReady(). You'll see this in most of the examples in this chapter and throughout the project. Simply, Ext.onReady() tells Ext JS what function you want called when the DOM is loaded. This is *before* the typical onLoad event fires but also *before* images are loaded. This function is handy because it allows you to execute code without waiting for the entire page, and all dependent resources, to load. This helps your application load faster and makes it more responsive for the user.

Function

The Function class adds a number of methods to every single Function object in JavaScript. Let's begin with a look at the createSequence() method:

```
function add(num1, num2) {
  alert(num1 + num2);
}
function subtract(num1, num2) {
  alert(num1 - num2);
}
add(2, 2);
subtract(5, 3);
var doBoth = add.createSequence(subtract);
doBoth(10, 8);
```

The createSequence() method allows you to create a single function call that is actually two (or more) function calls executed in sequence. When this code is executed, four alert() messages appear in turn. The first says 4, since 2 + 2 = 4. The second says 2, since 5 – 3 = 2. The third and fourth are *both* a result of calling doBoth(). First, add() is called, passing it the parameters 10 and 8, so the alert() says 18. Then, subtract() is called, and the alert() message shows 2, since 10 – 8 = 2. The function passed to createSequence() is called with the same arguments as the Function createSequence() is called with.

Another interesting method is createInterceptor(). This provides a rudimentary form of aspect-oriented programming (AOP) whereby you can have a given function called before another is. For example:

```
var addMult = add.createInterceptor(function(num1, num2) {
  alert(num1 * num2);
});
addMult(6, 7);
```

Now, when addMult() is called, first the function defined inline in the call to createInterceptor() is executed, multiplying the two arguments and showing the result via alert(), 42 in this case. Then, add() is called, and we see 13 in a second alert() message. This is nice because you're tying two functions together in a loose way. The alternative would be to have add() call the inline function (which would be defined like any other function is in that case) before doing its own work, which makes them tightly coupled. The sort of loose coupling that createInterceptor() allows for is much cleaner, though.

■**Note** The createSequence() and createInterceptor() at first glance look quite similar, but there is one key distinction: with createInterceptor(), if the function passed to createInterceptor() returns false, then the function that createInterceptor() is called on will not be called. In this case, if the inline function returns false, then add() will not be called.

Next we'll talk about the defer() method, which allows you to execute the function you call it on after some period of time. This is a nice abstraction of the usual timeout() mechanism in JavaScript. In practice you would do something like this:

```
add.defer(3000, this, [8, 9]);
```

After three seconds (1,000 milliseconds per second, so 3,000 = 1,000 * 3), the add() function will be called, and the parameters 8 and 9 will be passed to it, so we'll see an alert() message saying 17. The argument this defines the object for which the scope is set. Also note that the call to defer() returns a number that is the ID of the timeout() created. This allows you to do a clearTimeout() before the function executes if you wish.

A BRIEF ASIDE ON ASPECT-ORIENTED PROGRAMMING

Aspect-oriented programming (AOP), sometimes called aspect-oriented software development (AOSD), is the technique whereby you identify so-called cross-cutting concerns and externalize them from the code in question.

A commonly used example is that of logging. Frequently, you want to output a log statement every time a given function is called. Typically, you would include some sort of log statement directly in the function. This works well enough, but the problem you quickly see is that you have logging code strewn all over the code because In all likelihood you want to do this in many functions.

AOP enables you to do the equivalent of telling your runtime environment, "Hey, do me a favor, buddy; output a log statement every time function A is called," without you having to specifically include the code to do so in the function. This is also an example of separation of concerns because what your function actually does is separated from the logging concern.

How this AOP approach is accomplished depends on the AOP implementation you use. Some work by modifying your code at compile time; others do so at runtime. Some truly work at the environment level, meaning your code is not modified and the function calls are instead intercepted somehow. The implementation isn't terribly important; the underlying concept is.

Number

The Number class extends the intrinsic Number JavaScript class and provides a single addition: the constrain() method. This method allows you to determine if the current value of the Number object falls within a given range by specifying a minimum and maximum value. If it does not fall within the range, constrain() will tell you which side of the range was exceeded by returning to you the minimum or maximum value as appropriate. Here's how it works:

```
var n = new Number(22);
alert(n.constrain(10, 25));
alert(n.constrain(1, 14));
```

This will result in two `alert()` messages, the first saying 22, because 22 falls within the range 10–25, and in that case `constrain()` returns the value of the Number object. The second `alert()` will say 14 because 22 is obviously outside the range 1–14, and it's higher than the maximum of 14, so that's the side of the range it exceeds.

String

The `String` class adds a couple of static methods to the intrinsic JavaScript `String` class, as well as two instance methods. For starters, there's the `escape()` method:

```
alert(String.escape("This\\is'a test"));
```

This results in the `alert()` pop-up seen in Figure 1-14.

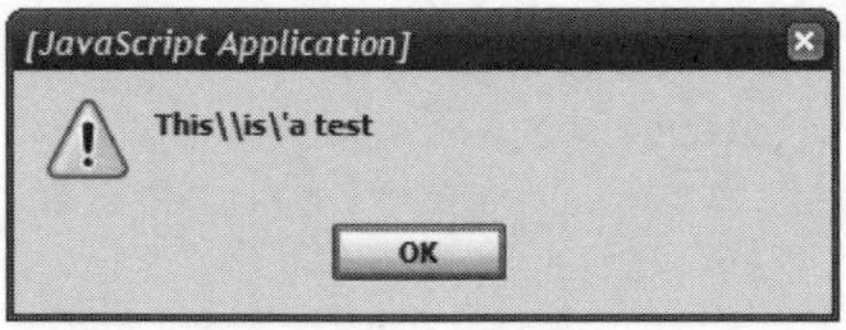

Figure 1-14. *The output of String.escape()*

The double backslash in the original string is itself escaped, so the content of the string would in fact be a single backslash. Then when the `escape()` method gets a hold of it, it's escaped, resulting in the double backslash you see in the output. The single quote is escaped as well.

The `format()` function is perhaps the handiest of all:

```
alert(String.format("Hello {0}, my name is {1}", "Barack", "Michelle"));
```

As you can see, it allows you to insert values into a string containing tokens. It's a simple positional insert, which means that subsequent arguments will be inserted sequentially into the target string, which is the first argument. So, "Barack" is inserted in place of token {0}, and "Michelle" into token {1}. The text in the `alert()` pop-up after that work is what you see in Figure 1-15.

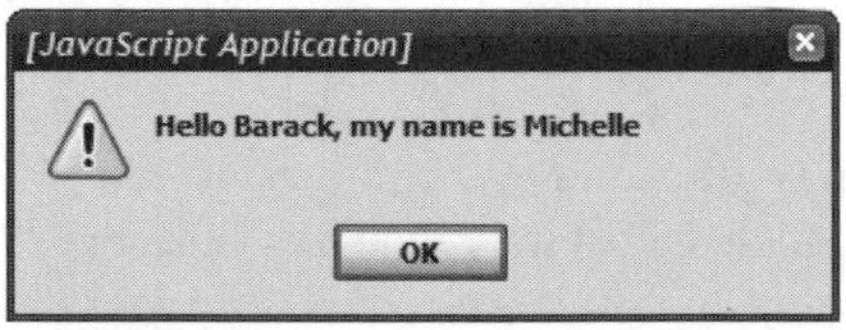

Figure 1-15. *The output of String.format()*

Next up is the `leftPad()` method, which gives you a convenient way to pad out values (most usually numbers, but not necessarily):

```
alert(String.leftPad("1234", 8, "0"));
```

The first argument is the value to pad out, and the second is the final length we want it to be. The final argument is the character to pad the first argument with, if its length initially is less than the second argument. So here the alert() message says "00001234," and if you don't believe me take a look at Figure 1-16!

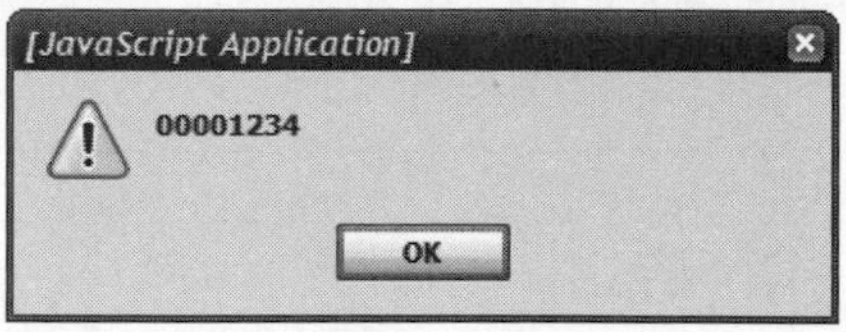

Figure 1-16. *The output of String.leftPad()*

The toggle() method is next, and it's a deceptively simple little function:

```
var s = "Republican";
alert(s.toggle("Republican", "Democrat"));
```

Here, the message in the alert() is as shown in Figure 1-17.

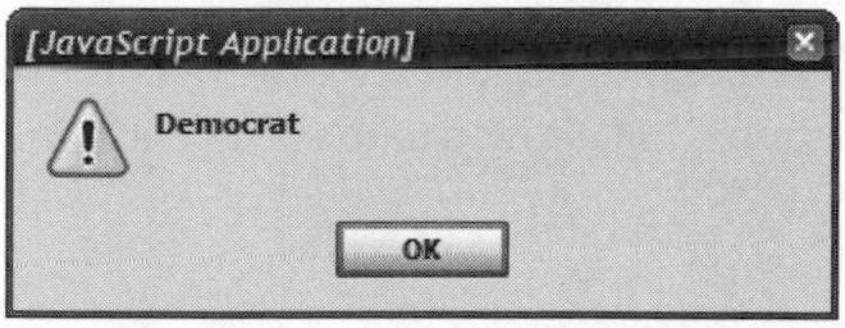

Figure 1-17. *The output of String.toggle()*

toggle() has compared the value of the string s to the literal string "Republican". If it matches, then it toggles the value and returns the second argument, "Democrat" in this case. If it was any other value it would have simply returned the current value of s. Note that the string s isn't altered by this call.

The final method in the String class is something I'm still surprised isn't built into JavaScript: the trim() method.

```
s = "    Trimmed String    ";
alert("\"" + s.trim() + "\"");
```

It's very simple but supremely helpful: given a string, trim whitespace from the start and end of it, leaving any spaces in the middle alone. You would imagine the next revision of JavaScript would finally eliminate the need for libraries to provide this function! Figure 1-18 shows the outcome of the example.

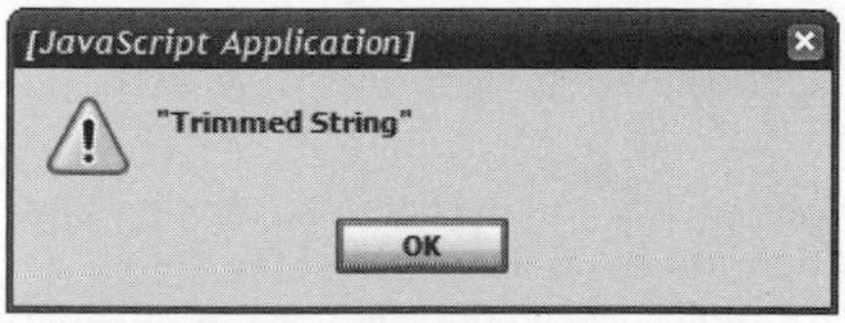

Figure 1-18. *The output of String.trim()*

> **■Note** There are a number of other classes in the global scope, including `CategoryAxis`, `NumericAxis`, `PieSeries`, `Series`, and `TimeAxis`. All of these are related to Ext JS's chart-generation capabilities. We'll touch on charting in Chapter 2 and then see it in action in Chapter 9, but since that is a somewhat more advanced topic I felt it better to not go into that stuff here. We're still getting our Ext JS "sea legs,"[10] so to speak, under us!

The Ext Namespace

The Ext namespace is chock-full of goodness, to put it mildly. As has been the case previously, it is not my intention to cover every single nook and cranny of it. My goal is to give you a solid overview of what's there, highlighting areas in more detail where I feel is warranted. So, without further ado, let's get to it!

Ext.Ajax

Ajax is, by most reckonings, the primary enabler of the whole RIA movement we are in the midst of. As such, you wouldn't expect any modern JavaScript library to not support it, and Ext JS is no exception. It provides a number of useful methods that allow you to fire asynchronous requests to a server. One of the simplest forms is this:

```
Ext.Ajax.request({
  url : "xxx", method : "post"
  params : { firstName : "Paul", lastName : "Newman" },
  headers : { fakeHeader : "someValue" },  disableCaching : true,
  success : function(opt, suc, res) {
    if (suc) {
      alert("The response was successful and was: " + res);
    }
  },
  failure : function(res, opt) {
    alert("Ajax failed: " + res);
  }
});
```

Here you can see the simple `Ext.Ajax.request()` method in action. It has a number of arguments that it accepts. The `url` argument tells the method what URL to request (xxx is obviously just a placeholder). The `method` argument, which defaults to `GET` but which I've overridden as `POST` here, specifies the HTTP method that will be used. The `params` argument is an object that includes extra parameters to include with the request. The `disableCaching` argument tells the method whether you want to ensure `POST` requests are never cached, which is

---

10   *Sea legs* is a term used to describe the ability of a person to walk steadily on the deck of a moving ship at sea. More informally, the term is often used to describe when you are in the process of learning something to mean that you aren't fully knowledgeable on the topic just yet, but you're working on it!

what true indicates. This appends a dynamic parameter onto the request to ensure a unique URL is requested no matter what. The success and failure arguments define callback functions to be executed when the request succeeds, or if it fails (communication failures, for instance). Each is passed the options (the opt argument) that were used to make the call, and the response (the res argument) that came back from the server. The success function also gets a Boolean argument (suc) that indicates whether the request succeeded. In addition, you can pass a form argument that names a form on the page from which parameters will be generated. There are also the xmlData and the jsonData arguments, which provide the method with an XML document or a JSON object, respectively, from which to generate parameters.

When you call this method, it returns a Number that is the transaction ID for the request. This is useful because you can then call the Ext.Ajax.abort() method, passing that transaction ID to it, to cancel the request if it is still in flight. Related to this is the Ext.Ajax.isLoading() method, which similarly accepts the transaction ID and tells you if the request is still outstanding.

As you saw, the form argument lets you serialize a form to generate parameters for the request. If you need to serialize a form without making an Ajax request, you can use the Ext.Ajax.serializeForm() method, which takes in the name of the form (or a reference to the form node in the DOM) and returns to you a URL-encoded string of parameters generated from it.

There are also a number of useful properties that you can set on the Ext.Ajax class. For example, the autoAbort property, when true, will cause any new request to abort any already in progress. The disableCaching property allows you to globally set whether all Ajax requests will include that cache-busting parameter that ensures unique URLs for every request. The method property allows you to set the default method (GET or POST) for all Ajax requests. The timeout property lets you tell Ext.Ajax how long it should wait for a request to return before it assumes it timed out (the default is 30,000, or 30 seconds).

In addition to all this, the Ext.Ajax class uses an event-driven model that lets you handle certain events globally. For example:

```
Ext.Ajax.on('beforerequest', function() { alert("About to do Ajax"); });
```

This hooks an event listener to the specified event and will cause an alert() pop-up to open before every Ajax request by calling the function passed as the second argument. The other events you can handle are requestcomplete, whenever a response comes back from the server, and requestexception, which occurs any time an HTTP error occurs.

You can also use the Ext.Ajax.hasListener() method to determine if there is currently a listener for a given event (pass the name of the event you want to check as the argument to it). You can use the Ext.Ajax.removeListener() to stop handling a given event (or use the Ext.Ajax.purgeListeners() to stop handling all events in one statement). There is an Ext.Ajax.suspendEvents() to temporarily stop handling all events, and there is even an Ext.Ajax.fireEvents() method that lets you fire a specific event without firing an Ajax request (pass it the name of the event to fire as the first argument and an object as the second that contains the parameters to pass to the listener for the event).

The Ext.Ajax class is an especially clean and simple, and yet powerful, Ajax implementation. It is very robust and yet extremely easy to use, essentially boiling down to a single method!

Ext.DomHelper

The Ext.DomHelper class is a handy utility class that allows you to easily create fragments of HTML and insert them into the DOM. If you've written code to work with the DOM methods, then you'll quickly realize how cool this class is (otherwise you'll just have to take my word for it!). Let's look at the complete source code for the example Ext_DomHelper.htm, shown in Listing 1-1.

Listing 1-1. *The Ext_DomHelper.htm Example*

```html
<html>
  <head>
    <title>Chapter 1 - Ext.util Namespace - EXT.DomHelper class</title>

    <script type="text/javascript" src="ext/adapter/ext/ext-base.js"></script>
    <script type="text/javascript" src="ext/ext-all.js"></script>

    <style>
      .cssTable {
        color : #ff0000;
        border : 1px solid #000000;
      }
      .cssCell {
        background-color : #eaeaea;
      }
    </style>

    <script>

    function testIt() {

      Ext.DomHelper.append("divTable", {
        id : "tblTable", tag : "table", cls : "cssTable", children : [
          { tag : "tr", id : "row1", children : [
              { tag : "td", cls : "cssCell", id : "row1_cell1", html : "1_1"},
              { tag : "td", cls : "cssCell", id : "row1_cell2", html : "1_2"},
              { tag : "td", cls : "cssCell", id : "row1_cell3", html : "1_3"}
            ]
          },
          { tag : "tr", id : "row2", children : [
              { tag : "td", cls : "cssCell", id : "row2_cell1", html : "2_1"},
              { tag : "td", cls : "cssCell", id : "row2_cell2", html : "2_2"},
              { tag : "td", cls : "cssCell", id : "row2_cell3", html : "2_3"}
            ]
          }
        ]
      });
```

```
        Ext.DomHelper.applyStyles(Ext.getDom("row2_cell2"), "color:#00ff00");
        Ext.DomHelper.insertAfter(Ext.getDom("tblTable"), {
          tag : "div", id : "divDiv1", html : "I am divDiv1"
        });
        alert(Ext.DomHelper.markup({
          tag : "div", id : "divDiv1", html : "I am divDiv1"
        }));

      }

      Ext.onReady(testIt);

    </script>

  </head>

  <body>
    <div id="divTable"></div>
  </body>

</html>
```

If you load Listing 1-1 in your browser, you will see a simple page that looks something like Figure 1-19.

When the page loads, because of the Ext.onReady() statement the testIt() method will execute. In this method we see the first use of DomHelper:

```
Ext.DomHelper.append("divTable", {
  id : "tblTable", tag : "table", cls : "cssTable", children : [
    { tag : "tr", id : "row1", children : [
        { tag : "td", cls : "cssCell", id : "row1_cell1", html : "1_1"},
        { tag : "td", cls : "cssCell", id : "row1_cell2", html : "1_2"},
        { tag : "td", cls : "cssCell", id : "row1_cell3", html : "1_3"}
      ]
    },
    { tag : "tr", id : "row2", children : [
        { tag : "td", cls : "cssCell", id : "row2_cell1", html : "2_1"},
        { tag : "td", cls : "cssCell", id : "row2_cell2", html : "2_2"},
        { tag : "td", cls : "cssCell", id : "row2_cell3", html : "2_3"}
      ]
    }
  ]
});
```

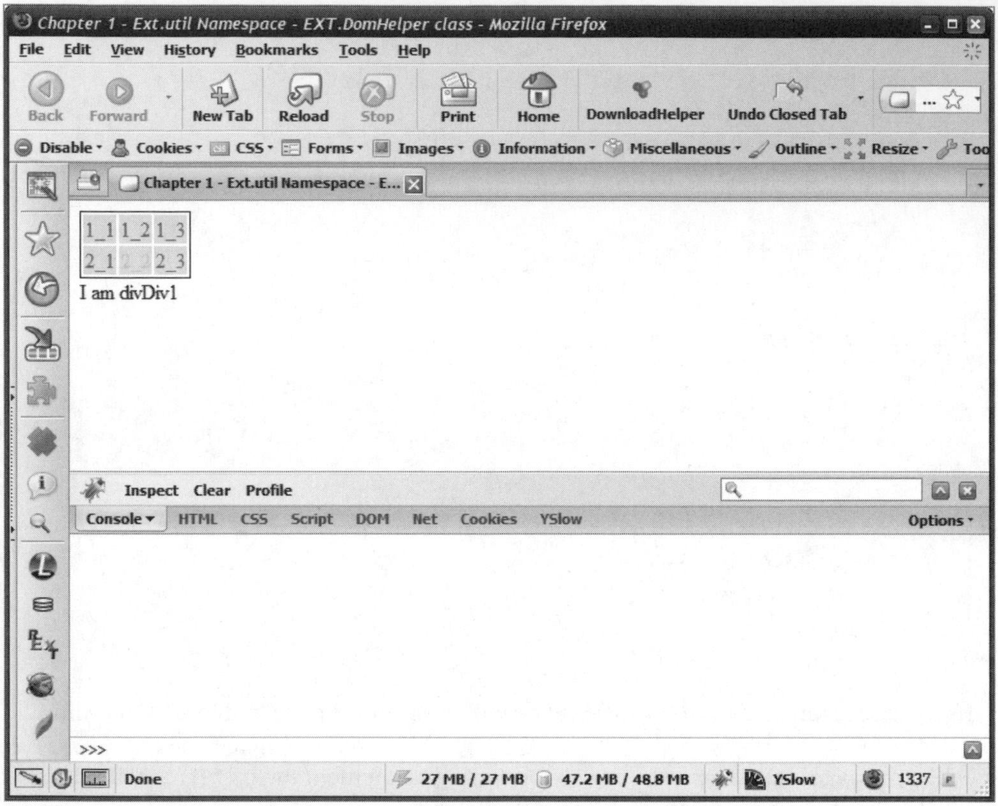

Figure 1-19. *The page you'll see when you load the page in Listing 1-1 in a browser*

This builds a table and inserts it into the `divTable` `<div>`. We use the `DomHelper.append()` method, and it's a simple enough beast. The first argument it takes is the ID of the DOM node to insert the generated HTML fragment into. The second argument is an object that describes the fragment to generate. First, we tell it what HTML tag we want to create, `table` in this case, using the tag `attribute`. We could create anything we want here, but a table is a good example because it allows us to see the `children` attribute in action. Even before that, though, we set an `id` of `tblTable` on the generated table, and we assign a style class of `cssTable` using the `cls` attribute.

Now, on to the `children` array. We can create as many children as we wish, and each child can itself have a `children` attribute. This allows us to create a hierarchy of elements as deep as we wish. The `html` attribute on each child is the content to insert in the element created.

In other words, you're simply creating some number of nested objects, each with the same attributes (`tag`, `html`, `cls`, `id`, and `children`) that describes a snippet of HTML in object form. `DomHelper` takes care of converting that into HTML and inserting it into the DOM.

It would probably be enlightening to jump ahead in the code a bit. The append() method isn't the only choice. We can also use insertBefore() method to insert the fragment before a given element. There is also insertAfter(), which inserts the fragment after the given element. You could also use insertFirst(), which inserts the fragment as the first child of the given element. In the example code you'll find an example of Ext.DomHelper.insertAfter() in action:

```
Ext.DomHelper.insertAfter(Ext.getDom("tblTable"), {
  tag : "div", id : "divDiv1", html : "I am divDiv1"
});
alert(Ext.DomHelper.markup({
  tag : "div", id : "divDiv1", html : "I am divDiv1"
}));
```

You'll also notice the Ext.DomHelper.markup() method is used. This returns the HTML fragment generated by a call to one of the insert methods. So, the alert() dialog here is what you see in Figure 1-20.

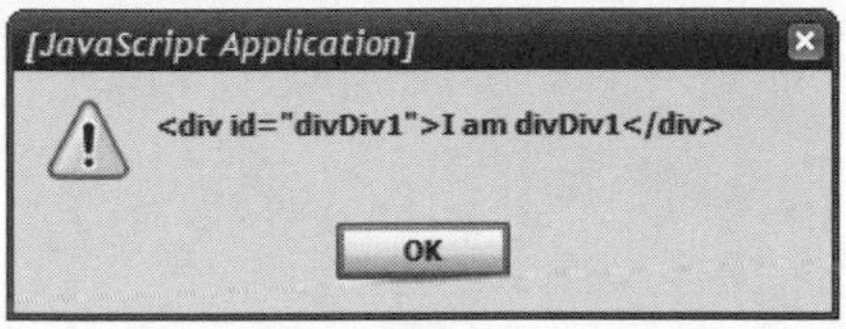

Figure 1-20. *The generated HTML fragment*

Hopefully that markup doesn't present any surprises, but it can be interesting to see what Ext JS is generating for us.

As an exercise, I suggest you insert a call to Ext.DomHelper.markup() and pass it the code in the first Ext.DomHelper.insert() call. This will show you the generated markup for the table. Go ahead, do that now—I'll wait!

The other method you can see in action here is Ext.DomHelper.applyStyles(), which, as its name implies, allows you to apply styles to a given DOM node. The first argument is the node itself, so I've used the Ext.getDom() method to get a reference to the second cell in the second row of the generated table. It then changes the text color to green, which you'll see if you load the page (you can't really tell from a black-and-white screenshot on the printed page obviously).

The DomHelper class, as you can see, is a handy tool indeed that saves you from having to mess around with the DOM API, which is frequently not a pleasant experience.

Ext.DomQuery

CSS selector queries are all the rage these days. The jQuery library is perhaps the main catalyst for this, but Ext JS provides a robust engine for CSS selector queries as well, encapsulated in the Ext.DomQuery class. In Listing 1-2 you can see examples of a number of its methods.

WHAT ARE CSS SELECTOR QUERIES?

In a nutshell, CSS selector queries are a mechanism for querying an HTML (or XML) document to retrieve one or more elements on the page in a collection, usually with the purpose of styling them in some way. The CSS3 selector spec is one way to query for elements, XPath is another, and Ext.DomQuery supports both.

Sometimes you want to manipulate a particular element on a page, and using `document.getElementById()` is a good choice, assuming the element is singular. But what if you want to, for example, style all the cells of all tables on the page so that their text is red, and you want to do this on the fly? Especially given that the contents of the table are possibly dynamically generated, you certainly don't want to try to retrieve each of them individually by ID. CSS selector queries allow you to do this succinctly.

Getting into constructing queries is a pretty extensive topic that I won't be covering in any detail in this book, so you may want to do some reading on that topic yourself. The Ext JS documentation for Ext.DomQuery has a decent summary, and a link to the official spec that includes more information and some good details.

Listing 1-2. *The DomQuery Class in Action*

```html
<html>
  <head>
    <title>Chapter 1 - Ext.util Namespace - EXT.DomQuery class</title>

    <script type="text/javascript" src="ext/adapter/ext/ext-base.js"></script>
    <script type="text/javascript" src="ext/ext-all.js"></script>

    <style>
      .cssRow1 {
        color : #ff0000;
      }
      .cssRow2 {
        color : #0000ff;
      }
      .cssCell {
        background-color : #00ff00;
      }
      .cssCellAlt {
        background-color : #eaeaea;
      }
    </style>

    <script>

    function testIt() {
```

```
        var query = "td[class=\"cssCell\"]";
        var elems = Ext.DomQuery.select(query);
        for (var i = 0; i < elems.length; i++) {
          console.log(query + " = elems[" + i + "].firstChild.nodeValue = " +
            elems[i].firstChild.nodeValue);
        }
        query = "td[class=\"cssCellAlt\"]";
        var f = Ext.DomQuery.compile(query);
        elems = f(Ext.getDom("row1"));
        for (var i = 0; i < elems.length; i++) {
          console.log(query + " = elems[" + i + "].firstChild.nodeValue = " +
            elems[i].firstChild.nodeValue);
        }
        query = "tr[class=\"cssRow2\"]";
        console.log("Ext.DomQuery.is(Ext.getDom(\"row2\"), " + query + ") = " +
          Ext.DomQuery.is(Ext.getDom("row2"), query));
        query = "td";
        elems = Ext.DomQuery.select(query);
        console.log("Filtered list = " +
          Ext.DomQuery.filter(elems, "td[class=\"cssCell\"]").length);

      }

      Ext.onReady(testIt);

    </script>

  </head>

  <body>
    <table border="1" cellpadding="2" cellspacing="2">
      <tr id="row1" class="cssRow1">
        <td class="cssCell">row1_cell1</td>
        <td class="cssCellAlt">row1_cell2</td>
        <td class="cssCell">row1_cell3</td>
        <td class="cssCellAlt">row1_cell4</td>
      </tr>
      <tr id="row2" class="cssRow2">
        <td>row2_cell1</td>
        <td>row2_cell2</td>
        <td>row2_cell3</td>
        <td>row2_cell4</td>
      </tr>
    </table>
  </body>

</html>
```

The first thing to take note of is the table structure in the <body> of the document. It is this structure that we'll be querying against. Note too the style classes applied to the elements. It is these settings specifically that are queried against.

If you open this page in Firefox with Firebug installed, Figure 1-21 will be the output in Firebug's console pane.

Note Of course, if you aren't using Firefox, or don't have Firebug installed… *why not?* Seriously, though, to run this example you'll need to replace the console.log() calls with suitable replacements; alert() should work fine in this case. The discussion that follows assumes you're using Firefox with Firebug installed.

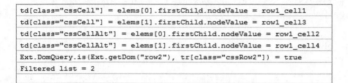

```
td[class="cssCell"] = elems[0].firstChild.nodeValue = row1_cell1
td[class="cssCell"] = elems[1].firstChild.nodeValue = row1_cell3
td[class="cssCellAlt"] = elems[0].firstChild.nodeValue = row1_cell2
td[class="cssCellAlt"] = elems[1].firstChild.nodeValue = row1_cell14
Ext.DomQuery.is(Ext.getDom("row2"), tr[class="cssRow2"]) = true
Filtered list = 2
```

Figure 1-21. *The console output for this page*

The first two lines of output are a result of this code:

```
var query = "td[class=\"cssCell\"]";
var elems = Ext.DomQuery.select(query);
for (var i = 0; i < elems.length; i++) {
  console.log(query + " = elems[" + i + "].firstChild.nodeValue = " +
    elems[i].firstChild.nodeValue);
}
```

First, a simple selector query is created. The query td[class="cssCell"] looks up all <td> tags on the page that have a class attribute setting of cssCell. This query is passed to the Ext.DomQuery.select() method, which returns an array of matching elements (you can pass a second optional argument, a reference to a DOM Element, that would limit the scope of the query, instead of querying the entire document as this example does). We can then iterate over that array and output the value of the cell. We have to drill down through the hierarchy a bit because each element of the array is a DOM Element object, and the firstChild of the Element is the text within the cell (it's actually a text node), and then the nodeValue attribute of that child is the actual text contents of the cell.

Now, being able to do queries with Ext.DomQuery.select() is neat enough, but it turns out to not be the most efficient thing out there. Precompiling the query when you know you're going to be doing it a lot is far more efficient, and Ext.DomQuery allows for that via the compile() method:

```
query = "td[class=\"cssCellAlt\"]";
var f = Ext.DomQuery.compile(query);
elems = f(Ext.getDom("row1"));
for (var i = 0; i < elems.length; i++) {
  console.log(query + " = elems[" + i + "].firstChild.nodeValue = " +
    elems[i].firstChild.nodeValue);
}
```

This time, we pass the query to `Ext.DomQuery.compile()`, which returns a `Function` object. We can then call on that function, passing in a root node to begin the search at (this is optional), and after that it works exactly as we saw before. The `Ext.DomQuery.compile()` method is important if you are going to be reusing the same query many times.

Something else that can come up is the need to determine if a given `Element` matches some query. You could perform a query and then see if you got any matches, but there's a more concise way to do it:

```
query = "tr[class=\"cssRow2\"]";
console.log("Ext.DomQuery.is(Ext.getDom(\"row2\"), " + query + ") = " +
  Ext.DomQuery.is(Ext.getDom("row2"), query));
```

The `Ext.DomQuery.is()` method allows you to pass in an `Element` (retrieve using `Ext.getDom()` here) and a query, and it will return `true` if the element matches the query and `false` if not.

Another commonly needed function is the ability to take an existing array of `Elements` and filter it based on a query. The code in the example that demonstrates looks like this:

```
query = "td";
elems = Ext.DomQuery.select(query);
console.log("Filtered list = " +
  Ext.DomQuery.filter(elems, "td[class=\"cssCell\"]").length);
```

First, a query is performed to get an array of all the `<td>` elements on the page (a total of eight). Next, `Ext.DomQuery.filter()` is used to get an array of only those `Elements` matching the query td[class="cssCell"]. That's why we get the display "2" in Firebug's console; only two `<td>` elements match that query. You can optionally pass a second boolean argument to `Ext.DomQuery.filter()`. If you pass `true`, you'll get only the elements that *do not* match the query.

Ext.Updater

Earlier we took a look at the `Ext.Ajax` class. Now we're going to look at another bit of Ajax functionality provided by Ext JS: the `Ext.Updater` class. This allows us to perform Ajax updates of a DOM element, and perhaps more importantly, allows us to do that periodically. Here's a simple example:

```
var u = new Ext.Updater("myDiv");
u.startAutoRefresh(30, "http://somedomain.com/somePage.jsp");
```

This will cause an Ajax request to fire every 30 seconds to the URL specified as the second argument to `u.startAutoRefresh()`. The results will be inserted into the DOM node with ID `myDiv` (presumably a `<div>`).

If you only need to update the element once as opposed to repeatedly, the `Ext.Updater.update()` method is available:

```
var e = Ext.get("myDiv");
var u = e.getUpdater();
u.update({
  url: "http://somedomain.com/somePage.jsp",
  params: { param1 : "Mister", param2 : "Softie" }
});
```

As you can see, passing parameters is available as well, so you can handle dynamic data easily. You can also see the `Ext.get()` method in use. This returns an `Ext.Element` object representing the specified DOM node. An `Ext.Element` object essentially "wraps" a DOM node and provides additional functionality to it, including methods like `getUpdater()`.

If you have an instance of `Ext.Updater()`, as via the `var u = e.getUpdater();` line in the example code but you no longer have a reference the DOM node it is bound to, you can call `getEl()` on the `Updater` to get such a reference. You can also call `abort()` on the `Ext.Updater` instance to abort any currently in-flight requests. The `isAutoRefreshing()` will return `true` if the `Ext.Updater` instance is set to automatically refresh and `false` if not. The `isUpdating()` method tells you if an update is currently in progress (`true`) or not (`false`). Finally, the `refresh()` method can be called on an `Ext.Updater` instance, even if it was a onetime update, to perform the update again.

The Ext.util Namespace

The `Ext.util` namespace contains a number of classes that provide some…wait for it… *utility*-type functions, hence the name! We're talking about general-purpose stuff here, and nothing specific to building UIs.

Ext.util.CSS

The `Ext.util.CSS` class is a singleton with a couple of useful methods for dealing with style sheets. The first is `Ext.util.CSS.createStyleSheet()`:

```
Ext.util.CSS.createStyleSheet(".cssDiv1{color:#ff0000;}", "ssDiv1");
```

Assuming you have an element on the page that has a class attribute value of `cssDiv1`, any text in that element will be turned red at this point because the `.cssDiv1` selector has been modified to change the color to red (`#ff0000`). You can modify that selector like so:

```
Ext.util.CSS.updateRule(".cssDiv1", "color", "#00ff00");
```

The first argument is the selector name, the second is the attribute to update, and the third is the new value. Once that code is executed you can get the contents of the selector like this:

```
var rule = Ext.util.CSS.getRule(".cssDiv1");
alert(rule);
```

This will display [object CSSStyleRule], which isn't terribly helpful. If you instead use the code

```
console.log(rule);
```

assuming you have Firebug installed in Firefox (and are running this code there!), you'll see the object displayed in the console. You can expand it to see the selectorText attribute, which displays .cssDiv1{color:#00ff00;} now after the color change, proving it worked. You can also use the Ext.util.CSS.getRules()to get all the rules active in the document. Optionally, you can pass true to that method, which will cause the rules cache to be refreshed, which is useful if you've made changes.

If down the road you want to entirely remove a style sheet—say you don't want that text to be green anymore—you can use the Ext.util.CSS.removeStyleSheet() method:

```
Ext.util.CSS.removeStyleSheet("ssDiv1");
```

The text will then turn back to the default color (black most likely).

Finally, with the Ext.util.CSS.getRules() method, there was that optional argument to refresh the rules cache. Although it didn't seem to be necessary in my testing, an Ext.util.CSS.refreshCache() method exists that can be called if you've dynamically added style sheets.

Ext.util.DelayedTask

The DelayedTask provides an abstraction around JavaScript's setTimeout() function. To use it, you use code that looks like this:

```
var t = new Ext.util.DelayedTask(
  function(inTime) {
    alert(inTime);
  }, this, [ new Date() ]
);
t.delay(3000);
```

After three seconds, an alert() pop-up will appear with the current date/time showing, as you can see in Figure 1-22.

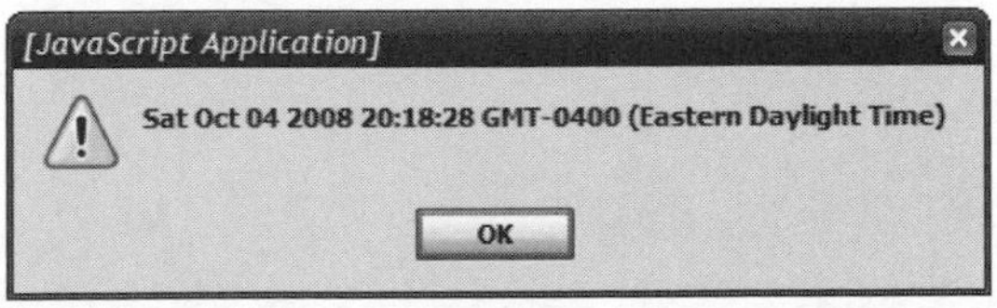

Figure 1-22. *The alert() seen after the delay period completes*

The first argument is obviously the function to execute. The second is the scope in which the function will execute, in this case the this keyword, and the third is an array of arguments to pass to the function. Note that the parameters are instantiated at the time of the call to `Ext.util.DelayedTask()`. In other words, the `Date` object created as part of declaring that array will show a time three seconds prior to when the `alert()` appears. Lastly, note that the function specified as the first argument will not fire until a call is made to `delay()`, because internally `setTimeout()` is used (presumably... I haven't examined the code to verify that, but it *acts* as if it is used, which is what matters). That call isn't made until `delay()` is called to define how long to wait until the function fires.

Ext.util.Format

The `Ext.util.Format` class contains a number of static methods for formatting values in one fashion or another. It has some methods that deal with strings, some that deal with numeric monetary values, and so on. Let's take a look at each, beginning with the `Ext.util.Format.capitalize()` method:

```
alert(Ext.util.Format.capitalize("this is a test"));
```

This results in an `alert()` pop-up that reads "This is a test", capitalizing the first letter, which you can see for yourself in Figure 1-23.

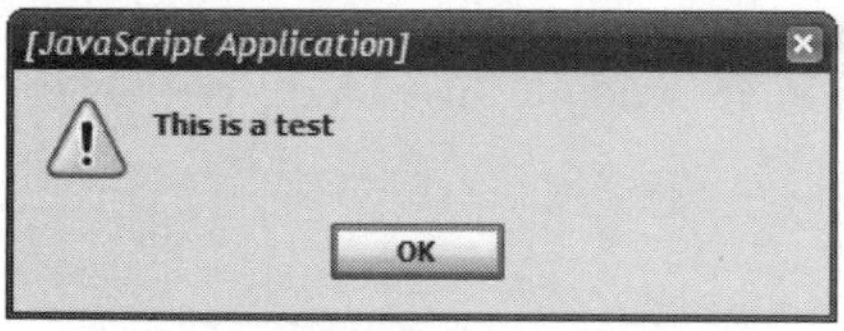

Figure 1-23. *The output of Ext.util.Format.capitalize()*

Similar to this is `Ext.util.Format.uppercase()`:

```
alert(Ext.util.Format.uppercase("this is a test"));
```

From that you wind up with Figure 1-24 on your screen. As you likely guessed, there is an `Ext.util.Format.lowercase()` method as well.

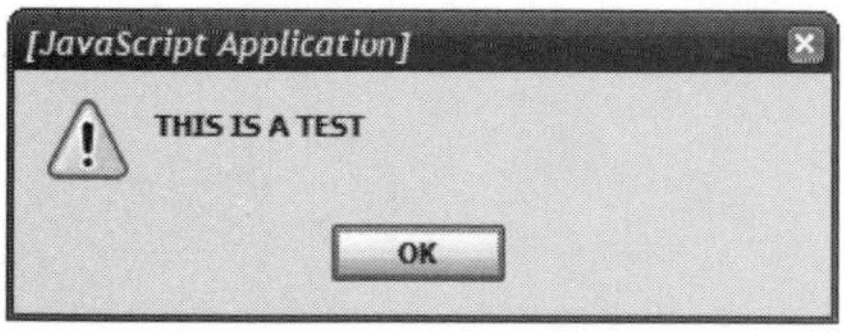

Figure 1-24. *The output of Ext.util.Format.uppercase()*

The `Ext.util.Format.date()`method formats a date:

```
alert(Ext.util.Format.date(new Date()));
```

The message seen here is something like "09/03/2008", depending on the date you run it of course, as in Figure 1-25. There is an optional second argument that specifies the format to use, but this example will use the default "m/d/y".

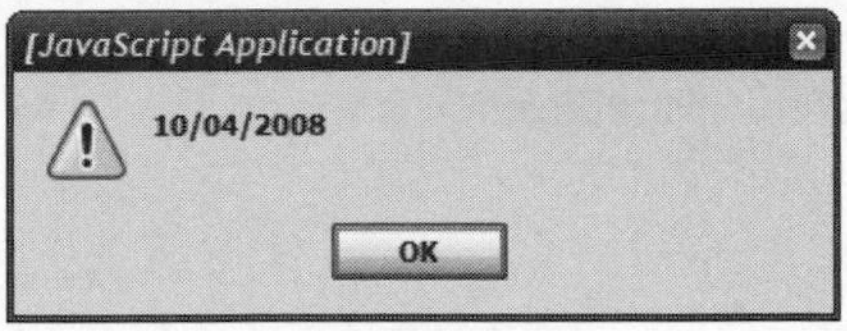

Figure 1-25. *The output of Ext.util.Format.date()*

The `Ext.util.Format.defaultValue()`method is interesting:

```
alert(Ext.util.Format.defaultValue("", "myDefault"));
```

The `alert()` message here is "myDefault", as you see in Figure 1-26, because the first argument (which is what's being checked by `Ext.util.Format.defaultValue()`) is empty— which is precisely what this method is for.

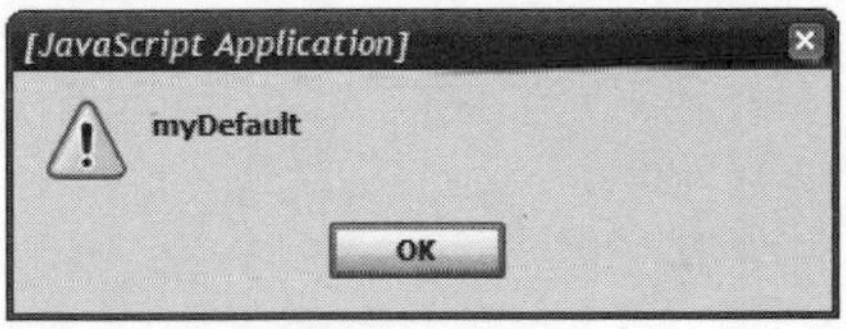

Figure 1-26. *The output of Ext.util.Format.defaultValue()*

Similar to this is the `Ext.util.Format.undef()` method, which returns an empty string if the passed-in argument is undefined. So, you'd get an empty string back from this example:

```
var z;
alert(Ext.util.Format.undef(z));
```

If z was instead defined in some way, you'd get the value of z back.
The `Ext.util.Format.ellipsis()` method is next:

```
alert(Ext.util.Format.ellipsis("I am way too long", 8));
```

This results in the string shown in Figure 1-27 because the first argument, a string to check, is greater than the length specified by the second argument, so it is truncated and an ellipsis is appended to the end.

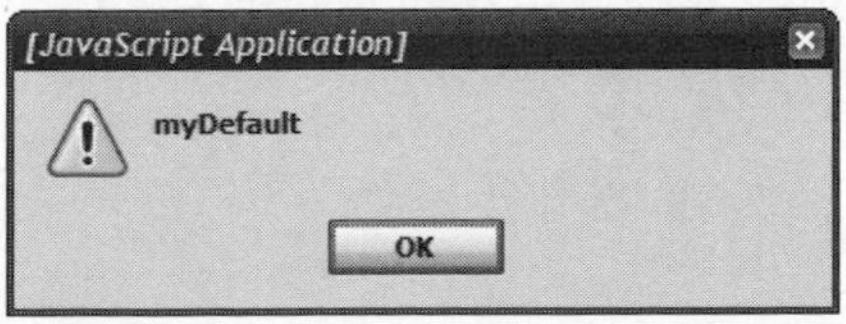

Figure 1-27. *The output of Ext.util.Format.ellipsis()*

Let's say you want to format the amount of space remaining on a hard drive for display to the user. Ext JS has you covered:

```
alert(Ext.util.Format.fileSize("187387234"));
```

Note that this method accepts a number or a string and either will be formatted properly (a string will be returned in both cases). The result of the example code is shown in Figure 1-28.

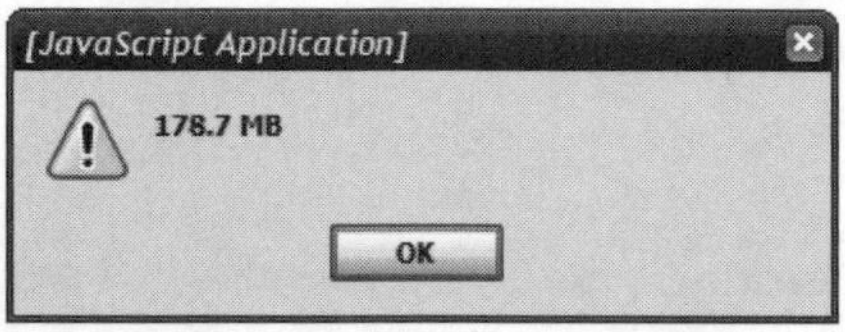

Figure 1-28. *The output of Ext.util.Format.fileSize()*

`Ext.util.Format.htmlDecode()` and `Ext.util.Format.htmlEncode()` are next, and their names pretty well tell you what they do:

```
alert(Ext.util.Format.htmlDecode("&lt;&gt;"));
alert(Ext.util.Format.htmlEncode("<>"));
```

This code gives you two alerts, shown in Figure 1-29 and Figure 1-30.

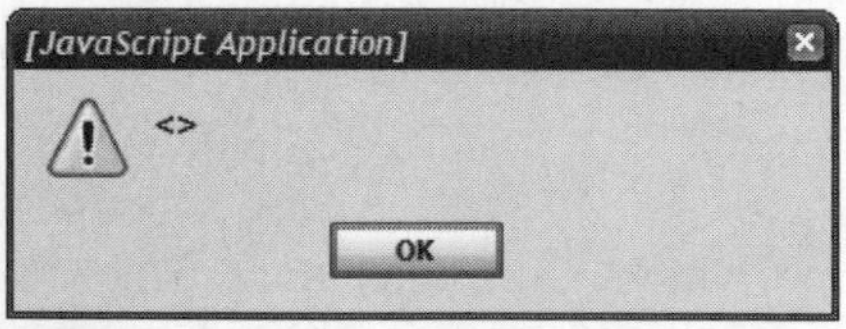

Figure 1-29. *The output of Ext.util.Format.htmlDecode()*

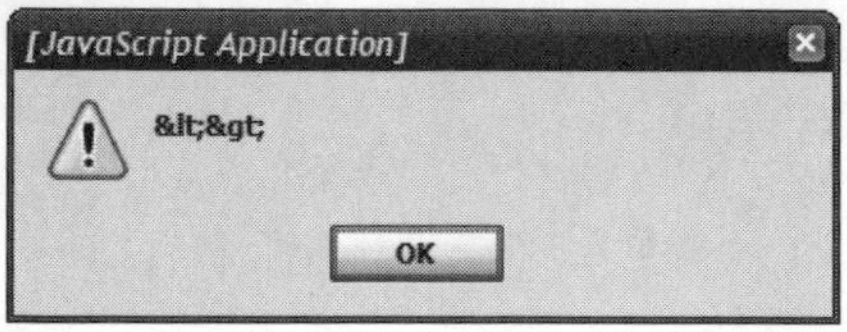

Figure 1-30. *The output of Ext.util.Format.htmlEncode()*

Ext JS supplies the usual `trim()` method in the form of `Ext.util.Format.trim()`, which I suspect doesn't need to be demonstrated. It simply strips leading and trailing space from a string you pass to it. There is also an `Ext.util.Format.substr()` method, which is used like this:

```
alert(Ext.util.Format.substr("JoanJessBess", 4, 4));
```

This code will display "Jess" because it grabbed four characters out of the string passed as the first argument, starting with the fourth character (1-based indexing here). Figure 1-31 proves that this is indeed the result.

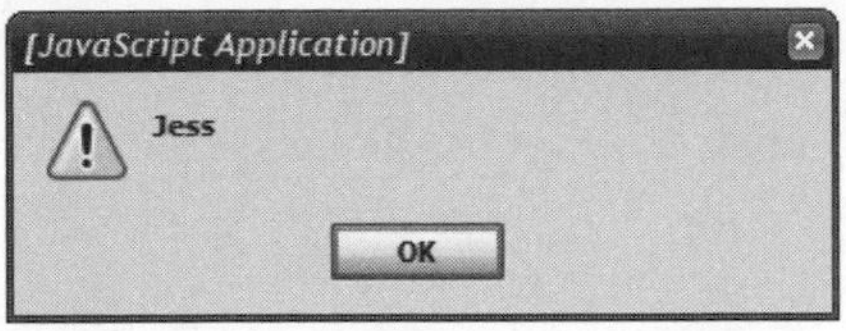

Figure 1-31. *The output of Ext.util.Format.substr()*

The next method to see in action is `Ext.util.Format.usMoney()`, which formats a string or numeric value based on US money formatting rules. For example:

```
alert(Ext.util.Format.usMoney("1234.56"));
```

This results in Figure 1-32.

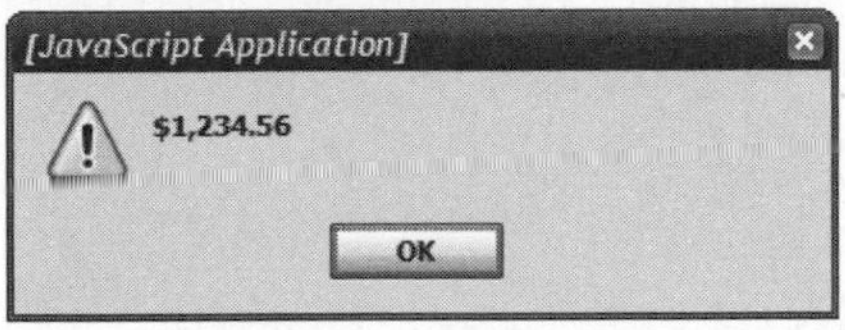

Figure 1-32. *The output of Ext.util.Format.usMoney()*

The last method we'll look at is `Ext.util.Format.stripTags()`. This method strips out HTML tags from a string, like so:

```
alert(Ext.util.Format.stripTags("<tag1>Tag1 stripped</tag1>"));
```

The displayed value will be simply what you see in Figure 1-33; the HTML tags have been removed.

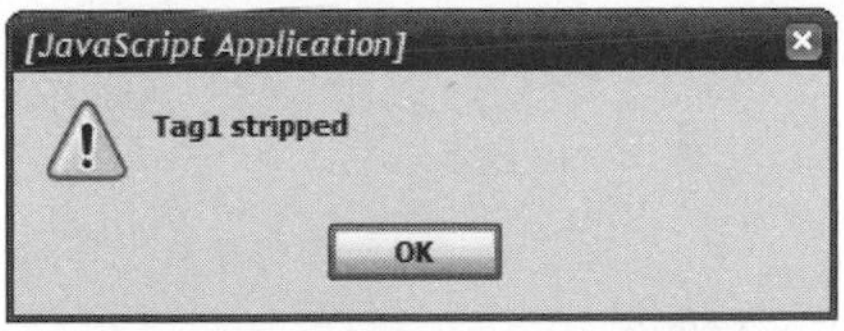

Figure 1-33. *The output of Ext.util.Format.stripTags()*

Ext.util.JSON

The `Ext.util.JSON` class is a pretty simple animal but a very useful one. It contains only two methods: `encode()` and `decode()`. Here are some working examples:

```
var o = Ext.util.JSON.decode(
  "{ firstName : \"Dudley\", lastName : \"Moore\" }");
alert(o.firstName + " " + o.lastName);
alert(Ext.util.JSON.encode(o));
```

The first `alert()` results in what you see in Figure 1-34 because the string of JSON was encoded to an object, from which the `alert()` references fields to generate the message.

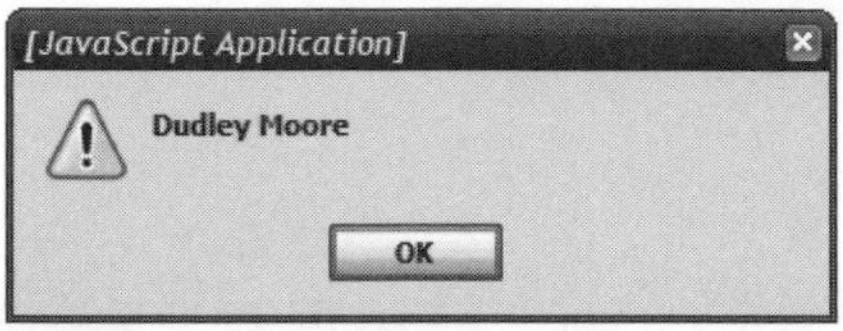

Figure 1-34. *The output of Ext.util.JSON.decode(), first alert()*

The second `alert()`, shown in Figure 1-35, shows the same (nearly) string that was passed to `Ext.util.JSON.decode()`. There are slight differences because `Ext.util.JSON.encode()` puts quotes around the field names as well as the values, but syntactically it's identical. Note that you can pass an array to `Ext.util.JSON.encode()` as well.

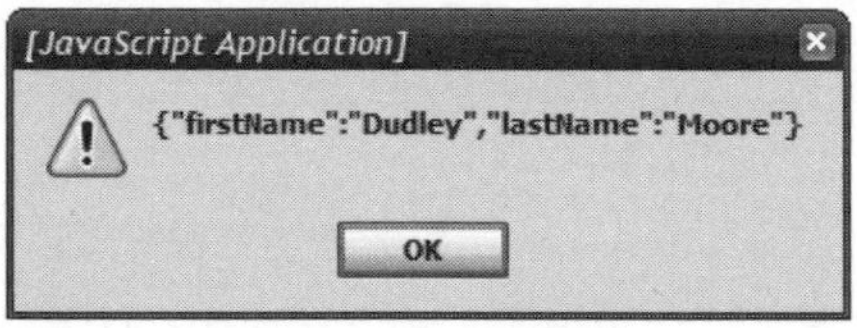

Figure 1-35. *The output of Ext.util.JSON.decode(),second alert()*

Ext.util.MixedCollection

The `Ext.util.MixedCollection` class is essentially a hybrid data structure that combines a `Map` with a `List`. As such, it contains methods that come from both of those structures, plus a few unique ones. Let's start with looking at how to instantiate an `Ext.util.MixedCollection` and how to add some items to it:

```
var mc = new Ext.util.MixedCollection();
mc.add("John", "Resig");
mc.addAll(
  { "Alex" : "Russell", "Joe" : "Walker", "Jack" : "Slocum" }
);
console.log(mc);
```

This adds four key/value pairs to the `Ext.util.MixedCollection`. The keys are "John", "Alex", "Joe", and "Jack", and the corresponding values are "Resig", "Russell", "Walker", and "Slocum" (the four giants of the JavaScript world I'd say, no disrespect to Brendan Eich or Douglas Crockford intended!). Assuming you run the code in Firefox and have Firebug installed, the `console.log(mc)` statement will result in the exploded view of the `Ext.util.MixedCollection` shown in Figure 1-36 (after you click on the line in the console).

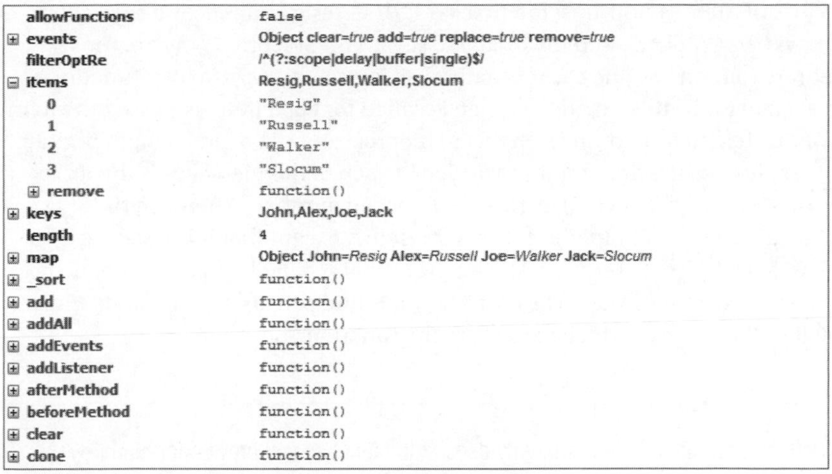

allowFunctions	false
⊞ events	Object clear=*true* add=*true* replace=*true* remove=*true*
filterOptRe	/^(?:scope|delay|buffer|single)$/
⊟ items	Resig,Russell,Walker,Slocum
0	"Resig"
1	"Russell"
2	"Walker"
3	"Slocum"
⊞ remove	function()
⊞ keys	John,Alex,Joe,Jack
length	4
⊞ map	Object John=*Resig* Alex=*Russell* Joe=*Walker* Jack=*Slocum*
⊞ _sort	function()
⊞ add	function()
⊞ addAll	function()
⊞ addEvents	function()
⊞ addListener	function()
⊞ afterMethod	function()
⊞ beforeMethod	function()
⊞ clear	function()
⊞ clone	function()

Figure 1-36. *The expanded view of the MixedCollection*

■**Note** Incidentally, something that threw me for a loop occurred here. If you run the entire example as presented in the source download for this book (Ext_util_MixedCollection.htm), you will likely see that the first console.log()'s output doesn't show all four items. This appears to be a timing issue because everything works as expected, but what you see in the console isn't right (at least that was the case on my PC). I don't know if this is a bug in Firebug or truly a timing issue of some sort, but it was disconcerting.

Now, let's say you want to see whether a given key is present in the Ext.util.MixedCollection or whether a given value is present. There are two methods specifically for doing both:

```
alert(mc.containsKey("John"));
alert(mc.contains("Walker"));
```

Both of these return true because there is indeed a value with a key of "John" and there is a value "Walker" present.

Now, what if you need to do something to each element in the Ext.util.MixedCollection? That too is easy to achieve, as you can see here:

```
mc.each(function(item, idx, len) {
  alert(idx + "/" + len + ": " + item);
});
mc.eachKey(function(key, item) {
  alert(key + " = " + item);
});
```

The each() method allows you to iterate over the collection of items in the Ext.util. MixedCollection. An item in this context really means the values, *not* the combination of key and value, which the term "item" might seem to imply. When the iteration using each()

executes, it results in four `alert()` pop-ups: the first says "0/4: Resig", the second says "1/4: Russell", the third says "2/4: Walker", and the final one says "3/4: Slocum". Why are those messages displayed? As you can see, the `each()` method accepts as an argument a function, which is called for each item. To this function, which is called for each item, is passed the item (value), the index of the item in the `Ext.util.MixedCollection`, and the overall length of the `Ext.util.MixedCollection`. So, the first number you see in each of the messages is the index value, which is zero-based, and the second is the length, or the number of items in the `Ext.util.MixedCollection`. The `eachKey()` method works the same, except that it is iterating over all the keys in the `Ext.util.MixedCollection`. The function that is called for each accepts the key and the value associated with the key. The `eachKey()` method can also accept a second argument that specifies the scope in which to execute the function.

■Note I actually found this behavior a little weird: why doesn't the function you provide for `eachKey()` receive an index value like the one for `each()` does? It seems to me that you might want the information there as well (ditto for the length). I'm sure there's some reason, but I found it a bit strange and thought it was worth pointing out.

If you were paying attention, you may have taken note of the index value that you get with `each()`. So far, `Ext.util.MixedCollection` has looked like a pretty typical `Map` in most regards. However, an index is typically associated with a `List` structure. This is why I said `Ext.util.MixedCollection` is a hybrid structure: it has characteristics of both. Now we're going to see how it's like a `List` (you could argue in fact that `each()` and `eachKey()` are `List`-like structures as well, since iterating over elements in a `Map`, while not totally unusual, isn't really typical either). So, let's say you want to know the index of a given key. That's easy:

```
alert(mc.indexOfKey("Joe"));
```

This will return 2 in our example, since that's where "Joe" appears. Because it's a `List`, to some extent order is maintained, which isn't usually a guarantee of a `Map`. Again, we see the hybridization here.

Now, how about if you want to retrieve a specific index? That too is easy:

```
alert(mc.get(1) + " - " + mc.get("Alex"));
```

The `get()` method accepts an index value and returns the associated value, so we get "Russell" in this case. I hedged a little bit here though because as you can see, `get()` can do more than that! You can also specify a key to get the associated value. So, in fact, the `alert()` message we seen here is "Russell – Russell". I've simply retrieved the same value two different ways, one `List`-like and one `Map`-like.

We saw at first how we can add items, but what if we want to replace the value of one? All it takes is a call to the `replace()` method:

```
mc.replace("John", "Sheridan" );
```

Now, the key "John" is associated with the value "Sheridan" instead of "Resig". You can outright remove items as well of course:

```
mc.remove("Joe");
mc.removeAt(0);
```

Again, you can do things the Map-like way, which means removing by key using the remove() method, or you can do it the List-like way, which means removing by index using the removeAt() method. The Ext.util.MixedCollection at this point contains only Alex=Russell and Jack=Slocum.

Ext.util.TaskRunner

The Ext.util.TaskRunner is a mechanism that allows you to run arbitrary tasks in a multi-threaded manner. Its usage is extremely simple, as this example illustrates:

```
var task1 = {
  run : function() {
    Ext.fly("divDT").update(new Date());
  }, interval : 500
}
var task2 = {
  run : function() {
    Ext.fly("divCount").update(count);
    count = count + 1;
    if (count == 5) {
      runner.stop(task1);
    }
    if (count == 10) {
      runner.stopAll();
    }
  }, interval : 750
}
runner = new Ext.util.TaskRunner();
runner.start(task1);
runner.start(task2);
```

A task is defined as an object with two attributes: run, which is a reference to a function to execute, and interval, which is how frequently to execute it (in milliseconds). So here, two tasks are created. The first executes every half a second and simply inserts the current date and time into the <div> divDT. The second task fires every three-quarters of a second and just increments a counter each time. These tasks are run by instantiating a new instance of Ext.util.TaskRunner, and then passing each task to the start() method.

The second task, when it reaches a count of five, will stop the first task by calling the Ext.util.TaskRunner.stop() method, passing a reference to the task to stop. When that task reaches a count of ten, it stops all tasks (which is just itself at that point) by calling the Ext.util.TaskRunner.stopAll() method. Believe it or not, that pretty much does it for this class! It's simple but an effective tool none the less.

IS THIS TRUE MULTITHREADING?

I don't think I would testify to this in court, but I suspect, without looking at the Ext JS source code, that this is not true multithreading. I say this because JavaScript is inherently single-threaded, and the only way to do "multithreading" is with timeouts and intervals.

Now, you can get something more akin to true multithreading by installing Google's Gears extension, which we'll get into later. You can also hold out for official, standard support for something called Web-Workers, which is multithreading for JavaScript. That technology is still working its way through standards bodies, however (for details see www.whatwg.org/specs/web-workers/current-work) so in the meantime Gears is probably the best choice.

This is all beside the point, though, to the extent that `Ext.util.TaskRunner` gives you a nice, clean approximation of multithreading in JavaScript, as close as you're likely to get with the current implementations and without any add-ons like Gears. It certainly does make working with intervals a breeze, if nothing else.

Ext.util.TextMetrics

The `Ext.util.TextMetrics` class gives you a handy mechanism to get information about the size of text. This might not sound like much on the surface, but it's actually a handy thing to be able to do. Oftentimes you need to know how much space, right down to the pixel, a certain amount of text will take up given a set of style settings. That's precisely what `Ext.util.TextMetrics` can do for you. Check out this code:

```
var tm = Ext.util.TextMetrics.createInstance(Ext.getDom("div1"));
var h = tm.getHeight("How tall am I?");
var s = tm.getSize("How big am I?");
var w = tm.getWidth("How wide am I?");
alert("getHeight() = " + h + "\n" +
  "getSize() = " + s.width + "/" + s.height + " (width/height)\n" +
  "getWidth() = " + w);
```

Assume too that there's a <div> on the page like so:

```
<div id="div1" style="font-size:32pt;">This is some text</div>
```

In Figure 1-37 you can see the resulting `alert()` pop-up.

Figure 1-37. *The alert() pop-up generated by running the Ext.util.TextMetrics example code*

You begin by instantiating an instance of `Ext.util.TextMetrics` and passing it a reference to a DOM node. This is necessary because the node gives the class information about the styles to use in its calculations. Then, it's a simple matter of calling methods like `getHeight()`, which tells you how tall in pixels the given text is, or `getWidth()`, which does the same but tells you how many pixels wide the text is. The `getSize()` method essentially gives you both combined in a single object, but it's based on the internal element's style and width properties. Note that if you are trying to get the height of a multiline bit of text, you will likely have to call `Ext.util.TextMetrics.setFixedWidth()`, passing it the width to set on the internal measurement element. This is necessary to get the correct values back from the other methods.

But…but…What About the Widgets?

As cool as all of that is, if you think this is all there is to Ext JS, you are very much mistaken. The widgets, which are probably the best part of Ext JS, are still left to be examined, and that's precisely what Chapter 2 will mostly be about. The `Ext` namespace is where all the UI widgets are located on top of all we've seen so far. Because there are a good number of them, and they are collectively what initially attracts most people to Ext JS to begin with, I felt it was better to wall them off and devote an entire chapter to them.

In addition to the widgets, I've left out a few more "advanced" topics to cover in Chapter 2. For example, Ext JS provides a very nice, robust data subsystem that allows you to abstract away your data storage mechanism. This is something I also felt was better held off until the next chapter.

One Last Tangential Thing: Ext Core

As of version 3.0, the Ext JS team has also released a separate, but very much related product called Ext Core. Ext Core contains much of what has been discussed in this chapter, but it *does not* include everything the full Ext JS library includes (widgets are the most obvious omission). Ext Core is intended to provide a consistent, fully cross-browser API for performing the most common tasks modern RIA developers need—tasks like DOM traversal and manipulation, CSS management, event handling, Ajax, and animations.

The nice thing about Ext Core is that it is licensed under the liberal MIT license, which is an open source license that allows a tremendous amount of freedom. Also, Ext Core is 100 percent free to use under that license, so all of the previous statements about licensing issues are null and void when it comes to Ext Core!

Ext Core is a real nice addition to the product offerings from Ext, LLC, and best of all, what is covered in this book applies to Ext Core as well! It may well be that as you look at your needs you discover that the full-blown Ext JS library has a lot more than you need, in which case Ext Core may be just the ticket, and a cheaper ticket at that!

Of course, the Ext team obviously hopes that people become enamored of Ext Core and eventually buy a full Ext JS license. This is, you have to remember, a business after all, so there's absolutely nothing wrong with that strategy. As good as Ext Core is, that's probably a good strategy on their part! In the end, though, Ext Core provides a *ton* of capabilities and a lot of power at no cost, which I think says a lot about the Ext team and their belief in the open source model.

■**Note** Ext Core 3.0 was released in beta as I was finishing up this chapter. Talk about a timely release!

Summary

In this chapter, we began our journey of exploration into the world of Ext JS by taking a step back and looking at the evolution of web application development. In fact, we took a step even *further* back than that and looked at what the term "web application" means in the first place. We looked at what an RIA is all about, and we talked about Ajax and why it's such an important development. We even looked at some other options for developing RIAs other than Ext JS. Finally, and most importantly for our purposes in this book, we looked at Ext JS itself! We saw what it has to offer, how it's structured, learned a bit about its history and philosophy, and we got started with the basics of using it.

In the next chapter we'll take the next step and look in much more detail at using Ext JS. We'll see more of its capabilities and get more familiar with it in general. All of this is meant to set the stage for the project chapters to follow. Also in the next chapter we'll look at something called Gears, which coupled with Ext JS will allow us to create those coming applications.

So get comfortable and move on—the best is yet to come!

■■■

CHAPTER 2

Widgets and Advanced Ext JS

In the previous chapter we began our look at Ext JS by seeing some of the basics of its usage, but we focused primarily on the general utility-type aspects of the library. We only touched on widgets in a limited way, and as it happens, Ext JS is primarily known for its widgets. So, in this chapter we'll focus almost entirely on the widgets. We'll look at some of the more "advanced," relatively speaking, topics in Ext JS. Here I refer to things like data handling and binding, drag and drop, and state management. Because all the applications in this book will make use of it, we'll also take a look at Google's Gears browser extension. While Ext JS is in no way tied or dependent on it, I think you'll see how Ext JS works *with* Gears very well and opens up a whole new world of possibilities for our development efforts.

Ext JS Widgets: An Overview

In many JavaScript frameworks and libraries you look at, you realize that each widget is completely independent of the others in terms of code. Because of this, you often find great disparity in what each widget offers. For example, getting the value of some sort of text field widget might require a call to its getValue() method, while a calendar widget might require a call to getSelectedDate(). One widget may have an option to have a border around it, while another will not.

In recent years, the "modern" libraries have taken things to a much higher level. A number of frameworks these days have a logical hierarchy to their widgets, so for example a text field widget is an extension of an editable widget, and an editable widget is an extension of a plain widget. This allows each subsequent child component to inherit the behaviors and capabilities of its ancestors.

Ext JS takes this tact, and it takes it to a fantastic extreme. In terms of overall structure, how clear it is, how logical it is, how efficient it is, Ext JS has no peers in the JavaScript library space. Some other libraries certainly do a good job too, but Ext JS, at least in the opinion of this author, takes it to another level.

■**Note** Please understand that what follows is not meant to be an exhaustive reference. As in the first chapter, I'll be discussing the things I think you'll find most interesting and useful. For individual widgets, I won't be listing every single config option, method, and event supported—that would just be reciting the Ext JS documentation. I'll try to note the parts I think you need to know about up front, but many other items will be introduced as we progress through the projects to come. Remember, the whole point of this book is learning by example and learning by seeing things in real use cases, so documenting every last detail would be the exact opposite of that. Besides, as rich and powerful as Ext JS is, it would take a heck of a lot more pages than this to do it right anyway!

The Hierarchy of Widgets

Most widgets have at their base of their inheritance hierarchy (not including the absolute base JavaScript Object) the Observable class. This is an abstract base class that provides a common interface for publishing events. In other words, it normalizes the mechanisms associated with events that any widget might expose or respond to. This means that the mechanism you use to make a button response to being clicked is the same underlying mechanism you use to make a grid column sort when clicked.

Extending from Observable is the Component class. The Component class endows an Ext JS component (or widget in other words) with some basic behaviors, such as the ability to be hidden and shown, enabled, or disabled. It also allows a component to be able to participate in the typical component life cycle that Ext JS provides for, including creation, rendering, and destruction. The Component class also allows all components to automatically be registered with the Ext.ComponentMgr so that you can later use the Ext.getCmp() method to get a reference to a named widget. In general, any visual widget should extend Component or its subclass BoxComponent, which adds automatic box model adjustments so that sizing and positioning is handled more or less automatically. (Not all widgets necessarily have to have a visible component, it seems.)

■**Note** You'll notice that I use the terms "widget" and "component" interchangeably in various places. Ext JS refers to UI widgets as components, which is not necessarily the same as the Component class (although many of the components are in fact subclasses of the Component class). Don't be confused, though: a widget is the same as a component in the context of Ext JS. In the cases where I'm referring to the Component class itself, I'll write it capitalized just like that and apply the special code font used throughout this book, but lowercase "component" when it refers to a widget.

Another inheritance path (there are more than one) still includes Component at its base, with BoxComponent above it, followed by Container extending from that. A component extending from Container is a component that can itself have child components. Something like a Button likely wouldn't have this capability (and doesn't because Button extends directly from Component). However, something like a TabPanel does, so TabPanel extends from Container.

As it happens, `TabPanel` isn't a direct child of `Container`—it's actually a child of `Panel`, but `Panel` is a direct child of `Container`. Because this is a rich inheritance hierarchy, it means that `TabPanel` is effectively a descendant of `Container` anyway.

As you look at what classes extend what, all of them descend from the JavaScript `Object` class. From that you find a couple of "inheritance paths" that all of the widgets follow. Each of these trees starts with a class that extends directly from `Object`.

Figure 2-1 depicts the entire inheritance tree with regard to components.

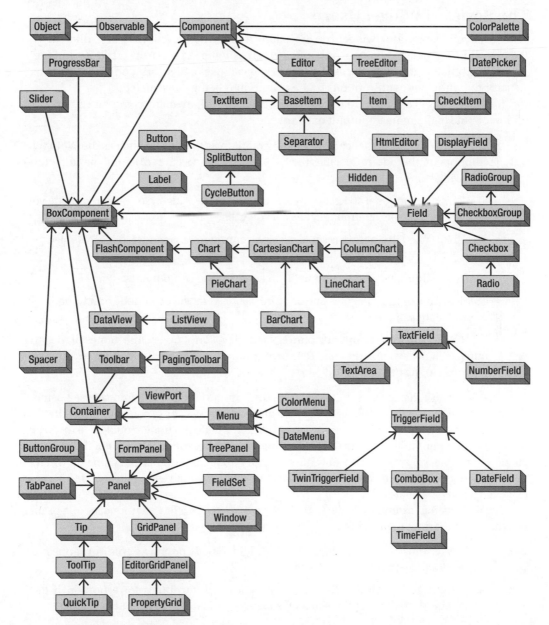

Figure 2-1. *Ext JS object model, extending from Observable*

Ext JS isn't just a series of components, and it's more than even a nice, logical, well-modeled object-oriented API. Ext JS wouldn't be nearly as powerful as it is if that's all it was. In fact, one of the things that make Ext JS so powerful is the concept of layout and layout-related components. To be more precise, the idea of layout is what allows you to take all these neat widgets and create a true user interface from them. We'll be looking at the concept of layout shortly, but before that, let's talk about some widget basics.

The Basics of Widget Usage

Whenever you instantiate a widget you are calling a constructor. This may be explicit in the case of using the `new` keyword, or implicit when using the `items` array attribute and the `layout` attribute. In any of these cases, though, you can pass a JavaScript object to the constructor that provides config options to the component being constructed.

Since all widgets extend from the `Component` class, they share many common config options. Some of the more important ones are:

- `applyTo`: For widgets that can use existing markup as their basis, such as the Window component, this option specifies the DOM node to use as the structural markup of the new widget.

- `cls`: This is an optional style class name to apply to the widget, so you can provide your own styling on a per-component basis if you wish.

- `disabled`: When this option is set to `true`, the component is rendered in a disabled state.

- `id`: This option specifies the unique ID to assign to the component.

- `plugins`: This option specifies one or more classes that will extend the functionality of the widget in some way. More on this later!

- `listeners`: The value of this attribute is itself a JavaScript object; the names of the attributes on it are event names and the corresponding values are functions to execute in response to the named event.

This is not an exhaustive list but it includes the options I think you'll find yourself using the most. Note that while all subclasses of `Component` will expose these config options, that doesn't necessarily mean that every single one of them will do anything. You'll have to check the Ext JS documentation to make that determination. In my experience, *most* of them are globally available, so you probably only have to worry about exceptions that come up when something doesn't do what you expect—you can normally assume everything works as expected across the board.

For widgets that extend from the `Container` class, there are a few additional config properties that are important to talk about:

- `activeItem`: Specifies the child item that should initially be active. This only applies to some containers, such as the `Accordion`.

- `autoHeight`/`autoWidth`: Sets the `height` and `width` style attributes correspondingly to 100%. These are those options that all subclasses will inherit but not all will honor.

- hideBorders: Set to true to hide the border of all child elements.

- layout: Specifies the xtype of the layout this Container should use.

- items: This is an array of JavaScript objects, each describing a child component of the Container.

Of these, layout and items are used nearly always when dealing with containers, and we'll be seeing a lot of them in action.

Now, making use of a widget requires one of two things: you either create a new one using the new keyword as you would any other class, or you define it in the items arrays of a container. What route you take depends on how you've chosen to write your code. You'll see plenty of examples of both throughout the projects. Keep in mind that in either case you'll be creating a config object to define the widget (in the case of passing an object as part of the items array, the object you're passing *is* the config object).

By way of example, here's one way you could create a new Window:

```
var win = new Ext.Window({
  width : 300,
  height : 300,
  title : "My First Window",
  html : "<b>I am some content</b>"
});
```

As you can see, the constructor accepts an object with four attributes: width and height are the horizontal and vertical size of the new Window, title is the text that will appear in the title bar, and html is the markup to use as the main content of the Window.

Now here's a similar example that uses the items array of a Panel to add an HtmlEditor widget to it:

```
new Ext.Panel({
  renderTo : "panelTarget", layout : "fit",
  title : "My First Panel",
  items : [
    { xtype : "htmleditor", height : 200 }
  ]
});
```

This comes from the ItemsExample.htm file included in the source code. When you run it, you'll see a <div> with a red border, as in Figure 2-2 (but in glorious Technicolor[1] in your browser!). Within it is the Panel, with the title "My First Panel," and within it is the HtmlEditor.

---

1 Around 1922, a company called Technicolor Motion Picture Corporation created a series of color file processes. Up until around 1952, Technicolor was the dominant technology in Hollywood for creating color motion pictures, and if you've ever watched an older movie you've no doubt seen the Technicolor logo splashed across the screen at some point.

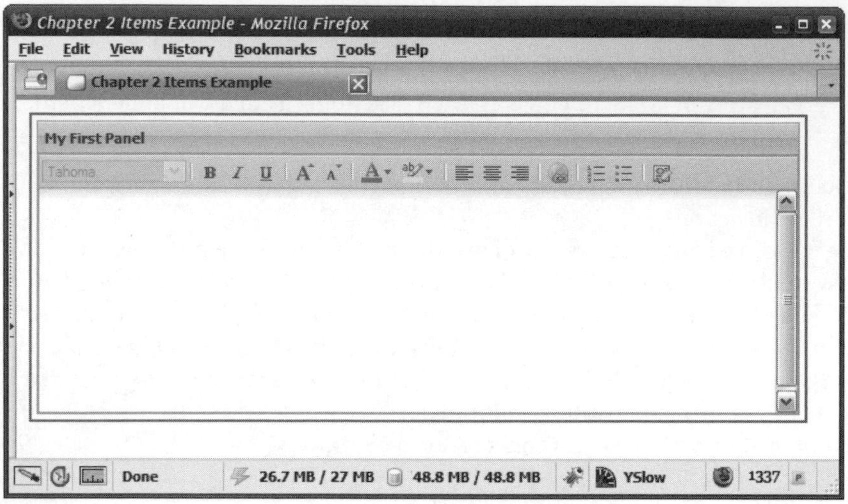

Figure 2-2. *Example of using the items array to create widgets*

Layout and Containers in Ext JS

When you get down to creating a UI with Ext JS, at the core of this is the concept of layout. More specifically, it's dealing at a high level with any of the classes in the `Ext.layout` namespace.

A layout is composed of some number of `Ext.Container` elements contained within it. Any Ext JS UI is a hierarchy of containers, and it's also very much possible for a given `Container` to itself have some sort of layout in it. It's this building up of layouts and `Containers` and layouts again (and `Containers` again!) within one another that results in the UI you see on the screen.

As a hierarchy, there must be some root element, some outer `Container` that all others are a child of. Indeed there is just such a thing in Ext JS: the `Viewport`.

■**Note** The screenshots you see in this discussion of layouts, viewports, panels, and so forth are taken from the examples you can find on the Ext JS web site. So if you'd like to see them in action, cruise on over there and check 'em out! It's always more enlightening to see them in a browser and play with them a bit.

Viewport

The `Viewport` is a `Container` (it extends from the `Container` class) that itself has a layout structure like any other `Container` does, but it holds a special place in Ext JS. The `Viewport` represents the whole of the area visible to the user, which means the browser window in other words (or to be more precise, not the *entire* browser window but just the portion where a web site renders, typically called the browser viewport).

When created, the Viewport automatically renders itself into the <body> of the document loaded in the browser and sizes itself so that it takes up the entire browser viewport. It also is aware of resizing events that can occur and reacts accordingly. If by this description you reason that there may be only a single Viewport per page, you can pat yourself on the back because that is absolutely true.

The Viewport is endowed with a specific layout structure, be it a BorderLayout, CardLayout, or what have you. A layout is some organization of Panels, so by virtue of having some layout on the Viewport you are defining the overall structure of your page. It's the act of adding Panels to the Viewport that adds the content.

You create a Viewport as shown in the example in Listing 2-1.

Listing 2-1. *Creating the Viewport*

```html
<html>

  <head>

    <title>Chapter 2 Viewport Example</title>

    <link rel="stylesheet" type="text/css" href="ext/resources/css/ext-all.css">
    <script type="text/javascript" src="ext/adapter/ext/ext-base.js"></script>
    <script type="text/javascript" src="ext/ext-all.js"></script>

    <script>

      Ext.onReady(function() {

        new Ext.Viewport({
          layout : "fit",
          items : [{
            title : "Hello there!", bodyStyle : "background-color:#ff0000",
            html : "I am some content",
          }]
        });

      });

    </script>

  </head>

  <body></body>

</html>
```

If you load Listing 2-1 in your browser, you'll find a title bar running across the top of the page with the words "Hello there!" in it, with the text "I am some content" below that. The rest of the page has a red background. The Viewport has filled up the whole browser viewport. The layout attribute passed to the Viewport constructor tells it what sort of layout to use. The value of this attribute is the xtype for the FitLayout (see the accompanying sidebar for an explanation of xtype). A FitLayout is a layout that has a single item that fills up the Container it is placed in. So, the Viewport has a single Container contained within it.

We then add children to the Viewport via the items array. Each object in this array is a Container. Since there's only a single Container in a FitLayout, there is likewise only a single Container in the items array. Since there is no type specified for the Container, we get a basic Container by default. The title attribute is the text for the title bar, and the html attribute is the markup content to put in the Panel.

This is a simple example. Most Ext JS-based UIs will be much more complex, as we'll see as we look at the projects. But, at the end of the day, that's the basic concept.

WHAT IS AN XTYPE?

An xtype, simply stated, is a symbolic name given to a specific class. In other words, it is a shorthand way to name a class in some context.

In older versions of Ext JS, before the 2.x series came to be, you had to instantiate all your UI widgets ahead of time. So, let's say your UI had ten Grids in it. That meant you had to instantiate all ten of them up front. But, what if nine of them weren't visible initially? That could be a lot of wasted memory and processor time to create all nine that you didn't even need at the time.

So, Ext JS 2.x introduced the idea of xtype. When you create a UI, as seen in the example in Listing 2-1, the xtype allows Ext JS to create the specified component in a lazy fashion—in other words, when it has to be displayed on the screen. In the example the layout is needed immediately, so there's no real difference.

Imagine, however, if we used a CardLayout, which layers Panels one on top of another so only one is visible at any given time. Further image that of three Panels created as part of the CardLayout, the two that aren't initially visible had Grids on them. There's no sense creating them all up front, so if we use an xtype instead, then they won't be rendered until needed.

Now, although "fit" here is an xtype, note that we're talking about the layout attribute. As you'll see later, in many instances there is literally an xtype attribute that you can specify in many instances. It's a semantic difference, though: here, the value of the layout attribute is an xtype value, just as it would be if the attribute name was literally xtype.

The Ext JS documentation lists all the possible xtype values for you, but you can also register your own if you like by using this code:

```
Ext.reg("myxtype", My.Class.Here);
```

If My.Class.Here was an instance of Component, it would be usable as an xtype just as any Ext JS component is.

As we explore the widgets, I'll list their xtypes so that you can quickly find them when you need them. Although I said previously this isn't intended as an exhaustive reference, I see no reason to not provide aspects of a reference to an extent if it makes life a little easier!

Panels

xtype : `panel`

I've mentioned the term `Panel` before, but I haven't defined it just yet. Along with the idea of layouts, and of the `Viewport` lording over everything, `Panels` are a fundamental building block of Ext JS-based UIs.

A `Panel` is a `Container`, but it has additional functionality that is geared toward making it an ideal building block for UIs. For example, a `Panel` contains toolbars at the top and bottom, and also has separate header, footer, and main content areas between them. In many cases these are optional components that you may not know are there unless you specifically deal with them, but all `Panels` have the capabilities in common nonetheless.

`Panels` also provide expand and collapse capabilities automatically, if you want them. `Panels` are meant to be dropped into other `Containers` or more usually layouts, and the Ext JS framework manages their life cycles.

There are many different types of `Panels`, and you'll be pretty much always working with descendants of the `Panel` class when you work with `Panels` at all. We'll discover various `Panels` as we go, but for now it's time to get back to the specific layouts that are possible.

FitLayout

xtype : `fit`

We already saw this layout in a previous example, so there's not a whole lot more to say about it. A `FitLayout` contains a single item that automatically expands to fill the `Container` it is placed in. You generally won't instantiate an instance of this class; you'll instead use its xtype as the value of a layout attribute on some `Container`.

Interestingly, `FitLayout` doesn't have any of its own config options, aside from those it inherits, which is always the case. When you want to have a `Panel` that fills the entire `Container` it's placed in, `FitLayout` is what you want. All you need to do is set the `layout` attribute of the `Container` to `fit` and add a single `Panel` to it and you're good to go. Note too that if you add multiple `Panels` to the `Container` with a layout of type `fit`, only the first added `Panel` will be shown.

BorderLayout

xtype : `border`

A `BorderLayout` is a relatively simple layout that also happens to be extremely common, perhaps even *the* most popular layout. It is a layout that has five regions: one along the top of the page, one on the left side, one on the right side, one on the bottom, and one between all of them in the middle. The four around the edges are referred to by compass directions (so the one on top is north, and so forth), while the middle section is the center.

The `BorderLayout` supports automatic split bars between the regions, allowing the user to resize them at will. It also supports expanding and collapsing of sections. Like `FitLayout`, the `BorderLayout` itself doesn't have of its own config options. The available options come from the children of `BorderLayout`, which are instances of `Ext.layout.BorderLayout.Region` or `Ext.layout.BorderLayout.SplitRegion`. These children are `Containers` into which you typically put some sort of `Panel`.

While there are five available regions in a BorderLayout, there's no requirement that you use them all. However, you cannot add regions after the BorderLayout has rendered, so you have to ensure that any regions you need are configured for use when you create the BorderLayout.

You don't explicitly instantiate an instance of Ext.layout.BorderLayout. Instead, you set the layout attribute of some Container to border (or the layout of the Viewport, which remember is just a special Container). For example, let's say you want to create a Panel to display that uses a BorderLayout to organize its content. Here's how you can do it:

```
var myPanel = new Ext.Panel({
  title : "This is my panel… there are many like it, but this one is mine",
  layout : "border",
  items: [{
    title : "North", region : "north", height:  200, minSize : 400, maxSize : 50
  },{
    title : "East", region : "east", width : 300
  },{
    title : "Center", region : "center"
  }]
});
```

Assuming this Panel filled the entire browser viewport, the layout would consist of a region running across the entire width of the browser viewport at top (north), with two sections below it. The section on the right (east) would have an initial width of 300 pixels while the region on the left (center) would fill the remainder of the browser viewport.

The width and height attributes set the initial size of a given region (height only makes sense for the north and south regions, while width only makes sense for the east and west regions; the center region always fills the remaining space). The minSize and maxSize attributes set the minimum size and maximum size the user is allowed to resize the region to via dragging the split bar.

In Figure 2-3 you can see a page using a BorderLayout. It's a bit more advanced than the example code, too, showing all regions in use.

As you can see, a BorderLayout allows you to create rather complex layouts in a fashion that is quite typical of GUIs. Once again, it's probably the primary layout you'll use in most cases.

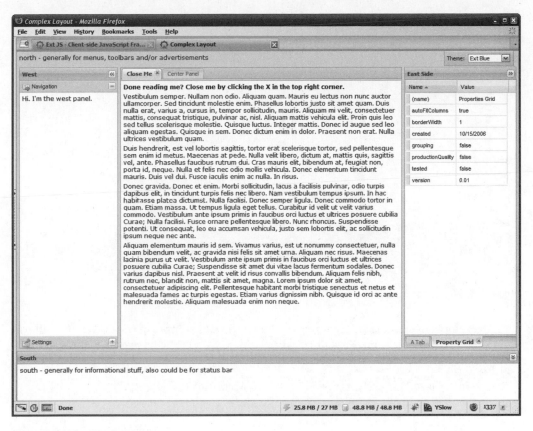

Figure 2-3. *The BorderLayout*

Accordion

xtype : `accordion`

The `Accordion` is in some ways like its own widget. In other libraries it actually is, but in Ext JS it is a type of layout (it's literally an extension of `FitLayout`). Simply stated, an `Accordion` is one in which you have a series of panes that can be selected by the user. The panes are stacked vertically (although some implementations allow horizontal stacking too) and usually include a nice animation effect when switching between them.

In Figure 2-4 you can see an example of an `Accordion`.

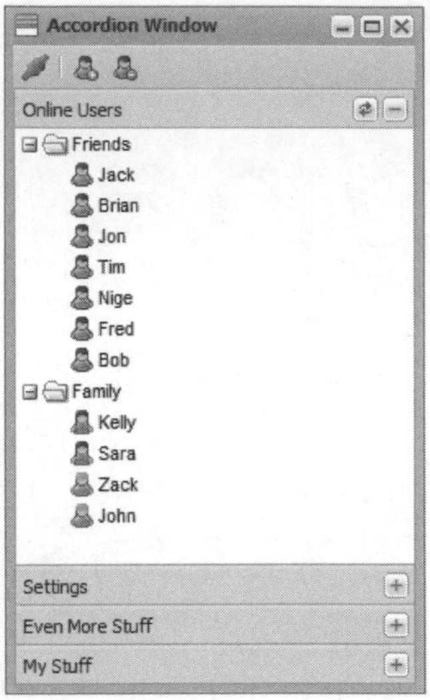

Figure 2-4. *The Accordion layout type*

An example of creating an Accordion can be seen in this snippet of code taken from the Accordion.htm example from the source code:

```
new Ext.Panel({
  renderTo : "panelTarget", title : "My First Accordion",
  layout : "accordion", height : 400, collapsible : true,
  layoutConfig : { animate : true },
  items: [{
    title : "Pane 1",
    html : "I am Pane #1"
  },{
    title : "Pane 2",
    html : "I am Pane #2"
  },{
    title : "Pane 3",
    html : "I am Pane #3"
  }]
});
```

So an instance of Ext.Panel is created here, with a layout value of accordion. We explicitly set a height so it fits in the <div> it's rendered into (panelTarget) and set collapsible to true to indicate that there should be an icon on the Accordion title bar that when clicked collapses the entire Accordion. The layoutConfig attribute is an object that contains settings specific to the chosen layout. You'll see this attribute a lot, but the attributes specified in it depend on the layout being used. In other words, it is essentially an object like what you would pass to the constructor of the Accordion class. Here, the animate attribute specifies that we want switching between the panes in the Accordion to be animated. This gives a nice sliding effect to the switching. Finally, the items array specifies the panes to be added, which by default are basic Panels. We give each a title and some html content and we have ourselves an Accordion!

CardLayout

xtype : card

The CardLayout is sort of like the FitLayout on steroids: it allows you to have multiple Panels fitted to the Container, but only allows a single one to be shown at a time. Things like wizard interfaces are typically implemented with CardLayout, as well as things like tabbed interfaces.

The single most important method exposed by the CardLayout is setActiveItem(). This allows you to show a new Panel in the CardLayout by either ID or index value. This is completely under your control as a programmer; the CardLayout doesn't even switch between Panels (or in response to user events, unless you write the code to do that), so there's nothing by default the user can click to switch as with an Accordion.

The CardLayout also supports a config option deferredRender, which, when true, tells the Container to only render a given Panel when it's actually shown. This is a good setting to keep in mind for efficiency of loading.

Here's a code example, taken from CardLayout.htm:

```
new Ext.Panel({
  renderTo : "panelTarget", title : "My First CardLayout",
  layout : "card", height : 400, id : "myCardLayout", activeItem : 0,
  items: [{
    title : "Panel 1",
    html : "I am Panel #1<br><br>" +
      "<input type=\"button\" value=\"Click to switch to #2\" " +
      "onClick=\"Ext.getCmp('myCardLayout')" +
      ".getLayout().setActiveItem(1);\">"
  },{
    title : "Panel 2",
    html : "I am Panel #2<br><br>" +
      "<input type=\"button\" value=\"Click to switch to #1\" " +
      "onClick=\"Ext.getCmp('myCardLayout')" +
      ".getLayout().setActiveItem(0);\">"
  }]
});
```

Here we have a CardLayout being rendered into our friendly neighborhood panelTarget <div>. We give it a title, specify the layout as card, and set its height to fill the <div>. Then we also assign an ID to the CardLayout. This is necessary because we'll need to be able to call its setActiveItem() method later, and this is how we can get it. We also specify that item 0 is initially active, which is the first Panel added in the items array.

Each of the Panels has some markup that contains a button. When one of them is clicked we use the Ext.getCmp() method, which is something you'll see a lot. This takes in an ID and returns a reference to the specified Component. On that returned reference we need to call the getLayout() method to get the CardLayout associated with the Container. This gives us back a reference to the CardLayout created implicitly by virtue of the layout attribute being set to card, and we can then call the setActiveItem() method to flip to the other Panel.

The CardLayout is a relatively simple animal, but we'll see it in use a lot. In Figure 2-5 you can see the example code in action. I've put two screenshots side by side so you can see each of the Panels. Just pretend the buttons were being clicked to jump back and forth between the two images and you'll get the idea (or simply run the example code!).

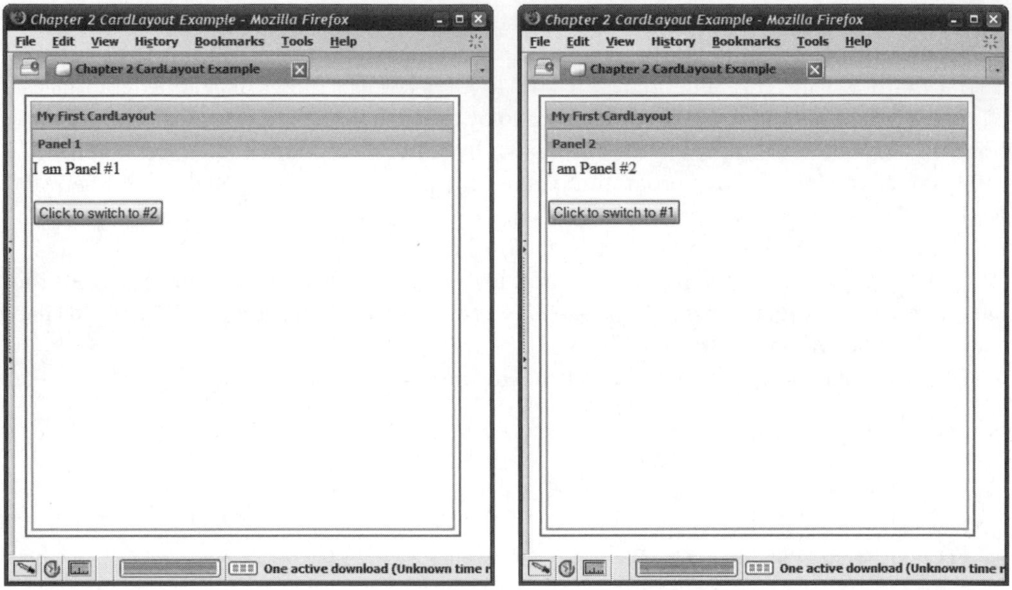

Figure 2-5. *The CardLayout in action (sort of)*

TableLayout

xtype : table

A TableLayout allows you to create table-based layouts with ease. In some ways it's conceptually similar to BorderLayout except that you are in control of what regions the layout has, how they span across others, and so forth.

A big difference between creating a layout using TableLayout and using plain old HTML tables (which TableLayout does behind the scenes) is that with TableLayout you don't concern yourself with tables and rows explicitly. You don't have to bother with nesting cells with rows and so forth. All you do is specify the total number of columns the TableLayout should have, and then start adding Panels to it, from left to right and from top to bottom. The TableLayout will figure out how to position each Panel based on that row count, in addition to any row span and column span settings you specify. If you're used to creating HTML tables, using TableLayout can be a little tricky to wrap your brain around, but once you do you quickly realize the flexibility it provides.

Figure 2-6 shows an example of a TableLayout. Here you can see there are two columns, and the first one is divided into two cells, one on top of the other. In HTML, you'd do something like this:

```
<table border="0">
  <tr>
    <td>Column 1, Cell 1</td>
    <td rowspan="2">Column 2</td>
  </tr>
  <tr>
    <td>Column 1, Cell 2</td>
  </tr>
</table>
```

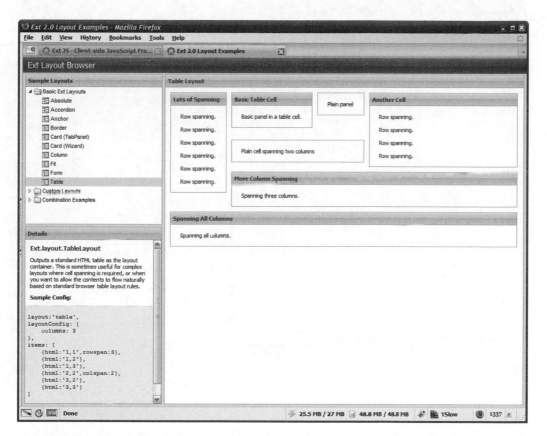

Figure 2-6. *The TableLayout*

With Ext JS and `TableLayout`, the same sort of thing is accomplished with this code:

```
new Ext.Panel({
  renderTo : "panelTarget", title : "My First TableLayout",
  layout : "table", height:400,
  layoutConfig: { columns : 2 },
```

```
    items: [
      { html : "Column 1, Cell 1", width : 200, height : 200 },
      { html : "Column 2", rowspan : 2, width : 200, height : 400 },
      { html : "Column 1, Cell 2", height : 200 }
    ]
});
```

The result of this, if you execute the TableLayout.htm example, is shown in Figure 2-7.

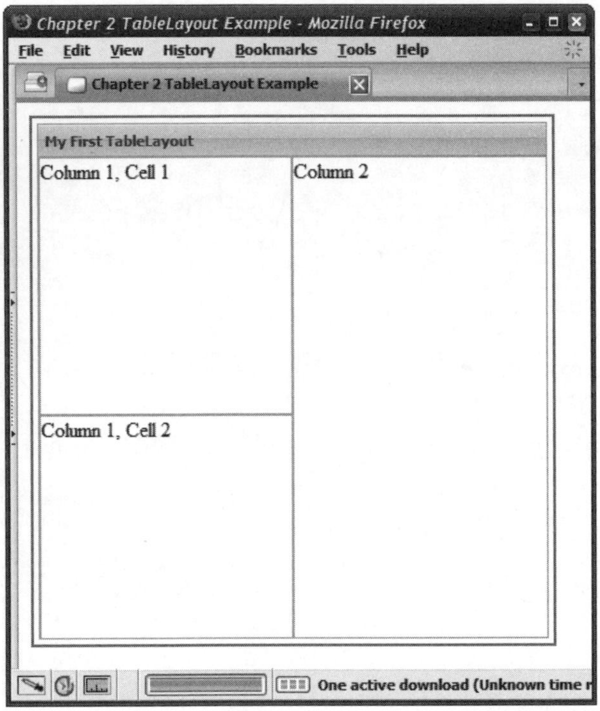

Figure 2-7. *Another TableLayout example*

As you can see, the number of columns is specified as part of the layoutConfig object, and then each Panel is added via the items array, each given the height and width to fill the area of the <div> it's supposed to. The second Panel has a rowspan of 2, just as it does in the plain HTML version.

AnchorLayout

xtype : anchor

An AnchorLayout is a layout that allows you to anchor contained elements relative to the containers' dimensions. In other words, if the Container is resized, either because the Container itself is resized or as an indirect result of its parent Container being resized, then all of the elements within it that have been anchored to it will be rerendered, and most importantly resized, according to the anchoring rules you supply.

It's not all about size, however: positioning can also be specified within the Container. Before we look at any code, take a look at Figure 2-8 to see what an anchored layout looks like.

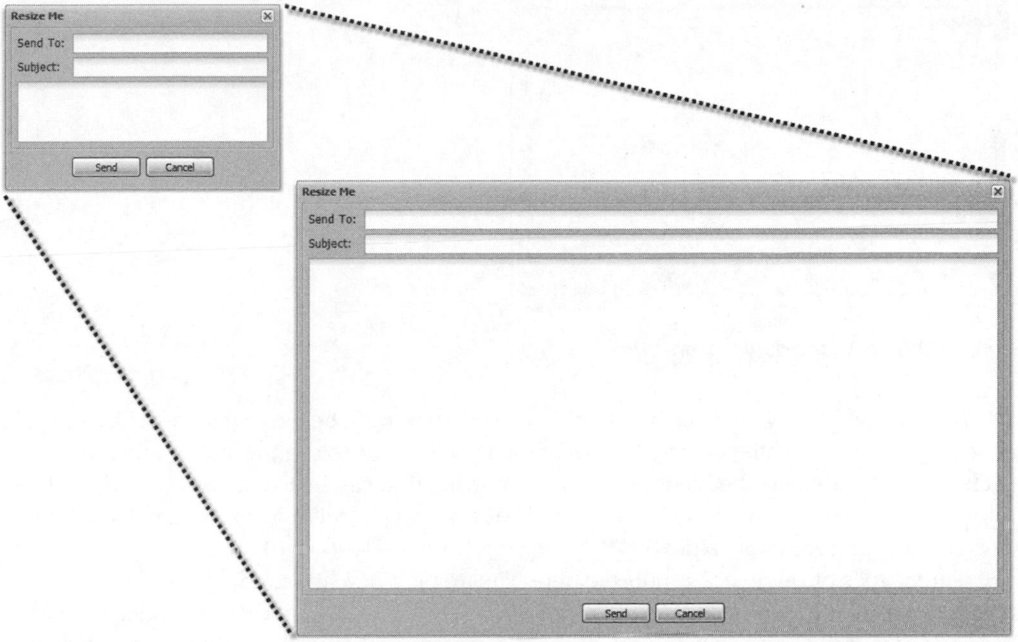

Figure 2-8. *A Panel using an AnchorLayout, at its minimal size and expanded to a larger size*

In Figure 2-8 you see the same Window with an AnchorLayout used internally to organize its children, in two different sizes. The larger version is a result of dragging the corner of the window to resize it. Notice how the text fields and labels are in the same relative position in each but have been resized to fill the Window.

What does the code for something like that look like? Well, it's not the exact code for the previous example, but it would look something like this:

```
new Ext.Window({
  resizable : true, layout : "anchor", title : "My First AnchorLayout",
  width : 200, height : 200,
  items: [
    { xtype : "textfield", anchor : "100%", value : "textfield1" },
    { xtype : "textfield", anchor : "100%", value : "textfield2" },
    { xtype : "textarea", anchor : "100% 60%", value : "textarea" }
  ]
}).show();
```

This code is taken from the AnchorLayout.htm example, which when run results in Figure 2-9.

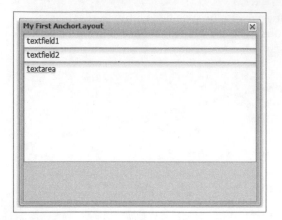

Figure 2-9. *The AnchorLayout, part deux*

In this case we have two text fields and one text area (we'll be looking at form fields in just a bit). The Window specifies an anchor layout, which allows us to use the anchor attribute on each element added via the items array. This is a string that can be used to specify anchoring rules. The value of this attribute is always in the form "xx yy"; xx is a horizontal anchor value and yy is a vertical anchor value.

Three types of values are supported here. The first is a percentage. So in the code, the text area specifically, the anchor attribute says that the text area should be expanded to fill the Window horizontally and that it should take up 60 percent of the height of the Window. You can also supply just a single anchor value as a percent, which Ext JS takes to be the width specification, and the height will default to a setting of auto.

You can also specify an offset value for the anchor attribute. This can be a positive or negative number. The first value is an offset from the right edge of the container, and the second is an offset from the bottom edge. So if we were to change the anchor attribute for the text area to –25 –75, that would tell Ext JS to render the item the complete width of the Window minus 25 pixels and the complete height of the Window minus 75 pixels. As with percentages, you can instead specify only a single value, and that will be taken as the right offset, with the bottom offset defaulting to 0.

You can also specify an anchor value of right, or r, or bottom, or b. In order for this to do anything, however, the Container must have a fixed size or must have an anchorSize config value defined at render time.

You can also mix and match anchor value types. For example, a value of –10 80% means that the element should render the full width of the Container minus 50 pixels from the right edge and 80 percent of the Container's height.

TabPanel

xtype : tabpanel

A TabPanel isn't actually a layout in the same way as the others are; it's a type of Panel. But since it is a way to lay out content on the screen, it fits in this section.

A TabPanel looks like what you see in Figure 2-10. Multiple tabs that allow the user to flip between different panes of content are present, and only one Panel within the TabPanel is visible at a time.

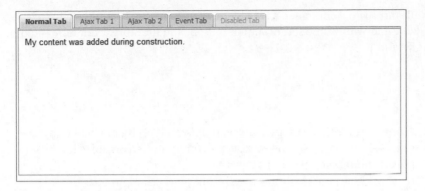

Figure 2-10. *The TabPanel*

The code that created the TabPanel in Figure 2-10 looks like this:

```
new Ext.TabPanel({
  renderTo : "panelTarget",
  activeTab : 0, width : 500, height : 200,
  items: [
    {
      title: "Normal Tab",
      html: "My content was added during construction"
    },
    { title: "Ajax Tab 1" },
    { title: "Ajax Tab 2" },
    { title: "Event Tab" },
    { title: "Disabled Tab", disabled : true }
    ]
});
```

You use this just like any of the other components we've looked at, so there's nothing new here. Here are some of the more interesting config options available:

- enableTabScroll, which when true adds a button to scroll through tabs if there are more than can be displayed across the TabPanel (the animScroll option goes along with this; when true it animates the scrolling of tabs)

- autoLoad, which should be a valid URL specification as described for the Ext.Updated.update() method and will cause an Ajax request to fetch that URL and put the response into the tab upon creation

- tabPosition, which accepts a value of top or bottom (the default is top) that specifies where the strip of tabs should be placed: above or below the tab bodies themselves

Form Widgets

Forms in Ext JS are in many ways similar to the usual <form> HTML elements, but as you might guess, with a lot more power, not to mention the fact that they look nicer! Creating forms is pretty simple too and follows a model similar to the type of code we've seen earlier.

As in HTML, it all starts with a container, a Form element of some sort, and then a bunch of input fields. It usually ends with some sort of submit button, and the story is not fundamentally different in Ext JS land.

FormPanel

xtype : form

In general, creating a form starts with creating a FormPanel. It is used pretty much like any other Panel type. Internally, FormPanel uses the FormLayout component to organize its children, which in this case are input fields of various types.

In its default state, a FormPanel internally has a BasicForm object that provides the basic functionality of a form, which includes submitting of the form via Ajax. You can override this to make the form submit in the way a normal <form> element does by setting its standardSubmit config option to true, but in the RIA world you probably want the Ajax method.

Here's some example code for a simple form that you can see in Figure 2-11:

```
var fp = new Ext.FormPanel({
  renderTo : "panelTarget", width : 400, height : 350, labelWidth : 120,
  bodyStyle : "padding:6px", url : "test.htm",
  items: [
    { xtype : "textfield", fieldLabel : "Your name", width : 250 },
    { xtype : "datefield", fieldLabel : "Your age" },
    { xtype : "checkbox", fieldLabel : "Married?" },
    {
      xtype : "textarea", fieldLabel : "About you", width : 250,
      height : 200
    }
  ],
  buttons: [{
    text : "Submit",
    handler : function() {
      fp.getForm().submit();
    }
  }]
});
```

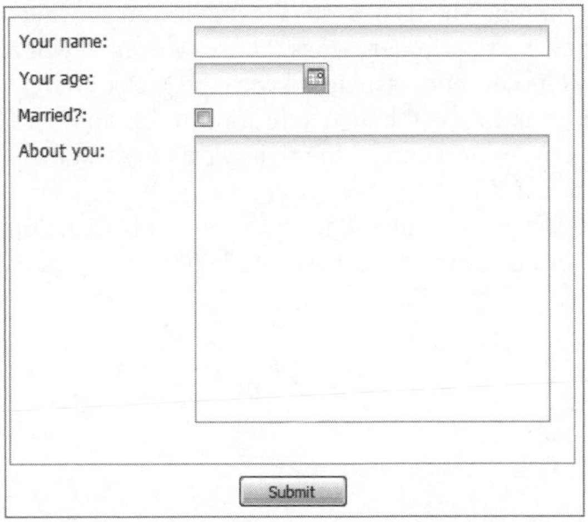

Figure 2-11. *A very simple form example*

It's a very simple form. The FormPanel is created and told to render to the panelTarget
<div>. We specify a width and height for the panel, as well as the labelWidth attribute, which
tells the form how wide a label for a field should be. I also added a bodyStyle attribute here to
keep the form fields and labels from bumping right up against the border of the FormPanel. The
url attribute specifies the URL that the form will be submitted to when the submit() method
is called. Then, a bunch of input fields are added via the items array, a textfield, a datefield,
a checkbox, and a textarea, all specified via xtype. As you can see, each field can have a label
as well, and even width values. (Remember, the width value is the width of the field itself, so
you have to subtract the width of the label to ensure the label plus the field isn't wider than the
FormPanel.) You can also specify a height, as I've done on the textarea.

Then a button is added to the footer of the FormPanel so the form can be submitted. It calls
the getForm() method of the FormPanel to get the underlying BasicForm, which we then call
the submit() method on. The form knows what URL to submit to, so our work is done at that
point. (Note that clicking the submit button will result in an error because you can't submit to
a local HTML file in most browsers due to security restrictions.)

Now we'll look at the individual fields that can be put on a form. While I suspect most of
them are familiar to you because they are much like their plain old HTML counterparts, a few
of them have no direct analogy, so they may be a bit more interesting to you.

TextField

xtype : textfield

The ubiquitous TextField is perhaps the most common form widget out there. Simply stated,
it is a box that allows the user to enter some text. Typically, the only real limitation placed on
the entry in a TextField is the maximum length, but there can be others.

For example, the TextField supports a maskRe config option whose value is a regular
expression that masks what the user can enter. For example, a single expression \D* will match
all non-numeric characters. So you could enter abc but not abc123 (and not abc123def either).

The TextField also has a maxLength config option, which specifies the maximum allowed length of the input, just like a plain <input type="text"> element does. The grow option, when true, allows the field to expand or contract to fit its content. Associated with the grow option are growMin and growMax. With grow set to true, growMin sets the field's minimum size and growMax sets the maximum size. The selectOnFocus option determines if any existing text in the TextField will be selected on focus (true) or not (false).

I'm going to go out on a limb here and assume you don't need to see a TextField in action. That being said, I'm going to do it anyway! Check out Figure 2-12 for a couple of TextFields.

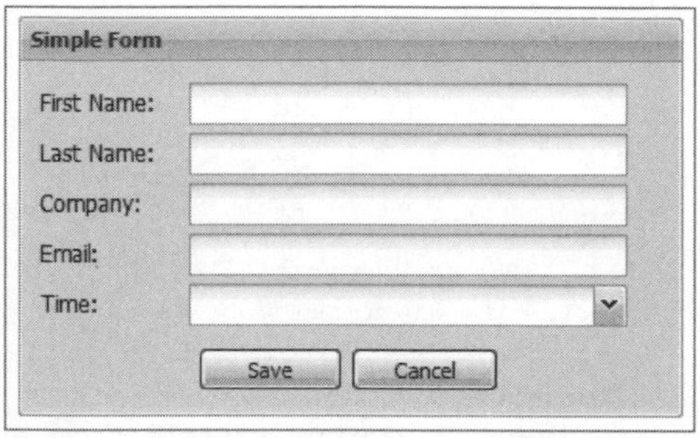

Figure 2-12. *The TextField*

Checkbox

xtype : checkbox

I won't spend much time on the Checkbox widget as you saw it in the previous example.

A Checkbox is used when users have a basic yes/no type of question that they need to answer. It has two config options: checked, which is either true or false and determines whether the check box starts off checked (true) or not (false); and readOnly, which when true makes the check box unclickable.

That about covers it! A Checkbox isn't exactly rocket science.

DateField

xtype : datefield

The DateField is a neat little widget that allows you to provide your users with a pop-up calendar so they can select a date value for a text input field. This allows you to ensure the value is entered in the format you need it to be in. It also tends to make it easier on the user (some people disagree; they say that hand-entering a date is always easier and quicker, and doubtless it is sometimes, but many people feel it generally isn't).

The DateField on the screen looks like what you see in Figure 2-13. The little calendar icon next to the text fields is what the user clicks to pop up the calendar. In this screenshot I've clicked the calendar next to the End Date field.

Figure 2-13. *The DateField*

The code behind this example is something along the lines of:

```
new Ext.FormPanel({
  renderTo : "panelTarget", width : 400, height : 350, labelWidth : 120,
  bodyStyle : "padding:6px", url : "test.htm", title : "Date Range",
  items: [
    { xtype : "datefield", fieldLabel : "Start Date" },
    { xtype : "datefield", fieldLabel : "End Date" }
  ]
});
```

HtmlEditor

xtype : htmleditor

The HtmlEditor widget is akin to what is usually called a rich editor in other libraries. It allows you to edit text that includes formatting, things like colors, fonts, font styles, lists, and so forth. I can only assume the Ext JS developers chose to call this thing an HtmlEditor because when you call its getValue() method, you get HTML representing the text, with all its formatting, that you have entered.

Well, whatever it's called and why it's called that, the widget appears in Figure 2-14; it's the large text area at the bottom and the toolbar above it.

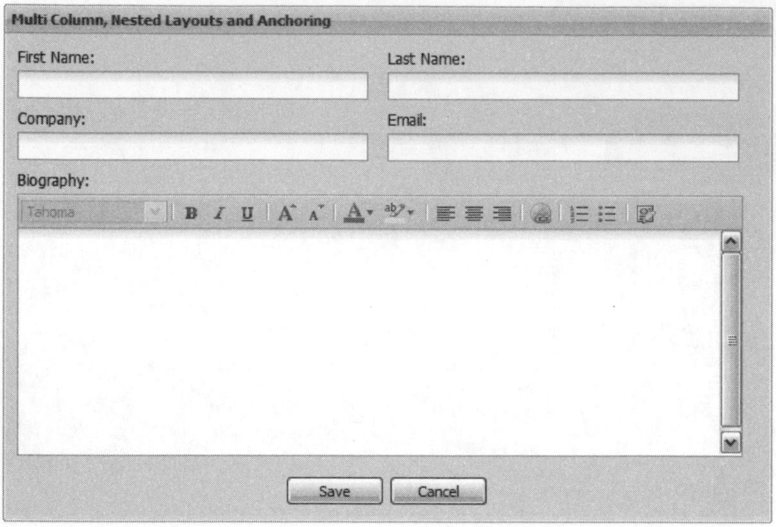

Figure 2-14. *The HtmlEditor*

The code for using an HtmlEditor is along these lines:

```
new Ext.Panel({
  renderTo : "panelTarget", layout : "fit",
  title : "HtmlEditor",
  items : [
    { xtype : "htmleditor", height : 200, id : "he" },
    {
      xtype : "button", text : "Get HtmlEditor Value", listeners : {
        click : function() {
          alert(Ext.getCmp("he").getValue());
        }
      }
    }
  ]
});
```

You'll notice the button on the bottom that when clicked calls the getValue() method of the HtmlEditor. Let's say the user entered Hello World in the HtmlEditor, and they made the text red and in bold. The alert() shown would contain this string:

```
<font color="#ff0000"><b>Hello World</b></font>
```

Now, you can argue that using a <font> tag is bad news, given our love of CSS these days. You might say the same for using the <b> tag. However, you can't deny that the HTML returned is indeed valid and matches the formatting applied to the text entered. That's the whole point of the HtmlEditor widget.

NumberField

`xtype : numberfield`

The NumberField is just like a TextField except that it has built-in numeric filtering. In other words, it'll only let you enter numbers. You can set the number of decimal places to show after the decimal point by specifying a value for the decimalPrecision config option (it defaults to 2). Note that you can enter more than the value specified by decimalPrecision, but when you blur off the field—that is, when focus leaves the field—it will be truncated back to that size. You can specify whether decimals are allowed in the first place by setting the allowDecimals config option to true or false. You can also specify a character to use as a decimal separator other than the default period by specifying it with the decimalSeparator config option (this can be a string of more than one allowed character if you wish). The allowNegative config option, similar to the allowDecimals option, determines whether the field will allow negative values (true) or not (false). The baseChars config option lets you set what characters are considered valid (it defaults to 0123456789). That's helpful if you want to allow entering of hexadecimal numbers, for example. The grow option, when true, allows the field to expand or contract to fit its content. Associated with the grow option are growMin and growMax. With grow set to true, growMin sets the field's minimum size and growMax sets the maximum size.

Since the NumberField is very similar to TextField, I don't think there's much more to say about it, or a need to show it here, so let's continue on with our survey of widgets.

TextArea

`xtype : textarea`

A TextArea is essentially a TextField that has more than one line of text available for the user to enter something into. It looks like what you see in Figure 2-15; it's the last field with the label Note.

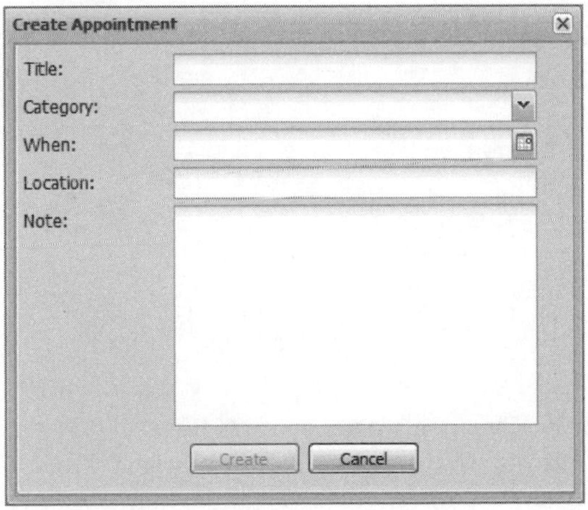

Figure 2-15. *The TextArea*

The TextArea widget supports a width and a height config option to specify its size. It also supports the grow, growMin, and growMax options previously discussed. It supports the regex option for validating the input against a regular expression, as well as a maxLength option for limiting the amount of text that can be entered.

The code for the FormPanel shows a TextArea being created, so there's no sense repeating that here.

Radio/RadioGroup

xtype : radio/radiogroup

A Radio, or radio button as it's frequently called, is a descendant of the Checkbox and is extremely similar. In contrast to a Checkbox, a stand-alone Radio button isn't generally seen; it is usually in a group. (The metaphor a Radio button seeks to implement is a multiple-choice question with a single correct but required answer, whereas a Checkbox is for multiple-choice questions where one or more answer may be given, or none at all.) You can in fact create a stand-alone Radio if you wish, but normally you you'll use the RadioGroup widget instead. Here are some examples:

```
new Ext.Panel({
  renderTo : "panelTarget", layout : "fit",
  title : "Radio Example",
  items : [
    { xtype : "label", text : "I am a radio:" },
    { xtype : "radio", name : "radio1" },
    { xtype : "label", text : "I am another radio:" },
    { xtype : "radio", name : "radio2" },
    { xtype : "label", text : "A more proper group of radios:" },
    { xtype : "radio", name : "radio3" },
    { xtype : "radio", name : "radio3" },
    { xtype : "label", text : "A real RadioGroup:" },
    { xtype : "radiogroup", columns : 1,
      items : [
        { boxLabel : "Item 1", name : "rg", inputValue : 1,
          checked : true },
        { boxLabel : "Item 2", name : "rg", inputValue : 2 }
      ]
    }
  ]
});
```

This code generates a total of six Radio buttons. The first two are solitary. If you click them you'll notice that while they become "checked," as you would expect, there's no way via the UI to deselect them. This is usually considered a flaw in a UI (alternatively there may be some button, or other trigger, that deselects it automatically, but that's not typically the right way to use a Radio button).

The third and fourth Radio buttons are also solitary, but notice that they have the same name. This tells Ext JS that they should be grouped and work as Radio buttons are meant to work: when you click one it is checked and the other is deselected. The two toggle each other, in other words, so only a single one is ever checked.

So, while you can have solitary Radio buttons that are essentially grouped via the name attribute, and while you may want to do this sometimes, it's often better to use the RadioGroup widget instead. The final two Radio buttons are created this way. One of the advantages that the RadioGroup gives you is that you can create columns of Radio buttons. The two grouped Radio buttons flowed straight down the page, and that would have continued it we'd added more. Sometimes this is what you want, but sometimes you have more than a few Radio buttons and you'd prefer to have two per line, side by side, just to save some space and make things look a little better. That's what you can do with RadioGroup. The columns config option tells the widget how many columns you want. Then, the items array specifies all the Radio buttons you want, and RadioGroup takes care of organizing them into columns.

Aside from the columns config option, there's little else specific to RadioGroup. Most of its other config options are from parent objects.

ComboBox

xtype : combo

A ComboBox is a combination of a TextField and a <select> from plain old HTML. Users can type a value in the TextField portion and have the <select> portion automatically match the value as they type. The ComboBox also can be used like a regular <select>, forgoing the ability for the user to type, whichever you need.

A ComboBox looks like what you see in Figure 2-16. There I've begun typing something and the ComboBox has found a match in the drop-down portion.

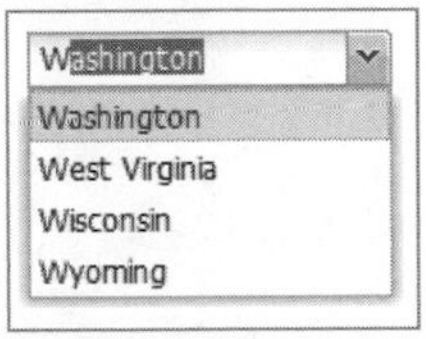

Figure 2-16. *The ComboBox*

There are a couple of ways to create a ComboBox, and we'll see some of the more useful ways in later chapters as we explore the projects. For now here's a very simple method:

```
new Ext.form.ComboBox({
  renderTo : "divTarget", style : "border:1px solid #000000",
  mode : "local", store : [
    "Ford", "Cadillac", "Chevy", "Chrysler", "Dodge",
    "Honda", "Hyundai", "Kia"
  ]
});
```

This creates a ComboBox with eight options in its drop-down section. By default you can type in the TextField portion, so if you type a C for example, you'll find that the drop-down opens up and shows Cadillac, Chevy, and Chrysler as the options. You could point to one and click right then and there, or you could continue to type. Type an H, so the TextField has CH in it, and you'll then see the list shrink down to just Chevy and Chrysler. Now type an E and Chevy will be the only remaining option. At this point if you press Enter or Return, the value Chevy will be copied into the TextField, and that becomes the value of the ComboBox that you can retrieve (which you can retrieve with the getValue() method).

If you want the ComboBox to work like a plain old <select>, you can set the editable config option to false. That's all it takes!

As I mentioned, there are some other more useful usages of the ComboBox, most notably the ability to hook it to a data store, which is a topic we'll discuss shortly. In the next chapter, you'll see an example of doing just that.

TimeField

xtype : timefield

Now that we've seen the ComboBox we can look at the TimeField. It may at first seem a little odd that a field meant for entering time values is related in any way to the ComboBox, but I think once you see Figure 2-17, the mystery will be solved.

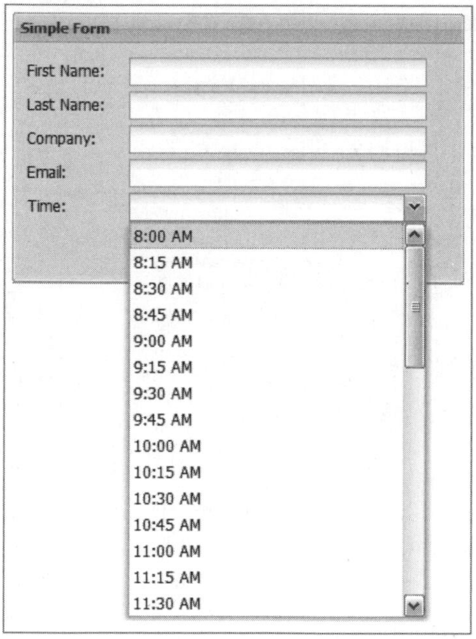

Figure 2-17. *The TimeField*

You create the TimeField just as you would any other widget, as you can see here:

```
Ext.onReady(function() {
  new Ext.form.TimeField( { renderTo : "divTarget" } );
});
```

In its default form, the `TimeField` has options in the drop-down portion starting with 12am and running to 11:45pm in 15-minute intervals. Also by default the `TimeField` works like a `ComboBox` in that the user can type a value and have it be autocompleted.

By default also, the `TimeField` will only allow the user to enter a value that matches one of the options in the drop-down portion. By setting the `forceSelection` config option to `false`, you can allow users to enter other valid time values, such as "11:53 PM."

Form Validation

One of the best things about forms in Ext JS is that they can have validation logic built into them without you having to so much as lift a finger! For example, check out the screenshot in Figure 2-18. Here, the two password fields do not match and the user has been alerted to that fact.

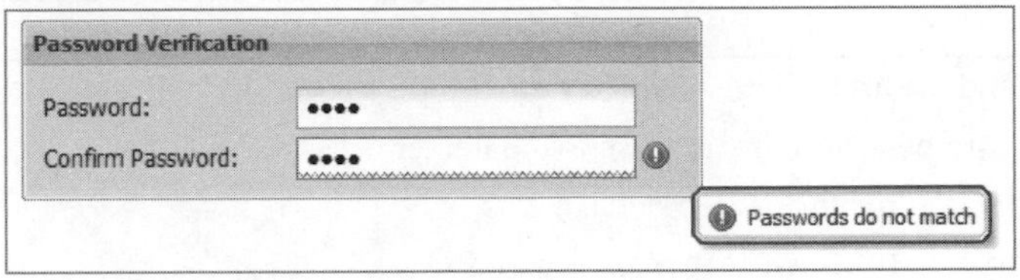

Figure 2-18. *An example of a form validation failure*

Think about this validation and what it would take to implement it. As another example, think about if you wanted the user to enter an e-mail address in a field and ensure it was in a valid form. If you're like me, visions of disgustingly complex regular expressions are dancing in your head right now, and that doesn't even take into account what would be required to highlight the field and show that little tooltip next to it. That's a fair bit of work all told!

In Ext JS, however, validating an e-mail address is as easy as adding a single config option to a `TextField`'s config object:

```
type : "email"
```

Add that, and voilà, any time the user exits the field the validation will be carried out and the tooltip will appear if the field is invalid! There is in fact one more piece to the puzzle to make that fully work, but that's what matters at the field level—we'll see the rest shortly.

Now there's more to it than that: what if, as is usually the case on forms, there is a submit button at the bottom, and we want the submit button to only be enabled when all fields in the form are valid? Again, I'm sure you can imagine the code required in order to pull this off, and while it's not all *that* complex, Ext JS makes it ridiculously simple! Add this config option to the `FormPanel`'s config object:

```
monitorValid : true,
```

This will cause the form to monitor itself to ensure all the fields within it are valid. You can manually check the status of the form at any time by calling the `getForm()` method of the `FormPanel`, and then calling the `isValid()` method on the `Form` object returned by `getForm()`.

However, as is the case with Ext JS most of the time, there is a more elegant solution. You can instead simply add a Button to the form with this config option:

formBind : true

From that point on, the Button will be disabled if any field on the form is invalid; otherwise it will be enabled. That's right—it's completely automatic!

In fact, that's the real beauty of Ext JS's form validation: it's all just some configuration options, after which it's all automatic!

Validating e-mail addresses isn't all Ext JS can do. The e-mail address validation is one of the built-in vtypes, which is short for "validation type." A number of other vtypes are available out of the box, as summarized in Table 2-1.

Table 2-1. *The Vtypes Available by Default with Ext JS*

Vtype	Description
alpha	Only allows letters and the underscore character
alphanum	Only allows letters, numbers, and the underscore character
email	Verifies that the entry is in the form user@domain.com
url	Verifies that the entry is in the form http://www.domain.com

As you can see, there are just some basics there; it's nowhere near all the vtypes you'd probably want and need in a complex application. Fortunately, the vtype system allows you to create your own vtypes very easily. Here's an example of doing just that:

```
Ext.QuickTips.init();
Ext.form.Field.prototype.msgTarget = "side";

Ext.apply(Ext.form.VTypes, {
  phoneMask : /[0-9-]/i,
  phoneText : "Phone number must be in the form 123-456-7890",
  phone : function(v) {
    if (v.length != 12) {
      return false;
    } else {
      return true;
    }
  }
});

var fp = new Ext.FormPanel({
  height : 100, bodyStyle : "padding:4px", monitorValid : true,
  items: [
    { xtype : "textfield", fieldLabel : "Phone #", vtype : "phone" }
  ]
});
```

```
fp.addButton( { text : "Submit", formBind : true } );

var w = new Ext.Window({
  title : "Test Custom VType", closable : false, modal : true,
  width : 310, height : 130, minimizable : false, resizable : false,
  draggable : false, items : [ fp ]
});
w.show();
```

First, we need to turn on the capability in Ext JS to display those tooltips (this is the other piece of the puzzle to get errors to display, as I hinted at earlier). The first two lines accomplish that. More precisely, the first line turns them on and the second globally sets where the icon showing an invalid field should be. In this case we tell Ext JS to put them to the right of the field.

The call to Ext.apply() adds the custom vtype to the Ext.form.VTypes class, which is the class that houses all the built-in vtypes, as well as any we create. Each vtype has three attributes: the *Mask attribute tells Ext JS the regular expression to use to mask off the input. Here, the expression says that only numbers and the dash symbol can be entered. Next is the *Text field, which is the text to be displayed when the field is invalid. Last is the function named after the vtype (which is also the value put in place of the asterisk in the other two attribute names). Here for example, the vtype is phone, so we have phoneMask, phoneText, and the phone() function. The function returns true if the passed-in value of the field, the variable v, is valid, and false if not.

After that, it's a simple matter of creating a FormPanel as we've seen before, making sure we set the monitorValid config option to true this time. The button is then added, with the formBind config option set to true. Finally, a Window is created with the FormPanel as a child of it. If you bring up this example (CustomVType.htm) and try typing in the field, if you press letters you'll notice the Submit button becomes disabled and the field is highlighted in red with the error icon next to it. Hovering over the icon reveals the error message.

You can do arbitrarily complex things in a vtype, even as far as making an Ajax call to a server to do some validation. You'll want to exercise caution doing something like that as it would be easy to destroy the performance of your application. But the basic mechanism is there for you to use (or abuse) as you see fit.

Menus and Toolbars (Oh My!)

Menus and toolbars are fundamental parts of modern GUIs, and Ext JS provides them of course! In Figure 2-19 you can see an example of a Toolbar. Interestingly, it is also an example of a Menu (as we'll discuss later). Notice that the Toolbar has quite a bit of capability built into it: aside from the usual icons, with or without text beside them, you can have toggle buttons, drop-downs, and much more.

Figure 2-19. *A Toolbar*

What I meant about this being a `Menu` as well as a `Toolbar` is that in Ext JS, there is no such thing as a separate menu bar for creating a menu on the top of a page, as is typical in many applications. Instead, you have to use the `Toolbar`, and then attach `Menu`s to buttons on the `Toolbar`. This isn't an optimal situation, and there is discussion on the Ext JS forums about what the future might hold, but this is the case for the current version. You can find at least one extension to Ext JS to give you a "proper" menu bar if you wish. However, as it happens, a `Toolbar` as a menu bar is pretty close to what you would want anyway—and in some ways might even be better.

Let's see how a `Toolbar` and a `Menu` are created:

```
var myMenu = new Ext.menu.Menu({
  items : [
    { text : "Menu Item 1" },
    "-",
    { text : "Menu Item 2", checked : true },
    "-", "<b class=\"menu-title\">Choose an OS</b>",
    { text : "Choose OS", menu : { items: [
      { text : "Windows", checked : true, group : "os" },
      { text : "Linux", checked : false, group : "os" }
    ]}}
  ]
});

new Ext.Panel({
  renderTo : "panelTarget", layout : "fit", border : false,
  items : [{
    xtype : "toolbar", items : [
      {
        text : "Toolbar Item 1", icon : "toolbarItem1.gif",
        cls : "x-btn-text-icon", handler : function() {
          alert("Toolbar Item 1 was clicked");
        }
      },
      { xtype : "tbspacer" },
      {
        icon : "toolbarItem2.gif", cls : "x-btn-icon",
        handler : function() {
          new Ext.Window({
            closable : true, modal : true, width : 300, height : 100,
            minimizable : false, resizable : false, draggable : false,
            html : "I am a window displayed from a toolbar button"
          }).show();
        }
      },
      {xtype:"tbspacer"}, {xtype:"tbseparator"}, {xtype:"tbspacer"},
      { text : "Click for Menu", menu : myMenu }
    ]
  }]
});
```

This is the code from the `ToolbarAndMenu.htm` example file. As you can see, two things are being created here: a `Menu` first, and then a `Toolbar` (within a `Panel`, so really three things). Let's start with the `Menu`.

A `Menu`, by itself, is just a container for other items. Take any menu bar in any application. When you click one of the words up top, like the typical File menu item in many applications, you get a pop-up window that happens to be anchored to that text, and this window has the menu items on it. This is a `Menu` object to Ext JS. You basically created these `Menu` objects, and then attached them to other elements (even the page, if you want a right-click context pop-up menu, for example). To create a menu bar, you would create a series of `Menu` objects and then attach them to a `Toolbar`. I'm getting ahead of myself here a bit!

Creating a `Menu`, of type `Ext.menu.Menu`, is little more than instantiating it and passing it the config object, in typical Ext JS fashion. This config object contains an `items` array, and each object in that array describes an item on the menu. For simple text items that can be clicked and that you can write code to react to, the object needs simply to have a `text` attribute, as you can see in the code with the first item in the array.

The second item is some literal text, and in this case it's a bit of text that Ext JS recognizes. A single dash means draw a divider line on the menu. You can put in any text you like, but it will become simply static text on the menu, good for headers and such. In fact, jumping ahead a bit, I've done exactly that with the fifth item in the array, "Choose an OS text." For that particular item I've also demonstrated that you can put arbitrary HTML in there, and I've used the `menu-title` CSS selector to style it (this selector is provided by Ext JS).

Going back a bit now, the third item in the array is a check box item. All it takes is adding the `checked` config option and Ext JS knows you want it to be a `CheckBox` item now. You can include a `checkHandler` attribute in the object as well, which is a reference to a function to execute when the item is checked (or unchecked).

The sixth item in the array shows that you can have submenus as well. You can then add any items you wish to it, and I've done so here. The items are this time `Radio` buttons because I've included the `group` attribute, which forces Ext JS not to make them `CheckBoxes`—as it would have done by virtue of the `checked` attribute—but to make them `Radio` buttons.

Now that we've created a menu, we can move on to creating the `Toolbar`. In this example I've made it a child of a `Panel`, and so I've used the `xtype` approach to create it. Just like a `Menu`, a `Toolbar` has an `items` array to describe each element to add to it. The first element I've added is a simple button that has an icon and some text next to it. The Ext JS-supplied `x-btn-text-icon` selector sets the styles appropriately for displaying both an icon and the text. The `icon` attribute tells Ext JS the name of the graphics file to use as the icon. The `handler` attribute is the function to execute when the item is clicked—here just displaying an `alert()` message.

The second element added with the `xtype` `tbspacer` is a spacer element that puts some blank space between elements. This allows you to make the `Toolbar` look just how you want.

The third element added is another button, this time one with just an icon. In this case the `x-btn-icon` selector is used to get rid of the text and the space otherwise reserved for it. The `handler` attribute is again used to react to the user clicking the button. This time around it displays a `Window`, which we've seen before but which we'll discuss further in a bit.

The fourth and sixth elements are again spacers, while the fifth element sandwiched between them is another special `xtype`, `tbseparator`. This draws a vertical line on the `Toolbar`, which is typically used to separate groups of icons.

The final element added is a simple text item, no icon or anything, but it has something new: the menu attribute. This refers back to the myMenu Menu created right before the Toolbar. Now when you click this button on Toolbar, the Menu we created will pop up below it. We've effectively made a Menu out of the Toolbar! You can imagine a series of these text-only buttons on the Toolbar, each with a Menu attached to it, and you can see how it would essentially simulate a menu bar.

The Toolbar can house a number of other elements, but I feel it would be better to introduce them as needed throughout the projects to come. With what you've seen here, you have the basics you need to understand those other capabilities; they build directly off what you've seen here.

Note One of the problems with using a Toolbar as a menu bar is that the buttons on the Toolbar have arrows next to them, which normal menus that we all know and love usually don't. As it happens, there is a way to get rid of the arrow (actually, there appears to be multiple ways). If you add this code to the Toolbar item with the menu attached, the arrow goes away:

```
listeners: { "render" : function(b) {
  b.el.child(b.menuClassTarget).removeClass("x-btn-with-menu");
}}
```

Not, perhaps, the best solution, but one that works.

Trees in Ext JS

Trees are another famous widget that you see all over the place. If you're a Windows user you are familiar with Trees as the list of folders on the left of Windows Explorer. Trees are great for displaying hierarchical data in a way that lets the user drill down into the data. In Figure 2-20 you can see an example of a Tree.

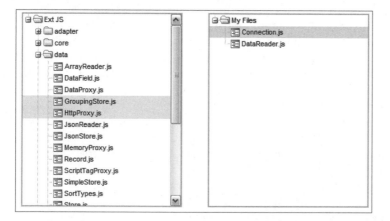

Figure 2-20. *Trees in Ext JS, two of them to be precise!*

Actually, that's *two* Trees! This example, from the Ext JS web site, shows one of the more advanced features of Trees: the ability to drag and drop items from one Tree to another!

For now, however, let's deal with a much simpler example by creating a Tree and populating it manually in code:

```
var treeData = [
  { authorName : "Stephen King", books : [
      "Carrie", "It", "The Stand", "Cujo"
    ]
  },
  { authorName : "Michael Crichton", books : [
      "Jurassic Park", "The Lost World"
    ]
  },
  { authorName : "Isaac Asimov", books : [
      "2001", "2010", "2069"
    ]
  }
];

var tree = new Ext.tree.TreePanel({
  renderTo : "panelTarget", layout : "fit", width : 250, height : 300,
  title : "Tree",
  root : new Ext.tree.TreeNode( { text : "Authors" } )
});

var rootNode = tree.getRootNode();
for (var i = 0; i < treeData.length; i++) {
  var node = rootNode.appendChild(new Ext.tree.TreeNode({
    text : treeData[i].authorName
  }));
  for (var j = 0; j < treeData[i].books.length; j++) {
    node.appendChild(new Ext.tree.TreeNode({
      text : treeData[i].books[j], listeners : {
        "click" : function(node) {
          alert("You clicked: " + node.text);
        }
      }
    }));
  }
}
```

Trees aren't something you deal with directly. Instead, you use the TreePanel. This is a Panel like any other, which means it can partake in all the layout magic Ext JS offers.

The code begins with some plain old JavaScript objects in an array. This is the data we're going to load into the Tree. Next, the TreePanel is instantiated. When you do this, you need to specify a root node (of type TreeNode) for the Tree, or things don't work. A TreeNode has a text attribute, which contains what is displayed on the page. You can also specify an id attribute for working with the nodes in the Tree later.

A TreeNode can have any number of child nodes, or it can be on its own, which is referred to as a leaf node. In this case we have the root node, which is a special case because, presumably, there will always be child nodes underneath it (otherwise a Tree wouldn't be much good!). Here, the root node represents authors.

Once the TreePanel is created and rendered, we can add some data to it. To do so, we first get a reference to the root node by calling getRootNode() on the TreeNode object. Then, we begin to iterate over the treeData array. Each element in the array is an object that contains an authorName attribute as well as a books attribute, which is an array of plain strings.

For each object in the treeData array, we create an Ext.tree.TreeNode, giving it the text taken from the authorName attribute. We use the appendChild() method of the root TreeNode object to add that node beneath the root node.

Then, we iterate over the books array for that author. For each we again create a TreeNode object with the text matching the next element in the books array, which is a book title. We append each of these TreeNode objects to the TreeNode for the author (to which we stored a reference in the node variable when we made the call to the appendChild() method). The net result is that we get a Tree with authors at the top, with three authors below it: Stephen King, Michael Crichton, and Isaac Asimov. Beneath each of those authors are a couple of book titles.

The user can now click each of the nodes to expand it and see what's below it. Clicking on Stephen King, for example, reveals four book titles: *Carrie*, *It*, *The Stand*, and *Cujo*. You'll also notice that when we created the TreeNode objects for each book, a listeners object was passed with a handler for the click event. So, if you click one of the book titles you'll get an alert() message saying you clicked the given title.

Loading a Tree like this is a little atypical. The more common way is via remote loading of data. Doing so is a simple matter. First, add a loader attribute to the config options of your Tree. This option points to an instance of Ext.tree.TreeLoader. You construct a TreeLoader like so:

```
var myTreeLoader = new Ext.tree.TreeLoader({
  dataUrl : "getMyData.jsp"
});
```

Now, assuming getMyData.jsp is on the same server that served the page this code is in, and assuming the returned data from that call is in the appropriate JSON form, the Tree will be populated automatically. The correct JSON form is this:

```
[
  { text: "Stephen King", children : [
    { text : "Carrie", leaf: true },
    { text : "It", leaf: true },
    { text : "The Stand", leaf: true },
    { text : "Cujo", leaf: true }
  ]},
  { text: "Michael Crichton", children : [
    { text : "Jurassic Park", leaf: true },
    { text : "The Lost World", leaf: true }
  ]},
```

```
{ text: "Isaac Asimov", children : [
  { text : "2001", leaf: true },
  { text : "2010", leaf: true },
  { text : "2069", leaf: true }
]}
]
```

This would generate the same Tree that we did via code, but without all that iterating over data and such we had to do ourselves. This is great if your data comes from a server-side source. But since that isn't always the case, knowing you can do it both ways is obviously good!

Grids in Ext JS

The Grid is one of the handiest widgets out there, and is about as common as a button is these days! A Grid is used to display columnar data that more times than not is a fairly large set of data and allows the user to scroll through that large set of data little by little. In Figure 2-21 is an example of a relatively simple Grid.

Company	Price	Change	% Change	Last Updated
3M CO	$71.72	0.02	0.03%	09/01/2008
Alcoa Inc	$29.01	0.42	1.47%	09/01/2008
Altria Group Inc	$83.81	0.28	0.34%	09/01/2008
American Express Company	$52.55	0.01	0.02%	09/01/2008
American International Group, Inc.	$64.13	0.31	0.49%	09/01/2008
AT&T Inc.	$31.61	-0.48	-1.54%	09/01/2008
Boeing Co.	$75.43	0.53	0.71%	09/01/2008
Caterpillar Inc.	$67.27	0.92	1.39%	09/01/2008
Citigroup, Inc.	$49.37	0.02	0.04%	09/01/2008
E.I. du Pont de Nemours and Company	$40.48	0.51	1.28%	09/01/2008
Exxon Mobil Corp	$68.10	-0.43	-0.64%	09/01/2008
General Electric Company	$34.14	-0.08	-0.23%	09/01/2008
General Motors Corporation	$30.27	1.09	3.74%	09/01/2008
Hewlett-Packard Co.	$36.53	-0.03	-0.08%	09/01/2008

Figure 2-21. *An example of a basic Grid*

The Grid in Ext JS is full featured, to say the least! For example, you can sort the data by clicking a column header. This is done on the client side and so is quite fast and doesn't impact your server infrastructure at all. You can also drag columns around, so if you wanted to see the Price field first, you could drag it and drop it before the Company column. Users can even turn columns off if they aren't interested in the data they contain.

You can resize the columns by dragging the vertical line between them. The Grid supports row striping, which is a slight color tint to the background of the row (usual gray) that makes it easier for users to track their eyes across the data.

The Grid can even have editable fields embedded within it, as you can see in Figure 2-22.

Edit Plants?				
Add Plant				
Common Name ▲	Light	Price	Available	Indoor?
Adder's-Tongue	Shade	$9.58	Apr 13, 2006	☑
Anemone	Mostly Shady	$8.86	Dec 26, 2006	☑
Bee Balm	Shade	$4.59	May 03, 2006	☑
Bergamot123	Shade	$7.16	Apr 27, 2006	☑
Black-Eyed Susan	Sunny	$9.80	Jun 18, 2006	☐
Bloodroot	Mostly Shady	$2.44	Mar 15, 2006	☑
Blue Gentian	Sun or Shade	$8.56	May 02, 2006	☐
Buttercup	Shade	$2.57	Jun 10, 2006	☑
Butterfly Weed	Sunny	$2.78	Jun 30, 2006	☐
California Poppy	Sunny	$7.89	Mar 27, 2006	☐

Figure 2-22. *An example of a Grid with editable fields embedded within it*

The `Grid` is always what's called a data-bound widget, which is a concept we'll be discussing very soon. In short, though, it means that you have some data, and the `Grid` is bound to it so that it is automatically populated from the data, and changes to the data *can* replicate back into the data automatically. This saves you from entering a lot of tedious code to populate the `Grid`.

■**Note** In fact, I wasn't able to find a way to manually add a row to a `Grid` at all. It seems that you always have to go through the data store (i.e., add some data to the store, and the `Grid` will automatically be refreshed). This makes working with a `Grid` very easy, and also consistent, since the data model is a concept that is used by other widgets. However, at the same time it's a little disconcerting at first because it seems as if you don't have as much control as you should. Rest assured; the data-binding capabilities in Ext JS more than make up for it!

`Grid`s can do even fancier things too. For example, in Figure 2-23 you can see a `Grid` that allows for grouping of elements. These groups can be expanded and contracted as the user desires.

Sponsored Projects				
Task	Due Date ▲	Estimate	Rate	Cost
☐ Ext Forms: Field Anchoring				
Integrate 2.0 Forms with 2.0 Layouts	06/24/2007	6 hours	$150.00	$900.00
Implement AnchorLayout	06/25/2007	4 hours	$150.00	$600.00
Add support for multiple types of anchors	06/27/2007	4 hours	$150.00	$600.00
Testing and debugging	06/29/2007	8 hours	$0.00	$0.00
(4 Tasks)	06/29/2007	22 hours	$112.50	$2,100.00
☐ Ext Grid: Single-level Grouping				
Add required rendering "hooks" to GridView	07/01/2007	6 hours	$100.00	$600.00
Extend GridView and override rendering functions	07/03/2007	6 hours	$100.00	$600.00
Extend Store with grouping functionality	07/04/2007	4 hours	$100.00	$400.00
Default CSS Styling	07/05/2007	2 hours	$100.00	$200.00
Testing and debugging	07/06/2007	6 hours	$100.00	$600.00
(5 Tasks)	07/06/2007	24 hours	$100.00	$2,400.00
☐ Ext Grid: Summary Rows				
Ext Grid plugin integration	07/01/2007	4 hours	$125.00	$500.00
Summary creation during rendering phase	07/02/2007	4 hours	$125.00	$500.00
Dynamic summary updates in editor grids	07/05/2007	6 hours	$125.00	$750.00

Figure 2-23. *An example not only of a more advanced Grid, but of the Ext JS plug-in capabilities*

The Grid even supports drag-and-drop capabilities, so the user can move rows around as they see fit (or drag them to other drag and drop–aware widgets). You can apply filtering to a Grid's data and make the filtering user driven. The Grid widget also has support for paging through large sets of data and for retrieving each page of data from a remote source, even across domains!

You'll notice that I haven't included any code example for this widget, and that's very much on purpose. If all those capabilities I mentioned earlier sounded a bit overwhelming, that's because they are! I believe that for this widget, you would be better served to have it revealed little by little during the course of dissecting the projects. We'll see plenty of Grid examples throughout the rest of the book, and many of these capabilities will be seen (but not all of them). I think that will make it seem less daunting than trying to demonstrate everything right here. Also, since a Grid is always bound to a source of data, and since we haven't really talked about that yet, it would be jumping the gun a bit and might wind up being confusing.

Rest assured, though, the Grid is going to be your friend by the end of this book, and you'll know it well!

The Other Widgets

There are a number of other widgets that sit in the main Ext namespace that I'd like to look at as well. Some of them fit conceptually with the others previously discussed (such as DatePicker, which logically fits with the form widgets), but others are off on their own. Some of these are special-purpose widgets that you probably won't use quite as much, others are perhaps a little controversial (some people feel they shouldn't be part of Ext JS at all), but still others are things you'll use very often.

ColorPalette

xtype : colorpalette

The ColorPalette widget is a relatively simple widget that has a highly specialized focus: allowing the user to choose a color. You've no doubt seen this in your favorite word processing program when you want to change the color of some text. You are presented, quite literally, with a palette of colors to choose from. Simply click one and you're good to go. The ColorPalette widget looks like Figure 2-24.

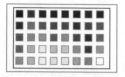

Figure 2-24. *The ColorPalette widget (which looks much better on a color monitor obviously!)*

The code for getting this up on the screen is pretty simple:

```
new Ext.ColorPalette({
  renderTo : "divTarget", style : "border:1px solid #000000",
  listeners : {
    select : function(inPalette, inColor) {
      alert(inColor);
    }
  }
});
```

The select listener fires when a color is clicked, and here I'm just displaying the color. So, for example, if you click a pure red square on the palette, the alert would say #ff0000, which is the hexadecimal RGB value corresponding to pure red.

I won't go into much more detail than this because, frankly, there's not a whole lot more to go into anyway. But more importantly, this is a specific use-case type of widget, so when you happen to need it you can look up the remaining few details.

DatePicker

xtype : datepicker

The DatePicker you've already essentially seen: the DateField form widget. The only real difference is that the DateField widget popped up the calendar when the user clicked an icon, and is specially designed to work within a form, whereas a DatePicker is basically the calendar portion of the DateField but stands on its own.

DatePicker is a good choice when you want to show a calendar to users all the time, not just when they click an icon. Figure 2-25 shows the DatePicker.

Figure 2-25. *The DatePicker widget*

The disabledDates config option allows you to specify an array of dates that should be disabled so the user can't select them. Similarly, the disabledDays option allows you to disable days of the week (0 for Sundays, 1 for Mondays, 2 for Tuesdays, and so on... so a value of [0,2,4] would disable Sundays, Tuesdays, and Thursdays). The minDate option allows you to specify the lowest date the user can select, which is useful if past dates are not valid inputs. The select event is probably the primary event you'll be interested in, and it fires when the user selects a date.

Window

xtype : window

If you've ever done any Microsoft Windows development, the concept of a Window is quite familiar to you. Check that: if you've ever simply *used* any modern GUI-based operating system, you are quite familiar with a Window!

In Ext JS, Windows are first-class citizens and have pretty much all the features a Window on a proper OS has. They can be minimized, maximized, resized, and dragged around; they can overlap other Windows and UI elements; they can host other widgets; and they can have animation effects when they open or are closed.

We've already seen at least one Window as part of the AnchorLayout example. Windows can have layouts applied to the elements displayed within them. In a sense, you can think of Windows as their own Viewports.

We'll be seeing plenty of Windows throughout the rest of this book, and you'll get to know them very well. For now I think taking a look back at the AnchorLayout code is enough (so, like, go ahead and flip back a few pages and check it out again if you want!).

Slider

xtype : slider

A Slider is another standard GUI widget that most of us know and love (or hate...some people are pretty adamant that a Slider shouldn't ever be used). A Slider is a good choice when you want the user to select a value within a specific range in discrete increments in a visual way. As you can see in Figure 2-26, the Slider in Ext JS is fairly robust.

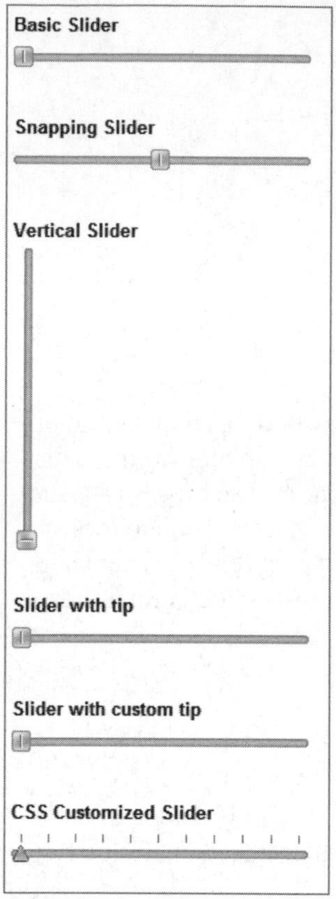

Figure 2-26. *A couple of variants of the Slider widget*

Creating a Slider is a piece of cake, as we've come to expect of all Ext JS widgets. Here's some simple code to demonstrate it:

```
new Ext.Panel({
  renderTo : "panelTarget", layout : "fit", width : 500,
  title : "Slider",
  items : [
    {
      xtype : "slider", value : 150, increment : 25,
      minValue : 0, maxValue : 500
    }
  ]
});
```

The Slider supports a couple of useful config options. First, the value option sets the initial value of the Slider. The increment option determines in what increments the user can change the value of the Slider. This is accomplished by simply clicking the knob, or handle, and dragging it left or right (or up or down in the case of a vertical Slider). The minValue and maxValue options determine the upper and lower limits of the range. While you may at some point see a Slider that allows the user to select something that is non-numeric, underneath it all the values are always numeric.

Note For example, in one of my previous books, *Practical Dojo Projects* (Apress, 2008), one of the projects was a game that used a Slider, which the Dojo library also offers, to allow the user to select a difficulty level. The values were easy, medium, and hard—at least, those were the values the user would see. Underneath the covers, though, each of those had a numeric value assigned to it, since that's what a Slider deals with behind the scenes.

The user can also click somewhere on the Slider's bar to change the value, which causes it to jump to the nearest incremental value. The clickToChange config option, which defaults to true, can be used to turn that off (set it to false). The vertical config option, when set to true, makes the Slider orient up and down, as you can see in Figure 2-26 with the third Slider. The getValue() method, likely the most important method available, is used to retrieve the current value of the Slider. There is likewise a setValue() method if you need to set the value after the Slider is created. Note that, as far as I can tell, there is no way to change the increment, maxValue, and minValue settings after creating a Slider, so you have to know those before you instantiate it.

ProgressBar

`xtype : progress`

Look, nobody likes to wait, least of all me! I want what I want, and I want it now!

Of course, life doesn't work that way, and unfortunately, neither does software. It is often the case that there is some task our computer needs to execute while we simply sit there and wait. A good application will give the user some indication that things are proceeding normally and how far along in the process things are. That's exactly what the ProgressBar is for. Take a look at Figure 2-27 to see what I'm talking about.

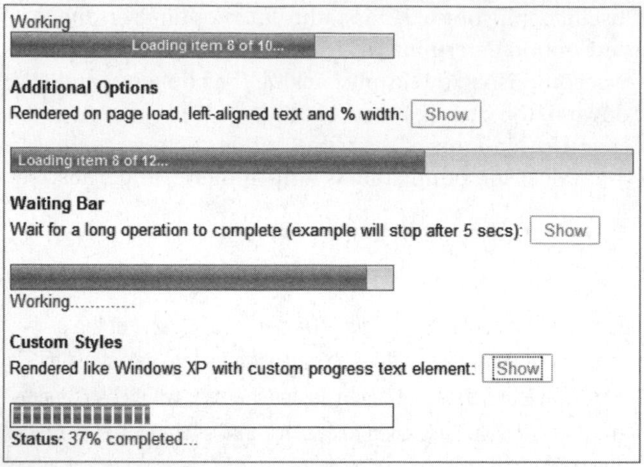

Figure 2-27. *Some variants of the ProgressBar widget*

There are a couple of ways to use this widget. Here's an example of one:

```
new Ext.Panel({
  renderTo : "panelTarget", layout : "fit", width : 500,
  title : "ProgressBar",
  items : [
    {
      xtype : "progress", id : "pb"
    }
  ]
});
Ext.getCmp("pb").wait({
  interval : 100, increment : 100,
  text : "Processing, please wait..."
});
```

Here we're creating a ProgressBar with an id of pb. Then, we get a reference to it via Ext.getCmp() and call its wait() method. This method allows us to use a ProgressBar in one of its two supported modes: auto-updating (manual updating is the other mode—more on this shortly). In this mode, the ProgressBar will simply go off and update itself over some period of time in some given increment step. This is a good choice if the operation the user has to wait for doesn't have predetermined "checkpoints." This way, users have something to look at that indicates the process is running.

In this mode, we pass a config object to the wait() method. This object, in this case, has three attributes. The first, interval, determines how often we want the ProgressBar to update itself, in milliseconds. So here we'll have ten updates per second. The increment attribute tells the widget how many progress update segments to fill in with each interval. How many update segments there will be depends on how wide the ProgressBar is. If the ProgressBar gets filled up, it will reset (i.e., empty) and start filling again. Finally, the text attribute determines what text to show within the ProgressBar as it is running.

In manual mode, it is your responsibility to update the value of the ProgressBar. This is the right way to go if you know, for instance, that the process that is running has five discrete parts to it. That way, you can update the ProgressBar when each part completes, thereby giving the user a true indication of how far along the process is. In this mode you would pass text as part of the config object passed to the ProgressBar constructor, and you would not call the wait() method. Instead, you would make calls to the updateProgress() method to set the value (and optionally new text) of the widget.

In general, you should use the manual mode any time you can because it has more true meaning to the user. Use the auto-updating mode when the process being waited on is more indeterminate.

Working with Data in Ext JS

Having all these widgets is great! It allows us to create some truly great web UIs with a minimum of effort. We can create applications that not only look fantastic but that expose advanced functionality to the user.

However, at the end of the day, nearly all applications have to have some data to operate on. It's one thing to be able to create a Grid, but a Grid isn't much good without information to put into it. With many other libraries, data is something that is left entirely to you. Sure, the library may give you an easy way to create a Grid, but putting data into it is your job.

With Ext JS, you can do things that way too. You can take control of every last detail and take all responsibility for populating widgets with data. However, if you're looking for something a bit better, Ext JS is there for you.

Data binding is the name of the game! The term "data binding" refers to a technique where something, often GUI widgets, is declaratively bound to a data source. This binding provides the capability to automatically update the widget when the underlying data changes. You don't have to poll the data source and update anything yourself, and you don't even have to tie into events and do some processing. True data binding gives you everything for free (or at least very close to free).

In Ext JS, two key concepts underlie data binding: Records and Stores (or data stores, if you want to be more pedantic). A Store is a client-side cache of Record objects. The data might have originated on the client, read in from cookies or some other mechanism (like Gears, which we'll be discussing shortly), or it may have come from a server-side data store.

A Record is a low-level description of the data. Let's jump right in and see some code:

```
var PersonRecord = Ext.data.Record.create([
  { name : "id", mapping : "id" },
  { name : "firstName", mapping : "firstName" },
  { name : "lastName", mapping : "lastName" }
]);
```

This code creates a type of Record. The Ext.data.Record class exposes a create() method that creates a constructor for a given record layout. In simpler terms, it creates a new subclass of the Record class itself. The object you pass into the create() method describes the structure of the data. It's a simple structure that mimics rows in a database table. In this example we have three fields that describe a person: id, firstName, and lastName. The mapping attribute maps a given field to some underlying JavaScript object. Ext JS seeks to abstract the underlying data store from its own data implementation, so at some point you will create a Record based on some JavaScript object. The fields in that object may not match the fields in the Record— in name, that is—so the mapping attribute allows you to map a Record field to an object field whose name may not match.

■**Note** In theory, the mapping attribute is only necessary if the fields of the Record don't match the names of the fields in the underlying object. In practice, however, I find that my code doesn't work if I don't explicitly include the mapping attribute, even when the field names are the same. I'm not sure why this is, so you may want to include the mapping attribute even when it isn't necessary. I don't see where there's any harm in doing so.

Once you have a Record, the next step is to create a Store for instances of that Record. While you could have Records that you put in simple arrays, or just have individual variables pointing to the Records, putting them in a Store is the most common approach. In addition, it provides a host of capabilities, such as filtering, retrieval, event-based updates, and more.

To create a Store, you write code like this:

```
var peopleStore = new Ext.data.Store({});
```

Yep, that's right: strictly speaking, that's all you need to do! There are a couple of different types of stores to choose from, but this gives you a plain-vanilla Store, which oftentimes is all you need. There is also a JsonStore, which includes built-in Ajax mechanisms for loading remote data in JSON form from a server. Also available is the GroupingStore, which adds capabilities for grouping Records based on a specified field. You will also see the SimpleStore floating around, which is an extended Store that makes loading data from JavaScript arrays a littler easier. In this book we'll primarily be dealing with your basic, run-of-the-mill Store, but at the end of the day the basic concepts are still the same.

Although most of the time you don't need to concern yourself with it, a Store will use some implementation of the Reader abstract class. A Reader knows how to take data in some underlying JavaScript form, be it an array or JSON string, and turn it into a Record object, as well as some metadata that the Store needs.

Another concept that you sometimes need to think about is the DataProxy. A DataProxy implementation (DataProxy is an abstract class) knows how to retrieve data in the underlying JavaScript form. In conjunction with a Reader, the DataProxy provides a batch of Records to a Store. Some available DataProxy implementations include the ScriptTagProxy, which allows you to read JSON-P data from a remote URL using dynamic <script> tag insertion; HttpProxy, which supports Ajax requests to retrieve data; and DataProxy, which accepts data during its construction and returns it when the Reader calls the proxy's load() method (which is the method always called by the Reader implementation to request data from the proxy).

Figure 2-28 illustrates the relationship between these components.

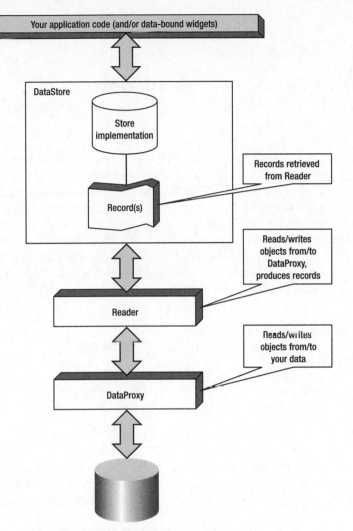

Figure 2-28. *Diagram of the components of the Ext JS data system*

In this book, we won't need to concern ourselves with DataProxys or Readers; we'll only focus on Records and Stores.

We saw how to create a type of Record, and we saw how to create a basic Store. So how do we load data into the Store? There are several ways; here's a simple one:

```
var people = [
  { firstName : "James", lastName : "Cameron" },
  { firstName : "Ron", lastName : "Howard" },
  { firstName : "Uwe", lastName : "Bole" }
];
```

```
for (var i = 0; i < people.length; i++) {
  peopleStore.add(
    new PersonRecord({
      id : new Date().getTime(),
      firstName : people[i].firstName, lastName : people[i].lastName
    })
  );
}
```

Here we have a basic JavaScript array of objects; each object contains a firstName and a lastName field. So, we simply iterate over this array and for each object we call the add() method of the Store. Passed to this method is a new instance of PersonRecord. The constructor to the PersonRecord accepts an object whose fields are mapped to the fields of the newly created Record based on the mapping attribute specified in the Record specification. The id field is autogenerated using the millisecond value of a Date object. That's all it takes! From this point on, we have a Store with three Records in it; each Record has the data taken from the array.

The next order of business is to take this populated Store and bind it to a widget. That's even simpler than you might think, as you can see for yourself:

```
new Ext.grid.GridPanel({
  store : peopleStore, renderTo : "panelTarget", width : 500,
  height : 150, autoExpandColumn : "lastName", title : "List of people",
  columns: [
    { header : "ID", width : 120, dataIndex : "id"},
    { header : "First Name", width : 150, dataIndex : "firstName" },
    { id : "lastName", header : "Last Name", dataIndex : "lastName" }
  ]
});
```

It literally takes only two things: the store attribute points to the data Store to use, and the elements in the columns array include a dataIndex attribute to specify which field in the Records returned by the Store each column maps to. Just like that, our Grid shows the Records in the Store!

Now, the neat thing is that if we modify a record in the Store, the Grid will automatically be updated! For example:

```
var record = store.getAt(0);
record.set("firstName", "Mike");
```

This will retrieve the first Record in the store, the one with the firstName "James" and the lastName "Cameron", and changes the firstName to "Mike" (thereby changing a famous movie director to a not-quite-as-famous baseball player[2]). Best of all, that change will instantly appear in the Grid, without our having to write any code or do anything at all. That, my friend, is the power of data binding!

Many Ext JS widgets include data-binding capabilities, but not all. Some that do include the ComboBox, DataView (which we'll look at next), and the Grid.

---

2 James Cameron is the famous director of such Hollywood hits as *Aliens*, *Titanic*, *The Abyss*, and *Terminator 2*. Mike Cameron on the other hand is a Major League Baseball player, an outfielder, who has played for such teams as the Chicago White Sox, Cincinnati Reds, and New York Mets.

The Template and XTemplate Classes

Templating used to be the purview of "grown-up" languages like Java, but nowadays, in the world of "professional" JavaScript, templating has found its way to the client as well.

Templating involves inserting dynamic data into static text to produce a final fragment of text, typically HTML for web development. Ext JS provides a robust templating mechanism via the Template and XTemplate classes.

The difference between the two is that the Template class provides a relatively bare-bones mechanism, whereas XTemplate provides more advanced features, such as conditional processing, comparison operators, subtemplates, basic math function support, and special built-in template variables. Let's look at an example of both, shown in Listing 2-2.

Listing 2-2. *The Madlib Example*

```
<html>

  <head>

    <title>Chapter 2 Template/XTemplate Example</title>

    <script type="text/javascript" src="ext/adapter/ext/ext-base.js"></script>
    <script type="text/javascript" src="ext/ext-all.js"></script>

    <script>

      function doMadlib1() {

        var t = new Ext.Template(
          "Dear {personName},<br><br>",
          "It is with great regret that I inform you that your ",
          "{color} {animalType} {petName} ",
          "has met with an unfortunate accident that caused their ",
          "{bodyPart} to be turned into a stalk of celery while {animalsName} ",
          "was at {place}.<br><br>",
          "Err, sorry 'bout that!<br><br>",
          "Sincerely,<br>",
          "Mom"
        );
        var vals = Ext.query("input[class=mlf1]");
        t.append("Madlib1Results", {
          personName : vals[0].value,
          color : vals[1].value,
          animalType : vals[2].value,
          petName : vals[3].value,
          bodyPart : vals[4].value,
          place : vals[5].value
        });
```

```
      }

    function doMadlib2() {

      var t = new Ext.XTemplate(
        "The robot overlords from planet {planetName} have declared that as ",
        "of this time, no human may acquire the following items:<br><ul>",
        "<tpl for=\"bannedItems\">",
        "<li>{itemName} - Reason: {noReason}</li>",
        "</tpl>",
        "</ul>"
      );
      var vals = Ext.query("input[class=mlf2]");
      Ext.getDom("Madlib2Results").innerHTML = t.applyTemplate(
        {
          planetName : vals[0].value,
          bannedItems : [
            { itemName : vals[1].value, noReason : vals[2].value },
            { itemName : vals[3].value, noReason : vals[4].value }
          ]
        }
      );

    }

  </script>

</head>

<body>

  <h1>Template/XTemplate-based Madlibs</h1>
  <table border="0" cellpadding="2" cellspacing="2">
    <tr>
      <td>
        <form name="Madlib1Form">
          A person's name: <input class="mlf1" type="text">
          <br>
          A color: <input class="mlf1" type="text">
          <br>
          A type of animal: <input class="mlf1" type="text">
          <br>
          A pet's name: <input class="mlf1" type="text">
          <br>
          A body part: <input class="mlf1" type="text">
          <br>
```

```
            A place: <input class="mlf1" type="text">
            <br><br>
            <input type="button" value="Create Madlib" onClick="doMadlib1();">
            <br>
          </form>
        </td>
        <td>
          <div id="Madlib1Results"
            style="border:1px solid #000000;width:400px;height:240px;"></div>
        </td>
      </tr>
      <tr>
        <td colspan="2">
          <br><hr><br>
        </td>
      </tr>
      <tr>
        <td>
          <form name="Madlib2Form">
            A planet name: <input class="mlf2" type="text">
            <br>
            An item: <input class="mlf2" type="text">
            <br>
            A reason to not allow it: <input class="mlf2" type="text">
            <br>
            Another item: <input class="mlf2" type="text">
            <br>
            Another reason to not allow it: <input class="mlf2" type="text">
            <br><br>
            <input type="button" value="Create Madlib" onClick="doMadlib2();">
            <br>
          </form>
        </td>
        <td>
          <div id="Madlib2Results"
            style="border:1px solid #000000;width:400px;height:240px;"></div>
        </td>
      </tr>
    </table>

  </body>

</html>
```

Do you remember those things called Mad Libs that you used to do as a kid? You are asked
for a noun, a verb, the name of an animal, a color, whatever, and they get plugged into some
text and it generates a mostly nonsensical little story? That's precisely what this example is.

If you look at the <body> section, you'll see some simple markup consisting of two forms laid out via a <table> (I know, it's evil to use tables for layout, but you know, if it works, why not?). Note that the fields in the forms don't have names associated with them. While it doesn't have anything to do with Template or XTemplate, there's a neat function in Ext JS that we'll see, the query() method, that allows us to deal with this situation.

Note that each form has a button that when clicked calls either doMadlib1() or doMadlib2(), depending on which form it was. For example, the button on the first form calls doMadlib1(), which is:

```
var t = new Ext.Template(
  "Dear {personName},<br><br>",
  "It is with great regret that I inform you that your ",
  "{color} {animalType} {petName} ",
  "has met with an unfortunate accident that caused their ",
  "{bodyPart} to be turned into a stalk of celery while {animalsName} ",
  "was at {place}.<br><br>",
  "Err, sorry 'bout that!<br><br>",
  "Sincerely,<br>",
  "Mom"
);
var vals = Ext.query("input[class=mlf1]");
t.overwrite("Madlib1Results", {
  personName : vals[0].value,
  color : vals[1].value,
  animalType : vals[2].value,
  petName : vals[3].value,
  bodyPart : vals[4].value,
  place : vals[5].value
});
```

A new Ext.Template object is instantiated, and a variable-length argument list (containing as many elements as you like) is passed to its constructor. The arguments are concatenated into one giant string, and that's our template text. You'll note that within the text are tokens in the form {xxx}. They will be replaced dynamically with the values from the form.

Now, how do we get those values? Again, this isn't related to templating, but the Ext.query() method is the answer. We use a simple CSS selector query that says to give us back all the <input> tags on the page that have a class attribute value of mlf1. If you look back at the markup, you'll see that all the <input> tags in the first form have such a class value, whereas all the <input> tags in the second form have a class or mlf2. So, the net result is that vals now holds a reference to an array, where each element of the array is one of the <input> tags in the first form.

So, now that we have a Template and we have the values from the form, it's time to merge them. There are a couple of methods you could execute on the Template object at this point. The apply() method would insert the data, which we pass to it as an object that presumably has fields matching the tokens in the template text. This would return an HTML fragment that we could do whatever we want with. We could also use the append() method, which works similarly but will append the fragment to the specified DOM node. Here, I've used the overwrite() method. This will overwrite the specified DOM node with the fragment.

One important aspect of the Template class is that if you are going to be reusing the Template often, you can call the compile() method on it. This will optimize its performance.

Now, the second Mad Lib form uses the doMadlib2() function, which uses an XTemplate instead of Template. That code looks like this:

```
var t = new Ext.XTemplate(
  "The robot overlords from planet {planetName} have declared that as ",
  "of this time, no human may acquire the following items:<br><ul>",
  "<tpl for=\"bannedItems\">",
  "<li>{itemName} - Reason: {noReason}</li>",
  "</tpl>",
  "</ul>"
);
var vals = Ext.query("input[class=mlf2]");
Ext.getDom("Madlib2Results").innerHTML = t.applyTemplate(
  {
    planetName : vals[0].value,
    bannedItems : [
      { itemName : vals[1].value, noReason : vals[2].value },
      { itemName : vals[3].value, noReason : vals[4].value }
    ]
  }
);
```

As you can see, it largely works the same as Template. However, there are a couple of important differences. First, in this case, we have a couple of objects contained in the bannedItems array in the data object. To display these objects, we need to iterate over this array. Within the template text you'll notice the <tpl for> tag. This is simply a for looping construct. It says to iterate over the elements in the bannedItems array and process the portion of the template between <tpl for> and </tpl> however many times there are elements in that array. The purpose is to generate an unordered list (<ul>). The other difference is that this time I decided to use the applyTemplate() method. This is an alias for apply(), and as such it does the same thing: it gives us an HTML fragment. So, I directly set the innerHTML attribute of the target <div> to that fragment.

■**Note** A fairly robust set of processing directives is available with XTemplate, and I'll introduce them here and there as required in various projects. Check out the Ext JS docs for full details.

Drag and Drop

The drag-and-drop metaphor is a common UI approach for various tasks, such as selecting items from a list. It's a more visual approach to the problem and is therefore popular in the GUI world.

Modern RIAs are expected to expose this sort of "advanced" UI metaphor, and any good library these days will provide the basics for you at a minimum. Ext JS is definitely no exception.

Take a peek at Listing 2-3. This is a full, working example of drag and drop.

Listing 2-3. *An Example of Drag and Drop with Ext JS*

```
<html>

  <head>

    <title>Chapter 2 Drag and Drop Example</title>

    <style>

      /* Style for a drop zone container. */
      .cssDDContainer {
        border : 1px solid #000000;
        width : 200px;
        height : 422px;
        background-color : #d0d0ff;
        overflow : auto;
        margin : 2px;
      }

      /* Style for a draggable item. */
      .cssDDItem {
        font-size : 8pt;
        font-weight : bold;
        font-family : arial;
        margin : 2px;
        border : 1px solid #000000;
        background-color : #ffd0d0;
        padding : 1px;
        cursor : move;
        z-index : 9999;
      }

      /* Style for when an item is hovering over a drop target. */
      .cssDDHover {
        background-color: #c0ffc0;
      }

    </style>

    <script type="text/javascript" src="ext/adapter/ext/ext-base.js"></script>
    <script type="text/javascript" src="ext/ext-all.js"></script>
```

```
<script>

  var presidents = [ "George Washington", "John Adams", "Thomas Jefferson",
    "James Madison", "James Monroe", "John Quincy Adams", "Andrew Jackson",
    "Martin Van Buren", "William Harrison", "John Tyler", "James Polk",
    "Zachary Taylor", "Millard Fillmore", "Franklin Pierce",
    "James Buchanan", "Abraham Lincoln", "Andrew Johnson",
    "Ulysses S. Grant", "Rutherford B. Hayes", "James Garfield",
    "Chester A. Arthur", "Grover Cleveland", "Benjamin Harrison",
    "Grover Cleveland", "William McKinley", "Theodore Roosevelt",
    "William Howard Taft", "Woodrow Wilson", "Warren Harding",
    "Calvin Coolidge", "Herbert Hoover", "Franklin Delano Roosevelt",
    "Harry S. Truman", "Dwight D. Eisenhower", "John F. Kennedy",
    "Lyndon B. Johnson",  "Richard Milhous Nixon",  "Gerald Ford",
    "Jimmy Carter", "Ronald Reagan",  "George Bush",  "Bill Clinton",
    "George W. Bush"
  ];

  // Override drag-and-drop events as necessary.
  Ext.override(Ext.dd.DDProxy, {
    // Event when the user starts dragging an item.
    startDrag : function(inX, inY) {
      // Show contents of item when dragging so it looks nicer.
      var item = Ext.get(this.getDragEl());
      var el = Ext.get(this.getEl());
      item.update(el.dom.innerHTML);
      item.addClass(el.dom.className + " dd-proxy");
    },
    // Event when an item hovers over a drop target.
    onDragOver : function(inElement, inTargetID) {
      // Only do something if item is over the drop target.
      if (inTargetID == "destinationContainer") {
        // Record this as the drop target for when dragging stops.
        var dropTarget = Ext.get(inTargetID);
        this.lastTarget = dropTarget;
        // Style the drop target.
        dropTarget.addClass("cssDDHover");
      }
    },
    // Event when an item leaves a drop target.
    onDragOut : function(inElement, inTargetID) {
      // Clear the recorded drop target.
      this.lastTarget = null;
      if (inTargetID == "destinationContainer") {
        // If leaving the destination container, remove the hover style.
        Ext.get(inTargetID).removeClass("cssDDHover");
      }
```

```
          },
          // Event when the user stops dragging an item.
          endDrag : function() {
            // Only do something if the item is over a drop target.
            if (this.lastTarget) {
              // Append the item to the drop target and remove the style.
              var item = Ext.get(this.getEl());
              Ext.get(this.lastTarget).appendChild(item);
              this.lastTarget.removeClass("cssDDHover");
              this.lastTarget = null;
            }
          }
        });


        /**
         * The appInit() function fires when the page loads.  It creates all the
         * draggable items and defines the drop zones.
         */
        function appInit() {

          // Create items that can be dragged and insert them into the DOM.
          var presidentsContainer = Ext.getDom("sourceContainer");
          for (var i = 0; i < presidents.length; i++) {
            var newDiv = document.createElement("div");
            newDiv.className =  "cssDDItem";
            newDiv.id = "president" + i;
            newDiv.innerHTML = presidents[i];
            presidentsContainer.appendChild(newDiv);
            var divElem = Ext.getDom("president" + i);
            divElem.dd = new Ext.dd.DDProxy("president")
          }

          // Register drop zone.
          var dz2 = new Ext.dd.DropZone("destinationContainer";

        } // End appInit().

        Ext.onReady(appInit);

      </script>

    </head>

    <body>
```

```
<!-- List of available presidents. -->
<div style="position:absolute;left:2px;top:2px;">
  <center><h2>U.S. Presidents</h2></center>
  <div class="cssDDContainer" id="sourceContainer">
</div>

<!-- List of presidents the user likes. -->
<div style="position:absolute;left:230px;top:2px;">
  <center><h2>The ones I like</h2></center>
<div class="cssDDContainer" id="destinationContainer">
</div>

</body>

</html>
```

Even though this isn't going to win the award for great-looking applications, let's have a look anyway, in Figure 2-29.

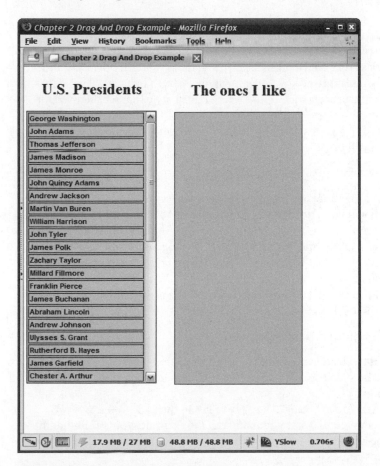

Figure 2-29. *The drag-and-drop example*

Let's not quibble over the fact that we're using styles and JavaScript in the same file as the markup, a practice generally frowned on these days. Sometimes it's nice to have a single HTML page that is all inclusive, and for a basic example like this I think it's fine.

Anyway… the way this works is pretty simple. First, we have two <div>s that are absolutely positioned. Inside each is another <div>. The inner <div>s will contain other <div>s, each representing a US president. All of them start out in the <div> on the left with the ID sourceContainer. Users can drag the ones they want over to the <div> on the right with the ID destinationContainer to indicate which presidents they like.

You create the <div>s for each president via code in the appInit() function:

```
for (var i = 0; i < presidents.length; i++) {
  var newDiv = document.createElement("div");
  newDiv.className =  "cssDDItem";
  newDiv.id = "president" + i;
  newDiv.innerHTML = presidents[i];
  presidentsContainer.appendChild(newDiv);
  var divElem = Ext.getDom("president" + i);
  divElem.dd = new Ext.dd.DDProxy("president" + i)
}
```

This is just some basic DOM manipulation code to create the <div>s and insert them as children of sourceContainer using the names of the presidents found in the presidents array. Note that each <div> has a class specified as cssDDItem (using the JavaScript className attribute name for the usual class attribute as it would appear on a <div> tag itself). This style is found in the <style> section and sets up such things as the cursor style that will be used for this element.

These are just plain old <div>s at this point, of course. The part that makes them draggable via Ext JS is the following line:

```
divElem.dd = new Ext.dd.DDProxy("president" + i)
```

An Ext.dd.DDProxy is an object that conceptually mimics the element you tell it to (the argument passed to it, which you've noticed works out at runtime to be the same value as that set for the id of the created <div>). More specifically, it creates an empty, bordered <div> that knows how to follow the mouse as you move it around after clicking on the element that it proxies (one of our president <div>s in this case). This is much more lightweight than trying to drag around the actual element.

The other task performed in appInit() is to register a drop target so that Ext JS knows where a draggable element can be dropped. This snippet does that:

```
var dz2 = new Ext.dd.DropZone("destinationContainer");
```

Once again we instantiate a class, Ext.dd.DropZone this time, that basically wraps a DOM node, destinationContainer here. Ext JS now knows that this element should react to draggable items dropped onto it.

But how exactly does it react to anything? The answer lies in the code in the Ext.override() call. If you removed that statement and ran the example, you'd find that the president items can be dragged, but you'd also see that dropping doesn't work. That's where the Ext.override() statement comes into play.

Ext.override() in general allows you to add a list of functions to the prototype of an existing class, overwriting any existing methods with the same name. One such object floating around is that Ext.dd.DDProxy class. This class contains a number of event handlers, and we need to override some of those to make everything work.

Four events in particular are of interest to us: startDrag, which fires when you click a draggable item and start dragging it around; onDragOver, which fires whenever a dragged item is hovering over a drop target; onDragOut, which is the opposite of onDragOver and thus fires when a draggable item leaves a drop target; and endDrag, which fires when the item is dropped.

First let's talk about the code that executes in response to the startDrag event. If you run the code with the Ext.override() statement removed, you'll notice that when you drag an item, all you see is a border being dragged—you don't see the contents of the original <div>. This may be fine in some cases, but wouldn't it be a little better if we saw what we were actually dragging? I think so! To accomplish this, we write the following code in the startDrag event handler:

```
var item = Ext.get(this.getDragEl());
var el = Ext.get(this.getEl());
item.update(el.dom.innerHTML);
item.addClass(el.dom.className + " dd-proxy");
```

The getDragEl() method returns a reference to the linked element (the <div> created by the proxy, in other words). Remember that this function is attached to the proxy, so the keyword this references the proxy itself. The getEl() method, on the other hand, returns a reference to the actual element being dragged. Then we set the contents of the empty proxy <div> using its update() method to the innerHTML of the real element. This allows us to see what we're dragging. Then we add the dd-proxy style class (supplied by Ext JS itself) to the object so it's styled properly. The addClass() method is good for this purpose (and is a handy method to remember since it is available on many objects when working with Ext JS).

So now that things *look* like we want, how do make it *work* like we want? It begins with the onDragOver event handler. When this event fires we have a relatively simple task: determine whether or not the dragged item is hovering over a valid drop target. To do this, we examine the ID of the target that is passed in to this event handler. If it matches the ID of our drop target, destinationContainer in this case, we get a reference to the Element underlying the drop target and store it in the lastTarget attribute of the proxy. We also add the cssDDHover class to it so the background color changes to indicate the item can be dropped there.

The next event to handle is endDrag. When the endDrag event fires, the code examines the lastTarget attribute to see if it's null. If it's not, that means the item is hovering over the drop target. In that case, we get a reference to the original <div>, and we then append it to the Element underlying the drop target. In other words, we move the DOM node from the sourceContainer <div> to the destinationContainer <div>. Finally, we remove the cssDDHover class from the drop target and make sure we clear the lastTarget attribute on the proxy.

The final event handler handles the onDragOut event. We have little to do here: set lastTarget to null so we know the item isn't hovering over a target, and if the target passed into the event handler is the destinationContainer, we also remove the cssDDHover class from it.

To see it all in action, take a look at Figure 2-30. In this screenshot you can see that I've dragged a few presidents over already and am in the process of dragging another. The destinationContainer is highlighted (you won't be able to see that too well on the printed page, although you may be able to discern a subtle difference in shades of gray).

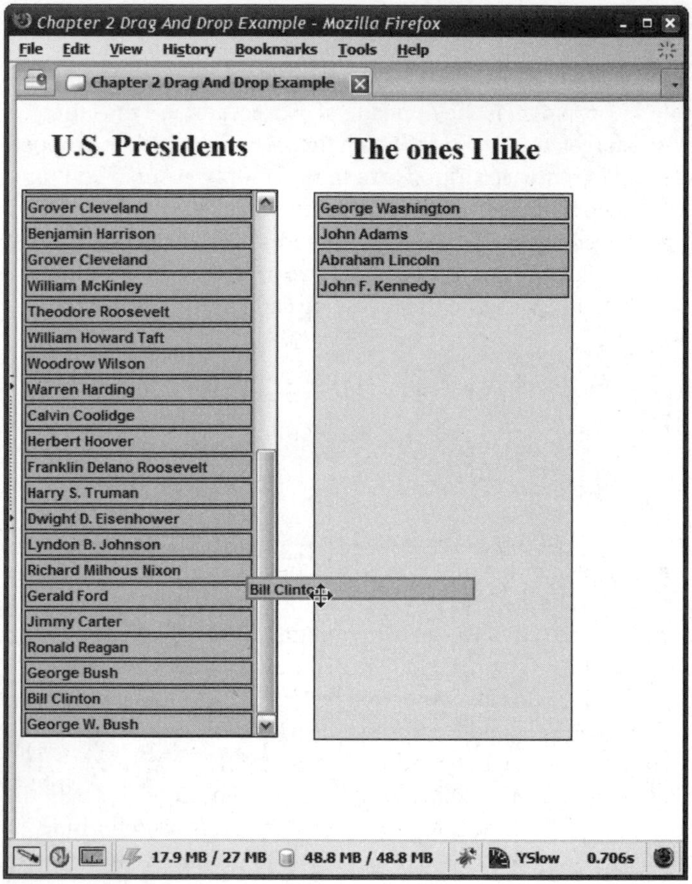

Figure 2-30. *The drag-and-drop example in action*

As you can see, implementing drag and drop with Ext JS is a piece of cake. You can build some powerful UIs with these simple capabilities, and they'll save you a ton of work along the way!

The "State" of Things

Another neat capability that most Ext JS widgets have is the ability to save their own state. For example, take this snippet of code:

```
var w = new Ext.Window({
  resizable : true, layout : "fit", title : "State-Saving Window",
  width : 200, height : 200,
  items: [
    { html : "Resize me, move me, reload the page!" }
  ]
});
w.show();
```

As you know by now, that code creates a Window that is 200 pixels wide and 200 pixels tall. It has a single default Panel in its content fitted to the entire size of the Window.

By default, the Window will appear in the center of the page. Also by default, the Window can be dragged around and resized. What happens, however, when you reload the page that code is a part of? The answer is that the Window will again be 200 pixels wide by 200 pixels tall and will appear in the center of the page.

Wouldn't it be nice if wherever users dragged the Window to, and however big or small they resized the Window to, it appeared that way when the page is reloaded? This is a typical function of most GUI applications, and since Ext JS is supposed to let us build rich UIs in a browser, shouldn't that be possible too?

Well, you may be thinking in that clever little brain of yours, "I can just hook up some event handlers to the resize and move events of the Window, use the getPosition() and getSize() methods to get that information, and then store it somewhere, maybe a cookie. Then, any time I create that Window I'll first grab that cookie, get the values from it, and set the Window's initial location and size dynamically. Problem solved!" Indeed, you could likely pull that off; it's not all that tough.

But you don't have to do all that work! Ext JS basically does it for you.

Look at this version of the previous code, with some slight additions:

```
Ext.state.Manager.setProvider(new Ext.state.CookieProvider());
var w = new Ext.Window({
  resizable : true, layout : "fit", title : "State-Saving Window",
  width : 200, height : 200, stateId : "window1", stateful : true,
  items: [
    { html : "Resize me, move me, reload the page!" }
  ]
});
w.show();
```

The first new line deals with something called the Ext.state.Manager. This is a singleton object that all Components consult with when they are created. If the Manager tells the Component that it has some state information about it stored, it hands it to the Component, which then uses it to do things like restore a Window's size and position.

You make a given Component state aware by adding the stateId and stateful config options to it. In fact, only the stateful option is necessary because the stateId defaults to the Component's id, which itself defaults to an automatically assigned value if you haven't specified it. That's all it takes! From then on, the Component will work in tandem with the Manager to store and restore state.

In order for the `Manager` to do its work, it needs to know how to store state information. In other words, it needs an implementation of the `Ext.state.Provider` interface. Ext JS provides the `CookieProvider` implementation that stores the state information in cookies. You can implement your own if you choose to do something more robust, such as making Ajax requests to a server to save and restore the information from a database.

State-saving for widgets is an extremely simple-to-use mechanism that provides a commonly expected feature of rich UIs. Say thank-you to the Ext JS developers for this!

For Your Date in the Boardroom: Ext JS Charting

A long time ago in a web application far, far away, charting was, shall we say, a bit of a challenge… maybe not so much a challenge as a hassle! To generate a chart, say a bar chart, you had to call on the server to generate some sort of image file, such as a JPEG, in real time. The image was based on some data that you either passed from the client or that already resided on the server. You then returned the image to the browser to be displayed. It wasn't perhaps the most difficult challenge in all of application development, but there were quite a few steps involved that had to all work together to get the chart in front of your users' eyes.

In the world of RIAs, where we endeavor to make the clients, rather than our poor servers, work their little tails off, we want those charts generated on the client. At this point in time there are a number of ways you can do that. One that has gained a lot of popularity is to use the nearly ubiquitous Flash plug-in. Since we're talking about Ext JS here, we don't want to deal with Flash directly, and Ext JS gives us just the abstraction layer we want.

The `Ext.chart` namespace is where we find this graphical goodness. Thanks to Ext JS, there's no heavy lifting for us to do. In fact, the charting capabilities Ext JS provides are built right on top of the data capabilities we've already seen, as well as the deeply object-oriented nature of the library.

For example, let's say we want to show a line chart to relay the relative awesomeness of the five seasons of my all-time favorite sci-fi series, *Babylon 5*. To do so, all we need to do is this:

```html
<html>
  <head>
    <link rel="stylesheet" type="text/css" href="ext/resources/css/ext-all.css">
    <script type="text/javascript" src="ext/adapter/ext/ext-base.js"></script>
    <script type="text/javascript" src="ext/ext-all.js"></script>
    <script>
      Ext.onReady(function() {
        var B5Store = new Ext.data.JsonStore({
          fields : [ "season", "awesomeness" ], data : [
            { season : "Signs And Portents", awesomeness : 10 },
            { season : "The Coming Of Shadows", awesomeness : 20 },
            { season : "Point Of No Return", awesomeness : 40 },
            { season : "No Surrender, No Retreat", awesomeness : 70 },
            { season : "The Wheel Of Fire", awesomeness : 15 }
          ]
        });
```

```
      new Ext.Panel({
        title : "The 'awesomeness' Of The Five Seasons Of Babylon 5 (line)",
        renderTo : "divLineChart", width : 700, height : 400, layout : "fit",
        items : [
          { xtype : "linechart", store : B5Store, xField : "season",
            yField : "awesomeness" }
        ]
      });
    });
  </script>
</head>
<body><div id="divLineChart" style="padding:10px;"></div></body>
</html>
```

Figure 2-31 shows the result.

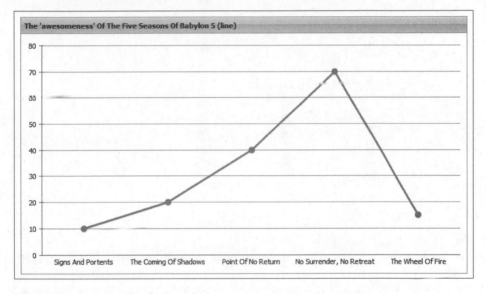

Figure 2-31. *An example of a line chart*

The Ext.data.JsonStore is used to read in some data, in JSON form. This produces B5Store, which we can bind to many different Ext JS components, such as Grids. We can also bind it to an Ext.chart.LineChart, which is nearly all we have to do to produce a line chart! We also need to tell the LineChart what fields in the data correspond to the x-axis (the seasons of the show) and the y-axis (the awesomeness of each). Ext JS takes care of all the messy Flash details. In this particular code, I've wrapped the LineChart in a Panel, just to make it look a little prettier (I gave it a title bar), and it is rendered to the divLineChart <div>.

■ **Note** All of these charts automatically have tooltips attached to the data points so that hovering over a dot on the line chart shows the value of that element, and hovering over a bar in the bar chart shows the value for the associated element. You can see an example of this in Figure 2-33 in a moment.

Now, let's say we determine a line chart isn't the best way to show this and decide instead that a column chart would be better. All we need to do is change the `xtype` to `columnchart` and we're off to the races, as you can see in Figure 2-32.

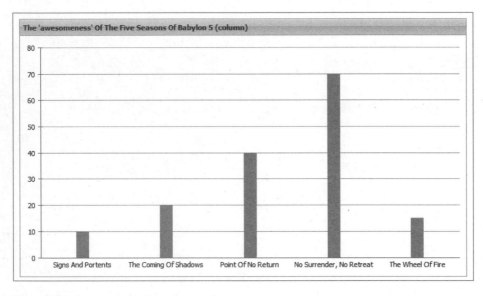

Figure 2-32. *An example of a column chart*

There is also a `barchart` `xtype`, but it's similar enough to `columnchart` that I have not demonstrated it here.

Now, let's say, hypothetically, that we're doing a fancy boardroom presentation for some television executives to convince them to let JMS[3] produce another season of *Babylon 5*. Further, we decide that a pie chart would probably impress the bean counters more. Have no fear; that's easy too—although it's not *just* an `xtype` change, but a whole lot more. We need to change the entire configuration of the component in the `items` array of the `Panel` to this:

```
{ xtype : "piechart", store : B5Store, categoryField : "season",
  dataField : "awesomeness" }
```

---

3   JMS stands for Joe Michael Straczynski, creator of *Babylon 5*. This series had a very interesting and tumultuous existence: it was planned as a five-year story arc, but was going to be cancelled after the fourth season. JMS rewrote a lot of the story to finish up the main arc in season four, but season five was then green-lighted, requiring some quick on-the-fly storytelling! As a related aside, while season five is generally considered not as strong as most others (as you can see in the charts!) it had a couple of top-notch episodes, most notably "The Fall of Centauri Prime," which was a very sad episode for one particular character!

Here, we have to tell the pie chart what field in the data corresponds to the categories—that is, the slices of the pie—and what field represents the values of each slice. Ext JS, in concert with Flash, then takes care of rendering the pie chart you see in Figure 2-33, including sizing each slice according to the relative value of each in the data.

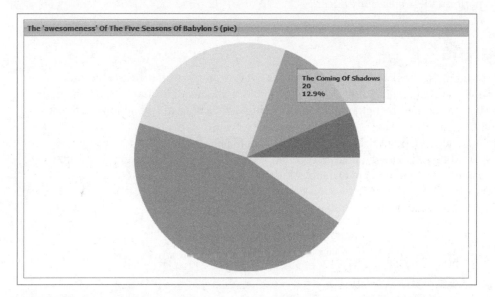

Figure 2-33. *An example of a pie chart*

As you can see, generating charts with Ext JS is a piece of cake and builds directly on top of the data mechanism, making it an extremely powerful and flexible solution. The downside is that Flash is required, but with something like 99 percent of all desktops with Flash already installed, that's not such a big deal.[4]

■**Note** One thing that doesn't seem possible with the pie chart is to show the category names on the slices. The tooltips *are* present, but that's not ideal. This is a capability I'd hope to see added to Ext JS in short order (and it possibly could be there in the currently released version).

You can see all of the charts described here by running the charts.htm file included in the download bundle for this book. If you load this file locally—that is, if you open your browser and simply open the file—you may see errors indicating that a connection between JavaScript and YUI Charts could not be established. This is a result of Adobe Flask blocking local content from communicating with remote servers, which the charting capabilities seem to require. To deal with this, you will need to tell the Flash plug-in that this communication is allowed.

---

4   The 99 percent figure is as of the writing of this chapter. Adobe keeps current statistics on Flash's penetration on this page: http://www.adobe.com/products/player_census/flashplayer/

To do so, visit http://www.macromedia.com/support/documentation/en/flashplayer/help/ settings_manager04.html. Select the Global Security Setting tab and either specify the location of charts.htm under "Always trust files in these locations," or select the Always Allow radio button. If you now reload charts.htm, you should see the glorious charts appear! You should have to perform these steps only once.

Plug-ins

By this point in this book I expect that you think Ext JS is pretty neat! It clearly has lots of functionality and capabilities, but does it do *everything* you need? Probably not. Fortunately, the Ext JS creators have thought ahead and have provided a plug-in system for you to use to extend the library.

In fact, there is a pretty robust ecosystem of Ext JS plug-ins available already. If you cruise on over to Ext JS web site—the page http://extjs.com/learn/Ext_Extensions in particular— you'll be able to see a number of available plug-ins.

For example, there is the Ext.ux.PowerWizard, shown in Figure 2-34. It allows you to create a nice wizard interface with no trouble at all.

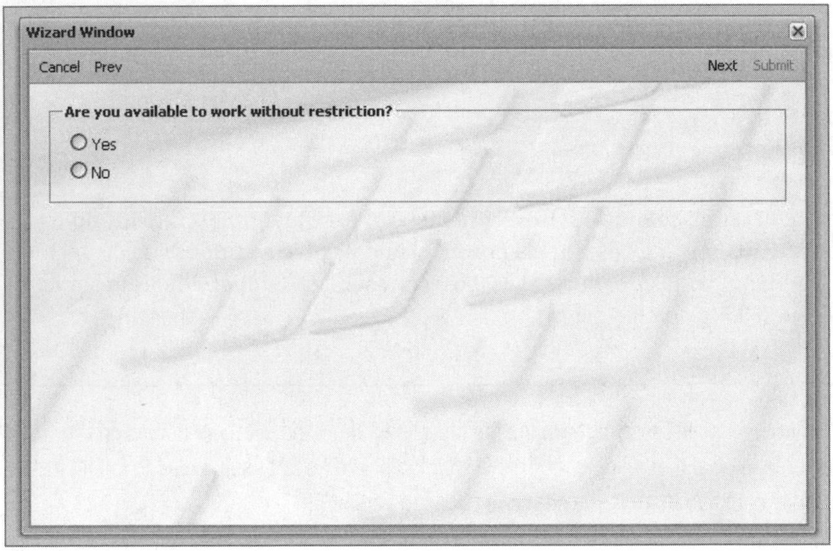

Figure 2-34. *The Ext.ux.PowerWizard plug-in*

The Ext.ux.MultiSelect is another fine example, as you can see in Figure 2-35. This plug-in allows you to choose from a number of options and "flip" them over into another box where you can reorder them.

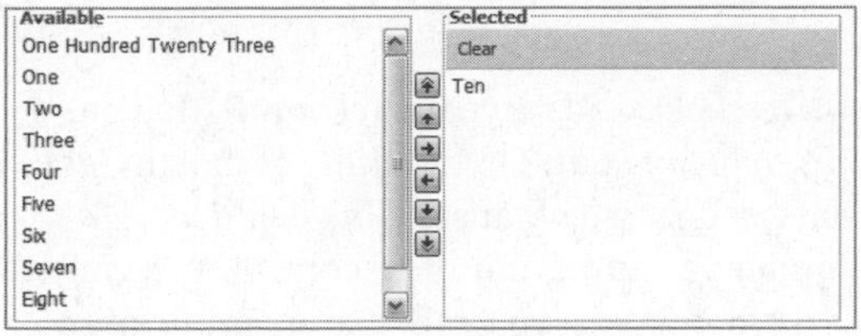

Figure 2-35. *The Ext.ux.MultiSelect plug-in*

All the extensions aren't even necessarily UI widgets, although most of them tend to be.

If you want to write your own widget, all it takes is creating a class that exposes an init() method. Usually, a plug-in extends the Observable class and extends an existing Component. When that Component is instantiated, you can specify the plug-in by adding it to the plugins config attribute, which is an array of plug-ins. Each plug-in's init() method will be called and will be passed the instance of the Component. The plug-in can do whatever it wishes at that point, including hooking into the various events the Component exposes, thereby allowing you to extend what the original Component does.

■**Note** Writing custom plug-ins won't be demonstrated in this book, so if it is a topic you would like to know more about, the Ext JS Learning Center (on the Ext JS web site) provides more details for you to explore.

These Are the Gears That Power the Tubes!

Gears (http://gears.google.com) is, in a nutshell, a browser extension that provides functionality in three distinct groups: LocalServer, Database, and WorkerPool. Gears is available for most major browsers and operating systems.

■**Note** Although Gears is still technically in beta, I think we all recognize Google's MO here: release something solid as beta; call it that for a good, long time; and then finally "flip the switch" to make it final years later (although as I write this Gmail is *still* beta, and it's more than a few years old!). Then make it gold years later, even though it's pretty much been that for a while. I suppose this is a lot better than the Microsoft "just release it and we'll fix it up later" approach.

LocalServer

The LocalServer component of Gears enables you to cache and serve the resources that go into rendering a web page from a local cache. This may not sound too exciting at first. In fact, your initial thought may be, "Browsers already have caches, so what's the big deal?"

The big deal, my friend, is that this cache is under your programmatic control. You can tell it what resources to cache and serve, and when. In other words, you can take an application "offline," assuming all its resources are in the cache, meaning a connection to the server is no longer required.

There is obvious potential in terms of performance too, although interestingly, that's a secondary concern at best. It's that ability to go offline and still have an application work that LocalServer is there to address.

The applications in this book won't be using LocalServer, so I won't go into anymore detail on it here. This is, after all, a book on Ext JS and not Gears! Go to http://gears.google.com to learn more if LocalServer is something that interests you.

WorkerPool

The WorkerPool component is another piece of Gears that is really very cool. You are no doubt familiar with how easy it is—thanks to the single-threaded nature of JavaScript—to lock up the browser with a while loop that never breaks or make similar programming gaffs. You are also no doubt aware that JavaScript doesn't provide threads as a language like Java does. JavaScript has timers and time-outs, which at least approximate threads, and we've seen how Ext JS abstracts this a bit more and makes it a little nicer for us, but a single thread of execution is still ultimately all there is in the interpreter at any given time; timers and time-outs are more an illusion than anything else.

With WorkerPool, Google has given us about as close to real threading as possible in Java-Script. It's especially useful if you have calculation-intensive operations to perform or input/output (I/O) operations in the background to run. There is at least one significant limitation to be aware of, however: threads in a WorkerPool, which are not surprisingly called Workers, can't access the DOM. This limits the Workers' usefulness quite a bit, but even with that limitation there's still plenty you *can* do with them.

WorkerPool, like LocalServer, isn't a part of Gears we'll get much use from, so we'll cut this discussion short and jump into the component we'll be using primarily: Database.

Database

Now, we *are* using the Database component of Gears in these applications. The Database component of Gears provides a client-side relational database system based on the SQLite (www.sqlite.org) engine, which is an open source database system. It essentially boils down to two simple classes: Database and ResultSet.

The architecture that Google talks about enabling with Gears provides for the ability to switch an application from "online" state to "offline" state at the flip of a switch. The way Google recommends doing this is shown in Figure 2-36.

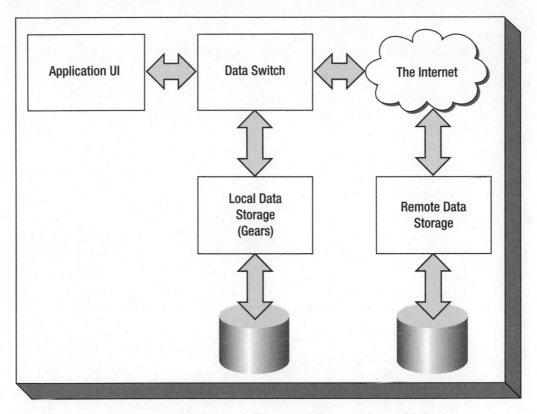

Figure 2-36. *The architecture behind online/offline capabilities made possible by Gears*

In this model, the Data Switch is some code in the client-side of your application that can determine whether the application is online or offline and which API your application reads and writes data to. In other words, you wouldn't directly use the Gears Database API. Instead, your application would use some API you provide that sits between the application code and the Gears Database API. Then, when you detect that your application is online, you write those data reads and writes to your server-side data store, typically via the Internet. When the application is offline, though, you use Gears API instead. When the application goes back online, the Data Switch is responsible for synchronizing the data in both directions.

Now, all the details about how you detect online versus offline status, and how data synchronization is done, are left to your discretion. With any luck, the JavaScript library you chose would help you out. Ext JS provides a robust event system that would potentially allow you to do this, but it doesn't itself deal with it.

As an example of using Gears, and the Database component in particular, consider the following HTML page:

```html
<html>
  <head>
    <script type="text/javascript" src="gears_init.js"></script>

    <script>

        db = google.gears.factory.create("beta.database", "1.0");
        db.open();
        db.execute(
          "CREATE TABLE IF NOT EXISTS test_table (" +
          "firstName TEXT, " +
          "lastName TEXT, " +
          "age INTEGER" +
          ");"
        );
        db.execute("INSERT INTO test_table " +
          "(firstName, lastName, age) values (" +
          "'Frank','Zammetti','35');");
        db.execute("INSERT INTO test_table " +
          "(firstName, lastName, age) values (" +
          "'Amanda','Tapping','42');");
        var rs = db.execute("select * from test_table");
        while (rs.isValidRow()) {
          alert(rs.field(0) + ", " + rs.field(1) + ", " + rs.field(2));
          rs.next();
        }
        db.close();

    </script>

  </head>
  <body></body>
</html>
```

Yep, that's all it takes! Now, if you have Gears installed and you save that HTML to a file and then load it in your browser, you should see two alert messages displaying the rows of the table. Obviously not rocket science by any stretch!

You may have noticed the import of the gears_init.js file. This is a bit of JavaScript provided by Google that takes care of initializing Gears and that provides the google and google. gears objects that you interact with.

Note To install Gears, which you'll need to do before you can play with the application in this chapter or the preceding example, go to `http://gears.google.com` and you should find a big button right there in front of your face to install it. Follow the rather simple instructions and you'll be good to go in no time! Also keep in mind that the first time you run Gears for a given application you will receive a security warning that you'll have to allow the application to use Gears.

We'll see much more of Gears, its `Database` component in particular, in all the projects to come, starting with the next chapter. So if this brief introduction seemed a little light, don't worry; you'll get your fill! Remember, though, we're here for Ext JS primarily, and that's where our focus will remain.

Summary

In this chapter we got a good look at the real stars of the Ext JS show: the widgets. We saw how they are part of a rich object-oriented hierarchy that endows these widgets with lots of common behaviors and properties, making our job of learning how to use them easy. We saw how the concept of layouts is at the core of what makes Ext JS so powerful. Then we moved beyond the widgets and saw how Ext JS provides for automatic data binding to many widgets and how it provides a rich event model to hook into in order to work with our data. We saw some other more "advanced" capabilities, such as drag and drop and state management. We looked at Gears (from Google), which will underlie all the applications in this book to provide a local database to stash our data.

In the next chapter we'll start with the project so you can see how Chapters 1 and 2 fit together. You will learn how to build some cool applications with very little effort.

PART 2

■ ■ ■

The Projects

The Internet is the most important single development in the history of human communication since the invention of call waiting.

—Dave Barry

Real programmers can write assembly code in any language.

—Larry Wall

You have that vacant look in your eyes that says "Hold my head to your ear, you'll hear the sea!"

—Londo Mollari (*Babylon 5*)

Well, believe me, Mike, I calculated the odds of this succeeding versus the odds I was doing something incredibly stupid…and I went ahead anyway.

—Crow (*Mystery Science Theater 3000*)

They've finally come up with the perfect office computer. If it makes a mistake, it blames another computer.

—Milton Berle

In view of the fact that God limited the intelligence of man, it seems unfair that he did not also limit his stupidity.

—Konrad Adenauer

I refuse to answer that question on the grounds that I don't know the answer.

—Douglas Adams

The pen is mightier than the sword…and considerably easier to write with!

—Marty Feldman

The ability to quote is a serviceable substitute for wit.

—W. Somerset Maugham

Ext JS for a Busy Lifestyle: OrganizerExt

Now that we've had a decent look at all Ext JS has to offer, it's time to dive right into our applications, starting with OrganizerExt. In this chapter we'll get our first real-world example of Ext JS in action. We'll learn how to construct a relatively complex UI, how to create data stores, and how to bind them to various UI components. We'll explore one way to structure an Ext JS application, and we'll get a taste of Gears in action underneath it all. In the end we'll have a fairly useful little application that should give you a good grounding in working with Ext JS in a realistic way.

What's This Application Do Anyway?

Look, we all have busy lives. What with work, spouses, children, bills, dogs, cats, and whatever else soaks up your time, it's difficult to keep track of it all. At least for me it is! I frequently forget where I'm supposed to be and when, what I'm supposed to get done and by when, who I need to talk to and how to contact them. True enough, my wife covers for me most of the time, but not everyone is lucky enough to be married to such a capable social secretary![1]

Wouldn't it be nice if we had some sort of device that could help us get organized? Some sort of electronic system where we could store information to help us through our busy day? Oh, if only humankind could get off their collective lazy butts and create such a wonderful invention!

Oh wait, we have just the thing: these computer things! Yes, that's right, computers are just the ticket. Of course, on their own they aren't everything we need: we need some software too, and that's precisely where OrganizerExt comes in.

OrganizerExt will give us the tools we need to bring structure to our crazy lives. How exactly, you ask? By providing the following functionality to its user:

- Four categories of information are provided: notes, tasks, contacts, and appointments.

- We'll be able to flip between the four categories quickly and easily using an `Accordion` layout.

- In each category we'll be able to view items in two ways: as icons or as a detailed listing in a grid.

---

1   I mean that in the best possible way, dear! Love ya!

- Also within each category, we'll be able to filter what items we see based on simple criteria, such as only showing notes in a specified category.

- We'll obviously be able to create items in all four categories as well as delete them. We won't be able to update existing items, though, for the sake of simplicity (and if you think that's a bit of foreshadowing of one suggested exercise afterwards, give yourself a high-five!). In regard to tasks, we'll be able to mark them as complete (which is a type of update, but is one specific case).

- We want a UI that is "fluid" in the sense that the user can expand and contract sections, as well as resize them, to ensure they can see what they are interested in. Fortunately, we get all of this for free with Ext JS!

- We'll be using Gears to store all this data client-side, and we'll use some Ext JS data mechanisms to minimize the amount of work needed to tie this underlying data to the UI.

If this all sounds a bit like Microsoft Outlook, just take a gander at the screenshot in Figure 3-1.

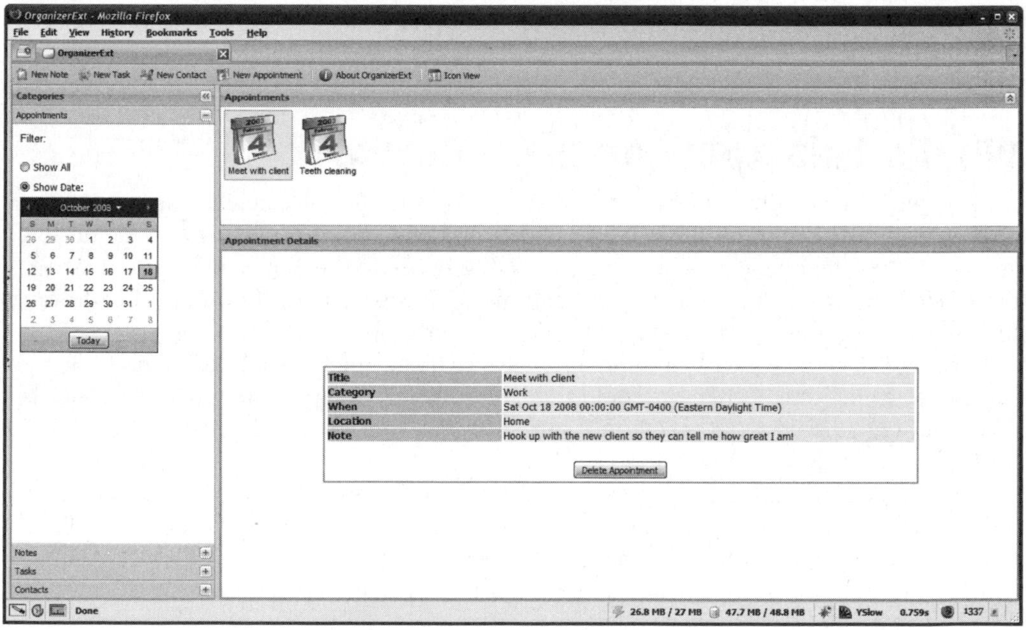

Figure 3-1. *Your first look OrganizerExt*

Yes, I most definitely took the basic structure from Outlook, but let's face it: it's a pretty simple and logical layout that lots of other applications have emulated (and probably many had long before Outlook hit the scene). So, I don't feel too badly about taking my inspiration from what Microsoft has already done.

This is, by and large, a fairly simple application and so makes for a good starting point. However, being simple doesn't make it… err… simple! What I mean is, while functionality-wise it's not too far-reaching, there's enough complexity in the code that it's quite interesting.

What you should take note of as we explore the code, however, is the code that's *missing*. Try to think what it would have taken to do many of the things that Ext JS is doing for us. It's sometimes downright amazing what a simple configuration parameter flag on a given widget can cause to happen.

But I've whetted your appetite quite enough at this point—let's get to it, starting with a look at the overall structure of the application and the files that make it up.

Overall Structure and Files

The directory structure of the application, and the files you'll find within it, is typical of all the applications in this book, and it follows the pattern you see in Figure 3-2.

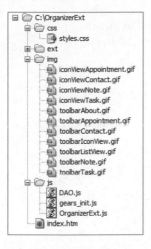

Figure 3-2. *The application's directory structure and constituent files*

In the root directory is the file index.htm. Since this is a sovereign web app (discussed in Chapter 1), this is the one and only page, and therefore it's obviously what gets loaded into the browser. Next is a css directory, which contains a single file, styles.css. This file contains all the styles for the application (those not provided by Ext JS itself, that is). Next is an img directory that contains any images needed by the application. In this case we've got a bunch that begin with icon, and these are the images shown in the icon view, one for each category of data. There are also those that start with toolbar, which are, I'm sure you've guessed, the images for the toolbar buttons. After that is a js directory that contains all the JavaScript that makes up the application. In this case we find DAO.js, which is our Data Access Object (DAO) class. This contains all the "low-level" code, so to speak, that interacts directly with Gears. There is also OrganizerExt.js, which is the main code of the application and is the code we'll be spending the most time with in this chapter. In addition there's gears_init.js, which is some code provided by Google to initialize Gears. We won't be looking at this in any sort of detail because it's largely outside the scope of this book, although we will see it being used in an indirect way.

There is also the ext directory, which of course contains Ext JS itself.

Now that we know what the directory structure looks like and what files make up the application, let's begin examining it, starting with the markup.

■**Note** The code printed in this chapter, as well as all subsequent chapters, has been condensed in the interest of space on the printed page. I have removed comments and tightened up line spacing in some cases, but the code itself is identical to what you'll find in the book's source code.

The Markup

As mentioned earlier, index.htm is the single HTML page that gets loaded into the browser. Since there is no page-to-page transition as with a typical web site, everything we need markup-wise is present in this single file.

To begin, let's check out the <head> of the document, which by and large is boilerplate-type content and holds no real surprises based on what we've seen in the previous two chapters:

```
<head>

  <title>OrganizerExt</title>

  <link rel="stylesheet" type="text/css" href="ext/resources/css/ext-all.css">
  <script type="text/javascript" src="ext/adapter/ext/ext-base.js"></script>
  <script type="text/javascript" src="ext/ext-all.js"></script>

  <script src="js/gears_init.js"></script>

  <link rel="stylesheet" type="text/css" href="css/styles.css">
  <script type="text/javascript" src="js/DAO.js"></script>
  <script type="text/javascript" src="js/OrganizerExt.js"></script>

  <script>
    Ext.onReady(organizerExt.init);
  </script>

</head>
```

First up, we find the usual Ext JS imports that we've seen previously—no surprises there. After that is the import of the gears_init.js file, which as we saw in Chapter 2 is all we need to do to allow us to use Gears (aside from having Gears installed, of course).

After that are the imports specific to this application, beginning with the style sheet in the styles.css file. Next are the two JavaScript source files, DAO.js and OrganizerExt.js. We'll get to all three of those shortly.

The last thing we see is a call to Ext.onReady(). Recall from previous discussions that this will occur when the DOM is fully loaded but potentially before all resources, such as images, are loaded. This is when you ideally want to build the UI because it makes the application more responsive sooner. Here we see that the init() method of the organizerExt object is called (organizerExt points to an instance of the OrganizerExt class).

Now we move on to the <body> of the document, and the first thing we find is the following line:

```
<div id="divSource" class="cssSource"></div>
```

This is the <div> that will serve as the source of window animations. I'll explain this in detail once we start looking at the style sheet for the application because it makes more sense in that context. So for now just stash this in the back of your brain for later analysis![2]

The next snippet of markup we see is that for our "initializing," or Please Wait dialog:

```
<div id="dialogPleaseWait" class="x-hidden">
  <div class="x-window-header">Please Wait</div>
  <div class="x-window-body">
    <table width="100%" height="100%" border="0" cellpadding="0"
      cellspacing="0" class="cssPleaseWait">
    <tr><td align="center" valign="middle">
      ... Initializing ...
    </td></tr>
    </table>
  </div>
</div>
```

This <div> uses a number of styles defined by Ext JS. The x-hidden selector is a relatively simple style that indicates that a given element should be hidden from view. Within the <div> you find a number of other <div>s. The first is given the style x-window-header and is essentially a marker that Ext JS uses when parsing this HTML (which, as we'll see later, is exactly what happens to create the dialog you see) to determine what the header of the dialog should be. Likewise, the x-window-body style marks the main content of the dialog. When we tell Ext JS we want to show the dialog, and we point it at the dialogPleaseWait <div>, Ext JS will use these markers to create the dialog for us. This is a fairly elegant way to create UI elements without having to write much code.

Within the <div> we are free to do whatever we like with the style x-window-body, and here you can see it's a simple table for centering that uses the cssPleaseWait selector (which we'll see shortly is defined in styles.css).

In Figure 3-3 you can see what this dialog window looks like when displayed.

---

2 Hopefully it's not like that nasty little fractal virus that Captain Picard had Data and La Forge create in the *Star Trek: The Next Generation* episode "I, Borg" to destroy the Borg collective… that's just the chance you'll have to take, I guess!

■**Note** You can create a number of UI elements this way, and we'll see this approach sporadically throughout the projects to come. By and large it's a choice you make between a more code-intensive approach and a more markup-based approach. You'll find that one approach works better in some situations than in others.

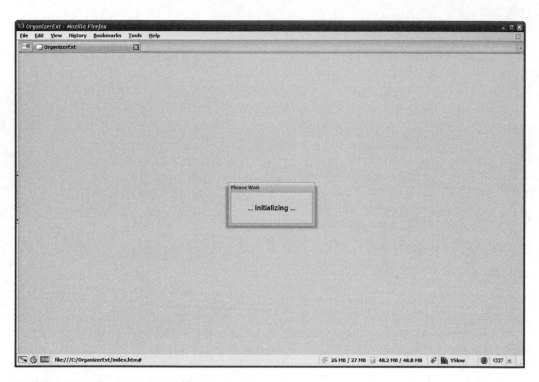

Figure 3-3. *The Please Wait initialization dialog*

The next snippet encountered is what you would see if Gears wasn't installed, and Figure 3-4 shows what that looks like (because I assume you have Gears installed by now and therefore wouldn't see this).

```
<div id="dialogNoGears" class="x-hidden">
  <div class="x-window-header">Gears Not Available</div>
  <div class="x-window-body" style="padding:8px;">
    <br>
    I'm sorry but Google Gears is not installed on your computer, or is
    unavailable for some reason (like you disabled the browser plugin for
    example).
    <br><br>
    If you do not have Gears installed, please visit
```

```
  <a href="http://gears.google.com/" target="new">the Gears home page</a>
  to install it.
  <br><br>
  If you do have it installed, please try enabling the plugin in whatever
  fashion is applicable in the browser you are using, and reload this
  application.
  </div>
</div>
```

This is pretty much the same as the Please Wait dialog definition, and it contains just
some simple markup, including a link to the Gears home page for users to click if they don't
have Gears installed already. That page opens in a new window on the off chance that a restart
of the browser isn't necessary (it generally is, but I did this just in case Google figures out a way
to do it without a restart down the road).

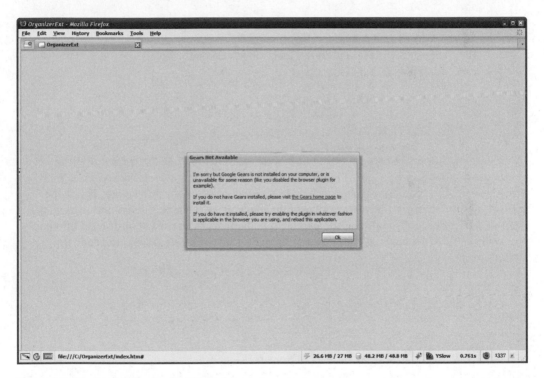

Figure 3-4. *The Gears Not Available dialog*

The "about" dialog is next, and it's once again just a simple bit of markup:

```
<div id="dialogAbout" class="x-hidden">
  <div class="x-window-header">About OrganizerExt</div>
  <div class="x-window-body">
    <table width="100%" height="100%" border="0" cellpadding="0"
      cellspacing="0" class="cssAbout">
      <tr><td align="center" valign="middle">
        OrganizerExt<br>
        Version 1.0<br>
        Frank W. Zammetti
        <br><br>
        Originally appeared in the book<br>
        &quot; Practical Ext JS Projects With Gears&quot;<br>
        Apress, 2008
        <br><br>
        All rights reserved<br>
        (and vigorously defended by an army of microscopic
        land-sharks with lasers mounted to their heads)
      </td></tr>
    </table>
  </div>
</div>
```

There's a little more content here, but otherwise there aren't any surprises after the previous two dialogs we've seen. Figure 3-5 shows what this dialog looks like on the screen. Note here how the content of the page behind the dialog window is grayed out. This is the typical "lightbox" effect that you see all over the place these days, and it's something you get with just a simple configuration option with Ext JS. Note too that the OK button isn't defined in this markup. We'll see how that button gets there soon, when we discuss the code in OrganizerExt.js.

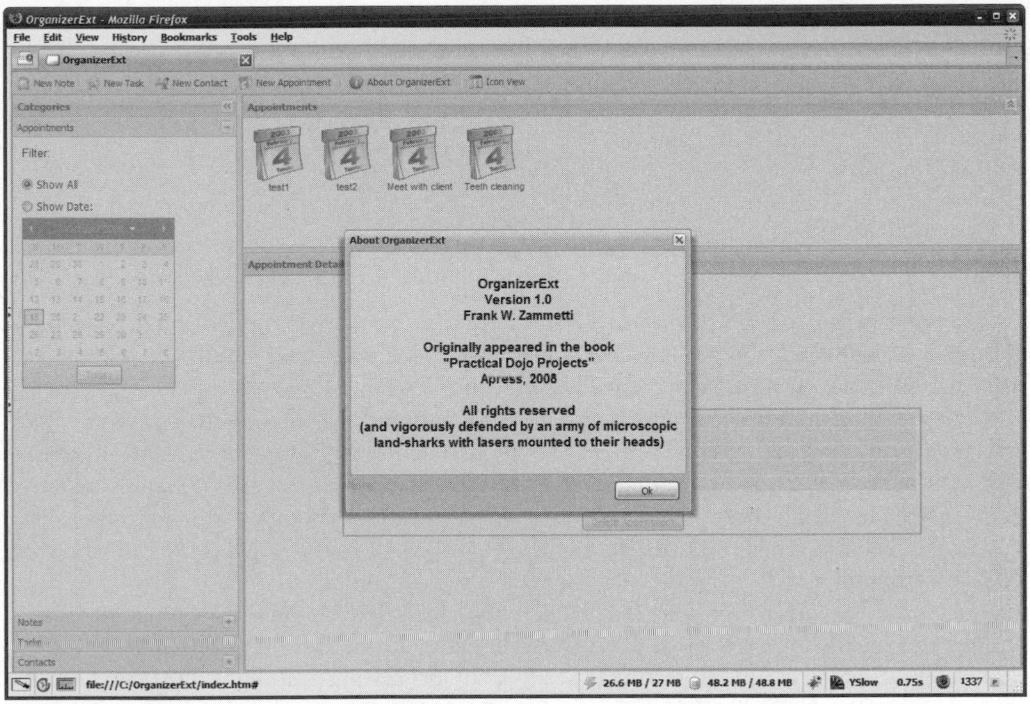

Figure 3-5. *The self-aggrandizing About dialog*

All that remains to be seen in index.htm are four chunks of HTML corresponding to the detail sections for each of the four categories. They are all essentially the same, so I've chosen one, tasks, to use as an example:

```
<div id="divTaskDetails" class="x-hidden">
  <table border="0" cellpadding="0" cellspacing="0" width="100%"
    height="100%">
    <tr><td align="center" valign="middle">
      <table border="0" cellpadding="2" cellspacing="2" align="center"
        width="75%" class="cssDetailsTable">
        <tr>
          <td class="cssDetailsLabel" width="30%">Category</td>
          <td class="cssDetailsData" id="task_category"></td>
        </tr>
        <tr>
          <td class="cssDetailsLabel" width="30%">Status</td>
          <td class="cssDetailsData" id="task_status"></td>
        </tr>
        <tr>
          <td class="cssDetailsLabel" width="30%">Content</td>
          <td class="cssDetailsData" id="task_content"></td>
        </tr>
```

```
        <tr><td colspan="2"> </td></tr>
        <tr>
          <td align="left" id="tdTaskDetailsDeleteButton"></td>
          <td align="right" id="tdTaskDetailsCompleteButton"></td>
        </tr>
      </table>
    </td></tr>
  </table>
</div>
```

As you can see, this is basically just an ordinary table structure wrapped in a <div>, which is initially hidden using the x-hidden selector. I make the assumption here that you can parse simple table markup on your own, since it's pretty basic stuff.

I went with a table here because (a) it's a simple approach to implement, (b) I didn't need anything more complex, and (c) I wanted to demonstrate how this was possible. An alternative would have been to create Ext JS widgets to do this, but that would have added some degree of code and made things a little more complex. More importantly, though, I wanted to show that you can indeed mix straight HTML like this into your Ext JS layouts, which is primarily how the UI is put together.

In Figure 3-6 you can see what this detail section looks like on the screen. Note that like the "about" dialog, the Delete Task and Complete Task buttons are added dynamically via code later on, which is also interesting to see (it's not just mixing in straight HTML with Ext JS widgets—it's also mixing Ext JS widgets in with straight HTML!). You can see, however, that there are two <div>s where the buttons will be inserted.

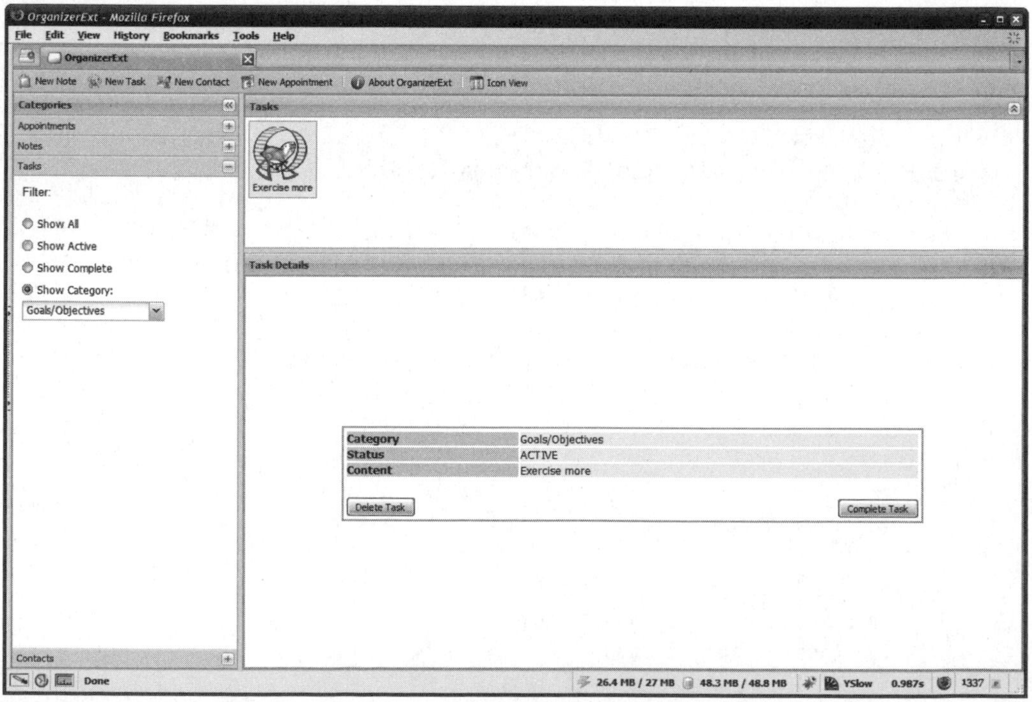

Figure 3-6. *Viewing the details of a selected task (note the filter in action too)*

As I said, the other three chunks dealing with appointments, notes, and contacts are by and large the same, but of course with differing fields. I suggest having a look at the full `index.htm` file to see this for yourself, but just looking at the tasks example pretty well gives you the full picture.

The Style Sheet

The `styles.css` file contains all the style information used in the application that isn't provided by Ext JS itself. There's not a whole lot here, and none of it is even remotely complex (unless CSS is new to you, in which case you probably want to make a quick detour into a CSS tutorial first). The first thing we encounter in this file is the following:

```css
.cssDefault {
  font-size : 10pt;
  font-family : arial;
}
```

The `cssDefault` selector is used to style the text seen in each of the four accordion panes. This just ensures a nice, consistent font styling across them all.

The `cssPleaseWait` selector is next:

```css
.cssPleaseWait {
  font-size : 12pt;
  font-weight : bold;
  font-family : arial;
}
```

This is the selector used to style the text in the Please Wait dialog. Here, the text is made a little bigger and styled in bold to make it stand out a little more.

After that we find the `cssAbout` selector:

```css
.cssAbout {
  font-size : 11pt;
  font-weight : bold;
  font-family : arial;
}
```

This is used to style the text of the About dialog. Once again it's nothing but some font settings, a little bigger than the font setting in the accordion panes (`cssDefault`) and a little smaller than the font setting in the Please Wait dialog (`cssPleaseWait`).

Next we come to `cssSource`, which is, for a change, not related to font styling and is a little more interesting:

```css
.cssSource {
  position : absolute;
  left: 1px;
  top : 1px;
  width : 1px;
  height : 1px;
}
```

When you run the application (you *have* run it, haven't you?), you'll notice that all the dialog windows don't just appear on the screen—they actually "fly" into view. Did you notice that they all fly in from the upper-left corner? If you were wondering how and why that is, cssSource is your answer, at least partially. You see, when you tell Ext JS to show a window, you can also give it the ID of some element on the page from which the window will fly into view. This can be anywhere you like, but in the case of this application I decided on the upper-left corner. The cssSource selector is the style given to the divSource <div>, as we saw when we looked at index.htm. This style puts that <div> in the upper-left corner of the page via absolute positioning. So, when we tell Ext JS to show a window and give it the ID divSource to use as the source of the animation, it's by virtue of this selector that the window flies in from that corner of the page.

■Tip Try changing the position values in this selector to see the windows fly in from other places on the page.

The cssDetailsTable selector is next:

```
.cssDetailsTable {
  border : 2px solid #99bbe8;
  padding : 2px;
}
```

This is the style given to the four tables used to display the details of a selected note, task, appointment, or contact. As you can see, it's really just a border specification and some padding—not exactly rocket science! The color was chosen to match the default Ext JS styling so it blends into the UI fairly well.

Within each of the details table are labels (like First Name, Last Name, and so on), and there is the data itself. For the labels, the following style is applied:

```
.cssDetailsLabel {
  background-color : #c7dffc;
  font-weight : bold;
  font-size : 10pt;
  font-family : arial;
}
```

This gives us a bluish background color, again chosen to blend in with the default Ext JS style sheet. It also sets the font style once again to a reasonable size and family.

As you would guess, the selector for styling the actual data is next:

```
.cssDetailsData {
  background-color : #f4f4f4;
  font-size : 10pt;
  font-family : arial;
}
```

This gives the cell a light-gray background and sets the font style once again. Note that the labels are bold but the data is not, which is a fairly typical thing to do (sometimes it's reversed, with the data bold and the labels not, but I personally find this way more visually appealing).

The following few styles are applied to the icon views for each of the four categories. The first is x-panel-body:

```
#listingCard .x-panel-body {
  background : white;
  font-size : 8pt;
  font-family : arial;
}
```

This defines the style applied to the body of a given item. Changing the background attribute, for example, will put a color behind each of the icons and their labels.

Next up is some styling that gets wrapped around the icons and their labels:

```
#listingCard .thumb-wrap {
  float : left;
  margin : 4px;
  margin-right : 0;
  padding : 5px;
}
```

This style ensures that the icons run horizontally across the page properly. This goes along with the following selector:

```
#listingCard .thumb-wrap span {
  display : block;
  overflow : hidden;
  text-align : center;
}
```

This ensures that the labels are centered on the icons and that if the text is too long it'll get cut off (which isn't a problem in this application because it's handled differently, as we'll see later).

The next selector is the style for when an icon is hovered over:

```
#listingCard .x-view-over {
  border :1px solid #dddddd;
  background : #efefef;
  padding: 4px;
}
```

It's not much more than a border and a background color change to give a nice highlighting effect. Related to this is

```
#listingCard .x-view-selected {
  background : #eff5fb;
  border : 1px solid #99bbe8;
  padding : 4px;
}
```

This is the style applied to an icon that has been selected, and once again it's little more than a different background color and border style (there's also padding defined on both of the previous selectors, but the color is what's important since that is what's apparent on the screen).

The last bit of style definition in this style sheet looks like this:

```
.x-form-field-wrap {
  position : static;
}
.x-form-field-wrap .x-form-trigger {
  position : static;
  top : auto;
  vertical-align : middle;
}
.x-form-field-wrap .x-form-twin-triggers .x-form-trigger {
  position : static;
  top : auto;
  vertical-align : middle;
}
```

These class definitions resolve a bug present in Ext JS v3.0 that causes the arrows on ComboBox elements to appear on the left side in some situations instead of to the right of the entry box portion. If nothing else, the fact that I was able to get an answer to this problem in under an hour is a testament to how good support for Ext JS is!

The Code

Now that we've looked at the markup and the style sheet involved, we can move on to the actual code. Let's begin by looking at the DAO class, which is in a sense a stand-alone entity to the extent that you could rewrite the entire application and still reuse this class with little or no change.

The DAO Class

Next we move on to the DAO class, contained within the aptly named DAO.js file. This class presents the API to the rest of the application through which all access to the underlying Gears database will be made. This gives us the possibility of storing the data in some other fashion later, perhaps on a server, without changing the application code, which is one of the primary benefits of the DAO pattern.

Let's begin by getting a bird's-eye view of this class via Figure 3-7, a UML class diagram of it.

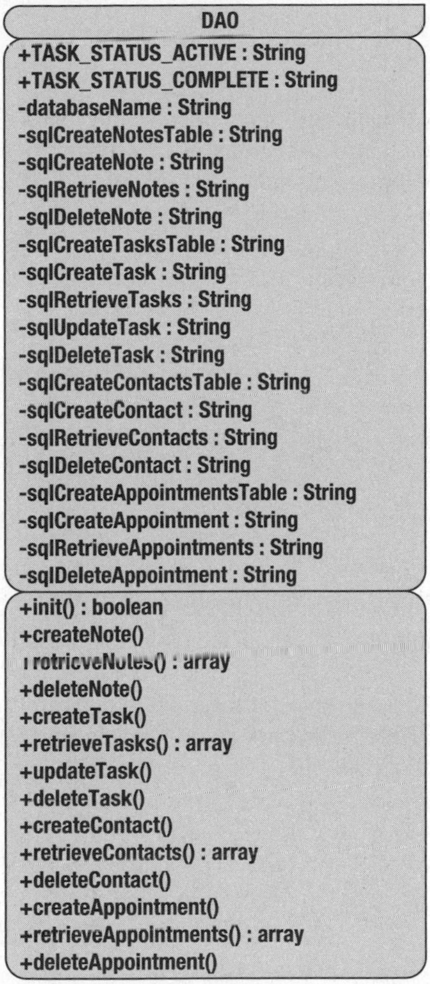

```
┌─────────────────────────────────────────┐
│                  DAO                      │
├─────────────────────────────────────────┤
│ +TASK_STATUS_ACTIVE : String              │
│ +TASK_STATUS_COMPLETE : String            │
│ -databaseName : String                    │
│ -sqlCreateNotesTable : String             │
│ -sqlCreateNote : String                   │
│ -sqlRetrieveNotes : String                │
│ -sqlDeleteNote : String                   │
│ -sqlCreateTasksTable : String             │
│ -sqlCreateTask : String                   │
│ -sqlRetrieveTasks : String                │
│ -sqlUpdateTask : String                   │
│ -sqlDeleteTask : String                   │
│ -sqlCreateContactsTable : String          │
│ -sqlCreateContact : String                │
│ -sqlRetrieveContacts : String             │
│ -sqlDeleteContact : String                │
│ -sqlCreateAppointmentsTable : String      │
│ -sqlCreateAppointment : String            │
│ -sqlRetrieveAppointments : String         │
│ -sqlDeleteAppointment : String            │
├─────────────────────────────────────────┤
│ +init() : boolean                         │
│ +createNote()                             │
│ +retrieveNotes() : array                  │
│ +deleteNote()                             │
│ +createTask()                             │
│ +retrieveTasks() : array                  │
│ +updateTask()                             │
│ +deleteTask()                             │
│ +createContact()                          │
│ +retrieveContacts() : array               │
│ +deleteContact()                          │
│ +createAppointment()                      │
│ +retrieveAppointments() : array           │
│ +deleteAppointment()                      │
└─────────────────────────────────────────┘
```

Figure 3-7. *UML class diagram of the DAO class*

First we see that there are two public fields:

```
DAO.TASK_STATUS_ACTIVE = "active";
DAO.TASK_STATUS_COMPLETE = "complete";
```

These are pseudo-constants that define the value that a task will have when it is active and when it is complete. Since JavaScript doesn't have the concept of a constant like most languages do, the best we can do is name them in a fashion that tries to indicate they are constants. There's a fairly standard way of doing that: all uppercase with underscores between words. This doesn't stop someone from changing the value of these fields, but by general convention most programmers will know they probably shouldn't just by looking at the name.

Next we find a private variable named databaseName:

```
var databaseName = "OrganizerExt";
```

This variable is used in the rest of the code to define the name of the database that Gears will store for us. This variable is optional since Gears will create a default name if you omit it, but it's cleaner to explicitly name something that makes sense. This value isn't needed outside the class; hence it's private to avoid any other code mistakenly changing it and breaking the application.

Following that is the definition of a couple of string variables:

```
var sqlCreateNotesTable = "CREATE TABLE IF NOT EXISTS notes (" +
  "id INT, category TEXT, content TEXT" +
")"
var sqlCreateNote =
  "INSERT INTO notes (id, category, content) " +
  "VALUES (?, ?, ?)";
var sqlRetrieveNotes = "SELECT * FROM notes";
var sqlDeleteNote = "DELETE FROM notes WHERE id=?";
```

This code defines some SQL statements related to notes, starting with a table creation statement. As you can see, it's a perfectly standard statement that creates the table if it doesn't yet exist (and does nothing if it does exist).

Following that is an SQL statement to create a new note. As you can see, dynamic parameters are present in the form of question mark placeholders. The actual values will be bound to these placeholders later when the statement is executed.

After that is the simple SQL statement to retrieve all notes. As it turns out, this is the only retrieval operation we'll need in this application, so it really is as simple as that.

Finally, there is an SQL statement used to delete a note. All this takes is an ID value for the note to delete, again using dynamic parameters.

THE U IN CRUD

If you've never heard the term CRUD before, now you have! CRUD stands for Create, Retrieve, Update, and Delete. These are the four basic operations that most database-driven applications need, and CRUD is a very common term in programming circles. It's also kind of fun to say, especially in place of more vulgar... er... vulgarities!

So, we can see here that there is a create SQL statement, a retrieve statement, and a delete statement for notes, but no update statement. The way I decided to code this application means that updating an item isn't necessary, at least in the case of notes, contacts, and appointments (tasks are a different story, as we'll see next).

In the interest of saving some space here I am not going to show the SQL statements for contacts, appointments, and tasks because they are, by and large, no different than what we just looked at, just with some different fields. Otherwise, they are the same, and there is a set of four SQL statements for contacts and appointments as well.

For tasks, however, there are five because there is an update query for them:

```
var sqlUpdateTask = "UPDATE tasks SET category=?, status=?, content=? " +
  "WHERE id=?";
```

Because a task can be updated in the sense that it can be marked as having been completed, we need such an update query. It works just the same as any of the others; it's just a slightly different query.

Before we continue looking at the code, I thought it would be a good idea to take a glance at the structure of each of the four tables (notes, tasks, contacts, and appointments). Seeing a slightly more graphical representation helps, so Figure 3-8 shows just such a representation of the `contacts` table.

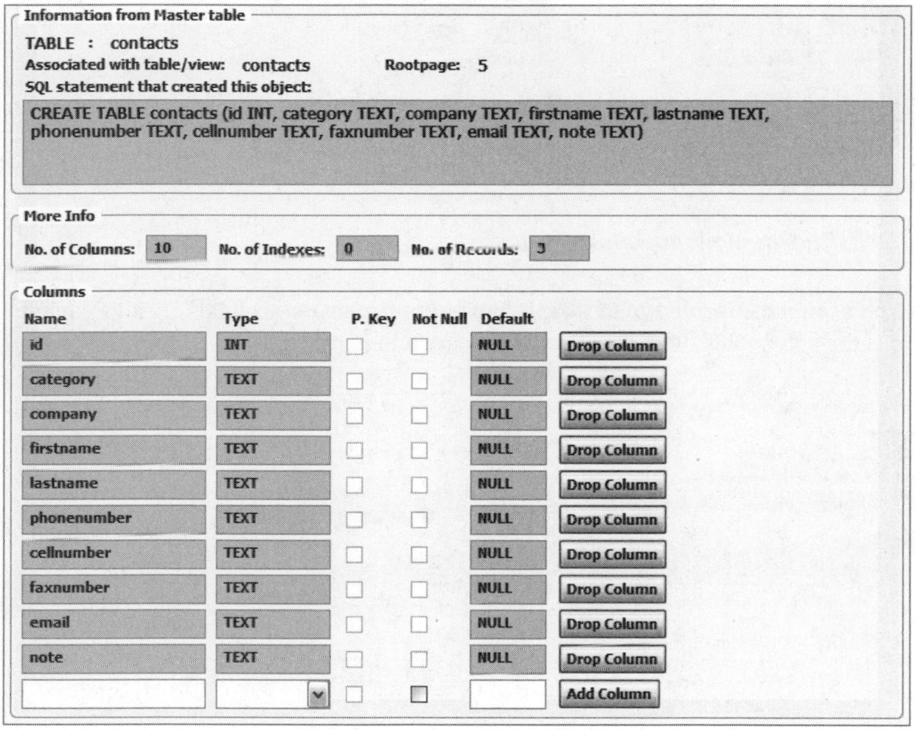

Figure 3-8. *Table structure of the contacts table*

A grand total of ten fields are present for each contact, all of them of type text, except for the ID. Pretty straightforward, I suspect.

In Figure 3-9 you can see the corresponding diagram of the `appointments` table.

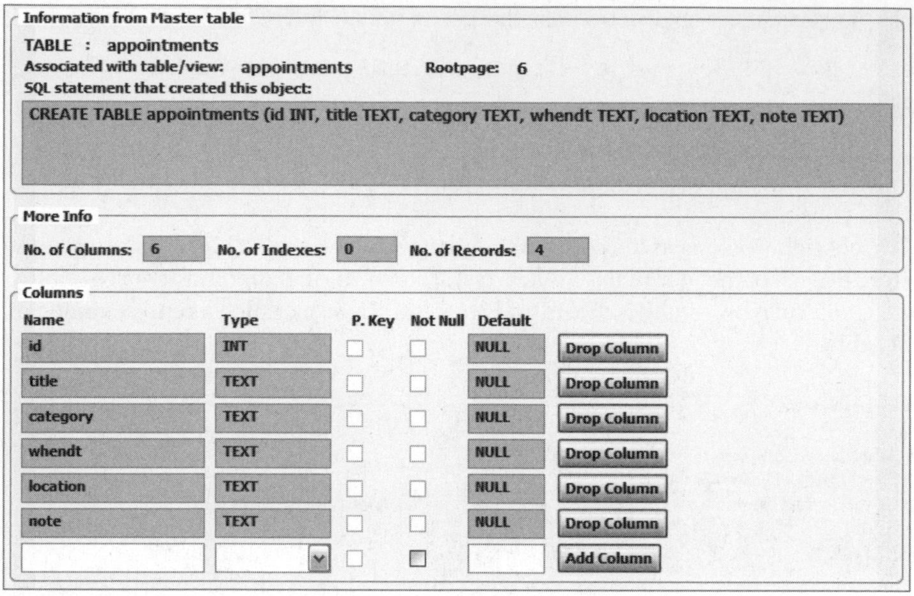

Information from Master table

TABLE : appointments
Associated with table/view: appointments   Rootpage: 6
SQL statement that created this object:

CREATE TABLE appointments (id INT, title TEXT, category TEXT, whendt TEXT, location TEXT, note TEXT)

More Info

No. of Columns: 6   No. of Indexes: 0   No. of Records: 4

Columns

Name	Type	P. Key	Not Null	Default	
id	INT	☐	☐	NULL	Drop Column
title	TEXT	☐	☐	NULL	Drop Column
category	TEXT	☐	☐	NULL	Drop Column
whendt	TEXT	☐	☐	NULL	Drop Column
location	TEXT	☐	☐	NULL	Drop Column
note	TEXT	☐	☐	NULL	Drop Column
	⌄	☐	☐		Add Column

Figure 3-9. *Table structure of the appointments table*

There isn't as much information to store for an appointment, so six fields are all we need. Next up is the notes table, with three fields, as shown in Figure 3-10.

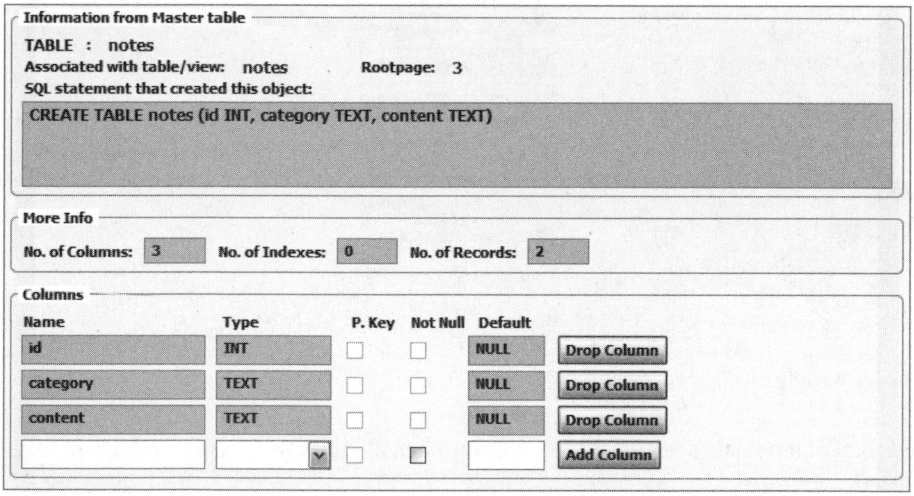

Information from Master table

TABLE : notes
Associated with table/view: notes   Rootpage: 3
SQL statement that created this object:

CREATE TABLE notes (id INT, category TEXT, content TEXT)

More Info

No. of Columns: 3   No. of Indexes: 0   No. of Records: 2

Columns

Name	Type	P. Key	Not Null	Default	
id	INT	☐	☐	NULL	Drop Column
category	TEXT	☐	☐	NULL	Drop Column
content	TEXT	☐	☐	NULL	Drop Column
	⌄	☐	☐		Add Column

Figure 3-10. *Table structure of the notes table*

To round things out, in Figure 3-11 is the same diagram for the tasks table. This is similar to the notes table, with the addition of the status field.

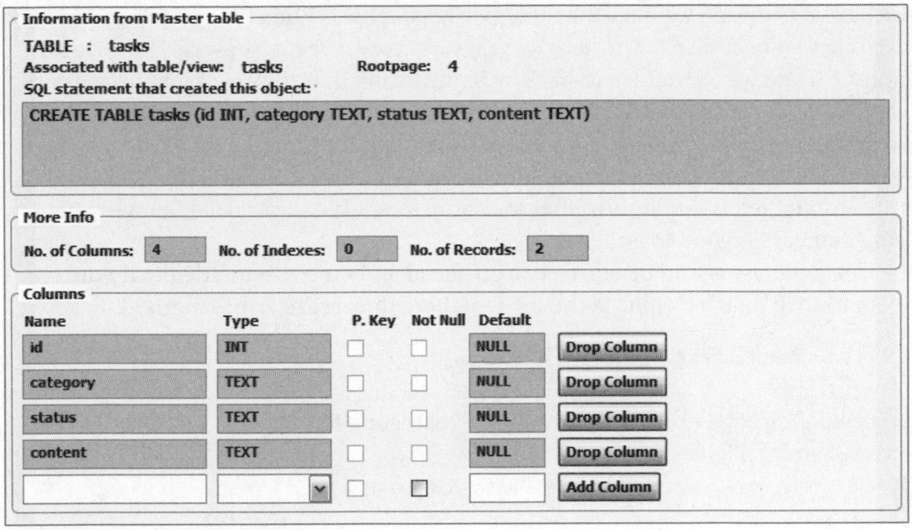

Figure 3-11. *Table structure of the tasks table*

Now, getting back to the code, we encounter our first method: `init()`. This method is responsible for some basic setup:

```
this.init = function() {

  var initReturn = true;
  if (!window.google || !google.gears) {
    initReturn = false;
  }

  var db = google.gears.factory.create("beta.database");
  db.open(databaseName);
  db.execute(sqlCreateNotesTable);
  db.execute(sqlCreateTasksTable);
  db.execute(sqlCreateContactsTable);
  db.execute(sqlCreateAppointmentsTable);
  db.close();

  return initReturn;

}
```

The first thing it does is ensure that Gears is installed and available. This will be the case if there is a `google` attribute on the `window` object and if there is a `gears` attribute on that `google` object. If either of those conditions isn't met, then the variable `initReturn` is set to `false`, which will be the variable returned from this method (we optimistically default its value to `true` in anticipation of no problems with Gears).

The next step is to ensure we have the tables we need. This is done by creating an instance of the beta.database object via a call to google.gears.factory.create(), as we've previously seen in Chapter 2. Then we open the database by name (using that private databaseName variable we saw earlier). After that we execute each of the four table creation SQL statements, one each for notes, tasks, contacts, and appointments. Recall that these statements will only have an effect when the tables don't already exist. Finally, we close the database (which is optional, but is good style nonetheless) and return that initReturn variable so the caller knows whether the underlying database is good to go.

Now that the database is initialized, we can go ahead and create items, delete them, and so on. In celebration of that, let's look at the next method, the createNote() method:

```
this.createNote = function(inNoteDesc) {

  if (inNoteDesc && inNoteDesc.id && inNoteDesc.category &&
    inNoteDesc.content) {
    var db = google.gears.factory.create("beta.database");
    db.open(databaseName);
    db.execute(sqlCreateNote, [
      parseInt(inNoteDesc.id), inNoteDesc.category, inNoteDesc.content
    ]);
    db.close();
  }

}
```

The inNoteDesc argument is an object that contains fields where the data for a note is stored. So, the first thing that's done is a check to ensure that we got an object for inNoteDesc (it's not null, in other words) and that the fields that are absolutely required for a note to be stored are not null either. In the case of a note, all of them are required, but that's not the case for other types of items. Once we do that verification, we again open the database and simply execute the sqlCreateNote query. Note the second argument to the db.execute() method: an array of data that will be inserted in place of those question mark placeholders we saw earlier. Gears will take care of properly escaping the inserted data, so this is a safe way to create a final SQL statement that avoids various hacking exploits that would otherwise be possible.

Now that we know how to create a note, seeing how to retrieve notes is the next logical step. Here's the code for that:

```
this.retrieveNotes = function() {

  var db = google.gears.factory.create("beta.database");
  db.open(databaseName);
  var rs = db.execute(sqlRetrieveNotes);
```

```
var results = [ ];
while (rs.isValidRow()) {
  results.push({
    id : rs.fieldByName("id"),
    category : rs.fieldByName("category"),
    content : rs.fieldByName("content")
  });
  rs.next();
}
rs.close();
db.close();

return results;

}
```

So once again the database is opened, and the sqlRetrieveNotes query is executed. From this we have a ResultSet object, so we begin to iterate over that. This is done by continually checking to see if rs.isValidRow() returns true, which indicates we have another row of data to process. For each row, we create an object consisting of three properties: id, category, and content. These are the data stored for each note. The values of these attributes are pulled from the row of data using the rs.fieldByName() method, which simply gets the value of the named field from the row. This created object is pushed into the array created before the iteration began. Finally, the ResultSet and database are closed and a simple array of objects is returned. Note that the array could be empty, but null would never be returned from this method, which makes writing code that uses this method a little cleaner since there is no null checking to be done.

■**Note** You may wonder why I didn't simply return the ResultSet to the caller. This would have worked, with some changes to the calling code, but the reason for not doing that is because it creates a "leaky abstraction." In other words, this DAO class is currently the only code in the application that knows we're working with Gears. If we return the ResultSet, which is a Gears-supplied class, the rest of the application has to "know about" Gears as well. Transferring the data to a simple array of simple objects means the application is abstracted from the underlying data store, which allows us to change to a different store down the road (imagine if this method actually made an Ajax request to a server to get the data instead).

Deleting a note is much the same, although it takes even less code:

```
this.deleteNote = function(inNoteDesc) {

  if (inNoteDesc && inNoteDesc.id) {
    var db = google.gears.factory.create("beta.database");
    db.open(databaseName);
    db.execute(sqlDeleteNote, [ inNoteDesc.id ]);
    db.close();
  }

}
```

To start with we have another quick check of inNoteDesc, ensuring it's not null and that there is an id specified on it. After that it's a simple execution of the sqlDeleteNote query, dynamically inserting the id value, and that's that!

At this point you've seen how create, retrieve, and delete works for notes. For contacts, appointments, and tasks, the code is virtually identical. The only differences are the SQL queries executed and the fields referenced. Therefore, we won't look at the methods for those items here, but I encourage you to have a look at the code yourself.

There is only one thing left to look at: the updateTask() method, which is used to mark a task as complete:

```
this.updateTask = function(inTaskDesc) {

  if (inTaskDesc && inTaskDesc.id && inTaskDesc.category &&
    inTaskDesc.status && inTaskDesc.content) {
    var db = google.gears.factory.create("beta.database");
    db.open(databaseName);
    db.execute(sqlUpdateTask, [
      inTaskDesc.category, inTaskDesc.status, inTaskDesc.content,
      inTaskDesc.id
    ]);
    db.close();
  }

}
```

There should by this point be little, if any, surprises. There is more verification this time around because there are a few more required fields. In fact, it's all of them, because when updating a task the code makes no effort to determine what fields changed—it simply writes out the values for all of them. Otherwise, this method is no different than what you've seen before.

The OrganizerExt Class

The OrganizerExt class is the heart and soul of the application; it's where all the best parts are! It's also a fairly lengthy piece of code, although as you'll see, much of it isn't what most people consider "code" per se—it's more configuration-type code.

Let's start by looking at a UML class diagram of OrganizerExt, as shown in Figure 3-12.

```
┌─────────────────────────────────────────┐
│            OrganizerExt                   │
├─────────────────────────────────────────┤
│ +currentCategory : String                 │
│ +notesStore : Ext.data.Store              │
│ +tasksStore : Ext.data.Store              │
│ +contactsStore : Ext.data.Store           │
│ +appointmentsStore : Ext.data.Store       │
│ +NoteRecord : Ext.data.Record             │
│ +TaskRecord : Ext.data.Record             │
│ +ContactRecord : Ext.data.Record          │
│ +AppointmentRecord : Ext.data.Record      │
│ +categoryList : String                    │
├─────────────────────────────────────────┤
│ +init()                                   │
│ +initMain()                               │
│ -testForGears() : boolean                 │
│ -createDataStores()                       │
│ -createRecordDescriptors()                │
│ -populateStores()                         │
│ -createNewNoteDialog()                    │
│ -createNewTaskDialog()                    │
│ -createNewContactDialog()                 │
│ -createNewAppointmentDialog()             │
│ -buildUI()                                │
│ +changeCategory()                         │
│ +changeViewMode()                         │
│ +showAppointmentDetails()                 │
│ +showNoteDetails()                        │
│ +showTaskDetails()                        │
│ +showContactDetails()                     │
└─────────────────────────────────────────┘
```

Figure 3-12. *UML class diagram of the OrganizerExt class*

There's certainly a fair bit there, but as I've done before I'm going to cut some of it out of our discussion on the grounds that what we *will* look at basically gives you the picture for the pieces I skip as well. As always, though, I encourage you to look at the complete code in the book's source code, if for no other reason than to keep me honest!

Class Fields

Let's begin by looking at the fields that are part of this class, beginning with currentCategory:

```
this.currentCategory = "appointments";
```

This field, which is public, is used when the user clicks the View Mode toolbar button. It is necessary to know which category of items is currently being shown to properly switch the view mode, and while it likely would have been possible to interrogate the accordion itself to determine what the selected pane is, how to do that wasn't readily apparent to me. More importantly, this approach offers greater efficiency.

Next we encounter a series of four public fields:

```
this.notesStore = null;
this.tasksStore = null;
this.contactsStore = null;
this.appointmentsStore = null;
```

These hold references to the data stores we'll be creating, one for each category. We'll see how the stores are created and manipulated in fairly short order, but for now let's move on to another group of four public fields:

```
this.NoteRecord = null;
this.TaskRecord = null;
this.ContactRecord = null;
this.AppointmentRecord = null;
```

These hold references to the Record classes we'll create that describe a type of item. The Record classes describe what fields a note Record in a data store has, for example. Note that these variables, as well as the previous data store variables, are all public because they will need to be accessible outside the scope of this class, as we'll see later.

The next field is categoryList:

```
this.categoryList = [
  "Competition", "Family", "Favorites", "Gifts", "Goals/Objectives",
  "Holiday", "Home", "Hot Contacts", "Ideas", "International",  "Key Custom",
  "Medical", "Meeting", "Miscellaneous", "Other",  "Personal", "Phone Calls",
  "Status", "Strategies", "Suppliers", "Time And Expenses", "VIP", "Waiting",
  "Work"
];
```

This too is public because it will be needed outside the scope of the class. Its purpose is to provide the list of categories under which an item can be saved. The items will be used to populate the combo boxes on the various create forms, as well as in the Accordion panes for filtering items.

The Initialization Code

Now that we've looked at the fields of the class, we can move right into the executable code. The first method we encounter is init(), which you'll recall from looking at index.htm is called when the DOM is loaded:

```
this.init = function() {

  new Ext.Window({
    applyTo : "dialogPleaseWait", closable : false, modal : true,
    width : 200, height : 100, minimizable : false, resizable : false,
    draggable : false, shadowOffset : 8, id : "dialogPleaseWait"
  }).show(Ext.getDom("divSource"));
  setTimeout("organizerExt.initMain()", 500);

}
```

First, an Ext JS `Window` is opened. The `applyTo` attribute is set to `dialogPleaseWait`; therefore, the markup in `index.htm` that contains the content of the `<div>` `dialogPleaseWait` will be used to form the `Window`. Recall that the special "marker" styles were used in that markup, and now we can see why: the `Window` class knows about those markers and so can determine what content in the specified DOM node is the header for the `Window`, what is the main content, and so forth. We specifically make the window static in the sense that it can't be minimized (`minimizable:false`), can't be resized (`resizable:false`), and can't be dragged around (`draggable:false`). We also make it modal (`modal:true`), which makes it a typical lightbox pop-up (everything else on the page is dulled out and the `Window` is front and center with the full focus of the user on it). In other words, it's pretty well there until we tell it to go away. The code here is interesting in that the `Window` object is created, and then we immediately show it via the chained call to its `show()` method (which is passed a reference to the `divSource` `<div>` so that the animation of the `Window` flying in starts from that location, which as you'll recall is the upper-left corner of the page). This chaining of method calls is pretty common in Ext JS programming, and in JavaScript in general. If you've used the popular jQuery library, you'll know that this can be taken to an extreme, but some people find it to be a much better style; it's up to your own tastes in the end.

Finally, we see that a timeout is started with an interval of 500 milliseconds (half a second). This is done to ensure that before the rest of the initialization procedure happens, the `Window` has completed its animation. This is important because JavaScript is always single-threaded, so if we continued with the rest of our code the `Window` very likely would not be visible, and almost certainly wouldn't properly complete its animation (at *best* it would probably happen in a choppy, visually displeasing fashion).

Once that timeout occurs, it fires the `initMain()` method of the `OrganizerExt` class, which is up for examination next:

```
this.initMain = function() {

  if (!testForGears()) { return; }

  createDataStores();
  createRecordDescriptors();
  populateStores();
  createNewNoteDialog();
  createNewTaskDialog();
  createNewContactDialog();
  createNewAppointmentDialog();
```

```
Ext.QuickTips.init();
Ext.form.Field.prototype.msgTarget = "side";

buildUI();

Ext.getCmp("dialogPleaseWait").destroy();

}
```

First, a call to the testForGears() method is made, so let's jump ahead slightly and look at that now:

```
var testForGears = function() {

  if (!dao.init()) {
    Ext.getCmp("dialogPleaseWait").destroy();
    var dialogNoGears = new Ext.Window({
      applyTo : "dialogNoGears", closable : false, modal : true,
      width : 400, height : 220, minimizable : false, resizable : false,
      draggable : false, shadowOffset : 8, closeAction : "hide",
      buttons : [{
        text : "Ok",
        handler : function() {
          dialogNoGears.hide();
        }
      }]
    });
    dialogNoGears.show(Ext.getDom("divSource"));
    return false;
  } else {
    return true;
  }

}
```

A call to the DAO class's init() method is made, which you'll recall returns true if Gears is good to go, and false otherwise. So, if we get false here we begin by destroying the dialogPleaseWait Window. Note that no animation occurs in this case—it's simply destroyed, which includes removing it from the screen straight away. After that, a new Window is created, this one using the contents of the dialogNoGears <div> as its template. For this Window there will be an OK button for the user to click to dismiss the Window. To do this we use the buttons configuration attribute to the Window constructor. This is a simple array of objects, where each object defines a button. We only have one button here, and when it's clicked we want to hide the Window (we could destroy it as well, but there's little different in this instance so I thought it would be nice to see something different than we saw with the Please Wait Window). One of the possible attributes on the object defining the button is the handler attribute, which is a reference to a function to execute when the button is clicked. In this case it's an inline function, since it's not needed anywhere else.

■**Note** We have a closure here: the dialogNoGears variable is a reference to the Window created, and it's still available to the callback function via closure. This makes for some clean, tight code, which is nice.

Finally, a call is made to the show() method of the new Window object. In this case I decided not to chain the method call as we saw previously, just to show a different syntax to you (see, I care about you, dear reader!)

A WORD ON CLOSURES

Although the assumption throughout this book is that the reader has a fair understanding of JavaScript, closures are one of those concepts that confuse the heck out of most developers until it finally just suddenly clicks. At that point, they see how very useful they are. Closures are not something that every developer has experience with, so I'll provide a brief description here.

A closure is an expression (typically a function) that can have free variables together with an environment that binds those variables (in other words, that "closes" the expression). Perhaps a simpler explanation is that functions in JavaScript can have inner functions. These inner functions are allowed to access all the local variables of the containing function, and most importantly, even after the containing function returns.

Each time a function is executed in JavaScript, an execution context is created. This is conceptually the environment as it was when the function was entered. That's why the inner function still has access to the outer function's variables even after return: the execution context of the inner function includes the execution context of the outer function.

Of course, if Gears was available, then the else branch would have hit, returning true, which gets us back into the main code of the initMain() method. In that case, a bunch of method calls execute. First is createDataStores(), which literally creates the four data stores, one for each category of items. Note that populating the stores with what may be in the Gears database is done later. Before that can occur, we need to create Record descriptors for notes, tasks, contacts, and appointments, and that's the result of calling the createRecordDescriptors() method.

Once those three methods complete, we have fully built data stores (although remember that they do not yet have data in them). Let's now we move on to creating the four dialog Window objects for creating notes, tasks, contacts, and appointments. There is a method call corresponding to each of them: createNewNoteDialog(), createNewTaskDialog(), createNewContactDialog(), and createNewAppointmentDialog(). We'll look at those shortly.

■**Note** I suppose, looking back on it now, creation of the data stores and Record descriptors could have been broken out into four separate methods like the creation of the Window dialogs are... I don't have any secret reason for doing it this way, but putting all the Window creation code together would have made for a much longer method!

Here are the next two lines of code:

```
Ext.QuickTips.init();
Ext.form.Field.prototype.msgTarget = "side";
```

This code configures Ext JS so that tooltips will work when validation failures occur on those four new item creation forms. It also indicates that, by default, the messages will be anchored to the side of the form elements. You can set this on a per-field or per-form basis, but doing so globally is better if you can, and in this case we can.

The final two tasks are to build the UI via a call to buildUI(), and to destroy the Please Wait Window. When that's done, the application is fully initialized and ready for user interaction.

The buildUI() is where most of the action is, but before we get to that we have a number of other methods to look at, starting with createDataStores().

The Data Stores

Creating the data stores isn't a big deal at all—in fact, it's another of those "if you've seen one, you've seen 'em all" situations. So, with that in mind, let's look at one:

```
organizerExt.notesStore = new Ext.data.Store({
  listeners : {
    "add" : {
      fn : function(inStore, inRecords, inIndex) {
        if (Ext.getCmp("dialogPleaseWait")) { return; }
        dao.createNote({
          id : new Date().getTime(),
          category : inRecords[0].get("category"),
          content : inRecords[0].get("content")
        });
      }
    },
    "remove" : {
      fn : function(inStore, inRecord, inIndex) {
        dao.deleteNote( { id : inRecord.get("id") } );
      }
    }
  }
});
```

A new Ext.data.Store() object is instantiated, and that might be the end of it except that we also need to add to it the ability to react to various events, namely adding Record objects to it and removing Record objects from it. This is done by including the listeners attribute in the configuration object passed into the constructor. The listeners attribute is an array of events, and objects contain information defining what happens in response to the event. So, the add event has an object that within it has a single attribute, fn. This is a reference to a function to execute when the add event fires. The signature of this callback method is defined in the Ext JS documentation for the add event. In this case it gets passed a reference to the data store itself, an array of Record objects being added (one or more Record objects can be added at a time), and the index at which the Record object will be added. For our purposes, we only care about that array of Record objects in actuality.

In the callback function itself, we do a quick check to see if the Please Wait Window is present. This is because *any* time a Record is added to the store, this function will execute. So, when the store is being populated initially, this will execute for each Record we add. Since at that point we know we don't want to save anything to the underlying database, we need to skip execution, and checking to see if that Window exists is an easy way to determine that. So, if the Window doesn't exist, all it takes is a call to the DAO class's createNote() method, passing it an object that contains all the data for a note, taken from the incoming inRecords array. In our use case, we know there's only one record and there's no iteration over the array to do, so we just go after the first, and only, element, directly.

When a Record is removed from the store, the same sort of thing occurs, but the remove event fires this time. In this case, we still pass an object to the DAO class's deleteNote() method, but this time it's only the id of the note to be deleted that we care about.

In order to make this clear, take a look at the sequence diagram[3] in Figure 3-13. This walks you through the flow for adding, deleting, and even updating Record objects in both the data stores and the underlying Gears database. Hopefully this figure helps you see how it all ties together because an event-driven model like this can sometimes be difficult to wrap your brain around.

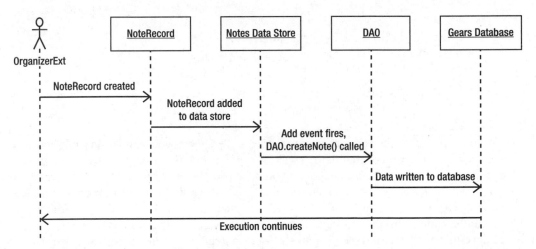

Figure 3-13. *Sequence diagram depicting the creation of a note*

Although I said that seeing one data store created is pretty much seeing how they're all created, I wanted to call out the tasksStore data store separately so you can see the update event handling in action:

---

3   I personally dislike sequence diagrams. I find that usually the degree to which they are useful is inversely proportional to the amount of time the creator spent on it, and they are virtually *never* as useful as you expect them to be. Hopefully this is one of the exceptions to disprove the rule!

```
organizerExt.tasksStore = new Ext.data.Store({
  listeners : {
    "add" : {
      fn : function(inStore, inRecords, inIndex) {
        if (Ext.getCmp("dialogPleaseWait")) { return; }
        dao.createTask({
          id : new Date().getTime(),
          status : inRecords[0].get("status"),
          category : inRecords[0].get("category"),
          content : inRecords[0].get("content")
        });
      }
    },
    "update" : {
      fn : function(inStore, inRecord, inOperation) {
        dao.updateTask({
          id : inRecord.get("id"), category : inRecord.get("category"),
          status : inRecord.get("status"), content : inRecord.get("content")
        });
        organizerExt.showTaskDetails(inRecord);
      }
    },
    "remove" : {
      fn : function(inStore, inRecord, inIndex) {
        dao.deleteTask( { id : inRecord.get("id") } );
      }
    }
  }
});
```

As you can see, the add and remove events are handled just as you saw a little while ago, but now we have the update event handled as well. It's not any different from the other event handlers, but I thought you'd like to see that for yourself! Note the use of new Date().getTime(), which returns a numeric value in milliseconds. This gives us a simple way to generate a unique identifier for a record that should be safe too. (If you change your PC's clock to a past date, or if you run the code so fast that multiple records are created in the same millisecond of time, a conflict could arise. But that seems unlikely in a JavaScript environment and especially so within the context of how this application works.)

■**Note** There are many events you can handle with regard to data stores, but here we only need these, and my suspicion is that most of the time these three events will be all you need. I'll name just a few others that might be of interest: clear (fires when the data cache is cleared), loadexception (occurs if an exception occurs in the proxy during loading) and datachanged (fires when the data cache has changed and a widget bound to the store should refresh its view). Consult the Ext JS documentation for the full list of events and the signatures for the callback functions to match.

The Record Descriptors

The record descriptors are instances of `Ext.data.Record`, and as such are a little more than simple value objects (VOs).[4] However, by and large, that's exactly how you can think of them. Figure 3-14 is a diagram showing the structure of each of the four types of `Record` classes we'll be creating.

```
organizerExt.NoteRecord
-id : float
-category : string
-content : string
-type : string
```

```
organizerExt.TaskRecord
-id : float
-category : string
-content : string
-status : string
-type : string
```

```
organizerExt.ContactRecord
-id : float
-category : string
-company : string
-firstname : string
-lastname : string
-phonenumber : string
-cellnumber : string
-faxnumber : string
-email : string
-note : string
-type : string
```

```
organizerExt.AppointmentRecord
-id : float
-title : string
-category : string
-whendt : datetime
-location : string
-note : string
-type : string
```

Figure 3-14. *The record descriptors in all their glory*

The way it works is that you instantiate an `Ext.data.Record` object by calling the static `create()` method of that class, feeding an array of field descriptors to the constructor, like so:

```
organizerExt.NoteRecord = Ext.data.Record.create([
  { name : "id", mapping : "id" },
  { name : "category", mapping : "category" },
  { name : "content", mapping : "content" },
  { name : "type", mapping : "type" },
]);
```

The result of this is the creation of a new class, `NoteRecord`, which we make a public member of the `OrganizerExt` instance. As you can see, we're specifying that this type of `Record` has four fields: `id`, `category`, `content`, and `type`. Each field is defined by an object in an array, and the object has two attributes: `name`, which is simply the name of the field in the `Record`, and

---

4 A VO is a construct that's seen most often in, but that's not limited to, the Java languages. It's simply a class designed for transferring data back and forth between two entities. This comes up in Java because you don't have structs like in C—classes are all there is. VOs usually contain no logic but just data fields, as well as accessor and mutator methods (a.k.a. getters and setters) for setting and accessing those fields.

mapping, which is the name of the attribute of the underlying data object. So for example, when we create an instance of a NoteRecord, we use this code:

```
var nr = new organizerExt.NoteRecord({
  id : 123, category : "myCategory", type : "Note", content : "myContent"
});
```

With the name and mapping attributes defined as such, the Record knows that the id attribute of the incoming object maps to the id field of the Record, and so forth. Note that the mapping attribute is optional if it's the same as the name attribute, or so says the Ext JS documentation. However, I had trouble with the code working if I left it out, so I included it. Also note that the value of the mapping attribute depends on what underlying Ext.data.Reader implementation is creating the Record. For example, if you were using the Ext.data.JsonReader, it's a JavaScript expression to reference the data, whereas for the Ext.data.XmlReader, it's an Ext.DomQuery path to the element to map to the Record field. An example would be E[foo=bar], which matches an attribute foo that equals bar (see the Ext JS documentation for full details).

The other three Record types are pretty redundant, aside from differing in the fields they contain, so take a look on your own and let's move on to some other things.

Populating the Data Stores

Populating the data stores from the Gears database, done once at startup, is a pretty trivial task, as you can see for yourself:

```
var retrievedNotes = dao.retrieveNotes();
for (var i = 0; i < retrievedNotes.length; i++) {
  organizerExt.notesStore.add(
    new organizerExt.NoteRecord({
      id : retrievedNotes[i].id,
      category : retrievedNotes[i].category, type : "Note",
      content : retrievedNotes[i].content
    })
  );
}
```

A call to one of the retrieval methods in the DAO, retrieveNotes() in this case, gets us all the data there is to get. Remember that we get back an array of simple objects here, so the next step is to iterate over that array. For each item we create the appropriate Record, a NoteRecord here, and pass that Record to the add() method of the corresponding data store. This is all done as one statement, just because it felt natural to me to do it this way. (The alternative would have been to create a NoteRecord, assign it to a variable, and pass it along to the add() method, but it's purely a style choice.) The other four data stores are similarly populated, so again we'll save some space and move on to some other things.

The "New Note" (and, Indirectly, the "New Task") Dialog

The next method we run into as we walk through this class is the createNewNoteDialog() method, which does precisely what its name implies it does:

```
var createNewNoteDialog = function() {

  var createNoteFormPane = new Ext.FormPanel({
    id : "createNoteFormPane", monitorValid : true,
    frame : true, labelWidth : 70, width : 400, autoheight : true,
    items : [
      {
        xtype : "combo", fieldLabel : "Category", name : "category",
        width : 280, allowBlank : false, editable : false,
        triggerAction : "all",
        mode : "local", store : organizerExt.categoryList, typeAhead : false
      },
      {
        xtype : "textarea",  fieldLabel : "Content",
        name : "content", width : 280, height : 230,
        allowBlank : false
      }
    ]
  });

  createNoteFormPane.addButton( { text : "Create", formBind : true},
    function() {
      var vals = Ext.getCmp("createNoteFormPane").getForm().getValues();
      var newNoteRecord = new organizerExt.NoteRecord({
        category : vals.category, content : vals.content, type : "Note",
        id : 0
      });
      organizerExt.notesStore.add(newNoteRecord);
      Ext.getCmp("dialogCreateNote").hide();
    }
  );
  createNoteFormPane.addButton("Cancel", function() {
    Ext.getCmp("dialogCreateNote").hide();
  });

  new Ext.Window({
    title : "Create Note", closable : true, modal : true,
    width : 400, height : 340, minimizable : false, resizable : false,
    draggable : true, shadowOffset : 8, items : [ createNoteFormPane ],
    closeAction : "hide", id : "dialogCreateNote"
  });

}
```

In the case of previous Windows, we created the Window and immediately showed it, but in this example we're creating the Window for later. This is a good technique when you know the Window (or other UI widget) is something you'll need over and over again. It's better to avoid the overhead of creation if you can by only creating it once and reusing it. That's precisely what we're doing here. We create a new Window, which starts off not visible.

Before we create the Window itself, though, we're creating a FormPanel. This is a widget that houses a form. On its own, a FormPanel, a descendant of the Panel class, doesn't do much. It has to be a child of some other widget to do much good. Here it's going to be a child of our Window.

Creating a FormPanel, and by extension a form, is not too tough. We start by instantiating an Ext.FormPanel object, passing into its constructor a configuration object. This object contains a number of fields, starting with id, which is pretty self-describing. Next is monitorValid, which is a neat option that tells the form to monitor itself to determine if it's "valid," whatever *valid* means in this context. This causes a looping event to occur whenever the valid state of the form changes. We can react to this state if we wish. More importantly, though, is that we can have other form elements tied to this state for free! Look down a bit in the code to where the Create button is created and note the formBind:true configuration option. This instructs the button to take part in that looping event so that whenever the form is not valid, the button is disabled, and when the form is valid, the button is enabled. This is precisely what you'd want to happen from a user interface perspective, and we got it without writing a lick of code. Very sweet!

Returning to the configuration of the FormPanel, we see the width and height specified, sized to fit nicely in our Window. We also see the frame:true attribute, which puts a nice frame border around the FormPanel, which just makes it look a little better within the Window. We also inform the FormPanel to set its height automatically (autoHeight:true) based on its contents. We also include a setting that specifies how wide the labels of our fields should be (labelWidth:70).

Following that is an array assigned to the items attribute. This will be the fields on our form. Each element of the array is an object that describes a given field. We start with the Category field. The xtype attribute tells us what kind of field this is going to be, a combo box in this case. We specify a label for the field via the fieldLabel attribute, and we assign a name to the field to retrieve its value later. The width attribute tells us how wide the field itself will be, minus the width of the label. (You'll notice the field is 280 pixels wide, and the label is 70 pixels wide, leaving 50 pixels in the width of the FormPanel and Window, which is enough to display the error icon when a field is invalid.) The allowBlank attribute, when set to false, indicates that this field is required in order for the form to be valid. This is how the mechanism enabled by monitorValid, and by extension the formBind attribute of the Create button, knows whether or not a given field is valid at a given point in time.

Setting the editable attribute to false indicates that the user should not be able to type a value into the combo box, which makes it work more like a traditional <select>.

■Note I encountered a problem while writing this code where once you select a value, the list of values no longer appeared. A user in the support forums on the Ext JS web site came to the rescue, indicating that the solution was to set `triggerAction` to `all`, as you see here. This essentially tells the combo box to re-query the data that is used to populate it any time the field is triggered—in this case, when the down arrow is clicked.

The `mode` attribute indicates whether the data for the combo box is coming from a remote source—a server in other words—or from local JavaScript. Here we have no server and a set list of options, so it's local. We also need to tell the `ComboBox` where the store of data is by specifying the `store` attribute. Here, it's simply pointing at the simple array referenced by the `categoryList` attribute of the `OrganizerExt` class.

A `TextArea` is next created for users to type their note into, which is where the xtype of `textarea` comes into play. Its attributes are obvious, given that we've seen them all already.

The `FormPanel` now has all the fields the user can enter, so all that remains is adding some buttons to it, one for actually creating the note and one for canceling, if the user changes his or her mind (after all, creating a note is a lifelong commitment, no?). The addButton() method of the `FormPanel` is made especially for this purpose. First the Create button is created. The first argument to this method is a configuration object, here specifying the text on the button and that formBind attribute discussed earlier.

The second argument of the addButton() method is a function to execute when the button is clicked. Here, this function doesn't have to do a whole lot: it gets a reference to the `FormPanel` via the `Ext.getCmp()` function, then gets the form contained within that `FormPanel`. It then calls the getValues() method of that form, which returns a simple object where the attributes correspond to the form fields, with their corresponding values assigned to the attributes. This object, reference by the `vals` variable, is used to create a `NoteRecord` object, which is then passed to the add() method of the notes data store. As we saw previously, this triggers the add event, which calls our `DAO.createNote()` method, which in turn writes the data to the Gears database. Did you notice how relatively little code we had to write to get the connection between the database, `DAO`, data store, and form? It probably amounts to 20 lines of code or so all totaled, which isn't much at all!

The cancel button is created similarly, and its function simply calls the hide() method on the `Window`. Remember, we're going to reuse this `Window`; hence we don't want to destroy it but just hide it.

The final step in this method is to create the actual `Window`. You've seen that a few times now, so it's nothing new. This time around, though, we specify the closeAction attribute, which is what will happen if the user clicks the close X icon on the `Window`. Again, we just want to hide it. One difference in the way this `Window` is created is that previously we saw how to create a `Window` based on some existing HTML, but this time around we're building it completely via code. So, the items attribute is used to attach various UI widgets to the `Window`, in this case our `FormPanel`, which contains all the content. Likewise, we have to explicitly specify a title for the `Window`.

In Figure 3-15 you can see the results of all this effort.

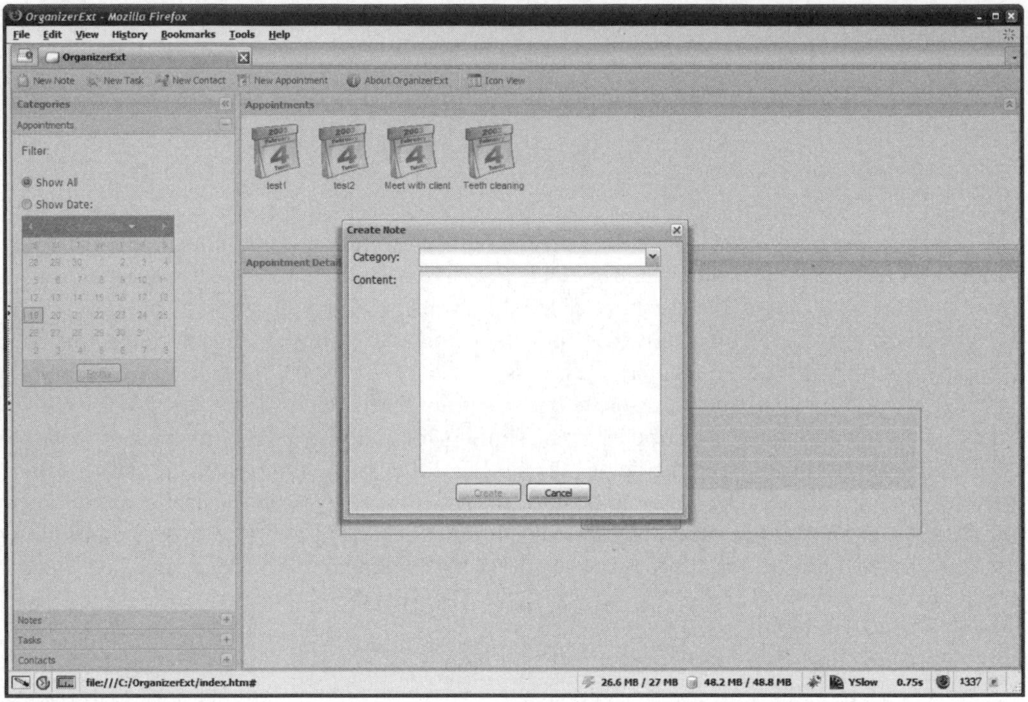

Figure 3-15. *The New Note window*

In Figure 3-16 you can see what happens when a form is not valid. The tooltip you see is a result of me hovering the mouse over the red exclamation bubble next to the field. Also notice that the Create button has been disabled. Again, note that we accomplished that with just some configuration options—we didn't have to write any code to do it.

If you play with the contacts creation `Window`, you'll notice that some other types of validations are present. For example, the e-mail address value must be a valid e-mail address. This too is something we can get automatically, like so:

```
{
  xtype : "textfield", fieldLabel : "eMail Address",
  name : "email", width : 250, vtype : "email"
}
```

This is the object in the `items` array that is specified for the `FormPanel` in the create contact `Window`. That `vtype` attribute, short for validation type, specifies a type of validation to occur for that field. Table 3-1 lists the other vtypes built into Ext JS.

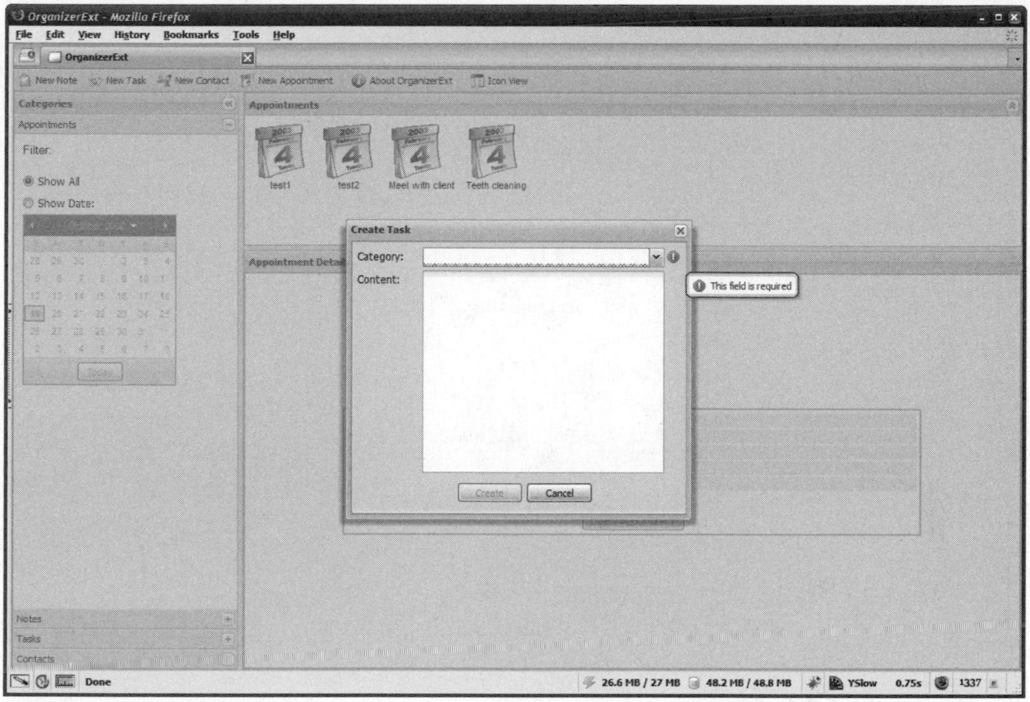

Figure 3-16. *The New Task window, with a validation failure and the associated tooltip*

Table 3-1. *Vtypes Available by Default in Ext JS*

Vtype	Description
email	Ensures the field's value is a valid e-mail format (i.e., `user@domain.com`)
url	Ensures the field's value is a valid URL format (i.e., `http://www.domain.com`)
alpha	Ensures the field's value only contains letters and the underscore character
alphanum	Ensures the field's value only contains letters, numbers, and the underscore character

It is also possible to create your own validation types, or extend these to meet your needs. You'll see an example of that in later chapters.

The New Appointment Dialog

Even though there's not much more to it than you've seen already, let's take a quick look at the New Appointment `Window`:

```
var createNewAppointmentDialog = function() {

  var createAppointmentFormPane = new Ext.FormPanel({
    id : "createAppointmentFormPane",
    frame : true, labelWidth : 100, width : 400, autoheight : true,
    monitorValid : true,
    items : [
      {
        xtype : "textfield", fieldLabel : "Title",
        name : "title", width : 250, allowBlank : false
      },
      {
        xtype : "combo", fieldLabel : "Category", name : "category",
        width : 250, allowBlank : false, editable : false,
        triggerAction : "all",
        mode : "local", store : organizerExt.categoryList
      },
      {
        xtype : "datefield", fieldLabel : "When",
        name : "whendt", width : 250, allowBlank : false
      },
      {
        xtype : "textfield", fieldLabel : "Location",
        name : "location", width : 250
      },
      {
        xtype : "textarea",  fieldLabel : "Note",
        name : "note", width : 250, height : 152
      }
    ]
  });

  createAppointmentFormPane.addButton( { text : "Create", formBind : true},
    function() {
      var vals = Ext.getCmp("createAppointmentFormPane").getForm().getValues();
      vals.whendt = Date.parseDate(vals.whendt, "m/d/Y");
      var newAppointmentRecord = new organizerExt.AppointmentRecord({
        title : vals.title, category : vals.category, whendt : vals.whendt,
        location : vals.location, note : vals.note, type : "Appointment",
        id : 0
      });
      organizerExt.appointmentsStore.add(newAppointmentRecord);
      Ext.getCmp("dialogCreateAppointment").hide();
    }
  );
```

```
createAppointmentFormPane.addButton("Cancel", function() {
  Ext.getCmp("dialogCreateAppointment").hide();
});

new Ext.Window({
  title : "Create Appointment", closable : true, modal : true,
  width : 400, height : 340, minimizable : false, resizable : false,
  draggable : true, shadowOffset : 8, items : [ createAppointmentFormPane ],
  closeAction : "hide", id : "dialogCreateAppointment"
});

}
```

The only thing really different here is the introduction of two new xtype values: datefield and textfield. The former creates a field with a calendar icon that, when clicked, presents a full calendar from which to choose a date. The textfield xtype is just like textarea except it is a single-line place for the user to type a value.

You can also here see the use of the Date.parseDate() method when getting the value of the When field. Because I wanted the data type of the whendt field in the AppointmentRecord to be a true JavaScript Date object, and since using getValues() on a form like this only gets you strings, I needed to parse that string into a Date object. That is exactly what parseDate() does for us. The second argument to this function indicates what the format of the input date string is, and gives us back a true Date object. Very nice!

■**Note** The call to getForm() on the FormPanel gives us back an Ext.form.BasicForm, which has a number of neat methods, getValues() among them. This is very much like an HTML form with all sorts of handy utility methods hanging off it, and I suggest you spend a few minutes with the Ext JS API documentation on the BasicForm class to become familiar with what it has to offer.

In Figure 3-17 you can see what the New Appointment Window looks like. I've even clicked the calendar icon next to the When field to show the calendar in all its glory.

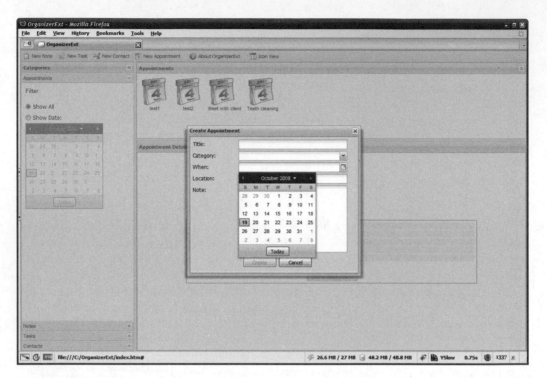

Figure 3-17. *The New Appointment dialog*

Building the User Interface: The buildUI() Method

As it happens, building the UI pretty well boils down to one massive JavaScript statement! You can take one of three approaches to building a UI with Ext JS. The first is what we'll see in this application: one giant statement. The second is to create a whole bunch of components programmatically and then stitch them together via code. The third is more of a declarative approach where you do as much as possible in markup, which is then used as the templates for the widgets created via code (which we've seen some of here). The bottom line is you're going to be writing code one way or another—it's just a question of how much and in what form.

Creating the Viewport

The first step is typically creating a `Viewport`. There is exactly one `Viewport` per page that takes up the entire browser window, and inside the `Viewport` goes various other `Container` components (usually `Panel` objects). Let's see how that `Viewport` is created first. Note that this begins that giant statement I mentioned, and all the code snippets that follow are parts of that statement.

```
var vp = new Ext.Viewport({
  layout : "border",
  items  : [{
```

The Ext.Viewport class is instantiated and passed a configuration object. The layout attribute specifies how the Viewport will organize its child components. A number of layouts are available, as you can see in Table 3-2. Note that these don't only apply to the Viewport; they can also in most cases be applied to children of the Viewport.

Table 3-2. *Layouts Available to the Viewport and Child Panels*

Layout Attribute Value	Description
absolute	This layout inherits the anchoring of Ext.layout.AnchorLayout and adds the ability for x/y positioning using the standard x and y component config options.
accordion	This layout contains multiple panels in an expandable accordion style so that only one panel can be open at any given time. Each panel has built-in support for expanding and collapsing.
anchor	This layout enables anchoring of contained elements relative to the container's dimensions. If the container is resized, all anchored items are automatically rerendered according to their anchor rules.
border	This is a multipane, application-oriented UI layout style that supports multiple nested panels, automatic split bars between regions and built-in expanding and collapsing of regions.
card	This layout contains multiple panels, each fit to the container, where only a single panel can be visible at any given time. This layout style is most commonly used for wizards, tab implementations, or other UI interfaces where multiple "pages" are present in the same area but only one is visible at a time.
column	This is the layout style of choice for creating structural layouts in a multi-column format where the width of each column can be specified as a percentage or fixed width but the height is allowed to vary based on the content.
fit	This layout contains a single item that automatically expands to fill the layout's container.
form	This layout is specifically designed for creating forms. Typically you'll use the FormPanel instead.
table	This layout allows you to easily render content into an HTML table. The total number of columns can be specified, and rowspan and colspan can be used to create complex layouts within the table.

There is also a basic Container layout, which is what you'll get for the Viewport if you supply no value for the layout attribute. In this case we're using a Border layout, since the structure of the application fits that model nicely: there's something on the top (the toolbar), something on the left (our Accordion category selector), and something in the middle (both the icon/list views and the details section). Note that you do not have to use all of the areas allowed for with a Border layout, you can skip any you like.

Creating the Accordion Pane

Once the Viewport is created and configured, we can start adding children to it, starting with the Accordion on the left where the user can flip between categories and filter listings. The code that begins creation of the Accordion looks like this:

```
region : "west", id : "categoriesArea", title : "Categories",
split : true, width : 260, minSize : 10, maxSize : 260,
collapsible : true, layout : "accordion",
defaults: { bodyStyle : "overflow:auto;padding:10px;" },
layoutConfig : { animate : true },
items : [
```

The region attribute specifies in what position of the Border layout this child should live in—in this example, the left side, or west area. An id can be assigned to this Accordion if you want to, as I've done here. You can set the title attribute to have a title bar present. The split attribute, when true, indicates that there is a split bar that the user can drag to resize this area. The width attribute specifies the starting width of the Accordion, and the minSize and maxSize attribute specify the minimum and maximum width the Accordion can have when the user resizes it. The collapsible attribute set to true includes the little arrow in the title bar of the Accordion that allows the user to quickly collapse this section of the layout. The defaults attribute specifies attributes to be applied to any component added to this Container. Here it applies some padding to the body of the content in each of the Accordion panes. The layoutConfig attribute is an object whose properties set attributes specific to the component being created. So here, for example, we're specifying that the Accordion should animate itself whenever the user flips between panes.

Once you have the Accordion all set up, you can begin to add components to it, and in this case I've done so using the items attribute.

The Appointments Accordion Pane

Each element of the items attribute array is an object that defines a component to be added to the Accordion, creating another pane in the Accordion. The first one here is creating the pane for appointments:

```
{
  listeners : {
    "expand" : {
      fn : function() { organizerExt.changeCategory("appointments"); }
    }
  },
  id : "appointmentsArea", title : "Appointments",
  items : [
    { xtype : "label", text : "Filter:" },
    { xtype : "label", html : "<br><br>" },
    {
      xtype : "radiogroup", columns : 1,
      items : [
```

```
      { boxLabel : "Show All", name : "appointmentsFilterType",
        inputValue : 1, checked : true,
        listeners : {
          "check" : function(inCheckbox, inChecked) {
            if (inChecked) {
              organizerExt.appointmentsStore.filterBy(
                function(inRecord, inIndex) {
                  return true;
                }
              );
            }
          }
        }
      },
      { boxLabel : "Show Date:",
        name : "appointmentsFilterType", inputValue : 2,
        listeners : {
          "check" : function(inCheckbox, inChecked) {
            var afcDatePicker =
              Ext.getCmp("appointmentsDatePicker");
            if (inChecked) {
              afcDatePicker.enable();
            } else {
              afcDatePicker.disable();
              afcDatePicker.setValue(new Date());
            }
          }
        }
      }
    ]
  },
  {
    xtype : "datepicker", id : "appointmentsDatePicker",
    disabled : true,
    listeners : {
      "select" : function(inPicker, inDate) {
        organizerExt.appointmentsStore.filterBy(
          function(inRecord, inIndex) {
            var whendt = inRecord.get("whendt");
            if (whendt.getMonth() == inDate.getMonth() &&
              whendt.getDate() == inDate.getDate() &&
              whendt.getFullYear() == inDate.getFullYear()) {
              return true;
            } else {
```

```
                return false;
            }
        }
    );
}
}
}
],
  border : false, cls : "cssDefault"
},
```

The first thing we see is that an event handler is defined by passing an array as the value of the listeners attribute. Each element in the array is an object with attributes named after events, as we've previously seen. Here, we call the changeCategory() method of the OrganizerExt class any time this pane is expanded.

After that we give an id and title to this particular pane, and then it's time to add some content to the pane. For that we use the items array once again.

The first two items added are xtype:label, which is just a simple string of text. Note that you can have HTML as the value here, and that renders as you'd expect it to. Following that is the addition of an xtype:radiogroup. This is some number of Radio buttons grouped together so that they function as mutually exclusive selections, just like Radio buttons should.

The columns attribute specifies how many columns should be used to render the Radio buttons, and this allows you to have matrixes of Radio buttons rather than just running right down the page vertically, as is the case here. Within the RadioGroup we again see an items array (this is a common thread if you haven't noticed by now!) where each element is a Radio button. Each Radio button has a boxLabel attribute, which is a fancy way of saying it's the text accompanying the Radio button, and a name attribute.

■Note The name attribute must match all the other Radio buttons in the RadioGroup; otherwise, they don't function in the expected way (i.e., only one selection allowed). This was frankly a little surprising to me; I expected that making the Radio buttons part of a RadioGroup made the name not matter, but that isn't the case.

The inputValue attribute allows you to assign a value to each Radio button, and the checked attribute determines which of the options is selected upon creation. Finally, we see another use of the listeners attribute to define some code to execute when the Radio button is selected by responding to the check event. In the case of the first Radio button, we filter the list currently being shown (although since this Radio button is the Show All option, "filtering" here means selecting all items from the store). Note that the check event fires when the item is checked or when it is unchecked, hence the reason the inChecked argument is taken into account: we only want this code to execute when the Radio button has been selected, not when it's been unselected.

■**Note** You may at first find the attribute checked, and the event named check, to be strange for a Radio button, since they don't really get "checked." However, a quick look at the Ext JS API docs clears it up: Radios extend from the Checkbox widget, and it inherits these items, among others. Remember, Ext JS is built based on a rich OOP foundation, and that shines through frequently like this.

In the case of the second Radio button, we need to enable the DatePicker if the Radio button has been checked, or disable the DatePicker if the Radio button has been unchecked. The call to Ext.getCmp("appointmentsDatePicker"); gets us a reference to the DatePicker, which we can then call enable() or disable() on as appropriate. Also, when the DatePicker is disabled, its date is set to today's date so that it's ready for the next time it's needed.

The DatePicker itself is the next item added to this Accordion pane using an xtype of datepicker. It starts out disabled (disabled:true) since the Show All Radio button is by default selected.

When the select event fires on the DatePicker, we execute some code to again filter the items shown in the list. The filterBy method of the target data store is used to filter the items. Recall that this method accepts a reference to a callback function that will be called for every Record in the store. The function returns true if the Record should be included, false if not. Because the appointments DataView objects are bound to the data store, they are updated automatically.

The Notes Accordion Pane

The Accordion pane for notes is conceptually very similar to the one for appointments, and the same is true for contacts and tasks. So, while I'll show the code for the notes pane here, I'm going to skip over much of it on the basis that you've already seen most of it, and I'll only be pointing out some differences for tasks and contacts.

```
{
  listeners : {
    "expand" : {
      fn : function() { organizerExt.changeCategory("notes"); }
    }
  },
  id : "notesArea", title : "Notes", border : false,
  cls : "cssDefault",
  items : [
    { xtype : "label", text : "Filter:" },
    { xtype : "label", html : "<br><br>" },
    {
      xtype : "radiogroup", columns : 1,
      items : [
```

```
            { boxLabel : "Show All", name : "notesFilterType",
              inputValue : 1, checked : true,
              listeners : {
                "check" : function(inCheckbox, inChecked) {
                  if (inChecked) {
                    organizerExt.notesStore.filterBy(
                      function(inRecord, inIndex) {
                        return true;
                      }
                    );
                  }
                }
              }
            },
            { boxLabel : "Show Category:",
              name : "notesFilterType", inputValue : 2,
              listeners : {
                "check" : function(inCheckbox, inChecked) {
                  var nfcCombo = Ext.getCmp("notesFilterCategory");
                  if (inChecked) {
                    nfcCombo.enable();
                  } else {
                    nfcCombo.disable();
                    nfcCombo.reset();
                  }
                }
              }
            }
          ]
        },
        {
          xtype : "combo", id : "notesFilterCategory", editable : false,
          mode : "local", store : organizerExt.categoryList,
          disabled : true, triggerAction : "all",
          width : 150, listWidth : 168,
          listeners : {
            "select" : function(inComboBox, inRecord, inIndex) {
              organizerExt.notesStore.filterBy(
                function(inRecord, inIndex) {
                  if (inRecord.get("category") ==
                    Ext.getCmp("notesFilterCategory").getValue()) {
                    return true;
                  } else {
```

```
            return false;
          }
        }
      );
    }
   }
  }
 ]
},
```

The primary difference between this and what we just looked at for appointments is that instead of a DatePicker we have a ComboBox for the user to choose a category to filter by. This uses an xtype of combo and is nearly the same as the ComboBox creations we saw earlier in the item creation dialogs. In fact, it is bound to the same basic array of data as those others were. Here, though, we have the addition of an event handler for the select event. The callback defined kicks off a call to filterBy() on the data store for notes, just as you'd expect. A simple comparison is all it takes to implement the required filtering logic.

In Figure 3-18 you can see what the ComboBox looks like in action.

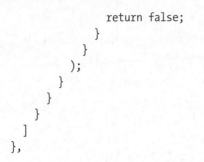

Figure 3-18. *The category being used to filter notes*

As you can see, it's basically the same as in the creation dialogs, just as you'd expect.

Filtering Tasks by Status

Within the configuration for the tasks pane is the callback executed in response to the check event of the Show Active Radio button. I'd like to point that out here:

```
{ boxLabel : "Show Active", name : "tasksFilterType",
  inputValue : 2,
  listeners : {
    "check" : function(inCheckbox, inChecked) {
      if (inChecked) {
        organizerExt.tasksStore.filterBy(
          function(inRecord, inIndex) {
            if (inRecord.get("status") ==
              DAO.TASK_STATUS_ACTIVE) {
              return true;
            } else {
              return false;
            }
          }
        );
      }
    }
  }
},
```

This code uses one of the pseudo-constants from the DAO class in the comparison, but aside from that it's just like what we've seen already.

Filtering Contacts by Last Name

Like the active task filtering, contacts have a slightly different filtering capability, which is the ability to filter by last name:

```
{ boxLabel : "Show last nams starting with A-C",
  name : "contactsFilterType", inputValue : 2,
  listeners : {
    "check" : function(inCheckbox, inChecked) {
      if (inChecked) {
        organizerExt.contactsStore.filterBy(
          function(inRecord, inIndex) {
            var firstLetter = inRecord.get(
              "lastname").charAt(0).toUpperCase();
            if (firstLetter >= 'A' && firstLetter <= 'C') {
              return true;
            } else {
```

```
          return false;
        }
      }
    );
  }
 }
}
},
```

This is the definition for just one of a number of Radio buttons, each corresponding to a group of letters (A–C here, the next is D–F, and so forth). When one of these is selected, the check event fires, and for each Record in the data store we check if the first letter of the lastname field starts with one of the letters in the selected group. If so, true is returned; if not, false is returned, and that gives us filtering by last name.

The Main Region

The main, or center region of the BorderLayout, is where you find the icon/grid views and the detail section for a given category. You can generally split up a given Container as many times as you wish using various layouts, so here we have the center Container split into multiple regions by using a BorderLayout again within it:

```
{
  id : "mainArea", region : "center", layout : "border",
  items : [
```

This means we have a BorderLayout nester inside the center region of another BorderLayout. That also means that we could have up to five Containers (north, south, east, west, and center) as part of the inner BorderLayout. As it turns out, we'll only need two, though.

The Icon and Grid Lists

The north region of this inner BorderLayout is where we'll put a series of Panels, eight of them: four Panels for the icon view of each of the four categories, and four Panels for the list view of each of the four categories. To achieve this we'll use a CardLayout in this region:

```
{
  xtype : "panel", region : "north", split : true,
  collapsible : true, id : "listingCard", layout : "card",
  activeItem : 0, title : "Appointments",
  height : 175, autoScroll : true,
  items : [
```

Again, all it takes is setting the layout attribute to card and we have what we want. A CardLayout stacks a number of Panels on top of one another so that only one is visible at a time. The activeItem attribute indicates which of the Panels is active to begin with using a simple 0-based index value. The autoScroll attribute set to true indicates that content larger than the area occupied by the CardLayout will be allowed to scroll. The region attribute tells the component that contains this CardLayout (the inner BorderLayout) what region this CardLayout should be rendered to—the north region in this case.

Now that we have a CardLayout, let's see how an icon view is created. We'll just look at one since—you guessed it—they are all virtually identical!

An Icon View

An icon view is a DataView, defined by using an xtype of dataview:

```
{
  xtype : "dataview", id : "dvAppointmentsIconView",
  store : organizerExt.appointmentsStore,
  tpl : new Ext.XTemplate(
    "<tpl for=\".\">",
      "<div class=\"thumb-wrap\">",
      "<div class=\"thumb\">" +
      "<img src=\"img/iconView{type}.gif\"></div>",
      "<span class=\"x-editable\">{title}</span></div>",
    "</tpl>",
    "<div class=\"x-clear\"></div>"
  ),
  singleSelect : true, overClass : "x-view-over",
  itemSelector : "div.thumb-wrap",
  listeners: {
    selectionchange : {
      fn : function(inDataView, inNodes) {
        var selectedRecord = inDataView.getSelectedRecords()[0];
        organizerExt.showAppointmentDetails(selectedRecord);
      }
    }
  }
},
```

A DataView allows us to display items however we choose by specifying a template to use to render each item. The tpl attribute specifies the Ext.XTemplate object to use for this purpose, and here we're creating a new one inline. As you can see, it consists of some basic HTML with the addition of some replacement tokens in it and some special processing tags. For example, the {title} token will be replaced with the title of a given appointment as entered by the user.

In addition to these tokens are some simple processing tags that can be used as part of the template. One such tag is <tpl for="."> (the quotation marks are escaped in the code, but this is the underlying statement). This special tag is equivalent to saying, "This template should be applied to all Records in the data store." More precisely, the template should never be applied to Records matched by the filterBy() method currently in effect, because the user could have chosen to filter the data based on some selected criteria from the Accordion panes.

After the template we find a few more configuration options. The singleSelect attribute, when true, indicates that only a single item in the DataView can be selected at a given time. The overClass attribute specifies the style class to apply to an item when the mouse is hovering over it. The `itemSelector` attribute indicates the style class to apply to the selected item. There is also the `listeners` attribute, as we've seen plenty of already. This time, we react to the `selectionchange` event, which results in the selected Record being retrieved via a call to `inDataView.getSelectedRecords()`. This method returns an array, but since we know only one item can be selected, it's the item at array index 0 that we're interested in. A call to `organizerExt.showAppointmentDetails()` is then made, passing along the Record object that was just retrieved. We'll see how those details are displayed soon, but first we need to look at a list view.

A List View

Creating a list view means creating a Grid, as you can see here:

```
{
  xtype : "grid", id : "gdAppointmentsListView",
  autoExpandColumn : "colTitle", minColumnWidth : 10,
  autoExpandMin : 10, autoExpandMax : 5000,
  store : organizerExt.appointmentsStore,
  columns : [
    {
      header : "Category", width : 50,
      sortable : true, dataIndex : "category"
    },
    {
      header : "Title", id : "colTitle",
      sortable : true, dataIndex : "title"
    },
    {
      header : "When", width : 90,
      sortable : true, dataIndex : "whendt"
    }
  ],
  viewConfig : { forceFit : true }, stripeRows : true,
  sm : new Ext.grid.RowSelectionModel({ singleSelect : true }),
  listeners: {
    rowclick : {
      fn : function(inGrid, inRowIndex, inEventObject) {
        organizerExt.showAppointmentDetails(
          inGrid.getSelectionModel().getSelected()
        );
      }
    }
  }
},
```

The grid xtype does the basic work for us, and then it's a matter of setting configuration options and defining the columns. The options are `autoExpandColumn`, which names the column that will expand to take up all the space in the grid; `minColumnWidth`, which is the smallest the user can make a column by dragging to resize it; autoExpandMin, which is the minimum space the column named by autoExpandColumn can take; and autoExpandMax, which is the maximum width of the column named by autoExpandColumn. The store attribute is the same as we've seen earlier: it binds the Grid to a particular data store, the one for appointments in this case.

After that is the columns attribute, which is an array of objects where each object defines a column in the Grid. Each object has a header attribute, which is the text to show in the column header; a width attribute, which is the initial width of the column; a sortable attribute, which indicates whether the user can click the column header to sort the data (true) or not (false); and dataIndex, which is the name of the field in a Record taken from the data store that we want displayed in that column.

Following the columns attribute are a few more configuration options (I probably should have grouped them all together, but Ext JS doesn't care, so it's purely a question of style). The first is viewConfig, which contains options that will be applied to the Grid's UI. The lone attribute within that object, forceFit, when true indicates that we want the Grid columns automatically expanded to fit the Grid in order to avoid horizontal scrolling. Next we see the stripeRows attribute set to true, and that does some color striping of the row to make it easier to read across its rows.

After that is the sm attribute, whose value should be (and is in this case) an instance of Ext.grid.RowSelectionModel. This defines how the user is allowed to select rows. Here, users can select only one at a time, so the singleSelect attribute of the config object passed to the constructor is set to true.

Finally, we have our friendly listeners attribute, and this time it's the rowclick event we're interested in. When a row is clicked, we need to show the details of the selected appointment via a call to organizerExt.showAppointmentDetails(). Passed to the callback for the event is inGrid, a reference to the Grid object; inRowIndex, literally the index number of the row that was clicked; and inEventObject, an object describing the event. The one we're interested in here is inGrid, because we can call the getSelectionModel() method to return the SelectionModel object we attached to the Grid, which contains a method for getting the Record associated with the clicked row via a call to getSelected(). That's all that is involved, aside from showing the details, which is coming up just a little later. For now, let's see how the areas where the details are shown are created, since that's obviously necessary before we can show details!

Item Details Panes

The details sections create another CardLayout, just like the Panel where the icon and list views are housed, one card for each category for which we might want to show details. Each of the four detail sections is defined by an object in the items array:

```
{
  xtype : "panel", region : "center", id : "detailsCard",
  layout : "card", activeItem : 0, autoScroll : true,
  title : "Appointment Details",
  items : [
```

```
      {
        autoScroll : true, xtype : "panel",
        html : Ext.getDom("divAppointmentDetails").innerHTML
      },
      {
        autoScroll : true, xtype : "panel",
        html : Ext.getDom("divNoteDetails").innerHTML
      },
      {
        autoScroll : true, xtype : "panel",
        html : Ext.getDom("divTaskDetails").innerHTML
      },
      {
        autoScroll : true, xtype : "panel",
        html : Ext.getDom("divContactDetails").innerHTML
      }
    ]
  }
]
},
```

Each of the detail sections is defined in index.htm as we saw earlier, and here we're setting the HTML that is to be displayed in a Panel. You see, it's not necessary to create Ext JS widgets and add them to a Panel; you can insert plain old HTML if you want via the html attribute. Since we already have the HTML we want to insert sitting on index.htm, all we need to do is get a reference to the appropriate <div> with a call to Ext.getDom() and get the innerHTML property. That becomes the value of the html attribute for the Panel, and voilà, we have content in the Panel!

Defining the Toolbar

Only one thing remains for us to define in our Viewport: the toolbar area up at the top. This is the closing section of that giant statement defining the Viewport that we started with, so let's dive right into it:

```
{
  id : "toolbarArea", autoHeight : true, border : false,
  region : "north",
  items : [{
    xtype : "toolbar", items : [
      {
        text : "New Note",
        handler : function() {
          Ext.getCmp("createNoteFormPane").getForm().reset();
          Ext.getCmp("dialogCreateNote").show(Ext.getDom("divSource"));
        }, icon : "img/toolbarNote.gif", cls : "x-btn-text-icon"
      },
```

```
{ xtype : "tbspacer" }, { xtype : "tbspacer" },
```

Thus begins the Toolbar definition. It lives in the north region of the main BorderLayout and has no border (it looks a little weird with the border present). The first item on the toolbar is the New Note button. When you click that button, the handler function is executed. Its job is to clear the form where the user enters note information. This requires a call to Ext.getCmp("createNoteFormPane") to get a reference to the FormPanel, followed by a call to getForm() to get a reference to the underlying form. Finally, reset() is called to do the actual dirty work of resetting the form. Once that's done, we can go ahead and show the Create Note Window.

```
{
  text : "About OrganizerExt",
  handler : function() {
    var dialogAbout = new Ext.Window({
      applyTo : "dialogAbout", closable : true, modal : true,
      width : 400, height : 320, minimizable : false,
      resizable : false, draggable : false, shadowOffset : 8,
      closeAction : "hide", buttons : [{
        text : "Ok",
        handler : function() {
          dialogAbout.hide();
        }
      }]
    });
    dialogAbout.show(Ext.getDom("divSource"));
  }, icon : "img/toolbarAbout.gif", cls : "x-btn-text-icon"
},
{ xtype : "tbspacer" },
{ xtype : "tbseparator" },
{ xtype : "tbspacer" },
```

We're putting the toolbar at the top of our BorderLayout, so we set the region attribute to north. The autoHeight attribute allows this Panel to set its height according to its contents, which is necessary for the toolbar to appear at all. We also indicate we don't want a border via border:false, since that would just look a bit wrong.

Next, the items array contains an object with an xtype of toolbar, and that's all it takes essentially to create a toolbar. The items array in that object then contains an object for each button to add, as well as spacers. For example, we see here how the New Note button is created. The text attribute is what you see on the screen. The handler attribute is the code to execute what the button is clicked. Here that's simply to get a reference to the form contained within the createNoteFormPane that we created earlier, resetting it via a call to its reset() method, and then showing the dialogCreateNote. Remember that this dialog Window was created but initially not shown, so we can use the Ext.getCmp(), which returns a reference to an existing Ext JS widget (Component, technically). We then just call show() on it, giving it a reference to our animation source <div>.

The `icon` attribute points to the image file to use as the icon for our button. This is optional, but we do want one because it spices up the toolbar a bit. Finally, the `cls` attribute is the style class to apply to the button, which here is supplied by Ext JS itself.

You'll also notice a number of objects with an `xtype` of `tbspacer`. These are just blank spaces you can use to spread things out a bit. Likewise, the `tbseparator` `xtype` puts a vertical line on the toolbar to break things up into logical groups, as you can see in Figure 3-19.

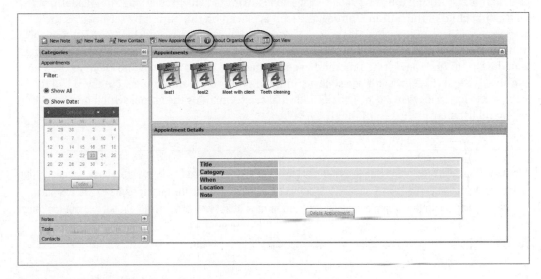

Figure 3-19. *An example of the tbseparator xtype*

The rest of the buttons are pretty similar to what we just saw. The button for switching between icon view and list view has a little more meat to it, so let's take a look at it:

```
{
    text : "Icon View", id : "tbViewMode",
    handler : function() {
      this.setText(this.getText().toggle("Icon View", "List View"));
      var iconImage = "url(img/toolbarIconView.gif)";
      if (this.getText() == "List View") {
        iconImage = "url(img/toolbarListView.gif)";
      }
      this.getEl().child("button:first").dom.style.backgroundImage =
        iconImage;
      organizerExt.changeViewMode(this.getText());
    }, icon : "img/toolbarIconView.gif", cls : "x-btn-text-icon"
  }
]
}]
}
```

While the button itself is defined in the same way, the click event handler has a bit more going on. First, we toggle the text shown on the button between icon view and list view. To do this we use the handy `toggle()` method that Ext JS added to the `String` class. This avoids an `if` statement or a trinary logic statement. Next we need to toggle the icon on the button as well. To do this we call `this.getText()`, which gives us the text currently on the button (which remember, we just changed!). Using this, we set the appropriate value for the image file to use. We do this by altering the `background-image` style attribute (`backgroundImage` in JavaScript) of the first child of the button. You see, the icon is placed on the button by setting it as the `background-image` of the `<div>` the button is contained within. By using `this.getEl()`, which returns the underlying `Ext.Element` object that represents this widget in the DOM, we can then call the `child("button:first")` method to get a reference to the appropriate DOM node. Then we simply set its `backgroundImage` style attribute to point to the new image. Finally, a call to `organizerExt.changeViewMode()`, a method we'll see soon, does the actual switch between icon view and list view in the rest of the UI.

Adding Buttons to the Detail Panes

Now that the UI has been largely constructed, there are a few loose ends to tie up to complete the UI. Recall that when we created the sections where item details are displayed, we left placeholders for the buttons, but we didn't create the buttons. Well, now it's time to turn around and do just that! All the detail panes have a Delete button, so let's look at just one as a representative example:

```
new Ext.Button({
  text : "Delete Appointment", renderTo: "tdAppointmentDetailsDeleteButton",
  handler : function() {
    var viewMode = "IconView";
    if (Ext.getCmp("tbViewMode").getText() == "List View") {
      viewMode = "ListView";
    }
    organizerExt.appointmentsStore.remove(
      Ext.getCmp("dvAppointments" + viewMode).getSelectedRecords()[0]
    );
  }, disabled : true, id : "btnAppointmentDeleteButton"
});
```

We instantiate the `Ext.Button()` class, passing it a configuration object during construction. This object has a couple of attributes. First, `text` is literally the text to display on the button. Second, `renderTo` gives the ID of a DOM node to put the button into; if you look back, you'll see that `tdAppointmentDetailsDeleteButton` is the ID of the placeholder `<td>` we created (remember that the Window was created from existing markup, which contained a table structure). The handler attribute gives a reference to a function, inline in this case, to execute when the button is clicked. The first thing we need to do in this handler is to determine whether the user currently sees the icon view or the list view. We do this by interrogating the text of the view switch toolbar button, just as we saw previously. This is necessary because we can then construct the proper ID of the DataView to reference, which we must do in order to ask it for a reference to the selected Record from the data store. With that Record in hand, it can be passed to the remove() method of the appointmentsStore for removal.

We also define the disabled attribute with a value of true so that the button begins disabled and remains so until we enable it (when an item is selected).

The tasks detail section also includes a button to mark a task as complete, and that's a bit different from the Delete buttons:

```
new Ext.Button({
  text : "Complete Task", renderTo: "tdTaskDetailsCompleteButton",
  handler : function() {
    var viewMode = "IconView";
    if (Ext.getCmp("tbViewMode").getText() == "List View") {
      viewMode = "ListView";
    }
    var record = Ext.getCmp("dvTasks" + viewMode).getSelectedRecords()[0];
    record.set("status", DAO.TASK_STATUS_COMPLETE);
  }, disabled : true, id : "btnTaskCompleteButton"
});
```

It is only different in the code of the handler, and then it's only different in that at the end we call the set() method of the Record to set the status field. This causes the update event to fire on the data store, and the data is saved via a call to the DAO.

■Note At the end of the buildUI() method you'll also notice this statement: vp.doLayout();. This instructs the viewport essentially to draw itself. Typically you don't need to do this; it happens automatically. However, I noticed an issue in the latest version of Firefox (3.0.3 at the time of this writing) where the titles of the icon view and the Accordion pane wouldn't show up unless I issued this statement. It does no harm to do so generally, although it's probably inefficient and certainly redundant even if Ext JS is smart enough to not do any extra work it doesn't have to do. Just remember, you shouldn't usually have to do this, but I wanted to point out the reason I did.

Making the Accordion Work: Changing Categories

We're very nearly at the end of the code of this application. We've seen how the data stores and Record descriptors are created, and we've seen how the dialog Windows for creating new items are created. In addition, we've seen how the UI is built and how most of it works. Along the way, we saw calls to a few methods of the OrganizerExt class, and those methods are what remain to look at.

First, recall that when the user clicks a pane in the Accordion, the changeCategory() method is called:

```
this.changeCategory = function(inCategory) {

  organizerExt.currentCategory = inCategory;

  var newActiveItem = null;
  var listingTitle = null;
  var detailsTitle = null;
  switch (inCategory) {
    case "appointments":
      newActiveItem = 0;
      listingTitle = "Appointments";
      detailsTitle = "Appointment Details";
    break;
    case "notes":
      newActiveItem = 1;
      listingTitle = "Notes";
      detailsTitle = "Note Details";
    break;
    case "tasks":
      newActiveItem = 2;
      listingTitle = "Tasks";
      detailsTitle = "Task Details";
    break;
    case "contacts":
      newActiveItem = 3;
      listingTitle = "Contacts";
      detailsTitle = "Contact Details";
    break;
  }

  var listingCard = Ext.getCmp("listingCard");
  listingCard.setTitle(listingTitle);
  listingCard.getLayout().setActiveItem(newActiveItem);
  var detailsCard = Ext.getCmp("detailsCard");
  detailsCard.setTitle(detailsTitle);
  detailsCard.getLayout().setActiveItem(newActiveItem);
  organizerExt.changeViewMode(Ext.getCmp("tbViewMode").getText());

}
```

Switching between categories entails switching the icon or list view, whichever mode the application is currently in, to the appropriate data store. That's what this method does, by and large. The inCategory argument is a string naming the category to switch to. The first thing we do is store the inCategory value in the currentCategory field of organizerExt, because we're going to need that value elsewhere.

So after that, we have a switch statement based on that argument. For each of the four possible values, we set three variables. The first, newActiveItem, will be the value of the activeItem attribute of the listingCard, the CardLayout containing the icon and list views. (If you're thinking ahead, you'll recall that there are eight cards in that CardLayout: four icon views followed by four list views… yet we only have four values here! Don't worry grasshopper, all will be revealed!)

The second variable is listingTitle, which is the text that will be displayed in the title bar above the listing section. Likewise, detailsTitle is the text to display in the title bar above the details section.

Once those variables are set, we move on to the common block of code following the switch block. First, we use the Ext.getCmp() method to get a reference to the listingCard, which is the CardLayout containing all four icon views and all four grid views. With that reference, we call setTitle() to set the title bar text. Next, we call the getLayout() method, which gives us a reference to the underlying ContainerLayout object for that Panel. This object exposes a setActiveItem() method, to which we pass the newActiveItem variable. This flips us over to the appropriate icon view for the category selected.

Next, we get a reference to the detailsCard, and likewise set its title and active item.

Now, at this point you've got to be saying to yourself, "Wait, what if we're currently in list view mode? Haven't we just flipped to an icon view?" Indeed we have, but that's where the call to organizerExt.changeViewMode() comes into play, which is our next destination.

Switching Between Icon View and List View

When users switch categories, or when they switch view modes, the changeViewMode() method gets called. In Figure 3-20 you can see an example of a switch to list view.

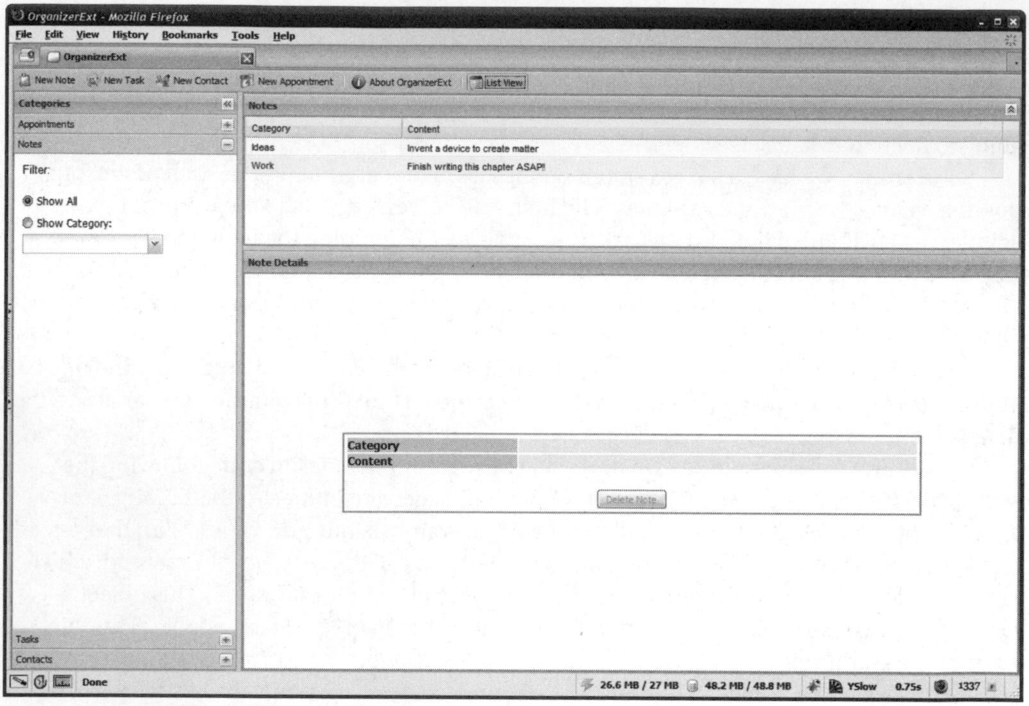

Figure 3-20. *The list view mode*

The code for this method is not terribly long, nor is it complex, as you can see for yourself:

```
this.changeViewMode = function(inMode) {

  var baseCardIndex = null;
  switch (organizerExt.currentCategory) {
    case "appointments":
      baseCardIndex = 0;
    break;
    case "notes":
      baseCardIndex = 1;
    break;
    case "tasks":
      baseCardIndex = 2;
    break;
    case "contacts":
      baseCardIndex = 3;
    break;
  }
```

```
var newActiveItem = null;
if (inMode == "List View") {
  newActiveItem = baseCardIndex + 4;
} else {
  newActiveItem = baseCardIndex;
}


var listingCard = Ext.getCmp("listingCard");
listingCard.getLayout().setActiveItem(newActiveItem);


}
```

Here, we're being passed a string that tells us what mode we're in. It happens to be
one of the two text strings displayed on the mode switch button, so either List View or
Icon View. The code begins by doing a switch based on the currentCategory, set back in the
changeCategory() method. We do this to determine the index of the card in the CardLayout
that is currently selected and store that in baseCardIndex. Since all four of the icon views were
added first, we know that at this point the index value is either 0, 1, 2, or 3 (remember that in
changeCategory() we always switched to an icon view, never a list view).

Next, we examine what view mode we're in. If we're currently in list view, we add four to
the value of baseCardIndex. Think about that for a moment. The four icon views have an index
value of 0, 1, 2, or 3. For example, the appointments icon view is index 0. The list views were
added to the CardLayout right after the icon views, so that means they begin at index 4. So the
appointments list view is at index 4. So by adding four to the baseCardIndex value, we now
have the correct index for the list view associated with the current category. Of course, if we're
in icon view mode, then baseCardIndex *is* the proper value already. In either case, the variable
newActiveItem is set to the appropriate value.

Then, we set the active item in the CardLayout to the value of newActiveItem. If we are in
icon view mode, then this effectively does nothing. But if we are in list view mode, we switch to
the list view. The user only sees a single switch because it happens so fast.

Showing Details of a Selected Item

The very last thing we need to look at is how the details of a selected item are displayed. I'm
definitely sounding like a broken record now, and I know it, but because all four of these methods (one each for notes, appointments, contacts, and tasks) are very similar, we only need to
examine one. I'll pick on appointments one last time for this:

```
this.showAppointmentDetails = function(inRecord) {

  if (inRecord) {
    Ext.getCmp("btnAppointmentDeleteButton").enable();
  } else {
    Ext.getCmp("btnAppointmentDeleteButton").disable();
    inRecord = new organizerExt.AppointmentRecord({
      category : "", title : "", whendt : "", location : "", note : ""
    });
  }
```

```
    Ext.getDom("appointment_category").innerHTML =
      inRecord.get("category");
    Ext.getDom("appointment_location").innerHTML =
      inRecord.get("location");
    Ext.getDom("appointment_note").innerHTML =
      inRecord.get("note");
    Ext.getDom("appointment_title").innerHTML =
      inRecord.get("title");
    var wdt = inRecord.get("whendt");
    Ext.getDom("appointment_whendt").innerHTML =
      Ext.isDate(wdt) ? inRecord.get("whendt").format("m/d/Y") : "";
}
```

First, the code checks to see if the inRecord argument was null or not. This is to cover the case where the user clicks a blank section of the icon or list view, deselecting all items. In that case, the else branch would kick in. This disables the Delete button and creates a new Record of the appropriate type with all blank fields.

Then, it's a simple matter of setting the innerHTML attribute of each of the detail fields, which we get via calls to Ext.getDom() to the applicable fields from the Record object. If inRecord is null, it effectively clears all the fields since we set all the fields to blank.

The whendt field is slightly different. We want to display the value as mm/dd/yyyy, but that can only be done (with the Date.format() method at least) if it's a Date. If no record is available, however, it's a string. So, we get its value, and then use the Ext.isDate() method to determine if it's a Date. If it is, we can go ahead and format it (using the m/d/y specification, which outputs a value such as 10/21/2008); otherwise we just output an empty string.

And with that, our exploration of this code is complete!

Suggested Exercises

I hope you found this application a fun one to dissect! I also hope you found it at least a little useful. It's obvious that Microsoft shouldn't be worried about competition with Outlook here! Clearly features are missing that would be nice to have, and with that in mind here's a list of suggested exercises that I believe will not only make the application more useful but more importantly will get you some good experience with Ext JS:

- First and foremost, implement the ability to modify existing items. I purposely left this capability out because I think if you did no other exercises, this would be a worthwhile one to do. Should you reuse the create dialogs to do maintenance as well? Should the detail sections be forms that are editable? Or is there another option? It's up to you, but any choice will lead to a good learning experience.

- Add a time component to appointments, and then have the application pop up an alert an hour before a given appointment.

- Add a web site field for contacts and allow the user to click on it and open the site in a Window (an Ext JS Window, that is, not a new browser window). Related to this, make the e-mail field clickable so that a new message can be composed (use a simple mailto: link).

- Do something a little different for the detail views. Perhaps allow multiple items to be opened at once by opening each in an Ext JS `Window` that is bound to the detail area.

- Allow the user to maintain his or her own list of categories for an item. Allow users to add and remove what they wish and update the combo boxes accordingly.

- Add some other view filtering capabilities, such as contacts by company or appointments for a specified range of dates.

Summary

In this chapter we saw how to construct a relatively complex Ext JS–based user interface. We saw a number of widgets in action, including the `Viewport`, `BorderLayout`, `CardLayout`, `Accordion`, `Grid`, `DataView`, `DatePicker`, `FormPanel`, and more. You saw how we can easily have validations on forms with little work on our part. You also learned how to create stores of data and have Ext JS automatically bind those to widgets. We explored a few utility-type functions from Ext JS in action, too. You also saw how Gears can be used as the underlying data store and can be integrated seamlessly into an Ext JS application.

In the next chapter we'll create another personal information management (PIM)-type application, a project timekeeping application. We'll see a couple of new widgets in action, more work with Gears and data stores, and a few more utility functions too.

CHAPTER 4

■ ■ ■

Making Project Management Cool: TimekeeperExt

I don't like to mince words, so here goes: I hate project management! To me, it's a rather dull endeavor. It's a lot of time spent bugging people on the phone, asking them what they've accomplished since the last time I bugged them. It's a lot of time writing status reports for stakeholders and explaining why this is late or why that is taking longer than anticipated. Given that, project management is an absolutely necessary evil, and I respect those who do the job—it isn't easy and requires great skill to do well. Still, project management, for me at least, isn't the most exciting job imaginable, but I see no reason not to make the chore as fun and sexy as possible! So, the goal of this chapter is to create a basic project management and time-tracking application using Ext JS (so we know it'll be fairly sexy automatically). As we develop this application, you'll see another approach to structuring an Ext JS application, and you'll meet a few more UI widgets in real usage. You'll see a few Ext JS utility functions in play, gain more experience with the data subsystem, and play with the database component of Gears a little more. In the end you'll wind up with a useful tool, albeit not quite on par with Microsoft Project, for tracking the status of a project.

What's This Application Do Anyway?

As I mentioned in the opening paragraph, Microsoft Project is one of the top tools in use today for project management. This feature-rich program tracks projects, tasks that are part of that project, resources assigned to the project, and much more. It provides numerous views of the project, including Gantt charts.[1] It allows you to perform resource leveling[2] and

---

1   A Gantt chart is a specialized type of bar chart that graphically describes a project's schedule. It provides an at-a-glance summary of a project's status in a visual way (for those that can make sense of them!).

2   Resource leveling is a project management task focused on resolving conflicts that arise from tasks running in parallel that may contend for resources, or resources that are overallocated, or other sorts of resource allocation imbalances that can occur during project planning.

create critical path schedules[3] as well as critical chain[4] and event chain methodology[5] (by way of add-ons).

If all of this is foreign to you, count your blessings! Project management is actually an expansive area and a study that requires lots of, well, *study*, to master. I am in no way, shape, or form an accomplished project manager (PM for short), although I know the basics.

Fortunately, for the purposes of this book, the basics are all we need to worry about, and in fact we'll only be dealing with the most basic of basics. Managing a project boils down to three things: the project itself (obviously), tasks that make up the project, and resources (people, usually) assigned to the tasks. With these basics in mind, we can begin to outline what this application needs to do:

- The user should be able to create any number of projects. For each we should be able to specify a name, description, a starting date, an ending date, a number of hours allocated to the project, and the PM.

- We should be able to create tasks and allocate them to projects. To make things simple to implement, any given task can only be associated with a single project. (In real life, you might have tasks that are associated with multiple projects, but as far as using this application goes, it's not such a burden to have to create two copies of the same underlying task to manage, even if that strategy isn't quite ideal.) For each task we should be able to specify a name, description, a starting date, ending date, and number of hours allocated to the task.

- We should be able to create resources and assign them to tasks. Let's make another simplifying assumption here: a task can only be worked on by a single resource. This again isn't ideal or necessarily reflective of the real world, although I'd point out that some PMs believe this *should* in fact be the way it's done! For a resource we can specify a name and description and designate the resource as a PM (so they can be the PM of projects being tracked).

- We should be able to delete projects, resources, and tasks, subject to certain rules (such as not being able to delete a project that has tasks allocated to it).

- We should be able to modify projects, tasks, and resources as well. Pretty much everything can be modified except for the name, which we'll be using as a key for all three items.

- We should be able to book time against a task for a given resource. This will allow us to determine if a task is over its allocated hours, or close to it (within 10 percent of the allocated hours).

- We should be able to specify a completion percentage for tasks. We'll use this to show a graphical representation of how far along a task is.

---

3 The critical path is a mathematical algorithm used to schedule a set of tasks within a project. More often than not, though, you hear people talk about the critical path of a project in the context of the linear set of tasks that must be completed for a project to reach a successful conclusion.

4 The critical chain approach puts more of an emphasis on resources than on tasks and rigid schedules, as is the case with the critical path approach.

5 The event chain methodology focuses more on the events that occur during the lifetime of a project more so than on tasks and resources. This approach allows for a less rigid schedule that provides more flexibility to deal with uncertainty and the inevitable changes that occur as a project progresses.

- For projects, tasks, and resources, there will be a summary view that gives us the most pertinent information about each entity at a glance. We'll show some graphics to specify when a task is overdue, over hours, and so forth. We'll do the same for a project.

- We'll use a tree to show our projects, tasks, and resources all nicely nested so we can quickly see what tasks belong to what project and who is working on a given task. We'll have three different views, one each for projects, tasks, and resources.

As you can see, the basics are covered fairly well, and you can actually track work with this application, although it admittedly doesn't hold a candle to Microsoft Project. Before we begin tearing into the code, let's take a quick look at the application, starting with Figure 4-1, which shows the welcome screen.

Figure 4-1. *The TimekeeperExt welcome screen*

On the top we have a menu, and each of the main objects the application deals with: projects, resources, and tasks, each its own menu item. On the left is a tree view, and above it some radio buttons that allow us to switch the view. Here we're in the Project view, so the tree shows all the projects that have been created, with the tasks associated with each nested underneath them, and the resources assigned to each task below that. In the main portion of the page is the welcome message and application title, and that's also where we'll see those summary views I mentioned.

Speaking of those summary views, in Figure 4-2 you can see the Resource Summary of a resource I've selected out of the Resource view tree.

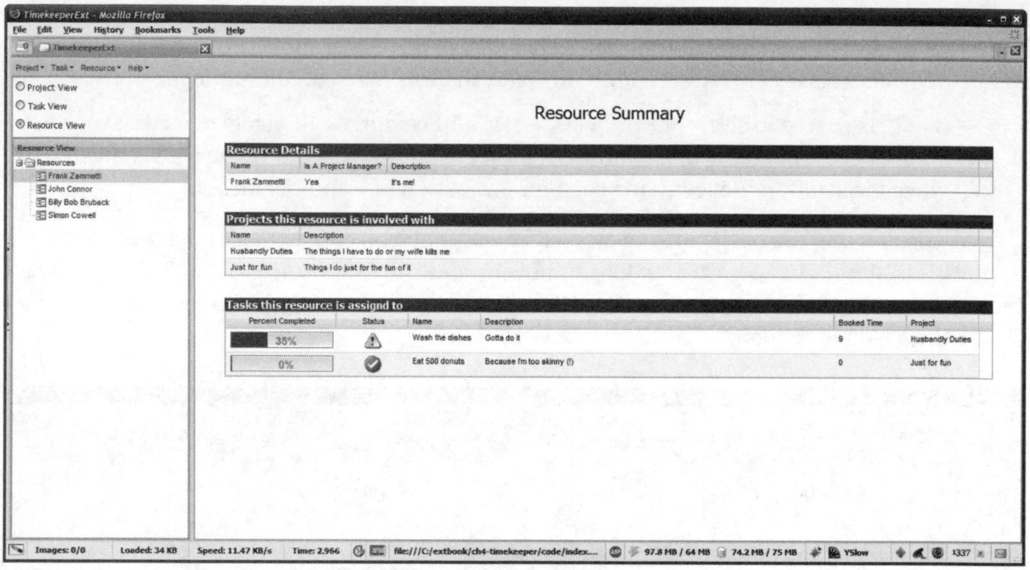

Figure 4-2. *The TimekeeperExt Resource Summary*

As you can see, three Grids are present in this summary view. The first contains some basic details about the resource. Below that is another Grid that lists the projects this resource is involved in (meaning they are assigned to work on a task allocated to the project). Finally, the third Grid shows all the tasks that the resource is currently working on. For each we see a bar graph that displays the task's percentage of completion, as well as an icon that tells us at a glance if the task is past due, under or over its allocated hours, or in danger of going over its allocated hours.

We'll see more of the application as we progress through the code, and you can play with it any time you like (now would be a good time!).

Overall Structure and Files

Let's begin by looking at the overall directory structure and the files involved in this application. By and large it's similar to the project in the previous chapter, and it's very similar to all the applications to come. Figure 4-3 shows the directory structure.

Figure 4-3. *The application's directory structure and constituent files*

In the root directory we have `index.htm`, the starting point for the application. The `css` directory contains the style sheet, `styles.css`, specific to this application. The `ext` directory is where Ext JS itself is—I haven't expanded it because it's rather large and at this point you should be fairly familiar with its contents. The `img` directory contains a bunch of images used in the application. The files `project.gif`, `resource.gif`, and `task.gif` are the icons seen in the tree views. The file `welcome.gif` is the image seen on the welcome screen. The remaining images, the ones beginning with `status`, are the status icons seen on the various summary views. Three types are present: the green check mark (representing under the allocated hours), the yellow warning sign (10 percent of allocated hours remaining), and the red stop sign (over the allocated hours). Each icon also has a version that has "PastDue" added to the end. These are the same icons but are animated GIFs so that the icon flashes to indicate the item is past due.

In the `js` directory are all our JavaScript files. In this application I've taken a fundamentally different approach than in the previous project. Recall in that project that there was a single monolithic JavaScript file (plus the `DAO` class in a separate file, but the majority of the code was in a single file). You'll also recall there that to build the UI I used a single huge JavaScript statement. This is far from the only way you can structure your code with Ext JS, and in this project we see another. Here, each of the unique UI objects is in its own file. The menu code is in `menu.js`, the code for the New Project dialog is in `NewProjectDialog.js`, the code for the projects tree is in `ProjectsTree.js`, and so on. We also find a `TimekeeperExt.js` file that contains some more general code that the application uses. As was the case with the previous project, there is also a `DAO.js` file where the database access code lives. The familiar `gears_init.js` file is also present.

■**Note** Which architecture you prefer is largely a matter of personal preference. Some argue that breaking up the code like this makes it easier to comprehend, while others argue that the mental gymnastics of jumping between multiple files negates that benefit. I personally have mixed feelings, so I generally try for a mixed solution: I tend to break things up to a certain extent, but I don't go overboard making things too granular. What you decide to do is neither right nor wrong—it's simply a design decision you have to make. I felt it was important to demonstrate both approaches in this book.

The Markup

The markup for this application, housed in `index.htm`, is actually fewer than 100 lines of code once you remove comments! Not much at all. Let's start by looking at the `<head>` of the document:

```
<head>
  <title>TimekeeperExt</title>
  <link rel="stylesheet" type="text/css" href="ext/resources/css/ext-all.css">
  <script type="text/javascript" src="ext/adapter/ext/ext-base.js"></script>
  <script type="text/javascript" src="ext/ext-all.js"></script>
  <script src="js/gears_init.js"></script>
  <link rel="stylesheet" type="text/css" href="css/styles.css">
  <script type="text/javascript" src="js/DAO.js"></script>
  <script type="text/javascript" src="js/StoresAndRecords.js"></script>
  <script type="text/javascript" src="js/TimekeeperExt.js"></script>
  <script type="text/javascript" src="js/Menu.js"></script>
  <script type="text/javascript" src="js/ProjectsTree.js"></script>
  <script type="text/javascript" src="js/ResourcesTree.js"></script>
  <script type="text/javascript" src="js/TasksTree.js"></script>
  <script type="text/javascript" src="js/NewProjectDialog.js"></script>
  <script type="text/javascript" src="js/NewTaskDialog.js"></script>
  <script type="text/javascript" src="js/NewResourceDialog.js"></script>
  <script type="text/javascript" src="js/DeleteProjectDialog.js"></script>
  <script type="text/javascript" src="js/DeleteTaskDialog.js"></script>
  <script type="text/javascript" src="js/DeleteResourceDialog.js"></script>
  <script type="text/javascript" src="js/ModifyProjectDialog.js"></script>
  <script type="text/javascript" src="js/ModifyTaskDialog.js"></script>
  <script type="text/javascript" src="js/ModifyResourceDialog.js"></script>
```

```
<script type="text/javascript" src="js/ResourceSummary.js"></script>
<script type="text/javascript" src="js/ProjectSummary.js"></script>
<script type="text/javascript" src="js/TaskSummary.js"></script>
<script>Ext.onReady(init);</script>
</head>
```

Most of this is old hat[6] by now. We begin by importing the usual Ext JS style sheet and base JavaScript files.

After the Ext JS–specific imports is a long line of JavaScript file imports. These are the JavaScript files containing the code for the application itself. We'll be looking at each of these individually. In addition there is the import of the main application style sheet, styles.css, as well as gears_init.js.

After that is the usual Ext.onReady() call, this time referencing a function named init. As it turns out, this function is nearly identical to what we saw in the OrganizerExt project, but don't worry—we'll be looking at it here shortly anyway.

With the <head> section concluded, we can move on to the body. The first thing you'll find is a <div> with an ID of divSource. (I won't show the <div> here because that would be redundant given that we saw it in the previous project.) This is the source element on the page to be used for animation of windows.

After that is a <div> with the ID dialogPleaseWait, which is the Window seen when the application starts up and is initializing. This too is just copied over from the previous chapter's project, so I'll save a little space here by not printing it. In fact, I won't even discuss it on the grounds that it would be redundant. Please do refer back to the previous chapter if you need a refresher.

Just like that dialogPleaseWait <div>, next is a <div> with the ID dialogNoGears. This again is just copied from the previous project; it specifies the contents of the Window to be displayed if Gears is not available.

Finally, we have one last <div>, this one with the ID dialogAbout. This specifies the contents of the About Window, and is just some plain text in a <table> (and, not to sound like a broken record, but it's just like in the last project!).

■**Note** Because of its inherent length, I condensed the source code as much as possible. This mostly amounts to removing all comments and blank lines, but I also reformatted some lines where possible. The actual executable code is unchanged, however.

The Style Sheet

Just like index.htm, the styles.css file for this project is particularly simple. In fact, here's the entire style sheet, minus the comment block at the top:

---

6 In case you're unfamiliar with the saying, "old hat" means something that is repeated too often, or is something very familiar.

```
.cssAbout { font-size : 11pt; font-family : tahoma,arial,verdana,sans-serif; }
.cssSource { position : absolute; left: 1px; top : 1px; width : 1px; height : 1px; }
.cssSummaryTitle {
  width : 100%;
  text-align : center;
  font-size : 18pt;
  font-family : tahoma,arial,verdana,sans-serif;
}
.cssSummaryTableHeader {
  background-color : #3f4d61;
  color : #ffffff;
  font-size : 11pt;
  font-weight : bold;
  font-family : tahoma,arial,verdana,sans-serif;
  padding-left : 2px;
}
.cssProgressBarFill {
  background : #3f4d61;
  border-bottom : 1px solid #3f4d61;
  border-right : 1px solid #3f4d61;
  border-top : 1px solid #3f4d61;
  float : left;
  height : 18px;
}
```

The cssAbout selector styles the text on the About Window, the cssPleaseWait selector styles the text on the Window seen during application initialization, and the cssSource selector styles the <div> used for the animation source for Window expand and collapse. We've seen all of this before, so I won't repeat the detailed explanations.

The next selector we find is cssSummaryTitle. This is used to style the title seen on the three summary views. It just gives us a nice, large, centered title. It's applied to a <div>, so setting width to 100% and text-align to center ensures the title text will wind up centered on the page, or more precisely within the center region of the BorderLayout that's the basic layout applied to the page.

The cssSummaryTableHeader selector is next, and it is the style applied to the text seen above each of the Grids in each of the summary views. It gives us a black(ish) bar across the page with medium-sized (relative to other text on the page) white text on it. It also adds some padding to the left so that it isn't bumping right up against the edge of the bar.

Finally, the cssProgressBarFill selector is, really, the only interesting style. As you saw in the earlier screenshots, a simple progress bar reveals the completion percentage of tasks. This style is used to help provide that progress bar. I think it makes more sense to discuss it in the context of understanding how the progress bars are done, so for now just remember this selector is here and we'll refer back to it when the time comes.

Now that we've gotten the markup and style sheet out of the way, let's get to some code!

The Code

The code for this application is organized into a number of JavaScript files that logically break the application down into pieces that we can digest more easily. I'm going to tackle these in a logical order, but there will necessarily have to be some jumping around and some "we'll get to this later" type of deferments. Let's start with the DAO.js file.

■**Note** As we examine this code, you will frequently see me add something like "This code is just like the others, so we're not going to look at all three." In fact, I suspect I'll sound like a broken record by the time this chapter is done! The reason for this is that large chunks of the code in this application are extremely similar to other chunks. In fact, when I wrote the code, I generally wrote the parts pertaining to projects, and then copied that code and modified it slightly to work for tasks and resources because conceptually they were identical, just with some relatively minor differences. In most cases it is sufficient to just examine the code for projects and have you look at the code for tasks and resources on your own. This saves space in what is already a fairly long chapter, and I don't believe you will miss anything by doing this—which ultimately to me is what truly matters!

DAO.js

If you've read this book in order, and I kind of make the assumption you have, then the DAO class isn't anything new or exciting. Because of this, I'll go through this very quickly. If by chance you jumped ahead to this chapter and skipped the previous OrganizerExt chapter, I suggest putting a bookmark on this page and going back to read that chapter.

If you're ready to move ahead, though, let's start by taking a look at the UML class diagram for the DAO class housed in the DAO.js file, seen in Figure 4-4.

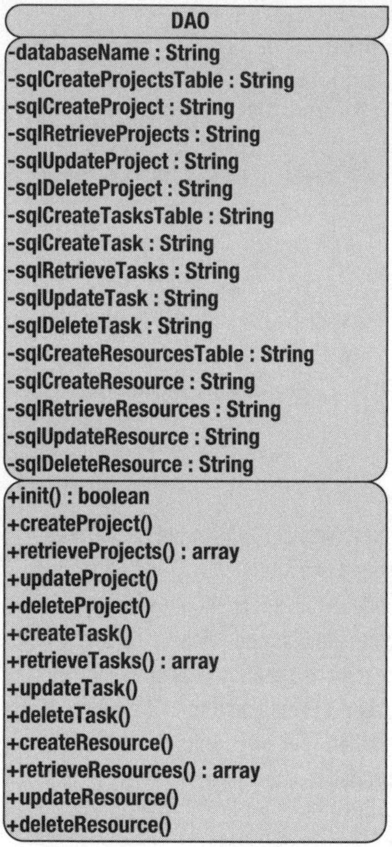

```
┌──────────────────────────────────────┐
│                  DAO                   │
├────────────────────────────────────────┤
│ -databaseName : String                 │
│ -sqlCreateProjectsTable : String       │
│ -sqlCreateProject : String             │
│ -sqlRetrieveProjects : String          │
│ -sqlUpdateProject : String             │
│ -sqlDeleteProject : String             │
│ -sqlCreateTasksTable : String          │
│ -sqlCreateTask : String                │
│ -sqlRetrieveTasks : String             │
│ -sqlUpdateTask : String                │
│ -sqlDeleteTask : String                │
│ -sqlCreateResourcesTable : String      │
│ -sqlCreateResource : String            │
│ -sqlRetrieveResources : String         │
│ -sqlUpdateResource : String            │
│ -sqlDeleteResource : String            │
├────────────────────────────────────────┤
│ +init() : boolean                      │
│ +createProject()                       │
│ +retrieveProjects() : array            │
│ +updateProject()                       │
│ +deleteProject()                       │
│ +createTask()                          │
│ +retrieveTasks() : array               │
│ +updateTask()                          │
│ +deleteTask()                          │
│ +createResource()                      │
│ +retrieveResources() : array           │
│ +updateResource()                      │
│ +deleteResource()                      │
└────────────────────────────────────────┘
```

Figure 4-4. *UML class diagram of the DAO class*

The class starts out with the databaseName field that names the Gears database we'll be using. The value in this case is TimekeeperExt. Following that we find 15 fields, the value of each of which is an SQL statement. There are three types of entities this application deals with: projects, tasks, and resources. The database schema is simple, as you can see in Figure 4-5, Figure 4-6, and Figure 4-7—one for each of the three tables corresponding to the three entities involved.

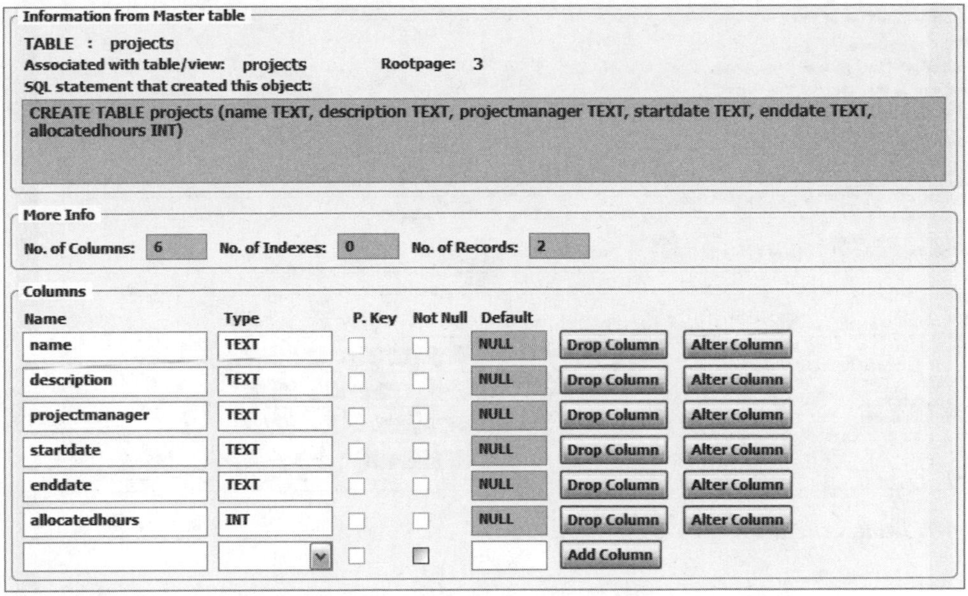

Information from Master table

TABLE : projects
Associated with table/view: projects   Rootpage: 3
SQL statement that created this object:

CREATE TABLE projects (name TEXT, description TEXT, projectmanager TEXT, startdate TEXT, enddate TEXT, allocatedhours INT)

More Info

No. of Columns: 6   No. of Indexes: 0   No. of Records: 2

Columns

Name	Type	P. Key	Not Null	Default		
name	TEXT	☐	☐	NULL	Drop Column	Alter Column
description	TEXT	☐	☐	NULL	Drop Column	Alter Column
projectmanager	TEXT	☐	☐	NULL	Drop Column	Alter Column
startdate	TEXT	☐	☐	NULL	Drop Column	Alter Column
enddate	TEXT	☐	☐	NULL	Drop Column	Alter Column
allocatedhours	INT	☐	☐	NULL	Drop Column	Alter Column
	∨	☐	☐		Add Column	

Figure 4-5. *Table structure of the projects table*

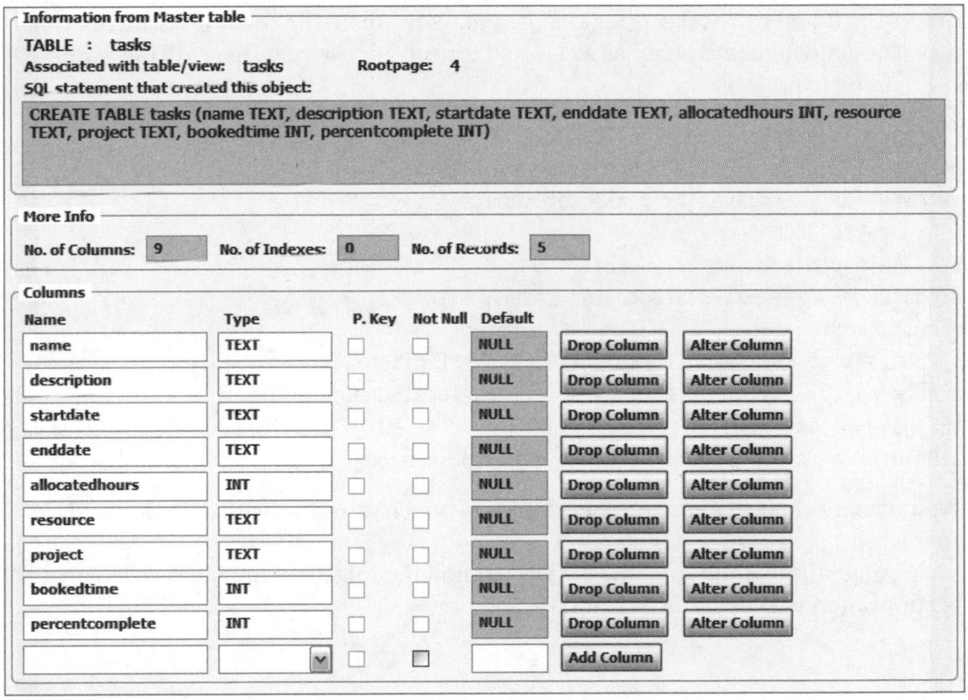

Information from Master table

TABLE : tasks
Associated with table/view: tasks   Rootpage: 4
SQL statement that created this object:

CREATE TABLE tasks (name TEXT, description TEXT, startdate TEXT, enddate TEXT, allocatedhours INT, resource TEXT, project TEXT, bookedtime INT, percentcomplete INT)

More Info

No. of Columns: 9   No. of Indexes: 0   No. of Records: 5

Columns

Name	Type	P. Key	Not Null	Default		
name	TEXT	☐	☐	NULL	Drop Column	Alter Column
description	TEXT	☐	☐	NULL	Drop Column	Alter Column
startdate	TEXT	☐	☐	NULL	Drop Column	Alter Column
enddate	TEXT	☐	☐	NULL	Drop Column	Alter Column
allocatedhours	INT	☐	☐	NULL	Drop Column	Alter Column
resource	TEXT	☐	☐	NULL	Drop Column	Alter Column
project	TEXT	☐	☐	NULL	Drop Column	Alter Column
bookedtime	INT	☐	☐	NULL	Drop Column	Alter Column
percentcomplete	INT	☐	☐	NULL	Drop Column	Alter Column
	∨	☐	☐		Add Column	

Figure 4-6. *Table structure of the tasks table*

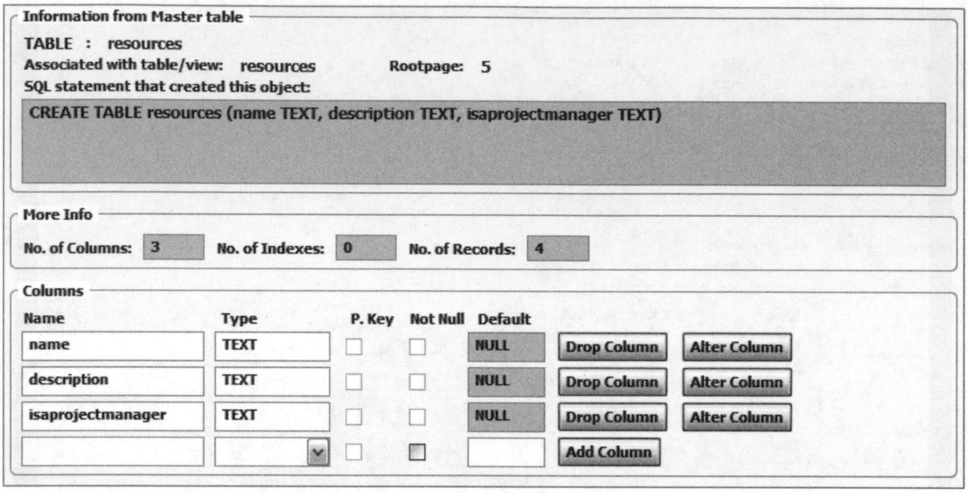

Figure 4-7. *Table structure of the resources table*

For each of the entities there are five SQL statements: one to create the associated table and one for each of the CRUD (Create, Retrieve, Update, and Delete) operations. So for example, there are sqlCreateProjectsTable, sqlCreateProject, sqlRetrieveProjects, sqlUpdateProject, and sqlDeleteProject fields, and there are five fields for tasks and five for resources. The statements are about as you would expect. For example, here are the statements pertaining to projects:

```
var sqlCreateProjectsTable = "CREATE TABLE IF NOT EXISTS projects (" +
  "name TEXT, description TEXT, projectmanager TEXT, " +
  "startdate TEXT, enddate TEXT, allocatedhours INT)"
var sqlCreateProject =
  "INSERT INTO projects (name, description, projectmanager, " +
  "startdate, enddate, allocatedhours) VALUES (?, ?, ?, ?, ?, ?)";
var sqlRetrieveProjects = "SELECT * FROM projects";
var sqlUpdateProject = "UPDATE projects SET description=?, " +
  "projectmanager=?, startdate=?, enddate=?, allocatedhours=? " +
  "WHERE name=?";
var sqlDeleteProject = "DELETE FROM projects WHERE name=?";
```

The statements for tasks and resources look very much the same, with different fields in the statements.

Moving on to the methods of the class, we first find the init() method. It is called once one the application start ups, and its code is as follows:

```
this.init = function() {
  if (!window.google || !google.gears) { return false; }
  var db = google.gears.factory.create("beta.database");
  db.open(databaseName);
  db.execute(sqlCreateProjectsTable);
  db.execute(sqlCreateTasksTable);
  db.execute(sqlCreateResourcesTable);
  db.close();
  return true;
}
```

As you can see, it first checks to be sure Gears is available and returns false if not. Once that is done, the three table creation statements are executed. They will only do something if the tables do not already exist. The method returns true when done, unless an exception is thrown by one of the database function calls.

After init() we find that there are four methods for each of the three entities we're working with, and each of the methods corresponds to one of the CRUD operations. Since each of these methods is just like its counterpart for the other two entities, let's just look at the four methods pertaining to projects because the ones for tasks and resources are just like them. Let's begin with the createProject() method:

```
this.createProject = function(inRecord) {
  var db = google.gears.factory.create("beta.database");
  db.open(databaseName);
  db.execute(sqlCreateProject, [
    inRecord.get("name"), inRecord.get("description"),
    inRecord.get("projectmanager"), inRecord.get("startdate"),
    inRecord.get("enddate"), parseInt(inRecord.get("allocatedhours"))
  ]);
  db.close();
}
```

In the OrganizerExt project you may recall that the methods of the DAO class took plain-old JavaScript objects, but here they are accepting Record objects—the Record objects used in an Ext JS data store. I did it that way because it keeps the DAO abstracter from Ext JS. If we decided to rewrite that project with, say, Dojo, then we wouldn't have to touch the DAO classes because they don't care that they are being called from an application based on Dojo or Ext JS or anything else. Here, however, the DAO essentially "knows" it's being used from an Ext JS application. This approach is conceptually perhaps a little simpler because it's more direct: there's never any transferring of data between objects; it's just always Record objects from end to end. The approach you prefer is a decision you'll have to make for yourself. Usually I tend to want to keep things abstracted, and most people feel that's a better approach architecturally, but I wanted to show you the alternative here.

The actual code of the method is pretty simple. Open the database and execute the appropriate SQL statement, passing in the replacement values as an array via the second argument of the call to db.execute(). Because we received a Record object, we have to use the get() method to get the values of the fields in the Record.

The retrieveProjects() method is next, and it too is pretty simple:

```
this.retrieveProjects = function() {
  var db = google.gears.factory.create("beta.database");
  db.open(databaseName);
  var rs = db.execute(sqlRetrieveProjects);
  var results = [ ];
  while (rs.isValidRow()) {
    results.push(new ProjectRecord({
      name : rs.fieldByName("name"),
      description : rs.fieldByName("description"),
      projectmanager : rs.fieldByName("projectmanager"),
      startdate : rs.fieldByName("startdate"),
      enddate : rs.fieldByName("enddate"),
      allocatedhours : parseInt(rs.fieldByName("allocatedhours"))
    }, rs.fieldByName("name")));
    rs.next();
  }
  rs.close(); db.close(); return results;
}
```

Executing the sqlRetrieveProjects statement gets us all the projects currently in the database. So, we iterate over the ResultSet and for each we create a new ProjectRecord and push() it onto the results array. Finally, that array is returned to the caller. Nothing to it!

Updating a project is also a simple matter:

```
this.updateProject = function(inRecord) {
  var db = google.gears.factory.create("beta.database");
  db.open(databaseName);
  db.execute(sqlUpdateProject, [
    inRecord.get("description"), inRecord.get("projectmanager"),
    inRecord.get("startdate"), inRecord.get("enddate"),
    inRecord.get("allocatedhours"), inRecord.get("name")
  ]);
  db.close();
}
```

The inRecord argument is a ProjectRecord, so all that's needed is to execute the sqlUpdateProject statement and pass to db.execute() as the second argument array the fields that could have been changed.

Last is deleting a project, which is implemented in the deleteProject() method:

```
this.deleteProject = function(inProjectName) {
  var db = google.gears.factory.create("beta.database");
  db.open(databaseName);
  db.execute(sqlDeleteProject, [ inProjectName]);
  db.close();
}
```

The name of a project is effectively its key (ditto for tasks and resources), so that's the argument to this method. Executing sqlDeleteProject is all it takes, the name passed into the method is inserted into the SQL and we're off to the races.

I'll remind you again that the four methods for tasks and the four for resources are nearly identical to these, but please do check the downloaded code nonetheless. Aside from the fields dealt with, the methods are pretty much carbon copies.

StoresAndRecords.js

The next piece of the puzzle to look at is the record types and data stores used in this application, which you'll find in the StoresAndRecords.js file. There are quite a few stores but only three types of records: ProjectRecord, TaskRecord, and ResourceRecord. These types are shown in Figure 4-8.

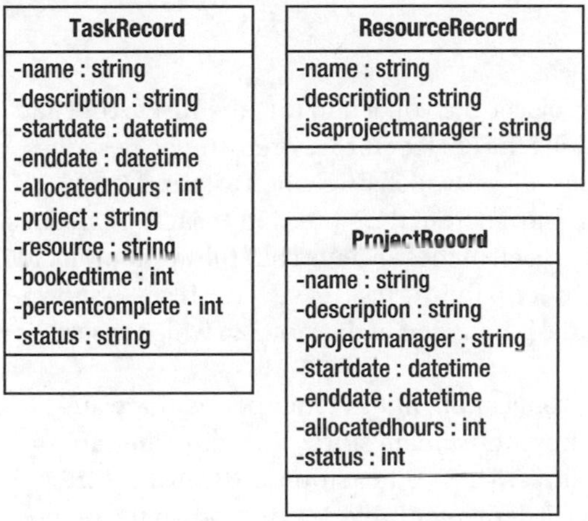

TaskRecord
-name : string
-description : string
-startdate : datetime
-enddate : datetime
-allocatedhours : int
-project : string
-resource : string
-bookedtime : int
-percentcomplete : int
-status : string

ResourceRecord
-name : string
-description : string
-isaprojectmanager : string

ProjectRecord
-name : string
-description : string
-projectmanager : string
-startdate : datetime
-enddate : datetime
-allocatedhours : int
-status : int

Figure 4-8. *The record descriptors in all their glory*

The status fields of the TaskRecord and ProjectRecord do not correspond to any field in the database tables; they are values that are calculated when a record is read and the value set on the Record. This is the Record field that is used to display the appropriate status icon in the summary view grids. All the other fields correspond to database table fields.

As I mentioned, there are quite a few stores in this application. Three are probably pretty obvious to you: a ProjectsStore, a TasksStore, and a ResourcesStore. These stores are populated from the corresponding database tables and literally just mimic the tables—all the records in the table have corresponding Records in the stores. These stores are populated when the application starts up, as we'll see, and any changes to them are replicated to the database.

This replication is an event-driven model, as you can see here:

```
var projectsStore = new Ext.data.Store({
  listeners : {
    "add" : { fn : function(inStore, inRecords, inIndex) {
        if (Ext.getCmp("dialogPleaseWait")) { return; }
        dao.createProject(inRecords[0]);
      } },
    "remove" : { fn : function(inStore, inRecord, inIndex) {
        dao.deleteProject(inRecord.get("name"));
      } },
    "update" : { fn : function(inStore, inRecord, inOperation) {
        dao.updateProject(inRecord);
      } }
  }
});
```

I'm again picking on the code pertaining to projects, but you'll find that the TasksStore and ResourcesStore is very much similar to this, so seeing the ProjectsStore pretty much describes the other two. As you can see, three events are hooked: add, which fires when a Record is added to the store; remove, which fires when a Record is removed from the store; and update, which fires when a Record obtained from the store is modified. Each of these events calls the appropriate DAO method. Note the check in the add event handler to see if the dialogPleaseWait Window is shown. If it is, then this event is firing as a result of the initial population of the store, in which case it would be a mistake to call the DAO method.

Those three stores are the main ones in this application, but as I mentioned there are quite a few others. All of them are derived from those three main stores, meaning they are populated from some subset of data from those three. These other stores are transitory in nature and are used as sources of data bound to UI elements. Table 4-1 runs down the other stores and describes their purpose. Note that all of them are created like so:

```
var projectManagersStore = new Ext.data.Store({});
```

They are empty and have no events hooked. Since anything done to them is meant to only be temporary, there are no events that need to be handled.

Table 4-1. *The Temporary Data Stores Used in This Application*

Store Name	Description
projectManagersStore	Project managers data store. This stores the ResourceRecords representing resources who are project managers. Although I group this store in with all the other temporary stores, it is in fact not quite temporary; it has data in it all along (assuming there are resources designated as project managers). But it is still derived from the ResourcesStore, so in that regard it's similar to the rest of the temporary stores.

Store Name	Description
availableTasksStore	Available tasks data store. This stores TaskRecords not associated with a project. The comment about not being a truly temporary store that applies to the projectManagersStore also applies to this one for the same reasons (although this one derives from the TasksStore instead of the ResourcesStore as projectManagersStore does).
tempAvailableTasksStore	This is a temporary store that will be a copy of the available TasksStore when the Modify Project dialog is shown.
tempAllocatedTasksStore	This is a temporary store used in the Modify Project dialog to show the tasks the project is using.
tempAssignedTasksStore	This is a temporary store used on the Modify Resource dialog to show the tasks assigned to the resource.
tempResourceSummaryDetails	This is a temporary store used in the Resource Summary view to show the details for the selected resource.
tempResourceSummaryProjects	This is a temporary store used in the Resource Summary view to show the projects the selected resource is involved with.
tempResourceSummaryTasks	This is a temporary store used in the Resource Summary view to show the tasks the selected resource is assigned to.
tempTaskSummaryDetails	This is a temporary store used in the Task Summary view to show the details for the selected task.
tempResourceSummaryResource	This is a temporary store used in the Task Summary view to show the details for the resource assigned to the task.
tempProjectSummaryDetails	This is a temporary store used in the Project Summary view to show the details for the selected project.
tempProjectSummaryTasks	This is a temporary store used in the Project Summary view to show the tasks allocated to this project.
tempProjectSummaryResources	This is a temporary store used in the Project Summary view to show the resources involved with this project.

As we explore the rest of the code, you'll see how and when these stores get loaded with data, and when and how they are bound to UI elements.

TimekeeperExt.js

Within the TimekeeperExt.js file is most of what I would call the "core" code of the application. It contains the code run to initialize the application, which includes loading data from the database and constructing the UI, as well as a number of functions that handle things like refreshing the various trees and displaying the various summary views.

A Custom RowSelectionModel

The first code we encounter is something we haven't seen before, but before we get to the code, let's take a look at another screenshot from the application (see Figure 4-9).

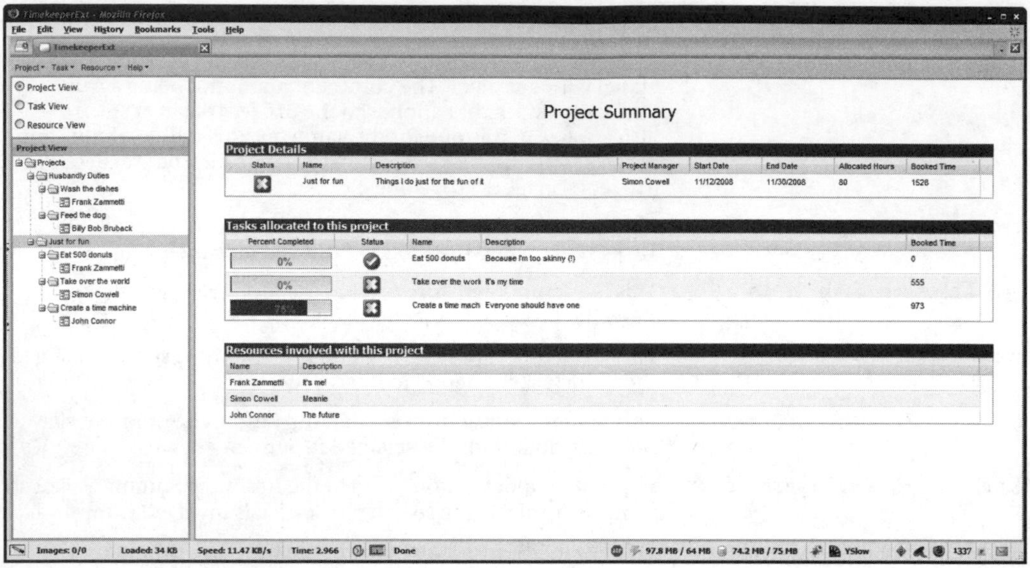

Figure 4-9. *The Project Summary view*

In Figure 4-9, the Project Summary view is shown. What's displayed here isn't too important just yet, except for one detail: the percent complete progress bars in the middle Grid showing the tasks allocated to this project. These progress bars give the user a visual representation of how far along a given task is. When we've seen Grids before, the cells have had just plain text in them. However, that's not a requirement of a Grid. We can put other widgets in them as well.

Doing this introduces a new concept, that of custom RowSelectionModels. A RowSelectionModel defines how data can be selected in a Grid, but more than that it allows us to determine how the contents of a given cell will be rendered. You can create a custom RowSelectionModel type by extending existing ones, as the code here shows:

```
Ext.grid.ProgressBarSelectionModel = Ext.extend(Ext.grid.RowSelectionModel, {
  header : "", sortable : true, fixed : true, dataIndex : "",
  baseCls : "x-progress", width : 150, renderer : function(inValue) {
    var textToDisplay = [ "", "" ];
    if (inValue <= 50) {
      textToDisplay[1] = inValue + "%";
    } else {
      textToDisplay[0] = inValue + "%";
    }
    return String.format(
      "<div class=\"x-progress-wrap\"><div class=\"x-progress-inner\">" +
      "<div class=\"cssProgressBarFill\" style=\"width:{0}%;\">" +
      "<div class=\"x-progress-text\" " +
```

```
        "style=\"color:#ff6060;font-size:11pt;width:100%;margin-top:2px;\">" +
        "{1}</div></div>" + "<div class=\"x-progress-text\" " +
        "style=\"color:#ff6060;font-size:11pt;width:100%;margin-top:2px;\">" +
        "{2}</div></div></div>", inValue, textToDisplay[0], textToDisplay[1]
    );
  }
});
```

The `Ext.grid.RowSelectionModel` is the default selection model for a `Grid`, so that makes it a good starting point. The `Ext.extend()` function provides a way to extend the existing `Ext.grid.RowSelectionModel` class, and we're adding the new type to `Ext.grid` so we can use it later. I'll jump the gun a bit and tell you that when you see this in use you'll find that the definition of the Percent Complete column of the `Grid` specifies a new instance of `Ext.grid.ProgressBarSelectionModel`, so many of the options you would typically specify on the column definition are defined here within the new class. For example, by default, a column using the `Ext.grid.ProgressBarSelectionModel` will be sortable (`sortable : true`) and cannot be resized by the user (`fixed : true`). It will also have a width of 150 pixels. You'll note that the `header` and `dataIndex` values, both of which we're familiar with, are empty strings. The reason they are empty strings is that the code creating an instance of this class is expected to populate them with values, whereas the other fields, while they could be overwritten, don't have to be. Since we have a specific use case here, and we know the values of most of these fields beforehand, setting their values as part of the class definition makes sense.

Now we come to the `renderer` attribute. This attribute references a function that will be called for every value in each row of the `Grid` in the column using the `Ext.grid.ProgressBarSelectionModel`. This allows us essentially to do whatever we want to render the contents of the cell. The value from the field in the `Record` being used to populate the `Grid` is passed in as `inValue`. The job of this code now is to create the markup for the progress bar.

The way this works is basically that the markup constructed uses the same basic structure as an Ext JS progress bar, and in fact you can see that many of the same styles are used. We have a template string with some replacement tokens present in it, three to be precise: the value (which is the percent complete in this case), plus two versions of the same value. If the value is less than or equal to 50 then the value, which has had a percent sign appended to it, needs to be styled differently and placed in a different `<div>` than if it's greater than 50. So, the value is put into an array as either the first or second element in the array, and the other element is a blank string. This is done so that there isn't any conditional logic in the markup template; it simply inserts the values from the array using the `String.format()` function that Ext JS provides.

The generated markup is returned, and will be inserted into the table cell. We could do whatever we wanted in this renderer function, which makes the model concept seen here extremely flexible and allows us to do much more in a `Grid` than you can by default.

■**Note** The original code that I derived this from was posted by an Ext JS user named EvilTed in the Ext JS support forums. I'd like to thank that user for sharing this code (although he informs me that his work was based on the work of someone else, so thanks to anyone else who had a hand in it too!).

A Few Variables for Good Measure

After that we find four global variables, which are summarized in Table 4-2.

Table 4-2. *Global Variables Defined in TimekeeperExt.js*

Variable	Description
currentProject	This is a reference to the ProjectRecord from the projectsStore that is currently selected, if any.
currentResource	This is a reference to the ResourceRecord from the resourcesStore that is currently selected, if any.
currentTask	This is a reference to the TaskRecord from the tasksStore that is currently selected, if any.
currentSummaryView	This contains the card index number of the currently visible summary view, or 0 for the welcome view.

Initializing the Application

Following that are two methods, init() and initMain(). They more or less work the same as in the OrganizerExt project, but they are structurally a little different, so let's have a look, starting with init():

```
function init() {
  new Ext.Window({
    applyTo : "dialogPleaseWait", closable : false, modal : true,
    width : 200, height : 100, minimizable : false, resizable : false,
    draggable : false, shadowOffset : 8, id : "dialogPleaseWait"
  }).show(Ext.getDom("divSource"));
  setTimeout("initMain()", 500);
}
```

Just like in OrganizerExt, this function is called via Ext.onReady(), as seen in index.htm. This displays the Please Wait Window and then fires off a timeout() that executes initMain(), which is this code:

```
function initMain() {
  if (!dao.init()) {
    Ext.getCmp("dialogPleaseWait").destroy();
    var dialogNoGears = new Ext.Window({
      applyTo : "dialogNoGears", closable : false, modal : true,
      width : 400, height : 220, minimizable : false, resizable : false,
      draggable : false, shadowOffset : 8, closeAction : "hide",
      buttons : [{
        text : "Ok",
        handler : function() { dialogNoGears.hide(); }
      }]
    });
    dialogNoGears.show(Ext.getDom("divSource"));
```

```
    return;
  }
  loadData();
  Ext.QuickTips.init(); Ext.form.Field.prototype.msgTarget = "side";
  buildUI();
  Ext.getCmp("dialogPleaseWait").destroy();
}
```

First, a call to dao.init() is made, and if false is returned then the No Gears Window is shown and application startup is aborted.

Assuming dao.init() returns true, initialization continues, beginning with a call to loadData(), which is responsible for loading all the data from the database for projects, tasks, and resources.

Loading the Data

The loadData() function is as follows:

```
function loadData() {
  var projects = dao.retrieveProjects();
  for (var i = 0; i < projects.length; i++) { projectsStore.add(projects[i]); }
  var tasks = dao.retrieveTasks();
  for (var i = 0; i < tasks.length; i++) { tasksStore.add(tasks[i]); }
  var resources = dao.retrieveResources();
  for (var i = 0; i < resources.length; i++) {
    resourcesStore.add(resources[i]);
  }
  populateProjectManagers(); populateAvailableTasks();
}
```

As you can see, a call is made to each of the retrieval methods in the DAO for the three entity types: projects, tasks, and resources. For each, the returned array is iterated over. These arrays contain ProjectRecord objects, TaskRecord objects, or ResourceRecord objects, depending on the type being worked on. For every element in the array a call to the add() method of the appropriate store is made. Finally, a call to populateProjectManagers() and a call to populateAvailableTasks() is made, which populates those two semi-temporary derived stores we saw earlier.

Populating the projectManagersStore

Here is the populateProjectManagers() function:

```
function populateProjectManagers() {
  projectManagersStore.removeAll();
  resourcesStore.each(function(inRecord) {
    if (inRecord.get("isaprojectmanager") == "Yes") {
      projectManagersStore.add(inRecord.copy());
    }
  });
}
```

First, we use the removeAll() method of the projectManagersStore to clear it out. This is necessary because this function will be used at other times, and we always need the store to be empty to begin with because the next step is to iterate over all the Records in the resourcesStore via the each() method. The function passed to each() is called for every Record, and that record is passed into the function as inRecord. The task here is to check the value of the isaprojectmanager field in the Record. If its value is Yes, then we add a copy of the Record to the projectManagersStore by calling the copy() method of the Record, which returns an identical copy of the Record it is called on.

■**Note** I had a nasty situation where originally I was simply calling add() on the projectManagersStore and adding the existing Record form the resourcesStore. The problem I discovered is that the update event would never fire for the Record after that, and the reason is that a Record can be associated with one and only one Store at any time in order for events to work properly. So, the simple solution was to use the copy() method of the Record object to add a copy to the projectManagersStore instead. The bad news is that changes to the resource now require updating the projectManagersStore as well, which is why I said this function will be called at other times. So remember, don't ever put the same Record in more than one Store if you expect events to work as expected! Learn from my hours of pounding my head on the desk!

Populating the AvailableTasksStore and Getting Back to initMain()

The populateAvailableTasks() is extremely similar and also pretty simple:

```
function populateAvailableTasks() {
  availableTasksStore.removeAll();
  tasksStore.each(function(inRecord) {
    if (inRecord.get("project") == "") {
      availableTasksStore.add(inRecord.copy());
    }
  });
}
```

The only real difference is that this time the project field is what we're interested in checking, and simply stated, if the field has no value then the task isn't assigned to a project, and thus is available to be added to a project.

Getting back into initMain(), after the call to loadData() returns, we initialize QuickTips as we saw in the last project so that we can have those pretty little validation error icons next to fields in our forms. After that, a call to buildUI() is made, which as the name implies, builds the user interface. Finally, the Please Wait Window is hidden.

Building the UI

The next thing to look at is that buildUI() function, and in stark contrast to the buildUI() method in the OrganizerExt project, which you'll recall was pretty darned lengthy, the one in this project is considerably smaller:

```
function buildUI() {
  new Ext.Toolbar(uioMenubar);
  new Ext.tree.TreePanel(uioProjectsTree);
  new Ext.tree.TreePanel(uioTasksTree);
  new Ext.tree.TreePanel(uioResourcesTree);
  var vp = new Ext.Viewport({
    layout : "border", items : [
      Ext.getCmp("mainMenu"),
      { region : "center", layout : "card", activeItem : 0, id : "mainCard",
        items : [
          { html :
            "<table width=\"100%\" height=\"100%\" border=\"0\" " +
            "cellpadding=\"0\" cellspacing=\"0\"><tr>" +
            "<td align=\"center\" valign=\"middle\">" +
            "<img src=\"img/welcome.gif\"></td></tr></table>" },
          new Ext.Panel(uioProjectSummary),
          new Ext.Panel(uioTaskSummary),
          new Ext.Panel(uioResourceSummary)
        ]
      },
      { region : "west", layout : "border", width : 250, split : true,
        items : [
          { region : "north", height : 84, bodyStyle : "padding:4px",
            items : [
              { xtype : "radiogroup", columns : 1,
                items : [
                  { boxLabel : "Project View", name : "viewMode",
                    inputValue : 1, checked : true,
                    listeners : {
                      "check" : function(inCheckbox, inChecked) {
                        if (inChecked) {
                          Ext.getCmp("vmCard").getLayout().setActiveItem(0);
                        }
                      }
                    }
                  },
                  { boxLabel : "Task View", name : "viewMode",
                    inputValue : 2, checked : false,
                    listeners : {
                      "check" : function(inCheckbox, inChecked) {
                        if (inChecked) {
                          Ext.getCmp("vmCard").getLayout().setActiveItem(1);
                        }
                      }
                    }
                  },
```

```
                { boxLabel : "Resource View", name : "viewMode",
                  inputValue : 3, checked : false,
                  listeners : {
                    "check" : function(inCheckbox, inChecked) {
                      if (inChecked) {
                        Ext.getCmp("vmCard").getLayout().setActiveItem(2);
                      }
                    }
                  }
                }
              ]
            }
          ]
        },
        { region : "center", layout : "card", activeItem : 0, id : "vmCard",
          items : [
            Ext.getCmp("projectsTree"), Ext.getCmp("tasksTree"),
            Ext.getCmp("resourcesTree")
          ]
        }
      ]
    }
  ]
});
populateProjectsTree();
populateTasksTree();
populateResourcesTree();
}
```

The reason it is so much shorter is that instead of defining the entire UI within one single statement, only the basic layout is defined while most of the components that go into it are defined in separate source files. For example, in the OrganizerExt project, recall that the menu was defined right there in buildUI(), so that was a hundred or so lines of code right there. Here, however, it's a single statement:

```
new Ext.Toolbar(uioMenubar);
```

The JSON that is fed to this constructor is contained in the Menu.js file, which we'll look at shortly, and which declares the variable uioMenubar, which is the configuration object, in JSON form, passed into the Ext.Toolbar constructor. This is a common theme repeated in this function a couple more times, for example, to construct the three view Trees seen on the left of the screen:

```
new Ext.tree.TreePanel(uioProjectsTree);
new Ext.tree.TreePanel(uioTasksTree);
new Ext.tree.TreePanel(uioResourcesTree);
```

Of course, there *is* some UI definition going on here, beginning with the Viewport definition. A BorderLayout is employed here to lay things out. The first item in the items array nested within the Viewport is the menu. The statement we just saw that instantiates the

Ext.Toolbar contains a region specification of north, which is where the menu bar should be in the BorderLayout, and it also defines an ID of mainMenu. So, the first item in the items array is simply a call to Ext.getCmp("mainMenu"), which effectively means that the menu bar is the first item (remember that you can create widgets and not render them immediately, but Ext JS still knows how to give you a reference to it by ID, assuming you gave the component an ID).

The next item in the items array is bound to the center region and is a Panel using the CardLayout type with the ID mainCard. The items array for it creates four nested items within this CardLayout, the first being some plain-old HTML for the welcome splash screen. The last three items are the three summary views, the configuration of which we'll look at later.

The next nested element in the BorderLayout is itself a BorderLayout in the west region. This is where the view selection Radio buttons and the trees are shown. Remember that you aren't obligated to use all the regions of a BorderLayout, and here only the north and center regions are used. In the north region we create the Radio buttons for selecting the view. This is just a RadioGroup, as we've seen before, and for each of the Radio buttons a check event handler is defined. The card showing in the vmCard component, which is created below the code for the view Radio buttons, is updated to show the appropriate Tree (each Tree is a card in the CardLayout shown in the center region of the BorderLayout in the west region of the main BorderLayout in use by the ViewPort).

As mentioned, the Trees themselves are each a card in a CardLayout, and this is defined below the Radio buttons.

Populating the Trees

Next up are three functions that have the responsibility of populating the three view trees. These functions are aptly named populateProjectsTree(), populateTasksTree(), and populateResourcesTree().

If by chance you've forgotten what a Tree looks like, take a gander at Figure 4-10.

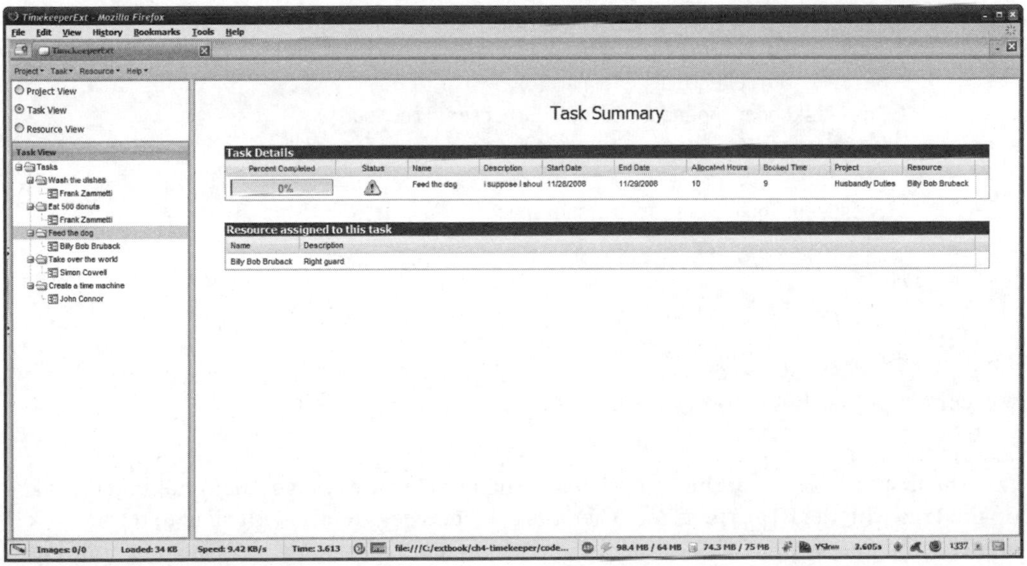

Figure 4-10. *The tree in the Task View*

Because of the similarities in these three functions, let's just take a look at one of them, populateProjectsTree(). This one is more complex and verbose than the other two, which is good because the other two are effectively a subset of this one, so understanding how populateProjectsTree() works means you'll understand the other two. Here's the code we're talking about:

```
function populateProjectsTree() {
  var newProjectNode = null; var newTaskNode = null;
  var pRootNode = Ext.getCmp("projectsTree").getRootNode();
  var delNode;
  if (pRootNode) {
    while (delNode = pRootNode.childNodes[0]) {
      pRootNode.removeChild(delNode);
    }
  }
  var assureUnique = 1;
  projectsStore.each(function(inProjectRecord) {
    newProjectNode = pRootNode.appendChild(new Ext.tree.TreeNode({
      id : "project~@~" + inProjectRecord.get("name"),
      text : inProjectRecord.get("name")
    }));
    tasksStore.each(function(inTaskRecord) {
      if (inTaskRecord.get("project") == inProjectRecord.get("name")) {
        newTaskNode = newProjectNode.appendChild(new Ext.tree.TreeNode({
          id : "task~@~" + inTaskRecord.get("name"),
          text : inTaskRecord.get("name")
        }));
        resourcesStore.each(function(inResourceRecord) {
          if (inTaskRecord.get("resource") == inResourceRecord.get("name")) {
            var newID = "resource~@~" + assureUnique + "~@~" +
              inResourceRecord.get("name");
            newTaskNode.appendChild(new Ext.tree.TreeNode({
              id : newID, text : inResourceRecord.get("name")
            }));
            assureUnique = assureUnique + 1;
          }
        });
      }
    });
  });
  pRootNode.expand();
}
```

The first task is to clear the Tree, which we do by using the Ext.getCmp() method to look up the Tree with the ID projectTree. Then the getRootNode() method is called to retrieve a reference to the root node. Then, we enter a while loop that keeps going until the root node has no more children. For each child node found, we call the removeChild() method on the root node, passing it a reference to the child node. I could find no single method to call to clear an existing Tree, and I also could find no simpler way to do it than this.

Once that's done, it is time to populate the Tree with the new data. The Project View Tree lists projects, with tasks nested below each, and resources nested below the tasks. So, we begin by iterating over all the projects in the projectsStore using its each() method. For each ProjectRecord in the store, we append a new Ext.tree.TreeNode to the Tree. A TreeNode has an id attribute and a text attribute, among other things. The id is a unique identifier, while text is what is seen in the tree by the user. The value for both of these comes from the name field of the ProjectRecord, but for the id the code prepends the string project~@~. The reasoning behind this will be explained in more detail when we look at the code behind the Tree itself, but simply stated, it allows other code to determine whether a project, task, or resource was clicked, and it also ensures all nodes in the Tree have a unique ID, which is a requirement.

The TreeNode also has an icon attribute that allows us to set the image seen next to the node. I have different icons for projects, tasks, and resources, so it is easy to differentiate them when looking at the tree.

Moving on, recall that tasks are nested beneath projects. Therefore, for each ProjectRecord, we also iterate over the TaskRecord objects in the tasksStore, and for each we check to see if its project field value matches the name field of the ProjectRecord. If it does, we add a TreeNode as a child of the newly created TreeNode for the project.

Likewise, for each task we need to nest resources underneath it, so again we iterate over the Records in a store, this time the resourcesStore. For each we check to see if the resource field on the TaskRecord object matches the name field of the ResourceRecord, and if so, a TreeNode is appended as a child to the new task TreeNode. For projects and tasks, since no two projects can have the same name, and the same goes for tasks, there is no risk of a conflicting id value for the TreeNode. However, this is not the case for resources, since the same resource could be assigned to multiple tasks. So, to ensure a unique id value, the value has a number appended to it that is incremented with each resource TreeNode added. As I mentioned, this will be explained a bit more shortly, but that gives you most of the information you need.

As a last step, the root node is expanded via a call to its expand() method. This just ensures that all projects are seen after the Tree is populated (by default, the root node would have been collapsed, and there's no point making users expand it when that's probably what they'd want to happen automatically anyway).

At this point I suggest looking at the populateTasksTree() and populateResourcesTree() functions, because going through them yourself is worth the time. However, as I previously mentioned, they are essentially just a subset of what we just looked at, so even if you don't, you won't be missing anything.

Showing Project, Task, and Resource Status

You may at this point have guessed how I wrote this code: I wrote a given function for projects, say the populateProjectsTree(), then took that function and modified it to work for tasks and resources. That's why I've said a few times now that seeing a single version of a given function is pretty well sufficient to understanding all three versions. Well, I'm about to say the same thing again! We're going to look at the three functions for displaying the project, task, or resource summary views. Once again, we'll take the showProjectSummary() function and look at it, leaving showTaskSummary() and showResourceSummary() for you to review on your own, or to skip entirely, since the two we won't look at here are similar to the one we will look at.

Speaking of the one we will look at, here it is:

```
function showProjectSummary() {
  if (currentProject) {
    Ext.getCmp("mainCard").getLayout().setActiveItem(1);
    currentSummaryView = 1;
  } else {
    Ext.getCmp("mainCard").getLayout().setActiveItem(0);
    return;
  }
  var projectBookedTime = 0;
  tempProjectSummaryTasks.removeAll();
  tasksStore.each(function(inRecord) {
    if (inRecord.get("project") == currentProject.get("name")) {
      var newRecord = inRecord.copy();
      newRecord.set("status", calculateStatus(inRecord.get("bookedtime"),
        inRecord.get("allocatedhours"), inRecord.get("enddate")));
      tempProjectSummaryTasks.add(newRecord);
      projectBookedTime = projectBookedTime + inRecord.get("bookedtime");
    }
  });
  tempProjectSummaryDetails.removeAll();
  var newRecord = currentProject.copy();
  newRecord.set("bookedtime", projectBookedTime);
  newRecord.set("status", calculateStatus(
    projectBookedTime, currentProject.get("allocatedhours"),
    currentProject.get("enddate")));
  tempProjectSummaryDetails.add(newRecord);
  tempProjectSummaryResources.removeAll();
  tempProjectSummaryTasks.each(function(inRecord) {
    var resourceRecord = resourcesStore.getById(inRecord.get("resource"));
    if (resourceRecord &&
      Ext.isEmpty(tempProjectSummaryResources.getById(resourceRecord.id))) {
      tempProjectSummaryResources.add(resourceRecord.copy());
    }
  });
}
```

The first check is to ensure that currentProject has a value, meaning it points to a ProjectRecord. If it's null, then the first card in the CardLayout mainCard is shown. As you'll recall, this is the CardLayout nested in the center region of the BorderLayout applied to the Viewport. The first card is the welcome screen, so this situation covers if the user clicks the root node of the projects Tree, in which case there is no active project, but this function will still be called because this function is called from the click event handlers on the Tree, as you'll see shortly.

If a project is selected, though, the second card is shown, which happens to be the Project Summary view card.

If you look at the Project Summary view, you'll see there are three Grids, the second of which shows all the tasks allocated to this project, so it needs to be populated first (and no, it's not a mistake, I skipped the first Grid on purpose… more to come). To do this, we need to populate a temporary store, appropriately named tempProjectSummaryTasks. Before this store can be populated, though, it needs to be cleared, which we accomplish with a call to removeAll(). Then, we begin to iterate over the TaskRecords in the tasksStore. For each, we see if its project field matches the name of the selectedProject, and if so, then a new Record is created that is a copy of the TaskRecord currently being examined. This gives us nearly all the data that we'll need to display in the Grid, except for one piece of information: the current status of the task. To fulfill that requirement, we use a function named calculateStatus(). The code for that function is present in TimekeeperExt.js as well, and here it is:

```
function calculateStatus(inBookedTime, inAllocatedHours, inEndDate) {
  var status = 0;
  var statusImage = "<img src=\"img/statusOK.gif\">";
  if (inBookedTime < inAllocatedHours &&
    inBookedTime >= (inAllocatedHours * .9)) {
    status = 1;
  } else if (inBookedTime > inAllocatedHours) {
    status = 2;
  }
  var endDate = Date.parseDate(inEndDate, "m/d/Y");
  if (new Date() > endDate) {
    if (status == 0) {
      statusImage = "<img src=\"img/statusOKPastDue.gif\">";
    } else if (status == 1) {
      statusImage = "<img src=\"img/statusDangerPastDue.gif\">";
    } else if (status == 2) {
      statusImage = "<img src=\"img/statusOverPastDue.gif\">";
    }
  } else {
    if (status == 1) {
      statusImage = "<img src=\"img/statusDanger.gif\">";
    } else if (status == 2) {
      statusImage = "<img src=\"img/statusOver.gif\">";
    }
  }
  return statusImage;
}
```

This function is used to calculate the status of both projects and tasks, and essentially it winds up returning a snippet of HTML for displaying the appropriate image in the Status column of a Grid. This function accepts three arguments: the total time booked to the project or task in hours, the number of hours allocated to the project or task, and the date the project or task was due to be completed.

The first task is to determine if the project or task is over its allocated hours, within 10 percent of its allocated hours, or has had less than that booked against it. The code begins by assuming that the project or task has had less than 90 percent of its allocated time booked again it, signified by the status variable having a value of 0 to begin with. Next, an if check is performed to determine if it is within 10 percent of the allocated hours, and if so, status is set to 1. If inBookedTime is greater than inAllocatedHours, then status is set to 2 to indicate an overage.

After that, it's time to determine whether the project or task is late. Before we go any further, I should explain that there are six images that can be displayed as a result of using this function. A green check mark indicates the project or task has had less than 90 percent of its allocated hours booked. A yellow warning sign indicates danger of going over hours (10 percent of allocated hours remaining), and a red X symbol indicates an overage. In addition, any one of these three can be blinking, indicating the project or task is past due. So, before the second if statement executes we know which of the three nonblinking images to display. The second if statement will then determine if one of the blinking versions needs to be returned.

So, the check is performed to see if the current date is greater than the inEndDate value. To do this comparison, we need to create a true Date object from a passed-in string, and the Date.parseDate() function that Ext JS provides is just the tonic for that! If the if branch is activated, then it examines the value of the status variable and selects the appropriate image based on it and creates the appropriate <img> tag markup. Likewise, if the project or task is not past due, then the else branch hits, and there we check if the project or task is in danger or is over hours, and select the appropriate blinking image there. (By default, the assumption is made that the project or task is both under hours/not in danger and is also not past due— that's why only two cases are checked for in the else branch: the third condition is the default.)

Getting back to the showProjectSummary() code, we've just completed population of the store for the middle task's Grid, save for one last detail. Note the line:

```
projectBookedTime = projectBookedTime + inRecord.get("bookedtime");
```

This line is the reason the Grids are not populated in the order they appear on the screen. In order to show a status for the project as a whole, we need to know how much time has been booked against it. Since that information is stored at the task level, we have to calculate it as we iterate over the tasks during population of that Grid.

Once we have that value, populating the project details Grid (the first one in the Project Summary view) is a pretty trivial matter. First, the tempProjectSummaryDetails store is cleared by a call to removeAll(). Then the currentProject Record is copied using its copy() method. Next, the bookedtime field of that Record is set to the value that was just calculated, and the status field is populated by making another call to calculateStatus().

Finally, the copy of the currentProject ProjectRecord is added to tempProjectSummaryDetails. The Grid automatically refreshes because it has been bound to that particular store (the same is true of all the Grids in all the summary views).

The last step is to populate the Grid showing resources working on this project. Since the only way to know this is by examining the tasks associated with this project, we use the each() method on the tempProjectSummaryTasks store (yet another reason it had to be done first) to iterate over its Records. For each we retrieve the ResourceRecord from the resourcesStore by looking it up based on the value of the resource field of the current TaskRecord being examined. Finally, a copy of the ResourceRecord is added to tempProjectSummaryResources, but only if the resource wasn't previously added. We determined this by using the `Ext.isEmpty()` function. Simply put, the code tries to look up the resource in `tempProjectSummaryResources`, and if `Ext.isEmpty()` returns `true`, then the resource hasn't been added yet and can be added now.

ProjectSummary.js, ResourceSummary.js, and TaskSummary.js

The three summary views, one each for project, task, and resource, are each housed in their own source file and are pretty simple config objects fed into an `Ext.Panel` constructor, as we saw in `TimekeeperExt.js`. As usual for this chapter, we'll just look at the `ProjectSummary.js` since the other two are simply variations on a theme. The code begins with this snippet:

```
var uioProjectSummary = {
  bodyStyle : "padding-left:40px;padding-right:40px;padding-top:30px;",
  autoScroll : true, items : [
```

The `uioProjectSummary` variable holds the JSON config information that defines the `Panel`. We have a `bodyStyle` that specifies some padding on the left, right, and top of the contents of the `Panel`, just to avoid bumping up against borders.

Next we have a chunk that describes the title:

```
{ border : false, html :
    "<div class='cssSummaryTitle'>Project Summary</div>" },
```

This winds up being a simple `Panel` that has some HTML displayed in it. We also remove the border so that it looks like a title and not a box with text in it!

Now we come to the first `Grid`, but before that is the header you see above the `Grid`:

```
{ border: false, bodyStyle : "padding-top:30px", html :
    "<div class='cssSummaryTableHeader'>Project Details</div>" },
```

This is again just a plain-old `Panel` with some plain-old HTML in it. The `bodyStyle` gives some padding on the top of the header and `Grid` so that there is space between it and whatever content is above it (the title in this case). Following that is the definition of the `Grid` itself:

```
{ xtype : "grid", id : "gdProjectSummaryDetails", trackMouseOver : false,
  store : tempProjectSummaryDetails, autoHeight : true, stripeRows : true,
  disableSelection : true, autoExpandColumn : "colDescription",
  columns : [
    { header : "Status", sortable : false, dataIndex : "status",
      align : "center" },
    { header : "Name", sortable : false, dataIndex : "name" },
    { header : "Description", sortable : false, dataIndex : "description",
      id : "colDescription" },
    { header : "Project Manager", sortable : false,
      dataIndex : "projectmanager" },
    { header : "Start Date", sortable : false, dataIndex : "startdate" },
    { header : "End Date", sortable : false, dataIndex : "enddate" },
```

```
      { header : "Allocated Hours", sortable : false,
        dataIndex : "allocatedhours" },
      { header : "Booked Time", sortable : true, dataIndex : "bookedtime" }
    ]
  },
```

This `Grid` is bound to the `tempProjectSummaryDetails` `Store`, which may be empty or may have data in it, depending on whether a project is currently selected. Data binding works either way, of course! For this `Grid` (and in fact all the `Grid`s on all three summary views), the `trackMouseOver` attribute is set to `false`, which means the rows of the `Grid` won't highlight when hovered over. Since these `Grid`s aren't meant to be interactive—they are just a method for displaying read-only data—this is a necessary setting. By extension, `disableSelection` makes sure the user can't select a row. The definition of the columns is, I suspect, pretty straightforward based on our previous experience with `Grid`s, as are the rest of the config options.

Next we find the second of the three `Grid`s, this one listing the tasks allocated to this project:

```
{ border: false, bodyStyle : "padding-top:30px", html :
    "<div class='cssSummaryTableHeader'>" +
    "Tasks allocated to this project</div>" },
{ xtype : "grid", id : "gdProjectSummaryTasks", trackMouseOver : false,
  store : tempProjectSummaryTasks, autoHeight : true, stripeRows : true,
  disableSelection : true, autoExpandColumn : "colDescription",
  columns : [
    new Ext.grid.ProgressBarSelectionModel({
      header : "Percent Completed", dataIndex : "percentcomplete",
      align : "center" }),
    { header : "Status", sortable : false, dataIndex : "status",
      align : "center" },
    { header : "Name", sortable : true, dataIndex : "name" },
    { header : "Description", sortable : true, dataIndex : "description",
      id : "colDescription" },
    { header : "Booked Time", sortable : true, dataIndex : "bookedtime" }
  ]
},
```

In this case I've listed the header and `Grid` definition together, since you now know what that header is all about from the last `Grid`. In fact, the `Grid` definition is pretty unremarkable too, except for one detail: within the `columns` array, the first column is an instance of `Ext.grid.ProgressBarSelectionModel`, which we saw defined in `TimekeeperExt.js`. This takes the value of the `percentcomplete` field of the `ProjectRecord` for each row in the `Grid`, plus the column header and an `align` value of `center`, and renders the progress bar as previously described.

The final Grid shows all resources involved with the project:

```
{ border: false, bodyStyle : "padding-top:30px", html :
    "<div class='cssSummaryTableHeader'>" +
    "Resources involved with this project</div>" },
{ xtype : "grid", id : "gdProjectSummaryResources", trackMouseOver : false,
    store : tempProjectSummaryResources, autoHeight : true, stripeRows : true,
    disableSelection : true, autoExpandColumn : "colDescription",
    columns : [
      { header : "Name", sortable : true, dataIndex : "name" },
      { header : "Description", sortable : true, dataIndex : "description",
        id : "colDescription" }
    ]
  }
 ]
};
```

At this point, that bit of code should be nothing new at all!

ProjectsTree.js, TasksTree.js, and ResourcesTree.js

Each of the trees that you see when you select Project View, Task View, or Resource View is
housed in its own source file. The Project View tree, for example, is in the ProjectsTree.js file.
The code you find in this file looks like this:

```
var uioProjectsTree = {
  layout : "fit", id : "projectsTree", title : "Project View",
  root : new Ext.tree.TreeNode( { id : "root", text : "Projects" } ),
  listeners : {
    click : function(inNode, inEvent) {
      if (inNode.id == "root") {
        Ext.getCmp("mainCard").getLayout().setActiveItem(0);
      } else {
        var splitVals = inNode.id.split("~@~");
        switch (splitVals[0]) {
          case "project":
            currentProject = projectsStore.getById(splitVals[1]);
            showProjectSummary();
          break;
          case "task":
            currentTask = tasksStore.getById(splitVals[1]);
            showTaskSummary();
          break;
          case "resource":
            currentResource = resourcesStore.getById(splitVals[2]);
            showResourceSummary();
          break;
        };
```

```
        var typeInCaps = Ext.util.Format.capitalize(splitVals[0]);
        Ext.getCmp("menu" + typeInCaps + "Delete" + typeInCaps).enable();
        Ext.getCmp("menu" + typeInCaps + "Modify" + typeInCaps).enable();
      }
    }
  }
};
```

Because each of these source files is so similar, just looking at this one will suffice. I suggest taking a look at them on your own, but you'll find that the TasksTree.js and ResourcesTree.js code are both a bit simpler and smaller than the ProjectsTree.js code because they in effect are a subset of what is in the code shown here.

As you can see, it's really just some JSON assigned to a variable named uioProjectsTree (uio stands for User Interface Object—just a prefix I invented). In TimekeeperExt.js you saw that this variable is passed to an Ext.tree.TreePanel constructor, so this JSON is defining that TreePanel. It specifies a fit layout so that the tree takes up the entire space allocated to its parent. It is given an ID of projectsTree so that we can address it later, and it has a title as well so that there is something between the view switch radio buttons and the tree itself.

Any time you construct a tree in Ext JS, it has to have a root node, even if you don't have data to put in it yet. This is a requirement during construction, so here we use the root attribute, the value of which is a new Ext.tree.TreeNode. The root node is no different from any other nodes—they are always TreeNode instances. We give the root a very uncreative ID of root and make the text that will be displayed next to the node Projects, since this is the Project View tree.

After that, event listeners are defined. In this case it's just a single one: the click event, which fires any time a node is clicked. Every time this event fires, the callback function is passed a reference to the node that was clicked as well as information about the event that occurred. The second argument is an instance of Ext.EventObject that provides information about the event such as X and Y location on the page of the event, character codes of pressed keys involved, and more.

For our purposes, however, it's only the first argument that matters to us, and that's a reference to the TreeNode object that was clicked. Most important is the id attribute of that object, which is the ID assigned to the clicked node. The first thing we do is see if the clicked node is the root node. If that is the case, the welcome screen is immediately shown by flipping to the first element in the list of cards underneath the CardLayout component with the ID mainCard, which we know is the CardLayout in the center region of the main BorderLayout that organizes the Viewport contents.

Once we determine that it wasn't the root node that was clicked, the next chore is to determine the type of node that was clicked, and the ID associated with the item the node represents. In the Project View tree, there are projects, there are tasks, and there are resources. However, to the tree itself, they are all just TreeNode objects; the tree doesn't know or care what they represent to the rest of our code. To give extra meaning to each node, I used a special string format for the ID. That format is xxx~@~yyy or xxx~@~yyy~@~zzz. The first format is used for projects and tasks, while the second is used for resources. The substring ~@~ is nothing but a delimiter. I used this instead of a comma or something more typical because I needed something that I could safely assume wouldn't naturally occur in entered data. This particular combination seemed to me pretty safe. In both formats, the xxx portion is the type of node, so the value is either project, task, or resource. For projects and tasks, the yyy portion is then the actual ID of the project or task. (Remember that the ID is really the name of the item, but it serves as a unique ID here.) In the case of resources, yyy is instead a unique value constructed based on the time the node was added, as you saw in TimekeeperExt.js, and zzz is the ID. This is necessary because a single resource can appear more than once in the tree since a resource can be assigned to more than one task. If all nodes in the tree don't have unique IDs, you'll find that the tree breaks, and things like hovering and selection don't quite work right. Doing this ensures those problems are avoided.

So, the ID of the clicked node is tokenized and broken into an array named splitVals that has either two or three elements. The first element of the array, which is the type of node, is used as the branch condition in a switch statement. Whatever the type is, the appropriate variable is set. For projects, the currentProject variable is set to the Record in the projectsStore associated with the clicked node. For tasks, the Record from the tasksStore is pointed to by the currentTask variable, and for resources the Record comes from the resourcesStore and is pointed to by the currentResource variable. This allows the summary views to know what Record to draw their displayed data from, and it allows the application to know what project, resource, or task should be dealt with when using the Modify or Delete menu items.

Speaking of Modify and Delete, the next task performed is to enable those menu items as appropriate. To do this, the first element in the splitVals array is capitalized using the Ext.util.format.capitalize() function, yielding one of the strings "Project", "Task", or "Resource", depending on the type of node that was clicked. With this string we are then able to construct the ID of the menu items that need to be enabled. For a project node, for example, the menu items with the IDs menuProjectDeleteProject and menuProjectModifyProject need to be enabled, so those IDs are constructed. We use the Ext.getCmp() function to get a reference to the menu item, and then its enable() method is called to activate it.

As I mentioned, the code found in TasksTree.js and ResourcesTree.js is nearly identical to this, but since in the Task View tree there can only be tasks and resources shown, there is one less case statement. In the case of tasks and resources, clicking on the root node does nothing, so there is a simple check that effectively ignores clicks on that node. Also, in the case of the Resource View tree, there's no need to do any of the mucking around with node types and IDs. Because there are only resources shown in that tree, and since resources must always have a unique name anyway, and since the name is effectively the ID of the nodes in the tree, there is no need to ensure uniqueness manually. It's already ensured naturally, so the code there has none of the branching involved. Have a look to verify I'm not making any of this up!

Menu.js

The main menu is how most of the functionality of TimekeeperExt is accessed. There is a menu item for each entity we deal with. For instance, there is a Project menu, as shown in Figure 4-11.

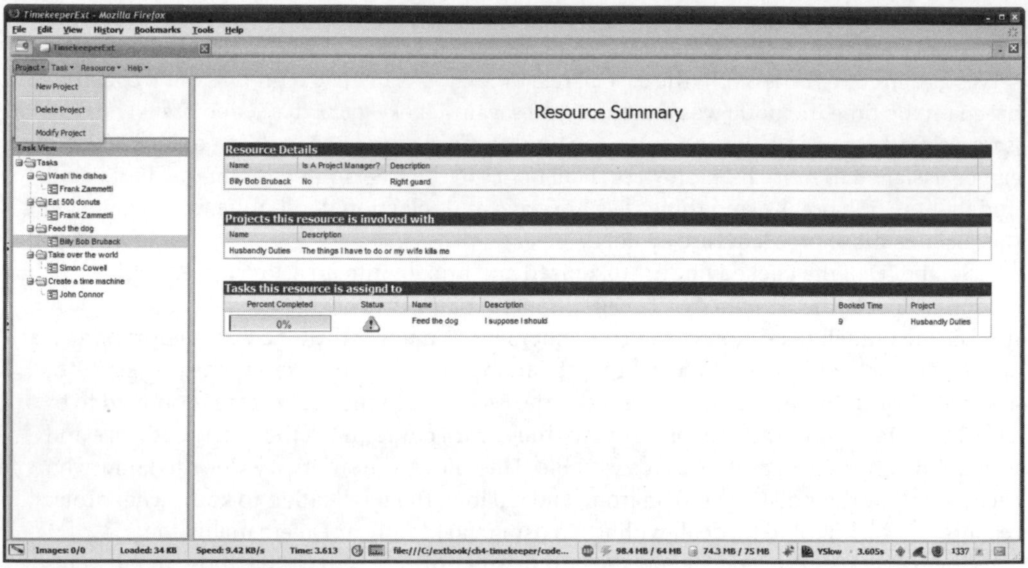

Figure 4-11. *The Project menu*

Likewise, there is a Task menu, which you can see in Figure 4-12. Each of the first three menus has three items: one to create a new project, task, or resource; one to delete the currently selected project, task or resource; and one to modify the currently selected project, task, or resource.

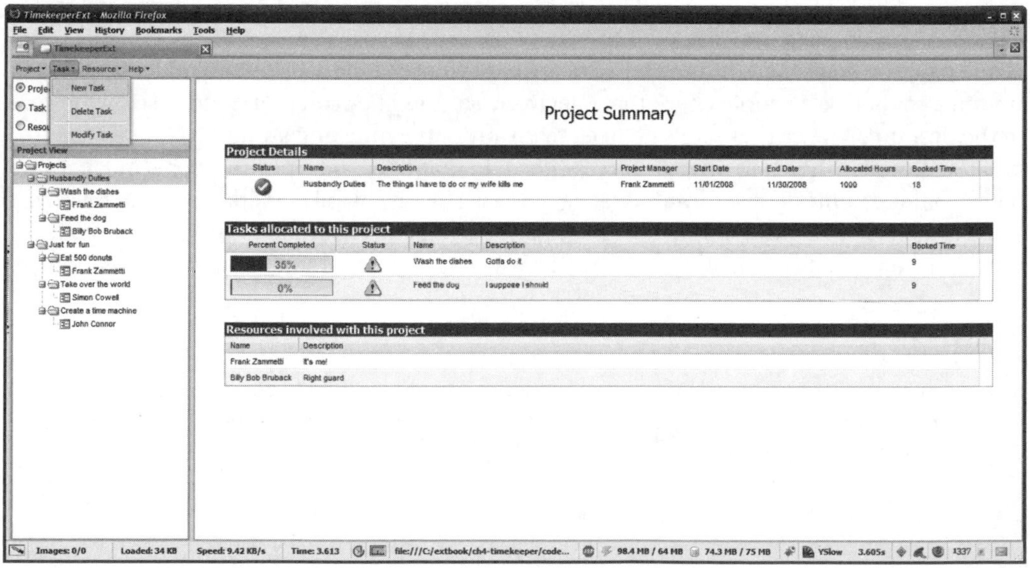

Figure 4-12. *The Task menu*

Before an item is selected, the Delete and Modify options are disabled, as you can see in Figure 4-13 where the Resources menu is shown.

Figure 4-13. *The Resource menu*

The final menu, the Help menu, contains a single option that shows an About dialog, similar to what we saw in the OrganizerExt project. To save some space I haven't shown a screenshot of that menu here, nor have I shown the About dialog or explained its code. Except for the text, it's the same as in OrganizerExt, so feel free to go back to that chapter and check it out if you need to.

The code behind the menu, how it is created, and how it reacts when clicked are all housed in the Menu.js file. This code is about 200 lines long, but a lot of very similar parts are repeated. So, let's look at just a small portion of it, that dealing with projects:

```
var uioMenubar = {
  id : "mainMenu", region : "north", height : 26,
  items : [ {
    text : "Project", menu : {
      items : [ {
        text : "New Project",
        handler : function() {
          var dialogNewProject = Ext.getCmp("dialogNewProject");
          if (!dialogNewProject) {
            dialogNewProject = new Ext.Window(uioNewProjectWindow);
          }
          dialogNewProject.show(Ext.getDom("divSource"));
        }
      },
```

```
          "-",
        { text : "Delete Project", disabled : true,
          id : "menuProjectDeleteProject",
          handler : function() {
            var dialogDeleteProject = Ext.getCmp("dialogDeleteProject");
            if (!dialogDeleteProject) {
              dialogDeleteProject = new Ext.Window(uioDeleteProjectWindow);
            }
            dialogDeleteProject.show(Ext.getDom("divSource"));
          }
        },
          "-",
        { text : "Modify Project", disabled : true,
          id : "menuProjectModifyProject",
          handler : function() {
            var dialogModifyProject = Ext.getCmp("dialogModifyProject");
            if (!dialogModifyProject) {
              dialogModifyProject = new Ext.Window(uioModifyProjectWindow);
            }
            dialogModifyProject.show(Ext.getDom("divSource"));
          }
        }
      ]
    },
    listeners : {
      "render" : function(b) {
        b.el.child(b.menuClassTarget).removeClass("x-btn-with-menu");
      }
    }
  }
},
…Code for the other three menus is here…
  ]
};
```

Recall in the buildUI() function that the uioMenubar variable is fed to the constructor of
an Ext.Toolbar() object. However, the reference to the created component was not stored.
Instead, in the config object for the Viewport we used the ID of the menu, mainMenu, to retrieve
a reference to the widget, and that was used in the items array of the Viewport. Now in the
definition of the menu you can see that the region attribute is set to north, because we used a
BorderLayout on the Viewport, so this attribute tells the BorderLayout where to put the menu.

The items array of the menu contains our top-level menus. The first one has a text value
of Project. The menu attribute then defines the menu itself, the child elements of the top-level
menu element. The value of the menu attribute is an object which, in this case, has a single
attribute: items. This is an array of the children that are part of that menu.

The first item is the New Project item, so that's the value of the text attribute. The handler
attribute defines the function that will be called when the item is clicked. You'll notice as
you scan down the code that the handler function is nearly identical to the handler function

for the other two menu items; the only difference is the dialog that is shown. A reference to the appropriate dialog is gotten by a call to Ext.getCmp(), in this case the ID we're looking for is dialogNewProject. Then, if the component wasn't found, a new Ext.Window object is created, passing it the config object defined that describes the Window for that dialog, uioNewProjectWindow in this case. This will only occur if this is the first time the dialog Window is being shown. The Windows for all the pop-up dialogs are never destroyed; they are only hidden, so the only time we won't get a reference to an existing component is the first time it is used. Finally, the show() method of the Window is called, passing it a reference to the divSource <div> where our animation starts from.

You'll also notice that between each of the three menu items is a single item that appears to be a plain-old string: a dash character. This is a special cue to Ext JS to put a divider line on the menu.

The other menus all have extremely similar code behind them, so we can move on to something a bit more exciting.

NewProjectDialog.js, NewTaskDialog.js, and NewResourceDialog.js

The New Project, New Task, and New Resource dialogs are all fairly similar, so we'll just look at the NewProjectDialog.js file here. Before that, let's take a look at the dialog itself, shown in Figure 4-14.

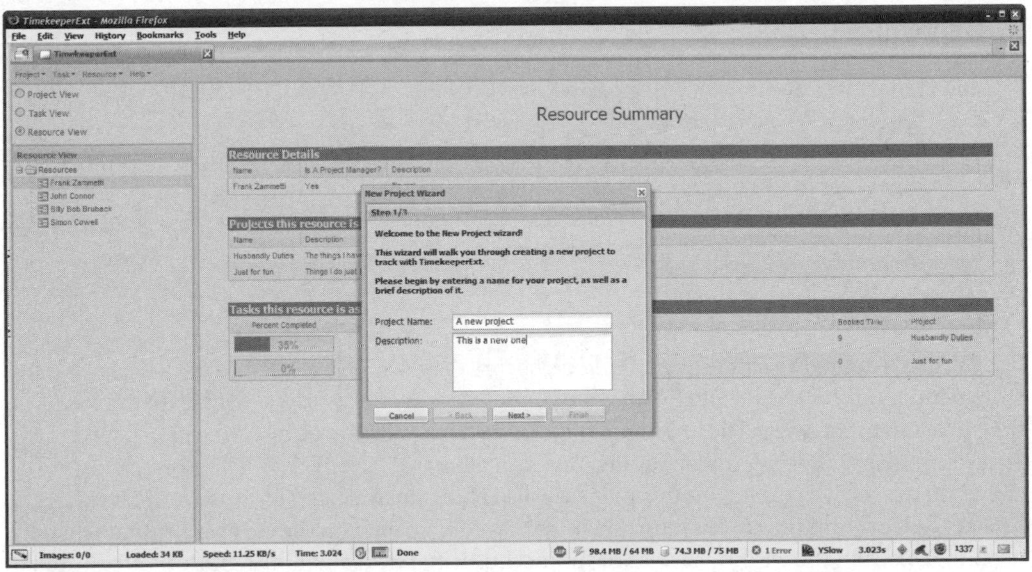

Figure 4-14. *Page 1 of the New Project Wizard*

The New Project and New Task dialogs are wizard-type dialogs, which Ext JS doesn't provide out of the box, but fortunately it's not difficult to implement at all. The first page of the wizard allows the user to enter a name and description of the project. We'll see the other two pages as we chug through the code.

■**Note** The New Resource dialog isn't a wizard flow because a single set of input fields is all it takes to define a resource.

Let's now look at the code behind the New Project dialog. I'll break this up into easily digestible pieces, in order:

```
var uioNewProjectWindow = {
  title : "New Project Wizard", closable : true, modal : true,
  width : 400, height : 340, minimizable : false, resizable : false,
  draggable : true, shadowOffset : 8, closeAction : "hide",
  id : "dialogNewProject",
```

Here we see the config information for a pretty ordinary Window. It has a width of 400 pixels and a height of 340 pixels. It cannot be minimized (minimizable:false), resized (resizable:false), or dragged (draggable:false), and it has slightly larger shadow than usual (shadowOffset:8). It is also modal (modal:true), so it acts like a lightbox. It has an id of dialogNewProject and a title of New Project Wizard. It is closable (closable:true), and when the close X is clicked it will be hidden (closeAction:hide) rather than destroyed.

Attached to this Window is a listeners object defining some event handlers:

```
listeners : {
  beforeshow : function() {
    Ext.getCmp("0newProject").getForm().reset();
    Ext.getCmp("1newProject").getForm().reset();
    Ext.getCmp("2newProject").getForm().reset();
    Ext.getCmp("dialogNewProjectCard").getLayout().setActiveItem(0);
    Ext.getCmp("newProjectNext").disable();
    Ext.getCmp("newProjectBack").disable();
    Ext.getCmp("newProjectFinish").disable();
  }
},
```

Well, it's actually a single event *handler*, beforeshow, which fires before the Window is shown but after it is constructed. This event handler resets three forms, which are the forms for each step of the wizard flow. We get a reference to the FormPanel by ID (0newProject, for example) and then get the underling form by calling getForm() on it. Then reset() is called on the form to reset it. At this point we also show the first step of the wizard by calling setActiveItem() on the Layout returned by getLayout() called on the CardLayout that will be used to construct the wizard. Also at this point the Next, Back, and Finish buttons are disabled.

Speaking of those buttons, they are defined next, starting with Cancel:

```
buttons : [
  { text : "Cancel", handler : function() {
      Ext.getCmp("dialogNewProject").hide(); }
  },
```

When Cancel is clicked, all that needs to be done is to hide this Window, so that's all you see here. The Window is hidden rather than destroyed so that when it's shown later we don't have to incur the overhead of creation a second time.

The Back button is defined next:

```
{ text : "< Back", disabled : true, id : "newProjectBack",
  handler : function() {
    var dialogCardLayout =
      Ext.getCmp("dialogNewProjectCard").getLayout();
    var currentStep =
      parseInt(dialogCardLayout.activeItem.getId().substr(0, 1));
    if (currentStep > 0) { dialogCardLayout.setActiveItem(currentStep - 1); }
    if (currentStep == 1) { this.disable(); }
  }
},
```

As I mentioned earlier, Ext JS doesn't provide a wizard by default; we have to build it ourselves. To do so, we use the handy CardLayout. Each step of the wizard is a card in that CardLayout, and we provide the functionality behind the Next and Back buttons that are typical of a wizard dialog. For the Back button, we begin by getting a handle to the CardLayout. Unfortunately, there is no easy way to ask a CardLayout which item is active, so you either have to keep track of that information yourself or figure it out dynamically. I wanted to minimize the number of "status tracking" variables used in this application, so I decided to get the value dynamically. We do this by getting the active item, which is available via the activeItem attribute of the CardLayout. We then get the ID of that item by calling getId(). The cards have IDs that begin with a number, 0–2, so we do a simple substr() to get the first character, and then use parseInt() to get it as a number. We now have a variable named currentStep with the value 0, 1, or 2, depending on which step of the wizard flow the user is on.

Next, if the currentStep is greater than 0, meaning users are on the second or third step, then moving back is a valid operation, and it's just a matter of calling setActiveItem() on the CardLayout and passing it the value of currentStep minus 1, which puts us on the previous step. If currentStep is 1, then the Back button is disabled at this point, which handles the situation where the user clicked Back and we just moved to the first step.

The Next button is, er, *next...*

```
{
  text : "Next >", disabled : true, id : "newProjectNext",
  handler : function() {
    Ext.getCmp("newProjectBack").enable();
    var dialogCardLayout =
      Ext.getCmp("dialogNewProjectCard").getLayout();
    var currentStep =
      parseInt(dialogCardLayout.activeItem.getId().substr(0, 1));
    if (currentStep < 2) { dialogCardLayout.setActiveItem(currentStep + 1); }
  }
},
```

This is very much along the lines of the Back button's code, except that here we need to ensure currentStep is less than 2, because Next doesn't work if we're on the final step.

The last button is the Finish button, which clearly has the most work to do:

```
{
  text : "Finish", disabled : true, id : "newProjectFinish",
  handler : function() {
    var vals0 = Ext.getCmp("0newProject").getForm().getValues();
    var vals1 = Ext.getCmp("1newProject").getForm().getValues();
    var vals2 = Ext.getCmp("2newProject").getForm().getValues();
    var doAdd = true;
    if (projectsStore.getById(vals0.newProjectName)) {
      alert("Project WAS NOT created " +
        "because a project already exists with that name");
        doAdd = false;
    }
    if (doAdd) {
      var newID = vals0.newProjectName;
      var newRecord = new ProjectRecord({
        name : vals0.newProjectName,
        description : vals0.newProjectDescription,
        projectmanager : vals1.newProjectPM,
        startdate : vals2.newProjectStartDate,
        enddate : vals2.newProjectEndDate,
        allocatedhours : vals2.newProjectAllocatedHours
      }, newID);
      projectsStore.add(newRecord);
      var rootNode = Ext.getCmp("projectsTree").getRootNode();
      rootNode.appendChild(
        new Ext.tree.TreeNode({
          id : "project~@~" + newID, text : vals0.newProjectName
        }));
      rootNode.expand();
    }
    Ext.getCmp("dialogNewProject").hide();
  }
}
],
```

The handler defined for the Finish button begins by getting a reference to all three of the forms, one on each page of the wizard flow. It then uses the getValues() method of the form to get an object for each that has fields corresponding to the values entered in the form. The next step is a check to ensure that no project currently exists in the projectsStore with the name that was entered. If that is the case, then a message is displayed via alert() to inform the user the project could not be added. Next, if the add is OK to continue, a new ProjectRecord is created, taking values from all three of the forms. The ID of the record is set to the same value as the name The ProjectRecord constructor, any Record constructor actually, takes two arguments. The first is an object that the DataReader reads to populate the ProjectRecord, and the second, which is optional, is the ID to assign to the ProjectRecord. Note that an id field on the Record is different from the ID the store knows the Record as. Supplying this second argument to the constructor gives each Record in the Store a unique ID that you can then use to retrieve the Record by later. Without an ID, you are left to scanning through all the Records to find what you want, which is inefficient and requires more work on your part.

Next, the new ProjectRecord is added to the projectsStore. This triggers the add event on the store, which calls the DAO's createProject() method to save the project to the database.

You might think that's the end of the story, but you'd be mistaken! Next, we need to add the project to the Project View Tree. To do this, we must get a handle to the root node, which we do by calling getRootNode() on the Tree itself. Next, we call appendChild() on that root node and pass it a new Ext.tree.TreeNode object. The TreeNode has two fields: text, which is the text seen in the Tree, and id, which is the internal ID the TreeNode is known by. We also pass a value for icon to specify the image to display next to the node. At this point we also call expand() on the root node so that all the projects are again visible.

Finally, the New Project Window is hidden and we're all done.

Moving on, we now come to this code:

```
items : [{
  layout : "card", activeItem : 0, id : "dialogNewProjectCard",
  items : [
    {
```

This is the definition of the CardLayout that houses the cards, each one of which is a step in the wizard. The first item in the items array looks like this:

```
xtype : "form", title : "Step 1/3", width : 400, height : 340,
id : "0newProject", bodyStyle : "padding:5px", monitorValid : true,
frame : true, labelWidth : 100, hideMode : "offsets",
items : [
  { html : "<b>Welcome to the New Project wizard!<br><br>" +
      "This wizard will walk you through creating a new project " +
      "to track with TimekeeperExt.<br><br>" +
      "Please begin by entering a name for your project, as " +
      "well as a brief description of it.</b><br><br><br>" },
  { xtype : "textfield", fieldLabel : "Project Name",
    name : "newProjectName", width : 220, allowBlank : false },
  { xtype : "textarea", fieldLabel : "Description",
    name : "newProjectDescription", width : 220, height : 80,
    allowBlank : false }
],
listeners : {
  clientvalidation : function(inFomPanel, inValid) {
    var dialogCardLayout =
      Ext.getCmp("dialogNewProjectCard").getLayout();
    var currentStep =
      parseInt(dialogCardLayout.activeItem.getId().substr(0, 1));
```

```
        if (currentStep == 0) {
          if (inValid) {
            Ext.getCmp("newProjectNext").enable();
          } else {
            Ext.getCmp("newProjectNext").disable();
          }
        }
      }
    }
  }
},
```

That's the definition for the first page of the wizard. It doesn't look much different than the previous FormPanels we've look at; however, there is one new attribute: hideMode. When set to offsets, as it is here, the FormPanel will be hidden by moving it off screen, rather than setting visible or display style attribute on it. This was necessary because without it the ComboBox on the second step didn't display right (the drop-down portion wasn't the same width as the text box portion). This has to do with Ext JS needing to get width values of various components, and that doesn't work if the element isn't visible. Fortunately, even if the element is positioned to, say, –1000 pixels to the left, which pushes it off the left side of the page, the browser considers it to still be visible even if the user can't see it, and those calculations work properly.

The first element in the items array is just some instructions to the user. After that are two form elements: a TextField for entering the project's name and a TextArea for entering a description.

Notice that both are defined as required (allowBlank:false). Also notice that the monitorValid config option was set to true. In the past, we've seen how we can have a button that enables and disables depending on the validity of the form. Here, we'd want the Finish button to work that way. Unfortunately, it doesn't seem to be possible to tie a button to the state of multiple forms, as we'd also need to do here. So instead, we use the listeners list and handle the clientvalidation event. This fires any time the validation state of the form changes. In this function, the code gets a reference to the currently active card, and if it's the first step and if the inValid argument was true, then the Next button is enabled. Notice that the Finish button isn't dealt with here. That's because the Finish button can only be activated on the last step of the wizard, and to get there the Next button would have to have been enabled on this step first.

Moving on, the second step of the wizard is shown in Figure 4-15.

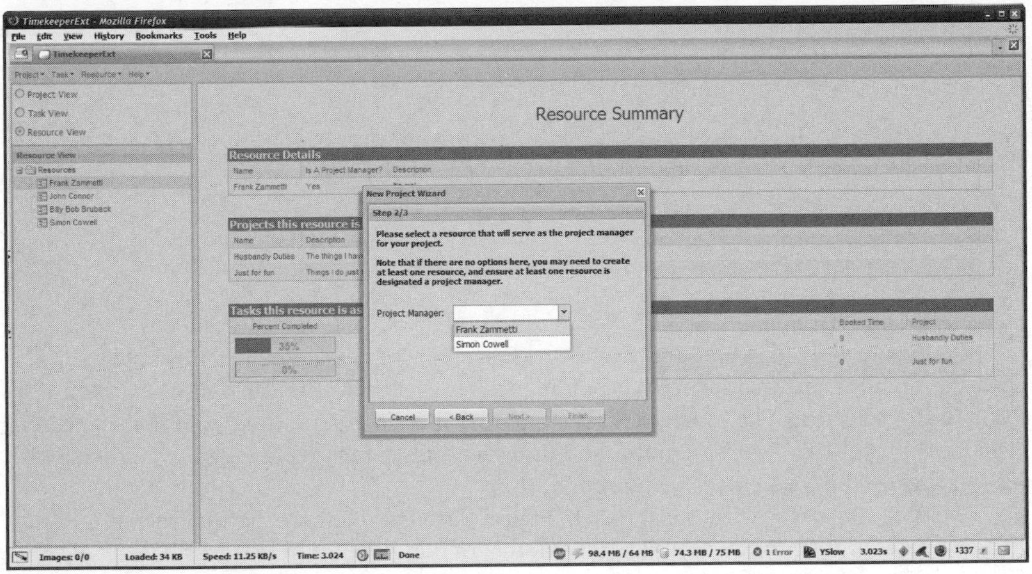

Figure 4-15. *Page 2 of the New Project Wizard*

All available PMs are presented in a `ComboBox`, which works well since only a single PM can be assigned to a project. Once the PM has been chosen, the user can move on to the third page of the wizard, where the user will select a start and end date for the project and declare how many hours are allocated to the project.

```
{
  xtype : "form", title : "Step 2/3", width : 400, height : 340,
  bodyStyle : "padding:5px", id : "1newProject", monitorValid : true,
  frame : true, labelWidth : 100, hideMode : "offsets",
  items : [
    { html : "<b>Please select a resource that will serve as the " +
        "project manager for your project.<br><br>Note that if " +
        "there are no options here, you may need to create at least " +
        "one resource, and ensure at least one resource is "+
        "designated a project manager.</b><br><br><br>" },
    { xtype : "combo", fieldLabel : "Project Manager",
      name : "newProjectPM", allowBlank : false,
      editable : false, triggerAction : "all",
      mode : "local", store : projectManagersStore,
      valueField : "name", displayField : "name" }
  ],
  listeners : {
    clientvalidation : function(inFomPanel, inValid) {
      var dialogCardLayout =
        Ext.getCmp("dialogNewProjectCard").getLayout();
      var currentStep =
        parseInt(dialogCardLayout.activeItem.getId().substr(0, 1));
```

```
            if (currentStep == 1) {
              if (inValid) {
                Ext.getCmp("newProjectNext").enable();
              } else {
                Ext.getCmp("newProjectNext").disable();
              }
            }
          }
        }
      },
```

It is largely defined in the same way as the first step; the only difference is that there is a ComboBox on this step. That ComboBox is bound to the projectManagersStore, so only PMs are available for selection. The ComboBox is set up to work like a regular <select>, so the user can't type anything in. This field is required, and the clientvalidation event is again handled and again activates the Next button, if appropriate.

The final step of the wizard is shown in Figure 4-16. This is where the user selects a start and end date for the project, as well as the number of hours allocated to the project.

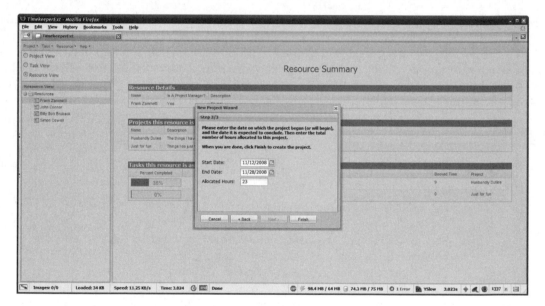

Figure 4-16. *Page 3 of the New Project Wizard*

Once again, the definition of this step doesn't deviate too much from the previous step, nor does the clientvalidation handler code:

```
          {
            xtype : "form", title : "Step 3/3", width : 400, height : 340,
            bodyStyle : "padding:5px", id : "2newProject", monitorValid : true,
            frame : true, labelWidth : 100, hideMode : "offsets",
            items : [
              { html : "<b>Please enter the date on which the project began (or " +
                  "will begin), and the date it is expected to conclude.  Then " +
                  "enter the total number of hours allocated to this project." +
                  "<br><br>When you are done, click Finish to create " +
                  "the project.</b><br><br><br>" },
              { xtype : "datefield", fieldLabel : "Start Date",
                name : "newProjectStartDate", allowBlank : false },
              { xtype : "datefield", fieldLabel : "End Date",
                name : "newProjectEndDate", allowBlank : false },
              { xtype : "numberfield", fieldLabel : "Allocated Hours",
                name : "newProjectAllocatedHours", width : 75, allowBlank : false }
            ],
            listeners : {
              clientvalidation : function(inFomPanel, inValid) {
                var dialogCardLayout =
                  Ext.getCmp("dialogNewProjectCard").getLayout();
                var currentStep =
                  parseInt(dialogCardLayout.activeItem.getId().substr(0, 1));
                if (currentStep == 2) {
                  Ext.getCmp("newProjectNext").disable();
                  if (inValid) {
                    Ext.getCmp("newProjectFinish").enable();
                  } else {
                    Ext.getCmp("newProjectFinish").disable();
                  }
                }
              }
            }
          }
        ]
      }]
};
```

Here, we have two DateFields for the user to choose a start and end date. The Allocated Hours field is a NumberField, so we know users are entering a valid numeric value by default. In the clientvalidation handler, it's time to enable the Finish button now, assuming the form on the step is valid. Also, we know at this point that the Next button can be disabled, so we do that as well.

Take some time now to look at the New Task and New Resource dialogs' code; they follow the same general model as this one. We will move on now to the dialogs for modifying existing entities (and because each of them is fairly different, we'll look at all three for a change!).

ModifyProjectDialog.js

Now that we've seen how new projects are created, it's time to see how existing ones are modified. The Modify Project dialog is not a wizard paradigm like the dialog for creating a new project; instead, it uses a simple tab-based UI metaphor. Take a look at Figure 4-17, which shows the Details tab of the Modify Project dialog.

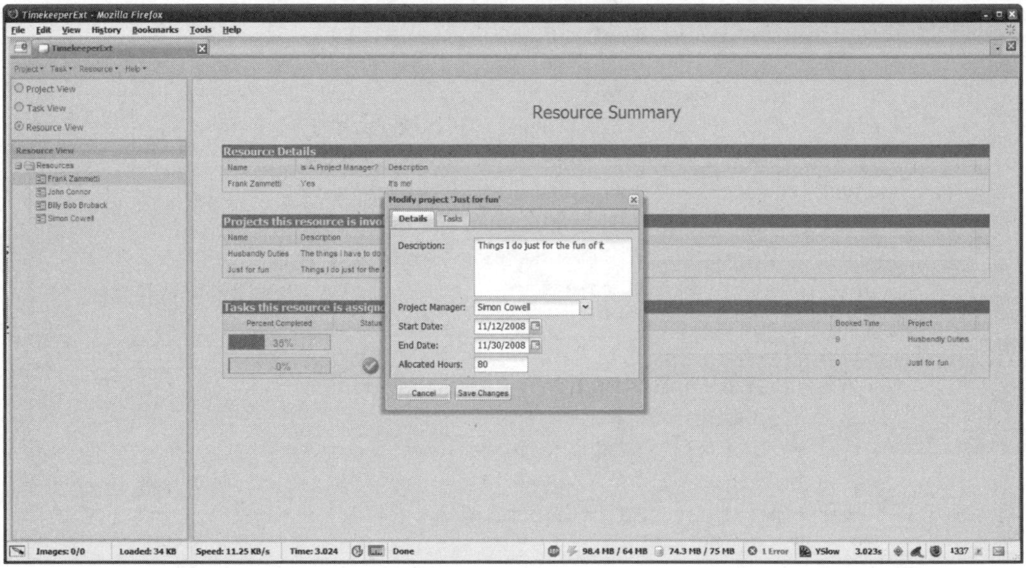

Figure 4-17. *The Modify Project dialog's Details tab*

There is also a Tasks tab where tasks are assigned to the project. Before we see that, though, let's get to the start of the code found in ModifyProjectDialog.js:

```
var uioModifyProjectWindow = {
  title : "", closable : true, modal : true, id : "dialogModifyProject",
  width : 360, height : 300, minimizable : false, resizable : false,
  draggable : true, shadowOffset : 8, closeAction : "hide",
```

This is the same sort of Window configuration we saw previously. A beforeshow event handler is defined in the listeners object, as you can see here:

```
listeners : {
  beforeshow : function() {
    this.setTitle("Modify project '" + currentProject.get("name") + "'");
    var detailsForm = Ext.getCmp("modifyProjectDetails").getForm();
    detailsForm.setValues({
      "modifyProjectDescription" : currentProject.get("description"),
      "modifyProjectStartDate" : currentProject.get("startdate"),
      "modifyProjectEndDate" : currentProject.get("enddate"),
      "modifyProjectPM" : currentProject.get("projectmanager"),
      "modifyProjectAllocatedHours" : currentProject.get("allocatedhours")
    });
```

```
    tempAvailableTasksStore.removeAll();
    availableTasksStore.each(function(inRecord) {
      tempAvailableTasksStore.add(inRecord.copy());
    });
    tempAllocatedTasksStore.removeAll();
    tasksStore.each(function(inRecord) {
      if (inRecord.get("project") == currentProject.get("name")) {
        tempAllocatedTasksStore.add(inRecord.copy());
      }
    });
  }
},
```

The job of this event handler is to first set the title of the Window to indicate the project being modified. Then, it populates the form that is present on the Details tab. To do so, we call Ext.getCmp("modifyProjectDetails") to get a handle to the FormPanel, and then call getForm() to get the underlying form. Ext JS provides us with a handy convenience method hanging off the form: setValues(), which takes as an argument a simple object. This object has fields with names matching the fields in the form. The setValues() method iterates over the fields in the form and sets the values from the fields in the object, if a matching field is found. That makes life a lot easier! Since we have currentProject pointing to the appropriate ProjectRecord, it's a simple matter to pull the data from that and put it in the object passed to setValues().

Once that's done we need to populate the tempAvailableTasksStore and the tempAllocatedTasksStore, which are used on the Tasks tab to populate the ComboBoxes. The former is the list of tasks not yet assigned to a project, and the latter is the list of tasks assigned to this project (if any). The removeAll() method is used first to clear each of the stores. Then, to populate tempAvailableTasksStore, we use the each() method of the availableTasksStore to iterate over its members. For each we create a copy of the Record and add it to tempAvailableTasksStore. For the tempAllocatedTasksStore, we iterate over the collection of Records in tasksStore. For each we see if its project field matches the name of currentProject. If so, a copy is added to tempAllocatedTasksStore.

Next we come to the definition of the buttons seen on the dialog, beginning with the Cancel button:

```
buttons : [
  { text : "Cancel", handler : function() {
    Ext.getCmp("dialogModifyProject").hide(); } },
```

Just like on the New Project dialog, all this button does is hide the dialog. The Save Changes button does a little more, as you can see for yourself:

```
{ text : "Save Changes", disabled : false, id : "modifyProjectSaveChanges",
  handler : function() {
    var valsDetails =
      Ext.getCmp("modifyProjectDetails").getForm().getValues();
    currentProject.beginEdit();
    currentProject.set("description", valsDetails.modifyProjectDescription);
    currentProject.set("projectmanager", valsDetails.modifyProjectPM);
    currentProject.set("startdate", valsDetails.modifyProjectStartDate);
```

```
        currentProject.set("enddate", valsDetails.modifyProjectEndDate);
        currentProject.set("allocatedhours",
          valsDetails.modifyProjectAllocatedHours);
        currentProject.endEdit();
        tempAvailableTasksStore.each(function(inRecord) {
          var record = tasksStore.getById(inRecord.get("name"));
          record.set("project", "");
        });
        tempAllocatedTasksStore.each(function(inRecord) {
          var record = tasksStore.getById(inRecord.get("name"));
          record.set("project", currentProject.get("name"));
        });
        populateProjectsTree();
        populateAvailableTasks();
        if (currentSummaryView == 1) { showProjectSummary(); }
        Ext.getCmp("dialogModifyProject").hide();
      }
    }
  ],
```

First, the values from the form named `modifyProjectDetails` are retrieved. Next, we call `beginEdit()` on `currentProject`. This is something we haven't seen before. As you'll recall, when you edit a `Record`, it fires an `update` event, and if you've written an event handler for it, your code will execute. That would be bad in this case because the `update` event handler calls a `DAO` method to save the updated data to the database. It would be inefficient to do that every time a single field was updated, which is precisely what would happen here. By calling `beginEdit()` on the `ProjectRecord`, the `update` event will not fire until the `endEdit()` method is called. You can think of it as batching of updates. Only a single `update` event will fire now, and therefore the `DAO` will only be called once, regardless of how much we modify the `ProjectRecord`.

Each of the fields that can be modified is updated, and the code is a little stupid to the extent that it doesn't do any "has this field changed?" sort of logic. Because we're batching all these updates it doesn't matter; it's a single hit on the database so it'll do no harm. It also seems that Ext JS is smart enough to not mark a field as changed that has been updated with the same value it currently has, so that's definitely good.

Once `endEdit()` is called, the `update` event fires, the `DAO` is called, and the modified data is written to the database. That's not all we need to have happen here, though. We also need to mark any tasks that are now allocated to this project as no longer available, and likewise we have to mark as available any task that was previously allocated this project but no longer is. To do this we iterate over the `Records` in the two temporary stores, beginning with `tempAvailableTasksStore`. For each `TaskRecord` in that store, we look up the `TaskRecord` in the `tasksStore` with the same `name` (remember, we only have a copy of that record in `tempAvailableTasksStore`) and set its `project` field to a blank string, which makes it available again. Similarly, we iterate over the `TaskRecords` in `tempAllocatedTasksStore` and for each, look up the `TaskRecord` with the same `name` in `tasksStore` and set its `project` field to the `name` of `currentProject`. The `update` event will fire for any modified `TaskRecord` and the change will be written to the database.

The other things we need to do here are update the Project View Tree and update the list of available tasks. The Tree needs to be updated to reflect changes in task allocations for currentProject. The availableTasksStore needs to be updated so that if the user tries to use the Modify Project dialog again, the list of available tasks accurately reflects these latest changes.

Also, if currentSummaryView's value is 1, which means the Project Summary view is showing, we need to call showProjectSummary() as well so that task allocation changes are reflected there immediately as well. That wraps up the Save Changes button!

Now we can look at the configuration that defines the UI of the Window:

```
items : [{
  xtype : "tabpanel", activeTab : 0, width : 360, height : 300, items : [
```

As mentioned earlier, a tabbed interface is used here, which means an xtype of tabpanel. The first tab is defined like so:

```
{ title : "Details", xtype : "form",
  id : "modifyProjectDetails", bodyStyle : "padding:5px",
  monitorValid : true, frame : true, labelWidth : 100,
  items : [
    { xtype : "textarea", fieldLabel : "Description",
      name : "modifyProjectDescription", width : 220, height : 80,
      allowBlank : false },
    { xtype : "combo", fieldLabel : "Project Manager",
      name : "modifyProjectPM", allowBlank : false, editable : false,
      triggerAction : "all", mode : "local", store : projectManagersStore,
      valueField : "name", displayField : "name" },
    { xtype : "datefield", fieldLabel : "Start Date",
      name : "modifyProjectStartDate", allowBlank : false },
    { xtype : "datefield", fieldLabel : "End Date",
      name : "modifyProjectEndDate", allowBlank : false },
    { xtype : "numberfield", fieldLabel : "Allocated Hours",
      name : "modifyProjectAllocatedHours", width : 75, allowBlank : false }
  ],
  listeners : {
    clientvalidation : function(inFomPanel, inValid) {
      if (inValid) {
        Ext.getCmp("modifyProjectSaveChanges").enable();
      } else{
        Ext.getCmp("modifyProjectSaveChanges").disable();
      }
    }
  }
},
```

This is all very much along the lines of what you've explored before. You can see again that the clientvalidation event is handled to enable and disable the Save Changes button as appropriate. This ensures that all required fields are filled in, and that those fields that have other types of validations are valid too.

Note In this case it probably would have been fine to bind the Save Changes button to the state of the `modifyProjectDetails` button, similar to what you saw in the OrganizerExt project. There isn't any master plan behind why I didn't do it that way here other than I was following the same pattern I'd used in the code for the New Project dialog. Take it as a demonstration of an alternative approach with no deeper meaning!

The second tab is where tasks are assigned to the project. Figure 4-18 shows what this tab looks like. You can see where I've expanded the Allocated Tasks (the tasks allocated to this project).

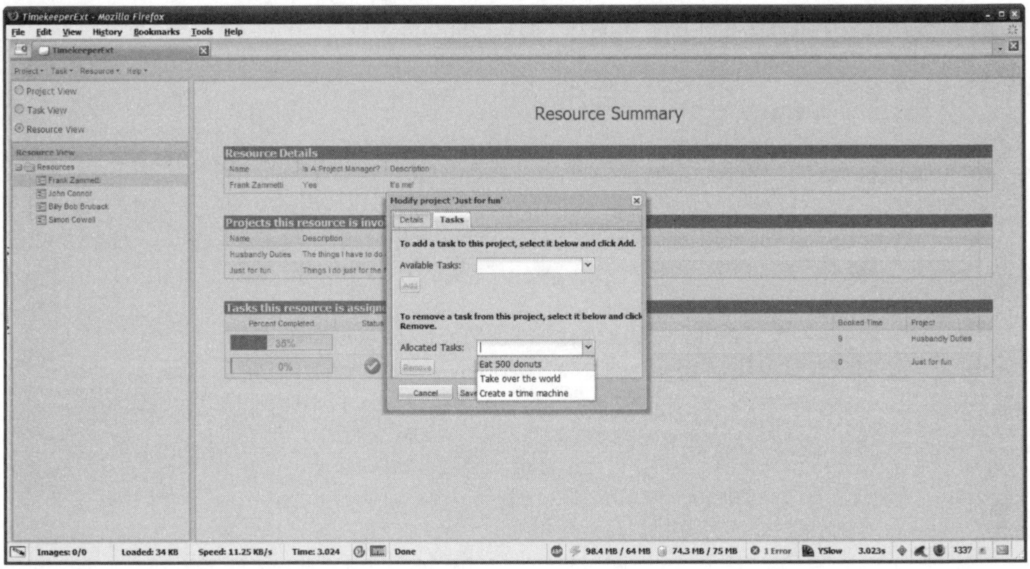

Figure 4-18. *The Modify Project dialog's Tasks tab*

The code that creates this tab's content is a little more complex than the Details tab, but is little more than an extension of things we've seen before:

```
{ title : "Tasks", xtype : "form", id : "modifyProjectTasks",
  bodyStyle : "padding:5px", frame : true, labelWidth : 100, items : [
    { html : "<b>To add a task to this project, select it below and " +
      "click Add.</b><br><br>" },
    { xtype : "combo", fieldLabel : "Available Tasks",
      name : "modifyProjectAvailableTasks", allowBlank : true,
      editable : false, triggerAction : "all", mode : "local",
      store : tempAvailableTasksStore, valueField : "name",
      displayField : "name", id : "modifyProjectAvailableTasks",
      listeners : {
        select : function(inComboBox, inRecord, inIndex) {
          Ext.getCmp("modifyProjectAddTaskButton").enable();
```

```
        }
      }
    },
    { xtype : "button", text : "Add", disabled : true,
      id : "modifyProjectAddTaskButton", handler : function() {
        var cb = Ext.getCmp("modifyProjectAvailableTasks");
        var taskName = cb.getValue();
        var taskRecord = tempAvailableTasksStore.getById(taskName);
        tempAllocatedTasksStore.add(taskRecord);
        tempAvailableTasksStore.remove(taskRecord);
        cb.clearValue();
        Ext.getCmp("modifyProjectAllocatedTasks").clearValue();
        this.disable();
      }
    },
    { html : "<br><br><b>To remove a task from this project, select it " +
      "below and click Remove.</b><br><br>" },
    { xtype : "combo", fieldLabel : "Allocated Tasks",
      name : "modifyProjectAllocatedTasks", allowBlank : true,
      editable : false, triggerAction : "all", mode : "local",
      store : tempAllocatedTasksStore, valueField : "name",
      displayField : "name", id : "modifyProjectAllocatedTasks",
      listeners : {
        select : function(inComboBox, inRecord, inIndex) {
          Ext.getCmp("modifyProjectRemoveTaskButton").enable();
        }
      }
    },
    { xtype : "button", text : "Remove", disabled : true,
      id : "modifyProjectRemoveTaskButton", handler : function() {
        var cb = Ext.getCmp("modifyProjectAllocatedTasks");
        var taskName = cb.getValue();
        var taskRecord = tempAllocatedTasksStore.getById(taskName);
        tempAvailableTasksStore.add(taskRecord);
        tempAllocatedTasksStore.remove(taskRecord);
        cb.clearValue();
        Ext.getCmp("modifyProjectAvailableTasks").clearValue();
        this.disable();
      }
    }
  ]
  }
}
]
}]
};
```

This code is interesting because the plain text sections are interspersed with the `ComboBox`es as well as the buttons. The first `ComboBox`, which is bound to the `tempAvailableTasksStore`, lists all tasks that aren't currently allocated to a project. Remember that a task can be allocated to only a single project, so a `ComboBox` is a good choice here. The user can select one of the tasks and click the Add button, which removes it from this `ComboBox` and adds it to the second Allocated Tasks `ComboBox`.

Notice that the two `ComboBox`es have a `select` event handler defined that enables the associated button. So, when an item is selected in the Available Tasks `ComboBox`, the Add button is enabled, and when an item is selected in the Allocated Tasks `ComboBox`, the Remove button is enabled. Then, each button has a handler defined, which is the function that is executed when it is clicked. For the Add button, that code gets a reference to the `modifyProjectAvailableTasks` `ComboBox` and calls its `getValue()` method. This gives us the name of the task being added to this project. The `TaskRecord` with that `name` is then added to the `tempAllocatedTasksStore`. It is then removed from the `tempAvailableTasksStore`. Finally, the value selected in both `ComboBox`es is cleared by calling `clearValue()` on each, and the Add button is disabled.

Similarly, the Remove button's handler removes the `TaskRecord` from the `tempAllocatedTasksStore` and adds it to the `tempAvailableTasksStore`. It then clears both `ComboBox`es and disabled the Remove button.

Note that none of these operations triggers any database modifications. That's the point of using copies of the `Record`s in these temporary stores: none of these changes hits the database, or even the canonical data stores, until Save Changes is clicked. If the user clicks Cancel, or clicks the `Window`'s X close icon, there is no harm; these temporary changes simply go away. No harm, no foul, as they say in basketball!

ModifyResourceDialog.js

I think it makes sense to look at some of the code for the Modify Resource dialog. While much of the code is similar to the Modify Project dialog, there are a few parts that are different. I'll cut out the really redundant parts and only look at the delta between them. First, though, let's get a glimpse of this dialog (see Figure 4-19).

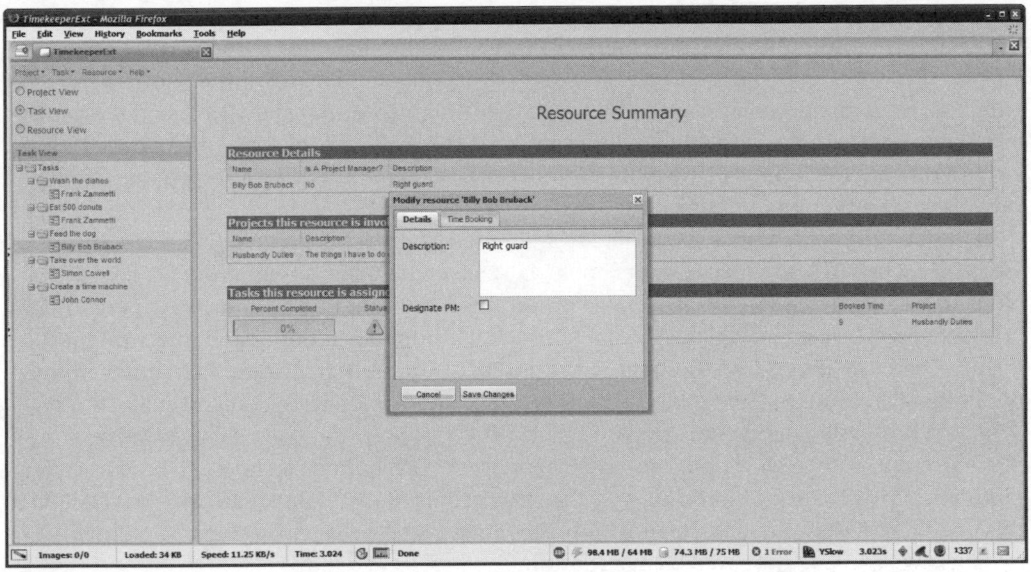

Figure 4-19. *The Modify Resource dialog's Details tab*

As with the Modify Project dialog, a tabbed interface is used. First, let's look at the beforeshow event handler for this dialog:

```
listeners : {
  beforeshow : function() {
    this.setTitle("Modify resource '" + currentResource.get("name") + "'");
    var detailsForm = Ext.getCmp("modifyResourceDetails").getForm();
    detailsForm.setValues({
      "modifyResourceDescription" : currentResource.get("description"),
      "modifyResourceIsAPM" :
        (currentResource.get("isaprojectmanager") == "Yes" ? true : false)
    });
    var modifyResourceHoursUsed = Ext.getCmp("modifyResourceHoursUsed");
    modifyResourceHoursUsed.setValue("");
    modifyResourceHoursUsed.disable();
    Ext.getCmp("modifyResourceBookButton").disable();
    tempAssignedTasksStore.removeAll();
    tasksStore.each(function(inRecord) {
      if (inRecord.get("resource") == currentResource.get("name")) {
        tempAssignedTasksStore.add(inRecord.copy());
      }
    });
    Ext.getCmp("modifyResourceAssignedTasks").setValue("");
  }
},
```

This code does the same sort of tasks as that of the Modify Project dialog. The title of the `Window` is set, and then the form on the Details tab is populated from the values in the `ResourceRecord` referenced by `currentResource`. Note the `modifyResourceIsAPM` form field, which I'll jump the gun a little and tell you is a check box. To set its value, we need to supply a `Boolean`, but the value stored in the isaprojectmanager field of the `ResourceRecord` is the string "Yes" or "No" (and it's one of those rather than a real `Boolean` because it made displaying this value easier on the summary views).

Next, on the Time Booking tab (Figure 4-20, a few pages hence) you'll find there is a `TextField` where the number of hours booked to a given task can be entered. This field is cleared, and disabled, and the associated Book button is disabled. The `ComboBox` where the task is selected will be cleared when the store to which it is bound is repopulated (more on that soon!). Therefore, these three fields are in a consistent state—that is, users can't enter a number for booked time until they've selected a task, and the Book button can't be enabled until a booked time value has been entered.

Next, the store to which the Assigned Tasks `ComboBox` is bound on the Time Booking tab is populated. This is done by iterating over the `TaskRecords` in the `tasksStore`. For each task that this resource is assigned to work on, a copy is added to `tempAssignedTasksStore`.

Next we come to the Save Changes button:

```
{ text : "Save Changes", disabled : false, id : "modifyResourceSaveChanges",
  handler : function() {
    var valsDetails =
      Ext.getCmp("modifyResourceDetails").getForm().getValues();
    var doSave = true;
    if (!valsDetails.modifyResourceIsAPM) {
      var resourceName = currentResource.get("name");
      projectsStore.each(function(inRecord) {
        if (inRecord.get("projectmanager") == resourceName) {
          alert("Resource WAS NOT modified " +
            "because PM designation cannot be changed while resource " +
            "is PM of a project");
          doSave = false;
        }
      });
    }
    if (doSave) {
      currentResource.beginEdit();
      currentResource.set("description",
        valsDetails.modifyResourceDescription);
      currentResource.set("isaprojectmanager",
        valsDetails.modifyResourceIsAPM ? "Yes" : "No");
      currentResource.endEdit();
      tempAssignedTasksStore.each(function(inRecord) {
        if (inRecord.dirty) {
          var taskRecord = tasksStore.getById(inRecord.id);
          taskRecord.set("bookedtime", inRecord.get("bookedtime"));
```

```
        }
      });
      if (currentSummaryView == 3) { showResourceSummary(); }
    }
    Ext.getCmp("dialogModifyResource").hide();
  }
}
],
```

First, all of the values on the form on the details are gotten, and the value of the modifyResourceIsAPM field is checked. This is a check box, which means it has a Boolean value, so if it isn't checked, the code checks to see if any project in the projectsStore has this resource assigned as its PM. If so, then the change is aborted because we can no longer make a resource a PM if they're assigned as PM on a project. A message is shown via alert() to indicate the failure and that's it; nothing else is done after that in this case.

If the change is going to proceed, we see the same sort of beginEdit() being called on the currentResource as we saw with Modify Project. The fields that can be updated are. Special care is taken with the isaprojectmanager field to translate from a simple Boolean to a string "Yes" for true and "No" for false. The endEdit() is called, and the changes trigger the update event and a call to the DAO.

Next, we use the each() method to iterate over the TaskRecords in the tempAssigned TasksStore. For each we look at the dirty field. This is a field—every Record has one—that will be set to true if the data in the TaskRecord has been modified. If it has, then we look up the canonical TaskRecord matching this task's name in tasksStore and set its bookedtime field to the value of the bookedtime field in the TaskRecord from tempAssignedTasksStore.

Next, if the Resource Summary is currently showing, it is refreshed to show any changes. Let's now look at the definition for the first tab, Details:

```
{ title : "Details", xtype : "form",
  id : "modifyResourceDetails", bodyStyle : "padding:5px",
  monitorValid : true, frame : true, labelWidth : 100,
  items : [{
      xtype : "textarea", fieldLabel : "Description",
      name : "modifyResourceDescription", width : 220, height : 80,
      allowBlank : false },
    { xtype : "checkbox", fieldLabel : "Designate PM",
      name : "modifyResourceIsAPM", allowBlank : false }
  ],
  listeners : {
    clientvalidation : function(inFomPanel, inValid) {
      if (inValid) {
        Ext.getCmp("modifyResourceSaveChanges").enable();
      } else{
        Ext.getCmp("modifyResourceSaveChanges").disable();
      }
    }
  }
},
```

I suspect this is very much as you'd expect. The `clientvalidation` event is used again to enable or disable the Save Changes button. Again, it is done this way just to follow a consistent approach throughout this project.

The Time Booking tab has a bit more meat on its bones, as you can see:

```
{ title : "Time Booking", xtype : "form",
  id : "modifyResourceTimeBooking", bodyStyle : "padding:5px",
  frame : true, labelWidth : 100, items : [
    { xtype : "combo", fieldLabel : "Assigned Tasks", editable : false,
      name : "modifyResourceAssignedTasks", allowBlank : true,
      id : "modifyResourceAssignedTasks",
      triggerAction : "all", mode : "local",
      store : tempAssignedTasksStore, valueField : "name",
      displayField : "name", listeners : {
        select : function(inComboBox, inRecord, inIndex) {
          Ext.getCmp("modifyResourceHoursUsed").enable();
        }
      }
    },
    { xtype : "numberfield", fieldLabel : "Hours Used", disabled : true,
      name : "modifyResourceHoursUsed", width : 75, allowBlank : true,
      id : "modifyResourceHoursUsed", enableKeyEvents : true,
      listeners : {
        keyup : function(inNumberField, inEventObject) {
          if (inNumberField.getValue() != "") {
            Ext.getCmp("modifyResourceBookButton").enable();
          } else {
            Ext.getCmp("modifyResourceBookButton").disable();
          }
        }
      }
    },
    { xtype : "button", text : "Book", id : "modifyResourceBookButton",
      disabled : true, handler : function() {
        var modifyResourceHoursUsed =
          Ext.getCmp("modifyResourceHoursUsed");
        var taskRecord = tempAssignedTasksStore.getById(
          Ext.getCmp("modifyResourceAssignedTasks").getValue());
        taskRecord.set("bookedtime", modifyResourceHoursUsed.getValue());
        modifyResourceHoursUsed.setValue("");
        modifyResourceHoursUsed.disable();
        Ext.getCmp("modifyResourceBookButton").disable();
```

```
                }
              }
            ]
          }
        ]
      }]
    };
```

First we see the modifyResourceAssignedTasks ComboBox, bound to the tempAssigned
TasksStore, which lists the task this resource is assigned to. Below that is a NumberField for
entering time booked against the selected task. The select event handler on the ComboBox
enables the modifyResourceHoursUsed NumberField when a task is selected. A keyup event
handler is then tied to the modifyResourceHoursUsed NumberField. Every time a key is pressed
the value of the field is examined. If it isn't empty, then the Book button is enabled; otherwise
it is disabled. This gives us a nice UI where as soon as a number is entered the Book button
becomes available. But if the users backspace and delete their entry, it becomes disabled. In
Figure 4-20 you can see how the Book button is enabled when a value has been entered.

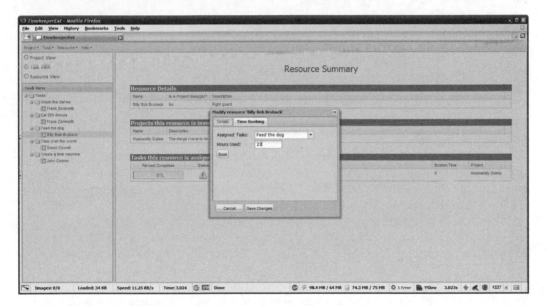

Figure 4-20. *The Modify Resource dialog's Time Booking tab*

Finally, the Book button has a handler defined. When clicked, it gets the value from
modifyResourceHoursUsed, and then looks up the TaskRecord from tempAssignedTasksStore
based on the value of the modifyResourceAssignedTasks ComboBox. It sets the bookedtime field
of that TaskRecord, and then clears the NumberField and ComboBox. Finally, it disables itself.

ModifyTaskDialog.js

The code in `ModifyTaskDialog.js` is similar to the previous two dialogs and thus it's probably not necessary to go over it here. The only real difference is that it's a bit simpler: as you can see in Figure 4-21, this dialog does not use a tab-based interface.

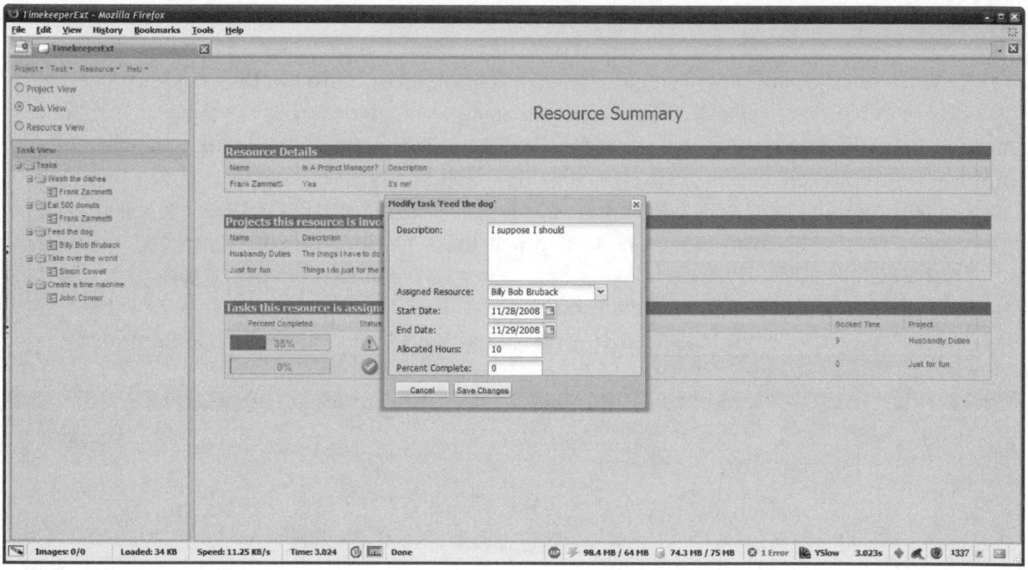

Figure 4-21. *The Modify Task dialog*

Since there's not as much information for a task that can be modified, a single `Panel` does the trick just fine. Everything we've seen before applies to this dialog. For example, there is a `beforeshow` event handler that populates the form in exactly the same way as the previous two dialogs. There is a temporary `Store` populated that the Project Manager `ComboBox` is bound to, and this `Store` is generated by copying records out of the `projectManagersStore`.

A `clientvalidation` event handler is attached to the form to enable the Save Changes button if all required form fields are filled in and if all fields are valid. Otherwise, it disables them.

The `TaskRecord` is updated in the same way as we've seen before, and the Task Summary view is refreshed if it is currently showing. Also, the Task View `Tree` and the Project View `Tree` are both refreshed because changes in this dialog could impact what should be displayed in them.

As usual, I suggest looking over the code in the download package. I wouldn't expect it would take more than a few minutes if you've read our discussion on the previous two dialogs.

DeleteProjectDialog.js, DeleteResourceDialog.js, and DeleteTaskDialog.js

The `DeleteProjectDialog.js`, `DeleteResourceDialog.js`, and `DeleteTaskDialog.js` files contain the configuration object for the three dialog `Windows` displayed when you want to delete a project, resource, or task. As with so much of the rest of this project, the task and resource code was created by copying the code for the project and making the appropriate changes.

Therefore, we'll just look at DeleteProjectDialog.js, secure in the knowledge that it is representative of the other two.

```
var uioDeleteProjectWindow = {
  title : "", closable : true, modal : true,
  width : 450, height : 200, minimizable : false, resizable : false,
  draggable : false, shadowOffset : 8, closeAction : "hide",
  id : "dialogDeleteProject", listeners : {
    beforeshow : function() {
      this.setTitle("Confirm deletion of project '" +
        currentProject.get("name") + "'");
    }
  },
  buttons : [
    { text : "No", handler : function() {
        Ext.getCmp("dialogDeleteProject").hide(); } },
    { text : "Yes",
      handler : function() {
        var doDelete = true;
        var projectName = currentProject.get("name");
        tasksStore.each(function(inRecord) {
          if (inRecord.get("project") == projectName) {
            alert("Project WAS NOT deleted " +
              "because it has tasks allocated to it");
            doDelete = false;
          }
        });
        if (doDelete) {
          projectsStore.remove(currentProject);
          Ext.getCmp("projectsTree").getNodeById(
            "project~@~" + currentProject.get("name")).remove();
          currentProject = null;
          showProjectSummary();
          Ext.getCmp("menuProjectDeleteProject").disable();
          Ext.getCmp("menuProjectModifyProject").disable();
        }
        Ext.getCmp("dialogDeleteProject").hide();
      }
    }
  ],
  items : [{
    html :
      "<table width=\"100%\" height=\"100%\" border=\"0\" cellpadding=\"0\" " +
      "cellspacing=\"0\"><tr><td class=\"cssAbout\" align=\"center\" " +
      "valign=\"middle\">Are you sure you want to delete the " +
      "selected project?</td></tr></table>"
  }]
};
```

In Figure 4-22 you can see what this dialog (indeed, all three of these dialogs) looks like.

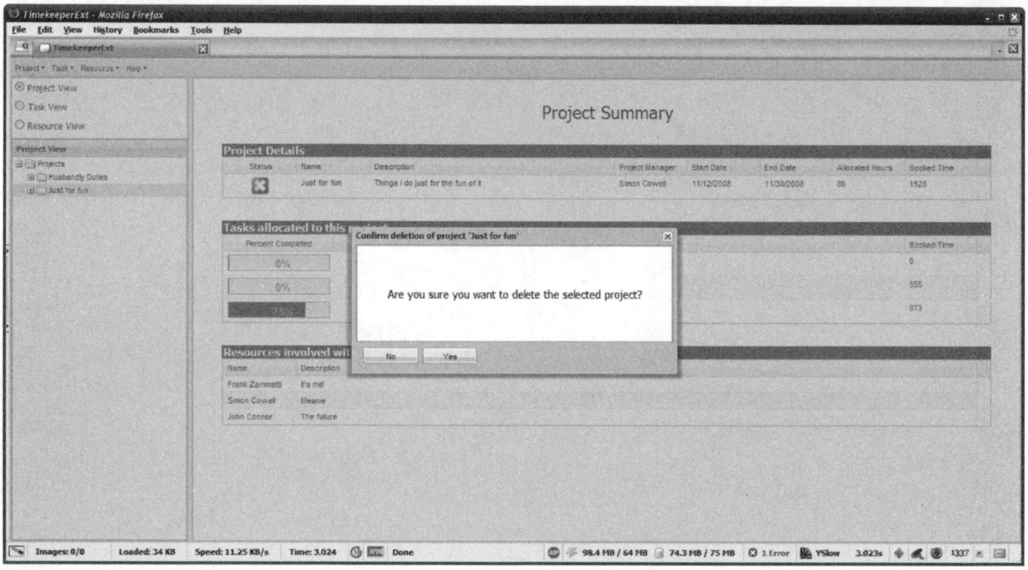

Figure 4-22. *The Delete Project dialog*

The code is pretty straightforward. The Window is defined as having an id of dialog
DeleteProject. It is defined as being closable (closable:true), modal (modal:true)—
so that it is effectively a lightbox—not minimizable, not resizable, and not draggable
(minimizable:false, resizable:false, and draggable:false). The Window is given a size of
450×200 (width:450 and height:200), and we make the shadow a little bigger by specifying
shadowOffset:8. Finally, the closeAction is set to hide so that when the user clicks the X to
close the Window, it will be hidden and not destroyed.

Also note that the title attribute is a blank string. This will be populated dynamically,
and in fact that's what we see next as part of the listeners object. The beforeshow event fires
before the Window is shown, and here we call the setTitle() method on the Window to set the
title to the value of the name field of the ProjectRecord pointed to by currentProject.

After that we find the buttons array, which defines the Yes and No buttons you see at the
bottom. The Window knows how and where to place these buttons; we only have to tell it what
kind of buttons we have. Each button has a text attribute and a handler attribute. The handler
attribute points to a function that is executed when the button is clicked. For the No button,
that's simply a call to the hide() method of the Window, once we get a handle to it by calling
Ext.getCmp().

The Yes button has a little more work to do, though. First, some validations must be
performed. For a project, that validation is simply to ensure the project doesn't have any
tasks allocated to it. While it would have been nicer if the application set the resource field
of all TaskRecords associated with the project to a blank string to make them available for

assignment again, this validation frankly makes the code simpler and shorter (but feel free to enhance the application in this regard as an exercise!). The validation requires the code to iterate over all `TaskRecords` in the `tasksStore` and look for any that have a `project` field value matching the `name` field of `currentProject`. If any are found, we use the `alert()` function to display a message saying the project cannot be deleted and why.

■**Note** Delete validations are one of the few differences between this and the resource and task delete dialogs. For resources, the validation is required to ensure the resource being deleted isn't assigned as the PM of a project, and to ensure the resource is not assigned to any tasks. Either situation causes the deletion to be aborted. For deletion of a task, the task cannot be deleted if it is assigned to a project. This is the only substantive differences between these three source files.

Once we confirm the project can be deleted, a couple of tasks are required. First, the project is removed from the `projectsStore` via the `remove()` method. You pass this a reference to the `Record` to be removed, which we have by virtue of `currentProject` pointing to it. Next, the node in the Projects `Tree` for the project has to be removed. This requires us to get a reference to the `Tree` itself, and then call its `getNodeById()` method to get a reference to the `TreeNode`. Remember that the ID of the node has the type appended to the front of it, so we need to do that here. Once we have a reference to that `TreeNode`, we have only to call the `remove()` method on it and the `Tree` is automatically updated.

Next, we set `currentProject` to `null` to indicate no project is currently selected, and we call `showProjectSummary()`, which will wind up showing the welcome screen again because `currentProject` is `null`.

Finally, the Delete Project and Modify Project menu items are disabled and the Delete Project dialog itself is hidden (but not destroyed).

The other part of this dialog's definition is what is displayed in the `Window`'s main content area, and that's done using the `items` array. It contains a single element that is just some plain-old HTML.

Now, if you replace the word `project` with `task` or `resource` everywhere in this code, you effectively have the Delete Task and Delete Resource dialogs' code, save for the validations we previously discussed. Take a look at them now just to be sure, but trust me: there are no surprises to be found!

Suggested Exercises

TimekeeperExt is a pretty useful little application. However, as I said in the beginning, it's certainly not on par with Microsoft Project or any number of other project management tools. There are plenty of features you could implement that would make it even better. I will list some of those to you as suggested exercises:

- Did you notice that the project itself doesn't have a percent complete indicator? That would be a nice addition, I think. You should be able to determine an overall percentage based on the percentages of all the constituent tasks.

- Here's a relatively quick and (probably) easy one: add a validation on start and end dates throughout the application to ensure the end date is after the start date. As it stands now, the application would allow that rather illogical situation (barring time-traveling visitors from Gallifrey[7] anyway!)

- Modify the application to allow more than one resource to be assigned to a given task, and also allow a given task to be associated with more than one project. Both of those are fairly significant changes, although they sound simple on the surface. You'll have to toy with the database structure, the UI, the core logic throughout, and more. This would be a challenge, but I believe you'd learn a ton by doing it.

- One key concept in project management is the idea of dependencies—that is, task B can't begin until task A has been completed. TimekeeperExt doesn't have any notion of dependencies at all, so it might be a good idea to add that! It might be as simple as being able to specify what task(s) a new task depends on, not allowing a start date that is before the end date of any of those tasks, and not allowing time to be booked against a task that cannot have started yet. You also probably would want to make the start date not required for a task that is dependent on another.

- The Ext JS tree supports drag-and-drop operations. How cool would it be to be able to drag tasks and resources around to assign them to projects and tasks correspondingly? As Eric Cartman[8] once said, HELLA-COOL! This is another fairly intensive suggestion, although it wouldn't require anywhere near the degree of code change as the previous suggestion, but it *would* require a fair bit of research on your part to figure out how to pull it off.

Summary

In this chapter we took a task that many people, including myself, find it hard to get too excited about, and we created an application that makes it just a little more fun than usual—and we have Ext JS to thank for that! We saw some new UI widgets in action, including the TreePanel, and we saw some others used a bit more, such as the Grid. We saw a different way to structure an Ext JS application, and a different approach to organizing our code. We saw some more action with Gears, focusing on its database component. You also probably learned more project management terminology than you ever wanted to know!

In the next chapter we'll create another handy application that will provide even more exposure to many of the UI capabilities of Ext JS. That project, a code cabinet, will provide a utility where we can stash snippets of code, retrieve them, search for them, and so on.

---

7 Gallifrey is the home world of the Doctor from the long-running British sci-fi show *Dr. Who*, a member of the now-extinct Time Lord race. If you don't know the show, or couldn't guess from the name of his race, the Doctor is a time traveler!

8 Eric Cartman is the obnoxious, overweight, and also hysterically funny kid from the long-running show *South Park*. In one early episode, Cartman uses the term "hella-cool" to describe something that is extremely cool. I'm not able to confirm if the term existed before Cartman uttered it, but it certainly came to prominence after that.

CHAPTER 5

■ ■ ■

A Place for Your Stuff: Code Cabinet Ext

In this chapter, we'll fulfill the need of our obsessive-compulsive personalities and develop an application to store our code snippets in.

As good developers, we quickly learn that "stealing" is better than creating. That is, the more you can find code that does what you need rather than writing it yourself, the better. This doesn't always mean stealing from others (and stealing is just an attempt at humor; it's not actually stealing, of course!). Especially after you do this programming thing for a while, you begin to steal from yourself more and more because you remember that you wrote that function to encrypt passwords a couple of projects ago, or you remember that algorithm you put together for processing account numbers, or whatever else.

Being able to find those snippets of code is a challenge, but it's a challenge we're here to meet! With the help of Ext JS and Gears, we'll create an application that lets us store our snippets, organize them, and even search for them. That's what this chapter is all about. In the process, you'll get some good experience with some new pieces of Ext JS that I think you'll find very interesting indeed!

Let's begin by looking at what we want to accomplish and what we want this application to be able to do.

What's This Application Do, Anyway?

A code cabinet, a virtual filing cabinet for our code snippets, should in many ways model an actual file cabinet. But what does that mean? Here are the bullet points:

- Like a real file cabinet, ours needs drawers. We'll call them categories here. We should be able to create categories with any name so we then have a mechanism with which to categorize our snippets. Being a virtual file cabinet, it will be allowed an unlimited number of drawers. In terms of user interface, let's use a Tree widget to display the categories (although we'll use it essentially like a list in that we won't allow for subcategories—and if you think that sounds like a hint for a suggested enhancement, you're right!).

- Within each category, we can add snippets of code. Each snippet will have pieces of information stored about it, including name, description, author, e-mail address (of the author, presumably!), and URL reference (that is, if we found the snippet online and want to remember the site we got it from). We'll also be able to store notes about the snippet and associated keywords with the snippet to make searching possible. We should also let the code and notes be entered in a rich way, not just in plain text.

- Speaking of searching, we want to be able to search for snippets based on several criteria, and in any combination of criteria. We'll include things like being able to search by name, description, author, keywords, and actual code content.

- Clearly the snippets need to be stored in a persistent way, so let's use Gears for this as we'll do throughout this book.

- We'll need to be able to delete categories and snippets because, hey, we're human and we screw up sometimes!

- By now we have seen two different approaches to architecting an Ext JS application, but why stop with just two? Let's look at a third way to structure things, a way that I for one feel is probably the best of the bunch.

- The entire user interface should be flexible—that is, we should be able to resize sections of it as we wish. Let's also allow the user to collapse and expand most sections. Finally, let's use Ext JS's state-saving capabilities so that the sizes they set persist across executions of the application.

All right, I think we've got enough here to get going, so off we go (if you're a child of the '80s feel free to start singing the theme to *The Great Space Coaster*[1] right about now!) Before we dive into the code, though, let's get an initial glimpse of Code Cabinet Ext, shown in Figure 5-1.

---

1   *The Great Space Coaster* (http://en.wikipedia.org/wiki/The_Great_Space_Coaster) was a children's television show from the early '80s that many of us in our mid-thirties grew up with. Most people tend to remember two things: Knock-Knock the bird, who naturally enough told knock-knock jokes, and Gary Gnu, who did the fake news reports ("No gnews is good gnews with Gary Gnu"). Of course, the theme song tends to stick in our heads too: "...get onboard, step inside, slowly for a magic ride... roaring towards the other side where only rainbows hide..." Ah, the memories!

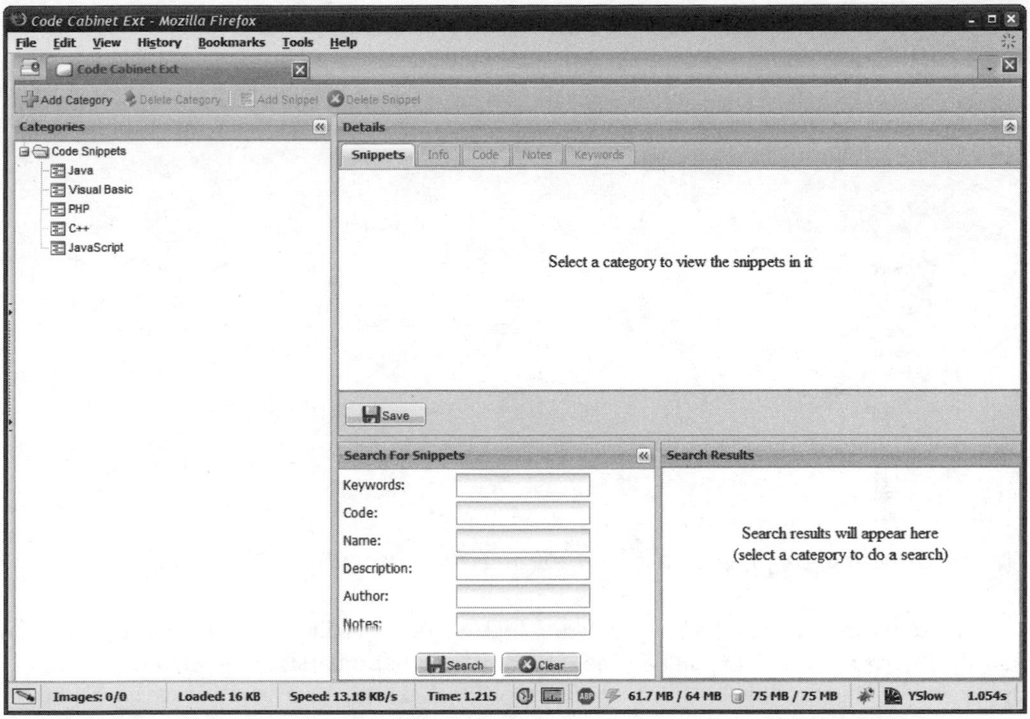

Figure 5-1. *Code Cabinet Ext, in all its (initial) glory*

See, just as described! You'll find the code to be fairly terse, again owing to the power Ext JS provides. In fact, there are number of new capabilities that add to the lack of verbosity of the code… but not, apparently, to the lack of verbosity of my writing, so enough setup, let's get to it, shall we?

Overall Structure and Files

With this project I decided to go with a different architectural approach, which will be discussed as we look at the code. At this point I want to emphasize that this approach is an extension of the previous project. That means we'll see a number of source files for individual UI elements, but there are fewer here, partially because the application itself is simply less complex but also as a result of the architecture. Figure 5-2 shows the breakdown of the application's directory structure.

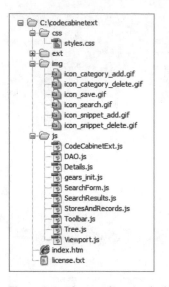

Figure 5-2. *The application's directory structure and constituent files*

We have the usual css directory with the single styles.css file in it, and as you'll see shortly, there's not much to that file. The ext directory is naturally still present, and in this application it is unmodified—that is, no theme or anything has been added as we did in the previous project. The img directory contains a couple of GIF files, all of them icons used on the toolbar and the buttons throughout the application, just to spice them up a little. In the js directory resides all our JavaScript source code. We have the gears_init.js file that we'd expect given that this application uses Gears (like all the others). CodeCabinetExt.js is our "main" source file, but as you'll see, it's fairly sparse. The DAO.js file is our data access object, and StoresAndRecords.js contains the definitions of all the Records and Data Stores we'll need. Each remaining file contains some configuration object that defines an element of the UI. The names I suspect are completely obvious, but if not have no fear; we'll be looking at each individually.

In the root directory we have index.htm, which is where we'll begin our exploration of the code.

■**Note** I may not have mentioned this previously, but all of the projects in this book are licensed under the GPL open source license. This fulfills the Ext JS licensing requirements, but I point it out because that's the reason you find the license.txt file in the root of all the projects and why the GPL license header is present in all the source files.

The Markup

The index.htm file in this application is a fair bit smaller than any of the others we've seen so far:

```html
<html>
  <head>
    <title>Code Cabinet Ext</title>

    <link rel="stylesheet" type="text/css" href="ext/resources/css/ext-all.css">
    <script type="text/javascript" src="ext/adapter/ext/ext-base.js"></script>
    <script type="text/javascript" src="ext/ext-all.js"></script>

    <script src="js/gears_init.js"></script>

    <link rel="stylesheet" type="text/css" href="css/styles.css">
    <script type="text/javascript" src="js/CodeCabinetExt.js"></script>
    <script type="text/javascript" src="js/StoresAndRecords.js"></script>
    <script type="text/javascript" src="js/DAO.js"></script>
    <script type="text/javascript" src="js/Viewport.js"></script>
    <script type="text/javascript" src="js/Toolbar.js"></script>
    <script type="text/javascript" src="js/Tree.js"></script>
    <script type="text/javascript" src="js/Details.js"></script>
    <script type="text/javascript" src="js/SearchForm.js"></script>
    <script type="text/javascript" src="js/SearchResults.js"></script>

  </head>

  <body onLoad="CodeCabinetExt.init();">

    <div id="divSource" class="cssSource"></div>

  </body>

</html>
```

I'd be willing to wager a minute's salary (because I'm clearly not a Las Vegas high-roller!) that this is probably pretty mundane by now. In fact, the only thing that may surprise you is the fact that I've used the plain-old onLoad event handler to call the init() method of the CodeCabinetExt object, which is the one and only instance of the object defined in the CodeCabinetExt.js file, and init() is what kicks off the application. The reason I did this is because, frankly, I couldn't get Ext.onReady() to work! I know we authors are supposed to have all the answers, but the fact is that part of what makes a "practical" book worth something, in my opinion anyway, is that you can read about the problems the author encountered writing the example code and learn how they got around them. This saves you time later because you don't have to spend that time figuring out what we've already figured out.

In this case, I am not sure why `Ext.onReady()` didn't work. As far as I can tell, it absolutely should have. The application never gets past the Please Wait `Window` when using it, though, and I'm not sure why. Falling back to onLoad works just fine, however. Keep in mind that the primary reason for using `Ext.onReady()` is to start your application's code executing as soon as possible and not have to wait for all resources to load first, as is the case with onLoad. Because of that, you can *usually* use the two approaches interchangeably, but `Ext.onReady()` will also *usually* give the appearance of better application performance. Here it probably isn't a big deal either way.

Note too that the only markup present here is the familiar `divSource` `<div>` for our `Window` animations. Because of some new functions used that we'll see soon, there isn't any need to define `Windows` in markup or anything else.

The Style Sheet

The style sheet in this application, like the markup in `index.htm`, is very limited. This is at least in part due to the way this application is constructed.

```
.cssPleaseWait {
  font-size : 12pt;
  font-weight : bold;
  font-family : tahoma,arial,verdana,sans-serif;
  color : #000000;
}

.cssSource {
  position : absolute;
  left: 1px;
  top : 1px;
  width : 100%;
  height : 1px;
}
```

The `cssPleaseWait` selector styles the text seen in the Please Wait pop-up during application startup. The `cssSource` selector is applied to the `divSource` `<div>`. Here, however, notice that it is different than in previous applications. Here, the width is 100%, whereas in previous applications it was 1 pixel, like the other attributes. This changes the effect you see when `Windows` appear. Instead of appearing to expand into view from the upper-left corner, they appear to "shrink into view," so to speak. In other words, the `Windows` fly in from the top, but they seem to shrink from a width across the entire page to their actual size. Check out the application in action to see this. It's a fairly subtle change, but one that I think looks quite a bit cooler!

The Code

Well, getting through the style sheet, markup, and directory structure didn't take very long, which means it's now time to jump right into the code! Let's begin with the DAO class, since that's largely something that stands on its own.

DAO.js

Recall in the previous application that I decided to feed Record objects to the DAO directly and to have the DAO return Records directly. I again decided to go with this approach because even though the argument against this—that the DAO code is in a sense tied to Ext JS—is valid, the simplicity of the code that results from this approach is highly compelling. With that in mind, take a look at the UML class diagram in Figure 5-3.

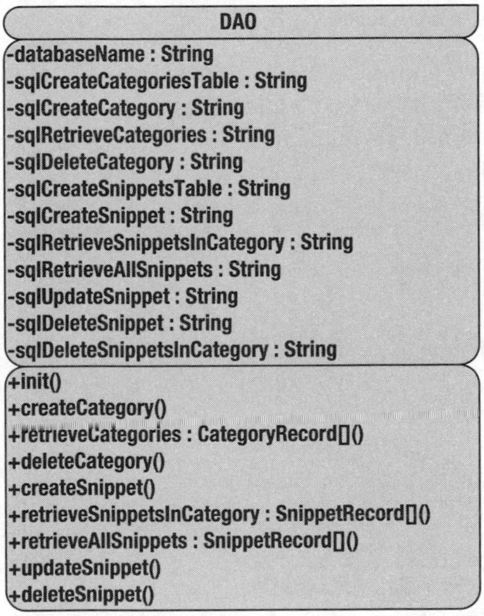

```
                         DAO
-databaseName : String
-sqlCreateCategoriesTable : String
-sqlCreateCategory : String
-sqlRetrieveCategories : String
-sqlDeleteCategory : String
-sqlCreateSnippetsTable : String
-sqlCreateSnippet : String
-sqlRetrieveSnippetsInCategory : String
-sqlRetrieveAllSnippets : String
-sqlUpdateSnippet : String
-sqlDeleteSnippet : String
-sqlDeleteSnippetsInCategory : String
+init()
+createCategory()
+retrieveCategories : CategoryRecord[]()
+deleteCategory()
+createSnippet()
+retrieveSnippetsInCategory : SnippetRecord[]()
+retrieveAllSnippets : SnippetRecord[]()
+updateSnippet()
+deleteSnippet()
```

Figure 5-3. *UML class diagram of the DAO class*

The diagram shows that the structure of the DAO is very much along the lines we've previously seen, and there's little surprise there: the structure makes a lot of sense, so why not stick with what works?

As we get into the code, however, we're immediately faced with something new and, presumably, exciting:

```
CodeCabinetExt.Data.DAO = new function() {
```

Previously we saw the DAO code beginning simply with:

```
function DAO() {
```

Later on, an instance of this class is created. Here, however, something else is going on. That something else is called "namespaces." I'm going to hold back on a full explanation at this point because it's easier to understand what's going on by looking at one particular line of code in CodeCabinetExt.js. At this point I'll simply tell you that the way this DAO code opens up is creating a DAO instance as well, but where that instance lives, so to speak, is quite a bit different.

Let's move on to the next thing we find in the DAO code:

```
var databaseName = "CodeCabinetExt";
```

As usual, we need a Gears database in which to store our application's data, and this field holds that name.

Next up we find a series of four SQL statements for dealing with categories:

```
var sqlCreateCategoriesTable = "CREATE TABLE IF NOT EXISTS categories (" +
  "name TEXT)"
var sqlCreateCategory = "INSERT INTO categories (name) VALUES (?)";
var sqlRetrieveCategories = "SELECT * FROM categories";
var sqlDeleteCategory = "DELETE FROM categories WHERE name=?";
```

This application deals with two entities: categories and snippets. A snippet is a child of a category at all times, but other than that we essentially have two simple tables to deal with, categories being the first. It's so simple that it only has a single name field (see Figure 5-4). I suspect the four SQL statements need no explanation.

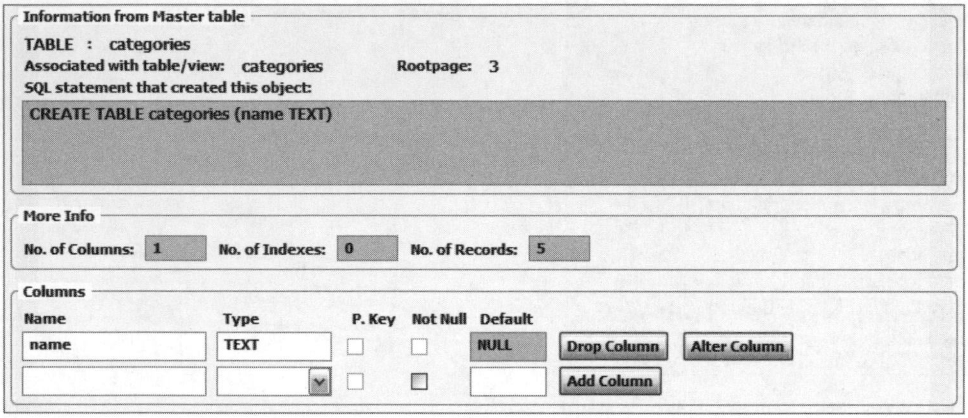

Figure 5-4. *Table structure of the categories table*

Dealing with snippets is a little more complicated, so we find that there are a few more SQL statements to look at:

```
var sqlCreateSnippetsTable = "CREATE TABLE IF NOT EXISTS snippets (" +
  "id TEXT, categoryname TEXT, name TEXT, description TEXT, author TEXT, " +
  "email TEXT, weblink TEXT, code TEXT, notes TEXT, keyword1 TEXT, " +
  "keyword2 TEXT, keyword3 TEXT, keyword4 TEXT, keyword5 TEXT)"
var sqlCreateSnippet = "INSERT INTO snippets (id, categoryname, name, " +
"description, author, email, weblink, code, notes, keyword1, keyword2, " +
"keyword3, keyword4, keyword5) VALUES (?, ?, ?, ?, ?, ?, ?, ?, ?, ?, ?, " +
"?, ?, ?)";
var sqlRetrieveSnippetsInCategory =
  "SELECT * FROM snippets where categoryname=?";
var sqlRetrieveAllSnippets = "SELECT * FROM snippets";
```

```
var sqlUpdateSnippet = "UPDATE snippets SET name=?, description=?, " +
  "author=?, email=?, weblink=?, code=?, notes=?, keyword1=?, keyword2=?, " +
  "keyword3=?, keyword4=?, keyword5=? WHERE id=?";
var sqlDeleteSnippet = "DELETE FROM snippets WHERE id=?";
var sqlDeleteSnippetsInCategory = "DELETE FROM snippets WHERE categoryname=?";
```

Even still, they are each individually pretty simple. There is more information to store about a snippet, however, and Figure 5-5 shows all of the fields involved. Note that the categoryname field is a foreign key to the name field of the categories table; other than that, the fields in the snippets table describe the snippet itself.

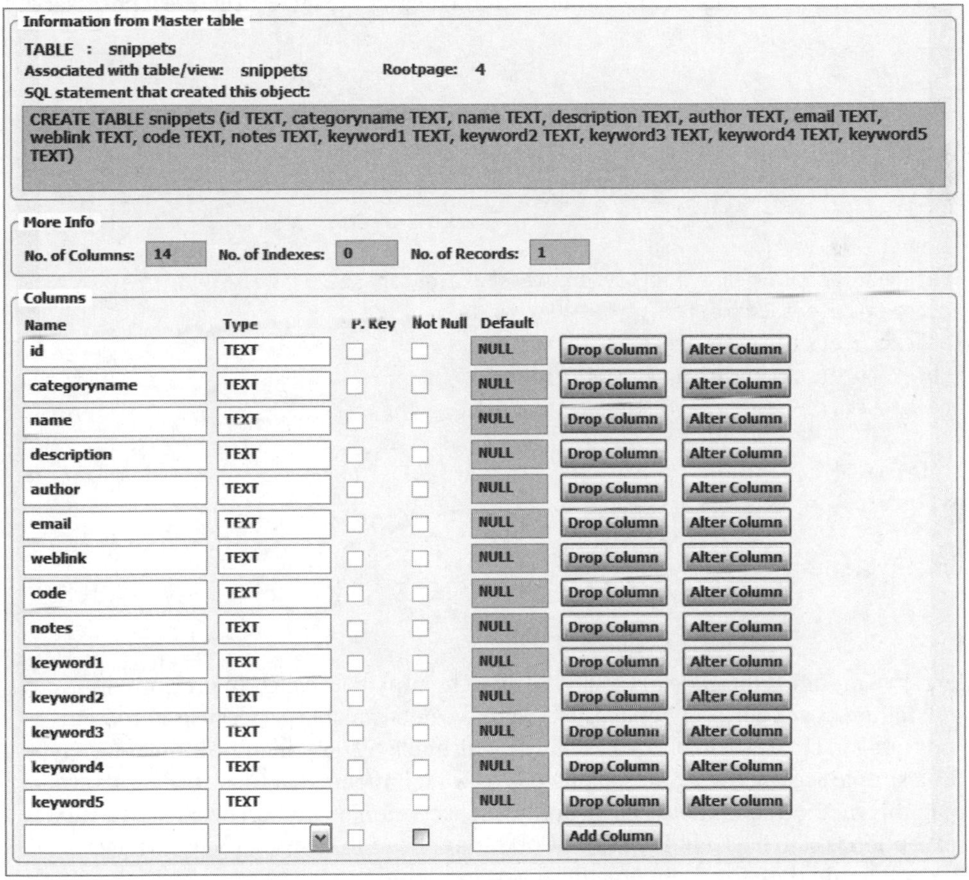

Information from Master table

TABLE : snippets
Associated with table/view: snippets   Rootpage: 4
SQL statement that created this object:

CREATE TABLE snippets (id TEXT, categoryname TEXT, name TEXT, description TEXT, author TEXT, email TEXT, weblink TEXT, code TEXT, notes TEXT, keyword1 TEXT, keyword2 TEXT, keyword3 TEXT, keyword4 TEXT, keyword5 TEXT)

More Info

No. of Columns: 14   No. of Indexes: 0   No. of Records: 1

Columns

Name	Type	P. Key	Not Null	Default		
id	TEXT	☐	☐	NULL	Drop Column	Alter Column
categoryname	TEXT	☐	☐	NULL	Drop Column	Alter Column
name	TEXT	☐	☐	NULL	Drop Column	Alter Column
description	TEXT	☐	☐	NULL	Drop Column	Alter Column
author	TEXT	☐	☐	NULL	Drop Column	Alter Column
email	TEXT	☐	☐	NULL	Drop Column	Alter Column
weblink	TEXT	☐	☐	NULL	Drop Column	Alter Column
code	TEXT	☐	☐	NULL	Drop Column	Alter Column
notes	TEXT	☐	☐	NULL	Drop Column	Alter Column
keyword1	TEXT	☐	☐	NULL	Drop Column	Alter Column
keyword2	TEXT	☐	☐	NULL	Drop Column	Alter Column
keyword3	TEXT	☐	☐	NULL	Drop Column	Alter Column
keyword4	TEXT	☐	☐	NULL	Drop Column	Alter Column
keyword5	TEXT	☐	☐	NULL	Drop Column	Alter Column
	▼	☐	☐		Add Column	

Figure 5-5. *Table structure of the snippets table*

Notice that there are two different retrieval statements. The sqlRetrieveSnippetsIn Category statement retrieves snippets in a given category and is used when a category is selected and we want to see the snippets within it. The sqlRetrieveAllSnippets statement returns all snippets across all categories and is used to perform searches. This hints at a slight architectural difference in this application as compared to the previous ones. In the others, all the data from the database is loaded at startup, and it's only updates (or deletes) that cause database access to occur again. Here, however, because of how the data is organized and how the application works, it makes more sense to do retrievals when necessary.

For instance, you could envision loading all the snippets at startup and them filtering down to the ones you need when a category is selected. However, why waste the memory doing that? It's more efficient to just read them in when needed. Since no network access is involved, there's no real concern about performance that might make you take a different approach.

Next up is the init() method. This serves the same purpose as all the other init() methods we've seen: it ensures that Gears is available, and creates the table structure if necessary:

```
this.init = function() {

  var initReturn = "ok";
  try {
    if (!window.google || !google.gears) {
      initReturn = "no_gears";
    } else {
      var db = google.gears.factory.create("beta.database");
      db.open(databaseName);
      db.execute(sqlCreateCategoriesTable);
      db.execute(sqlCreateSnippetsTable);
      db.close();
    }
  } catch (e) {
    initReturn = e;
  }
  return initReturn;

}
```

Here, I've modified the code to be slightly more helpful to its caller. In previous applications, a failure of any sort—either because Gears wasn't available or because a problem occurred trying to create the tables—was indistinguishable by the caller. Now the return type isn't just a simple Boolean—it's a string that tells us what happened. If Gears truly isn't available, then this method sends back "no_gears". If an exception of any sort occurs, then the text of the exception is sent back (and in the case of this application, is displayed to the user).

The next method we find is for creating a new category:

```
this.createCategory = function(inRecord) {

  var db = google.gears.factory.create("beta.database");
  db.open(databaseName);
  db.execute(sqlCreateCategory, [ inRecord.get("name") ] );
  db.close();

}
```

The inRecord argument is of type CategoryRecord. We'll see the definition of this shortly, but as I think you can surmise, it contains a single name field, and that's it.

Retrieving categories is a simple matter, and unlike snippets there's only a single retrieval method to get all of them:

```
this.retrieveCategories = function() {

  var db = google.gears.factory.create("beta.database");
  db.open(databaseName);
  var rs = db.execute(sqlRetrieveCategories);
  var results = [ ];
  while (rs.isValidRow()) {
    results.push(new CodeCabinetExt.Data.CategoryRecord({
      name : rs.fieldByName("name")
    }, rs.fieldByName("name")));
    rs.next();
  }
  rs.close();
  db.close();
  return results;

}
```

This is just like the retrieval methods in the DAO from the previous project. All it takes is executing the appropriate SQL statement, then iterating over the returned items and creating a CategoryRecord for each. Throw them all in an array, wrap it in a bow, and return it, good to go!

We can also delete a category, which is somewhat interesting:

```
this.deleteCategory = function(inCategoryName) {

  var db = google.gears.factory.create("beta.database");
  db.open(databaseName);
  db.execute(sqlDeleteCategory, [ inCategoryName ] );
  db.execute(sqlDeleteSnippetsInCategory, [ inCategoryName ] );
  db.close();

}
```

It's interesting because deleting a category also means deleting all the snippets within it, which arguably is not the way you'd want this application to work in an ideal world, but hey, feel free to enhance it! So, there are two SQL statements to execute, but otherwise this method works just like any other we've seen. In Figure 5-6 you can see where we nicely inform users of this when they try to delete a category.

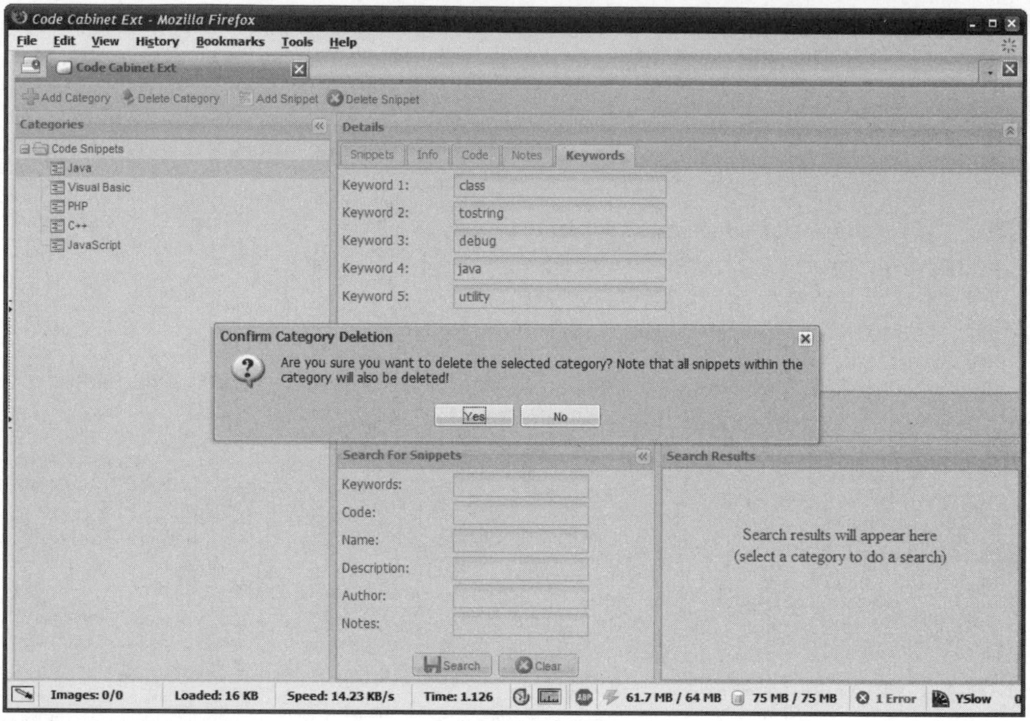

Figure 5-6. *The Confirm Category Deletion dialog*

Now we can move on to the methods for dealing with snippets, beginning with the ability to create a new snippet:

```
this.createSnippet = function(inRecord) {

  var db = google.gears.factory.create("beta.database");
  db.open(databaseName);
  db.execute(sqlCreateSnippet, [
    new Date().getTime().toString(), inRecord.get("categoryname"),
    inRecord.get("name"), inRecord.get("description"),
    inRecord.get("author"), inRecord.get("email"), inRecord.get("weblink"),
    inRecord.get("code"), inRecord.get("notes"), inRecord.get("keyword1"),
    inRecord.get("keyword2"), inRecord.get("keyword3"),
    inRecord.get("keyword4"), inRecord.get("keyword5")
  ]);
  db.close();

}
```

The inRecord argument is a SnippetRecord. It obviously has more fields than a Category Record, but is an ordinary Ext JS Record nonetheless. Note that when a snippet is created it is assigned an ID using the current time. This ensures uniqueness and also keeps our application code from having to generate its own key value for the snippet (the ID is the unique key of the table).

Retrieving snippets comes in two flavors, but both of them are implemented as part of the same method:

```
this.retrieveSnippets = function(inCategoryName) {

  var db = google.gears.factory.create("beta.database");
  db.open(databaseName);
  var rs = null;

  if (inCategoryName) {
    rs = db.execute(sqlRetrieveSnippetsInCategory, [ inCategoryName ] );
  } else {
    rs = db.execute(sqlRetrieveAllSnippets);
  }

  var results = [ ];
  while (rs.isValidRow()) {
    results.push(new CodeCabinetExt.Data.SnippetRecord({
      name : rs.fieldByName("name"), author : rs.fieldByName("author"),
      categoryname : rs.fieldByName("categoryname"),
      description : rs.fieldByName("description"),
      email : rs.fieldByName("email"), code : rs.fieldByName("code"),
      weblink : rs.fieldByName("weblink"), notes : rs.fieldByName("notes"),
      keyword1 : rs.fieldByName("keyword1"),
      keyword2 : rs.fieldByName("keyword2"),
      keyword3 : rs.fieldByName("keyword3"),
      keyword4 : rs.fieldByName("keyword4"),
      keyword5 : rs.fieldByName("keyword5")
    }, rs.fieldByName("id")));
    rs.next();
  }
  rs.close();
  db.close();
  return results;

}
```

Here, the inCategoryName argument names the category we want snippets for. However, that argument can be null, which means we want all snippets across all categories. The queries executed in both cases differ in that the one for retrieving queries from a category, sqlRetrieveSnippetsInCategory, requires the category name be dynamically inserted into it, while the sqlRetrieveAllSnippets does not. So, a little bit of conditional logic takes care of that, and the appropriate query is executed. In other cases we simply get back all available data and return an array of created SnippetRecord objects, so after that little bit of logic the code is identical. Note that each SnippetRecord is provided with the unique id value, but it is *not* one of the fields of the SnippetRecord itself—it is a separate property of the Record interface that Ext JS knows about.

Snippets can also be updated, and because each snippet has a unique ID—as opposed to previous projects, or even the categories in this one where the name is the key—the name field of a snippet can be updated as well, as you can see here:

```
this.updateSnippet = function(inRecord) {

  var db = google.gears.factory.create("beta.database");
  db.open(databaseName);
  db.execute(sqlUpdateSnippet, [
    inRecord.get("name"), inRecord.get("description"), inRecord.get("author"),
    inRecord.get("email"), inRecord.get("weblink"), inRecord.get("code"),
    inRecord.get("notes"), inRecord.get("keyword1"),
    inRecord.get("keyword2"), inRecord.get("keyword3"),
    inRecord.get("keyword4"), inRecord.get("keyword5"),
    inRecord.id
  ]);
  db.close();

}
```

Finally, snippets can be deleted too:

```
this.deleteSnippet = function(inID) {

  var db = google.gears.factory.create("beta.database");
  db.open(databaseName);
  db.execute(sqlDeleteSnippet, [ inID ] );
  db.close();

}
```

No surprises there!

StoresAndRecords.js

Now that we've seen the DAO code, it makes sense to see the Records and Stores involved in this application. The Records can be seen in Figure 5-7.

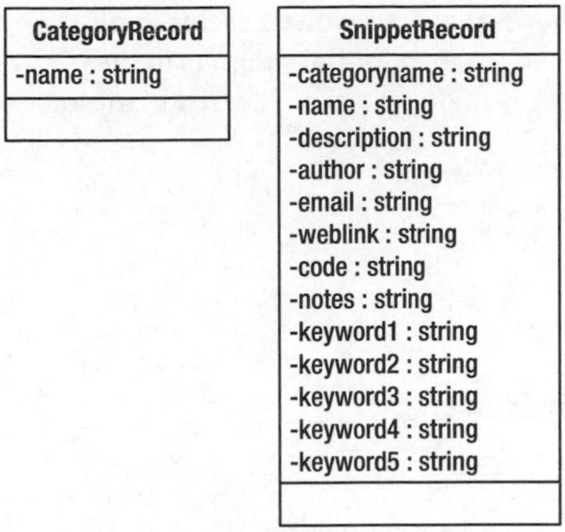

CategoryRecord
-name : string

SnippetRecord
-categoryname : string
-name : string
-description : string
-author : string
-email : string
-weblink : string
-code : string
-notes : string
-keyword1 : string
-keyword2 : string
-keyword3 : string
-keyword4 : string
-keyword5 : string

Figure 5-7. *The record descriptors in all their glory*

These Records are very simple animals, but let's see their definition anyway, starting with the CategoryRecord:

```
CodeCabinetExt.Data.CategoryRecord = Ext.data.Record.create([
  { name : "name", mapping : "name" }
]);
```

Yes, a single field, name, is all we need to make this whole rigamarole work! The SnippetRecord has a few more, though:

```
CodeCabinetExt.Data.SnippetRecord = Ext.data.Record.create([
  { name : "categoryname", mapping : "categoryname" },
  { name : "name", mapping : "name" },
  { name : "description", mapping : "description" },
  { name : "author", mapping : "author" },
  { name : "email", mapping : "email" },
  { name : "weblink", mapping : "weblink" },
  { name : "code", mapping : "code" },
  { name : "notes", mapping : "notes" },
  { name : "keyword1", mapping : "keyword1" },
  { name : "keyword2", mapping : "keyword2" },
  { name : "keyword3", mapping : "keyword3" },
  { name : "keyword4", mapping : "keyword4" },
  { name : "keyword5", mapping : "keyword5" }
]);
```

By the way, you can see here the same sort of "namespacing" going on as we saw with the DAO, so hold tight to your questions about that because we're nearly to that explanation. (I just hope I haven't built it up so much that it's a disappointment!)

With the Records out of the way, we can see the Stores that are involved in this application. As it turns out there are only three: one for categories, one for the snippets in the currently selected category, and one for any search results that may exist. The first of these is the CategoriesStore:

```
CodeCabinetExt.Data.CategoriesStore = new Ext.data.Store({
  listeners : {
    "add" : {
      fn : function(inStore, inRecords, inIndex) {
        if (Ext.MessageBox.isVisible()) { return; }
        CodeCabinetExt.Data.DAO.createCategory(inRecords[0]);
      }
    },
    "remove" : {
      fn : function(inStore, inRecord, inIndex) {
        CodeCabinetExt.Data.DAO.deleteCategory(inRecord.get("name"));
      }
    }
  }
});
```

This is where we store all the categories that currently exist. This Store is populated from the database once at startup and then all adds and deletes of categories are executed against it. As such we have an add and remove event handler defined to call the appropriate DAO method in each case.

In the add event handler we find something new: Ext.MessageBox.isVisible(). Recall that in previous applications we had some code to determine if the Please Wait Window was showing to avoid the add event firing during initial Store loading. Well, the same situation has to be accounted for here, but in this application there is no Please Wait Window. Instead, we're going to be using the Ext.MessageBox() feature. This allows us to display various sorts of dialogs without having to construct the Windows ourselves. We'll see the code for this a little later, but for now it's important to understand that using Ext.MessageBox() means we can have a single Window at a time opened, which means we can ask Ext JS if the Window is currently open by calling Ext.MessageBox.isVisible(). So, effectively, this serves the exact same purpose as the similar code seen in previous applications.

The SnippetsStore is next, and it is virtually identical to the CategoriesStore:

```
CodeCabinetExt.Data.SnippetsStore = new Ext.data.Store({
  listeners : {
    "add" : {
      fn : function(inStore, inRecords, inIndex) {
        if (CodeCabinetExt.populatingSnippetsStore) { return; }
        CodeCabinetExt.Data.DAO.createSnippet(inRecords[0]);
      }
    },
```

```
    "remove" : {
      fn : function(inStore, inRecord, inIndex) {
        if (CodeCabinetExt.populatingSnippetsStore) { return; }
        CodeCabinetExt.Data.DAO.deleteSnippet(inRecord.id);
      }
    },
    "update" : {
      fn : function(inStore, inRecord, inIndex) {
        CodeCabinetExt.Data.DAO.updateSnippet(inRecord);
      }
    }
  }
});
```

The only real difference is that the SnippetsStore has an update event handler as well since snippets can be updated, while categories cannot.

Finally, we find SearchResultsStore:

```
CodeCabinetExt.Data.SearchResultsStore = new Ext.data.Store({});
```

This is a temporary Store that is loaded with SnippetRecords matching the entered search criteria when the user wants to perform a search. At the start, though, it's just an empty Store, but defining it allows us to bind widgets to it, even though it's empty, so we can stick with a more declarative approach to defining our widgets that way.

CodeCabinetExt.js

All right then, now we find ourselves staring face to face with the CodeCabinetExt.js file, which I've described as the "main" source file. Each of the previous applications had a single JavaScript file that contained what you could call the "core" of the application. The CodeCabinetExt.js file is similar, but in this situation it's also quite a bit different. Let's begin by looking at the UML diagram for it, shown in Figure 5-8.

```
┌─────────────────────────────────────────┐
│              CodeCabinetExt               │
├───────────────────────────────────────────┤
│ +Data.CategoryRecord : Ext.data.Record    │
│ +Data.SnippetRecord : Ext.data.Record     │
│ +Data.CategoriesStore : Ext.data.Store    │
│ +Data.SnippetsStore : Ext.data.Store      │
│ +Data.SearchResultsStore : Ext.data.Store │
│ +populatingSnippetsStore : boolean        │
│ +UIObjects.Viewport : Ext.Viewport        │
│ +UIObjects.Toolbar : Ext.Toolbar          │
│ +UIObjects.Tree : Ext.tree.TreePanel      │
│ +UIObjects.Details : Ext.TabPanel         │
│ +UIObjects.SearchForm : Ext.form.FormPanel│
│ +UIObjects.SearchResults : Ext.Panel      │
├───────────────────────────────────────────┤
│ +init()                                   │
│ +buildUI()                                │
│ +UIEventHandlers.AddCategory()            │
│ +UIEventHandlers.DeleteCategory()         │
│ +UIEventHandlers.AddSnippet()             │
│ +UIEventHandlers.DeleteSnippet()          │
│ +UIEventHandlers.TreeClick()              │
│ +UIEventHandlers.RowClick()               │
│ +UIEventHandlers.SaveClick()              │
│ +UIEventHandlers.SearchClick()            │
│ +UIEventHandlers.ClearClick()             │
└───────────────────────────────────────────┘
```

Figure 5-8. *UML class diagram of the CodeCabinetEx, and its sub-namespaces class*

So, we can deduce that we're looking at a class here, and that's nothing we haven't seen before. What *is* new is how the class is defined. The answer happens to be the first line of executable code in this file, and it also happens to be what I've hinted at before: namespaces.

```
Ext.namespace("CodeCabinetExt", "CodeCabinetExt.UIObjects",
  "CodeCabinetExt.UIEventHandlers", "CodeCabinetExt.Data");
```

The Ext.namespace() function is something we haven't seen in action before. Here's what the Ext JS documentation has to say about it: "Creates namespaces to be used for scoping variables and classes so that they are not global." Here's what I have to say about it: it creates classes!

Remember that in JavaScript, a class is a function. Every function you create, because you can later create a new instance of it, is what you'd call a class in other languages such as Java. But you also hear this term "namespace" a lot in JavaScript circles. It's is really just another name for a function.

You can create functions within functions in JavaScript—there's no problem there. Each time you create a member of a function, it is local to that function; its scope is the function, in other words. That's what namespacing is all about: keeping elements out of global scope and instead putting them into some more private scope.

The Ext.namespace() function simply allows you to create these namespaces, these functions, these classes, whatever term you'd like to use, without having to write the associated JavaScript code yourself. It's a very handy function that takes any number of arguments you care to throw at it, and it creates the namespaces in that list. You can create nested namespaces, stand-alone namespaces, whatever you prefer.

So, in the call we see here, there is one namespace at the top of the heap: `CodeCabinetExt`. Then, it adds some namespaces within that namespace, namely `CodeCabinetExt.UIObjects`, which is where we'll put the configuration objects for all of user interface elements; `Code CabinetExt.UIEventHandler`, which is where we'll put the event handlers that are triggered by user interactions with various UI elements; and `CodeCabinetExt.Data`, which is where we'll put all our data-related items such as `Records`, `Stores`, and our DAO instance.

Speaking of the DAO, we saw this a little earlier in that code:

```
CodeCabinetExt.Data.DAO = new function() {
```

Now, that makes sense to me: in JavaScript remember that you can attach attributes to existing objects any time you wish, and that's exactly what's happening here. The call to `Ext.namespace()` created the `CodeCabinetExt` namespace, and then the `Data` namespace underneath it. Under the covers that means we have a function (`Data`) nested within another (`CodeCabinetExt`), and now in the DAO we're adding a DAO attribute to the `Data` function, which happens to be a reference to the function that is our DAO.

This is nice because it means the only thing we have in global scope in this application is the `CodeCabinetExt` object itself, regardless of all the source files we load (which foreshadows what you'll see: each of the JavaScript source files contains code that attaches new attributes to the namespaces created here). So we can bring in other libraries or code if we wish and be pretty well assured it won't conflict with ours.

Now that we know all about namespaces, let's see some of the attributes added to the `CodeCabinetExt` namespace:

```
CodeCabinetExt.currentCategory = null;
```

This is a reference to the currently selected `CategoryRecord`, if any.

```
CodeCabinetExt.currentSnippet = null;
```

This is similarly a reference to the currently selected `SnippetRecord`, if any.

```
CodeCabinetExt.populatingSnippetsStore = false;
```

This is a flag that tells us when the `SnippetsStore` is in the process of being populated. We'll see a bit later why this is important, but for now just remember this flag and that it indicates that `Store` is being populated.

The `init()`method that we saw called in response to the page's onLoad event is next:

```
CodeCabinetExt.init = function() {

  Ext.MessageBox.show({
    title : "Please Wait",
    msg : "<span class='cssPleaseWait'>... Initializing ...</span>",
    buttons : false, closable : false, animEl : "divSource"
  });
```

```
(function() {
  var daoInitResult = CodeCabinetExt.Data.DAO.init();
  switch (daoInitResult) {
    case "ok":
      Ext.state.Manager.setProvider(new Ext.state.CookieProvider());
      CodeCabinetExt.buildUI();
      Ext.MessageBox.hide();
    break;
    case "no_gears":
      Ext.MessageBox.show({
        title : "Gears Not Available", buttons : Ext.MessageBox.OK,
        msg : "<br>" +
          "I'm sorry but Google Gears is not installed on your computer, " +
          "or is unavailable for some reason (like you disabled the " +
          "browser plugin for example)." +
          "<br><br>" +
          "If you do not have Gears installed, please visit " +
          "<a href=\"http://gears.google.com/\" target=\"new\">" +
          "the Gears home page</a> to install it." +
          "<br><br>" +
          "If you do have it installed, please try enabling the plugin in " +
          "whatever fashion is applicable in the browser you are using, " +
          "and reload this application."
      });
    break;
    default:
      Ext.MessageBox.alert("DAO Initialization Failed",
        "Data access could not be initialized.  Reason: " + daoInitResult);
    break;
  }
}).defer(500);

};
```

First, as with the other applications in this book, we want to show a Please Wait message while the application initializes. In the previous projects we created our own Window and
showed it. Here we're saving some time and effort and instead using the Ext.MessageBox()
function. This function allows us to create a variety of pop-up dialog message windows, some
that accept input, some with progress bars on them, and so on. Here we just want a simple
text-only message similar to a plain-old alert() message.

There are a number of ways to get a message displayed, but one of the most flexible is to
use the show() method. This method accepts an object that provides configuration information describing what you want to show. In this case we specify the title attribute to set the
title of the Window, the msg attribute to set the message seen (and notice that you can include
markup here, which is how the cssPleaseWait selector is applied to the text), the buttons attribute (set to false) to indicate we don't want any buttons for the user to click, closable (set to
false) to indicate that the message can't be dismissed by clicking the close X icon, and finally

the `animEl` attribute, which specifies the element on the page to use as the animation source for showing and hiding the message.

Next is something else new. We've seen these five `init()` methods before, but this one is structured quite a bit differently. We are defining an anonymous function. This function contains all our initialization logic. Once that function is defined, we immediately call the `defer()` method on it. The `defer()` method is an embellishment that Ext JS adds to the prototype of JavaScript's function, meaning every function we create has this method available to it. All it does is say "wait some period of time (500 milliseconds in this case) and then execute the function `defer()` is called on." So, this is implementing the same sort of delay to give the Please Wait message time to appear that we've seen in other applications implemented with `timeout()`. This, I think you'll agree, is a bit more elegant.

MORE INFO ON PROTOTYPE THAN YOU EVER WANTED TO KNOW!

Functions in JavaScript are first-class citizens, meaning they are proper objects, extending directly from the `Object` class, and they have properties and methods like any object does. Because of this, they also all have common methods such as `apply()` and `call()` and properties such as `length` and `constructor`.

One other such property is `prototype`. Initially, its value is an empty object, so it's as if you wrote:

```
function foo() { };
foo.prototype = { };
```

The properties and methods of the object `prototype` points to have no impact on `foo` itself; they are not a part of it (directly at least; more on this shortly), but they will have an impact if you instantiate a new instance of `foo`. They will become a part of the new object directly. Take this code, for example:

```
function foo() { };
foo.prototype = {
  name : "test",
  sayName : function() { alert(this.name); }
};
var f = new foo();
try { foo.sayName(); } catch (e) { alert("no"); }
f.sayName();
```

The result will be two `alert()` pop-ups, one that says "no," and another that says "test." As you can see, the property `name` was added to the instance of `foo` pointed to by the variable `f`. However, the attempt to call `sayName()` on `foo` will fail, which is why it's in the `try...catch` block, because it isn't a part of `foo`.

Now, there is a way you can access the `name` property in `foo`, and here it is:

```
alert(foo.prototype.name);
```

Since the object `prototype` points to is a member of `foo`, you can still dig down through the hierarchy like that to get to it. However, the idea of `prototype` isn't to store data, as other properties of `foo` would be, but to define properties and methods that will become a part of any new instance of `foo`. It provides something of an inheritance mechanism in JavaScript.

The initialization logic itself is very much like we've seen before. First, the DAO's init() method is called. Remember that in this version of DAO.init(), it returns a string indicating what happened. So, the next step is to switch on that return value. If the value is ok, then we can continue initialization. Let's come back to that.

If the return is no_gears, then we know Gears wasn't available. So, we again use the Ext.MessageBox.show() function to display the same sort of message as seen in other applications. In those other applications the Window was defined in markup in index.htm, but here it's defined entirely in code. Note that the buttons attribute is not set here, nor is closable, as seen on the Please Wait pop-up. That means there will be a single OK button, which is the default state of Ext.MessageBox.show(), and the close X icon can be used. The message seen in this case is shown in Figure 5-9.

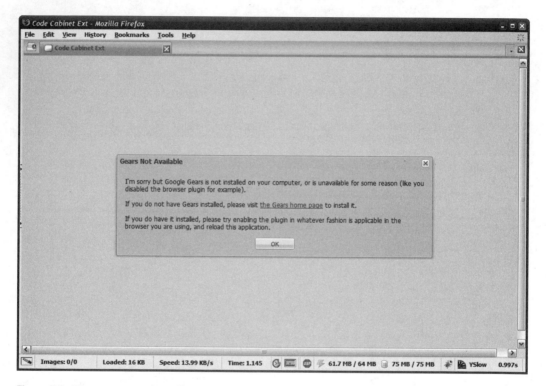

Figure 5-9. *Oops, gotta go install Gears I guess!*

The other possible outcome is some sort of exception. In that case, Ext.MessageBox. alert() is used. As it happens, Ext.MessageBox.alert() doesn't look a whole lot different than the Window seen in the "No Gears" pop-up, as you can see for yourself in Figure 5-10.

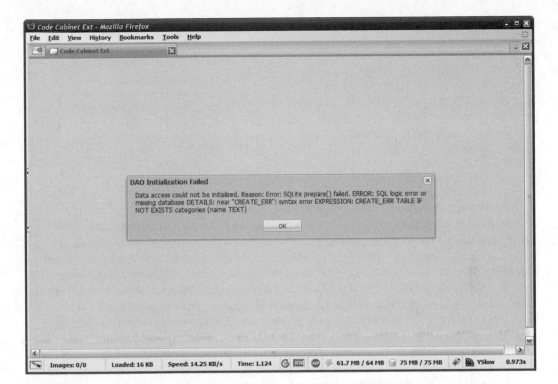

Figure 5-10. *Some unknown error occurred.*

Going back to the initialization that occurs when DAO initialization is successful, the first step is to set up for state saving. Remember the requirement for the user to be able to resize sections of the application and have the sizes persist across application executions? Well, to do that we need to tell Ext JS what kind of provider to use to store the information. We will use cookies, and so it's the Ext.state.CookieProvider() we want. No further information is needed; once the Manager is handed the provider instance to use, we're done.

The next step is to build the UI, and for that we need a call to the buildUI() method:

```
CodeCabinetExt.buildUI = function() {

  new Ext.Toolbar(CodeCabinetExt.UIObjects.Toolbar());

  new Ext.tree.TreePanel(CodeCabinetExt.UIObjects.Tree());

  new Ext.TabPanel(CodeCabinetExt.UIObjects.Details());

  new Ext.form.FormPanel(CodeCabinetExt.UIObjects.SearchForm());

  new Ext.Panel(CodeCabinetExt.UIObjects.SearchResults());

  new Ext.Viewport(CodeCabinetExt.UIObjects.Viewport());

  var rootNode = Ext.getCmp("Tree").getRootNode();
```

```
    var categories = CodeCabinetExt.Data.DAO.retrieveCategories();
    for (var i = 0; i < categories.length; i++) {
      CodeCabinetExt.Data.CategoriesStore.add(categories[i]);
      var categoryName = categories[i].get("name");
      rootNode.appendChild(new Ext.tree.TreeNode(
        { id : categoryName, text : categoryName }
      ));
    }
    rootNode.expand();

}
```

Well now, *that* certainly is a bit different, and in a couple of ways! First, we clearly aren't defining the entire UI in one giant JSON object—it's more like the TimekeeperExt project where things are broken up, individually constructed, and then put together. Let's see, we have a Toolbar being created, a Tree for our categories, a TabPanel where the tabs for our snippet details and snippets Grid will go, a FormPanel for our search form, a plain-old Panel where our search results Grid will live, and of course a Viewport to make it all work. What's a bit bizarre here, though, is we seem to be calling functions that must be returning configuration objects to use to construct each of those elements. As we'll see, that's precisely what's happening.

After all that, we're also loading up categories from the database and populating the Tree that was just constructed. That code looks fairly familiar to us, having seen it a couple of times in TimekeeperExt. The root node of the tree is expanded so that we can see all the categories, and buildUI() is done. Back in the calling code (that anonymous function from earlier whose execution was deferred) the Please Wait message box is hidden, and application initialization is complete.

Now, we should probably look in more detail and find out what those functions that were called to get the configuration objects for the UI elements are all about, and maybe understand why it's done that way (yes, hard to believe, but there is absolutely a method behind my madness!)

Viewport.js

A Viewport contains our UI, so defining one is obviously necessary in this application. In the init() method we just discussed, we saw that a call is made to CodeCabinetExt.UIObjects.Viewport(), which we surmised must be returning a configuration object describing the Viewport. Well, that function can be found in the aptly named Viewport.js file, and consists of this bit of code:

```
CodeCabinetExt.UIObjects.Viewport = function() { return ({
  layout : "border", items : [
    { region : "north", height : 28, items : [ Ext.getCmp("Toolbar") ] },
    { region : "west", layout : "fit", border : false, width : 300,
      split : true, title : "Categories", collapsible : true,
      items : [ Ext.getCmp("Tree") ] },
```

```
    { region : "center", layout : "border", items : [
      { region : "north", layout : "fit", border : false, height : 300,
        split : true, title : "Details", collapsible : true,
        items : [ Ext.getCmp("Details") ] },
      { region : "west", width : 300, split : true,
        title : "Search For Snippets", collapsible : true,
        items : [ Ext.getCmp("SearchForm") ]
      },
      { region : "center", layout : "fit",
        title : "Search Results", items : [ Ext.getCmp("SearchResults") ] }
    ]}
  ]
}); };
```

This isn't a whole lot different than anything we've previously seen, and there aren't any new attributes to describe, so I'd like to spend our time talking about the approach rather than the details.

You'll notice right away that many parts of the UI are obtained via calls to Ext.getCmp(), which is a technique we've seen before. As long as those elements are constructed before the Viewport, which is the case as we saw in the init() method a short while ago, then everything works as we expect.

However, what's the thinking behind this being a function call? Why not just have CodeCabinetExt.UIObjects.Viewport be an object definition? That way, you could do what you see in Listing 5-1 instead.

Listing 5-1. *The Viewport Defined As a JSON Object Not Wrapped in a Function Call*

```
CodeCabinetExt.UIObjects.Viewport = {
  layout : "border", items : [
    { region : "north", height : 28, items : [ Ext.getCmp("Toolbar") ] },
    { region : "west", layout : "fit", border : false, width : 300,
      split : true, title : "Categories", collapsible : true,
      items : [ Ext.getCmp("Tree") ] },
    { region : "center", layout : "border", items : [
      { region : "north", layout : "fit", border : false, height : 300,
        split : true, title : "Details", collapsible : true,
        items : [ Ext.getCmp("Details") ] },
      { region : "west", width : 300, layout : "fit", split : true,
        title : "Search For Snippets", collapsible : true,
        items : [ Ext.getCmp("SearchForm") ]
      },
      { region : "center", layout : "fit",
        title : "Search Results", items : [ Ext.getCmp("SearchResults") ] }
    ]}
  ]
};
```

Well, here's the problem with doing that: the object definition is interpreted at the time this file is imported into `index.htm`, which means that the order in which files are imported becomes important. For example, if we have a `Grid` that's bound to a `Store`, then we have to ensure that the code that defines the `Store` is imported before the file containing the `Grid` definition. This isn't a huge problem in a relatively small application such as this one, or TimekeeperExt, which suffers from this import order problem, but in a larger project it can quickly become a big hassle.

By wrapping the configuration object in a function call, however, the JSON won't be interpreted until the function is called. Assuming we only allow that to happen when the page is loaded, we can ensure that import order doesn't matter and our application is therefore much easier to maintain.

Note In my first attempt, this code, and the other source files that we'll see, were implemented as a string. In other words, I used what you see in Listing 5-1, except that each line of the JSON was wrapped in quotes, so a giant string of JSON was constructed. Then, instead of function calls to get the JSON I instead fed the string to `Ext.util.json.decode()` to get back the actual object to pass to the `Viewport` constructor. This approach also gets around the problem of ordering of imports because the string won't be interpreted (into a JSON object, I mean) until the `Viewport` is constructed. However, it has a number of drawbacks. First, you have to worry about escaping the JSON so as to not break the string construction, which can be a hassle. More importantly, though, code editors that do coloring and brace matching can't work in that situation, which means development can be more difficult. All in all, I like the function call-wrapping approach seen in this application. You don't have to worry about import order, you can define elements in separate files, and you can continue to use your editor of choice most effectively. FTW![2]

As you'll see, the configuration objects for all the other UI elements are similarly defined this way, and I think you'll find the rest of the projects in this book will use the same structure because I believe it is the best approach (at least, the best I've found!).

One other plus is that if you wanted to, you could replace the function calls with Ajax calls that retrieved the configuration objects from the server. This would allow you to change your UI structure pretty much on the fly (which could be a recipe for disaster as much as a really cool capability). I'm not sure you'd ever want to do this, if for no other reason than the fact that the extra round-trips involved from client to server would hurt performance, but it's nice to know the possibility exists. This approach of breaking up the UI elements into separate source files and then returning the configuration JSON from a function call allows you that flexibility.

---

2   FTW is one of many Internet abbreviations (see `www.netlingo.com/emailsh.cfm` for more details) which stands for "for the win." This can frequently be seen at the end of argument threads where someone is comparing a number of things and is making the argument that one of them is superior. FTW can also have another—less kind—meaning. I will leave you to find out what that is on your own, if you wish!

Toolbar.js

The next thing we'll look at is the definition of the Toolbar. You can see the Toolbar here in Figure 5-11, which also shows the Info details tab.

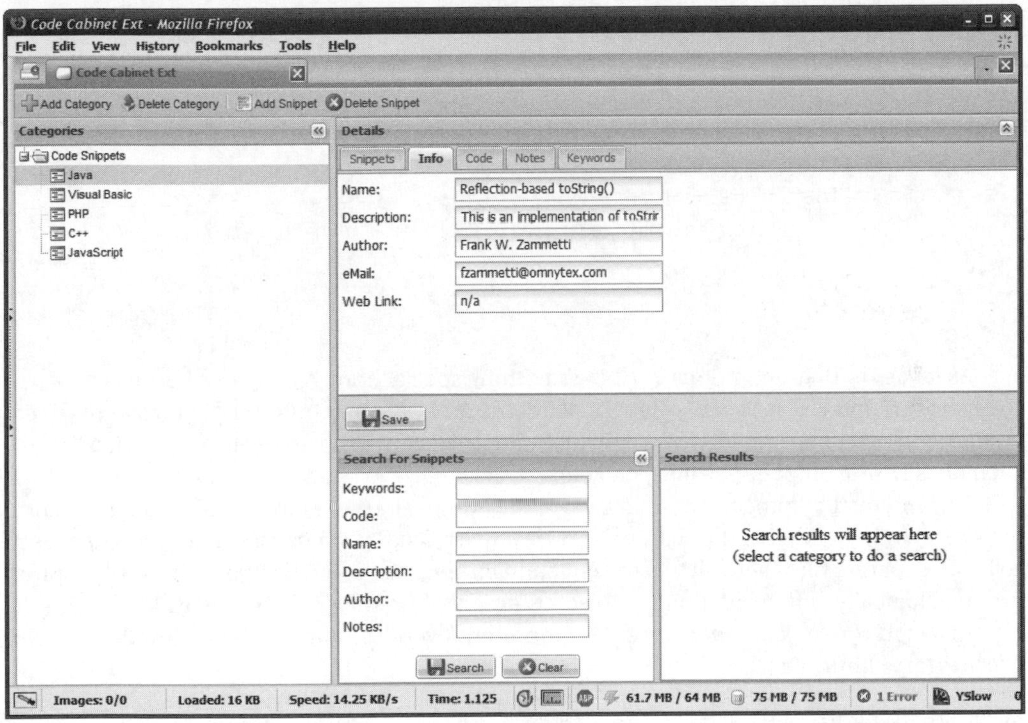

Figure 5-11. *The Toolbar (bask in its majesty!) and the Info details tab, as an added bonus!*

The configuration object for the Toolbar looks like this:

```
CodeCabinetExt.UIObjects.Toolbar = function() { return ({
  id : "Toolbar", items : [
    {
      text : "Add Category",
      handler : function() {
        CodeCabinetExt.UIEventHandlers.AddCategory();
      }, icon : "img/icon_category_add.gif", cls : "x-btn-text-icon"
    },
    {
      text : "Delete Category", id : "DeleteCategory", disabled : true,
      handler : function() {
        CodeCabinetExt.UIEventHandlers.DeleteCategory();
      }, icon : "img/icon_category_delete.gif", cls : "x-btn-text-icon"
    },
```

```
    { xtype : "tbseparator" },
    {
      text : "Add Snippet", id : "AddSnippet", disabled : true,
      handler : function() {
        CodeCabinetExt.UIEventHandlers.AddSnippet();
      }, icon : "img/icon_snippet_add.gif", cls : "x-btn-text-icon"
    },
    {
      text : "Delete Snippet", id : "DeleteSnippet", disabled : true,
      handler : function() {
        CodeCabinetExt.UIEventHandlers.DeleteSnippet();
      }, icon : "img/icon_snippet_delete.gif", cls : "x-btn-text-icon"
    }
  ]
}); };
```

As far as Toolbar definitions go, there's nothing special here. A couple of buttons, a tbseparator, and we're all set. Note that all but the Add Category button is defined as disabled to start; the others are enabled as contextually logical (i.e., when you select a snippet, only then does Delete Snippet become enabled).

One interesting thing here is that each of the buttons has an event handler attached that calls a function defined in the CodeCabinetExt.UIEventHandlers namespace. You might expect to find a separate file where all those event handlers live, but you'd be wrong. In fact, they are grouped logically with the definition objects themselves, so they're in this very file!

In fact, if you look out the right side of the aircraft you'll see one of them now, the AddCategory() button:

```
CodeCabinetExt.UIEventHandlers.AddCategory = function() {

  Ext.Msg.prompt("Add Category", "Please enter a name for the new category:",
    function(inButtonClicked, inTextEntered) {
      if (inButtonClicked == "ok") {
        if (CodeCabinetExt.Data.CategoriesStore.getById(inTextEntered)) {
          Ext.Msg.alert("Name not allowed",
            "A category with that name already exists.  " +
            "Please choose another."
          );
          return;
        }
        var categoryRecord = new CodeCabinetExt.Data.CategoryRecord(
          { name : inTextEntered }, inTextEntered
        );
        CodeCabinetExt.Data.CategoriesStore.add(categoryRecord);
        var rootNode = Ext.getCmp("Tree").getRootNode();
```

```
    rootNode.appendChild(
      new Ext.tree.TreeNode( { id : inTextEntered, text : inTextEntered } )
    );
    rootNode.expand();
    }
  }
);

};
```

This code is called when the Add Category button is clicked. I think it's nice to be able
to have this code right alongside the Toolbar definition, and the namespaces allow us to do
that (or at least, makes it easier to do so). The function of adding a category begins with a
new method of Ext.Msg. Whoa, wait, Ext.Msg? What's that? Simply stated, it's a pseudonym of
Ext.MessageBox; they can be used interchangeably. This time, it's the prompt() method we're
interested in. This works just like the plain JavaScript prompt() function, it allows us to get
some input from the user. The first argument is the title of the pop-up, and the second is the
prompt text. Just as with the plain prompt() function, you can optionally pass a default value
as well.

Unlike with the plain prompt() function, though, you can also pass a callback function
that will be executed when the pop up is closed. This function is passed the text of the button
that was clicked as well as the data that was entered. So, the code then checks to see what button was clicked. It's either going to be OK or Cancel, as you can see in Figure 5-12.

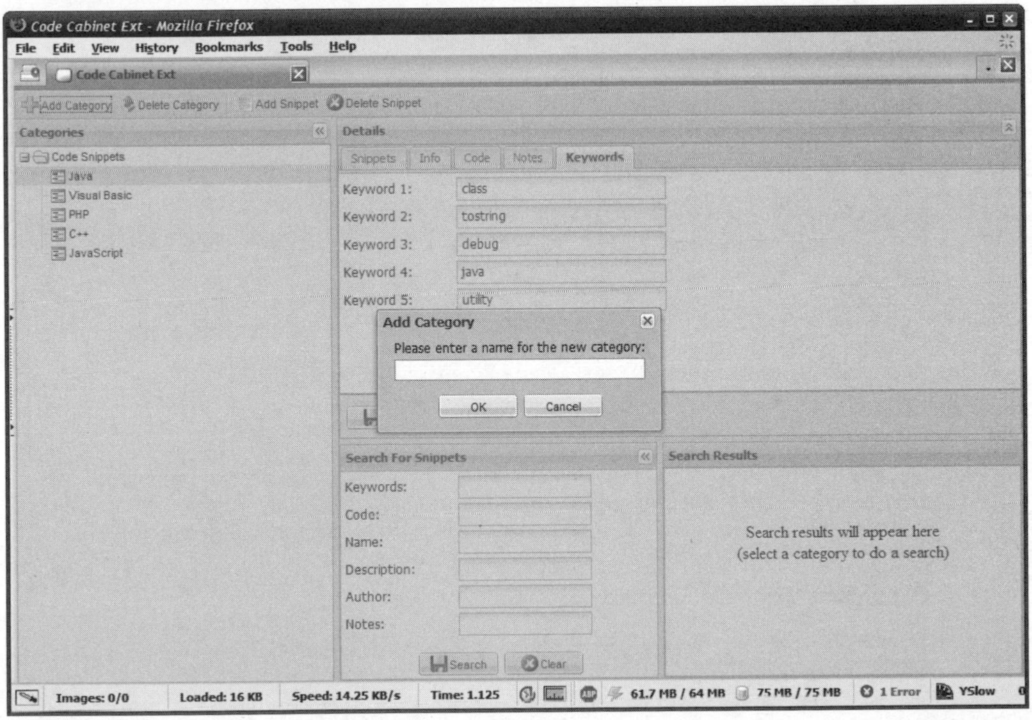

Figure 5-12. *The Add Category prompt*

Interestingly, it is always passed in all lowercase, so we don't have to do any converting here. If the value is ok, only then do we do some work, and that work begins with trying to retrieve the CategoryRecord from the CategoriesStore with the name that the user entered. If it is found, the addition is not allowed because the name must be unique. In that case, Ext.Msg.alert() is used to inform the user.

Assuming the name proves to be unique, it's a simple matter of creating a new Category Store with the entered name, adding the CategoryRecord to the CategoriesStore, which triggers the add event. The add event in turn calls the DAO.createCategory() method, which adds the category to the Tree. The details of this code are nothing new.

Next we find the Delete Category button's event handler:

```
CodeCabinetExt.UIEventHandlers.DeleteCategory = function() {

  Ext.MessageBox.confirm("Confirm Category Deletion",
    "Are you sure you want to delete the selected catalog? " +
    "Note that all snippets within the category will also be deleted!",
    function(inButtonClicked) {
      if (inButtonClicked == "yes") {

        var rootNode = Ext.getCmp("Tree").getRootNode();
        var categoryTreeNode = Ext.getCmp("Tree").getNodeById(
          CodeCabinetExt.currentCategory.get("name"));
        rootNode.removeChild(categoryTreeNode);

        CodeCabinetExt.Data.CategoriesStore.remove(
          CodeCabinetExt.currentCategory);
        CodeCabinetExt.currentCategory = null;

        CodeCabinetExt.Data.SnippetsStore.removeAll();

        Ext.getCmp("DeleteCategory").setDisabled(true);
        Ext.getCmp("AddSnippet").setDisabled(true);
        Ext.getCmp("DeleteSnippet").setDisabled(true);

        Ext.getCmp("Details").setActiveTab(0);
        Ext.getCmp("tabSnippets").getLayout().setActiveItem(0);
        Ext.getCmp("tabInfo").setDisabled(true);
        Ext.getCmp("tabCode").setDisabled(true);
        Ext.getCmp("tabNotes").setDisabled(true);
        Ext.getCmp("tabKeywords").setDisabled(true);

        Ext.getCmp("SearchForm").getForm().reset();
        CodeCabinetExt.Data.SearchResultsStore.removeAll();
```

```
      }
    }

  );

};
```

While deleting a category isn't too hard, there are a number of steps that have to be accomplished. First, we get the root node of the Tree and then use its getNodeById() method. We feed this method the name of the currently selected category (whose CategoryRecord the CodeCabinetExt.currentCategory field now points to) to get the TreeNode representing the category. Then we call removeChild() on the root node, passing it the TreeNode to remove. That takes care of our Tree.

Next, we call remove() on the CategoriesStore to remove the category. This triggers the remove event on the CategoriesStore, which calls the DAO.deleteCategory() method, so now the store and the underlying database is taken care of. We also set CodeCabinetExt. currentCategory to null to indicate no category is currently selected.

Next, we clear the SnippetsStore since there are no longer snippets to show.

After that, the Delete Category, Add Snippet, and Delete Snippet Toolbar buttons are disabled since they only become available when a category and/or snippet is selected, which obviously can't be the case if we just deleted the selected category!

Then, the details section is taken care of. This amounts to switching to the first tab, and then switching to the first card in the CardLayout that houses the content of that tab. This shows the "Select a category to view the snippets in it" message again, just like when the application starts up and no category is selected. Finally, all the other detail tabs are disabled, and at that point we're done.

The search form and results are cleared, just in case there were results from this category showing. It would be a Very Bad Thing™ if the user clicked a result and the category didn't exist any longer!

The Add Snippet button also has an event handler, shown here:

```
CodeCabinetExt.UIEventHandlers.AddSnippet = function() {

  if (!CodeCabinetExt.Data.SnippetsStore.getById("New Snippet")) {
    CodeCabinetExt.Data.SnippetsStore.add(
      new CodeCabinetExt.Data.SnippetRecord({
        categoryname : CodeCabinetExt.currentCategory.get("name"),
        name : "New Snippet", author : "",
        description : "A new snippet", email : "", code : "", weblink : "",
        notes : "", keyword1 : "", keyword2 : "", keyword3 : "", keyword4 : "",
        keyword5 : ""
      }, "New Snippet")
    );
  }

};
```

Adding a snippet is nothing more than adding a new SnippetRecord to the SnippetsStore. However, since we only want to allow one new snippet at a time, we first try to retrieve the snippet with the name "New Snippet." If it's not found, the addition can go ahead.

Finally, here's the Delete Snippet button's event handler:

```
CodeCabinetExt.UIEventHandlers.DeleteSnippet = function() {

  Ext.MessageBox.confirm("Confirm Snippet Deletion",
    "Are you sure you want to delete the selected snippet?",
    function(inButtonClicked) {
      if (inButtonClicked == "yes") {
        CodeCabinetExt.Data.SnippetsStore.remove(CodeCabinetExt.currentSnippet);
        CodeCabinetExt.currentSnippet = null;
        Ext.getCmp("DeleteSnippet").setDisabled(true);
        Ext.getCmp("Details").setActiveTab(0);
        Ext.getCmp("tabInfo").setDisabled(true);
        Ext.getCmp("tabCode").setDisabled(true);
        Ext.getCmp("tabNotes").setDisabled(true);
        Ext.getCmp("tabKeywords").setDisabled(true);
      }
    }
  );

};
```

Here we see yet another Ext.MessageBox (we're back to that instead of Ext.Msg, but remember, they're the same thing!). This time it's the Ext.MessageBox.confirm() function. This gives us a display like what you see in Figure 5-13.

This provides a nice Yes/No-type question to the user. Just as with the prompt() method, we get back the text of the clicked button, so we can branch accordingly. Only when the user clicks Yes do we have something to do, and it begins by deleting the snippet from the SnippetsStore. Once again, this triggers the delete event on the store, which calls the DAO.deleteSnippet() method to take care of the database.

The CodeCabinetExt.currentSnippet field is set to null, and then the Delete Snippet Toolbar button is disabled. All the other Toolbar buttons can remain as is, though, so the Toolbar is done.

Finally, the Details section needs to be updated, which involves switching to the first tab, which means we'll be looking at the (now updated) list of snippets in the category again. The other tabs are disabled, and that does it.

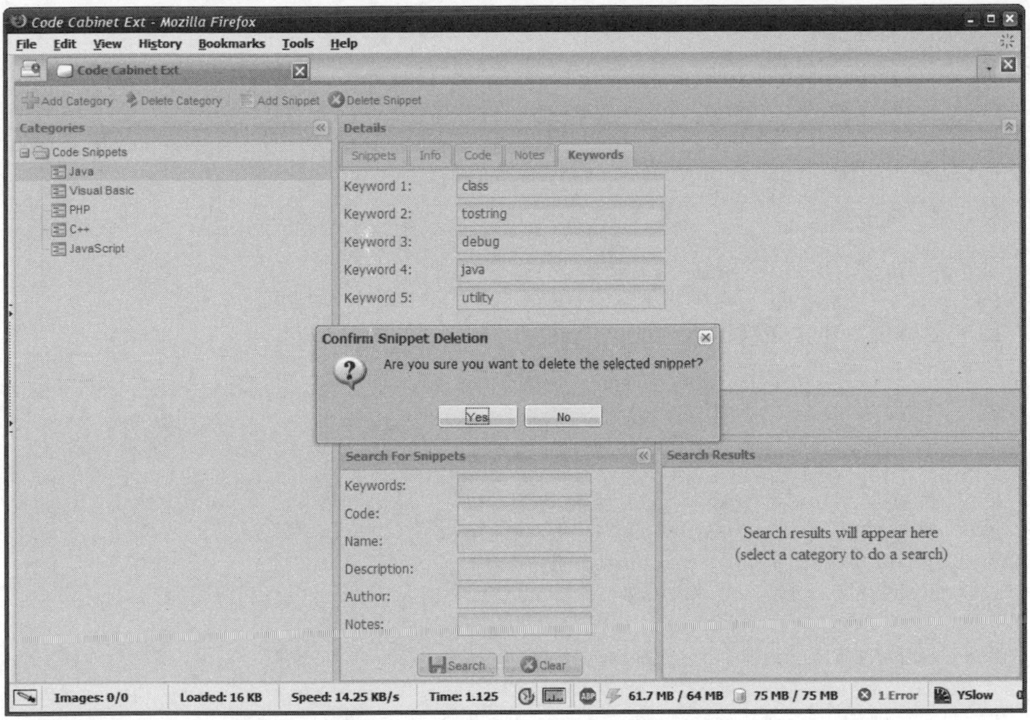

Figure 5-13. *The Delete Snippet prompt*

Tree.js

The code for the categories Tree is not much more than a small configuration object along with a single event handler. Let's look at that configuration object first:

```
CodeCabinetExt.UIObjects.Tree = function() { return ({
  id : "Tree", root : new Ext.tree.TreeNode(
    { id : "root", text : "Code Snippets" }
  ),
  listeners : {
    click : function(inNode, inEvent) {
      CodeCabinetExt.UIEventHandlers.TreeClick(inNode, inEvent);
    }
  }
}); };
```

Here we have a simple Tree definition with the single required root TreeNode present. It has a click handler attached to react to its nodes being clicked. That handler, which is where the more interesting stuff can be found, looks like this:

```
CodeCabinetExt.UIEventHandlers.TreeClick = function(inNode, inEvent) {

  var categoryRecord = CodeCabinetExt.Data.CategoriesStore.getById(inNode.id);
  CodeCabinetExt.currentCategory = categoryRecord;

  Ext.getCmp("DeleteCategory").setDisabled(false);
  Ext.getCmp("AddSnippet").setDisabled(false);

  Ext.getCmp("tabInfo").setDisabled(true);
  Ext.getCmp("tabCode").setDisabled(true);
  Ext.getCmp("tabNotes").setDisabled(true);
  Ext.getCmp("tabKeywords").setDisabled(true);
  CodeCabinetExt.currentSnippet = false;

 CodeCabinetExt.populatingSnippetsStore = true;
  CodeCabinetExt.Data.SnippetsStore.removeAll();
  var snippets = CodeCabinetExt.Data.DAO.retrieveSnippets(inNode.id);
  for (var i = 0; i < snippets.length; i++) {
    CodeCabinetExt.Data.SnippetsStore.add(snippets[i], snippets[i].id);
  }
  CodeCabinetExt.populatingSnippetsStore = false;

  Ext.getCmp("Details").getLayout().setActiveItem(0);
  var ts = Ext.getCmp("tabSnippets");
  ts.getLayout().setActiveItem(1);
  ts.show();

};
```

When a node in the Tree is clicked, the required action is to display the snippets in that category in the Grid found on the Snippets tab of the Details section, as seen in Figure 5-14. This requires a couple of steps.

First, the CategoryRecord associated with the clicked TreeNode is retrieved from the CategoriesStore via its getById() method. The ID being searched for is retrieved from the clicked node and passed into the handler function as the inNode argument by getting its id property. Next, CodeCabinetExt.currentCategory is set to the CategoryRecord.

Next, we enable the Toolbar Delete Category and Add Snippet buttons. Following that, the details section is set up. This means disabling all the tabs other than the Snippets tab (because no snippet is selected at this point). We also set CodeCabinetExt.currentSnippet to false at this point.

The next step is to populate the SnippetsStore with the snippets for this category. First, the CodeCabinetExt.populatingSnippetsStore field is set to true. Did you stash that in your memory as I suggested earlier? Good! Now we can see why this is necessary: the add and remove events of the SnippetsStore should *not* execute while the store is being populated, and that's where this variable comes in. When set to true, those two handlers do nothing. Once they are set to true, the removeAll() method can be called on the SnippetsStore to clear it. Next, a call to the DAO's retrieveSnippets() method is made, passing it the name of the category to get snippets for (remember that the ID of the TreeNode clicked is in fact the name of the category).

Once that method returns, we iterate over the array of `SnippetRecords`. We add each to the `SnippetsStore`, ensuring that we give it the appropriate ID as well. At the end of this loop we set `CodeCabinetExt.populatingSnippetsStore` to `false` so that the events on that `Store` can once again fire.

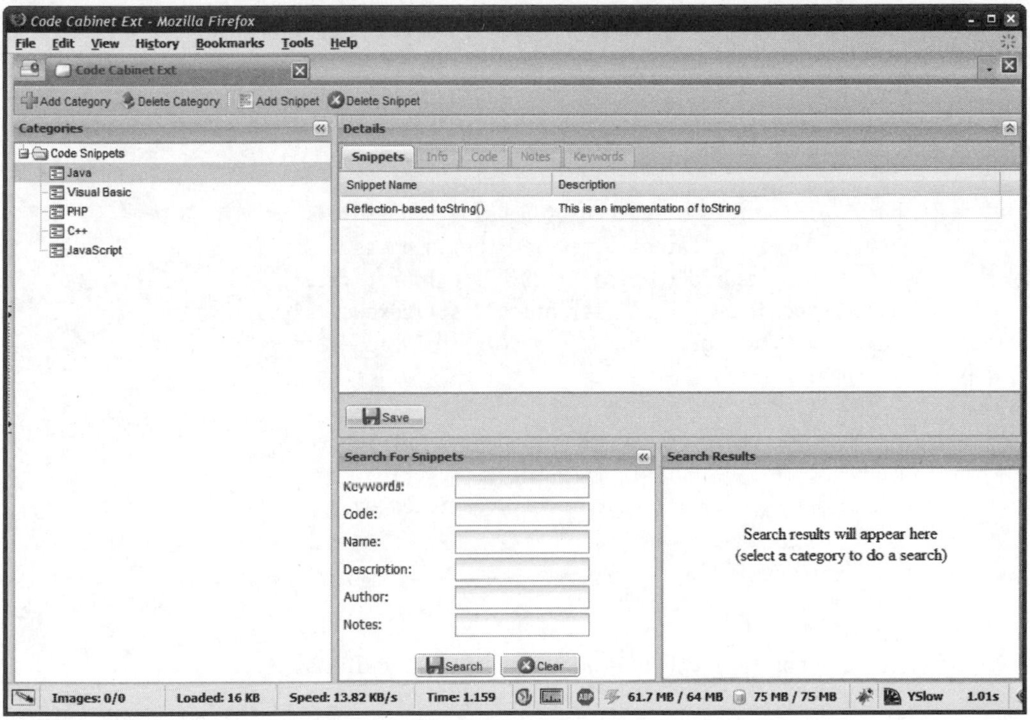

Figure 5-14. *With a category selected, the snippets within it can now be seen.*

The last thing to do is to switch to the snippets `Grid` on the Snippets tab by setting the active item of the `TabPanel` to 0 to ensure we're on the right tab, and then setting the active item of the `CardLayout` within that tab to 1 to show the `Grid`.

■**Note** I encountered an issue where the `Grid` wouldn't show up all the time. My solution was to call the `show()` method on the Snippets tab, which shouldn't be necessary, but seemed to do the trick in this case. It's good to know you can impose your will a bit and make Ext JS show something it has decided it wouldn't!

Details.js

The `Details.js` file is where we'll find the largest chunk of code in this application, and none of it is rocket science by any stretch of the imagination! This file contains all the code pertaining to the snippet detail tabbed section. I'll break this up into some smaller chunks, beginning with the configuration object for the first tab, the Snippets tab:

```
CodeCabinetExt.UIObjects.Details = function() { return ({
  buttons : [
    { xtype : "button", text : "Save",
      icon : "img/icon_save.gif", cls : "x-btn-text-icon",
      handler : CodeCabinetExt.UIEventHandlers.SaveClick
    }
  ],
  id : "Details", activeTab : 0, items : [
    { title : "Snippets", id : "tabSnippets", layout : "card",
      activeItem : 0, items : [
        { id : "SnippetsMessage", border : false,
          bodyStyle : "text-align:center;padding-top:75px;",
          html : "Select a category to view the snippets in it" },
        { id : "SnippetsGrid", xtype : "grid", border : false,
          autoExpandColumn : "colDescription", stripeRows : true,
          sm : new Ext.grid.RowSelectionModel( { singleSelect : true } ),
          listeners: {
            rowclick : {
              fn : function(inGrid, inRowIndex, inEventObject) {
                CodeCabinetExt.UIEventHandlers.RowClick(
                  inGrid.getSelectionModel().getSelected()
                );
              }
            }
          },
          store : CodeCabinetExt.Data.SnippetsStore, columns : [
            { header : "Snippet Name", sortable : true,
              dataIndex : "name", width : 200 },
            { header : "Description", sortable : true,
              dataIndex : "description", id : "colDescription" }
          ]
        }
      ]
    }
  ]
},
```

A single button is placed at the bottom for saving. This button remains visible on each of the tabs; that way, users can save their changes at any time from any tab. The handler for this button is called on the CodeCabinetExt.UIEventHandlers.SaveClick() method, which we will get to shortly as well.

This is where the snippets in the selected category are displayed in a Grid, or where the message telling the user to select a category is. This tab therefore contains a CardLayout within it, as you can see. The first card is the one containing the message. The value for the bodyStyle attribute uses some plain CSS to center the text horizontally and to push it down 75 pixels from the top.

The second card is where the Grid is, so it's a GridPanel (xtype:grid). This Grid is bound to the CodeCabinetExt.Data.SnippetsStore, which we know is populated when a node in the Tree is clicked. Row striping is turned on for visual appeal, and the Description column is set to auto-expand to fill up the space in the Grid. We define a RowSelectionModel so that only a single row can be selected at a time. Finally, a rowclick event handler is attached. This handler gets the selected row via the SelectionModel. It passes this row to the CodeCabinetExt.UIEventHandlers.RowClick() function, which we'll look at a bit later.

The code for the Info tab definition is next:

```
{ disabled : true, title : "Info", layout : "fit", id : "tabInfo",
  bodyStyle : "padding:4px", items : [
    { xtype : "form", id : "InfoForm", labelWidth : 100,
      border : false, items : [
        { xtype : "textfield", fieldLabel : "Name",
          id : "info_name", name : "name", width : 200 },
        { xtype : "textfield", fieldLabel : "Description",
          id : "info_description", name : "description", width : 200 },
        { xtype : "textfield", fieldLabel : "Author",
          id : "info_author", name : "author", width : 200 },
        { xtype : "textfield", fieldLabel : "eMail",
          id : "info_email", name : "email", width : 200 },
        { xtype : "textfield", fieldLabel : "Web Link",
          id : "info_weblink", name : "weblink", width : 200 }
      ]
    }
  ]
},
```

This is just a plain-old FormPanel with a batch of TextFields. The layout of the tab itself is set to fit so that the content stretches to fill it (which you can't really tell with this particular tab anyway). This is in fact the case for all the rest of the tabs. Each field is given a unique id as well.

■**Note** During technical review, it was discovered that adding and updating snippets had, shall we say, issues? The solution that I came up with was to assign each form field a unique ID and then not use the typical setValues() and getValues() method on the BasicForm they are a part of. After some research, I found that it seems to be a known bug in Ext JS that is being corrected in a future release. This was the simplest workaround I could find, but that's why there's still a name attribute as well: while it's not necessary now, it was there for using setValues() and getValues().

The next bit of code defines the Code tab:

```
{ disabled : true, title : "Code", layout : "fit", id : "tabCode",
  bodyStyle : "padding:4px", items : [
    { xtype : "form", id : "CodeForm", layout : "fit",
      items : [
        { xtype : "htmleditor", name : "code", hideLabel : true,
          id : "code_code" }
      ]
    }
  ]
},
```

In Figure 5-15 you can see this tab for yourself.

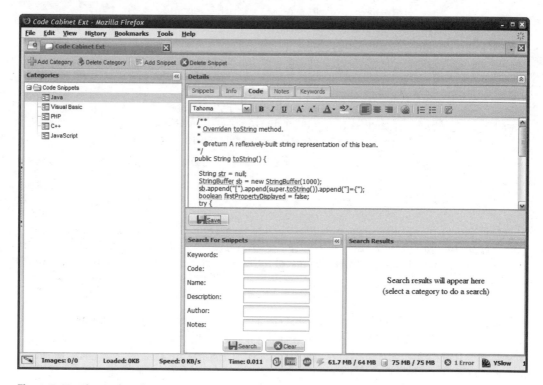

Figure 5-15. *The Code tab*

The interesting thing here is that instead of just a plain-old TextArea, which is what you would probably at first think is the appropriate widget here, I've used the HtmlEditor widget. This is a rich-text editor that allows users to format their text in a variety of ways, including colors, bold, and italics. I felt this was a good choice because as a developer it can be helpful to highlight parts of the code, or color-code things, and so on.

The hideLabel attribute is set to true on this widget. As its name implies, this attribute is used to hide the label that would otherwise be present on all form fields. Without this you would have seen whitespace to the left of the HtmlEditor, plus a colon, because the fieldLabel attribute by default is empty. So Ext JS displays it and then appends the colon. All of that is just ugly and entirely unnecessary given the existence of the hideLabel attribute!

The Notes tab is nearly identical to the Code tab, but just to prove it, here's the code:

```
{ disabled : true, title : "Notes", layout : "fit", id : "tabNotes",
  bodyStyle : "padding:4px", items : [
    { xtype : "form", id : "NotesForm", layout : "fit",
      items : [
        { xtype : "htmleditor", name : "notes", hideLabel : true,
          id : "notes_note" }
      ]
    }
  ]
},
```

And, as if that wasn't enough, Figure 5-16 shows you what it looks like, which is to say, just like the Code tab!

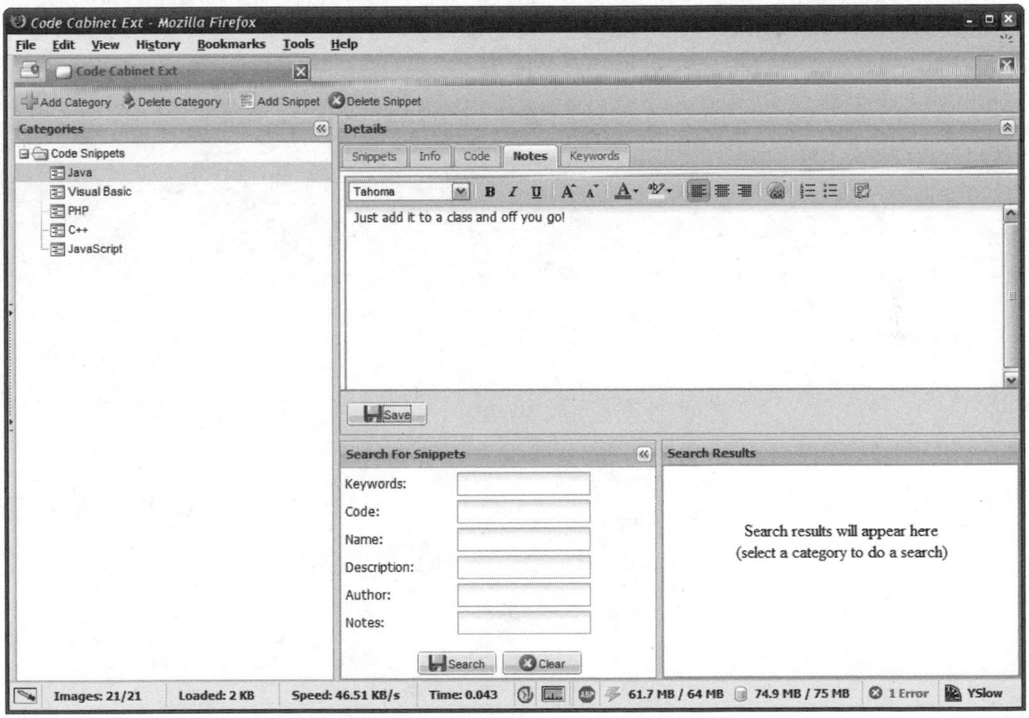

Figure 5-16. *The Notes tab (which could just as easily be the Code tab)*

The final tab to be defined is the Keywords tab, and it is very similar to the Info tab:

```
{ disabled : true, title : "Keywords", layout : "fit",
  id : "tabKeywords", items : [
    { xtype : "form", id : "KeywordsForm", labelWidth : 100,
      border : false, bodyStyle : "padding:4px", items : [
```

```
            { xtype : "textfield", name : "keyword1", id : "keywords_keyword1",
              fieldLabel : "Keyword 1", width : 200 },
            { xtype : "textfield", name : "keyword2", id : "keywords_keyword2",
              fieldLabel : "Keyword 2", width : 200 },
            { xtype : "textfield", name : "keyword3", id : "keywords_keyword3",
              fieldLabel : "Keyword 3", width : 200 },
            { xtype : "textfield", name : "keyword4", id : "keywords_keyword4",
              fieldLabel : "Keyword 4", width : 200 },
            { xtype : "textfield", name : "keyword5", id : "keywords_keyword5",
              fieldLabel : "Keyword 5", width : 200 }
          ]
        }
      ]
    }
  ]
}); };
```

Once again we have just a simple form with five TextFields on it, one for each keyword.
I felt five keywords would likely be sufficient in most cases, but feel free to disagree and modify
the application to allow for more if desired. Figure 5-17 shows what this tab looks like.

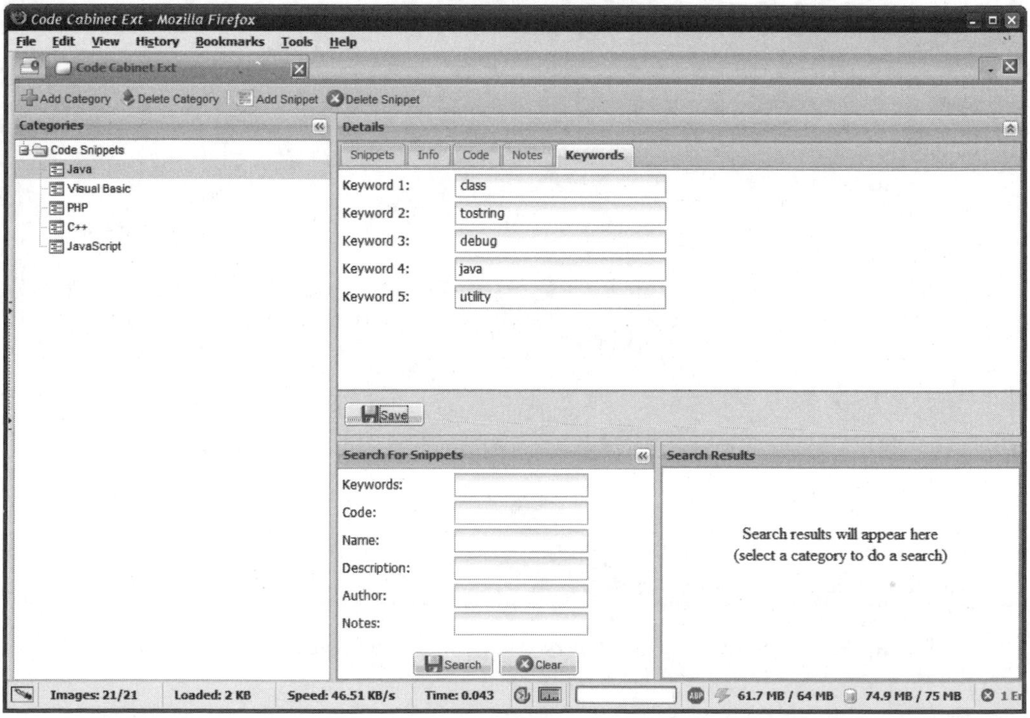

Figure 5-17. *The Keywords tab*

Now that we have the UI defined, we can go ahead and look those event handler functions we saw being called, starting with the SaveClick() method:

```
CodeCabinetExt.UIEventHandlers.SaveClick = function() {

  CodeCabinetExt.currentSnippet.beginEdit();
  CodeCabinetExt.currentSnippet.set("name", Ext.getCmp("info_name").getValue());
  CodeCabinetExt.currentSnippet.set("description",
    Ext.getCmp("info_description").getValue());
  CodeCabinetExt.currentSnippet.set("author",
    Ext.getCmp("info_author").getValue());
  CodeCabinetExt.currentSnippet.set("email",
    Ext.getCmp("info_email").getValue());
  CodeCabinetExt.currentSnippet.set("weblink",
    Ext.getCmp("info_weblink").getValue());
  CodeCabinetExt.currentSnippet.set("code", Ext.getCmp("code_code").getValue());
  CodeCabinetExt.currentSnippet.set("notes",
    Ext.getCmp("notes_note").getValue());
  CodeCabinetExt.currentSnippet.set("keyword1",
    Ext.getCmp("keywords_keyword1").getValue());
  CodeCabinetExt.currentSnippet.set("keyword2",
    Ext.getCmp("keywords_keyword2").getValue());
  CodeCabinetExt.currentSnippet.set("keyword3",
    Ext.getCmp("keywords_keyword3").getValue());
  CodeCabinetExt.currentSnippet.set("keyword4",
    Ext.getCmp("keywords_keyword4").getValue());
  CodeCabinetExt.currentSnippet.set("keyword5",
    Ext.getCmp("keywords_keyword5").getValue());
  CodeCabinetExt.currentSnippet.endEdit();

};
```

Since we'll be updating multiple fields on the SnippetRecord we need to call beginEdit() on the currentSnippet. That way, we conveniently have a reference to it and can update each of the fields. The values are retrieved from the individual fields (see the note a few pages back about why I didn't use getValues() here). Finally, endEdit() is called on the SnippetRecord, triggering a call to DAO.updateSnippet(), and we're done. Saving couldn't be easier!

The last bit of code to look at is the RowClick() method. It's fairly long in comparison to most of the others in this application but isn't any tougher to follow:

```
CodeCabinetExt.UIEventHandlers.RowClick = function(inRecord,
  inFromSearchResults) {

  if (inFromSearchResults) {
    var tree = Ext.getCmp("Tree");
    var node = tree.getNodeById(inRecord.get("categoryname"));
    node.select();
    tree.fireEvent("click", node, null);
  }
```

```
    CodeCabinetExt.currentSnippet = inRecord;

    Ext.getCmp("DeleteSnippet").setDisabled(false);

    Ext.getCmp("tabInfo").setDisabled(false);
    Ext.getCmp("tabCode").setDisabled(false);
    Ext.getCmp("tabNotes").setDisabled(false);
    Ext.getCmp("tabKeywords").setDisabled(false);

    Ext.getCmp("keywords_keyword1").setValue(inRecord.get("keyword1"));
    Ext.getCmp("keywords_keyword2").setValue(inRecord.get("keyword2"));
    Ext.getCmp("keywords_keyword3").setValue(inRecord.get("keyword3"));
    Ext.getCmp("keywords_keyword4").setValue(inRecord.get("keyword4"));
    Ext.getCmp("keywords_keyword5").setValue(inRecord.get("keyword5"));

    Ext.getCmp("notes_note").setValue(inRecord.get("notes"));

    Ext.getCmp("code_code").setValue(inRecord.get("code"));

    Ext.getCmp("info_name").setValue(inRecord.get("name"));
    Ext.getCmp("info_description").setValue(inRecord.get("description"));
    Ext.getCmp("info_author").setValue(inRecord.get("author"));
    Ext.getCmp("info_email").setValue(inRecord.get("email"));
    Ext.getCmp("info_weblink").setValue(inRecord.get("weblink"));

    Ext.getCmp("Details").getLayout().setActiveItem(1);
    Ext.getCmp("tabInfo").show();

};
```

This method is called from two different places: clicking a snippet in the snippets Grid, or clicking a snippet from the search results Grid (which we'll be looking at next). That's the reason for the first little if statement: the inFromSearchResults argument will only be true when this is called from the search results Grid. In that situation, since we aren't sure the category of the selected snippet is selected, we need to ensure it is. To do so we're going to simulate the user clicking on the appropriate Tree node. So naturally, the first step is to find the node in the Tree by getting a reference to the Tree and then using its getNodeById() method. Once we have the TreeNode, we call its select() method. Once that's done we can simulate the click by calling the fireEvent() method on the Tree, passing it the name of the event to fire, click in this case, as well as a reference to the node itself. This then causes all the UI setup and such that we previously saw.

After that, or if we're dealing with a click of a row in the snippets Grid and not the search results Grid, then we need to record the SnippetRecord as current by setting CodeCabinetExt.currentSnippet to point to it. The appropriate Toolbar items are then enabled.

Next, we have to populate all four of the detail tabs. So, for each, we get a reference to the fields on them using our dear friend Mr. Ext.getCmp(), and then the setValues() of the individual fields to set the value retrieved from the SnippetRecord.

Once all four of the tabs have been populated, a call is made to flip to the Info tab, and then we call the show() method on the tab. This again shouldn't be necessary, but without it the details didn't always appear.

SearchForm.js

The final two source files relate to the search capability. The first file, SearchForm.js, implements the form where you enter search criteria, beginning with the UI definition:

```
CodeCabinetExt.UIObjects.SearchForm = function () { return ({
  id : "SearchForm", labelWidth : 100, border : false,
  bodyStyle : "padding:4px", items : [
    { xtype : "textfield", fieldLabel : "Keywords",
      name : "keywords" },
    { xtype : "textfield", fieldLabel : "Code",
      name : "code" },
    { xtype : "textfield", fieldLabel : "Name",
      name : "name" },
    { xtype : "textfield", fieldLabel : "Description",
      name : "description" },
    { xtype : "textfield", fieldLabel : "Author",
      name : "author" },
    { xtype : "textfield", fieldLabel : "Notes",
      name : "notes" }
  ], buttons : [
    { xtype : "button", text : "Search",
      icon : "img/icon_save.gif", cls : "x-btn-text-icon",
      handler : CodeCabinetExt.UIEventHandlers.SearchClick },
    { xtype : "button", text : "Clear",
      icon : "img/icon_snippet_delete.gif", cls : "x-btn-text-icon",
      handler : CodeCabinetExt.UIEventHandlers.ClearClick }
  ]
}); };
```

The definition of the form is straightforward; there are no new fields to explain! One thing that is new, however, is that these buttons are jazzed up a little by placing icons on them. We do this using the icon and cls attributes. The icon attribute points to an image that we want to put on the Button, and the cls attribute is what makes that button show up. The x-btn-text-icon value is a style class supplied by Ext JS's base style sheet that makes the Button show the image along with a text label next to it.

The next method, SearchClick(), is by far the meatiest piece from the search feature. This method implements the logic behind the search itself. Because it's fairly lengthy, I'll break it down into small, more easily digestible chunks, starting with this one:

```
CodeCabinetExt.UIEventHandlers.SearchClick = function() {

  var searchVals = Ext.getCmp("SearchForm").getForm().getValues();
  searchVals.keywords = Ext.util.Format.trim(
    Ext.util.Format.lowercase(searchVals.keywords));
  searchVals.code = Ext.util.Format.trim(
    Ext.util.Format.lowercase(searchVals.code));
  searchVals.name = Ext.util.Format.trim(
    Ext.util.Format.lowercase(searchVals.name));
  searchVals.author = Ext.util.Format.trim(
    Ext.util.Format.lowercase(searchVals.author));
  searchVals.description = Ext.util.Format.trim(
    Ext.util.Format.lowercase(searchVals.description));
  searchVals.notes = Ext.util.Format.trim(
    Ext.util.Format.lowercase(searchVals.notes));
```

Here we're getting the values of each of the search criteria TextFields. This is done by getting a reference to the form via Ext.getCmp("SearchForm").getForm(), a construct we've seen numerous times, and then calling its getValues() method. The values are trimmed and converted to lowercase using the Ext.util.Format class and its trim() and lowercase() methods, respectively, so all our searches will be case-insensitive and there's no chance of not finding matches due to wayward whitespace around values. (This assumes that the fields of the SnippetRecords objects in which we try to find matches are similarly trimmed and lowercased, but that assumption is correct, as you'll see shortly.)

Once we have the values we can begin our work. Let's start with some validation to ensure only valid searches are attempted:

```
if (searchVals.keywords == "" && searchVals.code == "" &&
  searchVals.name == "" && searchVals.author == "" &&
  searchVals.description == "" && searchVals.notes == "") {
    Ext.MessageBox.show({
      title : "Unable to perform search", buttons : Ext.MessageBox.OK,
      animEl : "divSource",
      msg : "I'm sorry but you must enter at least one search criterion " +
      "in order to perform a search."
    });
  return;
}
```

The validation amounts to nothing more than assuring at least one of the search criteria has been entered. If not, we use our friend the Ext.MessageBox.show() method to show a fancier, Ext JS-based alert() pop-up.

Here's the next bit of code we encounter:

```
CodeCabinetExt.Data.SearchResultsStore.removeAll();
var snippets = CodeCabinetExt.Data.DAO.retrieveSnippets();
```

To find matches we need the snippets to search through, so a quick call to the DAO's retrieveSnippets() method does the trick. Note that no category name is passed to this method, so that argument is effectively null, which you'll recall from looking at the DAO code means all snippets in the database will be returned.

With those snippets in hand, we can go ahead and start trying to find matches:

```
var matchesFound = false;
for (var i = 0; i < snippets.length; i++) {
```

We then begin to iterate over the array of SnippetRecord objects returned from DAO.retrieveSnippets(). We have a variable matchesFound set to false initially. This will be set to true when we find that we have one or more matches. So, the next step is to process all the fields in the next SnippetRecord and do the same sort of trimming and case conversion that we did with the search criteria to ensure that we'll get matches, if there legitimately are any:

```
var snippetKeyword1 = Ext.util.Format.trim(
  Ext.util.Format.lowercase(snippets[i].get("keyword1")));
var snippetKeyword2 = Ext.util.Format.trim(
  Ext.util.Format.lowercase(snippets[i].get("keyword2")));
var snippetKeyword3 = Ext.util.Format.trim(
  Ext.util.Format.lowercase(snippets[i].get("keyword3")));
var snippetKeyword4 = Ext.util.Format.trim(
  Ext.util.Format.lowercase(snippets[i].get("keyword4")));
var snippetKeyword5 = Ext.util.Format.trim(
  Ext.util.Format.lowercase(snippets[i].get("keyword5")));
var snippetCode = Ext.util.Format.trim(
  Ext.util.Format.lowercase(snippets[i].get("code")));
var snippetName = Ext.util.Format.trim(
  Ext.util.Format.lowercase(snippets[i].get("name")));
var snippetAuthor = Ext.util.Format.trim(
  Ext.util.Format.lowercase(snippets[i].get("author")));
var snippetDescription = Ext.util.Format.trim(
  Ext.util.Format.lowercase(snippets[i].get("description")));
var snippetNotes = Ext.util.Format.trim(
  Ext.util.Format.lowercase(snippets[i].get("notes")));
```

With the fields of the next SnippetRecord to check suitably converted to lowercase and trimmed, we can begin looking for matches. Because we can enter multiple search criteria, that means we need to look for matches with whatever combination of criteria were entered. If the user enters a value in the Name field and enters a value in the Keywords field, it means we're looking for all snippets that have the name value in its Name field as well as the keywords specified. To do that, we have a variable named matched:

```
var matched = "";

if (searchVals.name != "") {
  if (snippetName.indexOf(searchVals.name) != -1) {
    matched += "T";
  } else {
    matched += "F";
  }
}
```

We'll then check each possible criterion in turn. Anytime a search criterion is in play, and anytime a match is found based on those criteria, we'll add a T to matched. If a given criterion is in play but there is no match, we'll add an F. That way, when we get to the end, if we have no Fs in the matched string, that means the snippet is a match on all criteria requested. Not only is this a simple approach, but it also enables us to extend the search facility by adding new criteria, without having to redesign the underlying matching mechanism.

You can see the first criterion being checked: the name. If searchVals.name, which is the value the user entered, is not a blank string, that criterion is in play. So, we do a simple indexOf() search to see whether the entered value appears anywhere in the name field of the SnippetRecord. If it does, we consider that a match; otherwise, it's not a match.

The code, author, description, and notes search criteria are all essentially identical to the name code, so just have a look at them; I won't bore you by describing them:

```
if (searchVals.code != "") {
  if (snippetCode.indexOf(searchVals.code) != -1) {
    matched += "T";
  } else {
    matched += "F";
  }
}

if (searchVals.author != "") {
  if (snippetAuthor.indexOf(searchVals.author) != -1) {
    matched += "T";
  } else {
    matched += "F";
  }
}

if (searchVals.description != "") {
  if (snippetDescription.indexOf(searchVals.description) != -1) {
    matched += "T";
  } else {
    matched += "F";
  }
}

if (searchVals.notes != "") {
  if (snippetNotes.indexOf(searchVals.notes) != -1) {
    matched += "T";
  } else {
    matched += "F";
  }
}
```

Now, the keywords are just slightly different:

```
if (searchVals.keywords != "") {
  var a = searchVals.keywords.split(",");
  var foundAny = false;
  for (var j = 0; j < a.length; j++) {
    var nextKeyword = Ext.util.Format.trim(a[j]);
    if (nextKeyword != "") {
      if (snippetKeyword1 == nextKeyword ||
        snippetKeyword2 == nextKeyword || snippetKeyword3 == nextKeyword ||
        snippetKeyword4 == nextKeyword || snippetKeyword5 == nextKeyword) {
        foundAny = true;
      }
    }
  }
  if (foundAny) {
    matched += "T";
  } else {
    matched += "F";
  }
]
```

Here we split() the keywords the user entered. We then iterate over the resultant array. The next token from the string is trimmed, and as long as it's not blank, we see whether that value appears anywhere in the keyword fields of the SnippetRecord. If so, we again have a match on this search criterion.

Finally, all the search criteria that are in play having been checked, we now see whether there are any Fs in the matched string. If there aren't, we have ourselves a match!

```
if (matched.indexOf("F") == -1) {
  matchesFound = true;
  CodeCabinetExt.Data.SearchResultsStore.add(snippets[i]);
}

}
```

The SnippetRecord is added to the SearchResultsStore, which is bound to the Grid in the search results area. Only one task remains at this point:

```
if (matchesFound) {
  Ext.getCmp("SearchResults").getLayout().setActiveItem(2);
} else {
  Ext.getCmp("SearchResults").getLayout().setActiveItem(1);
}

};
```

If there were any matches at all found, then the third card in the CardLayout in the search results area needs to be shown, which contains the Grid; otherwise, the second card is shown, the one that informs the user that no matches were found.

One last method can be found in this source file, and it's a simple one:

```
CodeCabinetExt.UIEventHandlers.ClearClick = function() {

  Ext.getCmp("SearchForm").getForm().reset();

};
```

I think it's obvious to you that this one is called when the clear button is clicked. A simple reset() call on the search form is all it takes.

SearchResults.js

We saw how the search form is put together, so now it would probably be a good idea to see how the results are put together. Before that, though, it's been a while since our last screen-shot, so take a gander at Figure 5-18, where you can see the search form and some results that have been pulled up based on my search criteria.

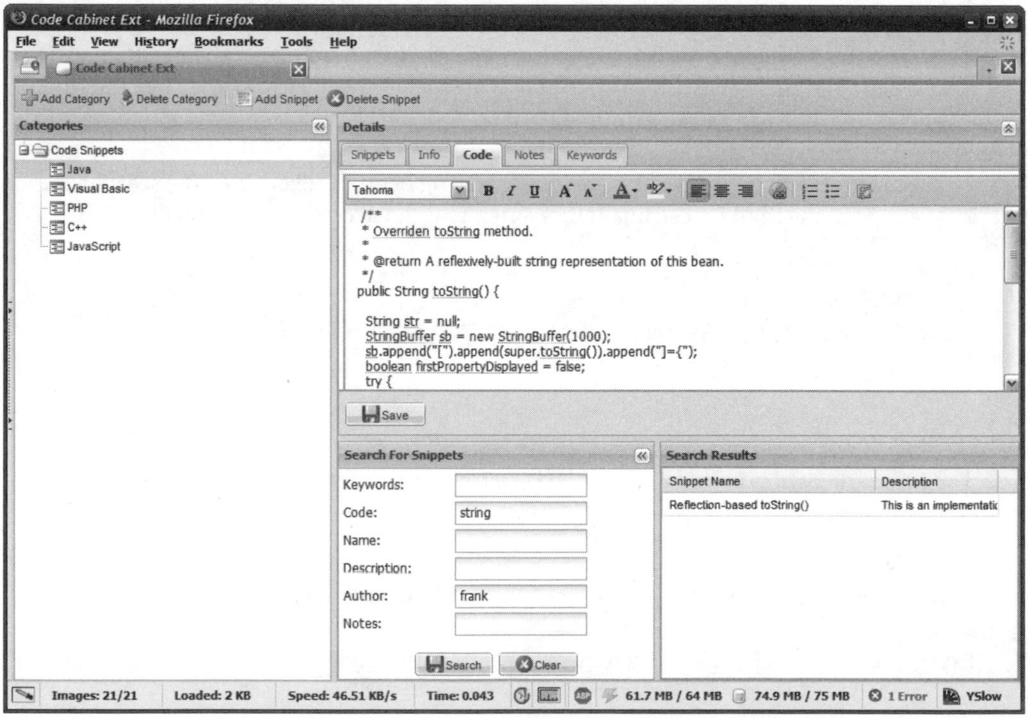

Figure 5-18. *A search, having been executed, has returned results (just one, but it still counts!).*

The code behind the results section is this:

```
CodeCabinetExt.UIObjects.SearchResults = function() { return ({
  id : "SearchResults", layout : "card", activeItem : 0,
  deferredRender : false, items : [
    { border : false, bodyStyle : "text-align:center;padding-top:50px;",
      html : "Search results will appear here<br>" +
      "(select a category to do a search)" },
    { border : false, bodyStyle : "text-align:center;padding-top:50px;",
      html : "No snippets were found matching your search criteria" },
    { border : false, store : CodeCabinetExt.Data.SearchResultsStore,
      xtype : "grid", autoExpandColumn : "colDescription",
      stripeRows : true,
      sm : new Ext.grid.RowSelectionModel( { singleSelect : true } ),
      columns : [
        { header : "Snippet Name", sortable : true, width : 200,
          dataIndex : "name" },
        { header : "Description", sortable : true,
          id : "colDescription", dataIndex : "description" }
      ],
      listeners : {
        rowclick : {
          fn : function(inGrid, inRowIndex, inEventObject) {
            CodeCabinetExt.UIEventHandlers.RowClick(
              inGrid.getSelectionModel().getSelected(), true
            );
          }
        }
      }
    }
  ]
}); };
```

So, we've got ourselves another CardLayout, similar to the Snippets tab in the Details section, because there is a message when there are no search results, and also a message when no matches are found, and finally a Grid for displaying the matches.

The first two cards are the messages, and they are just like what you saw on the Snippets tab. The third card is the Grid, and it isn't much different either from the snippets Grid on the Snippets tab. It even uses the save RowClick handler, which we explored earlier.

In fact, this whole chunk of code, taken as a whole, is kind of like the episode "Mirror, Mirror" of *Star Trek: The Original Series*. You know, the one when Kirk gets accidentally sent to a mirror version of the universe, except everyone is evil? There's evil Spock, evil Sulu, and so forth. Now, I'm not sure which bit of code is the evil twin, but the point is they are mirror images of one another, with just some minor differences. And yes, I am officially the master of stretched analogies here!

And with that one last pop-culture reference we've officially completed our exploration of this project and its code!

Suggested Exercises

I think the code cabinet as it is presented in this chapter is pretty useful, but as usual I've left some things out. Here are just a few suggestions, all of which would make it a more useful application, not to mention giving you a lot of good experience working with Ext JS:

- Allow for subcategories. Say I want to have a Java category, and below that I want to have a category for string-related snippets, one for math-related snippets, and one for UI-related snippets. As it stands today, I'd have to create three separate Java categories, all at the same level in the tree hierarchy. Allowing for subcategories would make the organizational capabilities of the application that much more robust.

- How about adding a field to the Info tab for the date the snippet was added? For bonus points, use the `DatePicker` widget, and for even more bonus points, add it to the search function.

- This one's a little bigger but would really make the application nice: history capabilities. In other words, every time you make a change to a snippet, record the state of the snippet before the change. Whether you simply duplicate the entire snippet record or try to do a fancy-pants diff mechanism is up to you. Add a tab that lists all the history records and allow one to be clicked so you can see the state of the snippet at that point. This would give this application a source control system type of feel to it.

- Add a Copy button below the code editor that when clicked copies the code to the clipboard maintained by the operating system (there is JavaScript code to do this; just Google for it). This is just a minor enhancement but could be a fairly significant convenience for the user. (To be honest, I thought of this only after this chapter was nearly all wrapped up. I feel a little silly for not thinking of it earlier, but hey, it gives me a chance to offer another suggested exercise to you, my dear reader!)

- Here's a fun one: remember how the `Windows` "shrink into view" from the top? How about adding a different source `<div>` for each `Window` in the application, each with its own style selector so that one "shrinks in" from the top, one from the left, one from the right, and one from the bottom. The selector you'd need for the bottom and right are tricky because you only know some of their positional values at runtime, you'd have to calculate them on the fly, and you'd also have to recalculate them if the `Window` is resized. The results would look pretty cool, though!

I suspect those suggestions will keep you busy for a while. They will not only make the application more useful but will definitely sharpen your skills in the process, so a definite win-win situation! What are you doing still reading? Get to work!

Summary

In this chapter, we developed an application for coding code snippets. We used a few new widgets and features in the process, got some further experience with the `Ext.data` package, and even played with Gears a bit more. We saw a whole new way to architect our applications, one that is probably the best and cleanest that we've seen so far. In the process, we created an application that we can use for a real purpose!

In the next chapter we'll introduce a server-side component in the form of JSON-P Web Services, and we'll see how Ext JS allows us to do that with incredible ease.

CHAPTER 6

∎ ∎ ∎

When the Yellow Pages Just Isn't Cool Enough: Local Business Search

Sit right back and you'll hear a tale, a tale of a big yellow book…I know, it doesn't quite fit the melody of the *Gilligan's Island* theme, but work with me here!

You kids today (hey, get off my lawn!) with your Internets and your iPhones[1] and your Tellmes,[2] you don't know what it was like! Back in the day, if you wanted to find a business in your hometown, you either asked a neighbor or pulled out this huge yellow book called, very creatively, the Yellow Pages. In this book, you could flip through an alphabetically sorted listing of all sorts of businesses in your vicinity. It was a manual process: you actually had to turn pages! You couldn't just type something into a computer and have it spit out a list of businesses; you had to burn some calories and expend some mental effort.

Ah, but I like progress as much as the next guy, so now I get to play the part of the old curmudgeon and tell these stories about how we used to walk to school in the snow, uphill, both ways, and use the Yellow Pages. I also get to write books and show how the world is much better now that we can write an application to save us from all that work, which is something I strive to avoid every chance I get!

That's precisely what this chapter is all about: we'll be writing an application that enables us to search for local businesses. We'll be able to see a map of where the business is located, along with some details about it. We'll also have the ability to store a business as one of our favorites so that, if you can believe it, we'll be able to expend even less energy next time to find it again! Ext JS will make all of this a piece of cake, of course, and we'll have a pretty useful little application by the time we're finished.

---

1 During the 2000 United States presidential campaign, George W. Bush uttered the term "Internets." Clearly, the Internet should never be pluralized like that; it was a typical Bushism, as it's known, which is why people now use this phrase in a humorous context (and sometimes in an insulting way, depending on how it's used).

2 Tellme (www.tellme.com) is a voice-activated service that enables you to call a 1-800 number and get information such as weather, sports scores, business listings, and more, all just by speaking into the phone. It's a very handy service to have at the ready in your cell phone's contact list.

What's This Application Do Anyway?

Let's get the silly terminology out of the way first, shall we? What we're actually creating here is called a mashup. A mashup, as these types of web apps have come to be known, is basically a web site or application that takes content from multiple sources (usually via some sort of public programmatic interface—a remote API, in other words), and integrates it all into a new experience—that is, a new application.

The term *mashup* might sound a bit silly (it does to me!), but it's the term that's been applied to what is at its core an extremely powerful vision: people provide various services and data over the Internet via a well-defined programmatic interface, and anyone can come along and combine them to create applications. In other words, we're talking about a relatively simple, open, platform-agnostic service-oriented architecture (SOA).

MORE ON SOA

The idea of SOA has been gaining steam over the past few years. Most notably, the concept of web services has been evolving rapidly over that time. However, the meaning of that term has been evolving as well. People now often consider things such as the Yahoo! services, which will be used in this application, to be web services, even though they don't use the full web services stack (that is, SOAP, WS-Security, and all the other specifications that can go along with it).

Whatever line of demarcation you choose to use, the bottom line is that you're developing using a SOA, which means you have loosely coupled components that expose a remote service interface that, usually, is platform- and language-agnostic and can therefore be married together in nearly limitless ways.

The benefits of this approach are numerous. The simple fact that you aren't generally tied to any particular technology or language is a big one. The ease with which updates can be done, assuming the interface doesn't change, is another big one (this is the same reason people love web apps in general). The ability to use all sorts of automated tools to both create and consume services is another (although this isn't always a good thing, if those tools become a crutch that allows you to not understand what you're doing). Realizing the goal of building your application on top of established standards is another. Reusing existing assets and therefore increasing the speed with which solutions can be delivered is another (some would argue this is the biggest benefit). There are plenty more; these are just some that come to mind immediately.

You've almost certainly heard the term *web services* before too. Web services are sometimes involved in mashups. However, web services, as most people mean when they use the term, can be pretty complicated beasts! SOAP; Universal Description, Discovery, and Integration (UDDI) directories; Web Services Description Language (WSDL) documents—not to mention a whole host of other specifications—are the types of things you deal with in working with web services. Although there's nothing that says that stuff can't be involved when writing a mashup, typically they aren't. There are other techniques available for writing mashups, as we'll soon see.

Today, the term mashup can also refer to a web app that, by and large, runs within your browser. In fact, for many people, mashup implies a JavaScript-based application that can run locally with no server interaction (aside from loading it in the first place, which is actually optional too) and calling on remote servers. The term mashup has generally come to mean browser-based JavaScript clients aggregating content through public APIs from various companies and vendors to form new applications. These APIs are often referred to as web services, and even though they may not truly be web services in the sense of using the full technology stack—the whole alphabet soup of terms I threw around in the preceding paragraph—they still fulfill the same basic goal as those types of web services. They provide services and function over a network (specifically, the Web), so calling them web services isn't too far-fetched anyway.

Many companies are getting into the API business, including companies you've certainly heard of: Google, Yahoo!, Amazon, and eBay, just to name a few. Google and Yahoo! have led the charge, and Yahoo!, in particular, originated a neat trick that will be central to the application we'll build in this chapter: the dynamic <script> tag trick, or <script> injection trick (it's sometimes referred to both ways). Now with the preliminaries out of the way, let's go ahead and spell out what this application is going to do:

- By using a remote service, we will be able to perform a search for businesses given an address or some components of a location. We'll be able to see a list of search results, page through large result sets, and select one to view in more detail, including the address, phone number, web site, and average user ratings.

- We'll also be able to view a map of the location around the business and be able to zoom in and out of that map.

- We can save a selected business as a favorite so that we can quickly call up its details later. These favorites will naturally be stored in a local database via Gears.

- The application will need something like a toolbar at the top, but we've seen that a bunch of times before so let's see if we can use some of the visual effect functions Ext JS provides to do something a little cooler, roughly emulating the Mac OS doc.

- The address used for a search can be saved as the default location to save time later, and we'll do this via cookies, just for something different.

Let's kick things off with Figure 6-1, depicting the application as it's seen at startup.

Here you can see that I have some favorites already stored, and the search form is cleared, all ready to receive my search criteria to look up more pizza parlors to feed my face at!

Now let's have a look at the web services we'll use to pull this off, and look at how we're going to be calling on them.

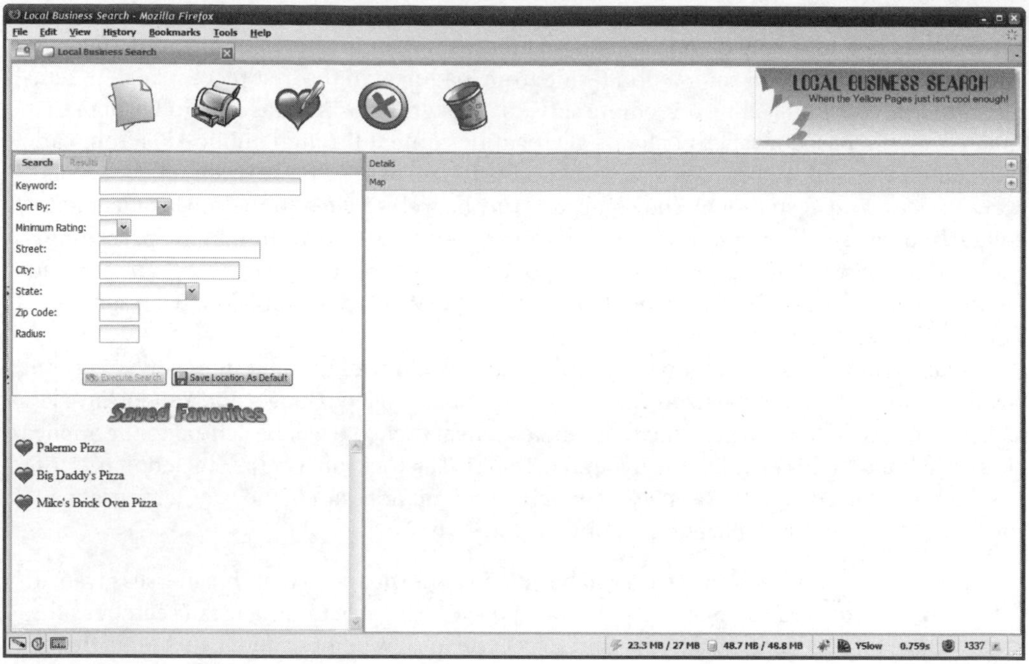

Figure 6-1. *The Local Business Search application as it appears at startup*

The <script> Tag Injection Technique and JSON-P

Yahoo! did something very cool a little while ago, and it is this one cool thing that makes the application in this chapter possible. Before we can explore that, though, we have to discuss what was going on before the coolness occurred.

For a while now, many companies, Yahoo! among them, have been exposing public APIs for people to use. For instance, you could perform a Yahoo! search remotely, or you could get a Yahoo! map from your own application, and so on. These APIs, these "web services," if you will, typically used XML as their data transport mechanism. You would post some XML to a given URL, and you would get an XML response back. It was (and still is) as simple as that. These types of services don't require all the web service technologies such as SOAP, UDDI, WSDL, and the like. It's a simple HTTP POST operation where the result returned by the server just happens to be XML.

If you wanted to use these APIs from a JavaScript-based client running in a browser, you quickly ran into a major stumbling block, though. Ajax, using the XMLHttpRequest object, has what's known as the same-domain security restriction in place. This means that the XMLHttpRequest object will not allow a request to a domain other than the domain from which the document the object is a part of was served. For instance, if you have a page named page1.htm located at http://www.omnytex.com, you can make requests to any URL at www.omnytex.com. However, if you try to make a request to something at www.yahoo.com, the XMLHttpRequest object won't allow it. This means that the APIs Yahoo! exposed aren't of much use to you if you try to access them directly from a browser. Because Ajax is the only way (apparently!) to make an asynchronous call from a browser that doesn't result in the full page being reloaded, it seems we're up a stream of feces without a means of locomotion! Even if you use a library such as Ext JS, it can't work around the limitations imposed by the underlying browser technology, so there's no relief to be had there.

There are ways around this same-domain restriction. Probably the most common is to write a server-side component on your own server that acts as a proxy. This enables your code to make requests via `XMLHttpRequest` to something like www.omnytex.com/proxy, which makes a request to something at www.yahoo.com on behalf of the calling code and returns the results. This is very cool, but it requires your own server in the mix, which is limiting.

Wouldn't it be so much more useful if the JavaScript running in the browser could make the request directly to Yahoo! and not need a server-side component? Yes, indeed it would be! And as you probably have guessed, there is a clever way to do it. Take a look at the following bit of plain-old JavaScript:

```
var scriptTag = document.createElement("script");
scriptTag.setAttribute("src", "www.yahoo.com/someAPI");
scriptTag.setAttribute("type", "text/javascript");
var headTag = document.getElementsByTagName("head").item(0);
headTag.appendChild(scriptTag);
```

So, what we have here is a new `<script>` tag being created. We set the `src` attribute to point to some API at Yahoo! (which at the end of the day is just a specific URL), and finally we append that new tag to the `<head>` of the document. The browser will go off and retrieve the resource at the specified URL, and then evaluate it, just as it does for any imported JavaScript file.

To understand this fully, keep in mind that anytime the browser encounters a `<script>` tag in the HTML document that it is parsing, it stops, retrieves the code at the URL specified by the `src` attribute of the `<script>` tag, and evaluates it, right then and there, meaning any global-scope code is executed immediately. Fortunately, if you create a `<script>` tag and insert it into the `<head>` as this code does, the browser does the same thing: it goes off and retrieves the JavaScript resource and evaluates it.

Now, in and of itself, that isn't too useful, for our purposes anyway. As I said, the Yahoo! APIs return XML and XML being evaluated by the browser won't do much. (Some browsers may generate a DOM object from the XML, but even still, that on its own isn't of much use.) Unlike with the `XMLHttpRequest` object, you don't get any events to work with, callback functions that can act on what was returned, and so on.

Now we come to the bit of coolness that Yahoo! came up with that I mentioned before. Let's say we have some XML being returned by a Yahoo! service, like so:

```
<name>Frank</name>
```

It may not be very interesting, but it's perfectly valid XML. Now let's ask the probing question: what is the JSON equivalent to that XML? It's nothing more than this:

```
{ "name" : "Frank" }
```

Okay, now suppose that we pass that JSON to a JavaScript function, like so:

```
someFunction( { "name" : "Frank" } );
```

What is the parameter passed to someFunction()? As it turns out, it's an object constructed from the JSON. (Remember that JSON stands for JavaScript Object Notation: it is literally a notation format that defines an object.) This means that if someFunction() looks like:

```
function someFunction(obj) {
  alert(obj.name);
}
```

...the result is an alert() pop-up that reads "Frank".

Are you starting to see what Yahoo! might have done? If you are thinking that the service returns something like this:

```
someFunction( { "name" : "Frank" } );
```

...then give yourself a big round of applause because you just came to the same wonderful discovery that Yahoo! did a while ago!

What Yahoo! came up with is the idea of returning JSON in place of XML from an API service call, and wrapping the JSON in a function call. When you call the API function, you tell it what the callback function is. In other words, you tell the remote service what JavaScript function on your page you want passed the JSON that is returned. So let's say you wanted to interact with some Yahoo! API that returns a person's name. Your page might look something like this:

```
<html>
  <head>
    <title>Dummy Yahoo API Test</title>
    <script>
      function makeRequest() {
        var scriptTag = document.createElement("script");
        scriptTag.setAttribute("src", "www.yahoo.com/someAPI?callback=➡
myCallback&output=json");
        scriptTag.setAttribute("type", "text/javascript");
        var headTag = document.getElementsByTagName("head").item(0);
        headTag.appendChild(scriptTag);
      }
      function myCallback(inJSON) {
        alert(inJSON.name);
      }
    </script>
  </head>
  <body>
    <input type="button" value="Test" onClick="makeRequest();">
  </body>
</html>
```

When you click the button, makeRequest() is called, and it uses that dynamic <script> tag trick to call the Yahoo! API function. Notice the URL, which specifies the name of the callback function and also specifies that we want to get back JSON instead of the usual XML. Now, when the response comes back, the browser evaluates what was inserted into the document via the `<script>` tag, which would be this:

```
myCallback( { "name" : "Frank" } );
```

`myCallback()` is called at that point, with the object resulting from evaluation of the JSON being passed to it. You can load this page from any domain, and it will work. Hence, we've done what the `XMLHttpRequest` object does (in a basic sense, anyway), and we've gotten around the same-domain limitation. Sweet!

Yahoo! was the first to use this hack (that I am aware of), but many others, such as Google, have begun to follow suit because what this allows is purely client-side mashups and API utilization. No longer do you need a server-side proxy. You can now make the requests across domains directly. This is an extremely powerful capability that leads to some cool possibilities, such as the type of application in this chapter.

■Note While this technique is useful because it allows you to make direct requests to any server you want, it also has the potential for malicious code to be introduced. Remember that what is being returned is script that winds up executing with the same privileges as any other script on the page. This provides a potential for scams including stealing cookies, spoofing, phishing, and so on. You therefore want to take care in your choice of services and organizations. Accessing APIs from Yahoo! or Google, for instance, isn't likely to present any security issues, but less-well-known companies may not be quite as safe.

The approach to web services where JSON is returned wrapped in a JavaScript function call has come to be known as JSON with Padding, or JSON-P. It is also sometimes referred to as JSON-based web services. Whatever the term, it all means the same thing.

The example we just looked at is nice, and not too complicated code-wise, but as I'm sure you can guess, Ext JS makes it even easier. Ext JS provides the `Ext.data.ScriptTagProxy` for this purpose:

```
new Ext.data.ScriptTagProxy(
  { url : "http://www.yahoo.com/someAPI" }
).load(
  { output : "json" },
  new (Ext.extend(new Function(), Ext.data.DataReader, {
    readRecords : function(inObject) {
      return inObject;
    }
  }))(),
  function(inObject) {
    alert(inObject);
  }
);
```

We'll get into the details of this later, but essentially you create an instance of `Ext.data.ScriptTagProxy` and pass its constructor an object that provides the URL of the remote service. Then, you call its `load()` method. The first argument to this method is an object that contains parameters to pass to the service, in this case the `output` parameter specifying `json`. The second argument is an instance of `Ext.data.DataReader`; here a custom descendent of it created right then and there, because a `DataProxy`, which `ScriptTagProxy` is a type of, needs a `DataReader` to do something with the response from the server. Typically this would be parsing `inObject`, which is the JSON returned from the server, and generating `Record` objects and returning them. Here, however, we just literally return the object resulting from evaluating the JSON returned by the server. Finally, the third argument is the callback method, which is passed what the `DataReader.readRecords()` method returns. Note that Ext JS takes care of the details of the callback, meaning you don't explicitly tell the remote service the name of the callback; it's generated by Ext JS and passed to the service under the covers. Very clean, very simple, typical Ext JS!

JSON-P AND ERROR HANDLING—THAT IS, THE LACK THEREOF!

JSON-P is a really handy technique. However, to call it anything other than a trick, even a hack, would mean we aren't being quite honest! It's most definitely thinking outside the box, that's for sure!

As neat a trick as it is, it has one significant flaw: error handling. That is to say, there really is none. There is no error callback as with a typical Ajax request, no interrogating HTTP status codes, or any of that. Your script simply doesn't do something you expected it to do. Oh, you may well see a failed outbound request in a debug tool such as Firebug, but that's about it, and that won't generally help your end users.

I'm talking here about "hard" errors—in other words, HTTP errors. Anything the remote service can handle is okay because the service will usually define some sort of error element(s) in the JSON for you to check for. But for the "hard" failures, it's a whole different ballgame.

There is one way you can get at least some degree of "hard" error handling: use a time-out. In other words, you fire off a request, and you start a JavaScript time-out, say to fire some function in 5 seconds. In the callback to the JSON-P request, you cancel the time-out. So, if the request takes longer than 5 seconds to execute, you take that to mean that the call failed, and the function the time-out fires is essentially your error handler. (If the response comes back in less than 5 seconds, that function will never fire because the timeout is canceled first.) This clearly isn't ideal: who's to say the request didn't just go long and is taking a little more than 5 seconds to complete? In fact, you could arguably make matters worse because you might flash an error message and then a short time later process a completed request that you just told the user had failed! You could code for this possibility too and avoid it with a system of status flags, but hopefully you see that in any case, this simply isn't a robust error-handling mechanism.

Even with Ext JS in the mix, it can't overcome the underlying limitation of the `<script>` tag injection technique that underlies `ScriptTagProxy`. So, as an FYI, in this application I took the tact that because the error-handling scheme is pretty poor anyway, I simply went with none at all—no timer tricks, nothing. If a service call hangs, the application hangs with the Please Wait dialog box showing. Not great by any stretch of the imagination, but such is the difficulty with the `<script>` injection technique underlying this all.

Meet the Yahoo! Web Services

Before you go looking at the web services we'll use to build this application, you need to get some paperwork out of the way first.

Most API services require you to register to use their APIs, and Yahoo! is no exception. Every time you make a Yahoo! service call, you need to pass an `appid` parameter. The value of this parameter is a unique identifier assigned to your application. Not passing this value, or passing an invalid value, will result in the call failing. Before you can play with the application in this chapter, you will have to register and get your own `appid`. It's a painless process that you can go through by accessing the following page:

```
http://api.search.yahoo.com/webservices/register_application
```

You should plug your own `appid` into the `LocalBusinessSearch.js` file (in the aptly named `appID` field) before you spend time with the application, just so you are playing nice with Yahoo!. I'll use XXX in the following sections when referencing `appid` to indicate that you should plug your ID in there.

There are some limitations associated with using the APIs in terms of request volume, but the upper limit is so high as to not be a realistic concern for your adventures with this application. In any case, the limits are based on requests made from a given IP address over a 24-hour period, so even if you run over the limit just try again tomorrow and you should be good to go. If you are intent on building a production-level application by using these services, you will need to consult with Yahoo! for other registration options that allow for high volumes. Again, for our purposes, the number of requests allowed is more than sufficient.

The Yahoo! Local Search Service

Yahoo! offers some very nice search services that you can play with, and one of them is the Yahoo! Local search service. It enables you to search for businesses in a given geographic location. For each search result, the service provides a plethora of information, including the business location, contact information (phone number, web site, and so forth), and user rating information.

Using this service requires you to access a given URL, for example:

```
http://local.yahooapis.com/LocalSearchService/V3/localSearch?appid=XXX&➥
query=pizza&zip=94306&results=2
```

The `query` parameter enables you to specify a keyword to search for, `zip` is just a US zip code to center the search around, and `results` is the maximum number of results you want to return. The `appid` is an ID you get when you register for the services, as discussed in the previous section. If you go ahead and paste that into the address bar of your web browser, assuming you replace the XXX `appid` with a valid ID, you'll see the following response:

```
<?xml version="1.0"?>➥
<ResultSet xmlns:xsi=http://www.w3.org/2001/XMLSchema-instance➥
xmlns="urn:yahoo:lcl" xsi:schemaLocation="urn:yahoo:lcl➥
http://api.local.yahoo.com/LocalSearchService/V3/➥
LocalSearchResponse.xsd" totalResultsAvailable="459"➥
```

```
totalResultsReturned="1" firstResultPosition="1"><ResultSetMapUrl>➥
http://maps.yahoo.com/broadband/?q1=Palo+Alto➥
%2C+CA+94306&amp;tt=pizza&amp;tp=1</ResultSetMapUrl➥
><Result id="28734629"><Title>➥
Patxi's Chicago Pizza</Title><Address>➥
441 Emerson St</Address><City>Palo Alto</City>➥
<State>CA</State><Phone>(650) 473-9999</Phone><Latitude>➥
37.445242</Latitude><Longitude>-122.163427</Longitude><Rating>➥
<AverageRating>4.5</AverageRating><TotalRatings>➥
30</TotalRatings><TotalReviews>21</TotalReviews>➥
<LastReviewDate>1203959693</LastReviewDate>➥
<LastReviewIntro>I'd give this place 4.5 Stars, but➥
since I can't tie goes to the Restaurant. This is➥
a good alternative to the legendary Zachary's with➥
the benefit that there isn't usually a wait. In➥
many ways I like this place better than Zachary's➥
since it seems to have figured out a way to do➥
Chicago deep dish without the heaviness of the➥
oils, It could be the sauce being more of a puree➥
instead of chopped tomatoes balances the oils out.➥
While I am mostly a NY Thin Crust kind of guy, this➥
is top notch pizza.</LastReviewIntro></Rating>➥
<Distance>2.67</Distance><Url>➥
http://local.yahoo.com/details?id=28734629&amp;➥
stx=pizza&amp;csz=Palo+Alto+CA&amp;➥
ed=5Ft25a160SwgYwogEsXfvFF62jUOrNK1trfxXbRawD4AClLt➥
Hub4_iH_GpomidnTfCwCqJBK</Url><ClickUrl>➥
http://local.yahoo.com/details?id=28734629&amp;➥
stx=pizza&amp;csz=Palo+Alto+CA&amp;ed=5Ft25a160➥
SwgYwogEsXfvFF62jUOrNK1trfxXbRawD4AClLtHub4_iH_➥
GpomidnTfCwCqJBK</ClickUrl><MapUrl>➥
http://maps.yahoo.com/maps_result?➥
name=Patxi%27s+Chicago+Pizza&amp;desc=6504739999➥
&amp;csz=Palo+Alto+CA&amp;qty=9&amp;cs=9&amp;➥
gid1=28734629</MapUrl><BusinessUrl>➥
http://www.patxispizza.com/</BusinessUrl>➥
<BusinessClickUrl>http://www.patxispizza.com/➥
</BusinessClickUrl><Categories><Category id="96926243">➥
Pizza</Category><Category id="96926236">Restaurants➥
</Category><Category id="96926237">➥
American Restaurants</Category>➥
<Category id="96926190">Italian Restaurants</Category>➥
</Categories></Result></ResultSet>

<!-- ws02.search.re2.yahoo.com compressed/?
chunked Fri Jul 25 22:45:33 PDT 2008 -->
```

To turn this into a JSON-P request, we have only to add two parameters to the request: output, with a value of json, and callback, with a value of the name of the function to call. So, if we do this:

```
http://local.yahooapis.com/LocalSearchService/V3/localSearch?appid=XXX&➥
query=pizza&zip=94306&results=1&output=json&callback=myCallback
```

…the response we get is now this:

```
myCallback({"ResultSet":{"totalResultsAvailable":"459",➥
"totalResultsReturned":"1","firstResultPosition":"1",➥
"ResultSetMapUrl":"http:\/\/maps.yahoo.com\/broadband\/➥
?q1=Palo+Alto%2C+CA+94306&tt=pizza&tp=1","Result":➥
{"id":"28734629","Title":"Patxi's Chicago Pizza",➥
"Address":"441 Emerson St","City":"Palo Alto","State":"CA","Phone":➥
"(650) 473-9999","Latitude":"37.445242",➥
"Longitude":"-122.163427","Rating":{"AverageRating":"4.5",➥
"TotalRatings":"30","TotalReviews":"21",➥
"LastReviewDate":"1203959693","LastReviewIntro":➥
"I'd give this place 4.5 Stars, but since I can't➥
tie goes to the Restaurant. This is a good alternative➥
to the legendary Zachary's with the benefit that there➥
isn't usually a wait. In many ways I like this place➥
better than Zachary's since it seems to have figured out➥
a way to do Chicago deep dish without the heaviness of➥
the oils, It could be the sauce being more of a puree➥
instead of chopped tomatoes balances the oils out. While➥
I am mostly a NY Thin Crust kind of guy, this is top notch➥
pizza."},"Distance":"2.67","Url":"http:\/\/➥
local.yahoo.com\/details?id=28734629&stx=pizza&➥
csz=Palo+Alto+CA&ed=5Ft25a160SwgYwogEsXfvFF62jUOr➥
NK1trfxXbRawD4AClLtHub4_iH_GpomidnTfCwCqJBK",➥
"ClickUrl":"http:\/\/local.yahoo.com\/details?➥
id=28734629&stx=pizza&csz=Palo+Alto+CA&ed=5Ft25➥
a160SwgYwogEsXfvFF62jUOrNK1trfxXbRawD4AClLtHub4➥
_iH_GpomidnTfCwCqJBK","MapUrl":"http:\/\/➥
maps.yahoo.com\/maps_result?name=Patxi%27s+➥
Chicago+Pizza&desc=6504739999&csz=Palo+Alto+➥
CA&qty=9&cs=9&gid1=28734629","BusinessUrl":➥
"http:\/\/www.patxispizza.com\/","BusinessClickUrl":➥
"http:\/\/www.patxispizza.com\/","Categories":➥
{"Category":[{"id":"96926243","content":"Pizza"},➥
{"id":"96926236","content":"Restaurants"},➥
{"id":"96926237","content":"American Restaurants"},{"id":"96926190",➥
"content":"Italian Restaurants"}]}}}});
```

It's not much to look at on the page, I admit, but it's golden in the code: if we called this by using the <script> injection trick, myCallback() would get called and passed an object with a bunch of data fields we can reference. For instance, the Latitude and Longitude fields tell us where this business is located, Rating tells us the average user rating, and Distance tells us how far away the business is. The set of data returned by the service is pretty large, and a lot of it won't be used in this application, but if you cruise on over to http://developer.yahoo.com/search/local/V3/localSearch.html, you can get all those details, plus a lot more, about this particular service.

The Yahoo! Map Image Service

Yahoo! is also going to be providing the maps that you can see on the Map pane of the application (yes, take a break and go play with the application a bit now!). Yahoo! Maps is a service that has been around for a while, even before a public JSON-P interface was provided for it. It enables you to get maps for a given address, as well as access other features, such as traffic and local places of interest. The API Yahoo! provides a number of different services, but for our purposes, we'll be focusing on the Map Image service.

The Yahoo! Maps Map Image API enables you to get a reference to a graphic of a map generated according to the parameters you specify in your request. You may specify latitude and longitude or address in your request (we'll be specifying longitude and latitude in the application itself, but in this discussion it'll just be an address, more precisely, a component of an address).

This service is referenced via a simple HTTP request, such as the following:

```
http://local.yahooapis.com/MapsService/V1/mapImage?appid=XXX&location=11719
```

The location parameter specified is just a US zip code, and the appid is once again your registered application ID. If you go ahead and paste that into the address bar of your web browser, you'll see the following response:

```
<?xml version="1.0"?>➡
<Result xmlns:xsi="http://www.w3.org/2001/XMLSchema-instance">➡
http://gws.maps.yahoo.com/mapimage?MAPDATA=n60ehud6wXUJUYM_tJcfOwsQpG9JUAzuPg➡
gQRTTce9N8zspONMdiDVuUVXTcOkJcBUZXUolGqZulnHzcPOkjcpYTF82_DXtJgf4ISRYS8gqVHa➡
BiWhmY3OqSK9C9PR4.k.HNxwaJJO2UQqOOexH6&amp;mvt=m?cltype=onnetwork&amp;.➡
intl=us</Result><!-- ws01.search.re2.yahoo.com compressed/chunked➡
Fri Jul 25 10:32:36 PDT 2008 -->
```

What you've gotten back includes a reference to an image now sitting on Yahoo's servers. If you pluck out the following URL:

```
http://gws.maps.yahoo.com/mapimage?MAPDATA=n60ehud6wXUJUYM_tJcfOw➡
sQpG9JUAzuPggQRTTce9N8zspONMdiDVuUVXTcOkJcBUZXUolGqZulnHzcPOkjcpYT➡
F82_DXtJgf4ISRYS8gqVHaBiWhmY3OqSK9C9PR4.k.HNxwaJJO2UQqOOexH6&amp;➡
mvt=m?cltype=onnetwork&amp;.intl=us
```

…and put that in the address bar of a web browser, you'll see an image that is a map of the Bellport/Mastic Beach area of Long Island, New York, as shown in Figure 6-2.

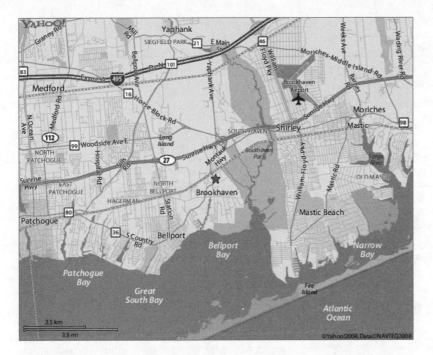

Figure 6-2. *The map resulting from assessing the URL in the example*

You can also add some parameters to the original request. For instance, you can specify that you want a GIF back (by default, you get a PNG file), and you can specify that instead of XML, you want JSON back. The URL would then look like this:

```
http://local.yahooapis.com/MapsService/V1/mapImage?appid=XXX&⮕
location=11719&image_type=gif&output=json&callback=myCallback
```

Now the response you get is this:

```
myCallback({"ResultSet":{"Result":"http:\/\/gws.maps.yahoo.com\/mapimage?⮕
MAPDATA=cxsuGud6wXXyiBJ69MPrKK..1HUkskJsw7lifuUcFkwxzQ4OjwJp.wHqkuSE⮕
pCr9RhHUtwrTtNO.b4WNfkBNid1D6TAblazXIF8anq5PqbaLIF5iAmHGbbh8LZtPjnvs⮕
LP8Ndkoiu1qWNWduAGHC&mvt=m?cltype=onnetwork&.intl=us"}});
```

A few other parameters are used in the application, and these are summarized in Table 6-1.

Table 6-1. *Some Yahoo! Map Image Service Parameters Used in This Application*

Parameter	Meaning
latitude	The latitude that is the center of the map.
longitude	The longitude that is the center of the map.
image_width	The width of the map image.
image_height	The height of the map image.
zoom	The zoom factor to apply to the map. This is a value in the range 1–12, where 1 represents street level and 12 represents regional level (a little wider than state level).

As with the local search service, I encourage you to examine the Yahoo! Maps APIs (http://developer.yahoo.com/maps/rest/V1) because they can definitely do more than this application demonstrates. This is about all we need for the purposes of this chapter, though, so you're now armed with all the knowledge you need to go forth and dissect this application!

Overall Structure and Files

This project uses the same basic architectural structure as the Code Cabinet project in Chapter 5. That decision means we'll see a number of source files for individual UI elements. Figure 6-3 shows the breakdown of the application's directory structure.

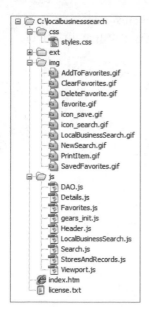

Figure 6-3. *The application's directory structure and constituent files*

The css directory, as with all the other applications so far, contains the lone styles.css file in it, and like the Chapter 5 project, it's pretty minimal. Our old friend the ext directory is still there obviously. The img directory contains a couple of GIF files which, in no particular order, are as follows: LocalBusinessSearch.gif, which is the logo you see in the upper-right corner of the application; icon_search.gif and icon_save.gif, which are icons used on the buttons on the search form; and favorite.gif, which is the heart icon shown next to my saved favorites. The remaining images are the images for the toolbar icons at the top. In the js directory is all our JavaScript source code. We have the gears_init.js file that we'd expect given that this application uses Gears like all the others. The LocalBusinessSearch.js is our "main" source file. The DAO.js file is our data access object, and StoresAndRecords.js contains the definitions of all the Records and Data Stores we'll need. The Details.js file contains the code pertaining to the detail Accordion pane. The Favorites.js file contains the code for dealing with the favorites list. The Header.js file contains the UI definition code for the top of the page, the toolbar and logo, plus the code that makes the icons actually do things when clicked. The Search.js file, which is where most of the action in this application is, deals with the search form and results and all the code related to that. Finally, the Viewport.js file contains the UI definition for the Ext JS Viewport.

In the root directory we have index.htm, which is where we'll begin our exploration of the code.

The Markup

The index.html file is the customary place to kick off the application, and as in past projects there's not a whole lot in it, as you can see for yourself:

```html
<html>
  <head>
    <title>Local Business Search</title>

    <link rel="stylesheet" type="text/css" href="ext/resources/css/ext-all.css">
    <script type="text/javascript" src="ext/adapter/ext/ext-base.js"></script>
    <script type="text/javascript" src="ext/ext-all.js"></script>

    <script src="js/gears_init.js"></script>

    <link rel="stylesheet" type="text/css" href="css/styles.css">
    <script type="text/javascript" src="js/LocalBusinessSearch.js"></script>
    <script type="text/javascript" src="js/StoresAndRecords.js"></script>
    <script type="text/javascript" src="js/DAO.js"></script>
    <script type="text/javascript" src="js/Viewport.js"></script>
    <script type="text/javascript" src="js/Search.js"></script>
    <script type="text/javascript" src="js/Favorites.js"></script>
    <script type="text/javascript" src="js/Details.js"></script>
    <script type="text/javascript" src="js/Header.js"></script>

    <script>Ext.onReady(LocalBusinessSearch.init);</script>

  </head>
```

```
<body>

  <div id="divSource" class="cssSource"></div>

  <div id="dialogPrint" class="x-hidden">
    <div class="x-window-header">Local Business Search Ext</div>
    <div class="x-window-body" style="background-color:#ffffff;padding:10px;">
      <br>
      Title: <span id="print_title"></span>
      <br><br>
      <img id="print_map">
      <br><br>
      Longitude: <span id="print_longitude"></span><br>
      Latitude: <span id="print_latitude"></span><br>
      Distance: <span id="print_distance"></span><br>
      Phone: <span id="print_phone"></span><br>
      Rating: <span id="print_rating"></span><br>
      Address: <span id="print_address"></span><br>
      City: <span id="print_city"></span><br>
      State: <span id="print_state"></span><br>
      Business Web Site: <span id="print_businessurl"></span><br>
    </div>
  </div>

</body>

</html>
```

We have the usual Ext JS imports, plus the Gears initialization JavaScript file. Following that is the import of the application style sheet and all the JavaScript files that make up the application itself. We again see Ext.onReady() being used to call the init() method of the LocalBusinessSearch object to kick-start the application.

The actual markup begins with the <div> that we've by now become used to, the source of our Window animations. Following that is some plain-old HTML that, based on the style classes that are applied, we can surmise is used to form a Window at some point. As it happens, this is the only Window in the application, and it is the one you see when you want to print a business, both its details and the currently showing map. In Figure 6-4 you can see what this window looks like.

Well, that's not *entirely* true. What Figure 6-4 shows is the Window with a MessageBox over it. This will become clear when we see how printing works, but for now let's take a look at Figure 6-5.

Now, *that* is what the print Window actually looks like, the Window defined by the markup in index.htm. It's simply maximized to take up the entire browser area, but it is still a Window. The markup itself is no big deal; most important are the <span> elements, which will be populated with the data about a selected business, with the map image mixed in.

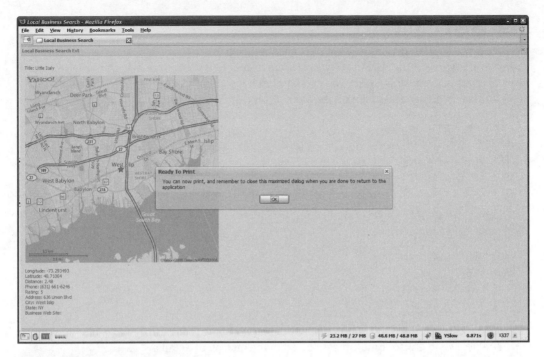

Figure 6-4. *Telling users they can print*

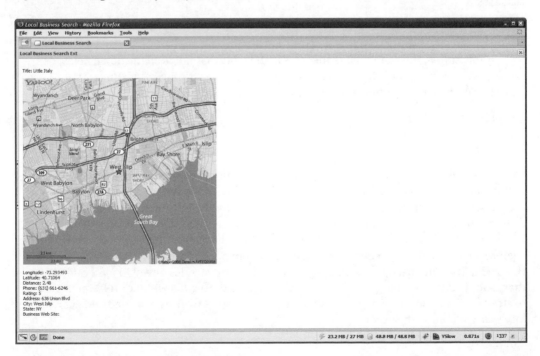

Figure 6-5. *What the user will see printed*

The Style Sheet

Let's now move on to the application style sheet housed in `styles.css`, which, similar to `index.htm`, is very simple. The first style class encountered is `cssSource`, which is one we've seen many times before so I'll skip an explanation here. I won't, however, skip the next two selectors for styling the text seen on the Details pane of the `Accordion`:

```
.cssDetailLabel {
  font-weight : bold;
  font-size : 12pt;
  font-family : arial;
}
```

The `cssDetailLabel` style is applied to the field label, so it's bolded to set it off from the data itself. Speaking of the data:

```
.cssDetailData {
  font-size : 12pt;
  font-family : arial;
}
```

As you can see, the only different is that the data itself isn't bold; otherwise it's the same. The next style is also something involved in the display of details:

```
.cssAltRow {
  background-color : #eaeaea;
}
```

Simply stated, this is applied to the rows in the table that holds all the detail fields, or more precisely, every *other* row in the table, so we get some striping going on.

The last style is something entirely new:

```
.x-table-layout {
  width : 100%;
}
```

As a quick experiment, try deleting this style and then reload the application. You'll see that the top header section doesn't stretch across the entire screen; it's all scrunched up on the left side only. That's because a `TableLayout` is used for the header, and a table with two cells is generated. The toolbar icons are in the first, and the logo is in the other. The toolbar icons should be left-aligned while the logo should be right-aligned, because I wanted them up against the edges of the screen. However, that won't happen by default because the table will be sized to its contents, not the page width. So, this style overrides one of Ext JS's built-in styles that is applied to the table generated by a `TableLayout`. Setting the width to 100% gets the table to stretch across the entire page, and then those alignments work as expected and everything looks as it should in the header.

The Code

As we've done in the past, we'll begin our exploration of the JavaScript portion of our show by looking at the DAO class.

DAO.js

You know the saying: if you've seen one DAO class, you've seen 'em all! This is very true here: this DAO is no different than any of the others we've looked at, so I won't go over every single detail here. But a high-level view is warranted, so let's start with Figure 6-6.

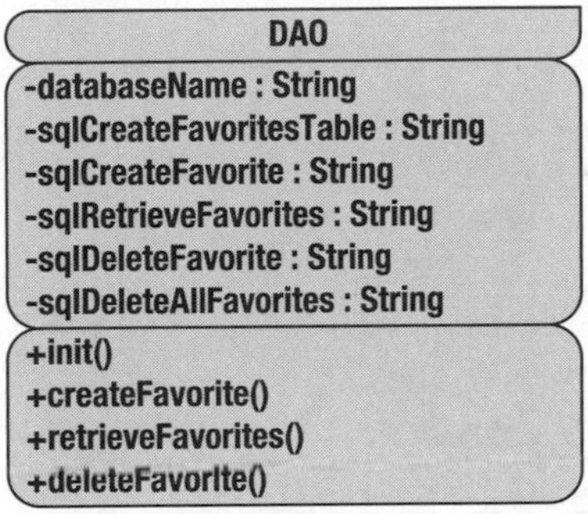

```
┌──────────────────────────────────────┐
│                 DAO                    │
├──────────────────────────────────────┤
│ -databaseName : String                │
│ -sqlCreateFavoritesTable : String     │
│ -sqlCreateFavorite : String           │
│ -sqlRetrieveFavorites : String        │
│ -sqlDeleteFavorite : String           │
│ -sqlDeleteAllFavorites : String       │
├──────────────────────────────────────┤
│ +init()                                │
│ +createFavorite()                      │
│ +retrieveFavorites()                   │
│ +deleteFavorite()                      │
└──────────────────────────────────────┘
```

Figure 6-6. *UML class diagram of the DAO class*

As you can see, we've got all the typical fields and methods, starting with databaseName, which in this application is LocalBusinessSearch. Then we have a couple of fields for the SQL queries. Table 6-2 summarizes everything.

Table 6-2. *The SQL Queries Contained in the DAO Class*

Field Name	Query	Description
sqlCreateFavoritesTable	CREATE TABLE IF NOT EXISTS favorites (id TEXT, title TEXT, distance TEXT, phone TEXT, rating TEXT, address TEXT, city TEXT, state TEXT, latitude TEXT, longitude TEXT, businessurl TEXT)	Creates the favorites table
sqlCreateFavorite	INSERT INTO favorites (id, title, distance, phone, rating, address, city, state, latitude, longitude, businessurl) VALUES (?, ?, ?, ?, ?, ?, ?, ?, ?, ?, ?)	Creates a record in the favorites table
sqlRetrieveFavorites	SELECT * FROM favorites	Retrieves all favorites
sqlDeleteFavorite	DELETE FROM favorites WHERE id=?	Deletes a given favorite
sqlDeleteAllFavorites	DELETE FROM favorites	Deletes all favorites

That's right, there is only a single table in the database, favorites, because that's all this application needs to store. This one table appears in the database, as seen in Figure 6-7.

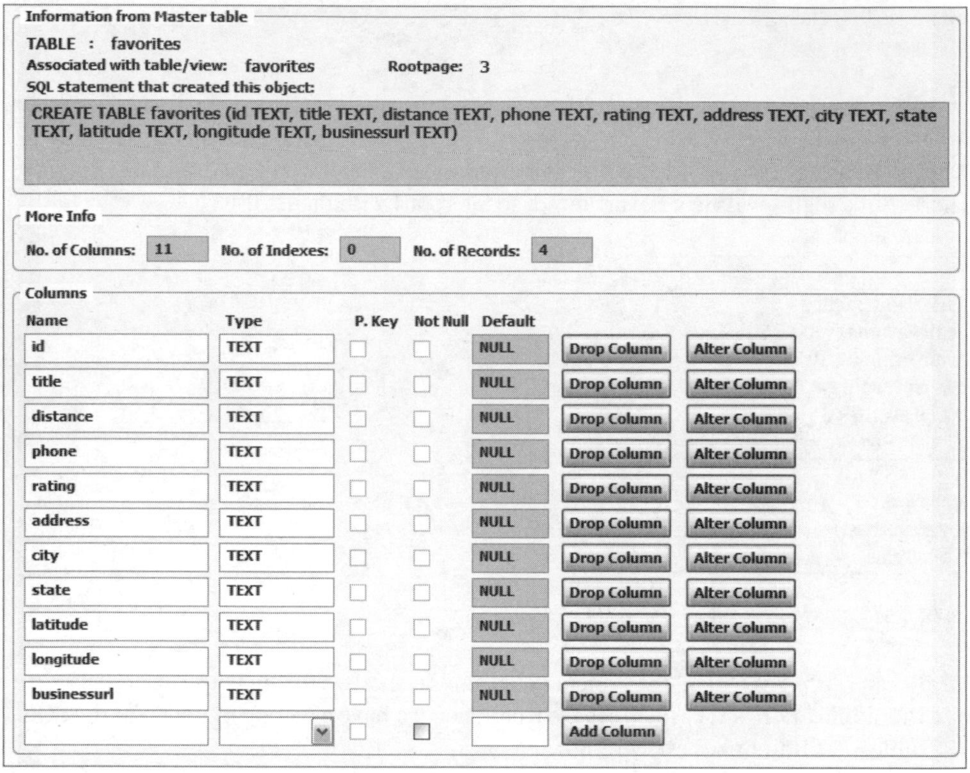

Information from Master table

TABLE : favorites
Associated with table/view: favorites   Rootpage: 3
SQL statement that created this object:

> CREATE TABLE favorites (id TEXT, title TEXT, distance TEXT, phone TEXT, rating TEXT, address TEXT, city TEXT, state TEXT, latitude TEXT, longitude TEXT, businessurl TEXT)

More Info

No. of Columns: 11   No. of Indexes: 0   No. of Records: 4

Columns

Name	Type	P. Key	Not Null	Default		
id	TEXT	☐	☐	NULL	Drop Column	Alter Column
title	TEXT	☐	☐	NULL	Drop Column	Alter Column
distance	TEXT	☐	☐	NULL	Drop Column	Alter Column
phone	TEXT	☐	☐	NULL	Drop Column	Alter Column
rating	TEXT	☐	☐	NULL	Drop Column	Alter Column
address	TEXT	☐	☐	NULL	Drop Column	Alter Column
city	TEXT	☐	☐	NULL	Drop Column	Alter Column
state	TEXT	☐	☐	NULL	Drop Column	Alter Column
latitude	TEXT	☐	☐	NULL	Drop Column	Alter Column
longitude	TEXT	☐	☐	NULL	Drop Column	Alter Column
businessurl	TEXT	☐	☐	NULL	Drop Column	Alter Column
	▼	☐	☐		Add Column	

Figure 6-7. *Table structure of the favorites table*

The remainder of the methods in the DAO class—init(), createFavorite(), retrieveFavorites(), and deleteFavorite()—are virtual copies of every other similarly named DAO method we've looked at. So let's move on to bigger and better things, although I do suggest taking a moment to peek at the code from this chapter's download nonetheless.

StoresAndRecords.js

This application also has a StoresAndRecords.js file containing… wait for it… DataStores and Records! To be more precise, there's a single Record, and it is the BusinessRecord, whose definition looks like this:

```
LocalBusinessSearch.Data.BusinessRecord = Ext.data.Record.create([
  { name : "title", mapping : "title" },
  { name : "distance", mapping : "distance" },
  { name : "phone", mapping : "phone" },
  { name : "rating", mapping : "rating" },
  { name : "address", mapping : "address" },
```

```
  { name : "city", mapping : "city" },
  { name : "state", mapping : "state" },
  { name : "latitude", mapping : "latitude" },
  { name : "longitude", mapping : "longitude" },
  { name : "businessurl", mapping : "businessurl" }
]);
```

Pretty boring, eh? Perhaps seeing it graphically would be a little more exciting? Let's give that a shot in Figure 6-8.

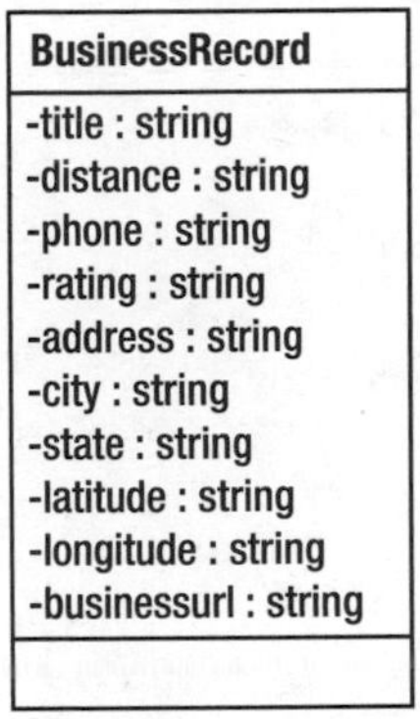

BusinessRecord
-title : string
-distance : string
-phone : string
-rating : string
-address : string
-city : string
-state : string
-latitude : string
-longitude : string
-businessurl : string

Figure 6-8. *Say hello to the BusinessRecord descriptor!*

Okay, yeah, you're right, not really any more exciting! We've seen a bunch of Records before this, so it isn't exactly earth-shattering at this point. However, what's coming next very well may be—the DataStore for storing search results:

```
LocalBusinessSearch.Data.ResultsStore = new Ext.data.Store({
  listeners : {
    beforeload : function(inStore, inOptions) {
      inStore.baseParams = LocalBusinessSearch.searchParams;
    }
  },
  proxy : new Ext.data.ScriptTagProxy(
    { url : LocalBusinessSearch.searchWebServiceURL }
  ),
  reader : new (Ext.extend(new Function(), Ext.data.DataReader, {
      readRecords : function(inObject) {
        if (inObject.Error) {
          LocalBusinessSearch.resultsTitle = inObject.Error.title;
          LocalBusinessSearch.resultsMessage = inObject.Error.Message[0];
          return { success : true, records : new Array(), totalRecords : 0 };
        }
        var totalResultsAvailable =
          parseInt(inObject.ResultSet.totalResultsAvailable);
```

```
        if (totalResultsAvailable == 0) {
          LocalBusinessSearch.resultsTitle = "No results";
          LocalBusinessSearch.resultsMessage =
            "The search criteria you provided returned no matches.";
          return { success : true, records : new Array(), totalRecords : 0 };
        }
        if (totalResultsAvailable > 200) {
          LocalBusinessSearch.resultsTitle = "Too many results";
          LocalBusinessSearch.resultsMessage =
            "The search criteria you provided returned more than 200 " +
            "matches.  Please narrow your search.";
          return { success : true, records : new Array(), totalRecords : 0 };
        }
        var recs = new Array();
        for (var i = 0; i < inObject.ResultSet.Result.length; i++) {
          var ratingVal = inObject.ResultSet.Result[i].Rating.AverageRating;
          recs.push(new LocalBusinessSearch.Data.BusinessRecord({
            title : inObject.ResultSet.Result[i].Title,
            distance : inObject.ResultSet.Result[i].Distance,
            phone : inObject.ResultSet.Result[i].Phone,
            rating : (isNaN(ratingVal) ? 0 : ratingVal),
            address : inObject.ResultSet.Result[i].Address,
            city : inObject.ResultSet.Result[i].City,
            state : inObject.ResultSet.Result[i].State,
            latitude : inObject.ResultSet.Result[i].Latitude,
            longitude : inObject.ResultSet.Result[i].Longitude,
            businessurl : inObject.ResultSet.Result[i].BusinessUrl
          }, inObject.ResultSet.Result[i].id));
        }
        return {
          success : true, records : recs, totalRecords : totalResultsAvailable
        };
      }
  }))
});
```

Wow, there's definitely some new stuff going on there! Even though the data that will populate this DataStore will be coming from a call to the Yahoo! search service (which is drastically different from the other applications we've seen so far), we still want to be able to use the same basic Ext JS data mechanisms. That means having a DataStore with events and being able to bind widgets to it. That's what all the code here is about: making this DataStore work just as any other even though it's calling a remote server.

Recall that a DataStore uses a DataProxy to retrieve data from some source, and then uses a DataReader to read that data to produce Records. So, skipping over the listeners element for just a moment, we see the proxy element pointing to an instance of an Ext.data. ScriptTagProxy. We talked about that briefly earlier, but generally it's a pretty simple animal:

construct an instance of it with a config object that includes a url attribute defining the URL to call to get a JSON-P response from, and that's about it. In the previous example we called its load() method to make the remote call and process the response. When it's the proxy for a DataStore, though, that all happens in the background, under control of the DataStore, so there's a bit less work here than we saw earlier.

The DataReader is next, and here we've got some funky syntax to deal with. The Ext. extend() method is used to extend a given class based on another. So, the line

```
reader : new (Ext.extend(new Function(),
  Ext.data.DataReader, { readRecords : { } });
```

creates a new instance of Function, extends it, adds the elements from Ext.data.DataReader to it, and then also overrides any elements, with the elements defined in the object passed as the third argument. The reader attribute is assigned to that new class. So in this case, a plain-old Function is extended, adding in all the fields and methods from Ext.data.DataReader, and then the readRecords() method is overridden.

The readRecords() method is called after the DataProxy retrieves the data. The response from that call—the object created by the JSON returned by the server—is passed into readRecords(). Its job is to produce an array of BusinessRecords (plus some other stuff) and return it. It's not conceptually complex, but there's a fair bit of work to do.

The first step is to determine if a "soft" error has occurred, things like "no matches found." To do so, we examine the Error element of the incoming object. If that element is present, then we need to cut things short! We grab the Error.title and Error.Message[0] elements for display, and we then return an object containing three elements: success, which indicates if the conversion to BusinessRecords was successful; records, which is an array of BusinessRecords; and totalRecords, which indicates the number of BusinessRecords. It may seem odd to set success to true in this case, but it is in fact the correct thing to do because as far as the rest of the DataStore code is concerned, readRecords() worked as expected, even in the case of a "soft" error. Therefore, we don't want any error-related events to fire, and success does that for us.

■**Note** Presumably you can get more than one error back at a time, given that Error.Message is an array. In practice I never saw this situation arise, and I can't imagine a scenario where it would happen given this application. So I think it's safe to just grab the first element of the array.

The error title and message are set on fields of the LocalBusinessSearch object, so essentially the work of readRecords() is done at this point.

Now, what happens if no errors were returned? In that case we need to do some processing. However, we must check for two other conditions first. I said earlier that an example of a "soft" error is "no matches found," but I actually lied there (consider it practice for my future political career!) because that is in fact *not* a "soft" error condition. Finding no matches is a perfectly valid response from the server, but we still need to handle it differently. So, we grab the ResultSet.totalResultsAvailable element from the returned object, and use parseInt() to get a number from it. If that number is 0, then we do a similar short-circuit end to readRecords() and return the same sort of object as we saw earlier. We set an error title and message on LocalBusinessSearch that reflects the fact that no matches were found. As I'm sure you can guess, we'll see some code later that knows how and when to display these error messages.

The other condition to check for is if there are more than 200 matches to the request search query. This is a problem because this application provides paging of large result sets. In other words, the user sees 10 matches at a time but can retrieve another 10 at any time. When dealing with the Yahoo! search service, you need to tell it what the number of the lowest search result you want is. So, if you want items 30–39 out of the 100 matches, then you tell it the lowest number you want is 30. The problem is that it won't accept a number higher than 250 here, even though it will happily find more than 250 matches! So, effectively, we're limited to 250 matches for any query because there's no way to display the matches above 250. I backed down to 200 instead of 250 to improve performance a little (fewer results to process means less time overall) and also to avoid any weird conditions that might occur if the numbers were off by one at any point. Besides, if you need more than 200 pizza parlors in an area, you're probably on your way to the hospital with a massive coronary anyway!

Once we pass through both those conditions, it is time to produce those BusinessRecords we need. Doing so is trivial: iterate over the ResultSet.Result array in the returned object and for each instantiate a new BusinessRecord object, populating its fields with the data from the returned object. Finally, an object is returned that now includes a populated array of BusinessRecords, plus the number returned.

Now we've seen how the DataStore for search results is put together. Later on we'll see how the loading of data (the remote service call, in this case) is triggered, but frankly, the truly interesting stuff is what we've just seen. It means we now have a DataStore, like any other, that we can bind to widgets, have events fire on, and so on. Speaking of events, we need to jump back to the listeners array for just a moment. You'll notice there that the beforeload event is handled. This event, as its name implies, fires just before the DataStore tries to load data, before it asks the DataProxy to get some data. To call on the Yahoo! search service, we're obviously going to need to pass the search criteria to use. Every time we ask the DataStore to load data, it passes the parameters stored in its baseParams field to the DataProxy, which will pass them along as HTTP request parameters (assuming the DataProxy is one that makes a request to a remote source). This is the mechanism used to pass the search criteria, which are stored between searches on the LocalBusinessSearch object. This is necessary because when we discuss how paging of data works, you'll see that this information isn't maintained automatically between paging requests. The Yahoo! web service requires it, so we have to get it to the DataProxy, and the beforeload event is perfect for that.

■**Note** Using baseParams for this seems a little wrong to me, but I couldn't get it to work any other way. It seemed to me that the DataProxy should use the same parameters as it did the last time it was called, which the Ext JS documentation seemed to indicate it should. In practice, though, that didn't work. So, by using baseParams in this way I was able to get everything to work as expected, and it didn't take much effort. It's not *that* big of a hack as far as I can tell, so I'm okay with it!

Next up we have another DataStore, but a considerably simpler one:

```
LocalBusinessSearch.Data.searchSortStore = new Ext.data.Store({});
var sortByVals = [ "Distance", "Relevance", "Title", "Rating" ];
for (var i = 0; i < sortByVals.length; i++ ) {
  LocalBusinessSearch.Data.searchSortStore.add
    (new Ext.data.Record( { optVal : sortByVals[i] } )
  );
}
```

searchSortStore is used to populate the Sort By ComboBox on the search form and provides some options. A ComboBox must be bound to a DataStore, so we can't just simply add elements to it manually. That's where this DataStore comes in. Here we see something new: since we know all the possible options for this DataStore up front, we can populate it right at the time it is created, and that's what we have here. The sortByVals array is iterated over, and for each element, a call to the add() method of the searchSortStore is made. Now, we can bind this DataStore to the ComboBox and we're good to go—it will be populated with the appropriate options, just like that!

There is also a searchMinimumRatingStore that is bound to the Minimum Rating ComboBox, and a searchStateStore that is bound to the State ComboBox. Aside from the data they are loaded with, they are the same as searchSortStore, so we'll skip looking at them here. Instead, let's look at the one remaining DataStore: FavoritesStore.

```
LocalBusinessSearch.Data.FavoritesStore = new Ext.data.Store({
  listeners : {
    "add" : {
      fn : function(inStore, inRecords, inIndex) {
        if (LocalBusinessSearch.skipFavoritesStoreEvents) { return; }
        LocalBusinessSearch.Data.DAO.createFavorite(inRecords[0]);
      }
    },
    "remove" : {
      fn : function(inStore, inRecord, inIndex) {
        LocalBusinessSearch.Data.DAO.deleteFavorite(inRecord.id);
      }
    },
    "clear" : {
      fn : function(inStore, inRecord, inIndex) {
        LocalBusinessSearch.Data.DAO.deleteFavorite();
      }
    }
  }
});
```

This too doesn't differ much from the DataStores we've seen in other applications. Here, we have our usual three events to deal with: add, which fires when a Record is added to this DataStore; remove, which is called when a Record is deleted; and clear, which fires when the removeAll() method is called on the DataStore. Each of these calls the appropriate DAO method, and only in the add event handler do we need to avoid doing anything in certain situations (for example, when the UI is being built, which you'll see in LocalBusinessSearch.js, the next stop on our code dissection train).

LocalBusinessSearch.js

The LocalBusinessSearch.js file contains the definition of the LocalBusinessSearch class. You can see the class outline in Figure 6-9.

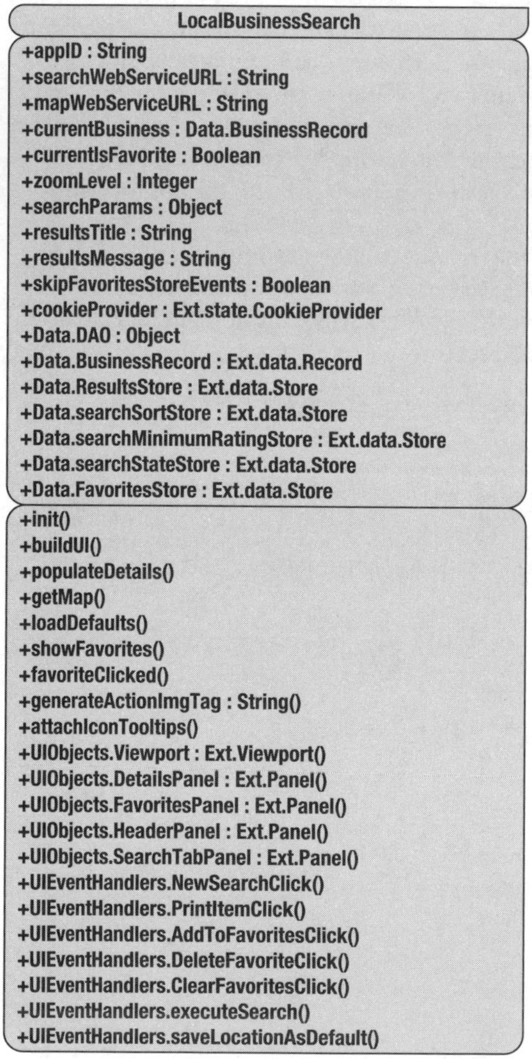

LocalBusinessSearch
+appID : String
+searchWebServiceURL : String
+mapWebServiceURL : String
+currentBusiness : Data.BusinessRecord
+currentIsFavorite : Boolean
+zoomLevel : Integer
+searchParams : Object
+resultsTitle : String
+resultsMessage : String
+skipFavoritesStoreEvents : Boolean
+cookieProvider : Ext.state.CookieProvider
+Data.DAO : Object
+Data.BusinessRecord : Ext.data.Record
+Data.ResultsStore : Ext.data.Store
+Data.searchSortStore : Ext.data.Store
+Data.searchMinimumRatingStore : Ext.data.Store
+Data.searchStateStore : Ext.data.Store
+Data.FavoritesStore : Ext.data.Store
+init()
+buildUI()
+populateDetails()
+getMap()
+loadDefaults()
+showFavorites()
+favoriteClicked()
+generateActionImgTag : String()
+attachIconTooltips()
+UIObjects.Viewport : Ext.Viewport()
+UIObjects.DetailsPanel : Ext.Panel()
+UIObjects.FavoritesPanel : Ext.Panel()
+UIObjects.HeaderPanel : Ext.Panel()
+UIObjects.SearchTabPanel : Ext.Panel()
+UIEventHandlers.NewSearchClick()
+UIEventHandlers.PrintItemClick()
+UIEventHandlers.AddToFavoritesClick()
+UIEventHandlers.DeleteFavoriteClick()
+UIEventHandlers.ClearFavoritesClick()
+UIEventHandlers.executeSearch()
+UIEventHandlers.saveLocationAsDefault()

Figure 6-9. *UML diagram of the LocalBusinessSearch class*

As with the previous application, the LocalBusinessSsearch.js file doesn't contain all the members you see in the UML diagram; many of them—most of them, in fact, in this application—are in other source files. But the basis for this class is constructed here, and it begins with this code:

```
Ext.namespace("LocalBusinessSearch", "LocalBusinessSearch.UIObjects",
  "LocalBusinessSearch.UIEventHandlers", "LocalBusinessSearch.Data");
```

As we've seen before, this code creates a top-level namespace (class), LocalBusinessSearch, with three nested namespaces within it: UIObjects, UIEventHandlers, and Data.

A number of fields are present in this class, and they are summarized in Table 6-3.

Table 6-3. *The Fields of the LocalBusinessSearch Class*

Field	Initial Value	Description
appID	You tell me!	This stores the application ID for the Yahoo! web services (don't forget to register for one or you won't be able to play with this application).
searchWebServiceURL	http://local.yahooapis. com/LocalSearchService/ V3/localSearch	This specifies the URL for the business search API.
mapWebServiceURL	http://local.yahooapis. com/MapsService/V1/ mapImage	This specifies the URL for the map image retrieval service.
currentBusiness	null	This is where the reference to the BusinessRecord currently being viewed is stored.
currentIsFavorite	false	This is a flag that tells whether the BusinessRecord currently being viewed is a favorite (because there's nothing about the BusinessRecord that can tell us this).
zoomLevel	null	This tracks the zoom level at which the map is currently being viewed.
searchParams	null	This stores the search parameters last used when calling the search service (needed for paging).
resultsTitle	null	This contains the MessageBox title for displaying errors occurring during a call to the web services.
resultsMessage	null	This contains the MessageBox message for displaying errors occurring during a call to the web services.
skipFavoritesStoreEvents	false	When set to true, this indicates that events on the FavoritesStore (add specifically) should not fire.

One more field is present, but I want to discuss it separately here:

```
LocalBusinessSearch.cookieProvider = new Ext.state.CookieProvider({
  expires : new Date(new Date().getTime() + (1000 * 60 * 60 * 24 * 365))
});
```

You've seen the `Ext.state.CookieProvider` before in previous projects with regard to storing the widget state. What I didn't tell you, however, is that you can use such an object to store arbitrary data in cookies as well! In this application I wanted to be able to store certain location-related fields from a search and make them default values. For instance, making your zip code a default value makes a lot of sense and saves time. Normally you would just instantiate `Ext.state.CookieProvider` and accept its default settings, but in this case I wanted those default values to persist for longer than the default of seven days. I wanted them to stick around for a year, and that's precisely what this does. It does so by specifying a value for the `expires` config attribute and setting its value to the current date (by getting its value in milliseconds via its `getTime()` method) and then adding one year's worth of milliseconds (calculated here rather than just plugging in the magic number of 31,536,000,000).

To set and retrieve cookies, you use the `set()` and `get()` methods of the `CookieProvider`. But let's not get ahead of ourselves—we'll see them in action soon enough!

Note You might be wondering why this default location information is stored in a cookie rather than in the Gears database. The answer is this: I wanted to demonstrate using the Ext JS cookie functions to you! You have already seen plenty of Gears interaction in this application and others, so I took this opportunity to go in a different direction and show off more of Ext JS. Feel free to rewrite the code to store it in the database if you wish; that wouldn't be a bad exercise.

The `init()` method is next, and this too is something we're quite familiar with. There are a few new parts in here to make it interesting:

```
LocalBusinessSearch.init = function() {

  var daoInitResult = LocalBusinessSearch.Data.DAO.init();
  switch (daoInitResult) {
    case "ok":
      Ext.form.VTypes["zipcode"] = /^\d{5}$/;
      Ext.form.VTypes["zipcodeMask"] = /[\d-]/;
      Ext.form.VTypes["zipcodeText"] = "Zip Code must be in the format of #####";
      Ext.QuickTips.init();
      Ext.form.Field.prototype.msgTarget = "side";
      Ext.state.Manager.setProvider(LocalBusinessSearch.cookieProvider);
      LocalBusinessSearch.buildUI();
      LocalBusinessSearch.loadDefaults();
      Ext.getDom("divFavorites").style.height = (Ext.getBody().getHeight() -
        110 - 300 - 58) + "px";
    break;
```

```
       case "no_gears":
         Ext.MessageBox.show({
           title : "Gears Not Available", buttons : Ext.MessageBox.OK,
           msg : "<br>" +
             "I'm sorry but Google Gears is not installed on your computer, " +
             "or is unavailable for some reason (like you disabled the " +
             "browser plugin for example)." +
             "<br><br>" +
             "If you do not have Gears installed, please visit " +
             "<a href=\"http://gears.google.com/\" target=\"new\">" +
             "the Gears home page</a> to install it." +
             "<br><br>" +
             "If you do have it installed, please try enabling the plugin in " +
             "whatever fashion is applicable in the browser you are using, " +
             "and reload this application.", animEl : "divSource"
         });
       break;
       default:
         Ext.MessageBox.alert("DAO Initialization Failed",
           "Data access could not be initialized.  Reason: " + daoInitResult);
       break;
   }

};
```

Before we discuss what's new, let's discuss what's missing: this code isn't being deferred as we've seen earlier, and there's no mention of a Please Wait message. These are interrelated and are not present for the same reason: I was experiencing some sort of timing issue with the Please Wait message that made the lightbox effect occasionally fail to go away when initialization was complete. I wasn't able to find the root cause (there's those darned deadlines again!), so I decided the better option was to remove all that entirely. Fortunately, initialization is very quick here so it's not a big loss.

Most of this code is just like what we've seen before, but there are some new things going on in the case "ok" code of the switch statement. The first thing is the definition of a custom vtype. The issue here is that when a user enters a value in the Zip Code field, we want to ensure it's in a valid format. It's always nice to use Ext JS's built-in form validation logic, but alas, there is no vtype out of the box for a zip code. Therefore, we have to create our own. In Chapter 2 you saw an example of creating a custom vtype, but there is an even simpler way, as you can see in this code. At least for types that only require a simple regex and no actual code behind it, all you need to do is add three elements to the VTypes array of the Ext.form object. The first element is named for the vtype you're creating, so we use zipcode. The other two then take that value as a base and append Mask and Text, so you get zipcodeMask and zipcodeText. The first element defines the regex to run against the entered value to determine whether it's valid, the zipcodeMask regex masks off the value for display, and the zipcodeText is the validation failure message seen when the value is not in a valid form.

The QuickTips and validation message location are then initialized, as seen previously, and the provider for the Ext.state.Manager is also set to the CookieProvider created earlier.

Next, `buildUI()` is called, which we'll skip for just a moment so we can finish looking through the `init()` code. Next, a call to `loadDefaults()` is made, which loads the stored default values, if any, from cookies and populates the search forms. We'll skip that for just a moment as well.

The final task is to size the area below the search form and results, where the users' stored favorites appear. This is necessary because there doesn't seem to be a way to have Ext JS do it automatically. The problem is that as the list grows, the area doesn't scroll. In order to have it scroll as you'd expect it to, we need to set the `overflow` style attribute to `auto` on it and the area the favorites are in needs to be sized so that its height is the height of the browser content area, minus the header, and minus the search area. We also subtract a few more pixels to account for borders and padding and such. That's what the final line in the `case "ok"` code does: it gets a reference to the `<div>` named `divFavorites` and sets its `height` style attribute. The body of the document is gotten via a call to `Ext.getBody()`, which, because it's an `Ext.Element` object, includes some utility methods, most importantly, `getHeight()`. This method gives us the total height of the browser content area. We take that value and subtract 110 (the height of the header) from it. Then we subtract 300 (the height of the search form and results area) and finally subtract 58 (a "magic number" reached by trial and error that accounts for the borders and padding and such). The result is that the `<div>` now fits in the area it is supposed to, and scrolling works as expected. As you'll see later, this same code executes whenever the browser is resized so that the `<div>` is always sized properly.

■Note Magic numbers are a *code smell*, that is, something that most programmers consider bad form. A magic number is a "naked" number statically present in code whose meaning and derivation isn't immediately obvious from the code. Generally, constants and/or variables are a better choice because they give the numbers some semantic meaning. For instance, I could have had a variable named `paddingAndBorders` and then used that in the expression to calculate the height. This arguably would have made the code more readable, but this was a good opportunity to point out what a magic number is. Magic numbers usually do make code harder to read, and you should therefore take this as an example of what you should *not* do in your own code! (Of course, there are always exceptions.)

Next up is `buildUI()`, which we skipped over a little while ago:

```
LocalBusinessSearch.buildUI = function() {

  new Ext.Viewport(LocalBusinessSearch.UIObjects.Viewport());

  LocalBusinessSearch.attachIconTooltips();

  LocalBusinessSearch.skipFavoritesStoreEvents = true;
  LocalBusinessSearch.Data.FavoritesStore.add(
  LocalBusinessSearch.Data.DAO.retrieveFavorites());
  LocalBusinessSearch.skipFavoritesStoreEvents = false;
  LocalBusinessSearch.showFavorites();

};
```

As is the case with much of the code here, this is just like what was in previous applications. The Viewport is first built, and again we're using the pattern of having methods that return the objects' config information. One thing that makes this different, however, is that the Viewport is all there is; in previous applications we've seen more than one object built here, such as toolbars and Accordions and the like. How is this possible? Well, it will be obvious when we look at Viewport.js, but in short, the calls to the methods to create the other objects are inlined with the Viewport code. This is a further enhancement to the architecture we've been slowly evolving with each project. (I don't know if there will be further evolutions... writing a book is as much an adventure as reading one!)

Once the Viewport is formed, which means all the subcomponents of it are as well, a call to attachIconTooltips() is made. If you play with the application you'll notice that the icons in the header have tooltips over them, text to tell you what they do when you hover over them. This isn't something you get for free; there is work involved in making that happen, and attachIconTooltips() is where that work is done. However, as that is part of the Header.js file, let's put aside those details for now and continue.

The next step is to load the favorites from the database. As the add() method is used to do that, we have the same situation as in other applications: the add event will be firing multiple times here, and we don't want that. So, the skipFavoritesStoreEvents flag is set to true, and the add event handler checks that and skips its work when it's true. A call to the DAO's retrieveFavorites() gets us an array of BusinessRecords, which is passed along to the FavoritesStore's add() method. Finally, the skipFavoritesStoreEvents flag is set to false, because from that point on we want that add event to fire. Finally the showFavorites() method is called, which is more code we'll defer looking at a little longer, but in short it generates the markup for the list of favorites seen in the bottom-left corner of the page.

The final method in this file is that loadDefaults() method I said we'd look at later. (See, I may put things off, but I get back around to them eventually!) Here's the code for that method:

```
LocalBusinessSearch.loadDefaults = function() {

  Ext.getCmp("searchStreet").setValue(
    LocalBusinessSearch.cookieProvider.get("defaultLocation_street"));
  Ext.getCmp("searchCity").setValue(
    LocalBusinessSearch.cookieProvider.get("defaultLocation_city"));
  Ext.getCmp("searchState").setValue(
    LocalBusinessSearch.cookieProvider.get("defaultLocation_state"));
  Ext.getCmp("searchZip").setValue(
    LocalBusinessSearch.cookieProvider.get("defaultLocation_zip"));

};
```

As I hinted at earlier, all it takes to retrieve a cookie is a call to the get() method of the cookieProvider. You pass in the key, or name, of the cookie, and it is retrieved (assuming it exists of course—you get a blank string if it doesn't). Then, each of the search form fields is set to the returned value, and that's how we see the saved default values in the form at application startup.

Viewport.js

Now we come to the Viewport.js file, which is something I said we'd get to soon... is this soon enough for you? Well, ready or not, here comes the code:

```
LocalBusinessSearch.UIObjects.Viewport = function() { return ({
  layout : "border", items : [
    { region : "north", height : 110, items : [
      new Ext.Panel(LocalBusinessSearch.UIObjects.HeaderPanel())
    ] },
    { region : "west", width : 440, items : [
      new Ext.TabPanel(LocalBusinessSearch.UIObjects.SearchTabPanel()),
      new Ext.Panel(LocalBusinessSearch.UIObjects.FavoritesPanel())
    ] },
    { region : "center", layout : "fit", items : [
      new Ext.Panel(LocalBusinessSearch.UIObjects.DetailsPanel())
    ] }
  ],
  listeners : {
    resize : function(inViewport, inAdjWidth, inAdjHeight, inWidth, inHeight) {
      var df = Ext.getDom("divFavorites");
      if (df) {
        df.style.height = (Ext.getBody().getHeight() - 110 - 300 - 58) + "px";
      }
    }
  }
}); };
```

As far as Viewports go, there are no surprises here. Once again we have our friend Mr. BorderLayout to thank for all the wonderfulness. In the north region is the header area, which contains the toolbar (well, not a *real* Ext JS toolbar, but still) and the application logo. In the west is a TabPanel that contains the Search and Results tabs, and below that is a plain-old Panel where our favorites are shown. In the center is where the details are, and it's a Panel as well, one using an Accordion layout. Notice that the center region has a layout of fit, so that the Accordion takes up the whole center region.

Of course, there is something exciting a new here: the fact that each of the components in the three regions is instantiated inline. This is that architectural evolution I talked about earlier. This lets the actual UI code be embedded in the Viewport definition, which I think makes more sense than instantiating an object and then including Ext.getCmp() in the Viewport definition, as we've seen previously. This way, even more ordering concerns are removed because we no longer have to ensure that all the components get created before creating the Viewport. It's a relatively minor change, but it makes things even cleaner than before.

There is also the small matter of the listeners array, and the one event handler contained within it, resize. Recall our earlier discussion when we looked at how the favorites section was sized properly during initialization. Well, this resizing needs to occur when the browser window is resized as well, and that's precisely the time at which the resize event fires. So, in it we do the same sort of math that we saw earlier. However, one problem exists: it turns out the `resize` event fires during initialization as well, and unfortunately it occurs before `divFavorites` is created. So, to avoid a nasty little error we need to check for its existence before resizing anything.

Header.js

The `Header.js` contains a lot of the code behind the functionality in this application, but the first part of it is pure eye candy (which there's nothing wrong with in my book, which this is, so eye candy it is!).

Have you ever used Mac OS? Or, have you ever seen a Fisheye list from libraries like Dojo? If not, I'll briefly explain. Picture a row of icons. As you mouse over an icon, it expands gradually (but rapidly). As you mouse off it, it contracts. The Mac OS doc is where this interface metaphor originated (to the best of my knowledge, and even if not, then certainly it's what made the effect famous). The Dojo toolkit has the Fisheye list as part of it, which provides this widget, but Ext JS does not. Fortunately, it's easy to replicate (at least roughly) and that's what I've done in the header, as you can see in Figure 6-10 (sort of). Of course, we're talking about animation here, so obviously this is something you need to play with the application to get a full appreciation for.

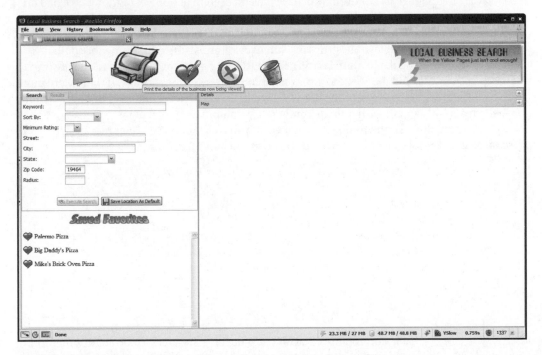

Figure 6-10. *The header with one of the toolbar icons being hovered over*

In this screenshot, my mouse is hovering over the print icon, which has expanded, and is also showing me a tooltip. So, how is this magic pulled off? Well, let's look at some code, shall we?

```
LocalBusinessSearch.UIObjects.HeaderPanel = function() { return ({
  layout : "table", border : false, layoutConfig : { columns : 2 }, items : [
    { border : false, bodyStyle : "padding-left:100px",
      html :
        LocalBusinessSearch.generateActionImgTag("NewSearch") +
        LocalBusinessSearch.generateActionImgTag("PrintItem") +
        LocalBusinessSearch.generateActionImgTag("AddToFavorites") +
        LocalBusinessSearch.generateActionImgTag("DeleteFavorite") +
        LocalBusinessSearch.generateActionImgTag("ClearFavorites")
    },
    { border : false, bodyStyle : "text-align:right",
      html : "<img src=\"img/LocalBusinessSearch.gif\">" }
  ]
}); };
```

This block of code is the UI definition for the HeaderPanel, and it contains two elements, the first being this Mac OS–like toolbar. (I'll simply be referring to it as the toolbar from now on… no sense giving Steve Jobs more credit than he deserves!) This HeaderPanel uses a TableLayout to organize its children, which we haven't seen in action yet, although we had an introduction to it in Chapter 2. In short, the TableLayout allows us to create an HTML table structure without all that pedantic messing about with HTML that is otherwise required.

In this case it's a simple table structure with two columns, one containing the toolbar and one containing the application logo. The layoutConfig element allows us to specify the number of columns, and the items array is essentially an array of table cells. If there were more than two elements in the items array, the table would flow onto a second row, but here we only have the two so it's a table with a single row and two columns.

In the first column is the toolbar, and for each icon a call to the LocalBusinessSearch. generateActionImgTag() method is called. This method looks like this:

```
LocalBusinessSearch.generateActionImgTag = function(inIconID) {

  return String.format(
    "<img id=\"{0}\" src=\"img/{0}.gif\" hspace=\"20\" " +
    "onMouseOver=\"Ext.get('{0}').scale(120, 100, { duration : .25 });\" " +
    "onMouseOut=\"Ext.get('{0}').scale(64, 64, { duration : .25 });\" " +
    "onClick=\"LocalBusinessSearch.UIEventHandlers.{0}Click()\">",
    inIconID);

};
```

As you can see, each icon requires that an <img> tag be generated. To do so, this method uses the String.format() method that Ext JS adds to the String class. This allows us to use token replacements to insert some dynamic data into static text. In this case, the dynamic data is the ID of the icon, passed into the generateActionImgTag() method, and if you look back at the HeaderPanel definition you'll see those values being passed in.

The actual markup returned by this method contains some new stuff for us. The onMouseOver event makes use of the Ext JS's visual effect (or FX as it is sometimes written) capabilities. What happens is that in the onMouseOver event handler, Ext.get() is used to retrieve the Ext.Element representing the <img> tag. Ext JS wraps all DOM elements in its own Ext.Element class that provides additional capabilities, and one of those capabilities is the scale() method (this method and all other animations are provided by the Ext.Fx class, but this is applied to the Ext.Element class, so effectively they become members of the Ext.Element class). This performs an animated scaling of the Ext.Element. The arguments to this method are the new width of the image, the new height, and an options object that here contains a single attribute, duration, which specifies the numbers of seconds the full animation should take. So here we're saying that the image should expand from its default size of 64 × 64 to 120 × 100 in a quarter second. Likewise, in the onMouseOut event handler, we scale the image back down to its original size. That's all it takes to fairly accurately emulate the Mac OS doc!

In the previous screenshot you can also see that each toolbar icon has a tooltip attached to it that shows up when you hover over it, but so far we haven't seen how that's done. Recall that in the init() method the LocalBusinessSearch.attachIconTooltips() was called after nearly everything else was done? Well, that's what does the deed, and now it's time to come face to face with that method:

```
LocalBusinessSearch.attachIconTooltips = function() {

  new Ext.ToolTip({
    target:"NewSearch", showDelay : 0, hideDelay : 0,
    html : "Start a new search"
  });
  new Ext.ToolTip({
    target:"PrintItem", showDelay : 0, hideDelay : 0,
    html : "Print the details of the business now being viewed"
  });
  new Ext.ToolTip({
    target:"AddToFavorites", showDelay : 0, hideDelay : 0,
    html : "Add the business now being viewed to your favorites"
  });
  new Ext.ToolTip({
    target:"DeleteFavorite", showDelay : 0, hideDelay : 0,
    html : "Remove the currently selected favorite from your favorites"
  });
  new Ext.ToolTip({
    target:"ClearFavorites", showDelay : 0, hideDelay : 0,
    html : "Clear your list of favorites"
  });

};
```

For each toolbar icon we create a new Ext.ToolTip object. This is a widget that is very easy to use: you simply feed a configuration object to the constructor containing a couple of elements, the first of which is target. This is the ID of the DOM node to attach the ToolTip to. You also supply the html attribute, which is the text of the ToolTip. You can also supply a number of other attributes; for this example the only two we're interested in are showDelay and hideDelay, which is the amount of time to take before a ToolTip is shown or hidden, respectively (here we want them to show up immediately, so 0 is the appropriate value).

The remaining methods in Header.js are the functions that are called when each of the toolbar icons is clicked. The first of these corresponds to the first toolbar icon, the one for starting a new search:

```
LocalBusinessSearch.UIEventHandlers.NewSearchClick = function() {

  Ext.getCmp("SearchForm").getForm().reset();
  LocalBusinessSearch.loadDefaults();
  LocalBusinessSearch.Data.ResultsStore.removeAll();
  Ext.getCmp("tabResults").disable();
  Ext.getCmp("SearchTabs").setActiveTab("tabSearch");
  Ext.getCmp("DetailsPane").collapse();
  Ext.getCmp("MapPane").collapse();

};
```

Just a couple of relatively simple tasks are required to accomplish this. First, the SearchForm is cleared in the usual manner. Next, the default values are loaded again, just like during initialization. Then, the ResultsStore is cleared and the Results tab is disabled. In addition, by calling setActiveTab("tabSearch") on the retrieved SearchTabs TabPanel, the Search tab is made current. Finally, both the Details and Map panes of the Accordion are collapsed. All of this sets up the UI just like it was when the application began (unless the user saved new default search values, in which case it'll be a little different).

The Print toolbar icon is next, and clicking it results in a call to PrintItemClick():

```
LocalBusinessSearch.UIEventHandlers.PrintItemClick = function() {

  if (LocalBusinessSearch.currentBusiness) {

    Ext.getDom("print_title").innerHTML =
      LocalBusinessSearch.currentBusiness.get("title");
    Ext.getDom("print_longitude").innerHTML =
      LocalBusinessSearch.currentBusiness.get("longitude");
    Ext.getDom("print_latitude").innerHTML =
      LocalBusinessSearch.currentBusiness.get("latitude");
    Ext.getDom("print_distance").innerHTML =
      LocalBusinessSearch.currentBusiness.get("distance");
    Ext.getDom("print_phone").innerHTML =
      LocalBusinessSearch.currentBusiness.get("phone");
    Ext.getDom("print_rating").innerHTML =
      LocalBusinessSearch.currentBusiness.get("rating");
    Ext.getDom("print_address").innerHTML =
      LocalBusinessSearch.currentBusiness.get("address");
```

```
      Ext.getDom("print_city").innerHTML =
        LocalBusinessSearch.currentBusiness.get("city");
      Ext.getDom("print_state").innerHTML =
        LocalBusinessSearch.currentBusiness.get("state");
      Ext.getDom("print_businessurl").innerHTML =
        LocalBusinessSearch.currentBusiness.get("businessurl");
      Ext.getDom("print_map").src = Ext.getDom("imgMap").src;

      var dialogPrint = new Ext.Window({
        applyTo : "dialogPrint", closable : true, modal : true,
        minimizable : false, constrain : true,
        resizable : false, draggable : false, shadow : false,
        autoScroll : true
      });
      dialogPrint.show();
      dialogPrint.maximize();

      Ext.MessageBox.show({
        title : "Ready To Print", buttons : Ext.MessageBox.OK,
        msg : "You can now print, and remember to close this maximized dialog " +
          "when you are done to return to the application",
        animEl : "divSource"
      });

  }

};
```

If no business is currently selected, then this method just ends and nothing is done. If a business is selected, however, the first task is to populate all of the fields that we saw in the markup in index.htm with the details from the current BusinessRecord. Next, a new Ext.Window is created, based on dialogPrint from index.htm. We define this Window as not being minimizable, resizable, or draggable (although it *is* closable); as not having a shadow; and as being constrained to the Viewport (constrain:true, which means that even if the Window was draggable you wouldn't be able to have part of it hanging off the screen... this is redundant given that the Window can't be dragged, but I thought you'd like to know about the constrain attribute, and it certainly doesn't hurt anything being there). Finally, the Window's autoScroll attribute is set to true so that we'll get scrollbars as necessary.

Once the Window is created, it's shown and then immediately maximized via its maximize() method. What you have at this point is a Window that overlays everything else on the page and takes up the entire browser content area. Finally, a MessageBox is shown telling users they can now print and to close the Window when they finish. It's the user's responsibility to print by clicking the browser's Print icon or menu option, and then to close the Window when done.

The next method we find lurking about is the AddToFavoritesClick() method, called when the Add to Favorites toolbar icon is clicked:

```
LocalBusinessSearch.UIEventHandlers.AddToFavoritesClick = function() {

  if (LocalBusinessSearch.currentBusiness &&
    !LocalBusinessSearch.currentIsFavorite) {

    LocalBusinessSearch.Data.FavoritesStore.add(
      LocalBusinessSearch.currentBusiness);

    LocalBusinessSearch.currentIsFavorite = true;

    LocalBusinessSearch.showFavorites();

    Ext.get("fav_" + LocalBusinessSearch.currentBusiness.id).highlight(
      "#ffff00", { attr : "background-color", endColor : "ffffff",
      duration : 1}
    );

    var tr = Ext.getCmp("tabResults");
    var sm = tr.getSelectionModel();
    if (sm.getCount() != 0) {
      sm.clearSelections();
    }

  }

};
```

The job of this method is to add the current BusinessRecord, assuming it is selected and assuming it isn't already a favorite (which happens to be the first check performed here) to the saved favorites. The add() method of the FavoritesStore is called, passing it the LocalBusinessSearch.currentBusiness, which triggers the call to the DAO's createFavorite() method. After that, LocalBusinessSearch.currentIsFavorite is set to true, since the business being viewed is in fact now a favorite, and a call to LocalBusinessSearch.showFavorites() is called, which updates the list of favorites on the screen. Now we use a little more Ext.Fx: a reference to the newly added favorite is obtained, and the highlight() method is used to do a Yellow Fade Effect.[3] This is an effect whereby you highlight a changed piece of information in yellow and then slowly fade it back to the nonhighlighted state. Of course, it does not have to be yellow, and it does not have to fade, but the underlying concept is the same: highlight changed information to provide a visual cue that something has happened (remember that changes caused by Ajax or other UI interactions can sometimes be subtle, so anything you can do to help people notice them will be appreciated). The highlight() method accepts as its first argument an RGB value specifying the color to highlight the item in. As its second argument, the method accepts an object that configures the item, including specifying the style attribute

---

3   The term "Yellow Fade Effect" seems to have originated with a company called 37signals, as seen in
    this article: www.37signals.com/svn/archives/000558.php.

to modify via the attr attribute, the ending color to fade to from the highlight color via the endColor attribute, and the duration in seconds the fade should take via the duration attribute. So here we're highlighting the new favorite in yellow (#ffff00), modifying its background-color style attribute, and fading from yellow to white (#ffffff) in one second's time. The effect can (sort of) be seen in Figure 6-11. Of course, like the toolbar, you have to see it in action for yourself, so fire up that browser and have a peek!

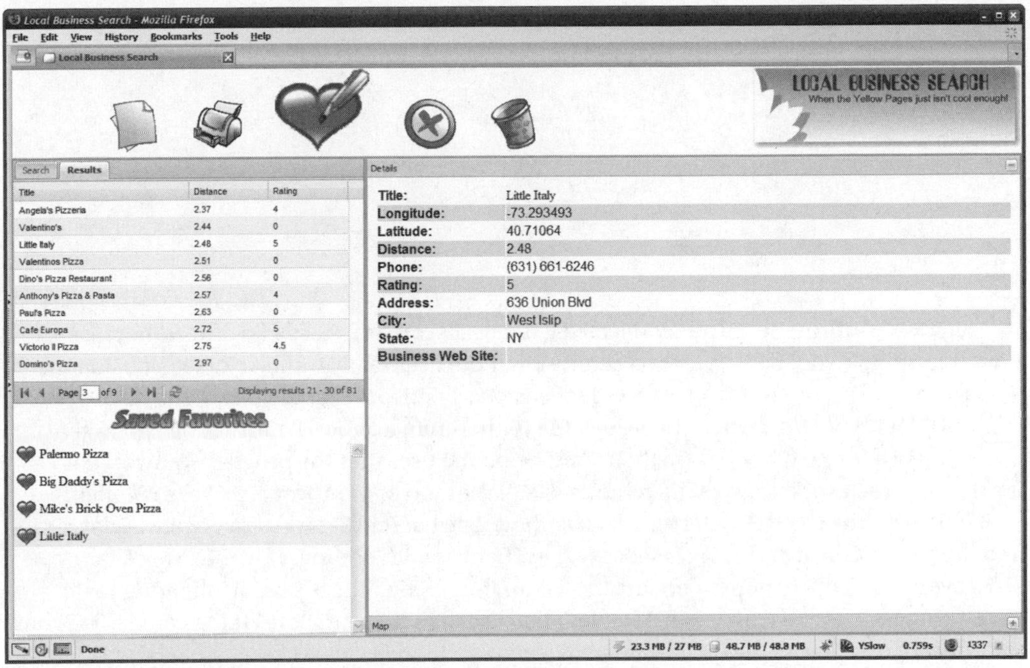

Figure 6-11. *A favorite has been added; notice it's fading in yellow? (What? All you see is black and white? Well, trust me, that's what it does!)*

Since we can add a favorite, it seems only reasonable to be able to delete one too, and that's what the next method is for:

```
LocalBusinessSearch.UIEventHandlers.DeleteFavoriteClick = function() {

  if (LocalBusinessSearch.currentIsFavorite) {

    Ext.MessageBox.confirm("Confirm Favorite Deletion",
      "Are you sure you want to delete the favorite '" +
      LocalBusinessSearch.currentBusiness.get("title") + "'?",
      function(inButtonClicked) {
        if (inButtonClicked == "yes") {
```

```
          LocalBusinessSearch.Data.FavoritesStore.remove(
            LocalBusinessSearch.currentBusiness);
          LocalBusinessSearch.currentBusiness = null;
          LocalBusinessSearch.currentIsFavorite = false;
          LocalBusinessSearch.showFavorites();
          LocalBusinessSearch.populateDetails();
          Ext.getCmp("DetailsPane").collapse();
          Ext.getCmp("MapPane").collapse();
          LocalBusinessSearch.getMap();
        }
      }
    );


  }

};
```

First we confirm the currently selected BusinessRecord is in fact a favorite; otherwise there's nothing to do. If it is, we then confirm that the user really wants to delete it using the MessageBox.confirm() function that we looked at earlier. Note that the text of the MessageBox contains the title of the favorite being deleted, rather than a generic message, which is generally better if for no other reason than convincing the user that the program knows what it's doing! If the user clicks yes, then the remove() method of the FavoritesStore is called, which fires off the deleteFavorite() DAO method. The currentBusiness reference is cleared, and the currentIsFavorite flag is set to false. Then, as with adding a favorite, we call on showFavorites() once more to update the list on the screen. There's no highlighting to do here, though, so there's none of that code. Then, a call to populateDetails() is made. This has the effect of clearing all the detail fields, since that method is smart enough to deal with the case where there is no BusinessRecord, as you'll see later. Then, the two Accordion panes are collapsed, and finally getMap() is called, which, like the call to populateDetails(), effectively clears out the Map pane of the Accordion. The confirmation dialog is shown in Figure 6-12.

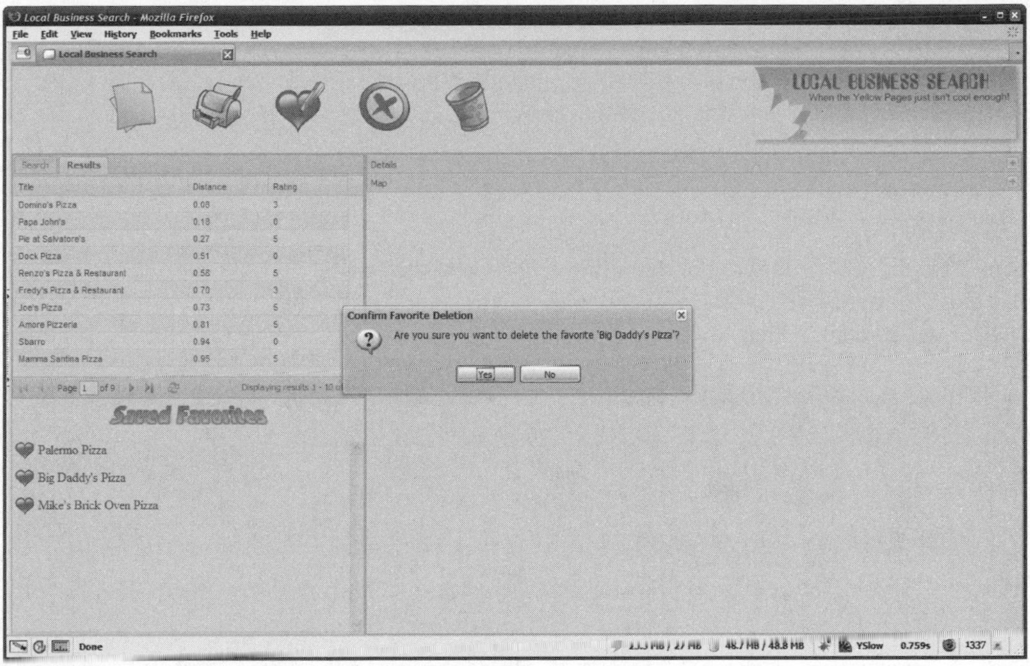

Figure 6-12. *Confirm Favorite Deletion prompt*

The final method we have to look at handles the case of users wanting to clear all their favorites in one go, and it's the aptly named ClearFavoritesClick() method:

```
LocalBusinessSearch.UIEventHandlers.ClearFavoritesClick = function() {

  Ext.MessageBox.confirm("Confirm All Favorites Deletion",
    "Are you sure you want to delete all your favorites?",
    function(inButtonClicked) {
      if (inButtonClicked == "yes") {
        LocalBusinessSearch.Data.FavoritesStore.removeAll();
        if (LocalBusinessSearch.currentIsFavorite) {
          LocalBusinessSearch.currentBusiness = null;
          LocalBusinessSearch.currentIsFavorite = false;
          Ext.getCmp("DetailsPane").collapse();
          Ext.getCmp("MapPane").collapse();
          LocalBusinessSearch.populateDetails();
          LocalBusinessSearch.getMap();
        }
        LocalBusinessSearch.showFavorites();
      }
    }
  );

};
```

This is very much like deleting a single favorite except that this time the removeAll() method of the FavoritesStore is called, which fires the clear event. This results in the deleteFavorites() method of the DAO being called with no favorite ID passed in, causing the sqlDeleteAllFavorites query to be executed. Otherwise, it works just like the DeleteFavoriteClick() method.

Details.js

The Details.js file contains the definition and code related to the center region of our Viewport's BorderLayout and is where details and the map for the currently selected business are shown, as seen in Figure 6-13.

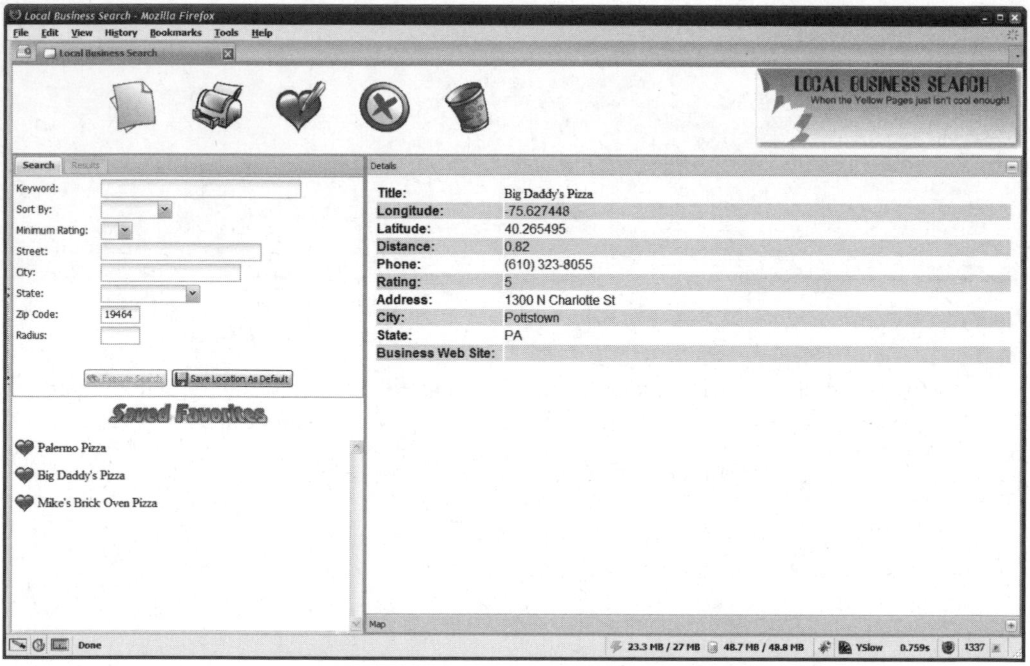

Figure 6-13. *The details of a business are displayed.*

This screen shows the details for a business and it is organized via an Accordion layout, so the details for the business are on a different pane than the map, which you can see in Figure 6-14.

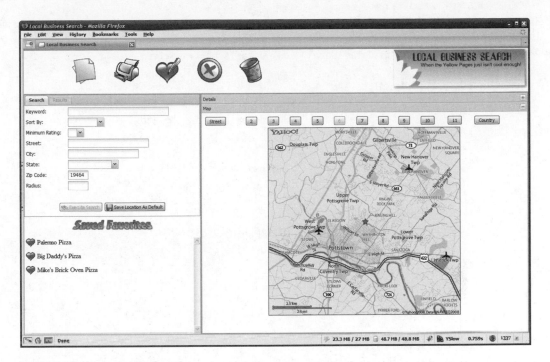

Figure 6-14. *A map is displayed.*

Let's first look at the UI configuration object:

```
LocalBusinessSearch.UIObjects.DetailsPanel = function() { return ({
  layout : "accordion", layoutConfig : { animate : true }, id : "Details",
  defaults: { bodyStyle : "overflow:auto;padding:10px;" }, items : [
    { title : "Details", id : "DetailsPane", collapsed : true, html :
      "<table width=\"100%\">" +
      "  <tr>" +
      "    <td width=\"20%\" class=\"cssDetailLabel\">Title: </td>" +
      "    <td class=\"cssDetailData\" id=\"details_title\"></td>" +
      "  </tr>" +
      "  <tr class=\"cssAltRow\">" +
      "    <td class=\"cssDetailLabel\">Longitude: </td>" +
      "    <td class=\"cssDetailData\" id=\"details_longitude\"></td>" +
      "  </tr>" +
      "  <tr>" +
      "    <td class=\"cssDetailLabel\">Latitude: </td>" +
      "    <td class=\"cssDetailData\" id=\"details_latitude\"></td>" +
      "  </tr>" +
      "  <tr class=\"cssAltRow\">" +
      "    <td  class=\"cssDetailLabel\">Distance: </td>" +
      "    <td class=\"cssDetailData\" id=\"details_distance\"></td>" +
      "  </tr>" +
```

```
    "    <tr>" +
    "      <td class=\"cssDetailLabel\">Phone: </td>" +
    "      <td class=\"cssDetailData\" id=\"details_phone\"></td>" +
    "    </tr>" +
    "    <tr class=\"cssAltRow\">" +
    "      <td class=\"cssDetailLabel\">Rating: </td>" +
    "      <td class=\"cssDetailData\" id=\"details_rating\"></td>" +
    "    </tr>" +
    "    <tr>" +
    "      <td class=\"cssDetailLabel\">Address: </td>" +
    "      <td class=\"cssDetailData\" id=\"details_address\"></td>" +
    "    </tr>" +
    "    <tr class=\"cssAltRow\">" +
    "      <td class=\"cssDetailLabel\">City: </td>" +
    "      <td class=\"cssDetailData\" id=\"details_city\"></td>" +
    "    </tr>" +
    "    <tr>" +
    "      <td class=\"cssDetailLabel\">State: </td>" +
    "      <td class=\"cssDetailData\" id=\"details_state\"></td>" +
    "    </tr>" +
    "    <tr class=\"cssAltRow\">" +
    "      <td class=\"cssDetailLabel\">Business Web Site: </td>" +
    "      <td class=\"cssDetailData\" id=\"details_businessurl\"></td>" +
    "    </tr>" +
    "</table>"
  },
  { title : "Map", id : "MapPane", collapsed : true, items : [
      { xtype : "panel", layout : "table", border : false,
        layoutConfig : { columns : 12 }, items : [
          { id : "btnZoom1", xtype : "button", text : "Street",
            handler : function() { LocalBusinessSearch.getMap(1); }
          },
          { id : "btnZoom2", xtype : "button", text : "2",
            handler : function() { LocalBusinessSearch.getMap(2); }
          },
          { id : "btnZoom3", xtype : "button", text : "3",
            handler : function() { LocalBusinessSearch.getMap(3); }
          },
          { id : "btnZoom4", xtype : "button", text : "4",
            handler : function() { LocalBusinessSearch.getMap(4); }
          },
          { id : "btnZoom5", xtype : "button", text : "5",
            handler : function() { LocalBusinessSearch.getMap(5); }
          },
          { id : "btnZoom6", xtype : "button", text : "6",
            handler : function() { LocalBusinessSearch.getMap(6); }
          },
```

```
        { id : "btnZoom7", xtype : "button", text : "7",
          handler : function() { LocalBusinessSearch.getMap(7); }
        },
        { id : "btnZoom8", xtype : "button", text : "8",
          handler : function() { LocalBusinessSearch.getMap(8); }
        },
        { id : "btnZoom9", xtype : "button", text : "9",
          handler : function() { LocalBusinessSearch.getMap(9); }
        },
        { id : "btnZoom10", xtype : "button", text : "10",
          handler : function() { LocalBusinessSearch.getMap(10); }
        },
        { id : "btnZoom11", xtype : "button", text : "11",
          handler : function() { LocalBusinessSearch.getMap(11); }
        },
        { id : "btnZoom12", xtype : "button", text : "Country",
          handler : function() { LocalBusinessSearch.getMap(12); }
        }
      ]
    },
    { border : false, bodyStyle : "text-align:center", html :
      "<img id=\"imgMap\" vspace=\"6\" " +
      "style=\"border:1px solid #000000;display:none;\">"
    }
    ]
  }
 ]
}); };
```

As expected, accordion is the layout value, and we specify that we want flipping between the panes to be animated by setting the layoutConfig object's animate attribute to true. I wanted there to be some padding around the content of all panes in the Accordion, so the defaults attribute comes into play, and the bodyStyle attribute within that object sets a padding style of 10 pixels. It also sets overflow to auto so that any scrolling, which can happen easily on the Map pane, kicks in as needed.

The items array contains two elements, one for each pane. The first pane is the Details pane, and it is defined using the html attribute and a giant constructed string. The markup itself is an unremarkable HTML table—nothing special there. Each cell in the table in the second column has an ID because that's where the detail information will be plugged in.

The second element in the items array is the Map pane, and it's slightly more interesting. It has an items array as well, and the first element in that array is a Panel that, once again, uses the TableLayout. This time, however, there are 12 columns, and there happens to be 12 Buttons created for the map-zooming functionality, so all the buttons are in a single row. This was necessary because if I hadn't used a TableLayout, the Buttons would render one under another, running down the screen, so that wouldn't work. A TableLayout was the simplest way to avoid that problem. The Buttons themselves are pretty simple—they just have a handler defined that calls the LocalBusinessSearch.getMap() method, passing what is basically a zoom factor.

The second element in the Map pane's items array is where the map itself goes, and it too is a plain Panel. All that's required here is to use the html attribute to create an <img> tag. The bodyStyle attribute on the Panel sets the text-align style attribute to center to center the <img> tag. The <img> tag isn't initially loaded with any image, so it is effectively empty. I put a border around the image and initially hide it.

That's it for the configuration; it is for the most part straightforward HTML wrapped by some Ext JS components.

The first method we find, populateDetails(), is called to show the details for a selected business:

```
LocalBusinessSearch.populateDetails = function() {

  var record = LocalBusinessSearch.currentBusiness ||
    new LocalBusinessSearch.Data.BusinessRecord({});

  Ext.getDom("details_title").innerHTML =
    Ext.util.Format.defaultValue(record.get("title"), "");
  Ext.getDom("details_distance").innerHTML =
    Ext.util.Format.defaultValue(record.get("distance"), "");
  Ext.getDom("details_phone").innerHTML =
    Ext.util.Format.defaultValue(record.get("phone"), "");
  Ext.getDom("details_rating").innerHTML =
    Ext.util.Format.defaultValue(record.get("rating"), "");
  Ext.getDom("details_address").innerHTML =
    Ext.util.Format.defaultValue(record.get("address"), "");
  Ext.getDom("details_city").innerHTML =
    Ext.util.Format.defaultValue(record.get("city"), "");
  Ext.getDom("details_state").innerHTML =
    Ext.util.Format.defaultValue(record.get("state"), "");
  Ext.getDom("details_latitude").innerHTML =
    Ext.util.Format.defaultValue(record.get("latitude"), "");
  Ext.getDom("details_longitude").innerHTML =
    Ext.util.Format.defaultValue(record.get("longitude"), "");
  Ext.getDom("details_businessurl").innerHTML =
    Ext.util.Format.defaultValue(record.get("businessurl"), "");

};
```

The first line ensures that we always have a BusinessRecord, whether it's the currently selected one referenced by LocalBusinessSearch.currentBusiness or a new empty one. This is required because, as you may recall, this method can be called at some points where the intent is to clear the detail fields. Rather than code special logic for that, I decided it was easier to just ensure I always had a BusinessRecord, and then I could use the Ext.util.Format. defaultValue() method during field population. So, for each detail field, a reference to it is retrieved via Ext.getDom(), and then its innerHTML property is set. The value set is determined by a call to Ext.util.Format.defaultValue(). If the first argument to that method is empty, meaning the field retrieved from the BusinessRecord is empty (which it would be if there is no current record), then a blank string is returned and set in the field on the screen. This not only covers the situation of clearing the detail fields but it also nicely deals with any missing fields returned by the web service (for instance, businessurl will frequently come back as null, and we wouldn't want to display null on the screen, which is what happens without Ext.util. Format.defaultValue() in there to effectively say "null means empty, so here's a blank string for ya" instead).

As mentioned before, the getMap() method accepts a zoom factor as an argument to it. This results in a new web service request being made and the map <img> tag updated to point to a map at the new zoom level. For example, if you zoom to country level, you'll get something that looks like Figure 6-15.

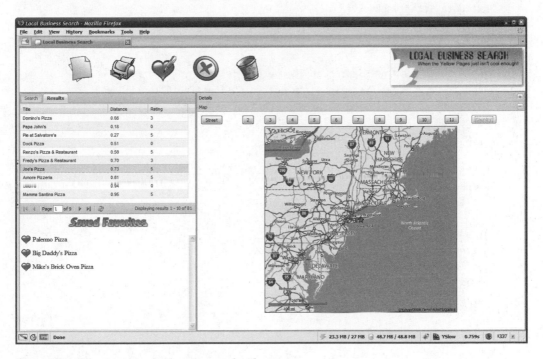

Figure 6-15. *The map, zoomed to country level*

The getMap() method looks like this:

```
LocalBusinessSearch.getMap = function(inZoomLevel) {

  if (!LocalBusinessSearch.currentBusiness) {
    var mapTag = Ext.getDom("imgMap");
    mapTag.style.display = "none";
    return;
  }

  if (inZoomLevel) {
    LocalBusinessSearch.zoomLevel = inZoomLevel;
  } else {
    LocalBusinessSearch.zoomLevel = 6;
  }
```

```
for (var i = 1; i < 13; i++) {
  var b = Ext.getCmp("btnZoom" + i);
  if (i == LocalBusinessSearch.zoomLevel) {
    b.disable();
  } else {
    b.enable();
  }
}

new Ext.data.ScriptTagProxy(
  { url : LocalBusinessSearch.mapWebServiceURL }
).load(
  {
    appid : LocalBusinessSearch.appID, output : "json",
    "longitude" : LocalBusinessSearch.currentBusiness.get("longitude"),
    "latitude" : LocalBusinessSearch.currentBusiness.get("latitude"),
    image_width : 480, image_height : 460,
    zoom : LocalBusinessSearch.zoomLevel
  },
  new (Ext.extend(new Function(), Ext.data.DataReader, {
    readRecords : function(inObject) {
      return inObject;
    }
  }))(),
  function(inObject) {
    var mapTag = Ext.getDom("imgMap");
    mapTag.style.display = "";
    mapTag.src = inObject.ResultSet.Result;
  }
);

};
```

Just like getDetails(), getMap() is also used to clear the Map pane. So, the first check done is to see if LocalBusinessSearch.currentBusiness is null, and if it is then the map <img> tag is hidden.

Next, we see if there was a zoom-level argument, and if not we set the default zoom level to 6, midway in the zoom range. Related to this is the task of resetting the buttons. So, we iterate over the buttons, and for each we check to see if it matches the zoom level. If it does, the button is disabled; otherwise it is enabled (no sense making the button for the current zoom level clickable).

After that comes the interesting bit: the web service call to get the new map image. Earlier we saw how the ScriptTagProxy can be tied to a DataStore to get data, but nothing says you *have* to use a ScriptTagProxy within the context of a DataStore. In this case, that's exactly what we need to do! So, a new ScriptTagProxy is instantiated, and the URL to the map service is passed via the config object's url attribute. Chained to that instantiation is a call to the load()

method. The load() method recall accepts an object that defines the parameters to pass to the service. So, we have our appid, which is needed for the service to accept our request, followed by the output specification of json, so we'll get a JSON-P response. Then we have longitude and latitude, pulled from the current BusinessRecord. The image_width and image_height attributes specify the size of the image we want back, and zoom is the zoom level.

The second argument to load() is an instance of a new DataReader, and this is similar-looking to what we saw earlier in terms of extending Function to include the methods of DataReader.

The third argument is the callback function, here inlined. So, the DataReader's readRecords() method fires, and here we're not doing anything with the response—we're simply returning it. Because this isn't in the context of a DataStore, there's no need to parse for Records or any of that, and while there is some error handling that could be done, as we did in ResultsStore, I decided to make things simple. We assume if a search result got a valid response, then so too would an image request. (This could be a favorite, which means the search service wouldn't have been previously called, but like I said, I went for simplicity here, not necessarily extreme robustness.)

Anyway, the callback executes and is passed the result of the call to readRecords(), which is just the object resulting from the JSON returned by the service. From it we grab the ResultsSet.Result element, which happens to be a URL to the image we requested. So we point the src attribute of the map <img> tag to it, and lo and behold, we have a zoomed image displayed, perhaps similar to what you see in Figure 6-16.

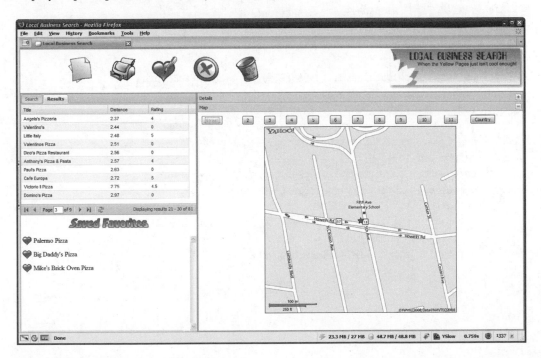

Figure 6-16. *The map, zoomed to street level*

Favorites.js

The next file to examine, Favorites.js, is a fairly small one compared to some of the others. This is where the functionality related to the favorites list is located, beginning with the configuration object for the FavoritesPanel, the area right below the search TabPanel:

```
LocalBusinessSearch.UIObjects.FavoritesPanel = function() { return ({
  border : false, bodyStyle : "padding-top:8px;", items : [
    { border : false,
      html : "<center><img src=\"img/SavedFavorites.gif\"></center><br>" },
    { border: false, bodyStyle : "overflow:scroll",
      html : "<div id=\"divFavorites\"></div>" }
  ]
}); };
```

Here we're simply defining two Panels, which will lay out horizontally (the default way Panels lay out). The first Panel contains some HTML for the Saved Favorites image. The second Panel houses the <div> where the generated list of favorites will go. Note that the bodyStyle of this Panel is set to scroll, so there will always be scrollbars, even when they aren't, strictly speaking, necessary. I felt this gave a more consistent look to the UI, especially considering the automatic height calculations we saw earlier.

The method that generates the list of favorites is up next, and its name is showFavorites():

```
LocalBusinessSearch.showFavorites = function() {

  Ext.getDom("divFavorites").innerHTML = "";

  LocalBusinessSearch.Data.FavoritesStore.each(function(inRecord) {
    Ext.DomHelper.append("divFavorites",
      { tag : "div", id : "fav_" + inRecord.id,
        style : "width:100%;margin-bottom:10px;cursor:pointer;",
        onclick : "LocalBusinessSearch.favoriteClicked(\"" +
          inRecord.id + "\");",
        onmouseover : "this.style.backgroundColor = \"#ffff00\";",
        onmouseout : "this.style.backgroundColor = \"\";",
        children : [
          { tag : "img", src : "img/favorite.gif", hspace : "4",
            align : "absmiddle" },
          { tag : "span", html : inRecord.get("title") }
        ]
      }
    );
  });

};
```

For each BusinessRecord in the ResultsStore, some code is executed, and within it are a few new tricks. First, the Ext.DomHelper.append() method is used to generate the markup. This method allows you to append some new HTML to an existing element, but it does so without you having to directly write that HTML. Think of this in comparison to the details code we looked at earlier where there was that giant string construction that built up some HTML. Here, we don't have to do that; we can take a more object-oriented approach and let Ext JS worry about the details. The first argument this method takes is the ID of the DOM node to insert the created element under. The second argument can be a straight string of HTML, so you can still do that if you prefer. You can also, as we've done here, pass in an object that defines the element to be inserted. You can also pass in an array of such elements if you're creating multiple things. Since we only have a single thing to create here, a single object it is! This object has only one required attribute: tag, which names the HTML tag you want to create. Here we're creating a <div>. Beyond that, the attributes you include depend on the tag you're creating and what you want to do with it.

So for instance, we saw earlier that after a favorite is added, this method will be called, and then the new item is highlighted. To do that highlighting, we need the items to have IDs associated with them, so id is one of the attributes. There's also some style setting to be done here, such as cursor:pointer, so that when the favorite is hovered over the user will get an indication via cursor change that it is clickable. There's also an onclick handler defined so that something happens when it is clicked, and ditto for onmouseover and onmouseout, which is how the background color is changed to yellow when the favorite is hovered over as well.

Another attribute that you can have is the children attribute. This allows you to create further elements as children of the new element. Here I'm creating an <img> tag for the little heart icon next to the favorite, as well as a <span> element where the title of the favorite is inserted from the BusinessRecord that is being operated on. Notice how the attributes for the <img> tag and the <span> tag are all different from the <div> tag being created, supporting what I said earlier about the attributes beyond the tag attribute, which is always present, being dynamic.

Now, when a favorite is clicked, we just saw that the favoriteClicked() method is called, and that's what we're looking at next:

```
LocalBusinessSearch.favoriteClicked = function(inID) {

  LocalBusinessSearch.currentBusiness =
    LocalBusinessSearch.Data.FavoritesStore.getById(inID);
  LocalBusinessSearch.currentIsFavorite = true;
  LocalBusinessSearch.populateDetails();
  Ext.getCmp("DetailsPane").expand();
  LocalBusinessSearch.getMap();

  var tr = Ext.getCmp("tabResults");
  var sm = tr.getSelectionModel();
  if (sm.getCount() != 0) {
    sm.clearSelections();
  }

};
```

Clicking a favorite requires a couple of things be done. First, the BusinessRecord for the favorite is pulled out of the FavoritesStore by ID using the getById() DataStore method. Next, we set the currentIsFavorite flag to true since we've seen where that's necessary to know. Then the details are populated, which we've also seen already. Next, the details

Accordion pane is expanded and the map is shown (remember that the default zoom level of 6 will be used here as per the getMap() method's logic when no zoom factor is passed in).

The last task that needs to be performed is to deselect any items in the search results Grid that might be selected. We do this just to make the UI consistent: when an item is selected from the Grid it is highlighted in the Grid, but here the business being shown isn't any that might be selected in the Grid, so it makes sense to clear those selections. Doing so requires that we get a reference to the Grid by using Ext.getCmp(), then get a reference to its SelectionModel via its getSelectionModel() method. Then, the getCount() method tells us if there are any selections they are cleared via a call to clearSelections().

■Note The call to clearSelections() is wrapped in the check of getCount() because if we fail to do so, and there are no items selected, then the call to clearSelections() results in an error. Figuring that one out had me running in circles for a good 20 minutes or so!

Search.js

The final source file we have to look at, Search.js, is one of the largest (although still not too large... thank you, Ext JS!). It's also where a good portion of the work of this application is done. Let's begin by looking at the UI configuration object. I'll split it in half to make it a little easier to digest, beginning with the part that defines the Search tab and form:

```
LocalBusinessSearch.UIObjects.SearchTabPanel = function() { return ({
  id : "SearchTabs", activeTab : 0, height : 300, items : [
    { title : "Search", lid : "tabSearch",
      bodyStyle : "padding:4px", items : [
        { xtype : "form", id : "SearchForm", labelWidth : 100,
          border : false, monitorValid : true, items : [
            { xtype : "textfield", fieldLabel : "Keyword",
              name : "query", width : 250, allowBlank : false },
            { xtype : "combo", fieldLabel : "Sort By", width : 90,
              name : "sort", editable : false, triggerAction : "all",
              mode : "local", valueField : "optVal", displayField : "optVal",
              store : LocalBusinessSearch.Data.searchSortStore },
            { xtype : "combo", fieldLabel : "Minimum Rating", width : 40,
              name : "minimum_rating", editable : false, triggerAction : "all",
              mode : "local", valueField : "optVal", displayField : "optVal",
              store : LocalBusinessSearch.Data.searchMinimumRatingStore },
            { xtype : "textfield", fieldLabel : "Street",
              name : "street", id : "searchStreet", width : 200 },
            { xtype : "textfield", fieldLabel : "City",
              name : "city", id : "searchCity", width : 175 },
```

```
          { xtype : "combo", fieldLabel : "State", width : 125,
            name : "state", editable : false, triggerAction : "all",
            mode : "local", valueField : "optVal", displayField : "optVal",
            store : LocalBusinessSearch.Data.searchStateStore,
            id : "searchState" },
          { xtype : "textfield", fieldLabel : "Zip Code", vtype : "zipcode",
            name : "zip", id : "searchZip", width : 50 },
          { xtype : "numberfield", fieldLabel : "Radius", width : 175,
            name : "radius", minValue : 5, maxValue : 1000, width : 50 }
        ],
        buttons : [
          { text : "Execute Search", formBind : true,
            icon : "img/icon_search.gif",
            cls : "x-btn-text-icon", handler : function() {
              LocalBusinessSearch.UIEventHandlers.executeSearch();
            }
          },
          { text : "Save Location As Default",
            icon : "img/icon_save.gif", cls : "x-btn-text-icon",
            handler :
              LocalBusinessSearch.UIEventHandlers.saveLocationAsDefault
          }
        ]
      }
    ]
  },
```

Now, in other applications we've had tabs, and we've had forms, and there's nothing here that we haven't seen before. The form uses validation to check a few things: that the Keyword field has a value and that the Zip Code field is in the appropriate format. Note the Zip Code field's use of the zipcode vtype that we saw defined early on. Speaking of that vtype, in Figure 6-17 you can see the result of that particular validation failing (it also shows the Keyword field as invalid since it has no value entered).

A number of the fields here are NumberFields, such as the Radius field, which allows us to ensure they too are in a proper format (a number of course!) and are in a valid range. Note that blank is in fact a valid value in those fields, so they don't have allowBlank set to false as the Keyword field does.

We have a couple of ComboBox fields as well. They are tied to the various DataStores we saw defined earlier.

Finally, two Buttons are attached to the form: Execute Search and Save Location As Default. The former is tied to the form's validation so it will be disabled when the form is not in a valid state. Both have icons on them, just to make them a little prettier, so the cls attribute has the value x-btn-text-icon to allow for that (and to still allow for text and to make sure it all looks right).

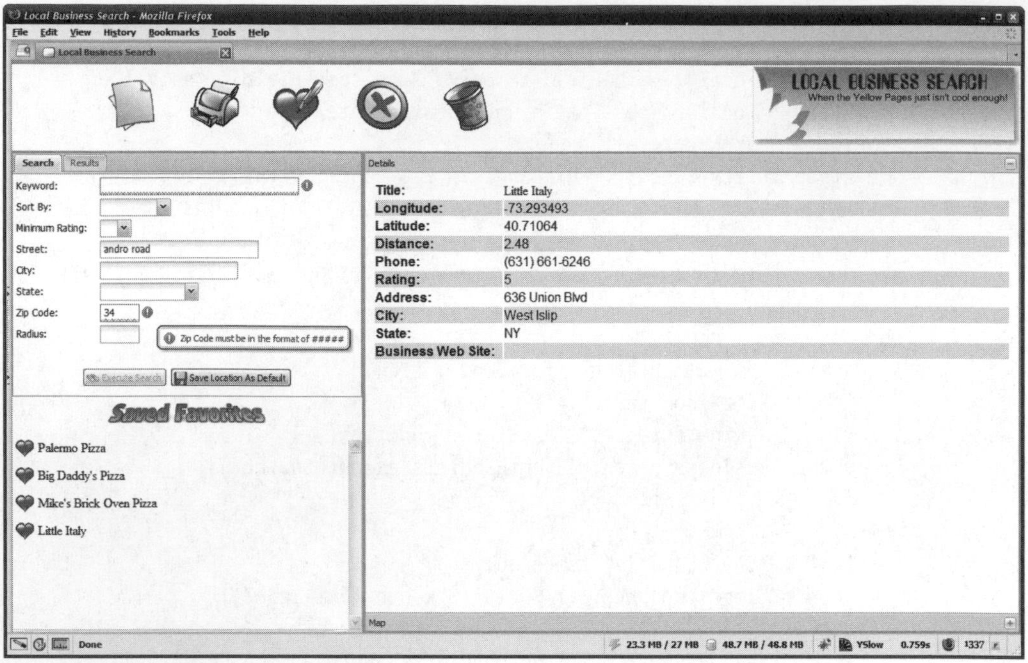

Figure 6-17. *The custom vtype in action*

Now let's move on to the Results tab, which has a few interesting and new things to talk about:

```
{ title : "Results", id : "tabResults", layout : "fit", disabled : true,
  xtype : "grid", autoExpandColumn : "colTitle", stripeRows : true,
  sm : new Ext.grid.RowSelectionModel( { singleSelect : true } ),
  listeners: {
    rowclick : {
      fn : function(inGrid, inRowIndex, inEventObject) {
        LocalBusinessSearch.currentBusiness =
          inGrid.getSelectionModel().getSelected();
        LocalBusinessSearch.currentIsFavorite = false;
        LocalBusinessSearch.populateDetails();
        Ext.getCmp("DetailsPane").expand();
        LocalBusinessSearch.getMap();
      }
    }
  },
  store : LocalBusinessSearch.Data.ResultsStore, columns : [
    { header : "Title", sortable : true,
      dataIndex : "title", id : "colTitle" },
    { header : "Distance", sortable : true, dataIndex : "distance" },
    { header : "Rating", sortable : true, dataIndex : "rating" }
  ],
```

```
    bbar : new Ext.PagingToolbar({
      pageSize : 10, paramNames : { start : "start", limit : "results" },
      store : LocalBusinessSearch.Data.ResultsStore,
      displayInfo : true, id : "bbar",
      displayMsg : "Displaying results {0} - {1} of {2}",
      emptyMsg : "No data to display"
    })
  }
]
}); };
```

Before we get into the code, though, have a look at Figure 6-18, where you can see some search results.

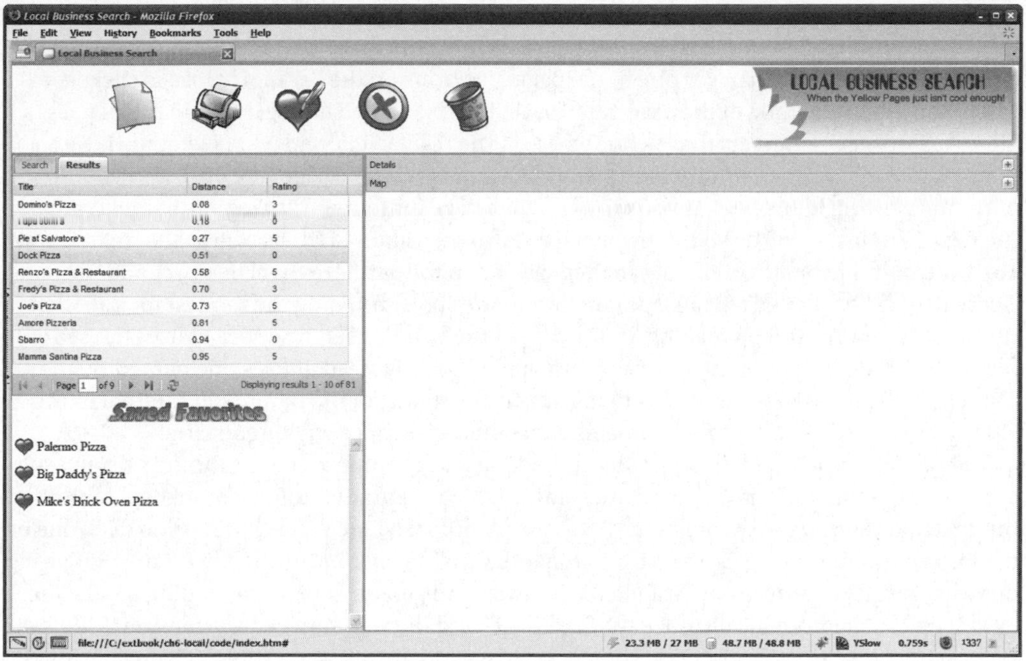

Figure 6-18. *Some search results, with the mouse hovering over a row*

First, this tab is disabled initially so that users can only flip to this tab when they've performed a search. This is to avoid a problem with the PagingToolbar that I'll talk about shortly (the PagingToolbar as well as the issue!).

The Grid is defined much like the others we've seen. It has a rowclick event handler that does the work that is similar to the work of the favoriteClicked() method we looked at in the previous section. This is no accident: the work necessary in this situation is basically the same as when a favorite is clicked, except that currentIsFavorite is set to false.

The new thing here is the bbar attribute, which we haven't seen on a Grid before. The bbar attribute defines a Toolbar to be placed at the bottom of the Grid (in fact, at the bottom of any Panel, of which GridPanel is one). The element defined by the object that is the value of bbar must be an `Ext.Toolbar`, or a descendant. One such descendant is the `PagingToolbar`. This is a specialized `Toolbar` that allows for paging through large result sets. To use it, you tie it to the same `DataStore` as the `Grid` using the `store` attribute, and then define a few other attributes. These attributes are as follows:

- `pageSize`, which determines how many results to show at a time in the `Grid`

- `displayInfo`, which when `true`, as it is here, displays information about what items are being shown

- `displayMsg`, which is the message to be displayed (this string is formatted using the braced numbers 0–2 as tokens that are replaced by the values for `start`, `end`, and `total`, respectively)

- `emptyMsg`, which is what will be displayed if there are no items to display

These messages are displayed in the `PagingToolbar` itself on the right.

There is one other attribute: `paramNames`. This attribute maps parameter names for load calls. Let me explain: whenever one of the paging buttons on the `PagingToolbar` is clicked, a call to the `load()` method of the associated `DataStore` is made. The `PagingToolbar` will pass along to it some parameters that define where in the results it is, and what elements it wants to display. For example, say there are 100 results and you have a `pageSize` of 10 and you're currently viewing items 1–10. If you click the Next Page button, the `PagingToolbar` will request the next 10 items; it will do so by specifying a starting position of 11, as well as the `pageSize` of 10. By default, the names of the parameters passed to the `DataStore` will be `start` and `limit`. These two will be passed as HTTP parameters to the server fulfilling the request for data that the `DataStore` will wind up making. In the case of the Yahoo! search service, it uses the `start` parameter, but it does not use a parameter named `limit`. Instead, it uses one named `results`. Therefore, the `paramNames` allows us to map `limit`, the name of the parameter internal to the `PagingToolbar`, to `results`, the parameter name the web service will understand.

I hope you realize at this point that something fairly complex, paging through result sets, was just implemented with nothing but some JSON configuration information! Well, nothing but that and the code we wrote in the `DataStore`… but still! I mean, every time you click one of the buttons on the `PagingToolbar`, Ext JS is handling all the behind-the-scenes work of figuring out what results to request and asking the `DataStore` to get the data. Data binding means the `Grid` is updated automatically once the `DataStore`, and the web service by extension, fulfills the request. If you've ever hand-coded something like that yourself, then you surely realize how much work this saves you (and yes, I'll stop calling you "Shirley[4]").

---

4   If you've never seen the movies *Airplane* and *Airplane II* I would say, first, what have you been doing all this time? Go out and rent or buy the DVDs now! If you have seen them, then you recognize the joke where someone says "Surely you can't be serious" and the reply comes back "Yes, I am serious, and stop calling me Shirley." This was used a couple of times in both movies to great comic effect, and most of us who have seen the movies use the line in real life every chance we get!

When the Execute Search button is clicked, I'll give you just one guess what method is executed! That's right, it's executeSearch(), and I'm going to break this into some chunks as well, starting with this one:

```
LocalBusinessSearch.UIEventHandlers.executeSearch = function() {

  LocalBusinessSearch.searchParams =
    Ext.getCmp("SearchForm").getForm().getValues();

  if (LocalBusinessSearch.searchParams.street == "" &&
    LocalBusinessSearch.searchParams.city == "" &&
    LocalBusinessSearch.searchParams.state == "" &&
    LocalBusinessSearch.searchParams.zip == "") {
    Ext.MessageBox.show({
      title : "Search Criteria Error", buttons : Ext.MessageBox.OK,
      msg : "You must enter a location to search around " +
      "(just zip code at a minimum)", animEl : "divSource"
    });
    return;
  }
  if (LocalBusinessSearch.searchParams.street != "" &&
    (LocalBusinessSearch.searchParams.city == "" ||
    LocalBusinessSearch.searchParams.state == "")) {
    Ext.MessageBox.show({
      title : "Search Criteria Error", buttons : Ext.MessageBox.OK,
      msg : "When street is entered you must also enter city and state",
      animEl : "divSource"
    });
    return;
  }
```

First, the values of the form are retrieved into searchParams, and then a couple of validations are performed (they could have been coded into the form, but I felt it was simply easier to implement them this way). The first check is to ensure some component of a location, Zip Code at a minimum, has been entered. A valid search can't be performed otherwise. If that test passes, then we need to ensure that if a Street Address is entered, so too is a City and State. While Zip Code alone is a sufficient location to perform a search, all of the other three must be entered in concert to be able to search. In Figure 6-19 you can see the results of a validation failure at this point.

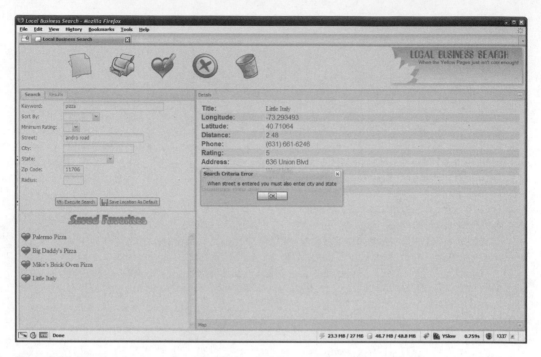

Figure 6-19. *Oops, gotta enter the right thing, dude!*

Next, a MessageBox is shown to indicate a search is in progress:

```
Ext.MessageBox.show({
  title : "Please Wait",
  msg : "<span class='cssPleaseWait'>... Searching ...</span>",
  buttons : false, closable : false
});
Ext.getCmp("tabResults").disable();
```

Also at this point, the Results tab is disabled. This is to account for the case where a previous set of search results is sitting there, and at this point I'll mention that problem with paging that I saw. This seems to be a known issue with the PagingToolbar, but there doesn't appear to be any simple way to reset the PagingToolbar or clear it, even if the DataStore is cleared. While researching this I came across a solution that, frankly, seemed like a whole lot more work than I'd like and seemed to me rather "hacky" in nature. Now, me and hacky solutions are good friends to be sure, but in this case there was a far easier solution: just disable the Results tab! As it turns out, loading the DataStore with new data resets the PagingToolbar, so when the next set of results comes in, everything will work as expected. Sometimes, hiding a problem is a perfectly valid solution!

Anyway, once the Please Wait window is showing, it's time to deal with some default search value issues:

```
if (Ext.isEmpty(LocalBusinessSearch.searchParams.sort)) {
  LocalBusinessSearch.searchParams.sort = "distance";
}
if (Ext.isEmpty(LocalBusinessSearch.searchParams.radius)) {
  LocalBusinessSearch.searchParams.radius = 5;
}
if (Ext.isEmpty(LocalBusinessSearch.searchParams.minimum_rating)) {
  LocalBusinessSearch.searchParams.minimum_rating = 0;
}
```

blank is a valid value in the Sort, Radius, and Minimum Rating fields because we're setting some default values for them. In addition to default values, there's some other static values to set:

```
LocalBusinessSearch.searchParams.appid = LocalBusinessSearch.appID;
LocalBusinessSearch.searchParams.output = "json";
LocalBusinessSearch.searchParams.sort =
  Ext.util.Format.lowercase(LocalBusinessSearch.searchParams.sort);
```

The appID is set on the searchParams, as is the output parameter. These are fed to the web service and, as you'll recall, are required to make the request work and to ensure we get a JSON-P response. Also, the sort parameter is set to lowercase using Ext.util.Format.lowercase() because the values in the ComboBox have capital letters in them so they look nice on the screen, but the web service doesn't take too kindly to the values not being all lowercase.

Once that's done, it's time to get some search results! Unlike with the paging toolbar where the load() method of the ResultsStore will be called automatically, there is no such automatic trigger here, so we have to do it ourselves, like so:

```
LocalBusinessSearch.Data.ResultsStore.load({
  params : { start : 0, results : 10 },
  callback : function(inRecords, inOptions, inSuccess) {
    if (inRecords.length == 0) {
      Ext.MessageBox.show({
        title : LocalBusinessSearch.resultsTitle, buttons : Ext.MessageBox.OK,
        msg : LocalBusinessSearch.resultsMessage, closable : true,
        animEl : "divSource"
      });
      return;
    }
    Ext.getCmp("tabResults").enable();
    Ext.getCmp("SearchTabs").setActiveTab("tabResults");
    Ext.MessageBox.hide();
  }
});

};
```

The first argument to this method is an object that sets some options for the load. Here we have only two: start and results, which you should recognize are the parameter names we specified in the paramNames attribute passed into the PagingToolbar's definition. To begin with, we want the first 10 records, so we start with item 0, and we want 10 results at a time.

The second argument to the load() method is a callback function to be called after the DataProxy fetches the data from the server and the DataReader has parsed the response into BusinessRecords. The first thing done in this callback is to see if we actually got any BusinessRecords back. If not, that means one of those "soft" error conditions we discussed earlier occurred, so in that situation we need to display the message using Ext.MessageBox. show(), and using the LocalBusinessSearch.resultsTitle and LocalBusinessSearch. resultsMessage attributes that we set in code in ResultsStore.

If we got results back, though, all we need to do now is enable that Results tab and flip over to it, and of course hide the MessageBox, which remember is the Please Wait message. The magic of data binding means the Grid now has the results showing, and paging is all ready to go!

The last method to look at is the method called when that Save Location As Default button is clicked:

```
LocalBusinessSearch.UIEventHandlers.saveLocationAsDefault = function() {

  var formVals = Ext.getCmp("SearchForm").getForm().getValues();
  LocalBusinessSearch.cookieProvider.set(
    "defaultLocation_street", formVals.street);
  LocalBusinessSearch.cookieProvider.set(
    "defaultLocation_city", formVals.city);
  LocalBusinessSearch.cookieProvider.set(
    "defaultLocation_state", formVals.state);
  LocalBusinessSearch.cookieProvider.set(
    "defaultLocation_zip", formVals.zip);

  Ext.MessageBox.show({
    title : "Default Location Saved", buttons : Ext.MessageBox.OK,
    msg : "This location has been saved and will be used automatically " +
    "next time you start the application", animEl : "divSource"
  });

};
```

Saving the default location isn't too tough: get the values of the search form and set some cookies. The cookieProvider we created earlier exposes a simple set() method that accepts a key, or name for the cookie, and the value of the cookie to set. Once all the location fields have been stored (whether they are blank or not doesn't matter), then a MessageBox is thrown up to indicate the location has been successfully saved. That's it!

Suggested Exercises

This is now my fifth book, and each one was an Apress "practical" book, which means I've written a whole lot of mini-applications over the past few years! I refer back to them when I have questions or need to remember how to do something. This application, however, is the first that I've found myself using on a pretty regular basis! I find it to be genuinely useful in my day-to-day life.

That being said, I think there are some things that could be added to make it even more useful, and I think they would be good learning exercises for you to undertake as well. So here are a few ideas:

- Add a link to the Yahoo! page with the details for the selected business. Look through the documentation for the local search service and you'll find that such a link is part of the data returned. This will enable you to see things like user ratings and reviews.

- Add a Google search pane to the Accordion. This will enable you to see a list of search hits for a given business as provided by Google. I say Google for two reasons: first, as for most of the planet, it is my search engine of choice because I find the results are generally better than other engines, and second, I want to prove that there's no inherent limitation on mashing up services from two sources. Google provides web APIs just like Yahoo! does, and while you could use Yahoo!'s web search services it might be fun to play with Google a little too.

- Store the last, say, three searches in the Gears database and provide a way to quickly pull them up. Store the search results, not just the search criteria. No sense pinging Yahoo!'s servers if you can avoid it!

- If you select an item in the search results Grid, you can then use the arrow keys to move up and down, but nothing changes on the right. It probably should, so how about you fix that?

- Add the ability to get directions to a selected business. You may have to look around for a service that gives you this capability; I'd check into what else Yahoo! offers first, and then perhaps Google's web API offerings.

- Use a slider in place of the zoom buttons on the Map pane. I wrote a version of this application for my last book on Dojo, and that's exactly what I did there. I ran into some issues with making it work with Ext JS, so time being tight I had to drop back and punt, and so using buttons was the answer. However, as an exercise, and heck, even if you can't make it work 100 percent, switching to a slider is a good exercise. The slider itself works just fine, but there were some relatively minor rendering issues I ran into that, while you could live with them as a result of an exercise like this, you wouldn't want to ship a book with them!

Summary

In this chapter, we looked at the concept of a mashup and saw how Ext JS provides some very nice functions for being able to call on remote web services, allowing you to develop a completely client-side mashup. We developed such an application and saw some of the services Yahoo! provides. We also learned about JSON-P, the technique underlying the functions Ext JS provides. We got to play with some more widgets and saw some more utility functions in action. We saw more of Ext JS's data subsystem than ever before. Plus, we wound up with what I think is a pretty useful application, which is definitely a win in my book!

In the next chapter we'll develop a tool that works with the Gears database, a very handy thing to have in your toolbox for sure!

■ ■ ■

CHAPTER 7

Your Dad Had a Workbench, Now So Do You: SQL Workbench

When I was a kid, I'd go into my dad's tool closet and take out a bunch of his tools, find the nearest electronic device, and proceed to take it apart. This didn't always make my parents too happy but at least they can rejoice in the fact that my son and daughter are doing the same thing on occasion to me! Looking inside something and figuring out what makes it tick is part and parcel of what we do as software developers, and just plain human beings. High-level abstractions and descriptions are often all we need, but diving into the nitty-gritty details is at other times exactly what we need.

We've been using Gears throughout this book, the database portion of it at least, but being able to peer into the databases themselves, unless you use the SQLite Manager add-on for Firefox, isn't something within our power. In this chapter we'll create an application that aims to alleviate that shortcoming!

We'll build ourselves an application called SQLWorkbench, and in the process we'll see a few new things in Ext JS. By the end of this chapter we'll have a handy tool that will prove valuable when we're using Gears for local database storage.

What's This Application Do Anyway?

If you use the Firefox browser—and you do in all probability if you're a (smart) developer—then I suggest getting familiar with the SQLite Manager add-on (`http://code.google.com/p/sqlite-manager/`). This is an especially great tool if you are doing Gears development, as we are in this book. This add-on is a utility for peeking directly into the SQLite databases that Firefox uses under the covers to store user data, as well as the databases created by Gears—in fact, any SQLite database you can name.

SQLite Manager was created by developer Mrinal Kant. It is a fabulous piece of work that makes dealing with SQLite vastly easier than it otherwise would be. You have already seen it in action without realizing it: all those screenshots where table structures have appeared throughout this book are a result of taking a snapshot of the table structure browser the add-on provides. Let's take a look at the full UI, though, shown in Figure 7-1.

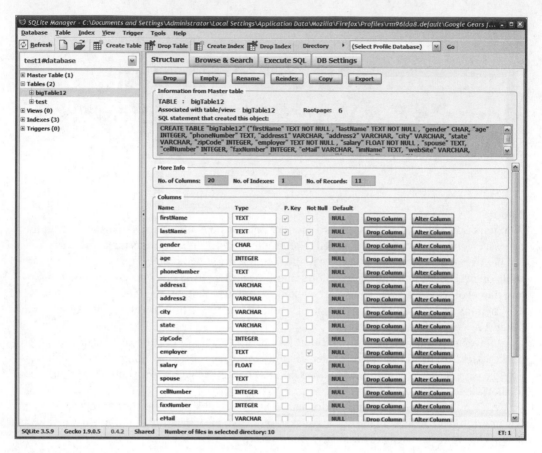

Figure 7-1. *The SQLite Manager Firefox add-on in all its glory!*

In short, the application we'll be developing in this chapter is largely modeled after SQLite Manager. In fact, when I started the project my intention was to use it nearly note for note, as the expression goes, and mimic what you see here. As I developed the application, though, I made some fairly large deviations from SQLite Manager, for better or worse, but most of the functionality is still taken from the add-on.

So, in more specific terms, what features are we going to provide and what tricks will we use to pull it off? Well, let's see…

- For this application we'll use an entirely different UI structure than we've previously used. There will be no master viewport like we've always had. Instead, everything will be a Window (except for the menu bar that we'll have at the top). In other words, it's a desktop metaphor.

- Users should be able to see a list of databases available to them, and they should be able to add and remove databases. This means not only adding and removing them from the list but adding and removing them physically from the file system as well.

- For any database selected, a list of the tables within it should be presented and we should be able to create new tables.

- The application should provide the ability to view the details of a selected table, including its structure and the data it contains, in a read-only browse mode.

- Common table operations should be available, including dropping the table, emptying the table of all data (but leaving the table structure intact), renaming the table, and copying the table (data and structure).

- There should be available to users a query tool that allows for arbitrary SQL statements to be executed against any database they wish.

That's a fair bit of functionality to implement, and is probably most of what you'd need in a tool like this. The advantage of building this application—aside from the obvious benefit of learning more about Ext JS, Gears, and SQLite—is that you can have the same basic capabilities that SQLite Manager provides outside of Firefox, say in Internet Explorer. To be fair, SQLite Manager is still the better tool overall, and it isn't my intent to compete with it, but as learning experiences go, this should be a good one, and the result of the work is a truly useful tool too. So let's get to it and build ourselves something useful!

Overall Structure and Files

The overall application structure is the same as that of previous applications, as you can see in Figure 7-2. Four directories exist in the root of the application: css, ext, img, and js.

Figure 7-2. *The application's directory structure and constituent files*

In the root we have the index.htm file as always, and the license.txt file that puts this application under the GPL license. In the css directory is the single styles.css file that we've come to expect housing the style sheet information for the application, and ext is Ext JS itself. Once again, this is a plain-vanilla Ext JS "installation," with no extra themes or other changes.

The `img` directory contains a batch of GIF files, all of which are icons used on various buttons throughout the application. Without exception, the name of the image file matches the caption of the button it appears on.

In the `js` directory we have the usual `gears_init.js` file that allows us to use Gears, and a main JavaScript file named after the application, `SQLWorkbench.js` in this case. This is where we'll find the `init()` method that, just like other applications, is essentially the entry point into the application code, as well as some other general code. There is also a `StoresAndRecords.js` file containing the definition of the `Records` and `Stores` used in this application.

The rest of the files correspond to individual `Windows` seen throughout the application and the code that goes along with them. So, the `Window` that shows the list of available databases is in the `DatabasesWindow.js` file, and the query tool's `Window` is in `QueryToolWindow.js` and so on. The `Help.js` file contains the three (sort of, as we'll see) `Windows` that you see when viewing help.

The Markup

As we've done with other applications, we'll begin with the basic markup found in `index.htm` that forms the basis of the application:

```html
<html>
  <head>
    <title>SQL Workbench</title>

    <link rel="stylesheet" type="text/css" href="ext/resources/css/ext-all.css">
    <script type="text/javascript" src="ext/adapter/ext/ext-base.js"></script>
    <script type="text/javascript" src="ext/ext-all.js"></script>

    <script src="js/gears_init.js"></script>
```

Nothing new here: we obviously need Ext JS to be imported (`ext-all.js`), along with its style sheet (`ext-all.css`) and we're using Ext JS in stand-alone mode so no third-party libraries are needed, so `ext-base.js` is the adapter we'll use.

Next up are the imports of the resources specific to this application:

```html
    <link rel="stylesheet" type="text/css" href="css/styles.css">
    <script type="text/javascript" src="js/SQLWorkbench.js"></script>
    <script type="text/javascript" src="js/StoresAndRecords.js"></script>
    <script type="text/javascript" src="js/CreateTableWindow.js"></script>
    <script type="text/javascript" src="js/DatabasesWindow.js"></script>
    <script type="text/javascript" src="js/TableDetailsWindow.js"></script>
    <script type="text/javascript" src="js/TablesWindow.js"></script>
    <script type="text/javascript" src="js/QueryToolWindow.js"></script>
    <script type="text/javascript" src="js/Help.js"></script>

    <script>Ext.onReady(SQLWorkbench.init);</script>

  </head>
```

No surprises there either! `Ext.onReady()` kick-starts the application by calling the `init()` method of the `SQLWorkbench` class—we'll get to that soon.

■**Note** In fact, `SQLWorkbench` is a namespace created on our behalf by a call to `Ext.namespace()`, as we've already seen. Since a namespace is nothing but a JavaScript function, which is how namespacing of code is generally achieved in JavaScript, it's quite natural to refer to a namespace as a class or even an object. As it happens, all three terms are correct, in addition to the term *function*, in this case since a namespace is a function is a class is an object in JavaScript!

For now, let's look at the HTML in the `<body>` of this document:

```
<body style="overflow:hidden;">

<div id="divSource" class="cssSource"></div>

<div id="divToolbar"
  style="width:100%;height:32px;position:absolute;left:0px;top:0px;"></div>
```

Setting the style attribute `overflow` to a value of `hidden` on the `<body>` tag ensures that we won't have scrollbars in the browser content area, which can happen in some browsers because of the way the `Toolbar` content is generated by Ext JS within the DOM. The `divSource` `<div>` is present once more for animation sourcing (i.e., where the `Windows` fly in from and fly to when closed).

There is also the `divToolbar` `<div>`. This is where the `Toolbar` will be inserted when we create it later. Note the `width` is set to 100% to stretch across the entire page, as a `Toolbar` typically does. Also note how it's positioned absolutely at pixel location 0, 0 so it's right there at the top of the page. I also set a `height` on it, although strictly speaking that isn't necessary since the `<div>` will expand to accommodate the content inserted into it. Still, I prefer to specify the height so that I always can count on the exact size when I try to position other elements relative to it (such as one particular `Window`, as we'll see in a bit).

The markup for the About `Window` is next:

```
<div id="dialogAbout" class="x-hidden">
  <div class="x-window-header">About SQLWorkbench</div>
  <div class="x-window-body">
    <table width="100%" height="100%" border="0" cellpadding="0"
      cellspacing="0" class="cssAbout">
    <tr><td align="center" valign="middle">
      SQLWorkbench<br>
      Version 1.0<br>
      Frank W. Zammetti
      <br><br>
      Originally appeared in the book<br>
      &quot;Practical Ext JS Projects With Gears&quot;<br>
      Apress, 2009
```

```
            <br><br>
            All rights reserved<br>
            (Rights?!?  What rights, you damned dirty ape?!?)
          </td></tr>
        </table>
      </div>
    </div>

  </body>

</html>
```

This is a simple Window definition in HTML, using the Ext JS-provided style classes to mark up the parts of the Window such as the header (x-window-header) and the body (x-window-body). Other than that, it's a simple table-based layout (I know, I'm evil for using a table-based layout...so sue me!).

As I mentioned earlier, one of the things I wanted to use was a whole different UI design paradigm with this application. Previously, all the applications you've seen used a BorderLayout to present the UI in discrete sections. This is a typical layout structure, one that works extremely well for all sorts of applications, which is why we've seen so much of it. However, it's far from the only paradigm you can use; another you could choose is the one employed in this application where everything you interact with is in its own separate Window.

This is essentially the same desktop metaphor your operating system itself uses (unless you're one of those masochistic personalities who prefer their Unix command line—I kid!). This is a good paradigm to choose when you have multiple elements to open and you don't know beforehand how many there may be. Since we allow a Window for each database to list its tables, that pretty much screams out "Windows!" In Figure 7-3 you can see what I'm talking about.

Here you can see we have the Databases Window, of which there is always a single one (although it can be closed too). Then there are two Table List Windows, one for each database. Finally, there is another Window opened that shows details of a selected table. I can open as many of these as I wish, drag them around, resize them or close them, and basically organize my workspace however I choose. This is fundamentally different from what you'd get with a BorderLayout, and in fact there *is no layout* in play here! There is no Viewport either, as you'll see as we go through the code. As it turns out, while a Viewport typically *is* used in an Ext JS application, there is no rule that says it *has* to be used, and this is such a case.

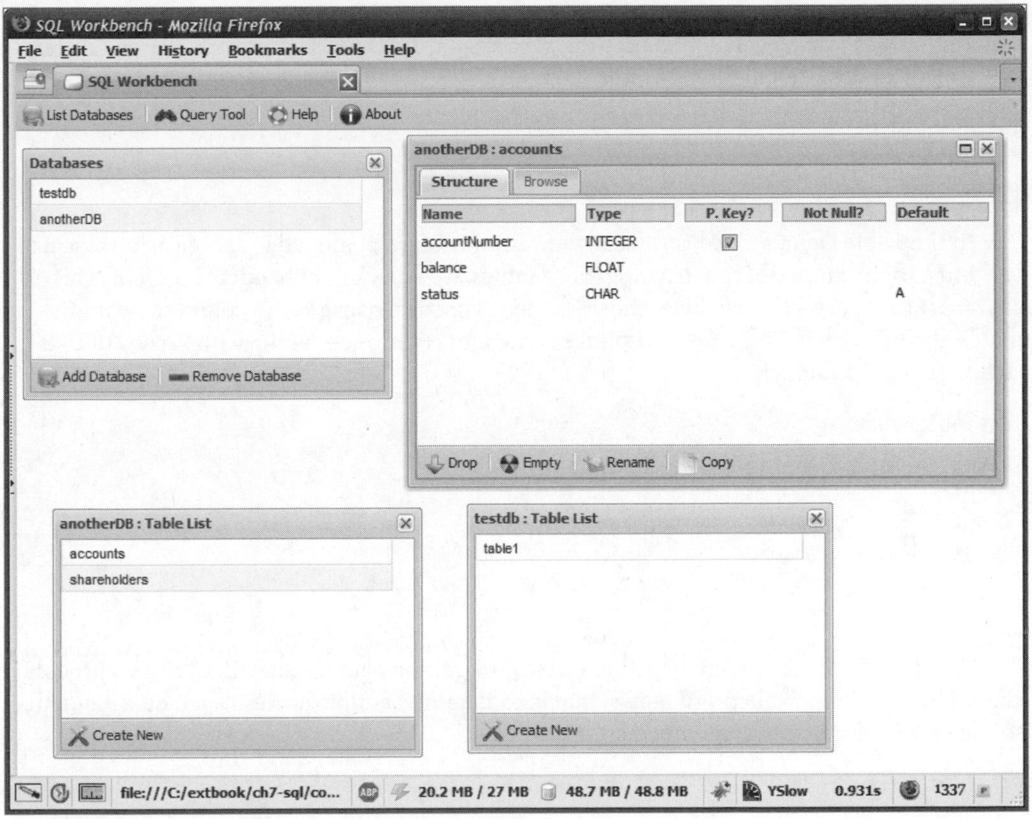

Figure 7-3. *An example of the multi-Window UI design this application is based on*

The Style Sheet

Next up is the style sheet, and we'll go through this quickly because it is by and large just repeating much of what we've seen in previous applications. Here's our constant companion, the cssSource class, which styles the divSource <div>:

```
.cssSource {
  position : absolute;
  left: 1px;
  top : 1px;
  width : 100%;
  height : 1px;
}
```

As the UI is built up, we need the TableLayouts used to stretch across their container, which they don't do by default. So here the x-table-layout, an Ext JS-provided class, is over-ridden to give the stretching we're after:

```
.x-table-layout {
  width : 100%;
}
```

In the Table Details Windows you can view the structure of the table, as well as browse its contents. In the course of constructing those tables, we need to put headers on them. This cssTableHeader class is what styles those headers. I chose a background color that would match the Ext JS default theme, and similarly the font styling goes along with Window title styling (at least roughly):

```
.cssTableHeader {
  color : #15428b;
  font-weight : bold;
  font-size : 11px;
  font-family : tahoma;
  padding : 4px;
}
```

The data that is displayed in the tables I just mentioned get styled with this cssTableCell class. The most important point here is that it adds some padding around each data element so the table doesn't appear all bunched up:

```
.cssTableCell {
  padding : 4px;
  font-size : 11px;
  font-family : tahoma;
}
```

Some of the cells in those same tables, namely the ones with Checkboxes in them, need to be centered to look right—that's what the cssTableCentered class is for. As you'll see, the cssTableCell class is still applied, but the cssTableCentered is added to give the centering. Keeping these as two separate classes allows for easily making a cell centered versus not centered while at the same time avoiding adding specific CSS classes for all the cases.

```
.cssTableCentered {
  text-align : center;
}
```

Finally, cssAbout is the style class applied to the text in the About Window:

```
.cssAbout {
  font-size : 11pt;
  font-family : tahoma,arial,verdana,sans-serif;
}
```

The Code

The code for this application is broken out into multiple source files, similarly to how the previous few applications have been in that each file, generally, relates to a particular UI element.

Naturally, though, the first one we're looking at doesn't!

SQLWorkbench.js

Now we start with the true code for this application, beginning with the contents of SQLWorkbench.js. You can see the UML diagram for this class in Figure 7-4. Its members include 8 fields and 17 methods. Many of these are not defined in SQLWorkbench.js, so my intention is to introduce each as they are encountered in whatever source file we happen to be examining at the time.

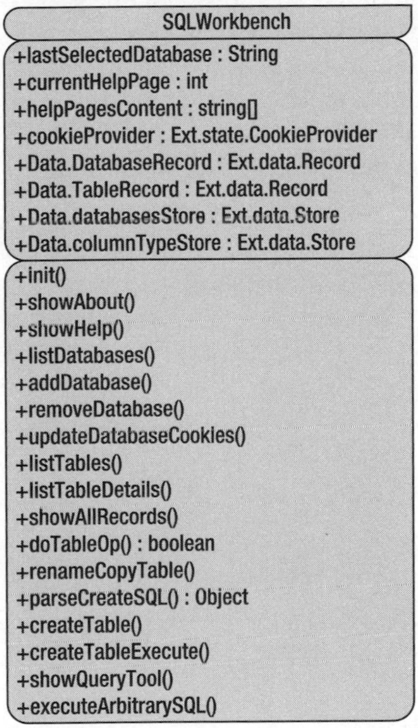

```
SQLWorkbench
+lastSelectedDatabase : String
+currentHelpPage : int
+helpPagesContent : string[]
+cookieProvider : Ext.state.CookieProvider
+Data.DatabaseRecord : Ext.data.Record
+Data.TableRecord : Ext.data.Record
+Data.databasesStore : Ext.data.Store
+Data.columnTypeStore : Ext.data.Store

+init()
+showAbout()
+showHelp()
+listDatabases()
+addDatabase()
+removeDatabase()
+updateDatabaseCookies()
+listTables()
+listTableDetails()
+showAllRecords()
+doTableOp() : boolean
+renameCopyTable()
+parseCreateSQL() : Object
+createTable()
+createTableExecute()
+showQueryTool()
+executeArbitrarySQL()
```

Figure 7-4. *UML class diagram of the SQLWorkbench class*

As I mentioned earlier, this "class" is actually a namespace, which you can see created with the first executable statement in this file:

```
Ext.namespace("SQLWorkbench", "SQLWorkbench.UIObjects",
  "SQLWorkbench.UIEventHandlers", "SQLWorkbench.Data");
```

Not only is the SQLWorkbench namespace being created, but so too are some subnamespaces nested underneath SQLWorkbench. These mimic what was seen in the previous applications. To reiterate, the SQLWorkbench.UIObjects namespace contains the config objects for the various UI components used in the application, `SQLWorkbench.UIEventHandlers` contains the JavaScript functions called in response to various UI events, and `SQLWorkbench.Data` is where we find things like `Record` and `Store` definitions.

In this application we list available databases that the user can play with, but within the context of this application it is unfortunately a fact that Gears does not allow you to get such a list automatically. Therefore, users have to tell us what database(s) they want to work with, and we probably should store that information somewhere. It felt a little odd to have to maintain a database to store a list of databases, though! So, I opted to go with cookies, and so we need an `Ext.state.CookieProvider` in this application:

```
SQLWorkbench.cookieProvider = new Ext.state.CookieProvider({
  expires : new Date(new Date().getTime() + (1000 * 60 * 60 * 24 * 365))
});
```

As you saw earlier, this defines a `CookieProvider` so that the cookies persist for one year. I suppose it's not too nice for users to have to reenter the names of all their databases every year, but it seems like a reasonable period of time (better than having to reenter them once a week for example, or even worse, every time the application is used).

Next up we have the `init()` method that we know is called via `Ext.onReady()` from `index.htm`. Its job is to "prime the pump," so to speak, to get the application up and running and ready for user interaction:

```
SQLWorkbench.init = function() {

  new Ext.Toolbar({
    id : "toolbar", renderTo : "divToolbar", items : [
      {
        text : "List Databases",
        icon : "img/ListDatabases.gif", cls : "x-btn-text-icon",
        handler : function() {
          SQLWorkbench.listDatabases();
        }
      },
      "-",
      {
        text : "Query Tool",
        icon : "img/QueryTool.gif", cls : "x-btn-text-icon",
        handler : function() {
          SQLWorkbench.showQueryTool();
        }
      },
      "-",
      {
        text : "Help", icon : "img/Help.gif", cls : "x-btn-text-icon",
        handler : function() {
          SQLWorkbench.showHelp(0);
        }
      },
      "-",
```

```
      {
        text : "About", icon : "img/About.gif", cls : "x-btn-text-icon",
        handler : function() {
          SQLWorkbench.showAbout();
        }
      }
    ]
  });

  SQLWorkbench.listDatabases();

}
```

First, the `Toolbar` is built. The `renderTo` attribute in the config object tells Ext JS to put this Toolbar into the `divToolbar` `<div>` we saw in `index.htm`. Again, while most of the applications in this book take a very Ext JS–specific approach (meaning the UI is built as an explicit hierarchy of components in JavaScript code), you can in fact build an entire UI this way instead. If you, for example, want to have a giant table structure on your page, or a CSS-based layout, and then simply create Ext JS components and insert them onto the page where you want, you absolutely can. You will, however, give up some of the power of Ext JS, things like users being able to dynamically resize page elements and things of that nature. But sometimes you don't need any of that, so the choice is often completely up to you.

CONTROVERSY/PHILOSOPHY: CODE-BASED LAYOUTS VS. MARKUP+CSS

Many people find the idea of designing the UI of an application in code to be controversial. I must admit, I do to some extent. The argument against it most often heard centers around the idea of page "designers" versus page "developers." The thought is that you have graphic artists doing the design, and often that means they are writing the simple markup and CSS that forms the structure of a page. Then, the developer comes along and adds the functionality to the layout.

This separation of concerns allows each group to focus on their core competencies. It's a compelling argument.

However, the reality is that not nearly as many development environments work that way as we might like. More often than not, it is the developer doing it all. There may still be guidance from a graphic artist, but it is still left to the developer to implement both the functionality and the layout.

The argument frequently heard is that creating a UI in code is intermingling things that shouldn't be intermingled. After all, markup defines the structure of how some data is presented, and CSS defines what it all looks like. If you have a database, and you want to display its data, you mark up the data using HTML's table features, and then style the table using CSS. The code's job is to get the data and present it to the HTML and CSS for display. This too is a pretty compelling argument.

However, using code to do layout allows for a level of dynamic ability that is hard to achieve otherwise. Markup and CSS are, for the most part, pretty static. JavaScript obviously is not. Therefore, a layout using JavaScript can allow for things that are difficult or impossible to achieve with just HTML and CSS—things like reflowing of content on resize events, or manipulation of layout, or dynamic creation of content.

In the end, I won't try to give you a right or wrong answer here mainly because I don't believe there is one. Obviously, writing a book on Ext JS implies I have an affinity for JavaScript-based layouts, and I suppose that's a fair supposition, but I've also publicly argued against them in the past. I could give the typical cop-out answer and simply say use the right tool for the job, and in fact, I think I'll do exactly that! I will say this, however: doing RIA development with the intent of mimicking desktop app–like functionality pretty well *requires* code-based UI layouts, so take that for what you will!

The About Window shown in Figure 7-5 is a result of executing the showAbout() method, which contains this code:

```
SQLWorkbench.showAbout = function() {

  var aboutWindow = Ext.getCmp("dialogAbout");
  if (aboutWindow) {
    aboutWindow.show(Ext.getDom("divSource"));
  } else {
    new Ext.Window({
      applyTo : "dialogAbout", id : "dialogAbout", closable : true,
      width : 400, height : 320, minimizable : false,
      resizable : false, draggable : false, closeAction : "hide",
      buttons : [{
        text : "Ok",
        handler : function() {
          Ext.getCmp("dialogAbout").hide();
        }
      }]
    }).show(Ext.getDom("divSource"));
  }

}
```

Recall in index.htm that this Window was described via markup. Of course, that in and of itself does nothing for us until we create an actual Window from it!

The first step is to see if the Window has already been created, and if it has, we simply call show() on it, passing it a reference to divSource. If it doesn't already exist, though, it is created here.

Linking the newly created Window to the markup in index.htm is a simple matter of pointing the applyTo config attribute of the Ext.Window constructor to the DOM node where the Window definition is. The Window is given an id of dialogAbout so that we can reference it later in the Ok Button's handler function to hide the Window by calling its hide() method. The Window is closable (closable:true) and cannot be minimized, resized, or dragged (minimizable:false, resizable:false and draggable:false correspondingly). Finally, it is given a size of 400 by 320 pixels and is shown immediately upon creation by calling show() and passing it a reference to the divSource <div> so we get our nice animation effect.

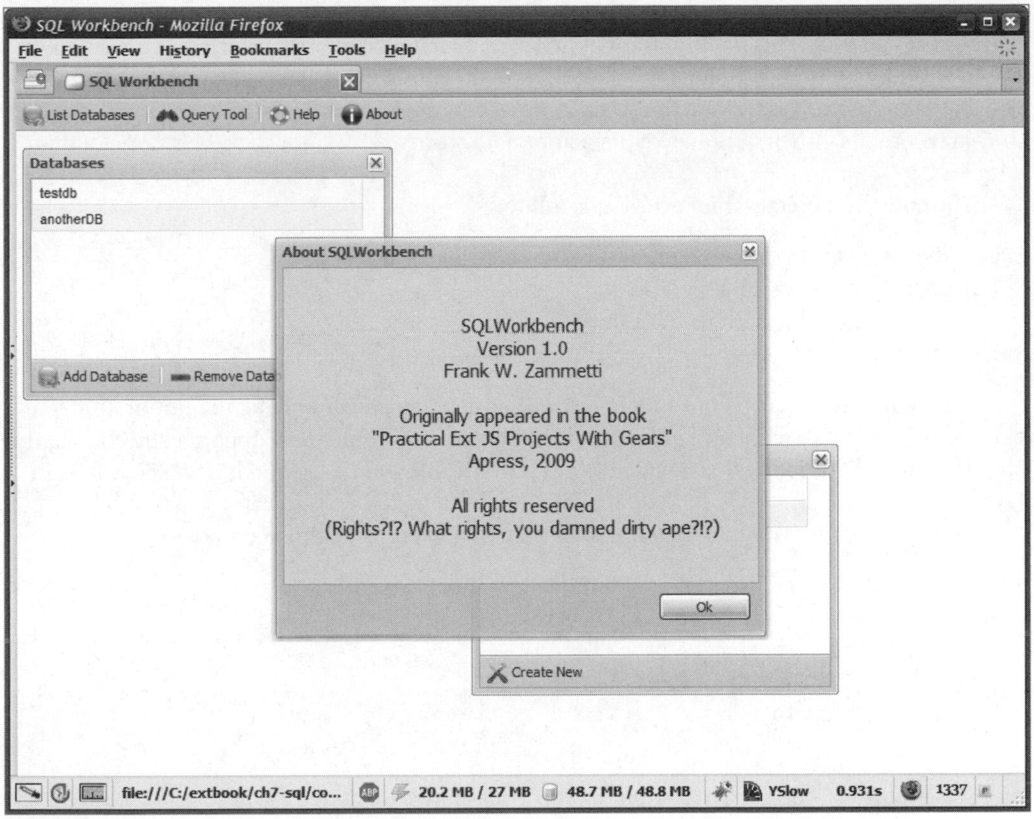

Figure 7-5. *The About Window*

StoresAndRecords.js

The StoresAndRecords.js file contains a couple of Record and Store definitions, although not too many in this particular application. In Figure 7-6 you can see the two Record types defined: DatabaseRecord and TableRecord.

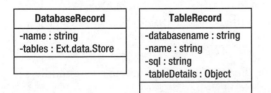

Figure 7-6. *They may not be much to look at, but the Record descriptors hide some interesting stuff!*

The DatabaseRecord describes an SQLite database. All we need is the name of the database and the tables it contains. The tables field is something new. Previously we've seen Record fields as simple types like strings and numbers, but here it's an Ext.data.Store, based on the diagram at least. There is no limitation on what types a field can be in a Record. A Store doesn't especially care, although it may not know what to do with some types, so you may have to write your own Store that does. In this case, however, these Records are only used with the UI; they aren't read from or written to a persistent data store of any kind, so there's none of that concern.

The code that creates this Record is as follows:

```
SQLWorkbench.Data.DatabaseRecord = Ext.data.Record.create([
  { name : "name", mapping : "name" },
  { name : "tables", mapping : "tables" }
]);
```

Notice that there is no type attached to either field, again supporting the notion that you can use any type you wish, and in true JavaScript form you could even dynamically change the "type" of a field (although that's typically not a smart thing to do, as much with Records as in JavaScript in general).

The TableRecord is similarly defined for describing a table within a database:

```
SQLWorkbench.Data.TableRecord = Ext.data.Record.create([
  { name : "databaseName", mapping : "databaseName" },
  { name : "name", mapping : "name" },
  { name : "sql", mapping : "sql" },
  { name : "tableDetails" }
]);
```

For a table we need to know what database it belongs to, hence the databaseName field, which maps to a given DatabaseRecord's name field. The name field itself is the name of the table, and the sql field is the SQL statement that was used to create the table. As we'll see later, this is a bit of information that we can coax out of SQLite and it is the key to making this whole application worth anything! Finally, the tableDetails field, similar to the tables field in the DatabaseRecord, isn't a simple type. It will have a value that is a JavaScript object that will contain information describing the table in detail (information that will be directly derived from the value of the sql field). There will be more to say on this last field later, but for now that gives you a good idea of what it and the others are for.

As you probably would have guessed, we need to have a Store for our DatabaseRecords to which we can bind the Grid used to display them in the Databases Window:

```
SQLWorkbench.Data.databasesStore = new Ext.data.Store({});
```

Again, since there's no requirement to persist these Records, there are no event handlers that need to be attached, so that single line of code is all we need.

■**Note** The database *names* are persisted via cookies, as I mentioned earlier. It would have been possible to use the event mechanism built into the Store to handle writing the cookies, but I chose to externalize it because I felt it made the code clearer. You could make the argument that using the events would be more in keeping with Ext JS best practices, and I wouldn't argue against that too much.

The final bit of code looks like this:

```
SQLWorkbench.Data.columnTypeStore = new Ext.data.Store({});
var columnTypeVals = [ "INTEGER", "DOUBLE", "FLOAT", "REAL", "CHAR", "TEXT",
  "VARCHAR", "BLOB", "NUMERIC", "DATETIME" ];
  for (var i = 0; i < columnTypeVals.length; i++) {
  SQLWorkbench.Data.columnTypeStore.add
    (new Ext.data.Record( { optVal : columnTypeVals[i] } )
  );
}
```

This is a Store with some hardcoded values that will be bound to the ComboBoxes used to select the type of a field when creating a table. The strings listed in the columnTypeValues array are the valid SQLite data types. That array is iterated over and add() is called on the columnTypeStore for each string. This all executes immediately when this file is loaded, as part of loading index.htm. Therefore, this Store is ready to go when the UI is built (which won't happen until the user decides to build a new table), so the ComboBoxes immediately have the values in them upon creation.

DatabasesWindow.js

Now that we have some of the groundwork laid, let's look at our first big piece of functionality: the Databases Window, the code for which is found in the aptly named DatabasesWindow.js file. This Window is what you see in Figure 7-7. Its job is to list all the databases that SQLWorkbench knows about that the user can work with and give that user the ability to choose one to work on, as well as add new ones and remove existing ones.

The first bit of code in this file is simply a field definition:

```
SQLWorkbench.lastSelectedDatabase = null;
```

Generally, once users select a database, this Window doesn't really care which one they selected. The code will open the Tables Window for the selected database and that's about the extent that the code in this file cares about database selection. One important exception is when the user wants to remove a database. In that case, obviously, the code needs to know which database was selected, and that's precisely what this field does: it stores the name of the last selected database.

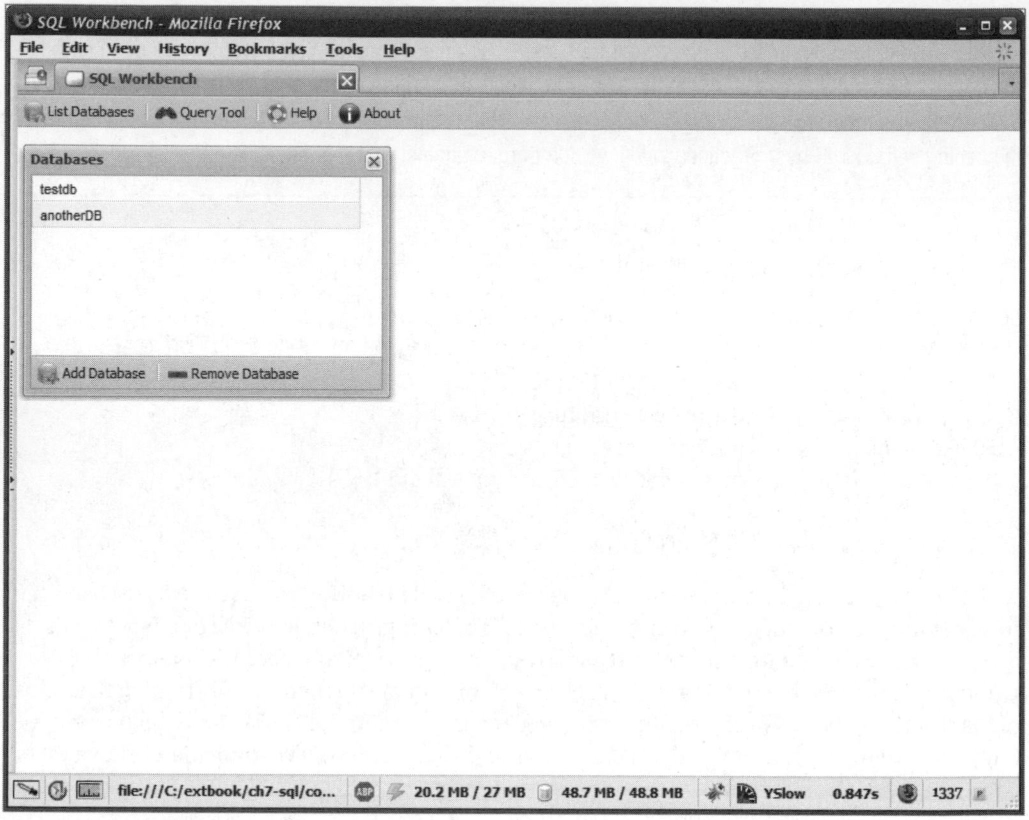

Figure 7-7. *The Databases Window*

Following that field definition is the listDatabases() method, which is called to display this Window and, you know, *list databases*!

```
SQLWorkbench.listDatabases = function() {

  var databasesWindow = Ext.getCmp("databasesWindow");
  if (databasesWindow) {
    databasesWindow.close();
  }
```

First, we check to see if the Window is already open, and if so, it is closed. In this way we have essentially a poor man's refresh function, and it means that whatever is displayed in this Window is current—at least since the last time this method was called.

The method continues thusly:[1]

---

1 Thusly? Who talks like that? It's like the expression "rue the day." Who talks like that? And yes, that's a Real Genius reference for those "in the know" For those "outside the know" (now *there's* an expression to use more often!), see http://www.imdb.com/title/tt0089886/.

```
SQLWorkbench.Data.databasesStore.removeAll();
var i = 0;
var nextCookie =
  SQLWorkbench.cookieProvider.get("SQLWorkbench_db_" + i);
while (!Ext.isEmpty(nextCookie)) {
  SQLWorkbench.Data.databasesStore.add(
    new SQLWorkbench.Data.DatabaseRecord(
      { name : nextCookie, tables : null }, nextCookie
    )
  );
  i = i + 1;
  nextCookie =
    SQLWorkbench.cookieProvider.get("SQLWorkbench_db_" + i);
}
```

This Window has a Grid within it, and that's where the databases are listed. So, we need a Store to contain DatabaseRecords that we can bind to that Grid. To do that, we begin by calling removeAll() on the databasesStore so we're starting with a clean slate. Next, we try retrieving a cookie with the name SQLWorkbench_db_0. This name is formed by appending an index value (starting with 0) to the static string SQLWorkbench_db. We use the Ext.isEmpty() function to see if the cookie was retrieved. If it was, then a new DatabaseRecord is created and the name field is set to the value of the retrieved cookie, which is stored in the variable nextCookie. Also, the id of the record is set to the database name. Then, we bump up the index counter and try to retrieve the next cookie. The loop continues until a cookie isn't found, which means we've read in all the previously saved databases from cookies.

Once that's done, we can go ahead and construct the Window:

```
new Ext.Window({
  title : "Databases", width : 300, height : 200, constrain : true,
  animateTarget : "divSource", id : "databasesWindow", maximizable : false,
  layout : "fit", x : 5, y : 40,
  bbar : [
    { text : "Add Database",
      icon : "img/AddDatabase.gif", cls : "x-btn-text-icon",
      handler : function() {
        SQLWorkbench.addDatabase();
      }
    },
    "-",
    { text : "Remove Database",
      icon : "img/RemoveDatabase.gif", cls : "x-btn-text-icon",
      handler : function() {
        SQLWorkbench.removeDatabase();
      }
    }
  ],
```

This is a straightforward `Window` definition. Note the use of the `constrain` config attribute, which ensures that the `Window` cannot be dragged off the edges of the page. Also note how the x and y attributes are used to position the `Window` in the upper-left corner of the page just below the `Toolbar` (which is why, if you recall from earlier, I explicitly set the height of the `Toolbar` even though I said it wasn't absolutely necessary... doing that allows me to know how far down the page I need to position this `Window` so as to not overlap the `Toolbar`). We use the `bbar` attribute to add some buttons to the bottom `Toolbar`. The two buttons added are for adding and removing a database from the list, which also do double duty by allowing the user to create or delete databases physically from SQLite. Clicking the Add Database button will add the database to the list if the database exists, but it will create the database in SQLite automatically if it doesn't exist. Likewise, clicking Remove Database not only removes the database from the list but actually removes it from the SQLite database. (There's no way to simply remove the database from the list, a point my diligent technical reviewer correctly made, so maybe that's your first enhancement challenge to tackle!)

The next part of the `Window` definition is the `Grid`:

```
items : [
  { xtype : "grid", border : false, stripeRows : true,
    store : SQLWorkbench.Data.databasesStore, hideHeaders : true,
    autoExpandColumn : "colName",
    sm : new Ext.grid.RowSelectionModel( { singleSelect : true } ),
    columns : [
      { header : "Name", sortable : true, dataIndex : "name",
        id : "colName" }
    ],
    listeners: {
      rowclick : {
        fn : function(inGrid, inRowIndex, inEventObject) {
          var databaseName =
            inGrid.getSelectionModel().getSelected().get("name");
          SQLWorkbench.lastSelectedDatabase = databaseName;
          SQLWorkbench.listTables(databaseName);
          inGrid.getSelectionModel().clearSelections();
        }
      }
    }
  }
]
}).show();

};
```

We've seen a bunch of `Grid`s before, so there aren't any surprises in the basic structure here. The `rowclick` event handler is different. Here we begin by getting the name of the selected database by first getting the selection model of the `Grid`, then calling its `getSelected()` method to get the `DatabaseRecord` for the row that was clicked, and then getting the `name` field of that record. Once we have that, we set the `lastSelectedDatabase` field to the database name so that we know which to remove if the user clicks that button. Then, the listTables() method is called, which will open a Window listing the tables in the selected database. Finally, the code clears the selection in this Grid. The purpose of this Window and Grid is for the user to select a database. However, since more than one database at a time can be open, leaving the last selected item in the Grid didn't quite feel right to me, and that's the reason this clearing of the selection is done.

Note I can certainly see the argument for not clearing the selection, and in a way it would simplify matters because you would no longer have to keep track of the last selected database with the lastSelected Database field—you could simply interrogate the Grid to see which item was selected at any given time. I just felt that the UI interaction didn't quite feel right going that route. Sometimes there's definitive right and wrong answers in UI design, other times it's simply a gut feeling, and this is one of those "go with your gut" times!

When the user clicks the Add Database button, the addDatabase() method is called (bet you didn't see that coming!). Here comes that method now:

```
SQLWorkbench.addDatabase = function() {

  Ext.MessageBox.prompt("Add Database",
    "Please enter the name of the database you wish to add.<br><br>Note that " +
    "if the database does not currently exist it will be created.<br>",
    function(inBtnID, inVal) {
      if (inBtnID == "cancel") { return; }
      if (inVal != null) { inVal = inVal.trim(); }
      if (!Ext.isEmpty(inVal)) {
        var db = google.gears.factory.create("beta.database");
        db.open(inVal);
        db.close();
        SQLWorkbench.Data.databasesStore.add(
          new SQLWorkbench.Data.DatabaseRecord({
            name : inVal
          }, inVal)
        );
        SQLWorkbench.updateDatabaseCookies();
        SQLWorkbench.listDatabases();
        Ext.MessageBox.hide();
      }
    }
  );

};
```

In Figure 7-8 you can see the result of this code, which starts by asking the user to supply the name of the database to add. This is done by using the `Ext.MessageBox.prompt()` method, similar to JavaScript's built-in `prompt()` method. If the user clicks Ok (clicking Cancel or manually closing the `MessageBox` aborts), then the name entered is trimmed and we simply open the database. Gears and SQLite are kind enough to create the database if it doesn't already exist, and if it does, no harm is done and we simply close the database right away. Once that's done, the only things left to do are to add a `DatabaseRecord` to the `databasesStore` for the new database, write out our cookies by calling the `updateDatabaseCookies()` method (which we'll look at shortly), and finally, call `listDatabases()` to re-create the Databases `Window`, but now with the new database listed in it.

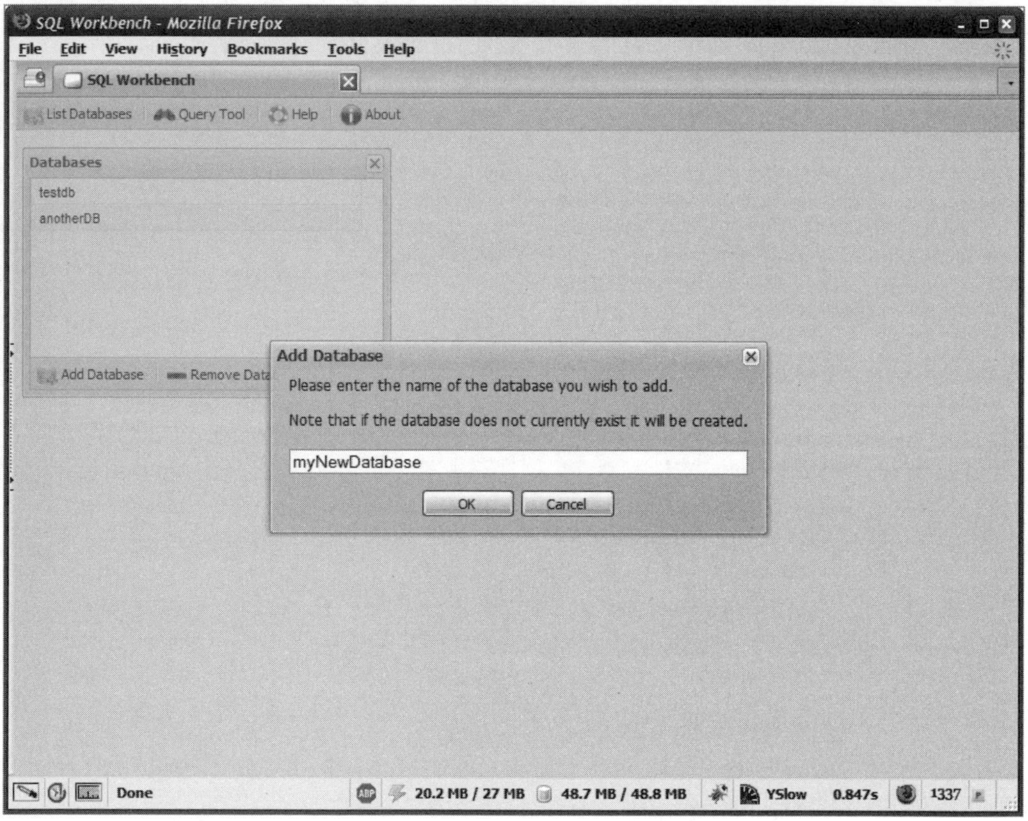

Figure 7-8. *The user is asked for the name of a database to add.*

The `removeDatabase()` method is next. It looks a bit complex at first but it isn't too bad:

```
SQLWorkbench.removeDatabase = function() {

  if (Ext.isEmpty(SQLWorkbench.lastSelectedDatabase)) { return; }
  Ext.MessageBox.confirm("Confirm Database Removal",
    "This will remove the " + SQLWorkbench.lastSelectedDatabase + " database " +
    "from the list of available database AND WILL ALSO physically remove the " +
```

```
    "database from the SQLite directory structure.  ALL DATA IN THE DATABASE " +
    "WILL BE LOST!  Are you absolutely sure about this?",
    function(inButtonClicked) {
      if (inButtonClicked == "yes") {
        var db = google.gears.factory.create("beta.database");
        db.open(SQLWorkbench.lastSelectedDatabase);
        db.remove();
        var tablesWindow =
          Ext.getCmp("tablesWindow~" + SQLWorkbench.lastSelectedDatabase);
        if (tablesWindow) { tablesWindow.close(); }
        var databaseRecord = SQLWorkbench.Data.databasesStore.getById(
          SQLWorkbench.lastSelectedDatabase);
        var tables = databaseRecord.get("tables");
        tables.each(function(nextRecord) {
          var tableDetailsWindow = Ext.getCmp("tableWindow_" +
            nextRecord.get("name")).close();
          if (tableDetailsWindow) { tablesDetailWindow.close(); }
        });
        SQLWorkbench.Data.databasesStore.remove(
          SQLWorkbench.Data.databasesStore.getById(
            SQLWorkbench.lastSelectedDatabase));
        SQLWorkbench.updateDatabaseCookies();
        SQLWorkbench.lastSelectedDatabase = null;
        SQLWorkbench.listDatabases();
        Ext.MessageBox.hide();
      }
    }
  );

}
```

First, we ensure that a database has been selected and abort if not. Next, we pop a confirmation using the Ext.MessageBox.confirm() method, which you can see in Figure 7-9. The text of the message asks users if they are sure they want to delete the database. If they click Yes, then we're off to the races. First, the database is opened and then the remove() method on it is called. This is a Gears-supplied method that takes care of destroying the currently opened database for us. So, that part is quite easy!

Next, we need to close the Tables Window for the database, if one was open. Ext.getCmp() is used and is passed the constructed ID of the Window. Assuming it is opened, the close() method is called on it and it's history.

Then we have to do the same thing for the Table Detail Windows that might be opened for the tables in this database, so we retrieve the DatabaseRecord from the databasesStore for the database being removed. This is done because we need to get at the tables field, which lists the tables in this database, if any. Once we have a hold of that store, we use its each() method to iterate over the TableRecords in it (remember that's the field that is itself a DataStore). For each we try to get a reference to the Table Details Window for that table, and if found we close it.

Once that's done we can go ahead and remove the DatabaseRecord from the databases Store. Then there's just some housekeeping to do: a call to updateDatabaseCookies() will cause the cookie for the database to be deleted; lastSelectedDatabase is set to null since the last selected database was just removed and therefore is no longer a valid value; and finally, listDatabases() is called to effectively refresh the Databases Window on the screen.

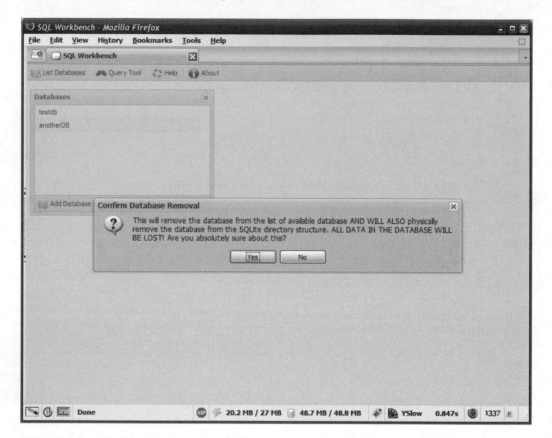

Figure 7-9. *The Confirm Database Removal prompt*

The last method in this source file is the one you've seen a couple of times now: updateDatabaseCookies(). As you can see, there's not much to it:

```
SQLWorkbench.updateDatabaseCookies = function() {

  var i = 0;
  var nextCookie =
    SQLWorkbench.cookieProvider.get("SQLWorkbench_db_" + i);
  while (!Ext.isEmpty(nextCookie)) {
    SQLWorkbench.cookieProvider.set("SQLWorkbench_db_" + i, null);
    i = i + 1;
    nextCookie =
      SQLWorkbench.cookieProvider.get("SQLWorkbench_db_" + i);
  }
```

```
  i = 0;
  SQLWorkbench.Data.databasesStore.each(function(nextRecord) {
    SQLWorkbench.cookieProvider.set("SQLWorkbench_db_" + i,
      nextRecord.get("name"));
    i = i + 1;
  });

}
```

The values corresponding to databases are stored in cookies named SQLWorkbench_db_x, where x is a number starting at 0. "Updating" the cookies, whether as a result of adding a new database or removing one, is a two-step process. First, a loop is entered into that keeps trying to get the next cookie in sequence. For each one found it is set to a value of null, which has the effect of removing it from the browser. Then, the databasesStore is iterated over using its each() method and for each DatabaseRecord a cookie is written out. In other words, the "update" is a cheat: it's really just re-creating *all* the cookies each time! I'm not sure there are too many alternate ways to pull this off if you're using cookies… you could just write out a single cookie with something like a comma-separated list of database names, but this way was more fun!

TablesWindow.js

The TablesWindow.js file contains all the code for the Tables Window (bet you didn't see that coming!). This Window, shown in Figure 7-10, is where the tables found in a selected database are listed.

Any table listed can be clicked to open a Table Details Window for it, and a new table can be created by clicking the Create New button on the bottom Toolbar. Let's take a look at the listTables() method, which is called when a database is selected from the Databases Window:

```
SQLWorkbench.listTables = function(inDatabaseName) {

  var tablesWindow = Ext.getCmp("tablesWindow~" + inDatabaseName);
  if (tablesWindow) {
    tablesWindow.close();
  }
```

First we check to see if a Tables Window is already opened for the selected database. The ID of any Tables Window is in the form tablesWindow~<databaseName>, where <databaseName> is replaced with the name of the selected database. If such a Window is already opened, we go ahead and close it. This makes clicking a database double as a refresh function.

The next step is to get the list of tables in the selected database. To do that we'll have to play with Gears and SQLite a bit:

```
  var db = google.gears.factory.create("beta.database");
  db.open(inDatabaseName);

  var rs = db.execute (
    "SELECT name, sql FROM sqlite_master where type='table';"
  );
```

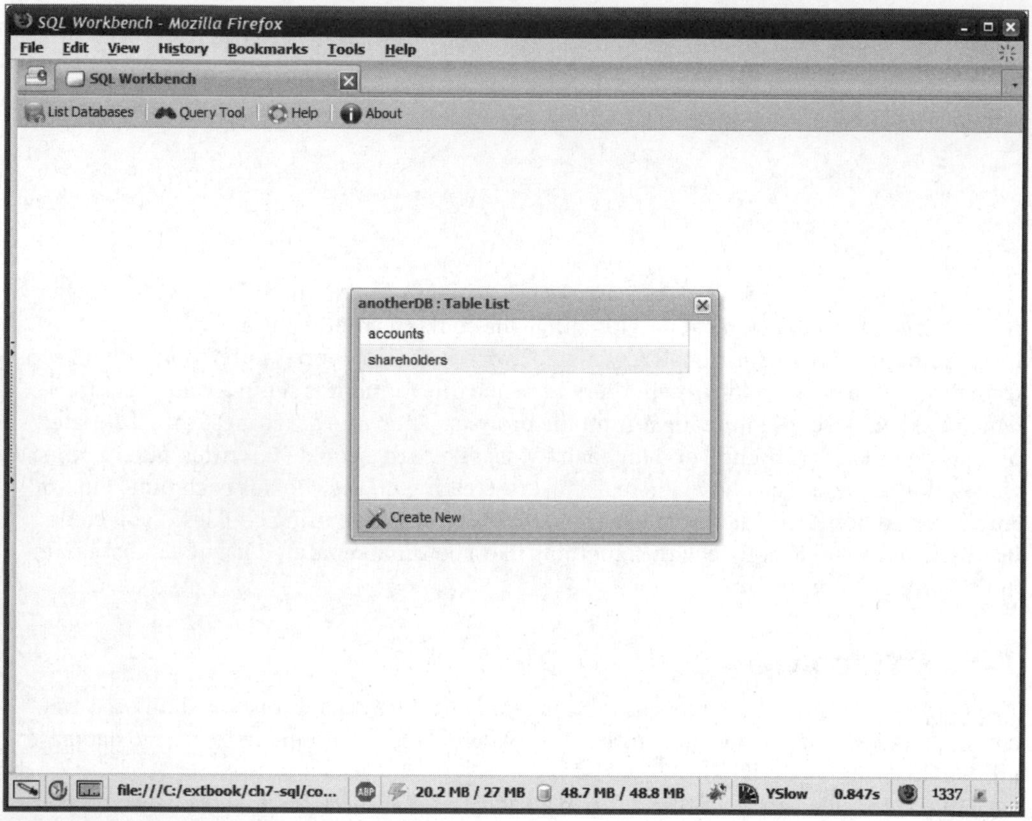

Figure 7-10. *The Tables Window*

Every SQLite database has a special read-only table named `sqlite_master` in it. The data in this table describes the database schema. The structure of this table is always what is shown in Table 7-1.

Table 7-1. *The Structure of the sqlite_master Table*

Field	Description
type	Tells the type of entity the record describes. For our purposes, the only value we care about is `table`.
name	Gives you the name of the entity the record describes. For our purposes, that means the name of the table.
tbl_name	When the value of type is `index`, the record is describing a table index. In that case, `tbl_name` gives the name of the table.
rootpage	I couldn't find definitive documentation of what this is anywhere, but I'm putting my money on it being the code page of the described table.
sql	This is the CREATE TABLE or CREATE INDEX query that created the described table or table index.

Since `sqlite_master` is just a table in the database, we can query it for information, and that's exactly what the snippet of code does: it queries for all records from `sqlite_master` where the type is `table` and it returns the `name` and `sql` fields, since that's all we care about here.

The next step is to get the `DatabaseRecord` associated with the database we just queried for tables:

```
var databaseRecord = SQLWorkbench.Data.databasesStore.getById(inDatabaseName);
var foundTables = databaseRecord.get("tables");
if (!foundTables) {
  foundTables = new Ext.data.Store({});
}
foundTables.removeAll();
```

The purpose behind this is that we're going to populate the `tables` field of the `Record`, which you'll recall from earlier is an Ext JS `DataStore`, with `TableRecord` objects. So, we request the `DatabaseRecord` from the `SQLWorkbench.Data.databaseStores` by using its `getById()` method, passing in the name of the database we want. Once we have that, we get its `tables` field. If the returned value is `null`, which happens the first time the database is selected from the Databases `Window`, we create a new `Ext.data.Store()`. If on the other hand we already have a `Store`, then we call `removeAll()` on it since we'll be repopulating it next, as you can see here:

```
while (rs.isValidRow()) {
  foundTables.add(new SQLWorkbench.Data.TableRecord({
    databaseName : inDatabaseName, name : rs.field(0), sql : rs.field(1)
  }, rs.field(0)));
  rs.next();
}
rs.close();
db.close();
```

We iterate over the `ResultSet` returned by the query of `sqlite_master` and for each row we create a new `SQLWorkbench.Data.TableRecord`. The `databaseName` field is set, as is the `name` and `sql` fields with the values returned by the query. The `TableRecord` is keyed by the table name as well so that we can retrieve it by name easily later. This `TableRecord` is added to the `foundTables` DataStore:

```
databaseRecord.set("tables", foundTables);
```

Finally, `foundTables` is added as the value of the `tables` field in the `DatabaseRecord` and we're good to go.

At this point we have all the information we need ready to go, so now it's just a matter of creating the `Window`:

```
new Ext.Window({
  title : inDatabaseName + " : Table List", width : 300, height : 200,
  constrain : true, animateTarget : "divSource", maximizable : false,
  layout : "fit", id : "tablesWindow~" + inDatabaseName,
  bbar : [
```

```
        { text : "Create New",
          icon : "img/CreateNew.gif", cls : "x-btn-text-icon",
          handler : function() {
            SQLWorkbench.createTable(inDatabaseName);
          }
        }
      ],
      items : [
        { xtype : "grid", border : false, stripeRows : true,
          store : foundTables, hideHeaders : true,
          autoExpandColumn : "colName",
          sm : new Ext.grid.RowSelectionModel( { singleSelect : true } ),
          columns : [
            { header : "Name", sortable : true, dataIndex : "name",
              id : "colName" }
          ],
          listeners: {
            rowclick : {
              fn : function(inGrid, inRowIndex, inEventObject) {
                SQLWorkbench.listTableDetails(inDatabaseName,
                  inGrid.getSelectionModel().getSelected().get("name"));
                inGrid.getSelectionModel().clearSelections();
              }
            }
          }
        }
      ]
    }).show();

};
```

The Window has a bottom Toolbar, courtesy of the bbar attribute, that has a single Create New button that calls the SQLWorkbench.createTable() method. The name of the database that was passed in to the listTables() method is now passed in to the createTable() method, which means we have a closure here, as discussed in Chapter 3.

The object in the items array, which winds up being the main content of the Window, is a GridPanel that is bound to the foundTables Store created previously. That's how we get the list of tables to show up. Clicking a row in the Grid results in the rowclick event firing and the handler defined here executing. This handler calls the SQLWorkbench.listTableDetails() method, passing in the name of the table to display details for, which is derived from the row that was clicked. We take the inGrid argument passed to the callback and call its getSelectionModel() method to get a hold of its SelectionModel. From there we can get the selected TableRecord by calling the getSelected() method, and then we just get the value of the name field to pass along to the listTableDetails() method.

CreateTableWindow.js

When users click the Create New button in the Tables `Window`, the Create Table `Window` appears, where they can enter the details for the new table they want to create. This `Window` is shown in Figure 7-11.

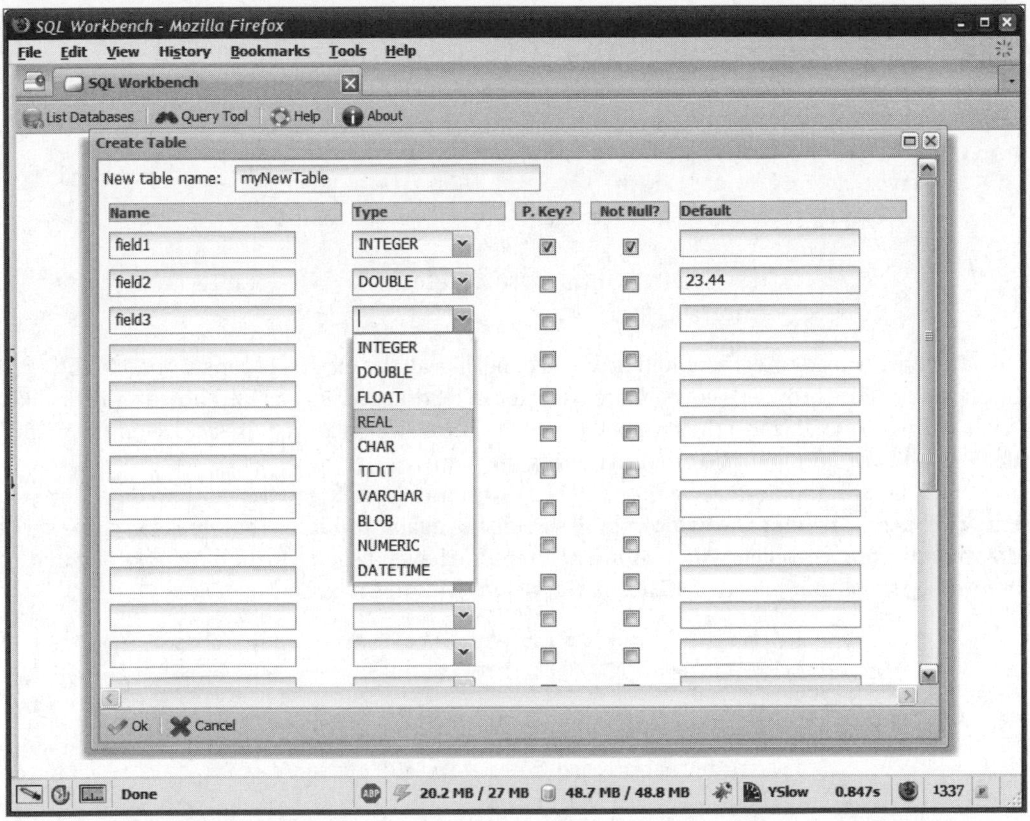

Figure 7-11. *The Create Table Window*

As you can see, users enter the name of the table at the top, and then enter details for up to 20 columns in the table. For each, they enter a name, the data type of the column, whether the column is the primary key field of the table, whether or not nulls are allowed in the column, and what the default value should be for that column.

■**Note** Twenty fields is an arbitrary limit; SQLite tables can have more. I limited it to 20 fields for two reasons. First, that way the `Window` doesn't take forever to appear, and second, doing so gave me at least one exercise to suggest at the end of the chapter!

When the user clicks the Create New button in the Tables `Window`, the `createTable()` method is called. I'll chunk-ify this method a bit so it's easier to digest:

```
SQLWorkbench.createTable = function(inDatabaseName) {

  var createTableWindow = new Ext.Window({
    animateTarget : "divSource", id : "createTableWindow", autoScroll : true,
    draggable : true, resizable : true, shadowOffset : 8, width : 700,
    height : 500, layout : "fit", constrain : true, title : "Create Table",
    maximizable : true,
    items : [
      { xtype : "form", labelWidth : 100, id : "createTableForm",
        bodyStyle : "padding:4px;overflow:scroll;",
        items : [
          { xtype : "textfield", width : 250, fieldLabel : "New table name",
            name : "createTableName" },
```

The basic `Window` is constructed first. This one, like all the others, is constrained to the boundaries of the browser's content area, but it can be dragged and resized however users like. It can even be maximized if they wish. Within this `Window` we create a `FormPanel`, and the first field we add is a simple `TextField` for entering the name.

Note, however, that you do not see the 20 rows corresponding to the column details we know the user can enter. If you look at the screenshot again, you'll see that this is in some sort of tabular layout, complete with column headers. We haven't seen a form that looks like that before, so how is that pulled off? The answer begins with this next chunk of code:

```
        { xtype : "panel", layout : "table", layoutConfig : { columns : 5 },
          id : "createTablePanel", border : false,
          items : [
            { html :
              "<div style='background-color:#dfe8f6;'>Name</div>",
              cellCls : "cssTableHeader" },
            { html :
              "<div style='background-color:#dfe8f6;'>Type</div>",
              cellCls : "cssTableHeader" },
            { html :
              "<div style='background-color:#dfe8f6;'>P. Key?</dv>",
              cellCls : "cssTableHeader cssTableCentered" },
            { html :
              "<div style='background-color:#dfe8f6;'>Not Null?</div>",
              cellCls : "cssTableHeader cssTableCentered" },
            { html :
              "<div style='background-color:#dfe8f6;'>Default</div>",
              cellCls : "cssTableHeader" }
          ]
        }
      ],
```

So, we're using the TableLayout to create a table, which makes sense given what you see in the screenshot. The interesting thing to note is that this Panel using the TableLayout is an element in the items collection of the FormPanel, so any form-type fields we add here are still part of the form, even though they are not directly nested under the FormPanel itself (i.e., not elements in the items array directly, as the TextField for entering the table's name is).

But even still, all we see here are some header definitions! Now, the header definitions are interesting because they are just simple elements with some HTML defined. Each is a <div> with a background-color set and a cssTableHeader CSS class applied to it. Some of them actually have two classes applied, cssTableHeader and cssTableCentered. If you look back at the CSS definition you'll see that cssTableCentered is the one with text-align set to center. So, the data in these columns will be centered, and since they're CheckBoxes it makes sense because they look better as centered than using the default left alignment.

So, while that's interesting, it *still* doesn't explain how those 20 rows of data entry fields get on the screen! I'll pull one of my "we'll get to that shortly" tricks... and in this case I do mean shortly, but first we have one more chunk to see:

```
  bbar : [
    { text : "Ok", formBind : true,
      icon : "img/Ok.gif", cls : "x-btn-text-icon",
      handler : function() {
        SQLWorkbench.createTableExecute(inDatabaseName);
      }
    },
    "-",
    { text : "Cancel", icon : "img/Cancel.gif", cls : "x-btn-text-icon",
      handler : function() { Ext.getCmp("createTableWindow").close(); }
    }
  ]
 }
]
});
```

This defines the bottom Toolbar on the Window where our Ok and Cancel buttons appear. Clicking Ok called the createTableExecute() method, passing it the name of the database this Window was opened for. We'll look at that method very soon as well. The Cancel button simply gets a reference to the Window and closes it.

So now we come to the mythical, magical beast that is responsible for those 20 rows we just *know* had to be here somewhere!

```
var createTablePanel = Ext.getCmp("createTablePanel");
for (var i = 0; i < 20; i++) {
  createTablePanel.add({ xtype : "textfield", hideLabel : true,
    width : 150, ctCls:"cssTableCell",
    name : "createTable_columnName_" + i });
  createTablePanel.add({ xtype : "combo", width : 100, editable : false,
    triggerAction : "all", mode : "local", valueField : "optVal",
    displayField : "optVal", store : SQLWorkbench.Data.columnTypeStore,
    ctCls : "cssTableCell", name : "createTable_columnType_" + i });
```

```
    createTablePanel.add({ xtype : "checkbox", hideLabel : true,
      ctCls : "cssTableCell cssTableCentered",
      name : "createTable_primaryKey_" + i });
    createTablePanel.add({ xtype : "checkbox", hideLabel : true,
      ctCls : "cssTableCell cssTableCentered",
      name : "createTable_notNull_" + i });
    createTablePanel.add({ xtype : "textfield", hideLabel : true,
      width : 150, ctCls : "cssTableCell",
      name : "createTable_defaultValue_" + i });
  }
```

The ability to dynamically add elements to an existing FormPanel is something we haven't seen before, but that's precisely what we have here. We have a loop with 20 iterations (ah-ha!) and within each we're adding five elements (hey, that's how many columns there are in the table!) to the createTablePanel Panel (the one using the TableLayout). The add() method allows us to add new Ext JS Components to another Component. You simply pass in the config object for the Component you want to create and it gets added.

The Components added here aren't too special; they're just basic form elements that we're already pretty familiar with. A couple of TextFields, a ComboBox, and some CheckBoxes are what we need. The ComboBox gets bound to the SQLWorkbench.Data.columnTypeStore that contains the list of valid SQLite data types.

Note that on all of these fields the hideLabel attribute is set to true since the headers of the table are effectively the field labels. We've manually done what Ext JS normally does for us automatically (the price to pay for a different sort of UI presentation). Also note that each gets a name value that has the index of the array appended to it. That allows us to easily retrieve them all later.

Now, these form elements aren't being added directly to the FormPanel; they're being added to the Panel with the TableLayout, which you'll recall was the Component directly under the FormPanel in its items array. The nice thing here is that these dynamically added Components still become part of the FormPanel, part of the underlying form, just as if they had been defined explicitly in the config object of the Window. Doing it this way saves you from having to have a ton more config information here: imagine 20 groups of five Component definitions statically within the Window's config object. Not pretty at all!

Once all the Components have been added, we have only to show the Window:

```
createTableWindow.show();
```

At this point users see the Window as they should, all created and ready for their use.

When users click the Ok button, it's time to create the table:

```
SQLWorkbench.createTableExecute = function(inDatabaseName) {

  var formVals =
    Ext.getCmp("createTableForm").getForm().getValues();

  if (Ext.isEmpty(formVals.createTableName)) { return; }

  var sql = "CREATE TABLE IF NOT EXISTS " +
    formVals.createTableName + " (";
```

First, the form is retrieved and, once we ensure users entered a table name, we begin to construct the SQL statement to execute, including the name of the table entered.

■**Note** Making sure a table name was entered is the extent of the checking done here. I'm sure that you, like me (and my technical reviewer who noted this) can point out about a billion ways you could break this statement, or wreak havoc on the database. This is one of those "Doc, it hurts when I bend my arm," "Well, don't bend your arm!" moments.

Next we can begin to deal with the columns of the table:

```
var columnCount = 0;
var primaryKeyCount = 0;
var primaryKeyNotNullFound = false;
for (var i = 0; i < 20; i++) {
  var columnName = formVals["createTable_columnName_" + i];
  var columnType = formVals["createTable_columnType_" + i];
  var primaryKey = formVals["createTable_primaryKey_" + i];
  var notNull = formVals["createTable_notNull_" + i];
  var defaultValue = formVals["createTable_defaultValue_" + i];
```

Since we know the names of the fields in the form used the index numbers, we can easily construct those names again to pull the appropriate fields out of the formVals object. So, we grab the values of each of the five fields for the row we're currently examining. Once we have them, we can do some checks:

■**Note** In all previous applications we've used code like formVals.fieldName to retrieve the fields' value. In JavaScript you can always access the elements of an object using dot notation *or* array notation, as we did here. Array notation is necessary when you're dynamically constructing the name of the field to access; object.field+i would be a syntax error since the plus sign is not a valid character in an object field name.

```
if (!Ext.isEmpty(columnName) && !Ext.isEmpty(columnType)) {
  if (!Ext.isEmpty(primaryKey) && !Ext.isEmpty(notNull)) {
    primaryKeyNotNullFound = true;
    break;
  }
  if (columnCount > 0) { sql += ", "; }
  columnCount++;
  sql += "\"" + columnName + "\" " + columnType;
```

```
      if (!Ext.isEmpty(primaryKey)) {
        primaryKeyCount++;
        sql += " PRIMARY KEY";
      }
      if (!Ext.isEmpty(notNull)) {
        sql += " NOT NULL";
      }
      if (!Ext.isEmpty(defaultValue)) {
        sql += " DEFAULT '" + defaultValue + "'";
      }
    }
  }
  sql += ");";
```

First we ensure that a name has been entered for the column and that a type has been selected. Those are the two required elements. Next, we check to see if the Primary Key and Not Null CheckBoxes were both checked, and if so, we set primaryKeyNotNullFound to true and break out of the loop. This is a simple error check that has to be done.

Next, we bump up the columnCount variable so we know we have enough information for this column to actually create it. Next, we construct more of the SQL statement. Remember, the SQL statement will be in the form:

```
CREATE TABLE IF NOT EXISTS <tableName> ("<fieldName>" <fieldType>);
```

So, first we see if a column has already been defined, and if so, we append a comma to the sql value. Next, we construct the "<fieldName>" <fieldType> portion of the string. Next, we see if the Primary Key CheckBox was checked. If so, the string PRIMARY KEY is appended. Note too that the primaryKeyCount field is incremented in this case. The same thing is done for Not Null. Finally, if a default value was supplied, we append it as well with the DEFAULT clause. All of that completes the definition of this table column.

Next we have some error checking to do:

```
  if (primaryKeyNotNullFound) {
    Ext.MessageBox.alert("Error",
      "Primary fields cannot be null.");
    return;
  }
  if (columnCount == 0) {
    Ext.MessageBox.alert("Error",
      "There were no columns to create.  Note that Column Name " +
      "and Column Type are both required for every column.");
    return;
  }
  if (primaryKeyCount > 1) {
    Ext.MessageBox.alert("Error",
      "Only a single column can be designated as Primary Key.");
    return;
  }
```

First, if that `primaryKeyNotNullFound` flag is set, then we have to tell the user that a primary key field cannot allow null values and abort creation of the table. Next we ensure that at least one valid column definition was found, meaning at least one column had a name and type selected. Finally, we ensure that only a single column is the primary key, which appears to be a limitation in SQLite.

Once all the validations have passed, we can get to the business of actually creating the table:

```
Ext.MessageBox.confirm("Confirm SQL Execution",
  "Are you sure you want to execute the following " +
  "SQL statement?<br><br>" + sql,
  function(inButtonClicked) {
    if (inButtonClicked == "yes") {
      var db = google.gears.factory.create("beta.database");
      db.open(inDatabaseName);
      try {
        db.execute(sql);
        db.close();
        SQLWorkbench.listTables(inDatabaseName);
        Ext.getCmp("createTableWindow").close();
        Ext.MessageBox.hide();
      } catch (e) {
        db.close();
        Ext.MessageBox.alert("SQL Execution Error", e);
      }
    }
  }
);

};
```

After we confirm that users want to execute the SQL we've constructed (and we very nicely show it to them!), then creating the table is a simple matter of opening the appropriate database, the name of which was passed in as `inDatabaseName`, and executing the SQL query. We wrap that all up in `try...catch` in case anything goes wrong, and if it does, we display the exception that was thrown. If no exception is thrown, we list the tables in this database again, which to the user appears as a refresh of the Tables Window, and then we close the Create Table Window and we're all done.

TableDetailsWindow.js

At this point we've looked at maybe half the code in this application, but where we find ourselves now is without question the biggest chunk to look at: the `TableDetailsWindow.js` file. This is all the code related to the Table Details Window, seen in Figure 7-12. As it turns out, the biggest chunk of functionality available in this application is found right here in this file.

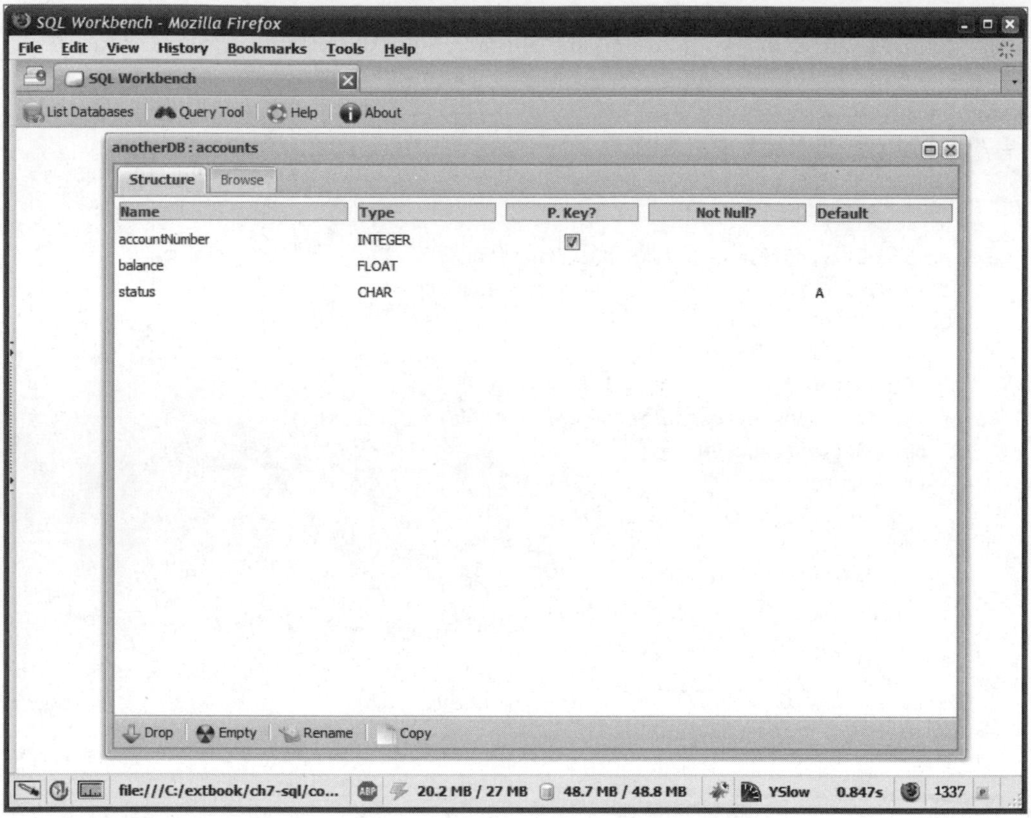

Figure 7-12. *The Structure tab of the Table Details Window*

Before we get to anything difficult, though, we have a bit of code that's very simple:

```
SQLWorkbench.listTableDetails = function(inDatabaseName, inTableName) {

  var tableWindow = Ext.getCmp("tableWindow_" + inTableName);
  if (tableWindow) {
    tableWindow.close();
  }
```

As you can see, the name of both the database and the table to display details for are passed in to this method as a result of the user clicking a table from the Tables Window. Using the table name specifically, we try to get a reference to a Window associated with this table, since one may already be opened. If one is found, we call its close() method, which results in it being destroyed. The next step is to create the Window, so by closing it first and then re-creating it we're effectively implementing a cheap refresh capability.

Defining the Window

Speaking of re-creating the Window:

```
tableWindow = new Ext.Window({
  title : inDatabaseName + " : " + inTableName, width : 700,
  height : 500, constrain : true, maximizable : true,
  animateTarget : "divSource", layout : "fit",
  id : "tableWindow_" + inTableName,
  items : [
    { xtype : "tabpanel", activeTab : 0, layoutOnTabChange : true,
      items : [
```

The title of the Window shows both the database and table names, which is pretty logical. The id value is created based on the table name, which is how we're able to get a reference to it prior to this. The items array begins with a Component of xtype tabpanel. If you look at Figure 7-12 again, you'll see there are two tabs, Structure and Browse. This is where the definition of those tabs begins. Note that I set the layoutOnTabChange config option to true. This causes the tabs to be laid out when switched to. This is often necessary to get Components that are children of a tab to be drawn properly.

Defining the Structure Tab

With the TabPanel started, we can begin to insert some tabs via its items array. The first is the Structure tab:

```
        { title : "Structure", layout : "table",
          id : "structureTablePanel_" + inTableName,
          layoutConfig : { columns : 5 }, autoScroll : true,
          items : [
            { html :
              "<div style='background-color:#dfe8f6;'>Name</div>",
              cellCls : "cssTableHeader" },
            { html :
              "<div style='background-color:#dfe8f6;'>Type</div>",
              cellCls : "cssTableHeader" },
            { html :
              "<div style='background-color:#dfe8f6;'>P. Key?</dv>",
              cellCls : "cssTableHeader cssTableCentered" },
            { html :
              "<div style='background-color:#dfe8f6;'>Not Null?</div>",
              cellCls : "cssTableHeader cssTableCentered" },
            { html :
              "<div style='background-color:#dfe8f6;'>Default</div>",
              cellCls : "cssTableHeader" }
          ],
          bbar : [
```

```
            { text : "Drop", icon : "img/Drop.gif", cls : "x-btn-text-icon",
              handler : function() {
                SQLWorkbench.doTableOp(inDatabaseName, inTableName, "drop");
              }
            },
            "-",
            { text : "Empty", icon : "img/Empty.gif", cls : "x-btn-text-icon",
              handler : function() {
                SQLWorkbench.doTableOp(inDatabaseName, inTableName, "empty");
              }
            },
            "-",
            { text : "Rename",
              icon : "img/Rename.gif", cls : "x-btn-text-icon",
              handler : function() {
                SQLWorkbench.renameCopyTable(
                  inDatabaseName, inTableName, "rename");
              }
            },
            "-",
            { text : "Copy", icon : "img/Copy.gif", cls : "x-btn-text-icon",
              handler : function() {
                SQLWorkbench.renameCopyTable(
                  inDatabaseName, inTableName, "copy");
              }
            }
          ]
    },
```

That was a fairly lengthy chunk of code, but it's not too complex and doesn't really contain anything new. A TableLayout is used within the tab to create a table where the details of the tables' structure will be displayed. The table is defined as having five columns (layoutConfig:{columns:5}), and autoScroll is set to true to ensure the user can scroll the content and not miss anything. After that, five elements with some simple HTML are added. These are the headers of the table. They are simply <div>s with a background color chosen to blend in with the rest of the Window, and with the cssTableHeader style class applied via the cellCls attribute. Two of the headers, P. Key and Not Null, also have the additional cssTableCentered class applied so that the text in the header is centered, which just plain looks better when the fields themselves are drawn below the headers because they contain CheckBoxes.

Next, the bbar attribute is used to define a Toolbar at the bottom of the tab. This includes a number of Buttons: Drop, for dropping the table from the database; Empty, for emptying the table but leaving its structure intact; Rename, for literally renaming the table; and Copy, for creating a copy of the table, including its data. The first two call on the doTableOp() method, and the last two call a third method named renameCopyTable. We'll be looking at those later, so don't worry about them just yet.

Defining the Browse Tab

The definition of the Browse tab, which you can see in Figure 7-13, is next, and it is surprisingly sparse.

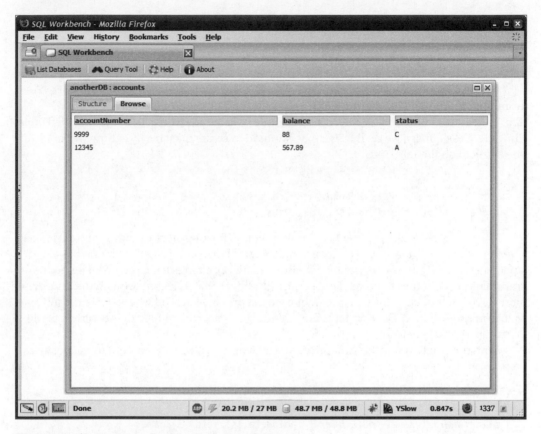

Figure 7-13. *The Browse tab of the Table Details Window*

```
        { title : "Browse", layout : "fit", id : "browseTab_" + inTableName,
          items : [ { id : "browseTablePanel_" + inTableName, html : "" } ]
        }
      ]
    }
  ]
});
```

Yep, that's it! The reason you don't see a bunch more here is that the actual content that will be shown is going to have to be built dynamically, and that's something we'll be looking at shortly.

Populating the Structure Tab

For now, though, the Window definition is complete and it's time to look at some executable code:

```
var databaseRecord = SQLWorkbench.Data.databasesStore.getById(inDatabaseName);
var tables = databaseRecord.get("tables");
var tableRecord = tables.getById(inTableName);
var sql = tableRecord.get("sql");
```

First, we retrieve the DatabaseRecord for the database name passed in as inDatabaseName from the databasesStore by using its getById() method. Once we have that, we grab the tables field from the DatabaseRecord, and then we grab the TableRecord for the specified table (inTableName). Finally, we get the SQL that was used to create the table by getting the value of the sql field on the TableRecord.

The next step is to do something with that SQL:

```
var tableDetails = SQLWorkbench.parseCreateSQL(sql);
tableRecord.set("tableDetails", tableDetails);
```

The parseCreateSQL() method is a fairly complex and long piece of code that we'll look at later. For the moment let me just explain what it does: it parses the SQL statement passed in and generates a simple JavaScript object from it that I call a table details record. This contains information about the structure of the table, including the fields it contains and the information about each, such as the type, whether each is a primary key, and whether any default values may be defined. Once we have the table details object, it is added to the TableRecord in its tableDetails field for later use.

With the details about the structure of the table in hand, we can move on to the business of populating the Structure tab:

```
var structureTablePanel = Ext.getCmp("structureTablePanel_" + inTableName);
for (var i = 0; i < tableDetails.fields.length; i++) {
  structureTablePanel.add({ html : tableDetails.fields[i].name,
    border : false, cellCls : "cssTableCell" });
  structureTablePanel.add({ html :
    Ext.util.Format.uppercase(tableDetails.fields[i].type),
    border : false, cellCls : "cssTableCell" });
  if (tableDetails.fields[i].primaryKey) {
    structureTablePanel.add(
      { xtype : "checkbox", checked : true, readOnly : true,
        ctCls : "cssTableCentered" }
    );
  } else {
    structureTablePanel.add({ html : " ", border : false });
  }
```

First we get a hold of the Panel using the TableLayout that was defined in the items array for the Window. This is the table we'll be building. Next, we iterate over the fields in the table details object. For each we're going to add a cell to the table, five in total, which completes a row in the table. The first one is the name of the field. All we need to do is use the add() method of the Panel and include the value to be displayed as the value of the html attribute. The cssTableCell class is assigned to the cell using the cellCls attribute, and the border is turned off, which makes it look better. For the field name and data type, that's all it takes.

For the columns that tell whether the database field is a primary key field or can be null, there is just a little more work to do. We begin by looking to see if the field is a primary key by checking the primaryKey field of the appropriate element in the fields array that is part of the tableDetails object. If the value returned is true, then a cell is added that contains a CheckBox that is checked. If the field is not a primary key field, then an empty cell is inserted (the   HTML entity is used to avoid the cell collapsing, as happens in some browsers).

■**Note** We used the ctCls attribute, which is an attribute of the Checkbox itself that applies to the container of the widget. This is different from the cellCls we've been seeing a lot of here. Centering didn't seem to work when applied to the table cell that the Checkbox was in, but applying it to the container of the Checkbox did—that's why the ctCls attribute is used here.

The same basic sequence of events is performed for the not null column as well:

```
if (tableDetails.fields[i].notNull) {
  structureTablePanel.add(
    { xtype : "checkbox", checked : true, readOnly : true,
      ctCls : "cssTableCentered" }
  );
} else {
  structureTablePanel.add({ html : " ", border : false });
}
structureTablePanel.add({ html : tableDetails.fields[i].defaultValue,
  border : false, cellCls : "cssTableCell" });
}
```

The final column added is the default value. This could be empty, which is fine.

Populating the Browse Tab

The next step is to populate the Browse tab and show the Window we just built:

```
SQLWorkbench.showAllRecords(inDatabaseName, inTableName);
tableWindow.show();
};
```

Don't worry, the showAllRecords() method is our next stop, and it's responsible for populating the Browse tab:

```
SQLWorkbench.showAllRecords = function(inDatabaseName, inTableName) {

  var databaseRecord = SQLWorkbench.Data.databasesStore.getById(inDatabaseName);
  var tables = databaseRecord.get("tables");
  var tableRecord = tables.getById(inTableName);
  var tableDetails = tableRecord.get("tableDetails");
```

The same bit of code that we saw just a short while ago is again executed to get the
DatabaseRecord, and the DataStore containing all the TableRecords associated with the database, and then the TableRecord for this specific table. In this case, however, we don't need
to parse the creation SQL because we already have the table details object sitting on the
TableRecord; all we need to do is retrieve it from the tableDetails field.

Next we need to get a reference to the Browse tab itself:

```
var browseTab = Ext.getCmp("browseTab_" + inTableName);
browseTab.remove("browseTablePanel_" + inTableName);
```

We also need to remove the Panel using the TableLayout that may exist, which fortunately
is easy: just call the remove() method of the Panel, passing it the ID of the Component to remove.
Since we'll be re-creating that now, no one will miss it!

Once that's done we can begin:

```
var browseTablePanel = new Ext.Panel({
  id : "browseTablePanel_" + inTableName, layout : "table", autoScroll : true,
  layoutConfig : { columns : tableDetails.fields.length }
});
for (var i = 0; i < tableDetails.fields.length; i++) {
  browseTablePanel.add({
    html : "<div style=\"background-color:#dfe8f6;\">" +
    tableDetails.fields[i].name + "</div>", cellCls : "cssTableHeader"
  });
}
```

First, a new Ext.Panel is created, which uses a TableLayout. The rest of this is very much
along the lines of the Structure tab and how its contents were created. However, with that tab
we know the columns in the table; they are static. Here however, the columns we have in the
table depend on the fields in the table itself. So, we begin by setting the columns attribute of the
layoutConfig object to the length of the fields field in the tableDetails object. That way, the
table will have a column for each field in the table.

Next we start to iterate over the fields in the table. For each we add a cell to the table,
just like we saw in the Browse tab code. Once the loop is complete, we have column headers
in the table.

The next step is to populate the actual data, so as I'm sure you can guess we need to go get
it first:

```
var db = google.gears.factory.create("beta.database");
db.open(inDatabaseName);
var rs = db.execute("SELECT * FROM " + inTableName);
```

A simple query is performed to get all the data in the table (and if you think this sounds like it could be a problem if the table is too long, you're right... see the suggested exercises at the end of the chapter).

Once we have all the data it's time to generate some stuff on the screen:

```
while (rs.isValidRow()) {
  for (var i = 0; i < tableDetails.fields.length; i++) {
    browseTablePanel.add({
      html : rs.fieldByName(tableDetails.fields[i].name),
      border : false, cellCls : "cssTableCell"
    });
  }
  rs.next();
}
db.close();
```

For each row returned we need to output the value for each field that we know is in the table, and it has to be done in the proper order so the data matches up with the column headers. So, we again loop through the elements in the `tableDetails.fields` array and for each add a cell to the table, taking the value of the `html` attribute from the current row of the `ResultSet`. Once that's done we have only to close the ResultSet and the Database and then:

```
browseTab.add(browseTablePanel);
```

Calling `add()` on the `browseTab` reference inserts the `Panel` we just built into the DOM (well, indirectly at least... it's handed to Ext JS's management, which then shoves it into the DOM) and voilà, we have a read-only browse view of the data in the table on the screen ready for the user to peruse!

Executing Various "Simple" Operations

As mentioned earlier, two of the `Buttons` on the Structure tab call the `doTableOp()` method, and as we'll find out, actually handle the other two `Buttons` as well! Here's the beginning of that method:

```
SQLWorkbench.doTableOp =
  function(inDatabaseName, inTableName, inOperation, inValue) {
```

As you can see, the method accepts the name of the database and table to operate on, which I think is pretty obvious, but it also accepts `inOperation`, which is literally the name of the operation to perform. Four values are understood: `drop`, `empty`, `rename`, and `copy`. The `inValue` argument is a value that will be used by the operation being performed. Two of the four operations, rename and copy, require this argument, the others do not.

The next thing this method does is some setup work:

```
var sql1 = null;
var sql2 = null;
switch (inOperation) {
  case "drop":
    sql1 = "DROP TABLE " + inTableName;
  break;
  case "empty":
    sql1 = "DELETE FROM " + inTableName;
  break;
  case "rename":
    sql1 = "ALTER TABLE " + inTableName + " RENAME TO " + inValue;
  break;
  case "copy":
    var databaseRecord =
      SQLWorkbench.Data.databasesStore.getById(inDatabaseName);
    var tables = databaseRecord.get("tables");
    var tableRecord = tables.getById(inTableName);
    var creationSQL = tableRecord.get("sql");
    sql1 = creationSQL.replace(inTableName, inValue);
    sql2 = "INSERT INTO " + inValue + " SELECT * FROM " + inTableName;
  break;
}
```

Based on the value of inOperation, the appropriate SQL query is constructed. All of them require the inTableName value, and that's all that the drop and empty operations require (inDatabaseName is used later). For rename, inValue is used because that's the new name of the table, so you can see it being appended as part of the SQL statement.

The copy operation is different and more complex than the rest. First, we get the Database Record corresponding to inDatabaseName in the same fashion as we've seen before. Then, we get the tables in the database, then the TableRecord for the specified table, and then the creation SQL statement. Next, we use the replace() method, an intrinsic method available on all JavaScript strings, to replace the name of the table with the value of inValue, which is the name of the copy of the table. Finally, we create a second SQL statement and assign it to the variable sql2 (all the others were assigned to sql1 notice, and sql2 started with a value of null).

All of that string manipulation gymnastics is required because there's no query, or function provided by Gears, to simply say "copy this table." To "copy" a table really means creating the new table and then copying the data from the old one. That's why we need the creation SQL for the source table and that's why two queries are involved in this operation.

Once that's done, we can go ahead and execute the query (or queries), once the user confirms it:

```
Ext.MessageBox.confirm("Confirm SQL Execution",
  "Are you sure you want to execute the following " +
  "SQL statement(s)?<br><br><br>" + sql1 + (sql2?"<br>"+sql2:""),
```

```
function(inButtonClicked) {
  if (inButtonClicked == "yes") {
    var db = google.gears.factory.create("beta.database");
    db.open(inDatabaseName);
    try {
      db.execute(sql1);
      if (sql2) {
        db.execute(sql2);
      }
      db.close();
```

Ext.MessageBox.confirm() is used to show users the SQL statement we're about to execute and requires them to confirm or deny the operation, as seen in Figure 7-14. If inButtonClicked, the argument passed to the callback function, is the value yes, then the operation can proceed. So, we open the database specified, and try to execute sql1. Then, if sql2 isn't null we execute that as well.

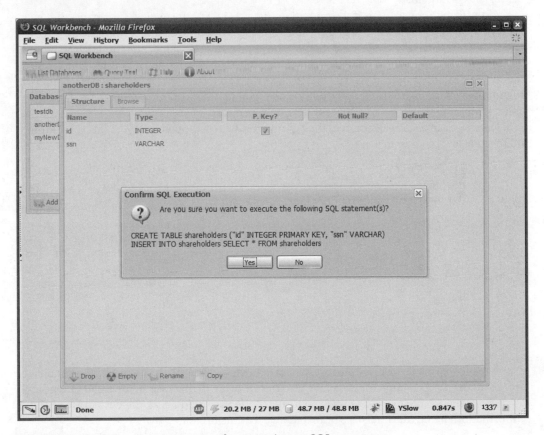

Figure 7-14. *Confirmation MessageBox for executing an SQL statement*

Once the queries have executed and the database has been closed, we have some UI work left to do:

```
SQLWorkbench.listTables(inDatabaseName);
Ext.MessageBox.hide();
if (inOperation == "rename") {
  Ext.getCmp("tableWindow_" + inTableName).setTitle(
    inDatabaseName + " : " + inValue);
} else if (inOperation = "drop") {
  Ext.getCmp("tableWindow_" + inTableName).close();
}
return true;
```

Calling the listTables() method causes the Tables Window for this database to be redrawn, which accounts for rename, drop, and copy operations to be reflected in the list since those result in new tables to show, or one old one no longer being shown. Then, the MessageBox is hidden.

After that we check to see if the operation that was just performed was a rename. If it was, then we need to change the title of the Table Details Window for that table. Ext.getCmp() allows us to get a reference to it, once we construct the appropriate ID value, and then the setTitle() method is called, passing in the name title that reflects the new name. Similarly, if the operation was a drop operation, then we need to close the Table Details Window, which is a simple matter of getting a handle to it and calling close() on it. At this point, we return true so the caller knows the operation was successful and we're done.

However, since the execution of the SQL queries were wrapped in try...catch, we know there's one last piece to this puzzle:

```
      } catch (e) {
        db.close();
        Ext.MessageBox.alert("SQL Execution Error", e);
        return false;
      }
    } else {
      return false;
    }
  }
);

};
```

Any exceptions thrown simply result in an Ext.MessageBox.alert() Window being shown that contains the exception message. We also return false in this case so the caller knows the operation failed. Note that false is also returned if the user didn't click the Yes button in the confirmation dialog (the final else branch here accounts for that).

Renaming and Copying a Table

Although we just saw that renaming a table and copying a table are functions the doTableOp()
method handles, that isn't the method that the Buttons on the Toolbar call directly. As it
turns out, there's a little bit of preparation to do before those functions can be executed by
doTableOp(), and that work is handled by the renameCopyTable() method:

```
SQLWorkbench.renameCopyTable =
  function(inDatabaseName, inTableName, inOperation) {
```

Similar to how doTableOp() accepts an inOperation argument, so too does this method.
Here, the supported values are rename and copy:

```
var windowTitle = "Rename Table";
var promptText = "Please enter the new name for the table";
if (inOperation == "copy") {
  windowTitle = "Copy Table";
  promptText = "Please enter the name for the new copy";
}
```

We start off assuming the operation will be rename, so the windowTitle variable reflects
that, as does the promptText variable. If inOperation is copy, though, we override the values for
windowTitle and promptText so they apply to a copy operation.

Then, an Ext.MessageBox.prompt() dialog is opened:

```
Ext.MessageBox.prompt(windowTitle, promptText,
  function(inBtnID, inVal) {
    if (inBtnID == "cancel") { return; }
    if (inVal != null) { inVal = inVal.trim(); }
    if (!Ext.isEmpty(inVal)) {
      SQLWorkbench.doTableOp(inDatabaseName, inTableName, inOperation, inVal);
    }
  }, null, false, inTableName
);

};
```

For both of these operations, the user is required to enter a value: the name to rename the
table to or the name of the copy of the table. We use the windowTitle and promptText variables
to set the title of the MessageBox and the text of the prompt message to the user accordingly.

The callback function passed to Ext.MessageBox.prompt() first checks to see if the Cancel
button was clicked, and if so, it just returns, no harm no foul. If that doesn't happen, we check
to make sure inVal, what the user entered, isn't null, and if not we trim() it. Then, if inVal has
a value, we call SQLWorkbench.doTableOp, passing in all the pertinent information.

Note too that the name of the table being renamed or copied is the default value in the
MessageBox, which is what that bit at the end with }, null, false, inTableName is all about.

Parsing the Creation SQL Statement

Warning! The following is not especially pretty code! I have no doubt that readers will write telling me a million different ways to do this part better, and that's cool, I look forward to hearing from you! In the meantime, while this code isn't going to win any awards for...well, anything probably, it *does* have the virtue of doing exactly what we need it to do: parse an SQL creation statement and get the details about the table from it. Unfortunately, there's no clean way to obtain this information from SQLite through Gears, so this general approach, whether the technique is great or not, is about the only path available to us.

```
SQLWorkbench.parseCreateSQL = function(inSQL) {

  var trimQuotes = function(inString) {
    return inString.replace(/^['"`]+|['"`]+$/g, '');
  };
  var replaceString = function(inSource, inReplace, inReplaceWith) {
    var start = inSource.toLowerCase().indexOf(inReplace.toLowerCase());
    while (start != -1) {
      inSource = inSource.substring(0, start - 1) +
        inReplaceWith + inSource.substring(start + inReplace.length);
      start = inSource.toLowerCase().indexOf(inReplace.toLowerCase());
    }
    return inSource;
  };
```

First, two utility functions are created (remember you can nest functions in JavaScript all you like). The first simply trims quotation marks from the ends of a string, which we'll need to clean up the value as we parse the incoming SQL string. The second replaces all occurrences of a given string within another.

```
  var tableDetails = {
    sql : inSQL,
    error : null,
    temporary : false,
    ifNotExists : false,
    tableName : null,
    databaseName : null,
    fields : [ ]
  };
```

The `tableDetails` structure is what we're ultimately trying to create here. The fields in this object are summarized in Table 7-2.

Table 7-2. *The Fields of the tableDetails Object*

Field	Description
sql	The table creation SQL statement passed into the method
error	If certain errors occur during parsing, this field will contain the failure reason
temporary	Tells us whether the table is a temporary table
ifNotExists	Tells us whether the if not exists clause was present in the SQL statement
tableName	The name of the table
databaseName	The name of the database the table belongs to
fields	An array of field descriptor objects, which is another plain JavaScript object with the following fields: name, the name of the field; type, the data type of the field; primaryKey, true if the field is a primary key; notNull, true if null is not allowed in the field; and defaultValue, the default value of the field

Next, the incoming SQL statement is trimmed:

```
inSQL = inSQL.trim();
```

Ensuring that there is no whitespace on either ends of the string makes parsing it easier. In fact, anything we can do to "normalize" things as we go makes the job easier, and you'll see a lot of that now.

The next step is one such normalization step:

```
var stringBefore = inSQL;
var stringAfter = inSQL.replace(/\s\s/g, ' ');
while (stringBefore != stringAfter) {
  stringBefore = stringAfter;
  stringAfter = stringAfter.replace(/\s\s/g, ' ');
}
inSQL = stringAfter;
```

What we're doing here is ensuring that throughout the entire string there are only single spaces. Since whitespace will be ignored when the SQL is executed, it's not an issue from a "does the SQL statement work" perspective, but it *does* make parsing things harder because we can't treat a space as a token delimiter. Ensuring there are only single spaces, however, allows us to do just that. So, a little regex magic later and the value of inSQL is guaranteed to only have single spaces.

The next step is to get the "prefix" portion of the SQL—that is, in an SQL statement like

```
CREATE TABLE "test" ("aaa" INTEGER PRIMARY KEY  NOT NULL , "bbb" TEXT)
```

the prefix is the portion before the field list, meaning the portion before the opening parenthesis. We can get this prefix pretty easily:

```
var prefix = (inSQL.substring(0, inSQL.indexOf("("))).trim();
```

Now that we have the prefix, we can do a quick validation:

```
if (prefix.toLowerCase().indexOf("create") != 0) {
  tableDetails.error = "create keyword not found";
  return tableDetails;
}
prefix = prefix.substring(7);
```

If we don't find the create keyword, then it's an error; we can't parse the incoming string, and the method aborts.

If this validation passes, then we know the first part of inSQL is create. So, by using prefix.substring(7), we get everything following the create keyword. With that, we check for a few other keywords:

```
if (prefix.toLowerCase().indexOf("temp ") == 0) {
  tableDetails.temporary = true;
  prefix = prefix.substring(5);
} else if (prefix.toLowerCase().indexOf("temporary") == 0) {
  tableDetails.temporary = true;
  prefix = prefix.substring(10);
}
```

If the keyword temp is present, then the table is a temporary table. It's also possible to have the keyword temporary in there, so we have to check for that as well. Fortunately, temp or temporary can only follow the create keyword, so the code doesn't have to be too clever (nor do I, thankfully!). Another substring() call gets us past whichever keyword was there, if any.

The next possible keyword is table, so we check for it next:

```
if (prefix.toLowerCase().indexOf("table") != 0) {
  tableDetails.error = "table keyword not found";
  return tableDetails;
}
prefix = prefix.substring(6);
```

In fact, it's not just possible; it *has* to appear next. Once you work past create and temp/temporary, table is the only valid keyword that can follow. So, if it's not found, it's another validation error that aborts the method. If it is found, then we can continue to parse the prefix.

```
if (prefix.toLowerCase().indexOf("if not exists") == 0) {
  tableDetails.ifNotExists = true;
  prefix = prefix.substring(14);
}
```

The if not exists clause is the next portion that can be present, so we check for that and set the flag in tableDetails if found.

The next step is to get the name of the table:

```
if (prefix.indexOf(".") == -1) {
  tableDetails.databaseName = null;
  tableDetails.tableName = trimQuotes(prefix);
} else {
  tableDetails.databaseName = trimQuotes(prefix.split(".")[0]);
  tableDetails.tableName = trimQuotes(prefix.split(".")[1]);
}
```

The complication here is that the SQL can have just the table name or the table name plus the database name in the form <databaseName>.<tableName>. So, we account for that by checking for a period. If not found, then all we have is a table name. However, it could have quotes around it, so now that trimQuotes() method we created earlier comes into play. If a period was found, then we split the prefix string on the period and trim both resulting array elements: the first is the database name, and the second is the table name.

The next step is to retrieve the list of field specifications:

```
var fields = inSQL.substring(inSQL.indexOf("(") + 1, inSQL.length - 1);
```

This is a simple matter of taking everything from the first character after the opening parenthesis to the end of inSQL, minus the last character.

However, we have a problem: the fields string could contain a primary key clause at the end. So, we check for that:

```
var primaryKeyListLocation = fields.toLowerCase().indexOf("primary key(");
var primaryKeyList = null;
if (primaryKeyListLocation != -1) {
  primaryKeyList = fields.substring(primaryKeyListLocation).trim();
  fields = fields.substring(0, primaryKeyListLocation).trim();
  fields = fields.substring(0, fields.length - 1);
}
```

If the test string primary key(is found, then we get everything from the point it's found, taking care to trim it. Then, it is removed from the fields string.

The next step is to scan through the list of field specifications and learn from each the information we need. To do so, we tokenize the string with the JavaScript string's split() method, using commas as the delimiter:

```
var fieldTokens = fields.split(",");
for (var i = 0; i < fieldTokens.length; i++) {
```

Then we iterate over the resulting array. For each element, which is a field in the table, we create a fieldDescriptor object:

```
var fieldDescriptor = {
  name : null, type : null, primaryKey : false, notNull : false,
  defaultValue : null
};
```

The next token, meaning the next field specification, is taken, trimmed, and converted to lowercase:

```
var field = fieldTokens[i].trim();
var testField = field.toLowerCase();
```

Then, we search for each of the valid SQLite data types within that string:

```
if (testField.indexOf("integer") != -1) {
  fieldDescriptor.type = "integer";
}
if (testField.indexOf("double") != -1) {
  fieldDescriptor.type = "double";
}
if (testField.indexOf("float") != -1) {
  fieldDescriptor.type = "float";
}
if (testField.indexOf("real") != -1) {
  fieldDescriptor.type = "real";
}
if (testField.indexOf("char") != -1) {
  fieldDescriptor.type = "char";
}
if (testField.indexOf("varchar") != -1) {
  fieldDescriptor.type = "varchar";
}
if (testField.indexOf("text") != -1) {
  fieldDescriptor.type = "text";
}
if (testField.indexOf("blob") != -1) {
  fieldDescriptor.type = "blob";
}
if (testField.indexOf("numeric") != -1) {
  fieldDescriptor.type = "numeric";
}
if (testField.indexOf("datetime") != -1) {
  fieldDescriptor.type = "datetime";
}
field = replaceString(field, fieldDescriptor.type, "").trim();
```

Whichever one is found, we set the appropriate value in the fieldDescriptor. Finally, we replace the data type in the token with a blank string, effectively removing it. This is another one of those "normalization" tricks to make the next part easier:

```
if (field.toLowerCase().indexOf("not null") != -1) {
  fieldDescriptor.notNull = true;
  field = replaceString(field, "not null", "").trim();
}
```

We check to see if the string not null appears in the token. If so, then we set the notNull field of the fieldDescriptor to true and delete the string from the token. Then we move on to a similar check for the primary key string that might be present:

```
if (field.toLowerCase().indexOf("primary key") != -1) {
  fieldDescriptor.primaryKey = true;
  field = replaceString(field, "primary key", "").trim();
}
```

After that, we have to see if there is a default value specified for the field:

```
var defaultValueKeywordStart = field.toLowerCase().indexOf("default");
if (defaultValueKeywordStart != -1) {
  var defaultValueStart = field.indexOf("'", defaultValueKeywordStart);
  var defaultValueEnd = field.indexOf("'", defaultValueStart + 1);
  fieldDescriptor.defaultValue =
     field.substring(defaultValueStart + 1, defaultValueEnd);
  field = field.substring(0, defaultValueKeywordStart).trim();
}
```

If the string default is found, then we look for the opening and closing single-quote characters that must be surrounding the default value. Once found, we use the substring() method to get the portion of the string in between them and record that as the defaultValue in the fieldDescriptor.

All that remains for dealing with the field is to get rid of any quotes around the name of the field, if they are present, and then push the fieldDescriptor onto the tableDetails.fields array:

```
  fieldDescriptor.name = trimQuotes(field);

  tableDetails.fields.push(fieldDescriptor);

}
```

The last task is to deal with that primaryKeyList that we pulled out earlier, if there is one:

```
if (primaryKeyList) {
  primaryKeyList = primaryKeyList.trim();
  primaryKeyList = primaryKeyList.substring(primaryKeyList.indexOf("(") + 1,
    primaryKeyList.indexOf(")"));
  var pkFields = primaryKeyList.split(",");
  for (var i = 0; i < pkFields.length; i++) {
    var pkFieldName = trimQuotes(pkFields[i]).trim();
    for (var j = 0; j < tableDetails.fields.length; j++) {
      if (pkFieldName.toLowerCase() ==
        tableDetails.fields[j].name.toLowerCase()) {
        tableDetails.fields[j].primaryKey = true;
        break;
      }
    }
  }
}
```

We start by trimming `primaryKeyList`, and then find the content between the opening and closing parentheses. With that portion of the string now in `primaryKeyList`, we split on comma again and iterate over the array. For each element, we get the value, trim quotes from the ends, and `trim()` it, just to be safe. At this point we have the name of the primary key field. So, we now iterate over the `tableDetails.fields` array and look for that field. Once found, we set `primaryKey` on that field descriptor to `true` and we're good to go.

```
  return tableDetails;

};
```

The method returns the `tableDetails` object and the caller has just what they want: an object containing details about the table, derived from the SQL that created it! Again, I apologize if you find this bit of code to be rather brute-force. The apology only goes so far, however, because, well, the code works! I have no doubt there's some magic regex, or fancy recursive algorithm that could do it cleaner, but hey, if the code works, it meets the first qualification for being decent, right?

QueryToolWindow.js

To paraphrase *Star Wars*: "Don't be too proud of this technological marvel you've created… the power to browse a database table is insignificant next to the power of naked SQL."[2]

Er, yeah, I realize that's a stretch. Ricky Henderson[3] stretching a single up the middle into a triple stretch.

But, stretch jokes aside, there's truth in the paraphrasing: this application lets us browse database tables, drop and empty tables, some other basic things, but if you have the ability to enter arbitrary, or naked, SQL statements and execute them, a ton more power becomes available to you. That's exactly what the Query tool, shown in Figure 7-15, is all about.

Here users can enter any SQL statement they want and it will be executed. If it's a query-type statement, then the results of the query will be shown at the bottom in tabular form. If it is instead an update-type query, then the number of rows affected will be shown instead. If any exceptions occur, that information will be displayed as well.

The code begins with the `showQueryTool()` Window, which does exactly what you think it does!

```
SQLWorkbench.showQueryTool = function() {

  if (Ext.getCmp("queryToolWindow")) {
    queryToolWindow.show();
    return;
  }
```

---

2 You certainly can't be considered a true geek if you need to read this, but the quote I'm paraphrasing is from *Star Wars* (and I mean the real *Star Wars*, not *Star Wars: A New Hope*, not the prequel trilogy, but the *real* one!). Spoken by Darth Vader, the original quote was, "Don't be too proud of this technological terror you've constructed. The ability to destroy a planet is insignificant next to the power of the Force."

3 Ricky Henderson is a Hall of Fame baseball player who is considered by most to be one of, if not *the*, best leadoff hitter in the history of the game. He is the all-time stolen base leader among other accomplishments and was known to frequently get more bases out of hits than other players could.

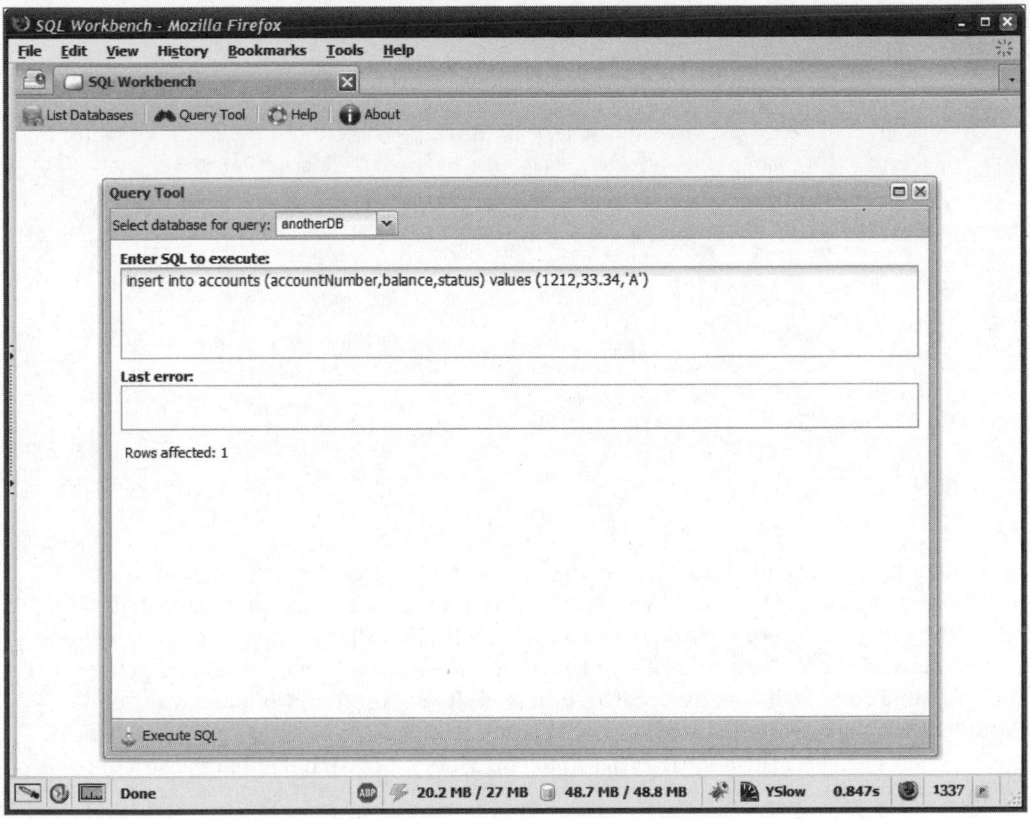

Figure 7-15. *An example of an update operation in the Query tool Window*

A quick check is first performed to see if the Query tool Window is already opened, and if so, it is shown, in front of all other open Windows. In that situation, this method is done, but if not, this code executes:

```
new Ext.Window({
    title : "Query Tool", width : 700, height : 600, constrain : true,
    animateTarget : "divSource", id : "queryToolWindow", maximizable : true,
    layout : "anchor", bodyStyle:"padding:8px;background-color:#ffffff",
    minWidth : 400, minHeight : 500,
```

The Window is defined with most of the usual config attributes, but the bodyStyle value is a little different. We've seen padding used before to ensure that the content of the Window doesn't bump right up against the borders, but what gives with setting the background-color? As it turns out, with the layout attribute set to anchor as we have here, the space around the content in the Window wasn't white—it was blue, which makes it not look very good, and not that much different either. So, by forcing the background color here to white, you can achieve the padding space you're looking for.

Next is the definition of two Toolbars, one on the top and one on the bottom of the Window:

```
tbar : [
  { xtype : "panel", baseCls: "x-window-header",
    html : "Select database for query: " },
  { xtype : "combo", width : 100, editable : false, id : "qtDatabase",
    triggerAction : "all", mode : "local", valueField : "name",
    displayField : "name", store : SQLWorkbench.Data.databasesStore }
],
bbar : [
  { text : "Execute SQL",
    icon : "img/ExecuteSQL.gif", cls : "x-btn-text-icon",
    handler : function() {
      SQLWorkbench.executeArbitrarySQL();
    }
  }
],
```

The top Toolbar contains two elements. The first is a plain-old Panel with some text
in it via its html property. Elements on a Toolbar don't necessarily have to be buttons; they
can be virtually any Component, of which a Panel is one. This allows for simple text labels and
such, as is done here. Setting the baseCls attribute to x-window-header ensures that the Panel
has the same color styling as the Toolbar; otherwise its background would be white and it
would stick out like a sore thumb. Following that is a ComboBox bound to the SQLWorkbench.
Data.databasesStore. Since the user has to tell the Query tool what database to run the query
in, this ComboBox is necessary.

The bottom toolbar simply has the single Execute SQL button that calls the
executeArbitrarySQL() method. After that is the items array:

```
items : [
  { html : "<b>Enter SQL to execute:</b>", anchor : "100% 4%",
    border : false },
  { xtype : "textarea", anchor : "100% 20%", id : "qtSQL" },
  { anchor : "100% 2%", border : false },
  { html : "<b>Last error:</b>", anchor : "100% 4%", border : false },
  { anchor : "100% 10%", id : "qtError" },
  { anchor : "100% 2%", border : false },
  { anchor : "100% 58%", border : false, id : "qtResult" }
]
}).show();

};
```

Recall that on the Window config object was the layout:anchor setting. This is the first use
of AnchorLayout in any project. Simply stated, an AnchorLayout allows you to define regions in
a container in such a way that they will dynamically resize along with the container. Imagine,
for example, a TextArea in a Window and when you resize the Window the TextArea expands and
contracts along with the Window.

Usually you specify percentage values within an AnchorLayout, but that's not always the case. In this example, though, it very much is. Each of the elements in the items array has an anchor attribute. This is in the form X Y, where X specifies the width of the element and Y the height (this isn't the only form actually, but for our purposes here it is, so if and when you decided to use an AnchorLayout on your own I'd hop on over to the Ext JS documentation, which lays this all out pretty well). Here, each of the elements should always stretch across the entire container so the X value is 100% for all of them. The Y value is some percentage such that the total height of all elements adds up to 100%.

So, what happens when the Window is resized? Well, the first element, which is just a simple text label, will be resized so that it takes up 4 percent of the total height of the Window. The TextArea where users enter their query will resize to take up 20 percent of the total height of the Window, and so on. This does leave open the possibility that the Window is resized too small and certain elements don't have enough space for their content. For example, making the Window too small will mean that 4 percent of its height is too small a space for the text to fit into and it will be cut off. That's exactly why the minWidth and minHeight attributes were specified on the Window config: the values (400 and 500 respectively) are about the minimum before Bad Things™ begin to happen to some portions of the UI.

This fluidity of layout is one of the major benefits of the code-centric approach to UI building that Ext JS provides.

Note that the borders are turned off on all the elements except the query entry box and the box where errors are reported (qtError). This is purely a "it looks better this way" thing.

So, when the user finally clicks the Execute SQL Button, the executeArbitrarySQL() method is called:

```
SQLWorkbench.executeArbitrarySQL = function() {

  var databaseName = Ext.getCmp("qtDatabase").getValue().trim();
  var sql = Ext.getCmp("qtSQL").getValue().trim();
  if (Ext.isEmpty(databaseName)) {
    Ext.MessageBox.alert("Error", "Please select a database");
    return;
  }
  if (Ext.isEmpty(sql)) {
    Ext.MessageBox.alert("Error", "Please enter a SQL query");
    return;
  }
```

First, we get the value from the qtDatabase ComboBox and trim it using the trim() method that Ext JS adds to the String class. Next, using Ext.isEmpty(), we make sure something was actually entered, and if not we display an alert using Ext.MessageBox.alert() and abort the method.

Next, a check is done to ensure users entered a query; they are notified and the method aborted if not.

With those validations out of the way, it's time to execute some SQL:

```
Ext.MessageBox.confirm("Confirm SQL Execution",
  "Are you sure you want to execute the following " +
  "SQL statement?<br><br><br>" + sql + "<br><br><br>...in database : " +
  databaseName,
  function(inButtonClicked) {
    if (inButtonClicked == "yes") {
      var queryToolWindow = Ext.getCmp("queryToolWindow");
      queryToolWindow.remove("qtError");
      queryToolWindow.remove("qtResult");
      var errMsg = "";
      var db = google.gears.factory.create("beta.database");
      db.open(databaseName);
      var resultTablePanel = null;
```

Well, *almost* time to execute some SQL! First we confirm that users want to do this by calling Ext.MessageBox.confirm() and showing the SQL to be executed and in what database it will be executed against. If they click the Yes button, which is determined by checking the value of the inButtonClicked argument to the callback (and remember the value is always lowercase regardless of the label on the button), then we can do our work.

That works begins by getting a reference to the Query tool Window. Then, using the remove() method available on it, we get rid of the elements seen in the items array with the IDs qtError and qtResults. These are the areas where errors are reported and where query results are shown. As you'll see, they are re-created during this process. Next, the errMsg variable is initialized to an empty string and then the database is opened. Note that this code is not wrapped in try…catch because if the database happens to not exist (which means it must have been deleted since the cookies were last read in), then it will simply be created.

Then, we try to execute the query:

```
try {
  var rs = db.execute(sql);
  var headersDone = false;
  while (rs.isValidRow()) {
    if (!headersDone) {
      resultTablePanel = new Ext.Panel({
        layout : "table", autoScroll : true, anchor : "100% 58%",
        layoutConfig : { columns : rs.fieldCount() }, border : false,
        id : "qtResult"
      });
```

This *is* wrapped in try...catch, however, because exceptions can most definitely be thrown at this point and we want to be able to display them to the user.

The next task is to begin constructing an HTML table structure for displaying the query results (we don't know if there are any yet, but I'm getting ahead of things!). This will look very similar to the Browse tab of the Table Details Window that we saw earlier. So first we check the ResultSet to see if we have a valid row. The only time the call to rs.isValidRow() will return false is if the query returned no results, which will come into play shortly. But for now let's assume it returns true.

In that case we're basically going to be iterating over the ResultSet. The first element encountered is special because, as we're building an HTML table here, we need some column headers. So, the headersDone variable is checked, and it starts off as false, so we hit the if branch of the check.

In that branch we build a new Panel that uses a TableLayout. Since we have to define the number of columns, we need to ask the ResultSet how many columns there are. Fortunately, the rs.fieldCount() method gives us exactly that information so our TableLayout can be built properly. Since this Panel will eventually be added to the items array of the Window, and since we already established that an AnchorLayout is used there, we need to include the anchor attribute on this new Panel so that it works properly when the Window is resized.

Next, we need to add a column to the TableLayout for each field in the ResultSet. The rs.fieldCount() is again used to perform a loop:

```
for (var i = 0; i < rs.fieldCount(); i++) {
  resultTablePanel.add({
    html : "<div style=\"background-color:#dfe8f6;\">" +
    rs.fieldName(i) + "</div>", cellCls : "cssTableHeader"
  });
  headersDone = true;
}
]
```

For each, we create a <div> with a background color and those <div>s have the cssTableHeader style class applied to give them padding. The value inserted into the body of the <div> is the name of the field, obtained by calling rs.fieldName() and passing it the index of the field. At the end we set headersDone to true so that for the next iteration of the loop (meaning the next row of data, if there is any), we'll skip a generation of the headers.

■**Note** rs.fieldCount() and rs.fieldName(), in other words, provide meta-information about the ResultSet, more specifically, about the fields returned by the query. Meta-information is a common concept when working with databases, and SQLite via Gears provides it as well.

So, that takes care of the headers. Remember at this point that we are already iterating over the records returned by the query, which means that we're currently processing the first real data that needs to be displayed. So, we need to generate table cells for the data in addition to the headers this time around:

```
for (var i = 0; i < rs.fieldCount(); i++) {
  resultTablePanel.add({
    html : rs.field(i), border : false, cellCls : "cssTableCell"
  });
}
rs.next();
}
```

It's the same sort of loop we used to generate the headers, but now we're just going after the field values in the normal `rs.field(i)` way that we've become used to. The `cellCls` attribute's value is now `cssTableCell` rather than `cssTableHeader`, but otherwise it's not much different. Figure 7-16 shows the result of all this hard work.

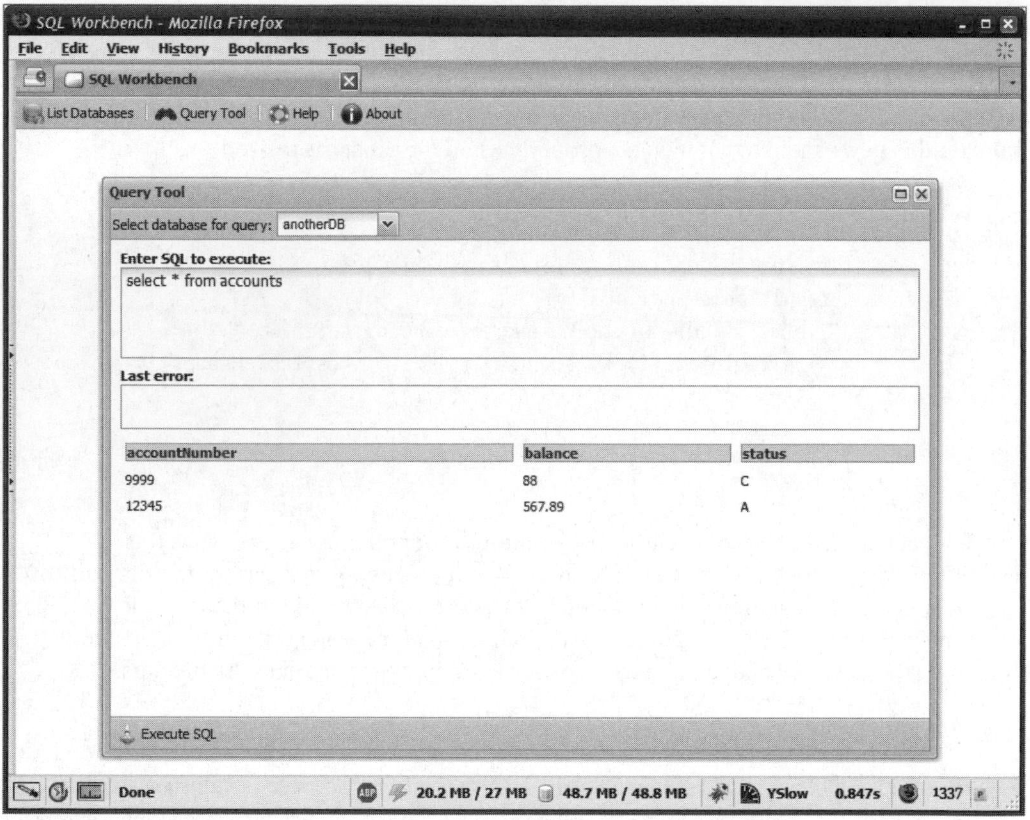

Figure 7-16. *An example of a select operation in the Query tool Window*

That concludes the iteration over the `ResultSet`. The next task is to account for queries that didn't return results. To do this, we simplify things a little and simply check to see if `headersDone` is `false`. If no results were returned, then `headersDone` would never have been set to `true`, and we're going to take that to mean that the query wasn't of a type that returned results (like a delete or update). This is a broken assumption, however, because a select query could return no results, in which case we'd be showing the "Rows affected" message in a case where it doesn't apply. Consider this an opportunity for you to enhance the application! But, it's probably *good enough* working this way anyway.

So, here's what happens when `headersDone` is `false`:

```
    if (!headersDone) {
      resultTablePanel = new Ext.Panel({
        layout : "table", anchor : "100% 58%", border : false,
        layoutConfig : { columns : 1 }, id : "qtResult"
      });
      resultTablePanel.add({
        html : "Rows affected: " + db.rowsAffected,
        border : false, cellCls : "cssTableCell"
      });
    }
```

We still need to create a table, but this time there's only a single column and it contains just a simple message telling how many rows were affected. The db.rowsAffected() method gives us that bit of metadata (notice that method is on the Database object and *not* the ResultSet object, as most of the others have been).

Once that's done, we have some minor cleanup to do:

```
    rs.close();
    db.close();
    Ext.MessageBox.hide();
  } catch (e) {
    db.close();
    errMsg = e;
  }
```

Close the ResultSet and Database and then hide the MessageBox that was prompting for confirmation, and we're done—well, unless an exception occurred. In that case, we set errMsg to the exception value.

The final task is to ensure all this stuff gets put on the screen! Here's that code:

```
    queryToolWindow.insert(4,
      { html : errMsg, anchor : "100% 10%", id : "qtError" }
    );
    queryToolWindow.add(resultTablePanel);
    queryToolWindow.doLayout();
  }
 }
);

};
```

First, we call the insert() method on the Window to insert a new Panel whose contents is errMsg (which may be a blank string of course, but that's perfectly fine). The insert() method accepts as its first argument an index value that indicates where in the items array this element should be inserted. If you look back at the Window definition, the qtError element was the fifth element in the items array, so that's an index value of 4 in a zero-based array. Now, contrast this to the addition of the results table. For that we're using the add() method, which simply appends the element to the end of the items array, which is always where the results should go. Finally, a call to doLayout() causes the Window to redraw itself, resulting in all these UI changes being shown as expected.

■**Note** If you have the table Window opened for the table you're doing an update-type operation on, you'll need to close the Window and open it again for the changes to be reflected on the Browse tab.

Help.js

The final file to look at is Help.js, which is where the online help resides. To begin with, we have a field:

```
SQLWorkbench.currentHelpPage = -1;
```

This records what page of help is currently being looked at. There are three pages that can be displayed and the user can cycle through them, as you can see in Figure 7-17. Each page is displayed in a Window and the Windows are created dynamically. Creating them, though, requires that we have some content to display, and that content is contained in the following array:

```
SQLWorkbench.helpPagesContent = [
  "<h1><i><u>Creating/modifying databases</u></i></h1>" +
  "<br>" +
  "The Databases window shows the list of databases you can work with.  You " +
  "can add a new database by clicking the Add Database button.  This will " +
  "prompt for the name of the database.  If the name you enter is a database " +
  "that already exists it will simply be added to the list.  If the database " +
  "does not exist then it will be created and added to the list.<br><br>" +
  "To remove a database, click it and then click the <b>Remove Database</b> " +
  "toolbar button.  The last database selected (since the last one to be " +
  "removed, if any) is the one that will be removed." +
  "<br><br>" +
  "Clicking a database opens the Tables window for that database, from which " +
  "you can work with tables.",
```

That's the first element of the array, and the value of the element is simply a giant string of HTML. This will become the content of the Window. There are similarly two more elements in the array, one for each page of help that there is, but there's probably no real benefit to displaying all the text here. Suffice it to say that they are defined just like the first element is: they too are just giant string concatenations where each formed string is the next element in the array.

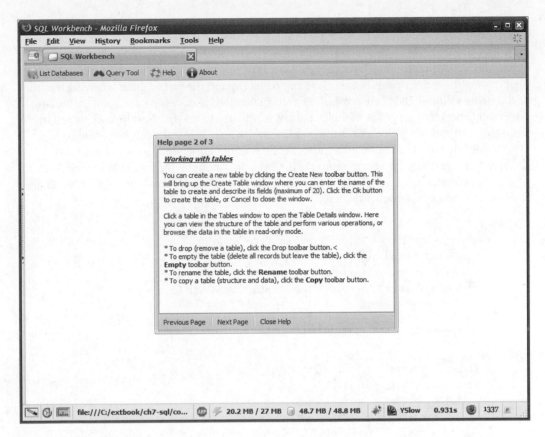

Figure 7-17. *A help page*

The code that is called in response to the user clicking the Help `Toolbar` button is the `showHelp()` method:

```
SQLWorkbench.showHelp = function(inPageToDisplay) {

  new Ext.Window({
    id : "dialogHelpPage" + inPageToDisplay, closable : false,
    width : 400, height : 320, minimizable : false, resizable : false,
    draggable : true, shadow : false, maximizable : false, layout : "fit",
    autoScroll : true,
    title : "Help page " + (inPageToDisplay + 1) + " of " +
      SQLWorkbench.helpPagesContent.length,
    items : [
      { html : SQLWorkbench.helpPagesContent[inPageToDisplay],
        bodyStyle : "padding:8px" }
    ],
```

This first chunk of code builds a Window with an id that has the page of help tied to it (so dialogHelpPage0 or dialogHelpPage1, for example). The Window is not closable, maximizable or minimizable, or resizable, but it *is* draggable. The layout type is fit so that the content we insert fills the entire Window. The autoScroll attribute is set ot true to allow for scrolling of long help pages (there aren't any, but this way you could expand the text without worrying about it not being visible). The title attribute is a string that tells users what page they are looking at. Finally, the items array has a single element within it: a Panel that has the contents of the helpPagesContent array element corresponding to the help page currently being viewed.

Going back to the id value for a moment, the number appended as part of it is taken from the inPageToDisplay argument to the method. So, when the Toolbar button is clicked, the value passed in would be 0. However, when the user clicks the Previous Page or Next Page button, the following code is executed:

```
bbar : [
  { xtype : "button", text : "Previous Page",
    handler : function() {
      if (SQLWorkbench.currentHelpPage > 0) {
        SQLWorkbench.showHelp(SQLWorkbench.currentHelpPage - 1);
      }
    }
  },
  "-",
  { xtype : "button", text : "Next Page",
    handler : function() {
      if (SQLWorkbench.currentHelpPage <
        (SQLWorkbench.helpPagesContent.length - 1)) {
        SQLWorkbench.showHelp(SQLWorkbench.currentHelpPage + 1);
      }
    }
  },
```

Here we have a bottom Toolbar defined via the bbar attribute. Each button does some bounds checking to ensure there is a next or previous page to display, then calls showHelp() again, passing in the new value for currentHelpPage. The Window for the next page to display is constructed, if necessary, but isn't yet shown… we'll get to that right after this break:

```
  "-",
  { xtype : "button", text : "Close Help",
    handler : function() {
      Ext.getCmp("dialogHelpPage" + SQLWorkbench.currentHelpPage).close();
      SQLWorkbench.currentHelpPage = -1;
    }
  }
]
}).show();
```

The Previous Page and Next Page buttons aren't the only ones on the bottom `Toolbar`. After a divider is inserted (just like the one I neglected to mention is between the Previous Page and Next Page buttons as well!), we have the Close Help button. This simply gets a reference to the currently opened `Window`, using the `id` value, and calls `close()` on it. Since only a single `Window` can be open at a time, that's all we need. In addition, the `currentHelpPage` field is set back to its starting value of `-1`, which strictly speaking isn't necessary, but I like having variables in known states whenever possible, so doing this satisfies that bit of obsessive-compulsive disorder on my part!

The next bit of code follows the `Window` construction and is responsible for showing the appropriate `Window`:

```
if (SQLWorkbench.currentHelpPage != -1) {
  Ext.get("dialogHelpPage" + SQLWorkbench.currentHelpPage).puff({
    duration : 1, remove : true
  });
}
```

Assuming we didn't just execute the code behind the Close Help button, then we get a reference to the `Window` currently being shown and use the puff effect on it to close it. The puff effect basically expands the `Window` and fades it out at the same time, like a puff of smoke does. Note that the call to the `puff()` method isn't blocking, so we can issue another effect at the same time, which comes into play next. By the way, the arguments to the `puff()` method specify that we want the effect to take one second to complete and that the element being puffed should be destroyed and removed from the DOM when the effect is completed.

Now, at the same time that the previous `Window` is puffed out of existence, the next `Window` to be displayed is faded in:

```
Ext.get("dialogHelpPage" + inPageToDisplay).fadeIn({
  duration : 1
});
SQLWorkbench.currentHelpPage = inPageToDisplay;

};
```

The `fadeIn()` method provides that effect, and again we do it over the course of one second. So, by the time the previous `Window` is gone, the new one is completely displayed, giving us a nice, smooth transition. Finally, the `currentHelpPage` is set to the new value provided by the `inPageToDisplay` argument, and the method is done.

■**Note** In Firefox at least, the combination of these two effects when the `Window`s overlap causes some sheering, a common graphical glitch seen in many games. In Internet Explorer ironically, which web developers enjoy bashing any chance they get, the transition is perfectly smooth (in IE7 at least). It's not a big deal in Firefox—it works as expected and doesn't look *too* bad—but for an anal retentive like me, it's more than a little annoying!

Suggested Exercises

Although this application nicely covers the basics (so say we all[4]!) there are certainly other capabilities that a tool of this nature can, and arguably even should, provide. Fortunately, that makes it pretty easy for me to suggest exercises to you:

- Add functions for dealing with indexes. Since this application is modeled largely on the SQLite Manager Firefox add-on, index features should be roughly the same, which means you'd want three new buttons on the Table Details `Window`: Create Index, Drop Index, and Reindex. The last one should be nothing more than a modification of the `doSimpleOp()` method in `TableDetailsWindow.js`. The Create Index and Drop Index functions will first require that you figure out how to retrieve the list of indexes for a table and then present a `Window` to enter the index details in the case of Create Index, or a list of existing indexes to choose from in the case of Delete Index. None of this is especially hard, and would make for a good exercise (hint: getting the list of indexes is a slight modification to the query to retrieve a list of tables in a database).

- The SQLite engine Gears uses has a full-text search capability, and it would be nice if there was a Text Search tool, similar to the Query tool, where that could be used.

- Provide the ability to add a new record from the Browse tab of the Table Details `Window`, as well as the ability to duplicate, edit, or delete the selected record.

- Allow more than 20 fields to be added in the Create Table `Window`. You can implement this however you choose; one way would be to dynamically add a new row to the form any time you detect that all existing rows have been populated.

- Talking about the Browse tab again, there is one major flaw there: what happens if there are more than a trivial number of rows in the table? It's going to grind the UI down to a halt, that's what! Therefore, you should implement some sort of paging mechanism. You could take several approaches here (at least, two that I can think of). The first would be to use the Ext JS Store/paging mechanism, which would be a fair bit of work to set up but at least you could get the paging for free. This would require determining what provisions SQLite has for paging (and honestly, I'm not sure what it does or doesn't provide). The other approach is to simply query for all records as we're already doing, then implement the paging capability yourself without using Ext JS's data mechanisms. This would probably wind up being easier to implement in an ironic way, and performance shouldn't be too bad (there's still the possibility of a locked UI if there's a *ton* of rows, but I suspect there would truly have to be thousands and thousands before it became an issue).

- Add the ability to limit the results seen in the Browse tab. I envision this as a list of the fields in the table and next to each is a `ComboBox` listing logic operations (equals, greater than, less, than, and so forth) and then a `Textfield` where a value is entered. Users can use as few or as many as they wish, and you simply build the `where` clause of the query.

---

4 If you read that and immediately "geeked out," as the saying goes, then I really don't need to say anything further. For those unfamiliar with the phrase "so say we all," that is the call to arms in the *Battlestar Galactica* television series. It basically means "We're all working toward the same stated goal as a unified front." On the show it seems to have a religious origin, but we'll skip getting into BSG canon, in the interest of not killing any more trees than we have to in order to print this book!

Summary

In this chapter we put together a handy little application for messing around with the SQLite databases that Gears produces. We saw a UI design different from other applications in that there is no central `Viewport` in play and no `BorderLayout` used, which we've seen a lot of before. Instead we developed this application using nothing but `Windows`, which is a perfectly viable way to do things and sometimes is the best UI design to choose. We saw how we can dynamically modify a `FormPanel`. We saw a few more cool effects that Ext JS provides to us, and we also saw the `TableLayout` in action quite a bit. We also got a little more experience with the Gears `Database` component, and although it's not directly Ext JS or Gears related, we even saw how to parse the SQL used to create a table in SQLite to get information about the table.

In the next chapter we'll take a break from all this seriousness and develop something entirely different than what has come before: a game! In the process we'll see more of Gears in action, aside from the `Database` component, and yet more Ext JS features in action. To boot, if we do things right, we'll have a handy little program we can use to waste time at work!

■ ■ ■

All Work and No Play: Dueling Cards

Look, life is pretty tough. I mean, even on a good day we all face those little trials and tribulations that drive some people crazy (and others to write web development books). That's why I try to inject some humor into my writing: as tough as life can be, it's a lot easier if you're going through it with a smile. That explains why video games are so important. They're an escape from the drudgery of everyday life, a way to forget our woes for a little while and enjoy ourselves.

So far in this book, all the applications have been pretty serious, with goals having to do with working more efficiently or providing some useful service. This chapter, however, and the project within it, is completely different. We're going to drop our business clothing for a while and replace it with t-shirts, jeans, and sneakers and write ourselves a good old-fashioned time-wasting game!

Ironically, writing a game is perhaps *the* best way to become a better developer too! You have to think in different ways than usual, confront different problems, and exercise your mind to an extent that traditional business-oriented programming doesn't always afford you. Plus, it's just plain fun!

So, we'll make a game here, and in the process we'll explore some new concepts, including Gears' WorkerPool (a way to get multithreading in JavaScript), new Ext JS effects, drag-and-drop, and DOM manipulation techniques. We'll see Ext JS and Gears in an entirely different way than any other project in the book has allowed, and in the end we'll have a fun little game to play instead of getting real work done—which can't be bad, can it?

What's This Application Do Anyway?

The game we're going to create is a relatively simple card game. I've personally never been a fan of solitaire and all its variants; in fact, I don't know the exact rules of a typical solitaire game off the top of my head! Still, I decided early on that a card game would be a good choice here because it would allow us to play with Ext JS's drag-and-drop support, which is something I think is very much worth spending some time with in this book.

So, without knowing the real rules of solitaire, and also because I wanted a way to demonstrate Gears' WorkerPool API (we'll get to that in a bit), I decided to mash up some concepts I've seen in various cards games and come up with something unique that I've titled Dueling Cards. So, rather than list the requirements for this application as I've previously done, I'll instead list the rules of the game:

- Ultimately, the goal of the game is pretty typical: get rid of all your cards before your opponent does.

- Four decks of cards with two jokers each are shuffled. From that total of 162 cards, we deal 30 cards to the player and 30 to his computerized opponent. Five of those 30 are showing; the rest are face-down in a stack. The remaining cards stay with "the dealer."

- Six more cards, termed "action" cards, are dealt from the dealer's stack to a spot between the player's and opponent's cards. Around each card are some indicators. The indicators can be a single arrow pointed up, a single arrow pointed down, or a double arrow pointed up or down. In addition, there can be an indicator above or below the arrows that appears as all the card suits are cycling.

- The way you play is to drag a card from your visible cards onto one of the action cards. Only valid drops can be made, and a drop's validity is determined by those indicators. For example, a single up arrow above a three of clubs means that the only card that can be placed there is a four of clubs. A double down arrow below a six of diamonds means that only a four of diamonds can be placed on it. If the cycling suit indicator is there, then the suit doesn't matter (so a four of any suit could be placed on the three of clubs or a four of any suit on the six of diamonds).

- Jokers are wild, so if a joker appears in the six action cards, then any card at all can be dropped on it. Likewise, you can drag a joker onto any action card at all.

- If you can find no valid drop, you can request six new action cards from the dealer. You can also click your own stack of cards to show five new ones.

- Your opponent is trying to make valid drops just like you. The difficulty of the game determines how fast your opponent makes moves. One advantage you have over your opponent is that your opponent *cannot* request new action cards from the dealer, so you're in control a bit there.

- One requirement per se that I'll spell out here is that, because it's a game, we want to have some "coolness" in this application. That means lots of animations, effects, and graphics. We'll also allow the user to choose from a couple of different card deck designs, and change the background image of the page as well. None of that impacts game play, but it's fun little things like that which make a game a game.

The game screen is laid out pretty much just like those rules suggest it would be, as you can see in Figure 8-1.

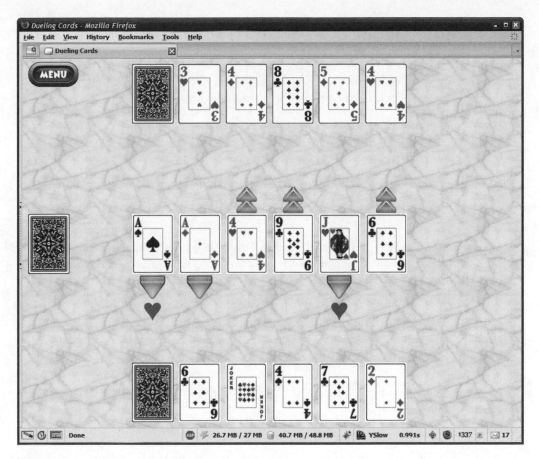

Figure 8-1. *Dueling Cards in action*

The cards on top are your opponent's cards, the cards in the middle are the action cards, and the cards at the bottom are your cards. The dealer's stack is on the left, and the button in the upper-left corner brings up the main game menu. So, as described in the rules, clicking the dealer's stack deals six new action cards and clicking your stack of cards to the left of your five visible cards brings up the next five cards in that stack. You can drag any of your visible cards onto any of the action cards, and if it's a valid drop, you will see a new card from your stack take its place among your visible cards (assuming you have any left in your stack). A new card will then be dealt from the dealer's stack.

So, it's a fairly straightforward game, but one that presents a bit of a challenge, given that your computerized opponent is quite good and pretty fast to boot, even on the easiest difficulty setting.

Now, before we tear into the code for this project we need to explore one new bit of Gears functionality that we haven't seen before: the WorkerPool component.

More Fun with Gears: WorkerPool, Worker, and Timer

You've probably heard on numerous occasions that JavaScript is inherently single-threaded. The main consequence of this is that a single long-running process can lock up the entire browser. For example:

```
var a = 1;
var b = 1;
while (true) {
  a = a + b;
  b = a;
}
```

A good old infinite loop like that is all it takes. This is the sort of thing that results in the infamous "unresponsive script" message seen in Firefox (Internet Explorer tends to simply hang in such cases).

If you keep up with the latest specification (spec) developments such as HTML 5, then you may be aware of a spec called Web Workers. This spec defines an API for JavaScript-based web applications to spawn background processes to provide something of a concurrent execution environment in JavaScript. While this spec is gaining a lot of support and looks on track to be adopted and (one would hope) implemented by the major browser vendors, it doesn't really help us today.

However, we do have something that is conceptually nearly identical to Web Workers, and that's the WorkerPool API of Gears.

Note In fact, if you check out the spec (http://www.whatwg.org/specs/web-workers/current-work/) and jump to the Acknowledgements section at the bottom, you'll see that the Web Workers spec is directly based on Gears' WorkerPool. As such, what you'll learn here will be very much applicable if and when that spec is finalized and adopted.

The WorkerPool provides a way to spawn new processes that do not share execution state. In many environments you have processes as well as threads. Threads are spawned by processes and share the execution state of their parent processes. Developers often use the term multithreaded when they really mean concurrent processes. The distinction is important to know, but at the end of the day it probably only really matters when you have both processes and threads to work with. If you only have one or the other, as with WorkerPool, then what you really mean is simply bits of code that can run concurrently. Whether you say processes or a thread almost doesn't matter in that context—only your computer science buddies are likely to make much of a fuss!

However, that part about no shared state is *very* important because it's the basis for the fact that the Workers, those bits of concurrently running JavaScript code, can only communicate with each other (or with the containing WorkerPool) via a well-defined message-passing mechanism.[1] Even simple things that you take for granted, such as being able to output a log message to Firebug's console via the `console.log()` function call, isn't available in a `Worker` because the `console` object isn't available to it (it exists in the execution state of the `WorkerPool`, but not of its child `Workers`). Likewise, the ubiquitous `window` object isn't available for the same reason (which makes it tricky to use `Workers`, as you'll see).

Since this whole project is about graphics, as most games are, I'll throw a graphic at you right now. Figure 8-2 shows the basic relationship of all these components (or it's the floorplan of Helm's Deep,[2] I'm not sure).

Web page

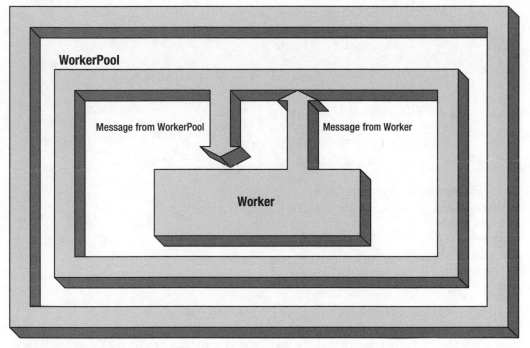

Figure 8-2. *Gears WorkerPool API, a graphical representation*

---

1   Oh, if only I could get away with communicating with my wife in this indirect kind of way…OUCH! Babe, don't smack my head while I'm typing!

2   In *The Lord of the Rings* series, Helm's Deep is a large valley in the White Mountains where the fortress of Aglarond, aka the Hornburg, could be found at the entrance to the Glittering Caves. This is the site of one of the epic battles against the forces of Saruman and Sauron during the War of the Ring in T.A. 3019 (T.A stands for Third Age… yes, I have way too much time on my hands!)

Some WorkerPool Code

So how do we use this WorkerPool thing and these Worker things? Here's a simple example:

```
<html>
  <head>
    <script src="js/gears_init.js"></script>
    <script>
      var workerPool = google.gears.factory.create("beta.workerpool");
      wp.onmessage = function(inMsgText, inSenderID, inMsgObject) {
        document.getElementById("workerResponse").innerHTML =
          "Worker #" + inMsgObject.sender + " says: " + inMsgObject.body;
      };
      var worker = workerPool.createWorker(
        "var wp = google.gears.workerPool;" +
        "wp.onmessage = function(inMsgText, inSenderID, inMsgObject) {" +
        "   var msg = inMsgObject.body[0] + ' * ' + " +
        "     inMsgObject.body[1] + ' = ' + " +
        "     inMsgObject.body[0] * inMsgObject.body[1];" +
        "   wp.sendMessage(msg, inMsgObject.sender);" +
        "}"
      );
      workerPool.sendMessage([3, 6], worker);
    </script>
  </head>
  <body>
    <div id="workerResponse"></div>
  </body>
</html>
```

So, the first thing we do is we create a new instance of a WorkerPool using the google.
gears.factory.create() method, which we've seen before when we dealt with database
access. The first thing to do once we have that instance is to register with it a function that will
act as a callback. This function will receive all messages sent by any Worker running within the
WorkerPool. This function accepts three arguments: the text of the message, the ID of the sending Worker, and an object that contains the message sent from the Worker.

■**Note** If this seems a little confusing, don't shoot the messenger! The folks at Google at some point
decided to change the API. Originally, that third argument wasn't present, but then they decided that was
the better approach. The current Gears documentation states that the first two arguments, inMsgText
and inSenderID, are actually deprecated and you should only work with the third inMsgObject argument. There are members within the object corresponding to the first two arguments (inMsgText is
inMsgObject.body and inSenderID is inMsgObject.sender).

The `inMsgObject` argument is the one we really care about. We can basically put whatever we like in it; it's completely up to us. Here we're just going to pass back a simple string from the `Worker`, so the attribute of `inMsgObject` that we'll look at is `body` (that's where the response always is located—it's just that in this case the `body` attribute is the entirety of the response, but it could be an object with its own set of attributes, for instance). This will be the string passed back from the `Worker`. The callback simply inserts the response string, concatenated with some other text, including the ID of the created `Worker`, into a `<div>` on the page.

The ID of the created `Worker` is returned by the call to `workerPool.createWorker()`. The `WorkerPool` exposes another method for creating `Workers`: `createWorkerFromUrl()`. `workerPool.createWorker()` takes a string of JavaScript and `createWorkerFromUrl()` takes a URL to a `.js` file. Either way the result is the same: some executable JavaScript is created in memory that is now called a `Worker`, and the ID of that `Worker` is returned.

Now, the `Worker` may or may not be doing anything at this point. In our example, it's actually not doing anything yet because it hasn't received any messages. So, in order to make it do something we need to send it a message. You'll notice (I hope!) that the `Worker`'s code included its own `onmessage` callback definition registered with the `WorkerPool` (which we got a reference to as the first statement in the `Worker`'s code). Remember that passing messages is the only way a `Worker` can communicate with the `WorkerPool` and the outside world, but it's also the only way a `Worker` can be communicated with by other code, be it another `Worker` or the `WorkerPool` and its environment. So, it needs to have a callback as well. This particular callback has the same signature as the first callback registered, and it basically works the same way. This callback simply multiplies two passed-in numbers and returns a string stating the result. The result string is returned by calling the `sendMessage()` method on the `WorkerPool`.

The `sendMessage()` method accepts two arguments: the message to send and the ID of the recipient. The `inMsgObject.sender` attribute provides the ID in this case, although it could be the ID of another `Worker`, if we had that information (it would have to have been passed it and stored at some point).

Remember that the `inMsgObject`'s `body` attribute can be anything we like, and in this case it's a string. However, take a look at the final line of JavaScript where we send a message to the `Worker`. In this case, it's an array. If you look again now at the callback within the `Worker` you'll notice that the values to multiply are extracted from the array exactly as you'd expect.

Limitations and Solutions

A single web page can spawn multiple `WorkerPools`, and they are completely isolated from one another, just like how Will Turner and Elizabeth Swann wound up in *Pirates of the Caribbean: At World's End*, except that there's not even the "they can be with each other every ten years" rule. But I digress.

`Workers` can be loaded across domains in a secure fashion, and you can then use the Gears-provided Ajax functions to communicate with the source domain. The `Worker` inherits the security constraint of the domain, so in other words you could have three different `Workers` loaded from three different domains, each capable of communicating with their source domain only.

As previously mentioned, Workers do not have access to certain objects such as Window. In fact, they don't have access to the DOM. This makes using them interesting in certain cases, as we'll see in this project (hint: you need cooperation between the Worker and the JavaScript outside of it based on messages being passed back and forth).

Because of this limitation, there is one important thing that Workers also do not have: access to timeouts and intervals. For the purposes of this project, that's a major problem. However, what Gears has taken away Gears has provided too! The Timer API provides an implementation of the WhatWG Timer specification and allows its use within Worker as well as in plain-old JavaScript on a page. Here's a simple example:

```
var t = google.gears.factory.create("beta.timer");
t.setTimeout(function() {
  alert("Fired via timeout 5 seconds later");
}, 5000);
```

There is a setInterval() method, as well as clearInterval() and clearTimeout(), as you'd expect.

So, that in a nutshell is the WorkerPool API. This will be the basis of how we implement the computer opponent in this project. I'll admit up-front that it's a bit of a forced usage because the opponent isn't really a long-running process, which is really what the WorkerPool is for.

Overall Structure and Files

The directory structure of Dueling Cards is very similar to all the previous applications, although there are a few differences, as you can see in Figure 8-3.

We have the usual styles.css file in the css directory and the index.htm file in the root directory. The primary difference between this and previous applications is the addition of a couple of directories under the img directory. The cardBacks directory contains images for the backs of the cards. You'll notice three different images: basicRed.gif, basicBlue.gif, and ashley.gif. The first two are, as their name implies, your basic, run-of-the-mill red and blue patterned card backs. The ashley.gif one gives you a more playful card back.

■**Note** In my previous book, *Practical Dojo Projects*, my son Andrew designed the levels for the game project presented there. My daughter Ashley, after seeing that, asked to play a role in this book somehow. My son is a few years older than my daughter, however (9 versus 6), and is starting to get into programming a little bit, while my daughter is the typical little princess with the dolls and tea parties and all that jazz and she doesn't really share my son's fledgling interest in programming (although she can use a computer just fine, better than some people I've seen at work!). So, I needed a task she could do that didn't involve coding, and a card back image turned out to be a good choice.

Figure 8-3. *The application's directory structure and constituent files*

The cardFaces directory, which I haven't expanded in the figure because it would be too long, is where you'll find 53 images, one for each card in a standard deck, plus one joker. The pageBacks directory contains a couple of images used as the background for the page, and users can switch those just like they can the card back in use.

The js directory contains all our code, and in this application I've structured it a little differently. This time, the files generally describe the functional area they belong to in the application rather than individual classes of UI component definitions. For example, the Data.js file contains the data fields that are a part of the DuelingCards namespace, which is defined in the DuelingCards.js file. The IndicatorsCode.js file contains code dealing with the indicator arrows around the action cards, and the MenuCode.js file contains the code related to the main menu. The OpponentCode.js file houses all the code that makes up the computer opponent you'll be trying to beat, and the SetupCode.js file contains code run at application startup.

The Markup

The index.htm file contains all the markup for this application, and it's at this point old hat since it only varies from the previous applications in two relatively minor ways. Have a look:

```
<html>
  <head>
    <title>Dueling Cards</title>

    <link rel="stylesheet" type="text/css" href="ext/resources/css/ext-all.css">
    <script type="text/javascript" src="ext/adapter/ext/ext-base.js"></script>
    <script type="text/javascript" src="ext/ext-all.js"></script>

    <script src="js/gears_init.js"></script>

    <script>
      Ext.namespace("DuelingCards");
    </script>

    <link rel="stylesheet" type="text/css" href="css/styles.css">
    <script type="text/javascript" src="js/DuelingCards.js"></script>
    <script type="text/javascript" src="js/Data.js"></script>
    <script type="text/javascript" src="js/SetupCode.js"></script>
    <script type="text/javascript" src="js/MenuCode.js"></script>
    <script type="text/javascript" src="js/IndicatorsCode.js"></script>
    <script type="text/javascript" src="js/OpponentCode.js"></script>

    <script>
      Ext.onReady(DuelingCards.init);
    </script>

  </head>

  <body
    style="overflow:hidden;background-image:url('img/pageBacks/marble.gif');">
    <div id="divSource" class="cssSource"></div>
  </body>

</html>
```

The first difference is that the namespace, DuelingCards, is defined here rather than in one of the .js files. I did this to allow maximum flexibility in the order of .js imports. Otherwise, I'd have to ensure that either the one file that defines the namespace was imported first or that each .js file tries to create the namespace if it doesn't exist, which seemed like a bit too much work to me, work being something I desperately try to avoid at all costs! So, the namespace is defined and *then* all the .js files are imported.

The other difference is that there's basically no markup here! The only markup is in fact the `divSource` `<div>` that we're quite familiar with by now. Everything else you see on the screen is under programmatic control from the get-go. Also note that the page background is set inline with the `<body>` element. The CSS purists out there will want to slap me for that, since inlining styles is generally frowned upon, but it frankly doesn't hurt my head in this case.

The Style Sheet

Similar to the markup in this application, the style sheet doesn't have much in it at all. It's like one of those small Dessert Shooters at Applebee's:[3] just enough to finish off a nice meal (yeah, I guess it's really nothing like that, but I'm hungry right now).

```
.cssDDNoHover {
  border : 2px solid #ffffff;
}

.cssDDHover {
  border : 2px solid #ff0000;
}

.cssSource {
  position : absolute;
  left: 1px;
  top : 1px;
  width : 100%;
  height : 1px;
}
```

The first two styles deal with drag-and-drop. The `cssDDNoHover` class is applied to cards that aren't being hovered over. It places a solid white border 2 pixels wide around the card. The `cssDDHover` class is applied to cards being hovered over, and it does the same thing but this time it's a red border. This gives a nice visual indication of when a card is being hovered over (it's also applied to the card being dragged for consistency).

The `cssSource` class is for our `Window` animation sourcing and is just a direct copy of what we've seen in the previous applications.

The Code

All of the code in this application exists within the `DuelingCards` namespace; Figure 8-4 shows the UML diagram of this namespace. As you can see, there are quite a few fields and methods there!

---

3 Applebee's is a company in the United States that owns and operates a chain of restaurants called Applebee's Neighborhood Bar and Grill. Some people love them, some don't, but their desserts are quite good: http://www.applebees.com/Menu_Desserts.aspx.

```
┌──────────────────────────────────────┐
│           DuelingCards                 │
├──────────────────────────────────────┤
│ +numActionCards : int                  │
│ +numPlayerOpponentCards : int          │
│ +numCardsDealt : int                   │
│ +viewSize : Object                     │
│ +pageBackground : string               │
│ +cDeck : string                        │
│ +contentEl : Element                   │
│ +actionCards : Array                   │
│ +playerCards : Array                   │
│ +playerStack : Array                   │
│ +dealerStack : Array                   │
│ +dealerStackY : int                    │
│ +initComplete : boolean                │
│ +lastTarget : Element                  │
│ +gameInProgress : boolean              │
│ +gamePaused : boolean                  │
│ +playerCardsRemaining : int            │
│ +opponentCardsRemaining : int          │
│ +opponentCards : Array                 │
│ +opponentStack : Array                 │
│ +workerPool : WorkerPool               │
│ +images : Object                       │
│ +imageSizes : Object                   │
│ +howToPlayShowing : boolean            │
├──────────────────────────────────────┤
│ +createCardDescriptor()                │
│ +startGame()                           │
│ +isValidDrop() : boolean               │
│ +dealerStackImgClick()                 │
│ +playerStackImgClick()                 │
│ +genRandom() : int                     │
│ +dealActionCard()                      │
│ +dealPlayerOpponentCard()              │
│ +doTitle()                             │
│ +handlePlayerDrop()                    │
│ +doEndGame()                           │
│ +genDecks()                            │
│ +createAndPositionIndicators()         │
│ +drawActionCardIndicators()            │
│ +setupMenu()                           │
│ +showMenu()                            │
│ +initOpponent()                        │
│ +opponentWorkerFunction()              │
│ +workerPoolCallback()                  │
│ +opponentStackImgClick()               │
│ +init()                                │
│ +preloadImages()                       │
│ +createCardDescriptors()               │
│ +createCardStackImages()               │
└──────────────────────────────────────┘
```

Figure 8-4. *UML class diagram of the DuelingCards class*

The trick in describing this application is exactly where to start from. I went back and forth a few times. In the end I decided that we should probably start with the data fields, housed in the Data.js file.

Data.js

Because of the sheer number of data fields present in the DuelingCards namespace, I decided to break them out into their own JavaScript file. I think you can better understand the rest of the code if you are first familiar with these fields (described in Table 8-1).

Table 8-1. *The Data Fields in the DuelingCards Namespace, Defined in the Data.js Source File*

Field Name	Description
numActionCards	This is how many action cards there are in the middle of the screen. Its initialized value is 6.
numPlayerOpponentCards	This is how many cards are visible for the player and computer opponent. Its initialized value is 5.
numCardsDealt	This is how many cards in total are dealt to the player and to the computer opponent. Its initialized value is 30.
viewSize	This is an Object that contains two attributes, width and height, which are the dimensions of the browser's content area. viewSize is used in calculations throughout the code and so is cached here for performance.
pageBackground	This indicates which of the page backgrounds is currently in use. Its initialized value is marble.
cDeck	This stores which of the card deck images is currently in use. Its initialized value is basicBlue.
contentEl	This is a reference to the document's body element, cached for performance.
actionCards	This is an array of cardDescriptor objects that describes each of the six action cards on the screen. We'll get into what a cardDescriptor is shortly.
playerCards	This is an array of cardDescriptor objects that describes each of the five visible player cards on the screen.
playerStack	This is an array of cardDescriptor objects that describes the 25 (or fewer) cards on the player's stack of cards.
dealerStack	This is an array of cardDescriptor objects that describes the cards on the dealer's stack.
dealerStackY	This is the calculated Y position where the dealer's card stack should appear on the screen.
initComplete	This flag is set to true once initialization tasks have completed.
lastTarget	This stores a reference to the Element that the player last dragged a card over and is used in drag-and-drop operations.
gameInProgress	This flag is set to true when there is a game in progress.
gamePaused	This flag is set to true when the game in progress is paused (the game being paused is different from a game being in progress, as you'll see later).
playerCardsRemaining	This stores the number of cards the player has left overall. When this reaches 0, the player wins.
opponentCardsRemaining	This stores the number of cards the computer opponent has left overall. When this reaches 0, the computer opponent wins.

Continued

Table 8-1. *Continued*

Field Name	Description
opponentCards	This is an array of cardDescriptor objects that describes each of the given visible computer opponent cards on the screen.
opponentStack	This is an array of cardDescriptor objects that describes the 25 (or fewer) cards on the computer opponent's stack of cards.
workerPool	This is the one and only Gears WorkerPool instance used to run our computer opponent's background Worker code.
howToPlayShowing	This flag is set to true when the How to Play instructions are currently showing.

In addition to the fields in Table 8-1, two others are present, but because they aren't just simple fields as the others are, I'll describe them separately.

Note You'll see where I've cached a number of DOM elements in these fields for "performance reasons." While this is generally true, especially in game development, because DOM access is relatively expensive and slow I'd be willing to bet the Ext JS is doing the caching anyway. Ext.getBody(), for example, is most likely caching the reference already (I didn't dig through the Ext JS code to confirm this, but knowing how smart the Ext JS developers are, it's a safe bet). However, storing the reference here does still have benefits because it trades a method call for a direct attribute access, which tends to be faster. The difference is usually not worth worrying about, but in game development, every little bit of speed helps, no matter how small.

The images field is an Object that contains a number of fields. You see, all of the graphics used in this game will be loaded during initialization to improve performance, and those images will be stored in this Object. So, you'll find the following fields in it:

- clubs, diamonds, hearts, spades: Each of these is an array of the card face images.

- joker: This is a single image of the joker card face.

- down1, up1, down2, up2: Each of these is one of the arrow indicator images: a single down arrow, a single up arrow, a double down arrow, and a double up arrow.

- suits_change: This is the animated suit change indicator image.

- menu0, menu1: The non-hover version of the menu button (menu0) and the mouseOver hover version (menu1).

- basicBlue, basicRed, ashley: Each of these is one of the card deck variation images.

- win, lose: The graphics seen when you win and lose the game, respectively.

- `title1`, `title2`, `title3`: These are the three images used in the title sequence.

- `pixelOfDestiny`:[4] A transparent 1×1-pixel GIF.

Going along with the `images` field is the `imageSizes` field, which is an object with fields that accompany the image references in the `images` field, where each field is an `Object` with a `width` and a `height` attribute that describes the dimensions of a given image. Here's the code for this field:

```
DuelingCards.imageSizes = {
  card : { width : 75, widthWithPadding : 85, height : 107 },
  arrowIndicator : { width : 48, height : 48 },
  suitChangeIndicator : { width : 32, height : 32 },
  menuButton : { width :  100, height : 50 },
  win : { width : 380, height : 104 },
  lose : { width : 387, height : 110 },
  title1 : { width : 386, height : 66 },
  title2 : { width : 310, height : 31 },
  title3 : { width : 204, height : 33 }
};
```

The `card` attribute describes the elements in the `clubs`, `diamonds`, `hearts`, and `spades` arrays in the `images` object, as well as the `joker` element and the `basicBlue`, `basicRed`, and `ashley` card deck design images. The `arrowIndicator` field describes the size of the `down1`, `up1`, `down2`, and `up2` fields in the `images` object. I believe all the rest are probably self-explanatory since they match the fields in the `images` object (except for `menuButton`, which describes both the `menu0` and `menu1` fields in the `images` object).

The last thing you'll find in the `Data.js` file isn't actually a data field but a method:

```
DuelingCards.createCardDescriptor = function() { return {
  suit : null,
  faceValue : null,
  elem : null,
  singleOrDouble : null,
  upOrDown : null,
  suitChangeable : null
}; };
```

The reason I put this method here is because it returns an instance of a `cardDescriptor`, and the `cardDescriptor` is defined only within this method, so in that sense it's still a data definition.

A `cardDescriptor` object is used throughout the code to describe a card. It has a number of fields to describe the card. First, the `suit` and `faceValue` fields tell you what suit (hearts,

---

4 "Captain Low-Rez and the Pixel of Destiny" is an Internet cartoon depicting the adventures of... well, if I tell you it'll ruin a pretty good humorous payoff! Take a look for yourself: http://www. kaizolabs.com/captainlowrez/episode1.html... rest assured, my use of "Pixel of Destiny" will make a lot more sense after you watch that!

clubs, spades, or diamonds) the card is and what value the card is from 2 to 14, where 11 is a jack, 12 is a queen, 13 is a king, and 14 is an ace. The elem attribute is a reference to the <img> Element that is displaying the card (this will be null for any card not currently visible). The singleOrDouble attribute, which can have a value of single or double, tells what indicator is currently around the card (so this only applies to action cards, as does the next two attributes). This upOrDown attribute, which can have a value of up or down, tells whether the arrow indicator is pointing up or down. The suitChangeable flag, a simple Boolean flag, tells us whether the cycling suit indicator is currently on this card.

SetupCode.js

The SetupCode.js file is where most of the application initialization logic is found. There are a few bits and pieces in other files, but the majority of it is here. The first bit of that logic is in the init() method:

```
DuelingCards.init = function() {

  DuelingCards.contentEl = Ext.getBody();
  DuelingCards.viewSize = DuelingCards.contentEl.getViewSize();

  DuelingCards.preloadImages();

  DuelingCards.setupMenu();

  DuelingCards.createCardStackImages();
  DuelingCards.createCardDescriptors();
  DuelingCards.createAndPositionIndicators();
```

The first line gets a reference to the document's body element so that we don't have to continually be calling Ext.getBody() over and over. Note that this returns an Ext JS Element object, which is a wrapper around a DOM element that provides a host of extra functionality, one of which is the getViewSize() method. This method returns an object containing a width and a height attribute, so we then know the size of the browser's content area, which we'll need later to position things properly.

The next line is responsible for preloading all the graphics used in the application so that we don't have a bunch of HTTP requests flying across the wire as the game runs (remember, you might be running this off a server where that sort of thing will have a negative impact). We'll be looking at this method, and the next few that are called, shortly.

The setupMenu()method really just creates the menu button and not much else. The createCardStackImages() takes care of creating the <img> elements for the five visible player cards, five visible opponent cards, and the six action cards. Finally, createAndPosition Indicators() creates the <img> elements for the arrow and suit change indicators and positions them on the page; since they will never actually move, they only have to be positioned once.

Next up is some code that you've seen before in Chapter 2: the definition of a custom DDProxy class.

```
Ext.override(Ext.dd.DDProxy, {
  startDrag : function(inX, inY) {
    var playerCard = Ext.get(this.getEl());
    playerCard.addClass("cssDDHover");
  },
  onDragOver : function(inElement, inTargetID) {
    if (inTargetID.indexOf("actionCard") != -1) {
      var dropTarget = Ext.get(inTargetID);
      DuelingCards.lastTarget = dropTarget;
      dropTarget.addClass("cssDDHover");
    }
  },
  onDragOut : function(inElement, inTargetID) {
    DuelingCards.lastTarget = null;
    if (inTargetID.indexOf("actionCard") != -1) {
      Ext.get(inTargetID).removeClass("cssDDHover");
    }
  },
  endDrag : function() {
    var playerCard = Ext.get(this.getEl());
    playerCard.removeClass("cssDDHover");
    if (DuelingCards.lastTarget) {
      DuelingCards.lastTarget.removeClass("cssDDHover");
      DuelingCards.handlePlayerDrop(playerCard.id.split("_")[1],
        DuelingCards.lastTarget.id.split("_")[1]);
      DuelingCards.lastTarget = null;
    }
  }
});

DuelingCards.initOpponent();

DuelingCards.doTitle();

}
```

I'm going to assume here that you didn't skip ahead to this chapter and did indeed read Chapter 2, in which case you should be fairly familiar with this. I'll just deal with the details pertaining to this specific project (and if you *did* skip ahead, well, thanks for being totally into the game project, but go back and read Chapter 2 before continuing, at least the part that discusses drag-and-drop back there).

First, let's see what we're talking about, courtesy of Figure 8-5. There you can see where I'm dragging the seven of spades onto the jack of diamonds. Note how the border of both cards is changed to red to indicate what is being dragged and what the drop target is.

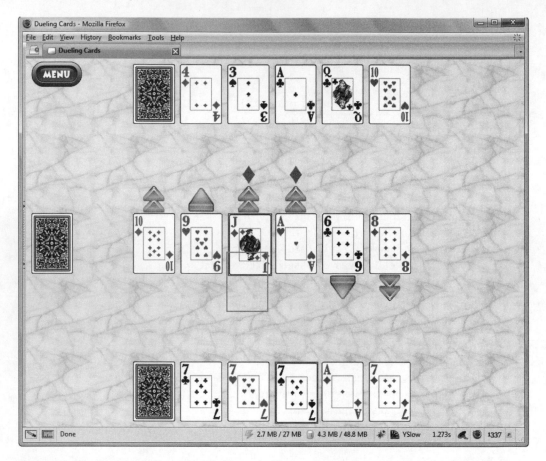

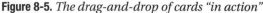

Figure 8-5. *The drag-and-drop of cards "in action"*

Now, how does this work? To begin with, the startDrag event is handled because we want to have a red border around the card being dragged. This is accomplished by adding the cssDDHover class (which you'll recall has a red border defined in it) onto the card being dragged. We can get a reference to that card by calling this.El(), which returns the Element for the <img> of the card being dragged.

The onDragOver event is then handled so that when we hover over an action card we can put a red border on it too. So, we check that the ID of the Element being hovered over is an action card by looking for that string in the ID. If it's found, then we first store a reference to the Element by the DuelingCards.lastTarget field and then add the cssDDHover class to it as well.

When the user drags a card off a previously hovered over card, the onDragOut event fires and the border is removed from the target card, if any. Also, we set lastTarget to null so that we know we no longer have an active drop target.

The endDrag event is then handled, and this is where the good stuff happens. First, we remove the red border from the card being dragged. Next, assuming we have an active drag target (which we may not, if the user just dropped the card on a blank area of the page), then we remove the cssDDHover class from the target action card. We then call the handlePlayerDrop() method, passing it the index of the action card that was dropped on, which is a number from 0 to 5. We'll look at this method later, but in short, it will determine if the drop was valid and do all the work necessary in that situation (or if it wasn't a valid drop).

The last two lines of the init() method initialize the computer opponent and then kick-start the title sequence, both of which are coming soon!

Preloading Images

As I previously mentioned, preloading images is something you have to do when writing a web-based game. Preloading is an old web development optimization in general as people tend to be more forgiving of startup delays than they are of constant little delays while using an application. In a game, though, where speed and performance are paramount, it's pretty much not even an optional thing to do!

The preloadImages() method, called from init(), takes care of preloading all the images used in the game. This is a fairly long method, but it's also a fairly redundant method. In it you'll find a bunch of blocks of code that are nearly identical to one another with only minor differences. Because of that redundancy, I'm only going to show one or two of those code blocks here, with the expectation that you'll review the entirety of the method on your own.

The first such block is actually a for loop that runs 2 to 14, which you'll notice happens to be the numeric face values of the cards in a deck, if you assign numbers to jack, queen, king, and ace of 11, 12, 13, and 14. Inside the for loop you'll find four blocks of code, one for each suit in a deck, that look like this:

```
var club = new Ext.Element(document.createElement("img"));
club.set({ src : "img/cardFaces/clubs" + i + ".gif" });
club.setSize(DuelingCards.imageSizes.card.width,
  DuelingCards.imageSizes.card.height);
DuelingCards.images.clubs.push(club);
```

The first step is to create an <img> tag, which we could do manually via standard DOM manipulation, but we're Ext JS fans around here, pal, so let's use it! You can create a new Ext.Element() object that wraps a new <img> element. This is nice because it provides all the handy methods and attributes on top of the basics. For example, we have a set() method we can call to set various attributes of our <img>, one of which is the src attribute. The filename is constructed using the suit of the card we're preloading and the index value of the for loop. Next, the setSize() method is called and passed to it are the width and height of the card image, which we find in the DuelingCards.imageSizes structure we saw earlier. Finally, the created Element is push()'d onto the end of the appropriate array, based on suit, in the DuelingCards.images object that we also saw earlier.

After the for loop ends, all the card images are loaded, save one: the joker. So, another block just like the block shown here is executed to load it.

Following that are blocks for loading the basicBlue, basicRed, and ashley card deck pattern images.

Next is another for loop, this one running from 1 to 2 (which seems a little pointless, but work with me here!). Within this loop the indicator images are loaded. Here's that code:

```
for (var i = 1; i < 3; i++) {
  var indicator = new Ext.Element(document.createElement("img"));
  indicator.set({ src : "img/up" + i + ".gif" });
  indicator.setSize(DuelingCards.imageSizes.arrowIndicator.width,
    DuelingCards.imageSizes.arrowIndicator.height);
  DuelingCards.images["up" + i] = indicator;
  indicator = new Ext.Element(document.createElement("img"));
  indicator.set({ src : "img/down" + i + ".gif" });
  indicator.setSize(DuelingCards.imageSizes.arrowIndicator.width,
    DuelingCards.imageSizes.arrowIndicator.height);
  DuelingCards.images["down" + i] = indicator;
}
```

The suit change indicator is then loaded after the loop.

Next, the two images for the menu button are loaded. There's one version for when the button is being hovered over and another for when it's not. A similar loop to the indicator images is done to minimize the actual code needed.

Next, the win and lose images are loaded, those displayed when you win or lose the game (Figure 8-6 shows the negative side of that equation!). This code is a little bit different, as you can see here:

```
var win = new Ext.Element(document.createElement("img"));
win.set({ src : "img/win.gif" });
win.setSize(DuelingCards.imageSizes.win.width,
    DuelingCards.imageSizes.win.height);
DuelingCards.contentEl.appendChild(win);
win.position("absolute", 5,
    (DuelingCards.viewSize.width - DuelingCards.imageSizes.win.width) / 2,
    (DuelingCards.viewSize.height - DuelingCards.imageSizes.win.height) / 2
);
win.hide();
DuelingCards.images.win = win;
```

An Element is created and its attributes set, but this time around we do an additional call to DuelingCards.contentEl.appendChild(), passing it the Element created. The other images are truly for preloading purposes, which means that at some point or another, the <img> Element will have its src attribute updated to the src attribute of one of these preloaded images. That, in a nutshell, is how image preloading works. However, in the case of the win and lose images, these *are* the <img> elements that will appear on the screen, so we have to insert them into the DOM. Recall that DuelingCards.contentEl is a reference to the document's <body> element, so here the <img> is appended to that element. Next, the position() method is called to place it on the screen absolutely. The value 5 passed in as the second argument is the z-index, which we set to be higher than everything else on the page. The X and Y coordinates are calculated by subtracting the width of the win image from the width of the browser's viewport and dividing by 2, which is the standard formula for centering an image. Finally, hide() is called so that the <img> is hidden.

Figure 8-6. *Your slap-in-the-face image (at least it's a pretty red with perspective on the screen!)*

■**Note** The position() method must be called *after* the Element is added to the DOM; otherwise, an error occurs.

The three graphics associated with the title are then loaded in a manner similar to the win and lose images. They are appended to the DOM immediately and centered on the page, but in a slightly different way than the win and lose images:

```
DuelingCards.images.title1 =
  new Ext.Element(document.createElement("img"));
DuelingCards.images.title1.set({ src : "img/title1.gif" });
DuelingCards.images.title1.setSize(5000, 5000);
DuelingCards.contentEl.appendChild(DuelingCards.images.title1);
```

```
DuelingCards.images.title1.position("absolute", 100,
  ((DuelingCards.viewSize.width - 5000) / 2),
  ((DuelingCards.viewSize.height - 5000) / 2)
);
```

Wow, 5000×5000… those images need a diet! In actuality, though, this allows for the title effect sequence. You see, the arguments to setSize() don't *have* to be the actual dimensions of the image. If they are larger or smaller, the image will be scaled accordingly. So, you have to visualize this in your head… we have an image that is 5000×5000 pixels in size, centered on the browser viewport; so what happens to the portion of the image that doesn't fit on the screen? Unless you have a massive monitor that covers an entire wall, that will certainly be the case. Simply stated, it gets clipped.

So now, if you played this game a bit before this point you'll know exactly what happens: the three lines of text that are the three title images, in sequence, quickly shrink down from their initial huge size to their real size, centered on the page. If you haven't run the code yet, now is definitely a good time. It's a relatively simple effect, but one that is pretty effective. We'll soon see how the actual animation is accomplished, but it's this initial sizing and positioning that makes it work right.

Finally, the infamous Pixel of Destiny is loaded, which is just a 1×1 transparent pixel image used as a placeholder in various spots—for instance, as the initial images for the indicator arrows, so they are effectively invisible.

Creating the Card Stack Images

With all the images preloaded, it's time to create some <img> elements for the three card stacks—that is, the stack of nonvisible cards for the player, opponent, and dealer. The code for creating each is, as you'd probably guess, all quite similar, so I'll just show one here, the one for the dealer, taken from the createCardStackImages() method:

```
DuelingCards.dealerStackY =
  (DuelingCards.viewSize.height - DuelingCards.imageSizes.card.height) / 2;
var dealerStackImg = new Ext.Element(document.createElement("img"));
dealerStackImg.set({
  src : DuelingCards.images[DuelingCards.cDeck].getAttributeNS("", "src"),
  id : "imgDealerStack", style : "cursor:pointer;"
});
dealerStackImg.setSize(DuelingCards.imageSizes.card.width,
  DuelingCards.imageSizes.card.height);
DuelingCards.contentEl.appendChild(dealerStackImg);
dealerStackImg.position("absolute", 3, 10, DuelingCards.dealerStackY);
dealerStackImg.addListener("click", DuelingCards.dealerStackImgClick);
```

First, we calculate the Y location for this image, which is midway down the page, using the same sort of basic formula for centering as we saw earlier but for vertical centering this time. Then, we create a new Ext.Element wrapped around an <img> element and set its src attribute to that of the preloaded current card deck pattern. Recall that the DuelingCards.cDeck field has a value of basicBlue, basicRed or ashley, which also happen to be the names of the fields in the DuelingCards.images object where the preloaded images are stored. So, using

DuelingCards.cDeck as an array index into the DuelingCards.images object retrieves the reference to the appropriate image. Then, it's just a matter of grabbing its src attribute.

Note Remember that you can always access object attributes via array notation or dot notation, and when you need to have the attribute you retrieve be dynamic, the array notation is the way to go. In cases where the attribute name is static, however, dot notation is more readable to most people.

Interestingly, though, you can't access the src attribute directly because that's simply not how it's done with an Ext.Element object. Instead, we have to use the getAttributeNS() method, which returns the value of a namespaced attribute from the element's underlying DOM node. The first argument to that method is the namespace to look the attribute up under, and the second is the name of the attribute.

The size of the image is then set, using the dimensions specified in the DuelingCards.imageSizes object, and then it is appended to the DOM. Next, it is positioned using absolute positioning, and given a z-index of 3.

Next, the addListener() method is called to attach a click event handler. In this case, clicking the dealer's stack image calls the DuelingCards.dealerStackImgClick() method, which we'll get to in a bit.

The opponent and player's card stack images are created in the same basic way, although the opponent's image does not have a click handler attached. The vertical positioning is also calculated a bit differently. The opponent's cards are positioned 10 pixels from the top of the page while the player's cards are positioned 10 pixels from the bottom. Have a look at the code that does that, just to see the math behind it, but I dare say it's quite simple and should be abundantly obvious. Other than that, the code is very much similar to what we've just discussed.

Creating cardDescriptors

Now that we have all the images preloaded and the card stack images have been created, we need to create cardDescriptor objects for the five visible player cards, five visible opponent cards, and the six action cards. First, let's create the action cards:

```
for (var i = 0; i < DuelingCards.numActionCards; i++) {
  var cardDescriptor = DuelingCards.createCardDescriptor();
  cardDescriptor.elem = new Ext.Element(document.createElement("img"));
  cardDescriptor.elem.set({ id : "actionCard_" + i });
  cardDescriptor.elem.setSize(DuelingCards.imageSizes.card.width,
    DuelingCards.imageSizes.card.height);
  DuelingCards.actionCards.push(cardDescriptor);
  DuelingCards.contentEl.appendChild(cardDescriptor.elem);
  cardDescriptor.elem.position("absolute", 2, 10, DuelingCards.dealerStackY);
  cardDescriptor.elem.hide();
  new Ext.dd.DropZone("actionCard_" + i);
}
```

A call to the createCardDescriptor() method that we saw earlier gets us a plain old JavaScript object that we call a cardDescriptor. In that object we need to set some attribute values. First is the elem attribute that points to the <img> element that is the visual representation of this card on the screen. This attribute's value is another Ext.Element wrapped around an <img> element. Next, its id attribute is set so that we can use that ID later, specifically the index number appended to the end, to determine which action card is being hovered over. Its size is also set as we've seen before, and it is then push()'d onto the DuelingCards.actionCards array. Next, it's appended to the DOM and positioned at the same location as the dealer stack image. Note that it has a lower z-index value than does the dealer's stack image, so all these card images will be obscured by the dealer's stack image (which is what you'd want since these cards will be showing face values rather than the back of the card as the stack image does). Finally, we create a new Ext.dd.DropZone() object wrapped around the <img> element in the DOM so that we can drop draggable objects here later.

The opponent and player cards are both created similarly, although the math behind determining the X location is a little different since we want the five cards, plus the image stack, to be centered on the screen. The only other difference is that the player cards are draggable, so the last line of their creation is:

```
new Ext.dd.DDProxy("playerCard_" + i);
```

This makes the <img> draggable, just as we need them to be. So, have a look at the code if for no other reason than to see how the horizontal positioning is done. You'll find it's all, once again, just like what you've seen here.

IndicatorsCode.js

Our next stop is the IndicatorsCode.js file, which contains two methods. The first is createAndPositionIndicators(), which is called from init() and whose job is to create the <img> elements for all the indicators and position them properly. The first task it performs is to figure out the X location of the first indicator on the left, as a starting point to base all the others off of, and to calculate the Y location where all the indicators will be. Here's that code:

```
var startX = (DuelingCards.viewSize.width -
  (DuelingCards.imageSizes.card.widthWithPadding *
  DuelingCards.numActionCards)) / 2;
var upArrowY =
  ((DuelingCards.viewSize.height - DuelingCards.imageSizes.card.height) / 2) -
    DuelingCards.imageSizes.arrowIndicator.width;
var suitChangeYTop = upArrowY -
  DuelingCards.imageSizes.suitChangeIndicator.height - 4;
var downArrowY =
  ((DuelingCards.viewSize.height - DuelingCards.imageSizes.card.height) / 2) +
  DuelingCards.imageSizes.card.height;
var suitChangeYBottom = downArrowY +
    DuelingCards.imageSizes.arrowIndicator.height + 4;
```

The startX variable is again just some centering logic, but this time it takes into account the number of action cards there are so that the entire group of them will be centered. It uses the `DuelingCards.imageSizes.card.widthWithPadding` field to account for a bit of space between the cards. Since the indicators are horizontally centered on each action card, this is the proper metric to use.

The Y locations are different depending on whether you're talking about the up arrows on the top of the cards (upArrowY) or the suit change icon when there's an up arrow by a card (suitChangeYTop), a down arrow below a card (downArrayY), or a suit change icon when there's a down arrow by a card (suitChangeYBottom). I think the math for all of these should be fairly self-explanatory, except perhaps for the number four pertaining to the suit change icons. This is simply an arbitrary number of pixels between the top or bottom of an arrow indicator and the suit change icon, to avoid them bunching up on the screen in an ugly way.

Once those values are calculated, the images themselves can be created, and this is done inside a loop:

```
for (var i = 0; i < DuelingCards.numActionCards; i++) {

  var img = new Ext.Element(document.createElement("img"));
  img.set({
    src : DuelingCards.images.pixelOfDestiny.getAttributeNS("", "src"),
    id : "upArrowIndicator_" + i
  });
  img.setSize(DuelingCards.imageSizes.arrowIndicator.width,
    DuelingCards.imageSizes.arrowIndicator.height);
  DuelingCards.contentEl.appendChild(img);
  img.position("absolute", 1, startX +
    (DuelingCards.imageSizes.card.widthWithPadding * i) +
      ((DuelingCards.imageSizes.card.width -
      DuelingCards.imageSizes.arrowIndicator.width) / 2),
    upArrowY);

  img = new Ext.Element(document.createElement("img"));
  img.set({
    src : DuelingCards.images.pixelOfDestiny.getAttributeNS("", "src"),
    id : "downArrowIndicator_" + i
  });
  img.setSize(DuelingCards.imageSizes.arrowIndicator.width,
    DuelingCards.imageSizes.arrowIndicator.height);
  DuelingCards.contentEl.appendChild(img);
  img.position("absolute", 1, startX +
    (DuelingCards.imageSizes.card.widthWithPadding * i) +
      ((DuelingCards.imageSizes.card.width -
      DuelingCards.imageSizes.arrowIndicator.width) / 2),
    downArrowY);
}
```

As you can see, there's a block of code for creating the next up arrow indicator and the next suit change indicator above an up arrow. There are two other blocks of similar code in this loop, one for creating the next down arrow and one for the next suit change indicator below a down arrow. To save space, I left them out here because they're not much different.

By this point you've seen a bunch of code like this already, so there's probably not much to be gained by going through it. But read through it on your own and make sure it all makes sense to you before continuing.

The next method in this source file is drawActionCardIndicators(). This method is called whenever one of the set of indicators around an action card needs to change and be updated on the screen:

```
for (var i = 0; i < DuelingCards.numActionCards; i++) {

  var card = DuelingCards.actionCards[i];
  if (inWhichToChange == null || inWhichToChange == i) {
    card.singleOrDouble = DuelingCards.genRandom(0, 1) == 0 ? "1" : "2";
    card.upOrDown = DuelingCards.genRandom(0, 1) == 0 ? "up" : "down";
    card.suitChangeable = DuelingCards.genRandom(0, 1) == 0 ? false : true;
  }

  Ext.get("upArrowIndicator_" + i).set({
    src : DuelingCards.images.pixelOfDestiny.getAttributeNS("", "src")
  });
  Ext.get("downArrowIndicator_" + i).set({
    src : DuelingCards.images.pixelOfDestiny.getAttributeNS("", "src")
  });
  Ext.get("topSuitChangeIndicator_" + i).set({
    src : DuelingCards.images.pixelOfDestiny.getAttributeNS("", "src")
  });
  Ext.get("bottomSuitChangeIndicator_" + i).set({
    src : DuelingCards.images.pixelOfDestiny.getAttributeNS("", "src")
  });

  var arrow = Ext.get("upArrowIndicator_" + i);
  if (card.upOrDown == "down") {
    arrow = Ext.get("downArrowIndicator_" + i);
  }
  arrow.set({
    src :
      DuelingCards.images[card.upOrDown + card.singleOrDouble].getAttributeNS(
        "", "src")
  });
```

```
  if (card.suitChangeable) {
    var suitChangeIndicator = null;
    if (card.upOrDown == "up") {
      suitChangeIndicator = Ext.get("topSuitChangeIndicator_" + i);
    } else {
      suitChangeIndicator = Ext.get("bottomSuitChangeIndicator_" + i);
    }
    suitChangeIndicator.set({
      src : DuelingCards.images["suits_change"].getAttributeNS("", "src")
    });
  }

}
```

First, a loop is begun, where each iteration will affect one of the action cards. With each iteration of that loop, we get a reference to the appropriate cardDescriptor from the DuelingCards.actionCards array. Next, we determine if this method passed a card number to update. If it was, then only that card is going to be updated. This accounts for the situation where a valid drop is made by the player or opponent and just that one action card needs to be replaced and the indicators changed. If null is passed in—which happens when the game starts up, for example—all of the indicators need to be changed. So, in either case, if this card is to be changed, we use a little utility method that we'll see when we look at DuelingCards.js called genRandom(). This method simply generates a random number between two defined values. So, the card.singleOrDouble field randomly gets a value of 1 or 2, the card.upOrDown field gets a value of up or down using some trinary logic, and the card.suitChangeable field gets a value of true or false.

The next step is to prepare for setting the appropriate image by clearing any existing images. This is done by setting the src attribute of each of the indicators around the current card being worked on to the src attribute of the preloaded Pixel of Destiny image. This is necessary to avoid double-indicators around cards. (Say a single up arrow is on the card now and randomly it was determined that there should now be a double down arrow; the single up arrow would still be set.) Keep in mind that all the indicator <img> elements are always visible on the page; it's just that some of them are showing transparent GIFs rather than actual indicators.

Once that's done, we set the appropriate arrow image. The code starts by assuming it's an up arrow and so gets a reference to the appropriate <img> element. If it's actually a down arrow, then the reference is overridden with a reference to the down arrow <img>. Next, the set() method is used to set the src attribute to that of the appropriate preloaded image.

Once the arrow is done, the last step is to similarly set the appropriate image for the suit change indicator. This is only done if card.suitChangeable is true; otherwise, the indicator <img> is already showing the Pixel of Destiny, so there's nothing to do.

MenuCode.js

Next we'll examine the menu code. What does the menu look like, you ask? See Figure 8-7 for the answer.

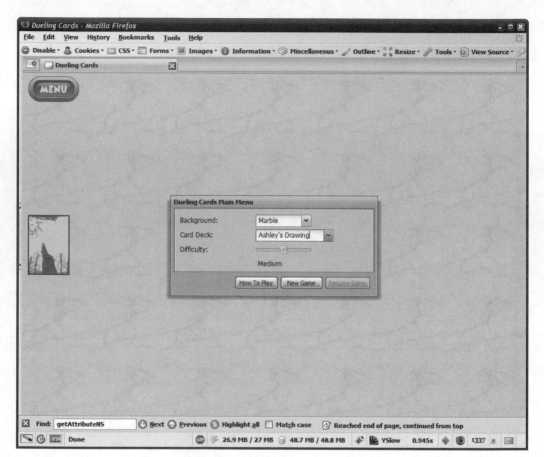

Figure 8-7. *The main menu as it initially appears*

The code behind the menu is actually one of the few places where you'll find rather mundane and altogether plain Ext JS code! It's the type of stuff you've seen tons of times before, beginning with the `setupMenu()` method:

```
var menu = new Ext.Element(document.createElement("img"));
menu.set({
  src : DuelingCards.images.menu0.getAttributeNS("", "src"),
  style : "cursor:pointer"
});
menu.setSize(DuelingCards.imageSizes.menuButton.width,
  DuelingCards.imageSizes.menuButton.height);
```

```
DuelingCards.contentEl.appendChild(menu);
menu.position("absolute", 99, 5, 5);
menu.addListener("mouseover", function() {
  if (DuelingCards.initComplete) {
    this.set({ src : DuelingCards.images.menu1.getAttributeNS("", "src") });
  }
});
menu.addListener("mouseout", function() {
  if (DuelingCards.initComplete) {
    this.set({ src : DuelingCards.images.menu0.getAttributeNS("", "src") });
  }
});
menu.addListener("click", function() {

  if (DuelingCards.initComplete) {
    if (DuelingCards.images.title1.isVisible()) {
      DuelingCards.images.title1.puff({ duration : 1 });
      DuelingCards.images.title2.puff({ duration : 1 });
      DuelingCards.images.title3.puff({
        duration : 1, callback : DuelingCards.showMenu
      });
    } else {
      DuelingCards.showMenu();
    }
  }
});
```

First, the menu button <img> is created in much the same way as we've seen before. This time, however, the addListener() method is used twice. The first time it is used to add a mouseover event handler. When this event fires, the src attribute of the <img> is changed to point to the preloaded menu1 image cached in the DuelingCards.images object. This makes it red with yellow lettering to give a nice active look to it. The mouseout event handler, which is the second time addListener() is used, resets the src attribute to the original menu0 image src value.

A click handler is also attached (which it would have to be; otherwise this button wouldn't do anything!). When the button is clicked, we check to see if initialization has completed by interrogating the DuelingCards.initComplete field. This field is set to true at the end of the init() method, so this keeps the user from prematurely clicking the button and showing the menu. In point of fact, the mouseover and mouseout event handlers perform the same check for the same reason.

Assuming initialization is complete, another check is performed to see if the first title image, referenced in the DuelingCards.images.title1 field, is visible. This is determined by using the isVisible() method supplied by the Ext.Element wrapper. If it's true, then we need to first get rid of the title. We do this by calling the puff() method on all three of the title images. The puff effect is a really nice effect that gives the appearance of a puff of smoke vanishing. So, all three title graphics simultaneously, over the course of one second, expand a bit and fade out at the same time.

The third title image has a callback handler attached that calls the DuelingCards.showMenu() method when the effect completes. If the title wasn't showing in the first place, then that method is called directly instead of applying the effect, which accounts for the menu being shown a subsequent time.

The next method in this source file is showMenu(), and this is where that boring old Ext JS code comes into play. In fact, it's so boring (and fairly long) that I'm not going to print it all here; otherwise, you'd be reading through about six straight pages of code. Instead, bring it up in your favorite text editor and follow along, and I'll call out bits and pieces of it as necessary.

The first block of code you'll find is this:

```
if (DuelingCards.gameInProgress) {
  DuelingCards.gamePaused = true;
  DuelingCards.workerPool.sendMessage({
    msg : "game_paused"
  }, DuelingCards.opponentWorker);
}
```

Setting the gamePaused field to true when a game is currently in progress allows code downstream to temporarily turn itself off, the background player code specifically, as we'll see. Once that's done, we need to inform that background Gears Worker that the game has paused because, as you'll recall, the Worker can't see the gamePaused field. So, we use the sendMessage() method of the created WorkerPool to send the "game_paused" message to the Worker referenced by the DuelingCards.opponentWorker field. Don't worry about the details of what this does now; we'll be looking at that code in a moment.

After that, we attempt to get a reference to the Window with the ID menuWindow by using the usual Ext.getCmp() method. If the Window exists, we simply call show() on it, but if it doesn't exist, then it needs to be created.

The Window is defined just like all the others you've already seen. One interesting thing is that it has a beforeshow event handler attached:

```
beforeshow : function() {
  Ext.getCmp("menuForm").getForm().setValues({
    pageBackground : DuelingCards.pageBackground,
    cardDeck : DuelingCards.cDeck
  });
  if (DuelingCards.gameInProgress) {
    Ext.getCmp("resumeGameButton").setDisabled(false);
  }
}
```

The pageBackground and cardDeck form fields are the two ComboBoxes that allow the user to change the page background image or the style of card deck they want to use. The values of those form fields are set to whatever the current values are so that they reflect reality. Also, the resumeGameButton is enabled when a game is in progress.

Three Buttons are then defined, one of which is the How to Play Button (the other two are the New Game and Resume Game Buttons, which we will discuss in a moment). Let's look at the handler function defined for the How to Play button:

```
if (DuelingCards.howToPlayShowing) {
  DuelingCards.howToPlayShowing = false;
  var w = Ext.getCmp("menuWindow");
  w.setPosition(w.getPosition()[0], w.getPosition()[1] + 110);
  w.setHeight(180);
} else {
  DuelingCards.howToPlayShowing = true;
  var w = Ext.getCmp("menuWindow");
  w.setPosition(w.getPosition()[0], w.getPosition()[1] - 110);
  w.setHeight(400);
}
```

The menu `Window` looks like Figure 8-8 when the How to Play instructions are visible, and it's a direct result of the `else` branch executing.

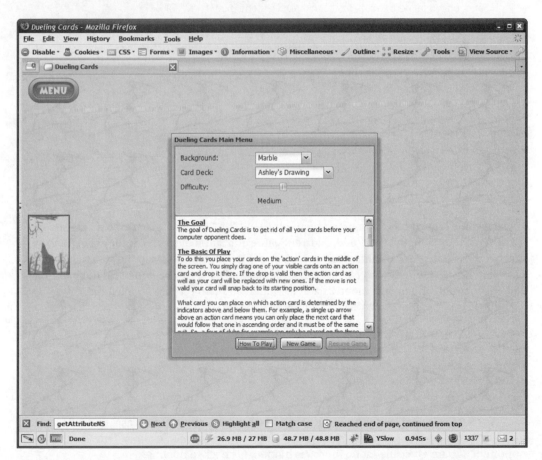

Figure 8-8. *The main menu as it appears when How to Play instructions are being viewed*

As you can see, the height of the `Window` expands to allow the instructions to be displayed. If that's all we did, though, the `Window` wouldn't now be centered on the page; it would be down, quite possibly cut off on the bottom, and that just wouldn't be cool. So, the else branch gets a reference to the Window, adjusts its size to allow for the area where the instructions are, and then moves the Window up 110 pixels, which allows it to remain centered. The if branch handles the case where the How to Play Button is clicked when the instructions are currently showing. In that case, the Window is resized to its original size, which effectively hides the instructions because it gets clipped by the bottom of the Window's main content area. The Window's vertical position is also reset.

The New Game Button is defined next. Its handler function looks like this:

```
if (DuelingCards.gameInProgress) {
  Ext.MessageBox.show({
    animEl : "divSource",
    buttons : Ext.MessageBox.YESNO, closable : false,
    msg : "There is a game in progress.  Click YES to abort it " +
      "and begin a new game, or click NO to continue the " +
      "game in progress", title : "Start new game?",
    fn : function(inButtonID) {
      Ext.getCmp("menuWindow").hide();
      if (inButtonID == "yes") {
        DuelingCards.startGame();
      }
    }
  });
} else {
  Ext.getCmp("menuWindow").hide();
  DuelingCards.startGame();
}
```

If a game is currently in progress, then our friend Mr. Ext.MessageBox.show() is used to ask users if they want to abandon the current game and start a new one. If they click the Yes button, the menu Window is hidden and startGame() is called, which is in the source file we'll be looking at next. If they click No, the MessageBox simply goes away—no harm done. If no game is in progress, then the menu Window is hidden and startGame() is called right away.

The Resume Game Button is next; here's its handler:

```
DuelingCards.gamePaused = false;
DuelingCards.workerPool.sendMessage({
  msg : "game_resumed"
}, DuelingCards.opponentWorker);
Ext.getCmp("menuWindow").hide();
```

This Button is enabled only when a game is in progress. If that's the case, then all we need to do is flip the gamePaused flag back to false, and send the "game_resumed" message to the opponent Worker. Once the menu Window is hidden, it's back to dueling!

After the Buttons are defined, there are a couple of form field definitions. We have two ComboBoxes and a Slider, which is something new. Let's start with the ComboBoxes first. We'll just look at one, since the other is very similar. Here's the ComboBox for selecting a page background:

```
{ xtype : "combo", width : 100, editable : false, border : false,
  triggerAction : "all", mode : "local", valueField : "val",
  displayField : "disp", name : "pageBackground",
  fieldLabel : "Background", store : new Ext.data.SimpleStore({
    fields : ["val", "disp"], data : [
      [ "goldRuffles", "Gold Ruffles" ],
      [ "grey", "Grey" ],
      [ "marble", "Marble" ],
      [ "party", "Party" ],
      [ "sky", "Sky" ]
    ]
  }),
  listeners : {
    select : function(inComboBox, inRecord, inIndex) {
      DuelingCards.pageBackground = inRecord.get("val");
      Ext.getBody().setStyle("background-image",
        "url('img/pageBacks/" + DuelingCards.pageBackground +
        ".gif')");
    }
  }
}
```

This is a pretty typical ComboBox definition, although having the data inline like this is something a bit different. A SimpleStore is created as part of the ComboBox definition, and the data attribute passed as part of its config object contains the actual items to be displayed. The fields attribute defines the names of the fields—that is, the names assigned to each element of the data array—which allows us to reference them via the usual valueField and displayField attributes.

The listeners object contains a select event handler. When an item is selected, we need to update the background-image style attribute of the body of the document and point it to the newly selected image.

As I mentioned, the card deck image ComboBox is pretty similar to this. When an item is selected there, however, the card stack images that we have a reference to in the DuelingCards.images object are updated to point to the selected preloaded image.

The difficulty Slider is the next form field, and this is the first time we've seen a Slider in action. There's not really much to know about it. Have a look for yourself:

```
{ xtype : "slider", fieldLabel : "Difficulty", width : 100,
  value : 2, increment : 1, minValue : 1, maxValue : 3,
  isFormField : true,
  listeners : {
    change : function(inSlider, inValue) {
      var dt = Ext.getCmp("difficultyText");
      switch (inValue) {
        case 1:
          dt.setValue("Easy");
        break;
```

```
        case 2:
          dt.setValue("Medium");
        break;
        case 3:
          dt.setValue("Hard");
        break;
      }
    }
  }
}
```

The `increment` attribute tells the `Slider` how much change in its value there is for each tick of the slider. The `minValue` and `maxValue` define the lower and upper bounds of the `Slider`'s value, and the `value` attribute defines its initial value. This game provides three difficulty levels—easy, medium, and hard—so there are just three ticks on this `Slider`. Each time the value of the `Slider` is changed, its `change` event fires, and we have a handler set up for that. Its job is to update the `TextField` right below the `Slider` to display a textual representation of its value.

■**Note** The `Slider` isn't by default a form field, which means it won't recognize the `fieldLabel` attribute and the `Slider` would actually appear where the field label should be. To make it work as a form field, you have to provide the `isFormField` attribute set to `true` in its config object.

Speaking of the `TextField`, that's actually a bit interesting. Let's have a look:

```
{ xtype : "textfield", readOnly:true, fieldLabel : " ",
  style : "background:#dfe8f6;border:0px solid #ffffff",
  labelSeparator : " ", id : "difficultyText",
  value : "Medium" }
```

My goal was to put the difficulty text right below the `Slider`, which turned out to not be as straightforward as you might think. In order to do it I used a `TextField` set up in such a way that you can't tell it's a `TextField`. Specifically, this means making sure `readOnly` is set to true, that the `fieldLabel` is a blank string (but using the HTML nonbreaking space entity so that it's still displaying *something* for a field label), setting the background color to match the background of the `Window`, making sure it has no border, and finally specifying a blank space for the `labelSeparator` too. The effect is you just see plain old text below the `Slider`, just like I wanted—you can't tell it's a `TextField`.

The last item in this `Window` is a simple `Panel` that contains a boatload of text via its `html` attribute. This provides the How to Play instructions. The `autoScroll` attribute is set on this `Panel` to true, and its background color is set to white, but otherwise it's nothing but a plain `Panel`.

DuelingCards.js

The DuelingCards.js file contains what could rightfully be called the main set of methods for this project. It contains a number of utility methods that support the rest of the methods, and it encapsulates much of the core game logic, aside from the opponent's code.

Starting a New Game

The first method you find as you look at this source file is startGame(). Of course, this will only be executed if a game isn't in progress, or if the user decided to start a new game when presented with the prompt shown in Figure 8-9.

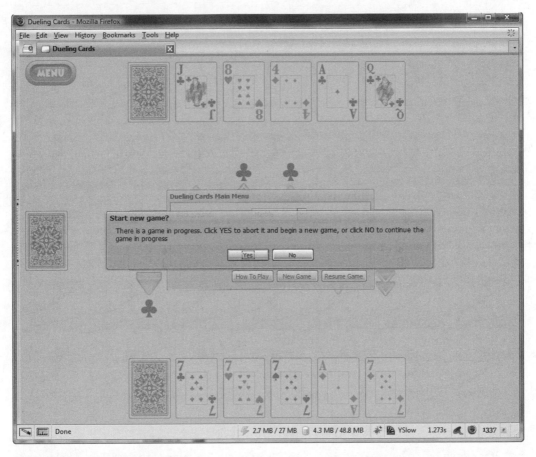

Figure 8-9. *Dueling Cards in action*

Let's step through the startGame() method:

```
Ext.get("imgPlayerStack").show();
Ext.get("imgOpponentStack").show();
Ext.get("imgDealerStack").show();
for (var i = 0; i < DuelingCards.numActionCards; i++) {
  try {
    Ext.get("upArrowIndicator_" + i).show();
    Ext.get("downArrowIndicator_" + i).show();
    Ext.get("topSuitChangeIndicator_" + i).show();
    Ext.get("bottomSuitChangeIndicator_" + i).show();
    DuelingCards.actionCards[i].elem.show();
    DuelingCards.opponentCards[i].elem.show();
    DuelingCards.playerCards[i].elem.show();
  } catch (e) {
    // Squelch exceptions since we know they might occur and it's fine.
  }
}
```

The first task is to ensure that all our images are showing because many of them would be hidden to start with. So, first the player and opponent's stack images are shown, which is a simple matter of getting a reference to them via a call to Ext.get(), then calling the show() method on them (Ext.get() returns an Ext.Element object, remember). Then we start a for loop that iterates for the number of action cards specified by DuelingCards.numActionCards. Within this loop we show all the arrow indicators, all the suit change indicators, all the action cards, and all the player and opponent's visible cards. This is all wrapped in a try…catch block, though, specifically because of the player and opponent cards. The value of DuelingCards.numActionCards is 6, but there are only five visible player and opponent cards, so this loop would throw an exception. So, we catch that exception and simply ignore it. This is basically a lazy way to write this code so that we don't need two additional loops, one for the player's cards and one for the opponent's cards, that have the appropriate terminator values. We don't need to build logic into this loop, either. It's perhaps a little lazy, but it makes the code more compact.

The code then hides the images for winning and losing the game, which is done if a game has just ended and the user is starting a new one.

Next, the difficulty setting the user chose is retrieved:

```
var dForm = Ext.getCmp("menuForm").getForm().getValues();
var selectedDifficulty = dForm.difficultyText.toLowerCase();
```

It is converted to lowercase because we're retrieving the value of the TextField below the Slider, which has the difficulty level in proper capitalization, so lowercasing it ensures our comparisons work properly.

Next, we send a message to the opponent Worker thread via the WorkerPool.sendMessage() method. The message sent is "start_game", and it also includes the difficulty level, since the Worker code needs to know that in order to configure itself, as we'll see.

Next, the DuelingCards.gameInProgress flag is set to true and DuelingCards.gamePaused is set to false.

Generating a "Shuffled" Deck of Cards

After that, the genDecks() method is called, which we'll actually jump ahead to right now:

```
DuelingCards.dealerStack = new Array();
for (var i = 0; i < 4; i++) {
  var choosen = new Array(54);
  var cardCount = 0;
  while (cardCount < 54) {
    var nextNumber = DuelingCards.genRandom(1, 54);
    if (!choosen[nextNumber]) {
      choosen[nextNumber] = true;
      var card = DuelingCards.createCardDescriptor();
      if (nextNumber >= 1 && nextNumber <= 13) {
        card.suit = "clubs";
        card.faceValue = nextNumber + 1;
      } else if (nextNumber >= 14 && nextNumber <= 26) {
        card.suit = "diamonds";
        card.faceValue = nextNumber - 12;
      } else if (nextNumber >= 27 && nextNumber <= 39) {
        card.suit = "hearts";
        card.faceValue = nextNumber - 25;
      } else if (nextNumber >= 40 && nextNumber <= 52) {
        card.suit = "spades";
        card.faceValue = nextNumber - 38;
      } else if (nextNumber >= 53 && nextNumber <= 54) {
        card.suit = "joker";
        card.faceValue = 2;
      }
      DuelingCards.dealerStack.push(card);
      cardCount = cardCount + 1;
    }
  }
}
```

The job of this method is to create four full decks of cards and "shuffle" them together. So, a new array is instantiated, and we start a loop from 0 to 3. Each tick of the loop creates another array to store the cards that have already been chosen. We also create a variable cardCount that will keep tabs on how many cards have been selected from the current deck being shuffled. While cardCount is less than 54, we call the genRandom() method to choose a number between 1 and 54, the number of cards in the deck (the usual 52 plus 2 jokers). Then, we look up in the chosen array to see if that card has already been chosen. If it has, then another will be chosen since cardCount won't be incremented with this iteration. If it hasn't been chosen, though, we enter a big if statement to determine the suit of the card.

Think of a deck of cards. You have four suits, and within each suit you have 13 cards. Therefore, each group of 13 that you can count off starting from 1 to 52 marks a suit change boundary. Put another way, the cards numbered 1–13 are clubs, 14–26 are diamonds, 27–39 are hearts, and 40–52 are spades. That leaves 53–54, which are the jokers. That's what the big if statement determines.

A cardDescriptor is created out of this with the suit and faceValue set accordingly, and the cardDescriptor is appended to the end of the DuelingCards.dealerStack array. The value of cardCount is incremented, and the loop continues. When four of these loop iterations have completed, we've got ourselves four decks of cards' worth of cardDescriptors, all nicely randomized.

Speaking of randomizing, let's take a quick peek at that genRandom() method we've referred to a couple of times. As it happens, it's literally a single line of code:

```
return Math.floor((inMax - (inMin - 1)) * Math.random()) + inMin;
```

This is a pretty typical piece of JavaScript for generating a random number in a given inclusive range refined by the inMin and inMax method arguments.

Starting a New Game Part Deux

Getting back to the startGame() method where we left off, the next bit of code you see after the call to genDecks() is this:

```
for (var i = 0; i < DuelingCards.numCardsDealt; i++) {
  DuelingCards.opponentStack.push(DuelingCards.dealerStack.shift());
  DuelingCards.playerStack.push(DuelingCards.dealerStack.shift());
}
```

From the dealer's stack of cards we take some number of cards, 30 actually, as defined by the DuelingCards.numCardsDealt field, and move them over to the array for the opponent and player. The shift() method removes the first item off the dealerStack array and returns it, and this returned cardDescriptor object is then push()'d onto the arrays for the opponent and player.

Following that, the DuelingCards.playerCardsRemaining and DuelingCards.opponentCardsRemaining fields are set to DuelingCards.numCardsDealt so that we can examine these values and determine when either the player or the opponent has won the game.

Finally, this code executes:

```
DuelingCards.dealerStackImgClick();
DuelingCards.playerStackImgClick();
DuelingCards.opponentStackImgClick();
```

These three methods are called when one of the stack images is clicked to show the next five cards for the player or opponent, or to deal six new action cards off the dealer's stack. In the case of the opponent's stack image, literally clicking the image does nothing, but for the sake of consistent naming I created an opponentStackImgClick() method anyway, which does the same thing as if the image were actually clickable.

Dealing New Action Cards

The `dealerStackImgClick()` method is the next one you find, and it's the one responsible for dealing six new action cards. This method begins with a quick check:

```
if (!DuelingCards.gameInProgress) { return; }
```

Obviously if a game isn't in progress, then clicking the dealer's stack image shouldn't do anything, and this takes care of that.

If a game is in progress, this code is executed:

```
for (var i = 0; i < DuelingCards.numActionCards; i++) {
  if (DuelingCards.actionCards[i].suit &&
    DuelingCards.actionCards[i].faceValue) {
    var card = DuelingCards.createCardDescriptor();
    card.suit = DuelingCards.actionCards[i].suit;
    card.faceValue = DuelingCards.actionCards[i].faceValue;
    DuelingCards.dealerStack.push(card);
  }
  DuelingCards.dealActionCard(i);
}
DuelingCards.drawActionCardIndicators();
```

We have a loop that goes for six iterations, as defined by `DuelingCards.numActionCards`. With each tick of the loop we examine the action card that is currently visible. If it has a `suit` and `faceValue`, then that action card is still in play—that is, the player or opponent hasn't made a valid drop on it, so it's going to need to be returned to the bottom of the dealer's stack. The trick here, however, is that we have a `cardDescriptor` for each of the visible action cards, so if we were to put that object onto the dealer's stack array, we'd no longer have a `cardDescriptor` for the visible action card! Therefore, we create a new `cardDescriptor` and copy its `suit` and `faceValue` fields over from the existing action card. Then, it is *that* new object that is `push()`'d onto the dealer's stack array.

Next, a call is made to `dealActionCard()`, passing in the number of the action card being worked on this loop iteration. This method, yet to come, deals a new action card to replace the specified one. Finally, since all six action cards are being replaced in this case, we need to randomly choose new indicators around all of them and update the graphics on the screen, which is the job of the `drawActionCardIndicators()` method that we saw earlier.

The last step this method has to perform is to inform the opponent `Worker` about the new action cards. Since the `Worker` doesn't share state with this code, it can't see the `DuelingCards.actionCards` array that it needs to. We therefore have to send a message and tell it exactly what the action cards now are:

```
var ac = new Array();
for (var i = 0; i < DuelingCards.actionCards.length; i++) {
  ac.push({
    suit : DuelingCards.actionCards[i].suit,
    faceValue : DuelingCards.actionCards[i].faceValue,
```

```
      singleOrDouble : DuelingCards.actionCards[i].singleOrDouble,
      upOrDown : DuelingCards.actionCards[i].upOrDown,
      suitChangeable : DuelingCards.actionCards[i].suitChangeable
    });
  }
DuelingCards.workerPool.sendMessage({
  msg : "update_action_cards", actionCards : ac
}, DuelingCards.opponentWorker);
```

Simply passing a reference to the DuelingCards.actionCards array won't work, nor will passing a new array containing the cardDescriptors from DuelingCards.actionCards because, again, that would constitute sharing state. Therefore, we have to create a new array that contains copies of the action card's cardDescriptors. Once we build that array it's a simple matter of sending a message to the Worker, passing in the array.

Dealing New Player Cards

When the player's card stack is clicked, the playerStackImgClick() method is called. It's a lot simpler than the dealer's version of this method. It begins with the same check of gameInProgress that we saw earlier; then this bit of code follows:

```
for (var i = 0; i < DuelingCards.numPlayerOpponentCards; i++) {
  DuelingCards.dealPlayerOpponentCard("player", i);
}
```

Here, all we need to do is call the dealPlayerOpponentCard() method, passing in whether we're dealing from the player's or the opponent's deck, and which card is being dealt. Doing this call five times, as defined by DuelingCards.numPlayerOpponentCards, results in five new cards from the player's stack being shown.

Dealing a New Action Card

Earlier I referred to the dealActionCard() method that was used when the dealer's stack image was clicked. This replaces one of the action cards with the next card on the dealer's stack. This method is as follows:

```
var yPosition = (DuelingCards.viewSize.height -
  DuelingCards.imageSizes.card.height) / 2;
```

The first step is to determine the vertical position the card will be placed at. This is the same centering code we've seen many times before. After that comes this code:

```
var card = DuelingCards.actionCards[inCardNumber];
var cardType = DuelingCards.dealerStack.shift();
card.suit = cardType.suit;
card.faceValue = cardType.faceValue;
card.elem.set({ src :
  DuelingCards.images[card.suit][card.faceValue-2].getAttributeNS("", "src")
});
```

This gets a reference to the appropriate `cardDescriptor` for the action card being updated, and then gets the next card off the dealer's stack via the `shift()` method. Then, the action card's `cardDescriptor`'s `suit` and `faceValue` fields are updated to match the card pulled from the stack. Finally, the `src` attribute of the underlying `<img>` element is updated to the appropriate image. The `DuelingCards.images` object has four elements, one for each of the suits, so we reference the appropriate one with array notation. Then array notation is again used to get the appropriate face value. Remember that each of these suit elements is a zero-based array, but the `faceValue` is a two-based value, so we need to subtract 2 from `faceValue` to get the appropriate array index.

Next, we determine the horizontal position of the card:

```
var startX = (DuelingCards.viewSize.width -
  (DuelingCards.imageSizes.card.widthWithPadding *
  DuelingCards.numActionCards)) / 2;
```

This determines the starting X position of the first card, which we'll base the position of this card off of, as you can see:

```
card.elem.position("absolute", 2, 10, DuelingCards.dealerStackY);
card.elem.moveTo(
  startX + (DuelingCards.imageSizes.card.widthWithPadding * inCardNumber),
  yPosition,
  { duration : .5 + (inCardNumber * ..5) }
);
```

The card is positioned at the same place as the dealer's stack image, but then the `moveTo()` method is used, which provides an animated movement from the current position of an element to a specified position. The specified position in this case is the `startX` value, plus the width of a card (with padding) times the number of the action card being updated. That, plus the previously calculated Y position value, gives the `moveTo()` method the appropriate destination coordinates. The duration of the animation is calculated based on which card is being updated. The cards further from the dealer's stack image take just a little longer to arrive, which is physically consistent with a real person dealing cards.

Dealing a New Card for the Player or Opponent

The `dealPlayerOpponentCard()` method is called when a valid drop has been made, or when the player's stack image is clicked, or when the game code simulates clicking the opponent's stack image. Its job is to take the next card off the player's or opponent's stack and replace the specified visible card with it.

So, the first step is to get a reference to the `cardDescriptor` of the visible card:

```
var card = DuelingCards[inWhich + "Cards"][inCardNumber];
```

The `inWhich` variable is a method argument that will have a value of either `player` or `opponent`. So, array notation is used to access the appropriate array within the `DuelingCards` namespace, and then it's just plain old array access to get the right `cardDescriptor`.

Next, we have to deal with one edge condition:

```
if (DuelingCards[inWhich + "Stack"].length == 0) {
  card.elem.hide();
  return;
}
```

If there are no cards left on the player or opponent's stack, then we're almost done here. The only thing left to do is to hide the card image instead of changing its image since this essentially means the game is over and we don't want the last card hanging around on the screen!

Assuming there's at least one card left to be dealt, though, we next determine where this card will be on the screen:

```
var startX = ((DuelingCards.viewSize.width -
  (DuelingCards.imageSizes.card.widthWithPadding *
  DuelingCards.numActionCards)) / 2) +
  DuelingCards.imageSizes.card.widthWithPadding;
var yPosition = null;
if (inWhich == "player") {
  yPosition = DuelingCards.viewSize.height -
    DuelingCards.imageSizes.card.height - 10;
} else {
  yPosition = 10;
}
```

The horizontal position is the same old boring calculation that we've seen before. The vertical position is different depending on the value of inWhich. We always want the card to be 10 pixels from the top of the screen for the opponent's cards or 10 pixels from the bottom of the screen for the player's cards, as you can see in Figure 8-10. That's the reason for the if block. For the opponent's cards, the else block, it's just a static value, but for the player's cards we have to base it off the height of the browser viewport, which we cached earlier in the DuelingCards.viewSize object.

Next, we have to (possibly) put the current card on the bottom of the stack:

```
if (card.suit && card.faceValue) {
  var savedCard = DuelingCards.createCardDescriptor();
  savedCard.suit = card.suit;
  savedCard.faceValue = card.faceValue;
  DuelingCards[inWhich + "Stack"].push(savedCard);
}
```

If the current cardDescriptor has a suit and faceValue, then it's still in play, which happens when the player clicks their stack image. In that case, we make a copy of the cardDescriptor, for the reasons previously discussed, and push() it onto the stack array. If this method was called as the result of a valid drop, then the cardDescriptor will have null values for suit and faceValue and it won't be put back on the stack.

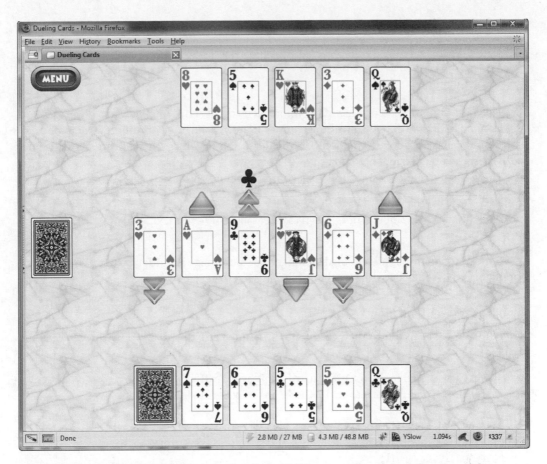

Figure 8-10. *Notice the spacing between the player and opponent cards and the edge of the screen.*

Now we have to get the next card off the stack:

```
var nextCard = DuelingCards[inWhich + "Stack"].shift();
card.suit = nextCard.suit;
card.faceValue = nextCard.faceValue;
card.elem.set({ src :
  DuelingCards.images[card.suit][card.faceValue-2].getAttributeNS("", "src")
});
```

The shift() method gets the first item from the array, and we then take its suit and faceValue and set it on the cardDescriptor for the visible card image. We also have to update the <img> src as necessary, and with the same sort of code we saw earlier.

Next, because we're trying to make a visually pleasing game here, we want to throw an animation in:

```
card.elem.show();
card.elem.position("absolute", 2,
  startX + (DuelingCards.imageSizes.card.widthWithPadding * inCardNumber),
  yPosition);
card.elem.slideIn();
```

The slideIn() method fires an effect where an element slides into view at a given location. All you need to do is ensure it's positioned appropriately, using the coordinates calculated earlier, and call the slideIn() method. The default duration values and such are perfectly fine in this case, so no need for any of that.

There's just one more minor task to accomplish before we leave this method:

```
if (DuelingCards[inWhich + "Stack"].length == 0) {
  Ext.get("img" + Ext.util.Format.capitalize(inWhich) + "Stack").hide();
}
```

If there are no more cards to be dealt, then the stack image is hidden so the player (or opponent) knows they have only their visible cards left to get rid of.

Handling a Player Card Drop

When the player drops one of their cards onto an action card, the handlePlayerDrop() method is called:

```
var playerCard = DuelingCards.playerCards[inPlayerCardIndex];
var actionCard = DuelingCards.actionCards[inActionCardIndex];

if (DuelingCards.isValidDrop(playerCard, actionCard)) {
  DuelingCards.playerCardsRemaining = DuelingCards.playerCardsRemaining - 1;
  playerCard.suit = null;
  playerCard.faceValue = null;
  if (DuelingCards.playerCardsRemaining == 0) {
    playerCard.elem.hide();
    DuelingCards.doEndGame("win");
    return;
  }
  DuelingCards.dealActionCard(inActionCardIndex);
  DuelingCards.dealPlayerOpponentCard("player", inPlayerCardIndex);
  DuelingCards.drawActionCardIndicators(inActionCardIndex);
}
```

Into this method is passed two arguments: inPlayerCardIndex, which is the number of the player's card that was dropped (0–4) and inActionCardIndex, the number of the action card it was dropped on (0–5). From these we go get a reference to the appropriate cardDescriptor. Next, the isValidDrop() method is called, passing these cardDescriptors. We'll be looking at that method next, for now just know that it returned true if the drop is valid, false if not.

If the drop was valid, we decrement the count of player card remaining. Then, we set the suit and faceValue fields to null, and if you think back to the previous methods we've looked at you'll see that was a condition that was checked for to trigger certain code branches.

Next, we see if there are no cards remaining for the player. If so, then the card is hidden, and the doEndGame() method is called, passing it a value win to indicate the player win graphic should be shown. In this situation, the method terminates.

If the player hasn't yet won, we need to deal a new action card to replace the one that was just matched by calling dealActionCard() and passing it the number of the card to replace. We then deal a new card from the player's stack to replace the one that was dropped by calling dealPlayerOpponentCard(). Finally we randomly draw new indicators around the new action card by calling drawActionCardIndicators().

Determining Player Drop Validity

As you just saw, the handlePlayerDrop() method needs to determine if a player card dropped on an action card is valid or not, so it calls isValidDrop(), which we'll look at now:

```
if (inDroppedCard.suit == "joker" || inActionCard.suit == "joker") {
  return true;
}
```

This first quick check handles the case where a joker is the card being dropped, or is the card being dropped on. In either case, the move is automatically valid so true is returned.

Barring that initial quick check, there's more work to be done:

```
var actionCardFaceValue = inActionCard.faceValue;
if (inActionCard.singleOrDouble == "1" && inActionCard.upOrDown == "up") {
  if (actionCardFaceValue == 14) { actionCardFaceValue = 1; }
  if (droppedCardFaceValue != (actionCardFaceValue + 1)) { return false; }
}
```

This first check deals with the case where the action card has a single up arrow above it. In this case, we have to essentially "normalize" the faceValue of the action card. The check, which is the last if statement, is very simple: increment the faceValue of the action card and see if it matches the dropped card's faceValue. The problem is, if the action card was an ace, then adding 1 to its value of 14 would result in 15, a value that isn't a valid faceValue. So, if the action card is an ace, then we change its faceValue to 1, which means that when the next if statement executes and increments it, it's a 2, which is the next card in sequence since we do a logical wrap-around from ace to 2 (or from 2 to ace if it was a down arrow). This sort of normalizing is done in the next couple of code blocks as well, and I'll skip the in-depth description in those cases.

The next case is for a double up arrow:

```
actionCardFaceValue = inActionCard.faceValue;
if (inActionCard.singleOrDouble == "2" && inActionCard.upOrDown == "up") {
  if (actionCardFaceValue == 13) { actionCardFaceValue = 0; }
  if (actionCardFaceValue == 14) { actionCardFaceValue = 1; }
  if (droppedCardFaceValue != (actionCardFaceValue + 2)) { return false; }
}
```

It's the same sort of logic, except that there's two "wrap-around" cases this time because a 2 is the next card in sequence for a king, and a 3 for an ace.

I'll save a few lines on the page here and tell you that there are two more code blocks that follow these that account for the down-arrow situations. They look and work just the same except that they're obviously doing subtractions rather than additions.

The final step is to deal with the suit of the cards. Remember that the method would have terminated already if the drop wasn't valid in terms of faceValue. Now, we check the suit, which is easy:

```
if (!inActionCard.suitChangeable && inActionCard.suit != inDroppedCard.suit) {
  return false;
}
```

If the suit change indicator isn't present, and if the suits of the dropped card and the action card don't match, then the move isn't valid; otherwise, it is.

The last line of this method returns true, which we'll only get to if all the validations were passed.

Ending the Game

As you saw in the handlePlayerDrop() method, when players use all their cards they win the game. This results in a call to doEndGame(), which displays the graphic shown in Figure 8-11.

The code for the doEndGame() method is as follows:

```
DuelingCards.gameInProgress = false;

Ext.get("imgPlayerStack").hide();
Ext.get("imgOpponentStack").hide();
Ext.get("imgDealerStack").hide();
for (var i = 0; i < DuelingCards.numActionCards; i++) {
  try {
    Ext.get("upArrowIndicator_" + i).hide();
    Ext.get("downArrowIndicator_" + i).hide();
    Ext.get("topSuitChangeIndicator_" + i).hide();
    Ext.get("bottomSuitChangeIndicator_" + i).hide();
    DuelingCards.actionCards[i].elem.hide();
    DuelingCards.opponentCards[i].elem.hide();
    DuelingCards.playerCards[i].elem.hide();
  } catch (e) {
    // Squelch exceptions since we know they might occur and it's fine.
  }
}

switch (inOutcome) {
  case "win":
    DuelingCards.images.win.fadeIn({ duration : 1 });
  break;
  case "lose":
    DuelingCards.images.lose.fadeIn({ duration : 1 });
  break;
}
```

Figure 8-11. *Your reward for a game well played… is it really worth it?*

First, we mark the game as being over by setting DuelingCards.gameInProgress to false. Next, we hide all three stack images. Then, all of the indicator images are hidden, along with all the player and opponent cards. We use the same sort of try…catch laziness we saw earlier to avoid having to write more code. Finally, we switch on the inOutcome value. If it's win, then we show the win image; otherwise, it's the depressing lose image. Just displaying it would be boring, so we instead use the fadeIn() method, which gradually, over the course of one second as specified, fades the graphic into view. That's all there is to it!

Showing the Title Sequence

The title sequence is a nice little animation sequence that obviously doesn't have the same impact on the printed page as on a real screen, but in Figure 8-12 you can see the final result of the sequence.

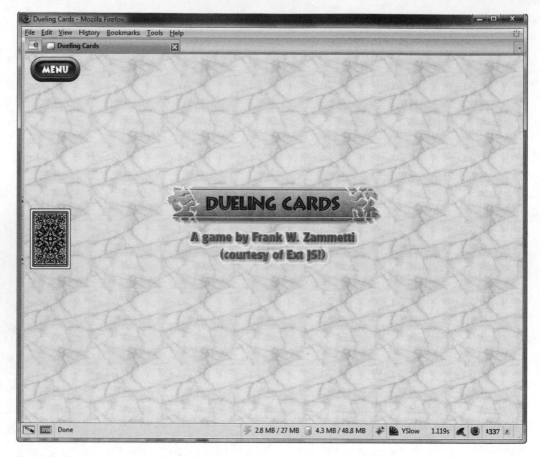

Figure 8-12. *Trust me, it looks much cooler on the screen!*

Earlier we saw how the three title graphics are created at a monstrous 5000×5000 pixel size, and I told you at that point that this sizing factors into how the title sequence works. Well, now it's time to see how, as implemented in the doTitle() method. That method goes a little somethin' like this:

```
var imgTitle1 = DuelingCards.images.title1;
var imgTitle2 = DuelingCards.images.title2;
var imgTitle3 = DuelingCards.images.title3;
```

Three variables are created that reference the images in the DuelingCards.images array for no other reason than I didn't feel like typing DuelingCards.images.title1 over and over again!

There are three lines of title graphics, and each of them starts out huge, as you know, and then shrinks down to its real size. These "shrinks" are done in sequence starting with the first graphic. Therefore, you're about to see three blocks of code, one for each of the graphics, beginning with this one:

```
imgTitle1.scale(DuelingCards.imageSizes.title1.width,
  DuelingCards.imageSizes.title1.height, { duration : 1 });
imgTitle1.moveTo(
  ((DuelingCards.viewSize.width - DuelingCards.imageSizes.title1.width) / 2),
  ((DuelingCards.viewSize.height -
    DuelingCards.imageSizes.title1.height) / 2) - 60,
  { duration : 1, callback : function() {
```

The scale()method does just what its name implies: it scales an image from its current size to the specified size. The specified size here is the real size of the graphic as defined in DuelingsCards.imageSizes.title1. This scaling finishes in one second's time.

Now, as the image is scaling, it also has to be moved to keep it centered on the screen. This can be rather hard to visualize, so as a quick exercise I suggest you modify this code by commenting out everything in this method after the first scale() call, and then load the page. You'll pretty quickly see the problem! So, the move() animation is set up to occur simultaneously with the scale() animation so that the image is continually shifted to keep it centered. I also subtract an arbitrary amount, 60, from the vertical position to pull up from the center of the page a bit. This is to account for the remaining two lines of the title because you want all three graphics *as a group* to be centered, not just each individual image.

The callback function then fires:

```
imgTitle2.show();
imgTitle2.scale(DuelingCards.imageSizes.title2.width,
  DuelingCards.imageSizes.title2.height,
  { duration : 1 });
imgTitle2.moveTo(
  ((DuelingCards.viewSize.width -
    DuelingCards.imageSizes.title2.width) / 2),
  ((DuelingCards.viewSize.height -
    DuelingCards.imageSizes.title2.height) / 2),
  { duration : 1, callback : function() {
```

As you can see, it's the same sort of thing we did for the first image. Here, however, the image is literally centered vertically on the page, which looks right when all three images are shown.

Speaking of the three images, here's the callback that fires the third image's appearance:

```
imgTitle3.show();
imgTitle3.scale(DuelingCards.imageSizes.title3.width,
  DuelingCards.imageSizes.title3.height,
  { duration : 1 });
imgTitle3.moveTo(
  ((DuelingCards.viewSize.width -
    DuelingCards.imageSizes.title3.width) / 2),
  ((DuelingCards.viewSize.height -
    DuelingCards.imageSizes.title3.height) / 2) + 30,
  { duration : 1, callback : function() {
      DuelingCards.initComplete = true;
```

Once again, it's the same basic idea, but this time the image is pushed down 30 pixels so it doesn't overlap the first or second images.

The `callback` here simply sets `initComplete` to `true` so that the rest of the code knows when it can react to user clicks, the menu button in particular.

And that, my friends, is how we do a cool little title animation with as little *real* work on our part as possible!

OpponentCode.js

The last source file we have to look at is `OpponentCode.js`, which is where all the code pertaining to our computerized component lives (well, *most* of it anyway). This is also where most of the Gears `Worker`/`WorkerPool` stuff is.

Constructing the Worker

The first thing you'll find when you open that file is the `initOpponent()` method, which as we saw earlier is called from the `init()` method. Here it comes now:

```
DuelingCards.workerPool.onmessage = DuelingCards.workerPoolCallback;
var s = DuelingCards.opponentWorkerFunction.toString();
s = s.substr(14);
s = s.substring(0, s.length - 2);
DuelingCards.opponentWorker = DuelingCards.workerPool.createWorker(s);
```

The first thing we do is register a callback with the `WorkerPool` instance reference by `DuelingCards.workerPool`. This is the function that will receive all messages sent *from* the `Worker` we're about to create.

Now, earlier when we talked about `WorkerPool`, you saw that you can pass a URL to the `createWorkerFromUrl()` method, or you can pass string to the `createWorker()` method. The latter is what we'll be doing, but in a different, more interesting way. What we have this time is an honest-to-goodness function named `opponentWorkerFunction()` that is a method of the `DuelingCards` namespace. We call `toString()` on that method. Yes, you read that right! Remember that in JavaScript a function is a first-class citizen; it's a proper object that literally extends from `Object`, which means it has a `toString()` method that returns the function as a string.

The unfortunate thing, though, is that it returns it fully, including the function `opponentWorkerFunction() {` part and the closing brace. So, the next two lines hack that stuff off the two ends of the string. This is admittedly a little brittle because if a particular browser implemented `toString()` differently, this code might not work. But it works fine in Internet Explorer and Firefox, which covers the majority of users, and since we're not writing code for a missile defense shield here, I can live with it if you can!

That string, containing just the code within the function, is then passed along to `createWorker()`,the `Worker` reference is stored in `DuelingCards.opponentWorker`, and the method is complete.

The OpponentWorker

We're now going to look at that opponentWorkerFunction(), beginning with the private variables that are a part of it, listed in Table 8-2.

Table 8-2. *The Private Variables within the opponentWorkerFunction()*

Variable	Description
opponentCards	The collection of opponent card cardDescriptor objects. This duplicates the DuelingCards.opponentCards collection internal to this Worker.
actionCards	The collection of action card cardDescriptor objects. This duplicates the DuelingCards.actionCards collection internal to this Worker.
difficulty	The difficulty level the game was started at: 7 = easy, 5 = medium, or 3 = hard.
timer	The Gears Timer object we'll use to process game loop events.
gameLoopInterval	Reference to the interval created to fire the gameLoop() method periodically.
sender	Reference to the message sender—that is, the WorkerPool outside this Worker.

The Message Handler Method

In the initOpponent() method, we saw that a message callback handler was registered with the WorkerPool to handle messages sent by the Worker. What about messages sent *to* the Worker? We need a function to handle that, too, and that's set up next:

```
google.gears.workerPool.onmessage = function(
  inMessageText, inSenderID, inMsg) {

  switch (inMsg.body.msg) {

    case "start_game":
      sender = inMsg.sender;
      if (inMsg.body.difficulty == "easy") {
        difficulty = 7;
      } else if (inMsg.body.difficulty == "medium") {
        difficulty = 5;
      } else if (inMsg.body.difficulty == "hard") {
        difficulty = 3;
      }
      gameLoopInterval = timer.setInterval(gameLoop, difficulty * 1000);
    break;

    case "end_game":
      timer.clearInterval(gameLoopInterval);
    break;
```

```
    case "game_paused":
      timer.clearInterval(gameLoopInterval);
    break;

    case "game_resumed":
      gameLoopInterval = timer.setInterval(gameLoop, difficulty * 1000);
    break;

    case "update_action_cards":
      timer.clearInterval(gameLoopInterval);
      actionCards = new Array();
      for (var i = 0; i < inMsg.body.actionCards.length; i++) {
        actionCards.push(inMsg.body.actionCards[i]);;
      }
      gameLoopInterval = timer.setInterval(gameLoop, difficulty * 1000);
    break;

    case "update_opponent_cards":
      timer.clearInterval(gameLoopInterval);
      opponentCards = new Array();
      for (var i = 0; i < inMsg.body.opponentCards.length; i++) {
        opponentCards.push(inMsg.body.opponentCards[i]);;
      }
      gameLoopInterval = timer.setInterval(gameLoop, difficulty * 1000);
    break;

  }

};
```

Since multiple messages are understood by this Worker, we begin by switching on the inMsg.body.msg value passed in. The first case is the "start_game" message. The first task is to store off the sender of the message, which is a reference to the WorkerPool. Since this message is the first one that will be received, and since we need to know the sender in order to send messages back to it, this is the right place to get that information and store it. Next, we take the difficulty level that is passed in, convert it to a numeric value, and store it. Finally, we use the Timer instance (which is created when the timer variable is declared) to start an interval that calls the gameLoop() method periodically, and the period is based on the difficulty level (every 7 seconds for easy, 5 seconds for medium, and 3 seconds for hard).

The next message handled is the "end_game" message, and there's nothing to do here but clear the interval so that gameLoop() won't be fired any further. In fact, the next message handled is "game_paused" and its code is identical to the code for "end_game".

■**Note** Yes, I know I could have let the cases fall through, but I generally dislike fall-through logic in `switch` statements because I've seen it have unintended side effects a few too many times. I prefer the more deterministic form of coding…most of the time!

The "resume_game" message is handled next, and all it needs to do is kick off the previously cleared interval again.

The next message to be handled is "update_action_cards". This message is sent when a change to the action cards occurs, like when the player makes a valid drop or the dealer's stack image is clicked. This is necessary because of that annoying "no shared state" thing again! So, this message is sent and along with it comes the list of `cardDescriptors` describing the action cards. Before anything is done with them, the interval calling `gameLoop()` is cleared. It would be a shame to try to execute the opponent's logic while the action cards are changing! In reality this probably isn't possible anyway due to JavaScript being single-threaded, but I'm not 100 percent sure if Gears opens up any possibilities in that area, and I certainly can't count on future browsers not doing that. So I figure it's safer to clear the interval and not have to worry about it. The code here then takes the `cardDescriptors` sent in, pushes them onto the internal `actionCards`, and restarts the interval.

Similarly, the "update_opponent_cards" message does the same thing for the cards the opponent is holding. This message is sent when the opponent makes a valid drop and the `Worker` has told the external code about it. The external code does some work, which results in the opponent's cards being updated, and then sends this message, along with the `cardDescriptors` for the opponent's cards. They are stored internally, just as the action cards are, and the message is fully handled.

The gameLoop() Method

The `gameLoop()` method is where most of the action really takes place; more specifically, it provides the core game logic that makes the computer opponent work. Figure 8-13 shows a graphical representation not only of this method but of the general flow of code within the opponent `Worker`, and the messages in and out of it.

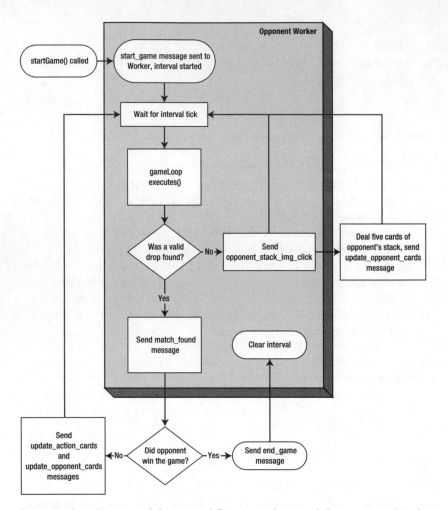

Figure 8-13. *A diagram of the general flow in and around the opponent Worker*

Let's step through this method bit by bit:

```
var usedCards = new Array(6);
var noMatchesFound = true;
for (var i = 0; i < 6; i++) {
  var faceValue = actionCards[i].faceValue;
```

The basic concept here is similar to how it works when the player drops a card on an action card, but essentially in reverse. In that case, the code has to figure out if the drop was valid, but here the logic is to figure out beforehand if there are any valid drops to be made for the opponent. To do this we iterate over the action cards. For each we get its faceValue and then do this:

```
if (actionCards[i].singleOrDouble == "1" &&
  actionCards[i] == "up") {
  if (faceValue == 14) { faceValue = 1; }
  faceValue = faceValue + 1
}
```

If this code looks a bit familiar to you then, well, I haven't lost your attention! This is nearly the same code that you saw in the isValidDrop() method in DuelingCards.js. Here, though, we're simply figuring out what the appropriate next card is based on the indicators around this action card. This block looks at the single up-arrow scenario. Following that we have the double up-arrow situation:

```
if (actionCards[i].singleOrDouble == "2" &&
  actionCards[i].upOrDown == "up") {
  if (faceValue == 13) { faceValue = 0; }
  if (faceValue == 14) { faceValue = 1; }
  faceValue = faceValue + 2;
}
```

After this are the other two blocks that look at the single and double down arrows, which I've skipped here. Feel free to take a look at the code on your own.

Once we know what the next card should be, we have to see if that card is one of the visible opponent cards. So, we start a loop:

```
for (j = 0; j < 5; j++) {
  if (!usedCards[j]) {
    var matchFound = false;
    if (opponentCards[j].suit == "joker" ||
      actionCards[i].suit == "joker") {
      matchFound = true;
    }
```

The way I've written this code, it's possible to have more than one valid drop result from the outer loop. So, we have to keep track of which opponent cards have been used already, and that's the purpose of the usedCards array. If the next opponent card checked in the loop hasn't been used, then we check to see if it, or the action card we're trying to find a valid drop for, is a joker. If either is a joker, then it's automatically a match. If it's not a joker, we have some more checking to do:

```
    if (opponentCards[j].faceValue == faceValue) {
      if (actionCards[i].suitChangeable ||
        actionCards[i].suit == opponentCards[j].suit) {
        matchFound = true;
      }
    }
```

If the faceValue matches, and if the suit matches *or* the suit change indicator is preset on this action card, then it's a match that way.

Once those checks have been done, we have some housekeeping work to do in case a match is found:

```
    if (matchFound) {
      noMatchesFound = false
      usedCards[j] = true;
      google.gears.workerPool.sendMessage({
        msg : "match_found",
        actionCard : i, opponentCard : j
      }, sender);
      break;
    }
  }
}}
```

The noMatchesFound flag is set to false since we now have at least one match resulting from the iteration over the action cards. Next, the element in the usedCards array corresponding to this opponent card is set to true so that we don't register a match for it twice during this processing. Finally, a "match_found" message is sent out of the Worker. As you'll see next, that's the other half of what makes this all work.

The final step is outside of the two loops:

```
if (noMatchesFound) {
  google.gears.workerPool.sendMessage({
    msg : "opponent_stack_img_click"
  }, sender);
}
```

When no valid drops are found, we send out the "opponent_stack_img_click" message, which will simulate the computer opponent clicking their card stack image to see if there are more cards on their stack that might match the action cards.

Handling Messages from the Opponent Worker

By this point we've seen that there are a couple of messages passed out from the Worker to the code that hosts the WorkerPool, and earlier we saw how that callback was registered with the WorkerPool. Now it's time to look at that callback function, the workerPoolCallback() method. This method, like the callback inside the opponent Worker, has a switch statement that branches based on the message received. The first message, "match_found", is without a doubt the more complex of the two, and it's up first:

```
var oCard = DuelingCards["opponentCards"][inMsg.body.opponentCard].elem;
var aCard = DuelingCards["actionCards"][inMsg.body.actionCard].elem;
oCard.moveTo(aCard.getX(), aCard.getY(), { duration : 2,
  callback : function() {
```

Recall that this message is sent as a result of a valid card being dropped by the opponent. In this case we need to do the move animation to simulate the opponent dragging and dropping the card. So, we get a reference to both the opponent card we want to drag and the action card it will be dropped on. With these in hand, we call the moveTo() method on the opponent card reference, and set the destination X/Y coordinates to the location of the action card.

The callback function fires when the animation completes:

```
var opponentCard =
  DuelingCards.opponentCards[inMsg.body.opponentCard];
DuelingCards.opponentCardsRemaining =
  DuelingCards.opponentCardsRemaining - 1;
opponentCard.suit = null;
opponentCard.faceValue = null;
if (DuelingCards.opponentCardsRemaining == 0) {
  DuelingCards.workerPool.sendMessage({
    msg : "end_game"
  }, DuelingCards.opponentWorker);
  opponentCard.elem.hide();
  DuelingCards.doEndGame("lose");
  return;
}
```

Here we're getting a reference to the cardDescriptor for the opponent card that was dropped. Next, we decrement the number of cards the opponent has left. Then the suit and faceValue fields are set to null in the cardDescriptor. The check on the value of DuelingCards. opponentCardsRemaining is next. If there are no cards left, we send the "end_game" message to the Worker so it can shut down the interval. Then the dragged card is hidden and the doEndGame() method is called, this time passing the value lose so the slap-in-the-face "you stink" graphic is displayed (just kidding; it simply says "You lose").

The following code executes when the opponent did not win and the game will continue:

```
DuelingCards.dealActionCard(inMsg.body.actionCard);
DuelingCards.dealPlayerOpponentCard("opponent",
  inMsg.body.opponentCard);
DuelingCards.drawActionCardIndicators(inMsg.body.actionCard);
```

The chore here is threefold. First, a new action card must be dealt to replace the one the opponent dropped their card on. Then, the opponent's dropped card must be replaced as well. Finally, a new random set of indicators needs to be drawn around the action card. We've already looked at the methods that accomplish all this, so there's really not much to add at this point.

Next we have a block of code whose job it is, partially at least, to tell the opponent Worker what the action cards now are:

```
var ac = new Array();
for (var i = 0; i < DuelingCards.actionCards.length; i++) {
  ac.push({
    suit : DuelingCards.actionCards[i].suit,
    faceValue : DuelingCards.actionCards[i].faceValue,
    singleOrDouble : DuelingCards.actionCards[i].singleOrDouble,
```

```
      upOrDown : DuelingCards.actionCards[i].upOrDown,
      suitChangeable : DuelingCards.actionCards[i].suitChangeable
    });
  }
```

We're again copying the DuelingCards.actionCards array so we can pass it in to the Worker. Similarly, the opponent's cards must be updated:

```
var oc = new Array();
for (var i = 0; i < DuelingCards.opponentCards.length; i++) {
  oc.push({
    suit : DuelingCards.opponentCards[i].suit,
    faceValue : DuelingCards.opponentCards[i].faceValue
  });
}
```

With those two arrays in hand, it's a simple matter of sending the two update messages that we saw handled before:

```
DuelingCards.workerPool.sendMessage({
  msg : "update_action_cards", actionCards : ac
}, DuelingCards.opponentWorker);
DuelingCards.workerPool.sendMessage({
  msg : "update_opponent_cards", opponentCards : oc
}, DuelingCards.opponentWorker);
```

When that's all done, the Worker is fully up to date and can continue to play the game properly.

The Faux Stack Click Method

At the risk of sounding like a broken record, you know by now that the dealer's stack card image is clickable, as is the player's. The opponent's, however, is not—at least, not by the player. The opponent can "click" their own stack to deal five new cards. Since Ext JS, as cool as it is, can't (yet) physically manifest an appendage out of the PC to actuate the mouse and physically click the image, we have to simulate it. As you saw a little while back, this occurs when the opponent finds no valid drops and needs to cycle their cards. The opponentStackImgClick() method is called in this situation:

```
for (var i = 0; i < 5; i++) {
  DuelingCards.dealPlayerOpponentCard("opponent", i);
}
var oc = new Array();
for (var i = 0; i < DuelingCards.opponentCards.length; i++) {
  oc.push({
    suit : DuelingCards.opponentCards[i].suit,
    faceValue : DuelingCards.opponentCards[i].faceValue
  });
}
```

```
DuelingCards.workerPool.sendMessage({
  msg : "update_opponent_cards", opponentCards : oc
}, DuelingCards.opponentWorker);
```

There are two steps to this. First, for each opponent card we call dealPlayerOpponentCard(). Then, we copy the DuelingCards.opponentCards array and send the "update_opponentCards" message, passing the copy of the array. Yep, that's all it takes! The Worker now knows about the five new visible cards and the game can continue.

Suggested Exercises

A game is perhaps the best kind of project for a book like this because there are literally limitless suggestions that could be made. I'll leave you with just a few:

- Use your well-practiced Gears database knowledge and allow for saving of high scores. Er, you'll have to implement high scores first of course! Maybe it's just the fastest winners or something like that, it's up to you!

- If you're really feeling daring, and you have some server-side coding chops, how about adding the ability to play against someone remotely? That's clearly a much bigger project, but it would let you play around with Ext JS's Ajax capabilities, something that was only briefly described in this book (on purpose, since this is a book focused on client-side development).

• Here's a relatively simple one: store the card deck and page background choices so that it gets set that way the next time the game is played. You could store this info in cookies, or you could go hog-wild and stash it in a Gears database.

- One flaw in this application is that if you resize the browser, nothing on the page repositions itself. I left that out on purpose because that would be a good exercise for you to do. My suggestion is to have a Viewport that takes up the whole page and hook into its resizing event, but the approach is up to you!

Summary

In this chapter we took a break from the ordinary and wrote ourselves a nifty little game. In the process we got our hands dirty with some non-widget goodness provided by Ext JS, including drag-and-drop, the Element wrapper class, and lots of UI effects. We also got to see the Gears WorkerPool in action, allowing us to implement an efficient multithreading mechanism in JavaScript.

In the next chapter, the final chapter of this book, we've put together an application for tracking our finances that will allow us to see a few new capabilities that we haven't seen before, including the charting capabilities Ext JS provides. Stick around—the final adventure is about to begin!

CHAPTER 9

■ ■ ■

Managing Your Finances: Finance Master

To quote the immortal words of Gordon Gekko:[1] "Greed, for lack of a better word, is good." Greed probably most frequently comes in the form of money, so therefore money is good. A big part of making money is simply being able to track your assets and liabilities and understand where your money is and how it's working for you in terms of return on investments.

With that in mind, the final project in this book is my special gift to you: a tool that will not only teach you more about Ext JS but will, hopefully, assist you in making boatloads of money. (This isn't completely altruistic, of course: you making more money means you'll have more to spend on your favorite author's future books!)

■Note I'm going to do something right up front that I really hate to do but that circumstances are forcing me to do: give a disclaimer for this project. While I strive to make all of the projects in my books cross-browser (at least Internet Explorer and Firefox on Windows at a minimum), this project gave me a lot of trouble in that regard. I was only able to get it to work reliably in Firefox. As far as I can tell, it's the fact that the charting support in Ext JS is new in version 3 and maybe still needs some work. But since the charting support is Flash based, it could very well be a Flash issue too. So, my strong suggestion is to only try running this app in Firefox to be safe, even though it should work in other browsers as well, and you may find it does.

What's This Application Do Anyway?

There are some top-notch financial tracking/planning software products out there. Quicken is probably the most well-known name. That product is developed by a team of dedicated engineers and has been developed over a very long period of time to be the polished, powerful solution it is today. At the end of the day, however, it all comes down to the relatively simple

---

1 Gordon Gekko is the main antagonist in the classic movie *Wall Street*. Gordon, a corporate raider played by Michael Douglas, embodies all that was wrong with those involved in the stock markct in the 80s (and now too it seems!).

concept of a diary[2] for your money! That's exactly what Finance Master is. It won't tell you how to invest your money and it won't balance your checkbook or simulate investment scenarios. What it *will* do is give you a nice, organized way to see where your money is, and to some extent, where it's been.

So, what's the feature set of this thing? The following is the list of what it'll do:

- It allows for the creation of multiple portfolios (a portfolio is a collection of accounts). Portfolios have a name that is meaningful to the user and are password protected.

- It lets you create and delete accounts of various types within a given portfolio.

- For a given account, activity can be stored and deleted. For checking and savings accounts, you can enter deposits or withdrawals and for other account types (investment, retirement and loan accounts), you can enter a new account balance. You can also enter a description and a date to go along with each activity item.

- The application should use a portal metaphor, meaning there are small modules, or portlets, that can be moved around on the screen as you desire. (Typically a portal allows for adding and removing of portlets, but here we'll just have four static portlets that are always present.) The portlets can be collapsed if you want.

- One portlet will be a portfolio overview that will show a list of accounts in the portfolio, their current balances, and their type. This will be displayed in a `Grid` that will group the accounts by type. This portlet will also provide the ability to add new accounts and delete existing accounts.

- Another portlet will be a portfolio distribution portlet that will show a pie chart that graphically represents how the assets in the portfolio are distributed across the various account types.

- A third portlet will be the account activity portlet that will show a `Grid` containing all the activity for the account. For each, you will see the date, deposit, withdrawal or new balance amount, and a description. This portlet will also let you add new activity and delete existing activity.

- The fourth and final portlet will be an account history portlet that will show a line chart illustrating the fluctuating balance of the account over time.

- You will be able to open a different portfolio at any time without reloading the application.

So, there are quite a few bullet points there, and it sounds like a lot, but in actuality it's really not. However, we'll definitely be seeing some new Ext JS stuff here, so let's open with a screenshot. In Figure 9-1 you see the initial Finance Master screen when the application is first launched.

---

2 My wife to this day refuses to use an actual checkbook. She instead opts for a simple spiral notebook where she keeps track of everything. I'm not saying that's good or bad; I'm just saying that we never seem to have money! Hmm…

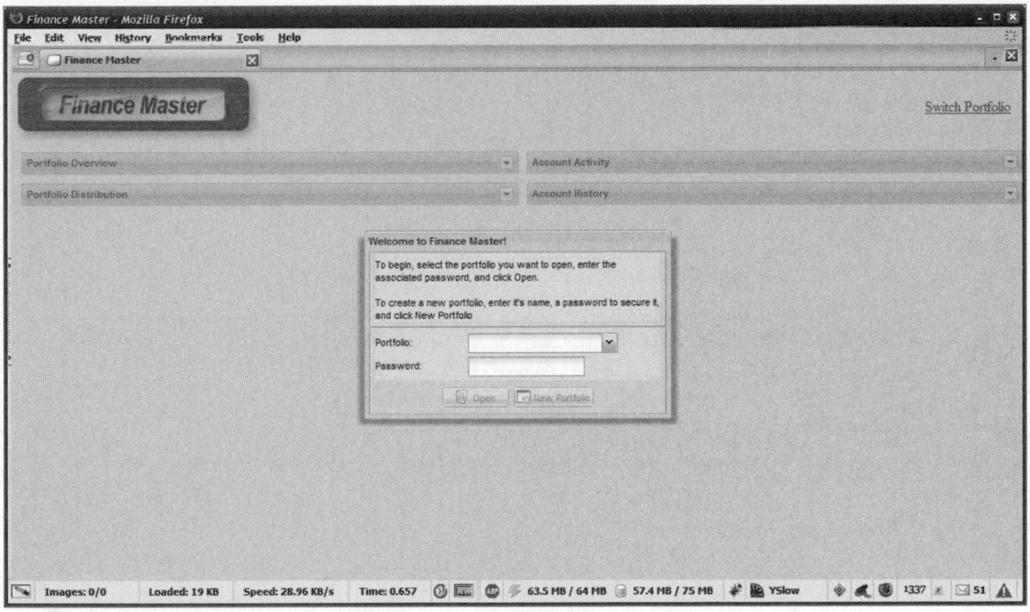

Figure 9-1. *Finance Master as it appears upon launch*

You can't tell from looking at the printed page, but this application has a different overall appearance than any we've seen thus far. That's thanks to a custom theme we've used. We'll see how to use a theme in an Ext JS project shortly, and as usual I think you'll be amazed at how very little work is involved on your part!

Anyway, that's jumping the gun a bit. Here we go, one more time!

■**Note** The theme used is the Gray Extended theme created by Jose Alfonso Dacosta Dominguez, a.k.a. galdaka, an Ext JS community member. Thank you, Jose, for giving this theme to the community! In case you are interested in more details, check out this thread in the Ext JS forums: http://extjs.com/forum/ showthread.php?t=65694.

A Warning About Warnings

Before we get going here, I need to point out a potential problem you may encounter the first time you run the application. You may wind up seeing something that looks like Figure 9-2.

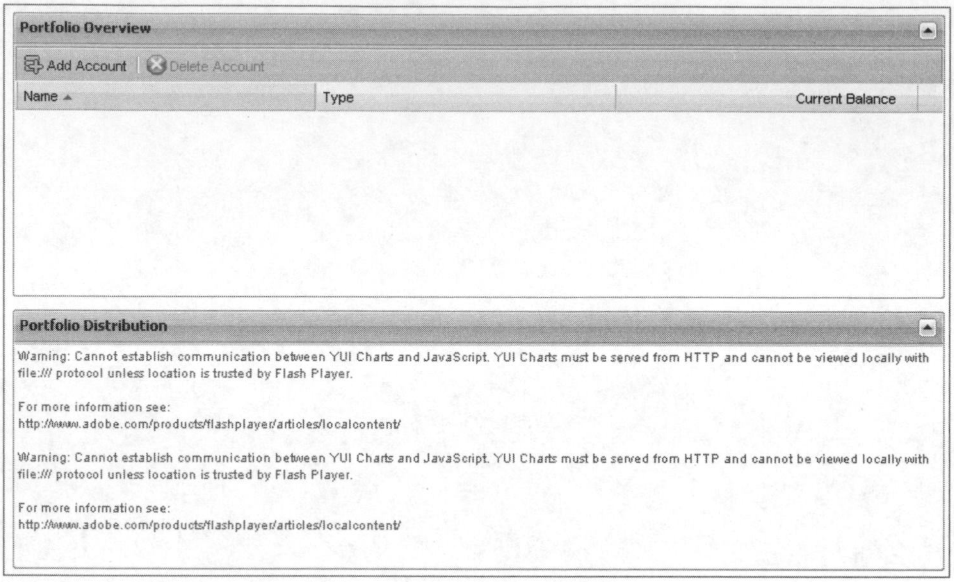

Figure 9-2. *A potential problem with the charting support*

If this happens, there are two things you can do, and the choice is entirely yours. One, as the message text implies, is to run the application on a server of your choosing. That should be all it takes to deal with this problem.

The other option, the one I personally went with, is to go into the Flash global security settings panel as described in previous chapters and specifically give permission to the location you have the project running from locally. This will allow JavaScript to talk to the Flash-based charts and everything should work as expected.

Depending on your Flash settings you may or may not experience this problem, but it happened to me the first time, so I give you the benefit of my experience!

Overall Structure and Files

The directory structure of Finance Master is not much different than previous applications, just with a few interesting JavaScript files, as you can see for yourself in Figure 9-3.

In the root, we have the usual index.htm, and license.txt files, and in the css directory we have the usual styles.css. There's also a portal.css file that is new, and this is the file that contains styles needed for the portal extension, which we'll get into as we examine the code in FinanceMaster.js.

In the img directory we have FinanceMaster.gif, which is the logo in the upper-left corner of the screen. We then have Add.gif, Cancel.gif, Delete.gif, New.gif, Ok.gif, and Open.gif, all of which are icons on various Buttons throughout the UI.

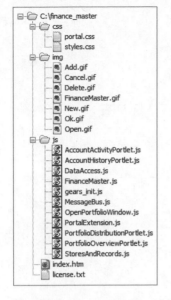

Figure 9-3. *The application's directory structure and constituent files*

The js directory contains FinanceMaster.js, our "main" JavaScript file, so to speak. We also find gears_init.js as always, and the StoresAndRecords.js file that we're pretty used to for our Ext.data.Store and Ext.data.Record definitions (although, as we'll see, in this application they aren't *all* in there). There's also DataAccess.js, which is basically like any of the DAO.js files we've dealt with before, but there is a reason it's named differently, as we'll see. There's also something called MessageBus.js, which is the source file that will give us our publish/subscribe architecture. Although we won't be looking at the contents of this file, on the grounds that looking at the code behind a given extension is beyond the scope of this book, we'll certainly see it get plenty of use, which is the big thing for us. The OpenPortfolioWindow.js is the code for the Window where a user opens (or creates, as it turns out) a portfolio. The PortalExtension.js contains an Ext JS extension providing a portal-based interface (we also won't be looking at the code in this file since I didn't write it, so it would be like looking at the Ext JS source code, which we haven't done either throughout this book). Finally, there are four other source files: AccountActivityPortlet.js, AccountHistoryPortlet. js, PortfolioDistributionPortlet.js, and PortfolioOverviewPortlet.js. If you said these files contain the code for a given portlet, then give yourself a pat on the back!

The Markup

The index.htm file is, as usual, our starting point, and it's at this point I think pretty boilerplate. Here it is, in its entirety:

```
<html>
  <head>
    <title>Finance Master</title>
```

```
<link rel="stylesheet" type="text/css"
  href="../../ext/resources/css/ext-all.css">
<link rel="stylesheet" type="text/css"
  href="../../ext/resources/css/xtheme-gray-extend.css">
<script type="text/javascript"
  src="../../ext/adapter/ext/ext-base.js"></script>
<script type="text/javascript" src="../../ext/ext-all.js"></script>

<link rel="stylesheet" type="text/css" href="css/portal.css">
<script src="js/PortalExtension.js"></script>

<script src="js/MessageBus.js"></script>

<script src="js/gears_init.js"></script>

<script>
  Ext.namespace("FinanceMaster");
  Ext.namespace("FinanceMaster.Portlets");
  Ext.namespace("FinanceMaster.Data");
</script>

<link rel="stylesheet" type="text/css" href="css/styles.css">
<script src="js/FinanceMaster.js"></script>
<script src="js/DataAccess.js"></script>
<script src="js/StoresAndRecords.js"></script>
<script src="js/OpenPortfolioWindow.js"></script>

<script src="js/PortfolioOverviewPortlet.js"></script>
<script src="js/PortfolioDistributionPortlet.js"></script>
<script src="js/AccountActivityPortlet.js"></script>
<script src="js/AccountHistoryPortlet.js"></script>

<script>Ext.onReady(FinanceMaster.init);</script>

</head>

<body><div id="divSource" class="cssSource"></div></body>

</html>
```

The usual Ext JS imports are present, but there's a surprise here. Remember earlier I mentioned that theme we're using to give us a gray UI look? There's just a single thing we need to do to activate that: import the appropriate style sheet, xtheme-gray-extend.css in this case. You're good to go, assuming you've put the files for the theme in the right place—which means you've put that style sheet file in resources/css under the ext directory, and also put the corresponding images directory containing all the graphic resources for the theme under `ext/resources/images`. As usual, things that would otherwise be complex are made exceedingly simple by Ext JS.

After that are a couple of imports for the portal extension: its `portal.css` and `PortalExtension.js` files. The `MessageBus.js` file is also imported, providing our publish/subscribe model, and of course things wouldn't be complete without `gears_init.js` being brought in.

Next, a couple of namespaces are created. I put these here because they must be present before the rest of the application code is loaded, so this seemed like a good place. Remember that the browser interprets things in the order they appear on the page, so these namespaces will be created before anything that needs them is.

After that comes a bunch of JavaScript imports that comprise the application code. Once all that is done, we have the typical `Ext.onReady()` call to bootstrap the application.

We also have the `divSource` `<div>` that we've seen numerous times, but as we'll see in a bit, I've managed to slightly change the way this is used this time around.

The Style Sheet

The style sheet for this application is extremely simple, and if you don't believe me, here's *the entire thing*:

```
.cssSource {
  position : absolute;
  left: 1px;
  width : 100%;
  height : 1px;
}
```

Yes, that's literally it! One class applied to the `divSource` `<div>` and nothing more. Notice that there's no `top` attribute for this, as we've usually seen in the past. I'll telegraph[3] this a bit and tell you that the `top` attribute's value will be dynamically applied, but we'll get to that in just a moment.

A few pages back we got our first look at Finance Master when it first loads, but that doesn't give you the full picture of the application. So, even though the code we've looked at so far is only the tip of the iceberg, let's get another, more complete look at Finance Master (see Figure 9-4).

Here you can clearly see the portal architecture, with four total portlets, two of which are currently expanded. You can also see the charting capabilities in action.

---

3 In professional wrestling, "telegraphing" a move is when one wrestler does something that gives a clue to their opponent what is coming, whether or not on purpose. When you telegraph something, in a more generic sense, it's a slang way of saying you're foreshadowing something that is coming soon.

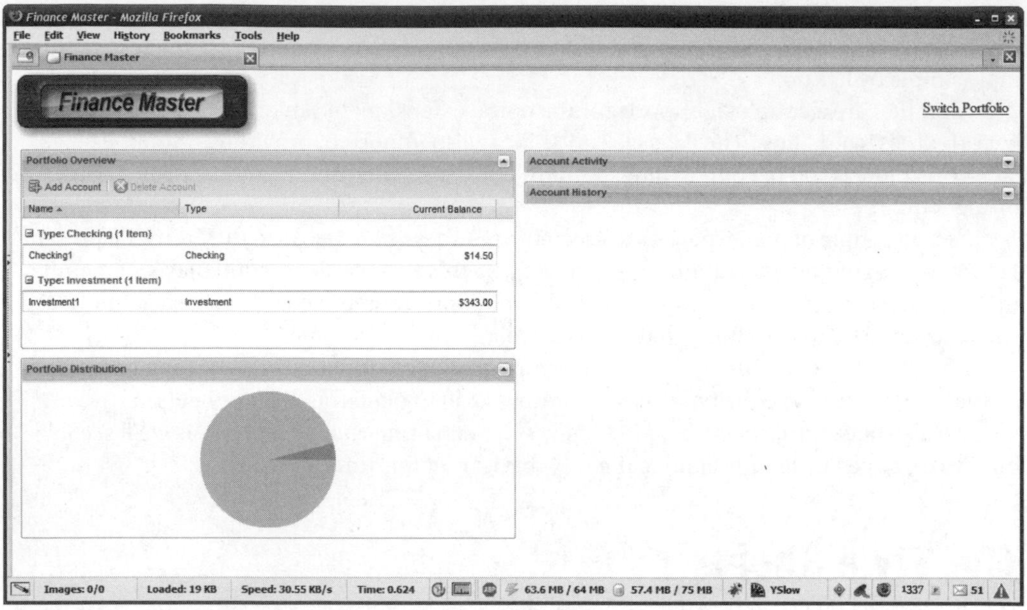

Figure 9-4. *Finance Master, after a portfolio has been opened*

Preliminaries Part I: A Brief History of Portals and Portlets (Apologies to Professor Hawking)

Before we get into the code of this application, I want to provide a context for what is to come. The first piece of business is to talk about the idea of a portal.

A *portal* is a way to organize the UI of an application so that there are small, discrete "modules" that can be displayed on the screen. Generally, these modules, which are called *portlets*, are rectangular in nature. Each portlet can provide some piece of functionality, and the user usually has control over which portlets are on the screen.

For example, if you were to create a news portal site, you might have a portlet for world news, another portlet for local news, one for sports, and one for financial news. You might also have a portlet where discussions among users about news stories could be found. The user could selectively show or hide any of these portlets, and usually they can be collapsed instead of removed from the UI. Users can also add other portlets as they wish to the UI to have other pieces of functionality available to them.

Portlets in a portal can also usually be arranged by the user. The interface to rearranging them can vary, but one fairly typical approach is to allow users to drag the portlets around and drop them where they want them to be.

The benefit to a portal architecture is that users are in control. They decide, from a list of choices, the available portlets in this case, what they see on the page, and how it's organized. A portal is an aggregation of different pieces of functionality encapsulated within the portlets it provides, so another advantage is that the user can have numerous, potentially very disparate sources of information in one consolidated view.

Portals are a popular choice for company intranet sites, personal information management (PIM) sites, and similar types of applications. In the Java world, there is a whole specification dedicated to the technology behind portals, and various vendors provide their own unique implementations of the specification with all sorts of value-added goodies such as cross-portlet authentication, preferences management, and out-of-the-box portlets for all sorts of things.

However, in the case of Finance Master, we don't have a full spec to support us. Instead, we have to go it alone. Thankfully, the Ext JS team created an example, one you can find on the Ext JS site that provides the basics of a portal application in JavaScript. Utilizing the extension code they wrote for that example, we can provide the same sort of interface design to Finance Master without much work at all.

One important consideration in portal creation, from a coding standpoint, is that since the portlets can be added and removed, expanded or collapsed, and arranged by the user, individual portlets have to be truly independent. They can't make assumptions about other portlets because it's easy to imagine a function call to a portlet that was removed leading to a quick JavaScript error. Fortunately, there is a rather easy solution to this problem: the publish/subscribe model.

Preliminaries Part II: The Publish/Subscribe Model

The publish/subscribe model, or pub/sub as it is often abbreviated, is a way to architect an application that is especially effective in asynchronous situations.

Let's do a little thought experiment[4] around the idea of portlets. Assume we have two portlets, A and B. Let's further say that portal A shows stock quotes in a typical animated ticker display while portlet B shows the stock price for a limited number of user-selected stocks. Now, assume we have a background process that polls some Internet-based source for stock prices. Every minute, this background process runs and gets the latest prices for all stock symbols available. Now, both portlets A and B will need to get this updated information. How exactly do they get that information?

Well, certainly the portlets could poll some common location that the background process updates, but that's pretty inefficient because the prices in the common location will frequently not be updated when the portlets check, so there's a lot of wasted CPU time there (and possibly network and storage bandwidth, depending on where the common location is). Alternatively, the background process could call some function that both portlets A and B expose to get the updated information. This will be efficient, but the problem here is that since this is a portal, one of the portlets, or both, may have been turned off by the user. So, we'll either get errors occurring, or at best we'll have some error handling that takes care of the errors, but that's a cop-out frankly.

The better approach in a situation like this would be a pub/sub model. Here, both of the portlets would "subscribe" to a given type of message that the background process would "publish." Here's the way it works. There is an entity, some sort of message processor, or

---

4 A *thought experiment* is a proposal for an experiment that would test a hypothesis. Thought experiments are a popular, and sometimes the only feasible, option to test theories in various scientific disciplines. Albert Einstein postulated most of general and special relativity based on little more than thought experiments!

message bus as it is often called, that has two methods, publish() and subscribe(). The two portlets call the subscribe() method. They pass to it the type of message they are interested in (usually by some sort of ID) and also a function to be called when the message is published. Then, the background process, which has some information it wants to share with anyone who has subscribed to a given message, calls the publish() method, passing in the ID of the message being published along with any other information that interested subscribers might want. Then, the message bus goes through its list of subscribers to the published message and calls the specified function, passing the information that was published along to it.

This model is a fairly simple way to allow communications between entities in a loosely coupled way, meaning they don't need to know anything about each other to communicate. All they need is access to the common messaging bus, and knowledge of the messages that can be published or subscribed to. This is all done asynchronously, so there is no need for any sort of polling or background code running to send and receive messages (in other words, the message bus only does something when publish() or subscribe() is called). It is therefore a quite efficient way of doing things.

In a portal environment, this is the way you almost *have* to do things, or you don't allow cross-portlet communication at all. More than that, though, it's the best way to design things in terms of communication from the portal itself to the portlets it hosts, and from the portlets to the portal when necessary. This way, portlets can be added or dropped without any concern. As long as they subscribe to the appropriate messages, and as long as the portal publishes the appropriate messages, or vice versa, everything will work great.

Even if you've never heard of the pub/sub model before, you in fact have been dealing with it throughout this book: events are a form of pub/sub! Just plain JavaScript event handlers are essentially a pub/sub model. If you add an onClick handler to a Button, for example, that's essentially a way of saying the code in that handler is "subscribing" to the click "message." When the user clicks the button, the browser "publishes" a click message, and the handler gets notified of the message and does its thing. I admit that's a roundabout way of looking at it and that having a message bus with explicit publish() and subscribe() methods is certainly more obvious, but it's the same basic concept either way.

With all of that in mind, we can now jump headlong into the JavaScript behind Finance Master and be able to understand what's going on a lot better now. Let's start with the Stores and Records defined in, oddly enough, the StoresAndRecords.js file.

The Code

Now that the preliminary topics have been covered, we can now dissect the code of this application. We'll begin by looking at the data model the application uses, and then move on to the "main" code, followed by the code for each of the four portlets.

StoresAndRecords.js

As we've seen in past applications, we'll need a couple of data Stores and a couple of Record types to make this application work. Unlike in past applications, though, not *all* of them will be found in this file. Some are specific to a given portlet, so they will be defined in the source files for those portlets. However, a couple of basic types are necessary for all portlets to be able to use, so we'll define them at a higher level here. In Figure 9-5 you can see the three Record types and two common Stores in this FinanceMaster.Data namespace, defined in this source file (partly at least, which is why you'll notice the "part 1" in the figure caption).

```
FinanceMaster.Data
+PortfolioRecord : Ext.data.Record
+AccountRecord : Ext.data.Record
+ActivityRecord : Ext.data.Record
+portfoliosStore : Ext.data.Store
+accountsStore : Ext.data.Store
```

Figure 9-5. *The FinanceMaster.Data namespace (part 1)*

The FinanceMaster.Data namespace was declared in index.htm, so we're good to go, beginning with the definition of a PortfolioRecord:

```
FinanceMaster.Data.PortfolioRecord = Ext.data.Record.create([
  { name : "name" }, { name : "password" }
]);
```

Naturally enough, a PortfolioRecord defines a portfolio. It only needs two simple attributes: name and password. These will also be the names of the attributes in the JSON that we'll use to create instances this class, so there's no need for a mapping attribute. (This is a common theme throughout this project—it makes the code more concise and self-describing.)

Next up we have the AccountRecord, which describes a given account inside a portfolio:

```
FinanceMaster.Data.AccountRecord = Ext.data.Record.create([
  { name : "portfolio" }, { name : "name" }, { name : "type" },
  { name : "balance" }
]);
```

Since an account belongs to a portfolio, we'll need a reference back to the name field of the PortfolioRecord that the AccountRecord is associated with, and that's the portfolio attribute. The name attribute is the name of the account, while type is one of the types an account is allowed to be (checking, savings, loan, retirement, and investment). The balance attribute is the current balance of the account, and this field will be dynamically calculated, not stored in the database.

Finally, we have the ActivityRecord class, which describes a given bit of activity within an account:

```
FinanceMaster.Data.ActivityRecord = Ext.data.Record.create([
  { name : "id" }, { name : "portfolio" }, { name : "account" },
  { name : "date" }, { name : "pretty_date" }, { name : "amount" },
  { name : "new_balance" }, { name : "description" }
]);
```

Unlike a PortfolioRecord, where the name attribute is the unique key, and AccountRecord, where portfolio and name form a composite key, there is no such key for an ActivityRecord that comes naturally from the data (unless you wanted to make a composite key out of all the fields, but that seems overkill to me). Therefore, we have a unique id field that serves as the key. The `portfolio` attribute serves the same purpose as the `portfolio` attribute in `AccountRecord`, and the `account` attribute ties the `ActivityRecord` back to the `name` field of the `AccountRecord` it is associated with. The `date` field is self-explanatory I suspect, but `pretty_date` is not. The problem that we'll encounter later on is that when we generate the chart showing activity for the account, there's no way to format the real date attribute, so it'll show up in the chart in its long, default JavaScript `Date` object format, which is quite ugly. So, alongside the real `date` field we have `pretty_date`, which is just a nicely formatted version of `date` that looks good on the chart. The `amount` attribute stores the deposit or withdrawal amount for checking and savings accounts, while `new_balance` stores the balance of the account at the time the `ActivityRecord` is created for other types of accounts. Finally, `description` is just a freeform note about the `ActivityRecord` for the user's own purposes.

Now that we know the types of `Records` we're dealing with, there are two `Stores` we need to look at, beginning with `portfoliosStore`:

```
FinanceMaster.Data.portfoliosStore = new Ext.data.Store({
  listeners : {
    "add" : {
      fn : function(inStore, inRecords, inIndex) {
        if (FinanceMaster.processStoreEvents) {
          FinanceMaster.Data.createPortfolio(inRecords[0]);
        }
      }
    },
    "remove" : {
      fn : function(inStore, inRecord, inIndex) {
        if (FinanceMaster.processStoreEvents) {
          FinanceMaster.Data.deletePortfolio(inRecord.get("id"));
        }
      }
    }
  }
});
```

This stores the canonical list of portfolios currently available. We use the same sort of event-driven model here that we've seen before, hooking into the add and remove events to persist the changes to our database.

We also have an `accountsStore` to store the list of accounts in the current portfolio:

```
FinanceMaster.Data.accountsStore = new Ext.data.GroupingStore({
  sortInfo : { field: "name", direction: "ASC" }, groupField : "type",
  listeners : {
    "add" : {
      fn : function(inStore, inRecords, inIndex) {
        if (FinanceMaster.processStoreEvents) {
          FinanceMaster.Data.createAccount(inRecords[0]);
        }
      }
    },
```

```
      "remove" : {
        fn : function(inStore, inRecord, inIndex) {
          if (FinanceMaster.processStoreEvents) {
            FinanceMaster.Data.deleteAccount(inRecord.get("portfolio"),
              inRecord.get("name"));
          }
        }
      }
    }
  }
});
```

Although the portfoliosStore will generally remain unchanged while Finance Master runs (unless a portfolio is added or removed), the accountsStore will change any time a portfolio is opened by the user because the accounts for the portfolio will be loaded into it.

Here's a test of whether you were paying attention or not: did you notice that this isn't plain old Ext.data.Store as we've typically used? This time around we're instantiating something called a GroupingStore. A GroupingStore is a data Store that…wait for it…groups its data according to some criteria you specify. Here, we're saying that we want all the records in the Store grouped by their type fields. This means that when we bind this to a Grid, as we'll do soon, it will show the data in groups, so we'll have all our checking accounts together, all our savings accounts together, and so on. More than just grouping them together, the Grid will actually have divider lines between each group and a bit of text as a title of each group. Take a look at virtually any of the screenshots in this chapter where you can see the portfolio overview portlet and you'll know exactly what I mean.

DataAccess.js

The DataAccess.js file is akin to the DAO.js file we've seen in previous projects. The reason we don't have a DAO.js file this time around is that there is no DAO class as in other projects. Instead, we have methods and attributes added to the FinanceMaster.Data namespace. As we know from past project dissections, a namespace and a class are basically the same thing, since in JavaScript they are both functions. So in essence, what we have here isn't much different; it's just a different way of laying out the code. Figure 9-6 shows the members that are added to the namespace courtesy of this source file.

```
┌─────────────────────────────────────────┐
│            FinanceMaster.Data             │
├─────────────────────────────────────────┤
│ +databaseName : String                    │
│ +sqlCreatePortfoliosTable : String         │
│ +sqlCreatePortfolio : String                │
│ +sqlRetrievePortfolios : String             │
│ +sqlDeletePortfolio : String                │
│ +sqlCreateAccountsTable : String            │
│ +sqlCreateAccount : String                  │
│ +sqlRetrieveAccounts : String               │
│ +sqlDeleteAccount : String                  │
│ +sqlCreateActivityTable : String            │
│ +sqlCreateActivity : String                 │
│ +sqlRetrieveActivity : String               │
│ +sqlDeleteActivity : String                 │
│ +sqlDeleteActivityInAccount : String        │
│ +sqlGetSavingsCheckingBalance : String      │
│ +sqlGetOtherBalance : String                │
├─────────────────────────────────────────┤
│ +init() : String                           │
│ +createPortfolio()                         │
│ +retrievePortfolios() : array               │
│ +createAccount()                           │
│ +retrieveAccounts() : array                 │
│ +deleteAccount()                           │
│ +createActivity()                          │
│ +retrieveActivity() : array                 │
│ +deleteActivity()                          │
│ +getAccountBalance() : int                  │
└─────────────────────────────────────────┘
```

Figure 9-6. *The FinanceMaster.Data namespace (part 2)*

The first thing we find is the field holding the name of the database:

```
FinanceMaster.Data.databaseName = "FinanceMaster";
```

Nothing new there—every project so far has had the same thing. Once again, though, note that the field is fully qualified within the namespace, which as we'll see goes for everything else throughout the rest of the code as well.

Next up are a couple of SQL statements for working with portfolios:

```
FinanceMaster.Data.sqlCreatePortfoliosTable =
  "CREATE TABLE IF NOT EXISTS portfolios (name TEXT, password TEXT)";
FinanceMaster.Data.sqlCreatePortfolio =
  "INSERT INTO portfolios (name, password) VALUES (?, ?)";
FinanceMaster.Data.sqlRetrievePortfolios = "SELECT * FROM portfolios " +
  "ORDER BY name";
```

I've generally assumed that you have some familiarity with SQL and so won't go into excruciating detail here unless there's something unusual to point out. I dare say these three statements wouldn't fall in that category, though! You can see the table structure for the portfolios table in Figure 9-7.

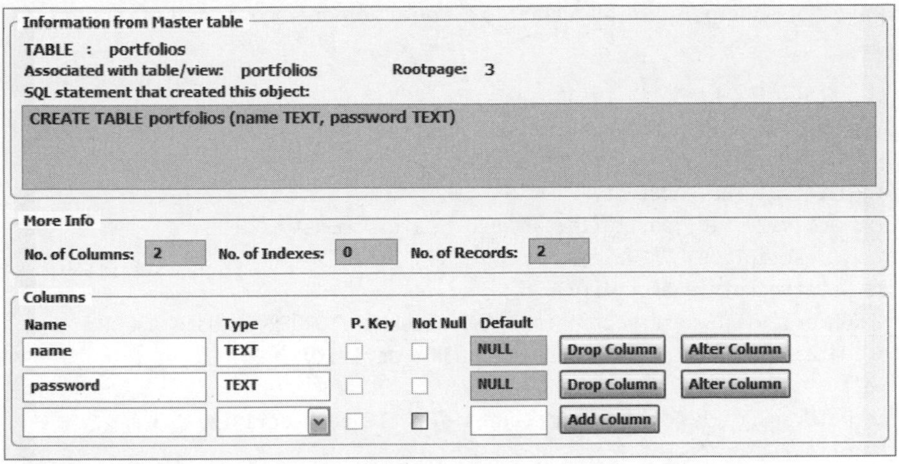

Figure 9-7. *The structure of the portfolios table*

Next up are a series of SQL statements for dealing with accounts:

```
FinanceMaster.Data.sqlCreateAccountsTable =
  "CREATE TABLE IF NOT EXISTS accounts (portfolio TEXT, name TEXT, type TEXT)";
FinanceMaster.Data.sqlCreateAccount =
  "INSERT INTO accounts (portfolio, name, type) VALUES (?, ?, ?)";
FinanceMaster.Data.sqlRetrieveAccounts =
  "SELECT * FROM accounts WHERE portfolio=? ORDER BY type, name";
FinanceMaster.Data.sqlDeleteAccount = "DELETE FROM accounts WHERE " +
  "portfolio=? AND name=?";
```

Figure 9-8 shows the corresponding accounts table structure.

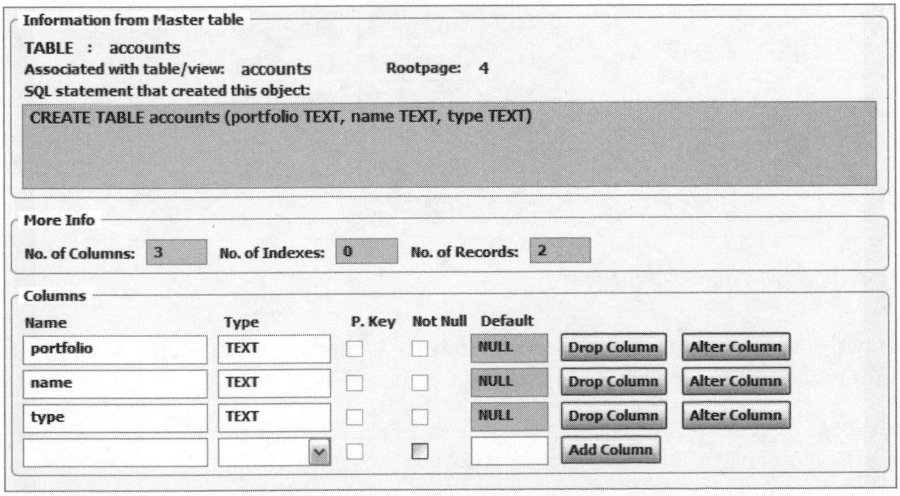

Figure 9-8. *The structure of the accounts table*

The next five SQL statements are all related to account activity records and the activity table:

```
FinanceMaster.Data.sqlCreateActivityTable =
  "CREATE TABLE IF NOT EXISTS activity (id INT, portfolio TEXT, " +
  "account TEXT, date INT, amount FLOAT, new_balance INT, description TEXT)";
FinanceMaster.Data.sqlCreateActivity =
  "INSERT INTO activity (id, portfolio, account, date, amount, " +
  "new_balance, description) VALUES (?, ?, ?, ?, ?, ?, ?)";
FinanceMaster.Data.sqlRetrieveActivity =
  "SELECT * FROM activity where portfolio=? AND account=? ORDER BY date ASC";
FinanceMaster.Data.sqlDeleteActivity = "DELETE FROM activity " +
  "WHERE id=?";
FinanceMaster.Data.sqlDeleteActivityInAccount = "DELETE FROM activity " +
  "WHERE portfolio=? AND account=?";
```

Figure 9-9 shows this table.

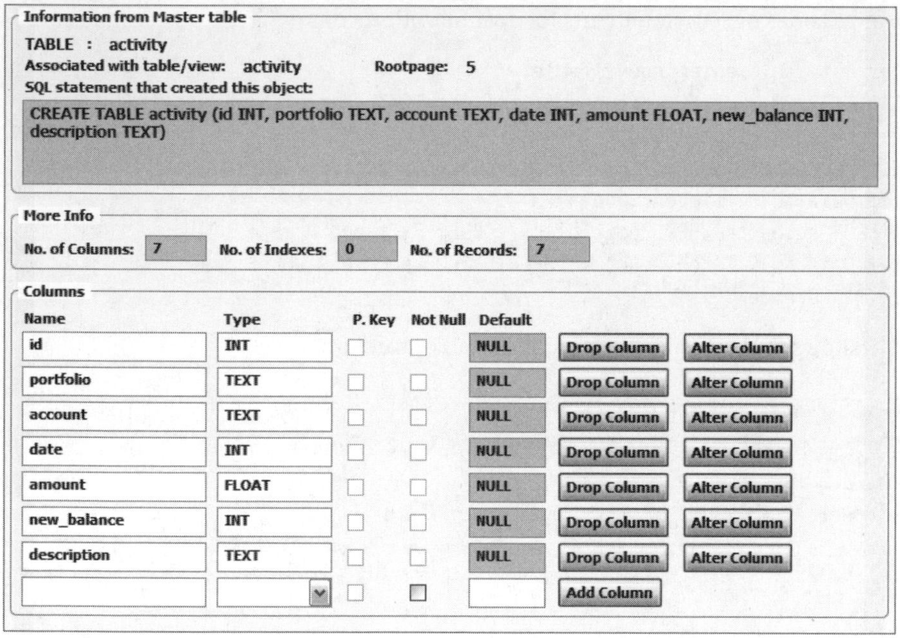

Figure 9-9. *The structure of the activity table*

The final two SQL statements are for two functions we'll need later that get the balance for a given account based on the type of account it is:

```
FinanceMaster.Data.sqlGetSavingsCheckingBalance = "SELECT SUM(amount) " +
  "AS balance FROM activity WHERE portfolio=? AND account=?";
FinanceMaster.Data.sqlGetOtherBalance = "SELECT new_balance AS balance " +
  "FROM activity WHERE portfolio=? AND account=? ORDER BY date DESC LIMIT 1";
```

There are two statements, one for getting the balance of a checking or savings account and the other for getting the balance of other types of accounts. The difference is that for a checking or savings account we need to sum the amount field for all activity records within the account. Since deposits are positive values and withdrawals are negative values in the amount column, this works exactly as expected, producing a single value that is the current balance of the account. For the other account types, however, what we really need to retrieve is the most current new_balance field value. To do so, we select that column, ordering the result set by date in descending order so that the newest record is the first, and then using the limit clause to return just a single record. Note that in both queries, the balance, whether calculated or otherwise, is named balance in the result set, so in both cases we have a common field to pull the value from and the code can therefore be pretty generic when getting the balance of an account.

Initializing the Data Access Layer

Now that we have the queries out of the way, let's look at the code that makes use of them, beginning with the init() method:

```
FinanceMaster.Data.init = function() {

  var initReturn = "ok";
  try {
    if (!window.google || !google.gears) {
      initReturn = "no_gears";
    } else {
      var db = google.gears.factory.create("beta.database");
      db.open(FinanceMaster.Data.databaseName);
      db.execute(FinanceMaster.Data.sqlCreatePortfoliosTable);
      db.execute(FinanceMaster.Data.sqlCreateAccountsTable);
      db.execute(FinanceMaster.Data.sqlCreateActivityTable);
      db.close();
    }
  } catch (e) {
    initReturn = e;
  }

  return initReturn;

};
```

This isn't any different than previous init() methods in DAO classes that we've looked at. It's just a quick check to be sure Gears is available, and if so we execute the table creation queries so that any tables not present are created. The value ok is returned if initialization is successful; otherwise the error that caused the failure is returned.

Working with Portfolios

Next up we have two methods for dealing with portfolios. Note that I'm going to breeze through these (and nearly all the other methods in this source file), because frankly you've seen them a number of times already and there are very few surprises. Let's start with the createPortfolio() method:

```
FinanceMaster.Data.createPortfolio = function(inRecord) {

  var db = google.gears.factory.create("beta.database");
  db.open(FinanceMaster.Data.databaseName);
  db.execute(FinanceMaster.Data.sqlCreatePortfolio, [
    inRecord.get("name"), inRecord.get("password")
  ] );
  db.close();

};
```

This method is called when the add event fires on the portfoliosStore, and as you can see it's a simple query execution using the PortfolioRecord passed in.

Next up is retrievePortfolios(), which is called once during application initialization:

```
FinanceMaster.Data.retrievePortfolios = function() {

  var db = google.gears.factory.create("beta.database");
  db.open(FinanceMaster.Data.databaseName);
  var rs = db.execute(FinanceMaster.Data.sqlRetrievePortfolios);

  var results = [ ];
  while (rs.isValidRow()) {
    results.push(new FinanceMaster.Data.PortfolioRecord({
      name : rs.fieldByName("name"), password : rs.fieldByName("password")
    }, rs.fieldByName("name")));
    rs.next();
  }
  rs.close();
  db.close();

  return results;

};
```

The array of PortfolioRecords we get from this method is used to populate the drop-down from which the user chooses an existing portfolio to open. This method is called directly as we'll see later, not as a result of any Store events firing.

Working with Accounts

Dealing with accounts is much the same as dealing with portfolios, although there are three methods to consider this time around. Let's start with createAccount(), which is called as a result of the add() method of the accountsStore firing:

```
FinanceMaster.Data.createAccount = function(inRecord) {

  var db = google.gears.factory.create("beta.database");
  db.open(FinanceMaster.Data.databaseName);
  db.execute(FinanceMaster.Data.sqlCreateAccount, [
    inRecord.get("portfolio"), inRecord.get("name"), inRecord.get("type")
  ] );
  db.close();

};
```

Once again we take in a Record, this time an AccountRecord; insert its attributes into the sqlCreateAccount query—and we're off to the races.

Once we can create accounts we can retrieve them, thanks to the retrieveAccounts() method:

```
FinanceMaster.Data.retrieveAccounts = function(inPortfolio) {

  var db = google.gears.factory.create("beta.database");
  db.open(FinanceMaster.Data.databaseName);
  var rs = db.execute(FinanceMaster.Data.sqlRetrieveAccounts, [ inPortfolio ] );

  var results = [ ];
  while (rs.isValidRow()) {
    results.push(new FinanceMaster.Data.AccountRecord({
      portfolio : rs.fieldByName("portfolio"), name : rs.fieldByName("name"),
      type : rs.fieldByName("type")
    }, rs.fieldByName("name")));
    rs.next();
  }
  rs.close();
  db.close();

  for (var i = 0; i < results.length; i++) {
    results[i].set("balance", FinanceMaster.Data.getAccountBalance(
      inPortfolio, results[i].get("name"), results[i].get("type") ));
  }

  return results;

};
```

Once again we find ourselves executing a query. For each returned row we create an AccountRecord and populate it from the data in the row. This time we have one additional task, however, and that's to get the balance for the account, since this isn't information stored in the database. So, once we have our array of AccountRecords we iterate over it and call the getAccountBalance() method for each. We'll see how that method works later, but for now it's enough to know that it returns the current balance of the account. We then insert the current balance into the balance field of the AccountRecord, and then return the array to the caller.

Deleting an account is the next function to cover, deleteAccount():

```
FinanceMaster.Data.deleteAccount = function(inPortfolio, inAccount) {

  var db = google.gears.factory.create("beta.database");
  db.open(FinanceMaster.Data.databaseName);
  db.execute(FinanceMaster.Data.sqlDeleteActivityInAccount, [
    inPortfolio, inAccount
  ] );
  db.execute(FinanceMaster.Data.sqlDeleteAccount, [ inPortfolio, inAccount ] );
  db.close();

};
```

Here we have two tasks to complete. First we delete the activity within the account, which we do by executing the sqlDeleteActivityInAccount SQL statement. Once that's done, we execute sqlDeleteAccount to wipe out the account itself.

Working with Activity Records

Activity in an account is stored in the activity table. There are two methods we use to maintain this table, starting with the createActivity() method:

```
FinanceMaster.Data.createActivity = function(inRecord) {

  var db = google.gears.factory.create("beta.database");
  db.open(FinanceMaster.Data.databaseName);
  db.execute(FinanceMaster.Data.sqlCreateActivity, [
    inRecord.get("id"), inRecord.get("portfolio"), inRecord.get("account"),
    inRecord.get("date").getTime(), inRecord.get("amount"),
    inRecord.get("new_balance"), inRecord.get("description")
  ] );
  db.close();

};
```

Creating an activity record is no different than creating a portfolio or account record as we've seen. Let's move on to retrieveActivity():

```
FinanceMaster.Data.retrieveActivity = function(inPortfolio, inAccount) {

  var db = google.gears.factory.create("beta.database");
  db.open(FinanceMaster.Data.databaseName);
  var rs = db.execute(FinanceMaster.Data.sqlRetrieveActivity, [ inPortfolio,
    inAccount ] );

  var results = [ ];
  while (rs.isValidRow()) {
    var d = new Date();
    d.setTime(rs.fieldByName("date"));
    results.push(new FinanceMaster.Data.ActivityRecord({
      id : rs.fieldByName("id"),
      portfolio : rs.fieldByName("portfolio"),
      account : rs.fieldByName("account"),
      date : d, pretty_date : d.format("m/d/Y"),
      amount : rs.fieldByName("amount"),
      new_balance : rs.fieldByName("new_balance"),
      description : rs.fieldByName("description")
    }, rs.fieldByName("id")));
    rs.next();
  }
  rs.close();
  db.close();

  return results;

};
```

Note here that when the ActivityRecord is created, its id field is used as the ID of the record in the Store as well (the second argument passed to the ActivityRecord's constructor). In fact, for portfolios and accounts it's the name field that becomes the ID of the record in the Store. This is important to note because it allows us a way to retrieve a specific record from a Store if we know the ID of the record we want. Assigning an ID like this is optional, but without it we'd have to iterate over the records in the Store looking for the one we want, so this is clearly better if we're going to need to retrieve individual records later.

Finally, deleting an activity is performed in the aptly named deleteActivity() method:

```
FinanceMaster.Data.deleteActivity = function(inID) {

  var db = google.gears.factory.create("beta.database");
  db.open(FinanceMaster.Data.databaseName);
  db.execute(FinanceMaster.Data.sqlDeleteActivity, [ inID ] );
  db.close();

};
```

No big deal I dare say and nothing that needs explaining at this point!

Getting the Balance of an Account

The final method in this JavaScript file is getAccountBalance(), which we saw being called earlier from retrieveAccounts(). Its job is to get the current balance of a specific account. Let's see how that works now, shall we?

```
FinanceMaster.Data.getAccountBalance = function(inPortfolio, inAccount,
  inType) {

  var sql = FinanceMaster.Data.sqlGetOtherBalance;
  if (inType == "Checking" || inType == "Savings") {
    sql = FinanceMaster.Data.sqlGetSavingsCheckingBalance;
  }
  var db = google.gears.factory.create("beta.database");
  db.open(FinanceMaster.Data.databaseName);
  var rs = db.execute(sql, [ inPortfolio, inAccount ] );

  var balance = 0;
  if (rs.isValidRow()) {
    balance = rs.fieldByName("balance");
  }
  rs.close();
  db.close();

  return balance;

};
```

As previously mentioned, how you get the current balance of an account depends on the type of account it is, which is why the third argument to the method is the type of the account. That, along with the name of the portfolio and account, gives us all the information we need. So, we start by assuming we'll be getting the balance of an account type other than a checking or savings account, which corresponds to the sqlGetOtherBalance SQL statement. We override this assumption if the account type is "Checking" or "Savings," in which case we'll need to use the sqlGetSavingsCheckingBalance SQL statement. We saw both of those SQL statements earlier, so you should have a good idea how they work. So, we execute whichever SQL statement is appropriate. We know that we'll get a single row back with a single field in it, the balance field, and it's that field's value that is returned from this method.

FinanceMaster.js

The next source file to look at is FinanceMaster.js. In the past, the file named after the project has been, in many ways, the "main" bit of code for the project. To the degree that initialization happens here, it's still sort of true in this project, but most of the real work is done outside this file, so it shouldn't take too long to get through this file. Let's begin in the customary way and check out the UML diagram in Figure 9-10.

```
┌─────────────────────────────────────────────────┐
│                  FinanceMaster                    │
├─────────────────────────────────────────────────┤
│ +msgBus : Ext.ux.MessageBus                       │
│ +cookieProvider : Ext.state.CookieProvider        │
│ +processStoreEvents : boolean                     │
│ +portletPositions : String[]                      │
│ +currentPortfolio : Ext.data.Record               │
│ +currentAccount : Ext.data.Record                 │
├─────────────────────────────────────────────────┤
│ +init()                                           │
│ +getPortlet() : Object                            │
└─────────────────────────────────────────────────┘
```

Figure 9-10. *The FinanceMaster namespace*

Earlier you'll recall that I talked about the pub/sub model and how that would be required to make this project work. Well, to make that model work requires only one thing:

```
FinanceMaster.msgBus = new Ext.ux.MessageBus();
```

The `Ext.ux.MessageBus` is an Ext JS extension that provides the common message processor we discussed earlier. This is the component that exposes the `publish()` and `subscribe()` methods this paradigm requires. We won't look at the code behind this extension because it's an extension after all and we should be able to drop it in and use it like we do Ext JS itself. But we'll see it in action plenty of times as we explore the code.

After that we have a custom storage provider, just like we've seen before:

```
FinanceMaster.cookieProvider = new Ext.state.CookieProvider({
  expires : new Date(new Date().getTime() + (1000 * 60 * 60 * 24 * 365))
});
```

This time around it's the positions of the portlets that we're interested in saving, and we'll keep them around for a year.

Just like in previous projects we have data `Stores` that react to various events, but we also have the situation during initialization where we don't want to process those events. So we again have a variable to tell us when the `Stores` should process those events and when they shouldn't:

```
FinanceMaster.processStoreEvents = false;
```

Next up we have a field named `portletPositions`:

```
FinanceMaster.portletPositions = [
  [ "PortfolioOverview", "PortfolioDistribution" ],
  [ "AccountActivity", "AccountHistory" ]
];
```

This field stores the positions of the portlets within the portal. Notice that this is a multidimensional array. Each of the elements in the top-level array is a column. The elements within each array are the name of a portlet in that column. The initial values here are the defaults before the user moves any portlets around.

The next two fields store a reference to the currently opened `PortfolioRecord` and `AccountRecord`, if any:

```
FinanceMaster.currentPortfolio = null;
FinanceMaster.currentAccount = null;
```

The next bit of code is something new and exciting! An annoying shortcoming (some would say) with Ext JS is that when you disable a form field, the label for that field is not similarly disabled. I prefer the label be disabled, and the way to accomplish that is to override the `enable()` and `disable()` methods on the `Ext.form.Field` class:

```
Ext.form.Field.prototype.disable =
  Ext.form.Field.prototype.disable.createInterceptor(function() {
  if (this.container) {
    this.container.parent().addClass("x-item-disabled");
  }
});
Ext.form.Field.prototype.enable =
  Ext.form.Field.prototype.enable.createInterceptor(function() {
  if (this.container) {
    this.container.parent().removeClass("x-item-disabled");
  }
});
```

In fact, we don't want to override what those methods do; we simply want to add some functionality to them. To do this, we wrap the invocation of those methods in an interceptor and add our code that way. It's a simple matter of adding or removing the `x-item-disabled` style class and we're good to go.

Initializing the Application

The next bit of code is the `init()` method. This is somewhat long, so I'll break it up into nice bit-sized chunks for your consumption, beginning with this one:

```
FinanceMaster.init = function() {

  var initResult = FinanceMaster.Data.init();
  switch (initResult) {
    case "ok":
    break;
    case "no_gears":
      Ext.MessageBox.show({
        title : "Gears Not Available", buttons : Ext.MessageBox.OK,
        msg : "<br>" +
          "I'm sorry but Google Gears is not installed on your computer, " +
          "or is unavailable for some reason (like you disabled the " +
          "browser plugin for example)." +
          "<br><br>" +
```

```
      "If you do not have Gears installed, please visit " +
      "<a href=\"http://gears.google.com/\" target=\"new\">" +
      "the Gears home page</a> to install it." +
      "<br><br>" +
      "If you do have it installed, please try enabling the plugin in " +
      "whatever fashion is applicable in the browser you are using, " +
      "and reload this application.", animEl : "divSource"
    });
    return;
  break;
  default:
    Ext.MessageBox.alert("Initialization Failed",
      "Data access could not be initialized.  Reason: " + initResult);
    return;
  break;
}
```

Here we're initializing data access as always and aborting initialization if any problems occur.

Once that's done, the next step is to retrieve a list of portfolios stored in the database so the user can choose one to open:

```
var portfolios = FinanceMaster.Data.retrievePortfolios();
for (var i = 0; i < portfolios.length; i++) {
  FinanceMaster.Data.portfoliosStore.add(portfolios[i]);
}
```

I think that probably doesn't need much explanation, but the next bit of code certainly does:

```
var columnConfigs = new Array();
columnConfigs[0] = new Array();
columnConfigs[1] = new Array();
for (var j = 0; j < 2; j++) {
  for (var k = 0; k < 4; k++) {
    var config = FinanceMaster.getPortlet(j, k);
    if (config) {
      columnConfigs[j].push(config);
    }
  }
}
```

To make it easier to build the UI we need to construct two arrays, one for each column in the UI. For each column we need to discover, based on what the user has done, which portlet is in each possible position. What I mean by *position* is that if you consider that you have two columns on the screen where portlets can live, and you have four total portlets, that means you could have any number of portlets in a given column, from zero to four. That means each column has four conceptual positions where a portlet can go. So, for each of the two columns we check to see what portlet is in each of the four possible positions, if any. The getPortlet() method does that for us. Let's break out of the init() method temporarily and get a look at getPortlet() right now:

```
FinanceMaster.getPortlet = function(inColumn, inPosition) {

  for (var i = 0; i < 2; i++) {
    var portletPositions = FinanceMaster.cookieProvider.get(
      "portletPositions" + i);
    if (portletPositions) {
      if (portletPositions == " ") {
        FinanceMaster.portletPositions[i] = new Array();
      } else {
        FinanceMaster.portletPositions[i] = portletPositions.split(",");
      }
    } else {
      FinanceMaster.cookieProvider.set("portletPositions" + i,
        FinanceMaster.portletPositions[i].join(","));
    }
  }

  var portletNamespace = FinanceMaster.Portlets[
    FinanceMaster.portletPositions[inColumn][inPosition]
  ];

  if (portletNamespace) {
    return portletNamespace.getConfig();
  } else {
    return null;
  }

};
```

This method begins by iterating over the two possible columns. For each it tries to retrieve a cookie named portletPositionsX, where X is either 0 or 1. If the cookie is found, we then need to see if its value is a single space character, which is a special case for when all the portlets are in the other column. If it is, then we instantiate a new empty array; if it's not, we split() the value of the cookie, which is a comma-separated list of portlet names present in that column. In either case we wind up with an array, which now becomes the value of the element in the portletPositions array corresponding to the column we're trying to load. If the cookie isn't found, the default value found in portletPositions will be used.

Finally, we read the element in portletPositions corresponding to the portlet position that the caller requested information on. Remember how this method is being called: in init() the code is requesting what portlet is present in a given position, and the position is denoted by the column number and position within the column. Using the value of the element from

portletPositions, we try to get a handle to the namespace associated with the portlet and call
the getConfig() method in it to return an Ext JS UI configuration object for a Panel. It's that
reference that is returned, or null if the namespace isn't found.

Now we can get back to init() itself. The next step is to create the Viewport:

```
var viewport = new Ext.Viewport({ layout : "border",
  items : [
    { region : "north", height : 80, border : false,
      html : "<table border=\"0\" width=\"99%\"><tr>" +
        "<td><img src=\"img/FinanceMaster.gif\"></td>" +
        "<td align=\"right\"><a href=\"javascript:void(null);\" " +
        "onClick=\"new Ext.Window(" +
        "FinanceMaster.OpenPortfolioWindow.getConfig(true))." +
        "show('divSource');\">" +
        "Switch Portfolio</a></td></tr></table>"
    },
```

Our friend Mr. BorderLayout is back once more, and the first thing we have defined is a
north region. Its content is just some simple HTML, a table to be precise, where we have the
application logo on the left and a link to open a new portfolio on the right.

Following that is the required center region, and that's where the portal itself sits:

```
    { xtype : "portal", region : "center", border : false,
      items : [
        { columnWidth : .5, style : "padding:10px 0px 10px 10px",
          items : columnConfigs[0]
        },
        { columnWidth : .5, style : "padding:10px 10px 10px 10px",
          items : columnConfigs[1]
        }
      ],
```

The xtype portal is supplied by the portal extension in the PortalExtension.js file.
Like the MessageBus.js code, we won't be looking at the extension code in the same way that
you typically don't (often at least) look at the code behind the HashMap class in Java or the
LinkedList available in C++. We just want to be blissfully ignorant and make use of it, and
that's what we have here.

You define a layout as you see fit inside the portal. In this case, as I've mentioned before,
we have a two-column layout. Each column is given 50 percent of the width of the screen, and
some padding is added so things get spaced out nicely. The items array for each column is the
value of the columnConfigs we generated right before this, so as you know, what you have here
is an array of Panel config objects.

The result of all this can be seen in Figure 9-11, where the default layout of portlets is
shown.

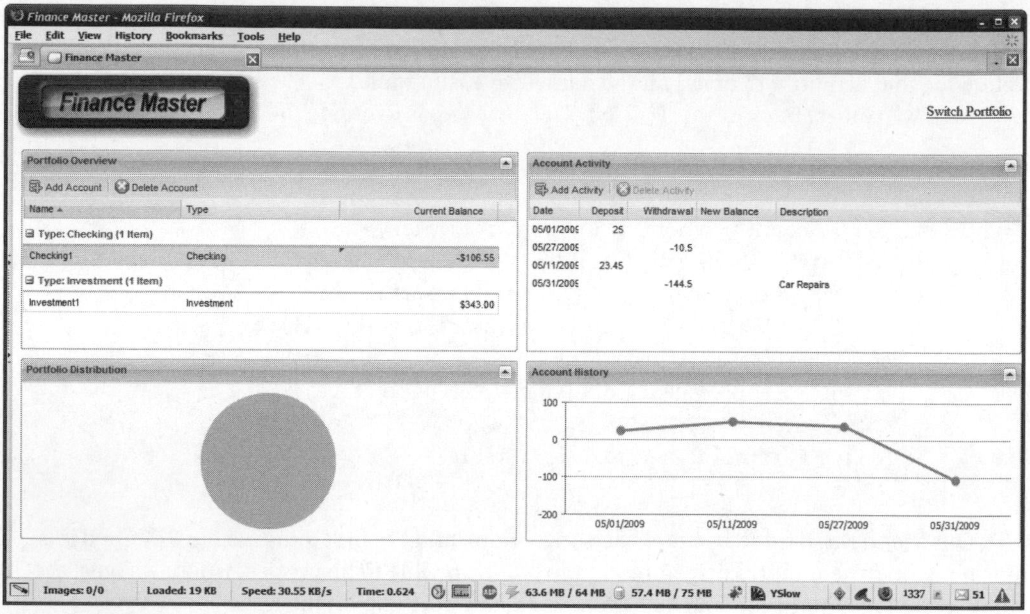

Figure 9-11. *The four portlets of the apocalypse*

With the layout defined, we have some further work to do to make this layout complete:

```
listeners : {
  resize : function(inComponent, inAdjWidth, inAdjHeight, inRawWidth,
    inRawHeight) {
    Ext.get("divSource").applyStyles(
      "top:" + Ext.getBody().getViewSize().height + "px;");
  },
```

Remember when we looked at styles.css that I said I managed to do something a little different with the divSource? Well, here it is! In this project, Windows zoom in from the bottom of the screen. To make this work, the top style attribute of divSource has to be set dynamically because we don't know the height of the browser window to begin with. So, we hook into the resize event of the Viewport, within which we can call Ext.getBody().getViewSize() to get the current dimensions of the browser's page area. Using this, we can use the applyStyles() method on the Ext JS Element wrapper object around divSource to set the top attribute accordingly. The resize event fires when the Viewport is first built, so we can ensure the value is set correctly right away, and it'll fire any time the user resizes the browser too so we know the value will stay up to date.

Another event we have to handle is the drop event, which is provided by the portal extension:

```
      drop : function(e) {
        for (var i = 0; i < 2; i++) {
          var j = FinanceMaster.portletPositions[i].indexOf(e.panel.id);
          if (j != -1) {
            FinanceMaster.portletPositions[i].splice(j, 1);
          }
        }
        FinanceMaster.portletPositions[e.columnIndex].splice(
          e.position, 0, e.panel.id);
        for (var k = 0; k < 2; k++) {
          var cookieValue = FinanceMaster.portletPositions[k].join(",");
          if (Ext.isEmpty(cookieValue)) {
            cookieValue = " ";
          }
          FinanceMaster.cookieProvider.set(
            "portletPositions" + k, cookieValue);
        }
      }
    }
  }
 ]
});
```

This event fires any time the user drags a portlet around and finally releases the mouse
Button to set the new position. When this occurs, we have a couple of tasks to complete. First,
we need to remove the portlet from its previous position in the portletPositions array. So, we
use the indexOf() method added to the array prototype by Ext JS to find out where it is, based
on the ID of the Panel that was dropped. Assuming it's found, the basic array splice() method
gets rid of it. After that we have to insert the portlet into its new position, and once again,
splice() does the trick. The next step is to write out the cookie values for the two columns.
To do this we take the element in portletPositions corresponding to each column and use
the array join() method to create a comma-separated value from it. Now, if this value winds
up being empty, as determined by Ext.isEmpty(), then we need to write out that special single
space character because both cookies must always have some value; otherwise the UI breaks
when it is built. Once the value is created we write out the cookie and the user's setting is now
persisted.

Completing Initialization

A few more miscellaneous tasks are required to complete initialization, beginning with this:

```
Ext.state.Manager.setProvider(FinanceMaster.cookieProvider);
```

The previous code sets our custom storage provider as the default for Ext JS's usage.

We're also very familiar with these two lines of code, setting up our validation message to
be displayed on form fields:

```
Ext.QuickTips.init();
Ext.form.Field.prototype.msgTarget = "side";
```

These three lines of code close out the `init()` method:

```
new Ext.Window(➥
  FinanceMaster.OpenPortfolioWindow.getConfig(false)).show("divSource");
FinanceMaster.processStoreEvents = true;
FinanceMaster.msgBus.publish("InitComplete");
```

The first shows the Open Portfolio `Window` as seen in previous screenshots. The second tells the data `Stores` they can begin processing events. The last one is the first time we're seeing the message bus used. Here we're publishing an "InitComplete" message. You'll see later that each of the portlets subscribes to this message so that they can do some first-time initialization, but keep in mind that the code in `init()` isn't directly calling on the portlets, since it doesn't know for sure which are present. That loose coupling (or *no* coupling really!) is the big advantage of the pub/sub model. In this case there isn't any data to pass to the subscribers, so only the message itself is passed to the `publish()` method.

OpenPortfolioWindow.js

The `Window` shown to the user to determine which portfolio to open (and doubling as the mechanism by which to create new portfolio) is found in the `OpenPortfolioWindow.js` file. You can see its diagram in Figure 9-12.

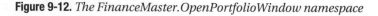

```
FinanceMaster.OpenPortfolioWindow

+getConfig()
+openClick()
+newClick()
+openPortfolio() : boolean
```

Figure 9-12. *The FinanceMaster.OpenPortfolioWindow namespace*

We begin with the `Window`'s config object, which I'll break up a bit to make it less overwhelming:

```
FinanceMaster.OpenPortfolioWindow.getConfig = function(inClosable) { return {

  closable : inClosable, modal : true, width : 350, height : 210,
  minimizable : false, resizable : false, draggable : false,
  id : "winOpenPortfolio", shadowOffset : 8,
  title : "Welcome to Finance Master!",
  items : [
    { frame : true,
      html : "To begin, " +
        "Select the portfolio you want to open, enter the associated " +
        "password, and click Open.<br><br>To create a new portfolio, " +
        "enter it's name, a password to secure it, and click New Portfolio"
    },
```

We start with a pretty basic `Window` config here. The `items` array begins with a `Panel` with some instructions telling the user what to do.

After that comes a `FormPanel`:

```
{ xtype : "form", id : "frmOpenPortfolio", frame : true,
  monitorValid : true,
  items : [
    { xtype : "combo", fieldLabel : "Portfolio",
      name : "name", allowBlank : false, editable : true,
      triggerAction : "all", mode : "local",
      store : FinanceMaster.Data.portfoliosStore,
      valueField : "name", displayField : "name"
    },
    { xtype : "textfield", fieldLabel : "Password", name : "password",
      allowBlank : false }
  ],
```

We have a `ComboBox` where the existing portfolios are listed. This widget is bound to the `portfoliosStore` we saw populated a while back in `init()`. Note that the `editable` attribute is set to `true`, which allows the user to type data in the text box area. This is required because this `ComboBox` does double duty: the user can select an existing portfolio or can enter the name of a new one. The `TextField` below that is where the user enters the password for the portfolio.

Notice that the form has `monitorValid` set to `true`, and also notice that both of the fields have `allowBlank` set to `false`. So, the `Buttons` on the bottom will be disabled unless there is a value in both form fields, as you can see here:

```
buttons : [
  { text : "Open", formBind : true, icon : "img/Open.gif",
    cls : "x-btn-text-icon",
    handler : function() {
      FinanceMaster.OpenPortfolioWindow.openClick();
    }
  },
  { text : "New Portfolio", formBind : true, icon : "img/New.gif",
    cls : "x-btn-text-icon",
    handler : function() {
      FinanceMaster.OpenPortfolioWindow.newClick();
    }
  }
]
    }
  ]

}; };
```

The `Buttons` themselves are like most we've seen before and just call out to some other methods in this namespace when clicked. First is the handler for the Open `Button`:

```
FinanceMaster.OpenPortfolioWindow.openClick = function() {

  var vals = Ext.getCmp("frmOpenPortfolio").getForm().getValues();
  if (FinanceMaster.OpenPortfolioWindow.openPortfolio(
    vals.name, vals.password)) {
    Ext.getCmp("winOpenPortfolio").close();
  }

};
```

Opening a portfolio is just a simple matter of calling the openPortfolio() method, passing it the portfolio name and password entered by the user. It may seem for a moment like this is a superfluous bit of indirection. After all, why not just call openPortfolio() directly from the Button's handler and do away with the need for openClick() at all? The reason is that the functionality provided by openPortfolio() is needed in two places, so doing it this way allows us to share that code and save our fingers some typing!

Assuming openPortfolio() returns true, the portfolio is successfully opened, then the Open Portfolio Window is closed. At that point the user is all set to begin making money. However, if the user fails to enter a valid password for the selected portfolio, the message in Figure 9-13 appears.

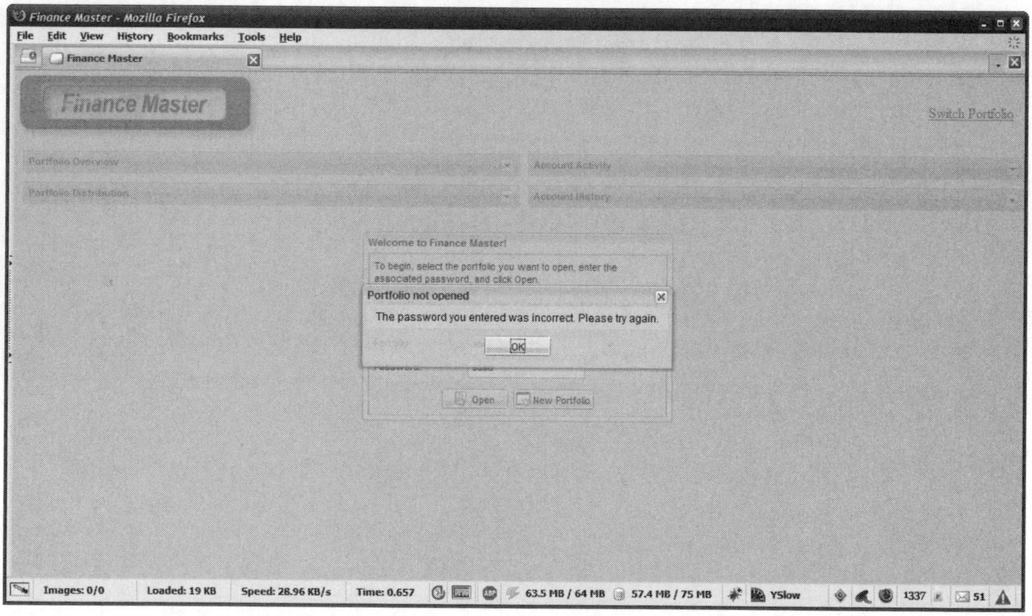

Figure 9-13. *Possible hacker, possible hacker, go away, come again some other day!*

The other Button, the one the user clicks to create a new portfolio, has its functionality fulfilled by the newClick() method:

```
FinanceMaster.OpenPortfolioWindow.newClick = function() {

  var vals = Ext.getCmp("frmOpenPortfolio").getForm().getValues();
  if (FinanceMaster.Data.portfoliosStore.getById(vals.name)) {
    if (FinanceMaster.OpenPortfolioWindow.openPortfolio(
      vals.name, vals.password)) {
      Ext.getCmp("winOpenPortfolio").close();
    }
  } else {
    var rec = new FinanceMaster.Data.PortfolioRecord({
      name : vals.name, password : vals.password
    }, vals.name);
    FinanceMaster.Data.portfoliosStore.add(rec);
    if (FinanceMaster.OpenPortfolioWindow.openPortfolio(
      vals.name, vals.password)) {
      Ext.getCmp("winOpenPortfolio").close();
    }
  }

};
```

The first thing we need to do is see if the name the user entered is already in use. The way I decided I wanted the application to handle this is to simply try to open the portfolio, rather than displaying an annoying message like "Hey moron, that name is already in use, try again!" So, the same call is made that we saw in openClick().

However, if the name isn't found in the list of existing portfolios, then we create a new PortfolioRecord with the entered name and password. That PortfolioRecord is then added to the portfoliosStore, which results in it being written to the database by virtue of the add event firing on the portfoliosStore. Finally, we call openPortfolio() to open it. Note that checking the return code should be pointless here because we know the portfolio exists and that the password here is correct, but we'll do it anyway, just in case some funkiness ensues.

The final method is openPortfolio() itself:

```
FinanceMaster.OpenPortfolioWindow.openPortfolio = function(inName, inPassword) {

  var rec = FinanceMaster.Data.portfoliosStore.getById(inName);

  if (rec) {
    if (inPassword == rec.get("password")) {
      FinanceMaster.currentPortfolio = rec;
      FinanceMaster.msgBus.publish("PortfolioOpened", rec);
      return true;
    } else {
      Ext.MessageBox.alert("Portfolio not opened",
        "The password you entered was incorrect.  Please try again.");
      return false;
```

```
      }
    } else {
      Ext.MessageBox.alert("Portfolio not opened",
        "The portfolio '" + inName + "' was not found.<br><br>" +
        "If you are trying to open an existing portfolio, please " +
        "select it from the list.  If you are trying to create a new " +
        "portfolio, please click the New Portfolio button.");
      return false;
    }

};
```

The first step is to try to retrieve the PortfolioRecord from the portfoliosStore. If the record is found, the password is then checked. Assuming the password matches, the currentPortfolio field is pointed to the PortfolioRecord and the "PortfolioOpened" message is published. This time we have some information to pass along, namely the PortfolioRecord itself. (There's no reason it *has* to be passed, since currentPortfolio points to it anyway and any subscriber could get to it that way. But I wanted to demonstrate data passing as part of a message.) If the password doesn't match, then the message we saw a little while ago is shown.

Figure 9-14 shows the result if the PortfolioRecord isn't found.

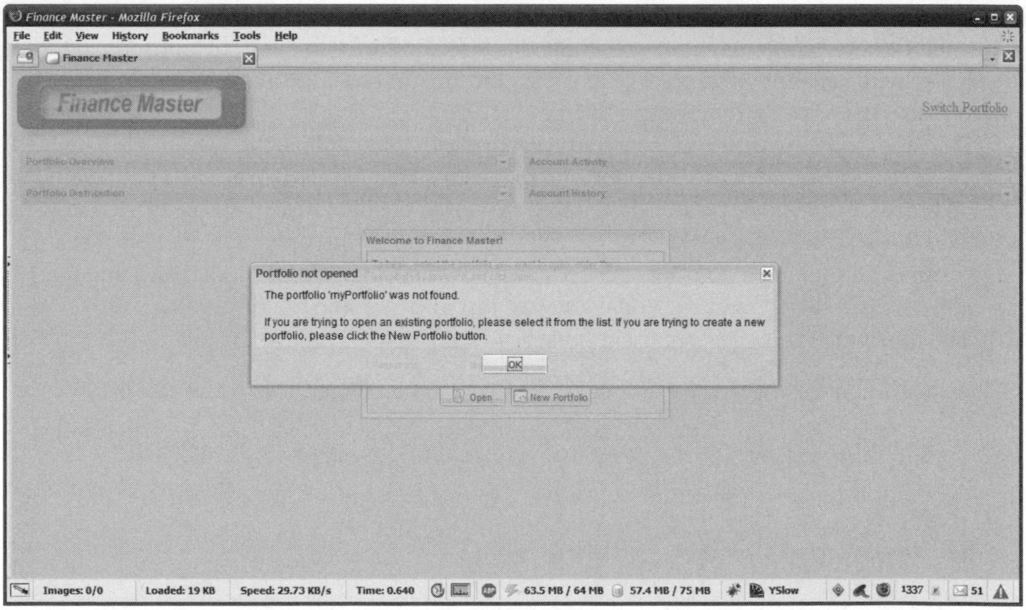

Figure 9-14. *The user entered a bogus portfolio name.*

We kindly give the user some helpful information on why this might have occurred and what they might be able to do to correct it (see, who says usability doesn't matter?).

PortfolioOverviewPortlet.js

Now let's look at the code for our first portlet. The portfolio overview portlet is the one that lists all the accounts in the portfolio and their balances. It is also where we can add and delete accounts. Although there are not a lot of members in the namespace, as Figure 9-15 shows, there's a fair amount of code in it nonetheless.

```
FinanceMaster.Portlets.PortfolioOverview
+accountTypesStore : Ext.data.Store
+accountTypeVals : String[]
+getConfig() : Object
+addAccount()
+deleteAccount()
```

Figure 9-15. *The FinanceMaster.Portlets.PortfolioOverview namespace*

We're going to have the ability to add accounts here, which means we need the ability to select an account. So, we'll need a Store that we can bind to a ComboBox for that purpose:

```
FinanceMaster.Portlets.PortfolioOverview.accountTypesStore =
  new Ext.data.Store({});
FinanceMaster.Portlets.PortfolioOverview.accountTypeVals =
  [ "Checking", "Investment", "Loan", "Retirement", "Savings" ];
for (var i = 0;
  i < FinanceMaster.Portlets.PortfolioOverview.accountTypeVals.length; i++) {
  FinanceMaster.Portlets.PortfolioOverview.accountTypesStore.add(
    new Ext.data.Record(
      { type : FinanceMaster.Portlets.PortfolioOverview.accountTypeVals[i] }
    )
  );
}
```

We do the same as in the past: by using an array as the source of data to populate the Store. This is pretty simple, clean, and effective.

Defining the Portlet's UI

Up next is the getConfig() method, called to get the configuration object for the Panel that is the portlet (any portlet is just a Panel, so we can do any Ext JS-ish stuff we want within it).

```
FinanceMaster.Portlets.PortfolioOverview.getConfig = function() { return {
```

```
  title : "Portfolio Overview", id : "PortfolioOverview", height : 200,
  layout : "fit",
```

This covers the basics for us. This particular portlet will be a GridPanel only, so using the fit layout ensures the Grid fills the Panel. After that we find the definition for the Grid itself:

```
items : [
  { xtype : "grid", store : FinanceMaster.Data.accountsStore,
    sm : new Ext.grid.RowSelectionModel( { singleSelect : true } ),
    id : "FinanceMaster.Portlets.PortfolioOverview.grdAccounts",
    columns : [
      { header : "Name", dataIndex : "name" },
      { header : "Type", dataIndex : "type" },
      { header : "Current Balance", align : "right",
        id : "FinanceMaster.Portlets.PortfolioOverview.grdAccounts_balance",
        dataIndex : "balance", renderer : Ext.util.Format.usMoney }
    ],
    view : new Ext.grid.GroupingView({
      forceFit : true,
      groupTextTpl : '{text} ({[values.rs.length]} ' +
        '{[values.rs.length > 1 ? "Items" : "Item"]})'
    }),
```

A couple of new things are shown here. First, the Current Balance column is right-aligned, which is typical of monetary fields. Second, that same field uses the renderer attribute. This attribute allows us to specify a function that will essentially intercept the value in the column for a given row before it is rendered and allows us to do whatever we like with it. Here, the Ext.util.Format.usMoney is actually an Ext JS–supplied function that will format a numeric value as a US currency value (making this application less than useful for users in other countries, but hey, there's a good exercise for you to undertake!).

The next step is to hook into the rowclick event:

```
listeners : {
  rowclick : function(inGrid, inRowIndex, inEventObject) {
    Ext.getCmp(
      "FinanceMaster.Portlets.PortfolioOverview.btnDelete").enable();
    FinanceMaster.currentAccount =
      inGrid.getSelectionModel().getSelected();
    FinanceMaster.msgBus.publish("AccountOpened",
      FinanceMaster.currentAccount);
  }
}
}
],
```

When an account is selected, the Delete Account Button is enabled, and the currentAccount field gets a reference to the AccountRecord that was selected. Finally, the "AccountOpened" message is published, which will cause the account activity portlet to load the activity for the account and the account history portlet to update its chart.

The Delete Account Button that was just enabled is part of a top toolbar on the Panel. Its definition begins with the definition of the other Button you see on the UI, the Add Account Button:

```
tbar : [
  { text : "Add Account", icon : "img/Add.gif",
    cls : "x-btn-text-icon",
    handler : function() {
```

The handler for this `Button` is where all the action is, as you can see for yourself:

```
new Ext.Window({
    closable : true, modal : true, width : 350, height : 170,
    minimizable : false, resizable : false, draggable : false,
    id : "FinanceMaster.Portlets.PortfolioOverview.winAddAccount",
    shadowOffset : 8, title : "Add an account",
    items : [
      { frame : true,
        html : "Enter a name for the new account, select its type, " +
          "and click Ok.  Click Cancel if you decide not to " +
          "add an account at this time."
      },
      { xtype : "form", frame : true, monitorValid : true,
        id : "FinanceMaster.Portlets.PortfolioOverview.frmAddAccount",
        items : [
          { xtype : "textfield", fieldLabel : "Name", name : "name",
            allowBlank : false },
          { xtype : "combo", fieldLabel : "Type",
            name : "type", allowBlank : false, editable : false,
            triggerAction : "all", mode : "local",
            store :
              FinanceMaster.Portlets.PortfolioOverview.accountTypesStore,
            valueField : "type", displayField : "type"
          }
        ],
        buttons : [
          { text : "Ok", formBind : true, icon : "img/Ok.gif",
            cls : "x-btn-text-icon",
            handler : function() {
              FinanceMaster.Portlets.PortfolioOverview.addAccount();
            }
          },
          { text : "Cancel", icon : "img/Cancel.gif",
            cls : "x-btn-text-icon",
            handler : function() {
              Ext.getCmp(
                "FinanceMaster.Portlets.PortfolioOverview.winAddAccount"
              ).close();
            }
          }
        ]
      }
    ]
}).show('divSource');
```

A `Window` is opened that contains a `FormPanel`. This form has two fields. The first is a `TextField` where the user enters the name of the account, and the second is a `ComboBox` where the user selects the type of the account. The `ComboBox` is bound to the `Store` we saw populated earlier. Both of these fields are required; therefore, they have `allowBlank` set to `false`, and the form itself has `monitorValid` set to `true`. Two `Buttons` are added to the form: the Ok `Button`, which has `formBind` set to `true` so that it will only be enabled when both fields have been entered, and Cancel, which the user clicks to abort adding a new account. This `Window` can be seen in Figure 9-16, where I've also expanded the `ComboBox`'s options for you to see.

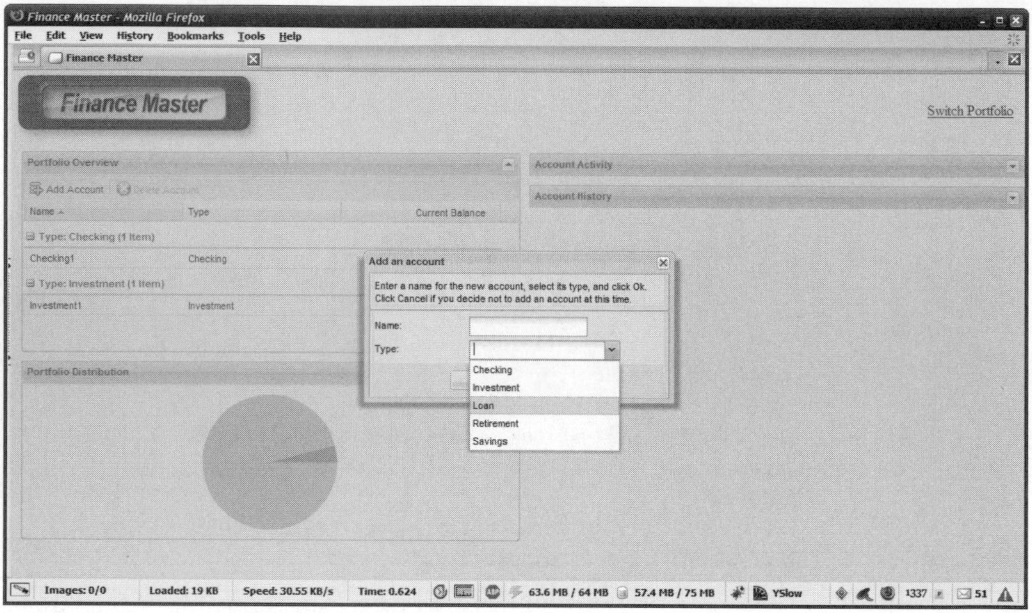

Figure 9-16. *Adding a new account and determining its type*

In Figure 9-17 you can see what happens when the user hasn't entered a value in the type field, and the user's mouse pointer hovers over the error indicator icon.

In a moment we'll look at the two methods that the Ok and Cancel `Buttons` call on when clicked, but for now let's continue looking at that toolbar definition. Next is the Delete Account `Button`:

```
{ text : "Delete Account", icon : "img/Delete.gif", disabled : true,
  cls : "x-btn-text-icon",
  id : "FinanceMaster.Portlets.PortfolioOverview.btnDelete",
  handler : function() {
    FinanceMaster.Portlets.PortfolioOverview.deleteAccount();
  }
 }
]

}; };
```

This is another simple `Button` definition, but of course it starts out disabled until an account is actually selected. The `deleteAccount()` method we'll see a bit later too. That actually concludes the UI config object for this `Panel`.

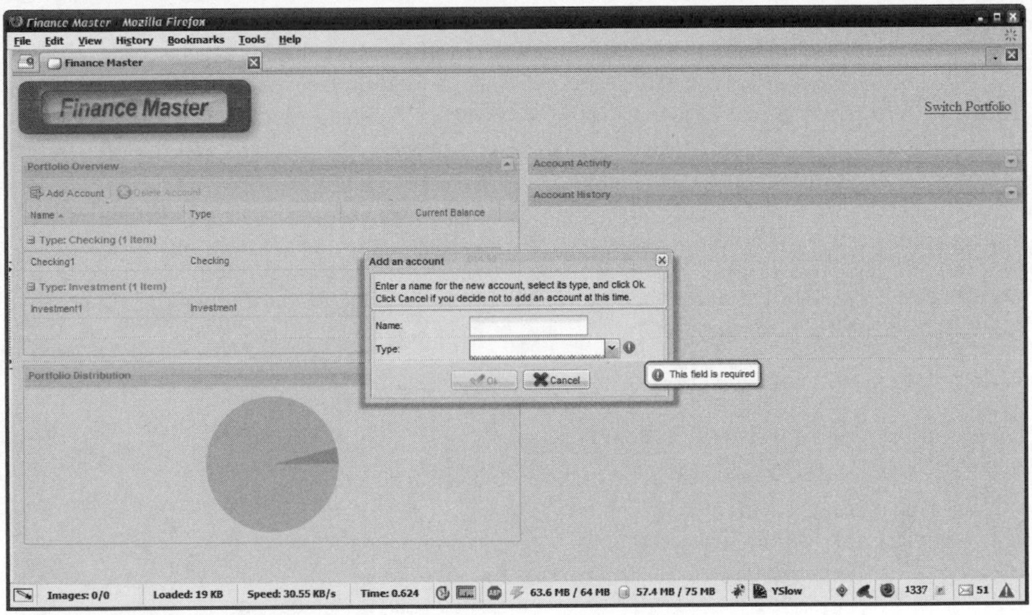

Figure 9-17. *Oops, try again, dude!*

Adding an Account

When the Ok Button in the add account Window is clicked, the addAccount() method is called:

```
FinanceMaster.Portlets.PortfolioOverview.addAccount = function() {

  var vals = Ext.getCmp(
    "FinanceMaster.Portlets.PortfolioOverview.frmAddAccount"
  ).getForm().getValues();
  var rec = FinanceMaster.Data.accountsStore.getById(vals.name);
  if (rec) {
    Ext.MessageBox.alert("Could not create account",
      "An account with the name '" + vals.name +
      "' already exists in this portfolio.  Please choose another name.");
    return;
  } else {
    rec = new FinanceMaster.Data.AccountRecord({
      portfolio : FinanceMaster.currentPortfolio.get("name"),
      name : vals.name, type : vals.type, balance : 0
    }, vals.name);
    FinanceMaster.Data.accountsStore.add(rec);
    Ext.getCmp(
      "FinanceMaster.Portlets.PortfolioOverview.winAddAccount").close();
  }

};
```

The first step, naturally enough, is to get the values of the form. Next, we attempt to retrieve the AccountRecord with the name the user entered. If it's found, we display a MessageBox to tell them the name is already in use. If the AccountRecord is not found, a new one is created and added to the accountsStore. This triggers the add events, which causes the data to be saved to the database. Finally, the add account Window is closed and the UI automatically gets updated based on the Store having a new record added.

Deleting an Account

Deleting an account isn't too tough, and it is a task handled by the well-named (if I do say so myself!) deleteAccount() method:

```
FinanceMaster.Portlets.PortfolioOverview.deleteAccount = function() {

  Ext.MessageBox.confirm("Confirm Deletion",
    "Are you sure you want to delete the selected account?",
    function(inButtonClicked) {
      if (inButtonClicked == "yes") {
        FinanceMaster.Data.accountsStore.remove(
          Ext.getCmp(
            "FinanceMaster.Portlets.PortfolioOverview.grdAccounts"
          ).getSelectionModel().getSelected()
        );
        Ext.getCmp(
          "FinanceMaster.Portlets.PortfolioOverview.btnDelete").disable();
        FinanceMaster.msgBus.publish("AccountDeleted");
      }
    }
  );

};
```

First we confirm that the user really wants to delete the account. Assuming the user clicks the Yes Button, we call the remove() method of the accountsStore, passing in a reference to the AccountRecord currently selected in the accounts Grid. That causes the remove event to fire on the Store, which results in a call to the deleteAcount() method in the data access layer, and the account (and all its activity records you'll recall) are removed from the database. We also need to re-disable the Delete Account Button. Finally, the "AccountDelete" message is published, since other portlets may need to update themselves based on this change (such as the account activity and account history portlets, which will collapse themselves in this case).

Reacting to Events

To complete this portlet, we need to handle a couple of messages, which is another way of saying we need to react to a couple of events (remember that messages being published is basically synonymous with events firing). The first that we'll begin with is the "InitComplete" message, which as you'll recall is published when the init() method completes. So, we have a subscribe() call on the message bus for that message:

```
FinanceMaster.msgBus.subscribe("InitComplete", function() {

  Ext.getCmp("PortfolioOverview").collapse();

});
```

The only task here is to collapse the portlet. This is done because I found there were sometimes rendering glitches if the portlet starts out collapsed, resulting from sizes not being calculated right because the element isn't visible at the time (a fairly common issue in any JavaScript-based UI construction). So I start them all out expanded and have them response to the "InitComplete" message by collapsing themselves. In addition to avoiding the rendering glitches, it starts the application in an "active" way, vis-à-vis, using some animation. This is just a somewhat more interesting startup transition, that's all.

The next message that needs to be handled is the "PortfolioOpened" message, called when the user selects a portfolio to open (or creates a brand-new one):

```
FinanceMaster.msgBus.subscribe("PortfolioOpened", function() {

  Ext.getCmp("PortfolioOverview").expand();

  var rec = arguments[0],

  var accounts = FinanceMaster.Data.retrieveAccounts(rec.get("name"));

  FinanceMaster.Data.accountsStore.removeAll();
  FinanceMaster.processStoreEvents = false;
  for (var i = 0; i < accounts.length; i++) {
    FinanceMaster.Data.accountsStore.add(accounts[i]);
  }
  FinanceMaster.processStoreEvents = true;

});
```

In this case, the first chore is to expand this portlet, since seeing the overview of the accounts in the portfolio is an obvious thing to do. Next, we grab the PortfolioRecord that is passed into the method. When a message is published on the message bus, you can pass any data you like after the message itself, and you can pass as much as you like. The function that is passed to the subscribe() method gets all of those arguments to the publish() method passed along to it (minus the message itself). Since every JavaScript function inherently has access to an arguments array, that's how we can get a hold of that data. Alternatively you could use named arguments; it would work just as well, but sticking with the arguments array enforces the idea that the list of arguments can be dynamic.

In any case, here we only have a single argument, the PortfolioRecord, so it's the first element in the arguments array. Once we have that, we can make a call to the FinanceMaster. Data.retrieveAccounts() method, passing it the name of the portfolio, to get the list of accounts for that portfolio. Once we have that, we can go ahead and iterate over that returned array and add each of the AccountRecord objects to the accountsStore. We have to be sure to (a) clear the accountsStore first by calling removeAll(), and (b) turn event processing off for the `Store` while we're loading the `AccountRecords`; otherwise, we'll get add events firing for each, which would result in duplicates added to the database.

PortfolioDistributionPortlet.js

The next portlet we'll look at is the portfolio distribution portlet. This is the portlet responsible for showing a pie chart that visually conveys how the assets in the portfolio are distributed between the various account types. Let's begin with some UML, as shown in Figure 9-18.

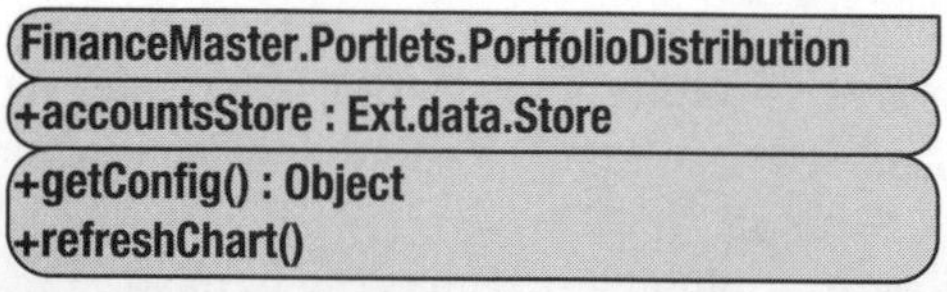

```
FinanceMaster.Portlets.PortfolioDistribution
+accountsStore : Ext.data.Store
+getConfig() : Object
+refreshChart()
```

Figure 9-18. *The FinanceMaster.Portlets.PortfolioDistribution namespace*

As you can see, this portlet is considerably simpler than the last. It begins with its own `Store`:

```
FinanceMaster.Portlets.PortfolioDistribution.accountsStore =
  new Ext.data.Store({});
```

This is the `Store` that will be bound to our pie chart. For now it is empty, but we'll see where and how it gets its data shortly.

Defining the Portlet's UI

First, though, let's see the UI configuration:

```
FinanceMaster.Portlets.PortfolioDistribution.getConfig = function() { return {

  title : "Portfolio Distribution", id : "PortfolioDistribution", height : 200,
  layout : "fit"

}; };
```

That's about as simple as it gets! You may be wondering where exactly the definition of the chart is. In point of fact, it is created dynamically a little bit downstream of here. Before we get to that, though, have a gander at Figure 9-19 to see what this portlet looks like.

You'll notice the tooltip showing details for the larger of the pie wedges. This appears when users hover over it with their mouse.

■Note It does not appear possible to put this information statically on a pie chart, which to me is a real shortcoming. I asked around on the Ext JS forums about this and no one could tell me how to do it. Reading through the documentation doesn't give any clues either, so it appears to not be possible. Hopefully a future version will provide this capability.

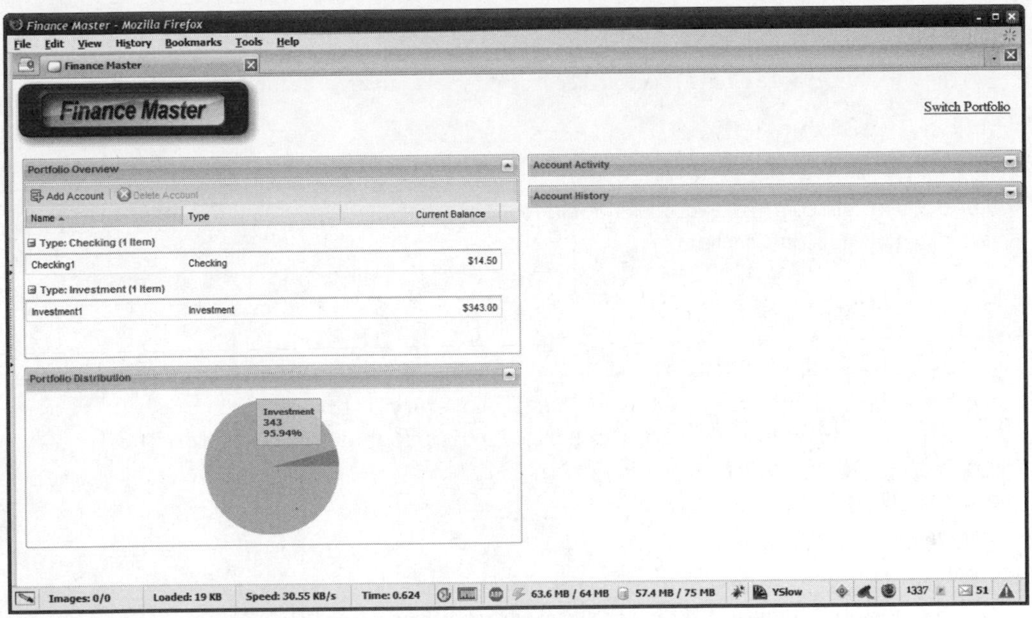

Figure 9-10. *Hovering over the chart to see the underlying data*

Refreshing the Chart

The real workhorse for this portlet is its refreshChart() method and, oh look, here it comes now:

```
FinanceMaster.Portlets.PortfolioDistribution.refreshChart = function(inRec) {

  FinanceMaster.Portlets.PortfolioDistribution.accountsStore =
    new Ext.data.Store({});

  var accounts = FinanceMaster.Data.retrieveAccounts(inRec.get("name"));

  var mc = new Ext.util.MixedCollection();
  for (var i = 0; i < accounts.length; i++) {
    var acctType = accounts[i].get("type");
    var balance = 0;
    if (mc.containsKey(acctType)) {
      balance = mc.get(acctType);
    }
    balance = balance + accounts[i].get("balance");
    mc.add(acctType, balance);
  }
```

```
mc.eachKey(function(inKey, inItem) {
  FinanceMaster.Portlets.PortfolioDistribution.accountsStore.add(
    new FinanceMaster.Data.AccountRecord({ type : inKey, balance : inItem })
  );
});

var p = Ext.getCmp("PortfolioDistribution");
var c = Ext.getCmp("pdChart");
if (c) {
  p.remove(c, true);
}
p.add(new Ext.chart.PieChart(
  { dataField : "balance", id : "pdChart", categoryField : "type",
    store : FinanceMaster.Portlets.PortfolioDistribution.accountsStore }
));
p.doLayout();

};
```

The first step is to clear out the accountsStore. Unfortunately, I ran into a nasty problem when I tried to do the more logical removeAll() on it: a JavaScript error kept things from working. I found that to get around it I had to re-create the Store entirely as done here. Annoying and inefficient, but it works!

The next step is to instantiate a MixedCollection that we'll populate with elements keyed by account type. For each we'll store the accumulated balance across all accounts of that type within the portfolio. Then, we iterate over the collection of accounts and for each we get its type. We attempt to retrieve the element in the MixedCollection for that type, and if it's there, we get the balance. If no such element is found, then this account must be the first of its type. In either case, we add the balance of the account to the accumulated balance and put the element back in the MixedCollection, overriding the previous element if it was there.

Once that's done, we need to populate the accountsStore, since that's what the chart is bound to and where it gets the data it's charting from, so we go through the MixedCollection and create an AccountRecord for each. This is effectively co-opting the AccountRecord, since what we're storing isn't actually an account. However, the type and balance fields are present, so it's a decent choice.

Next, we try to retrieve a reference to the chart. If it's found, we call the remove() method on its container, which destroys it. Then, we create a new PieChart and add it to the container. Finally, a call to the container's doLayout() method gets the chart drawn on the screen.

■**Note** This destroying and creating of the chart also seemed to be a necessary evil to make things work fairly consistently. While the charting support in Ext JS is very nice, powerful, and simple, my hope is that future versions solidify it a bit. In the meantime, I suggest you exercise a certain amount of caution in using it because you'll likely face little nagging issues like I experienced until a future release.

Reacting to Events

Only a few message subscriptions are left, and all of them are quite simple, beginning with the "InitComplete" message handler:

```
FinanceMaster.msgBus.subscribe("InitComplete", function() {

  Ext.getCmp("PortfolioDistribution").collapse();

});
```

Once again the portlet is immediately collapsed so that everything renders properly. The "PortfolioOpened" message is handled next:

```
FinanceMaster.msgBus.subscribe("PortfolioOpened", function() {

  var p = Ext.getCmp("PortfolioDistribution");
  p.expand();

  var rec = arguments[0];

  FinanceMaster.Portlets.PortfolioDistribution.refreshChart(rec);

});
```

The portlet is first expanded, and then the PortfolioRecord passed in is retrieved. The refreshChart() method is called and the chart is drawn as a result.

The "ActivityAdded" message also needs to be handled because the chart will have to change any time activity is added to any account in the portfolio:

```
FinanceMaster.msgBus.subscribe("ActivityAdded", function() {

  FinanceMaster.Portlets.PortfolioDistribution.refreshChart(
    FinanceMaster.currentPortfolio);

});
```

Once again, refreshChart() is called, but this time the PortfolioRecord wasn't passed in so we need to use currentPortfolio to do the same job.

Finally, the "ActivityDeleted" message also needs to be handled:

```
FinanceMaster.msgBus.subscribe("ActivityDeleted", function() {

  FinanceMaster.Portlets.PortfolioDistribution.refreshChart(
    FinanceMaster.currentPortfolio);

});
```

It's identical to the "ActivityAdded" handler, for obvious reason!

AccountActivityPortlet.js

The next portlet we'll examine is the account activity portlet, and you can see its UML diagram in Figure 9-20.

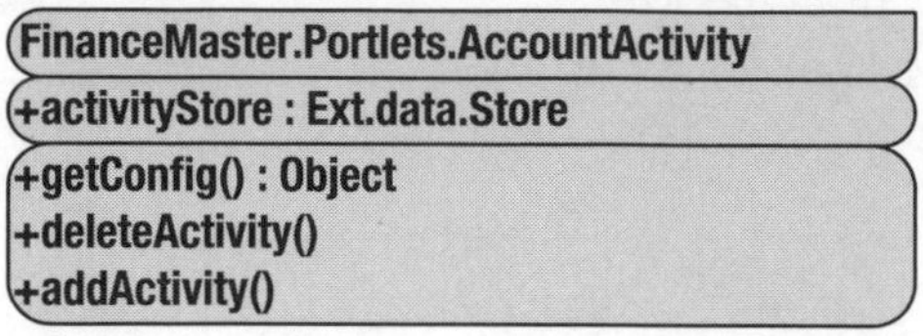

```
FinanceMaster.Portlets.AccountActivity
+activityStore : Ext.data.Store
+getConfig() : Object
+deleteActivity()
+addActivity()
```

Figure 9-20. *The FinanceMaster.Portlets.AccountActivity namespace*

This portlet begins with its own internal data Store, which is nearly identical to those we've seen elsewhere in this project and in other projects:

```
FinanceMaster.Portlets.AccountActivity.activityStore = new Ext.data.Store({
  listeners : {
    "add" : {
      fn : function(inStore, inRecords, inIndex) {
        if (FinanceMaster.processStoreEvents) {
          FinanceMaster.Data.createActivity(inRecords[0]);
        }
      }
    },
    "remove" : {
      fn : function(inStore, inRecord, inIndex) {
        if (FinanceMaster.processStoreEvents) {
          FinanceMaster.Data.deleteActivity(inRecord.get("id"));
        }
      }
    }
  }
});
```

As you can see, it's the typical basic Store with the add and remove events handled to tie it back into the data layer and eventual persistence in the Gears-based database.

Defining the Portlet's UI

The configuration object for this portlet's UI is fairly lengthy, so we'll go over it bit by bit so you can build up an understanding of it. We begin with this fairly sizable chunk:

```
FinanceMaster.Portlets.AccountActivity.getConfig = function() { return {

  title : "Account Activity", id : "AccountActivity", height : 200,
  layout : "fit",
  items : [
    { xtype : "listview", singleSelect : true,
      store : FinanceMaster.Portlets.AccountActivity.activityStore,
      id : "FinanceMaster.Portlets.AccountActivity.grdActivity",
      columns : [
        { header : "Date", sortable : true, dataIndex : "date", width : .1,
          tpl : '{date:date("m/d/Y")}'
        },
        { header : "Deposit", sortable : true, dataIndex : "amount",
          width : .1, hidden : true, align : "right",
          tpl : '<tpl if="amount &gt;= 0">{amount}</tpl>'
        },
        { header : "Withdrawal", sortable : true, dataIndex : "amount",
          width : .1, hidden : true, align : "right",
          tpl : '<tpl if="amount &lt; 0">{amount}</tpl>'
        },
        { header : "New Balance", sortable : true, dataIndex : "new_balance",
          width : .1, hidden : true,
          tpl : '<tpl if="new_balance &gt; 0">{new_balance}</tpl>'
        },
        { header : "Description", sortable : true, dataIndex : "description" }
      ],
      listeners: {
        click : function(inListView, inSelections) {
          Ext.getCmp(
            "FinanceMaster.Portlets.AccountActivity.btnDelete").enable();
          return true;
        }
      }
    }
  ],
```

This is the Grid for displaying the list of ActivityRecords for the account. Oh, but wait, it's not exactly a Grid now, is it? Here we're using a new Ext JS component called a ListView. A ListView is a more lightweight and efficient version of the Grid. It doesn't have all the capabilities that the Grid does, but it's faster and more memory-efficient and is a great choice when you don't need all the capabilities a Grid provides but you still have data to display in a table-like format. The ListView also does *not* provide horizontal scrolling as the Grid does. Instead, the widths of the columns are initially proportioned by percentage based on the container width and the number of columns.

As you examine the configuration you'll see it looks an awful lot like a Grid that we know and love. In the case of the ListView, however, the columns have width attributes that are fractions of 1. So .1 as you see on the first three columns means the initial width of the column will be one tenth, or 10 percent, of the total width of the ListView.

Here we also have some formatting to do on each of the columns. To do so we supply the tpl attribute, an XTemplate template format specification.

For the first column we use the date operator to format as m/d/Y the date field of the ActivityRecord being rendered.

For the other three columns, we need to do some conditional logic to determine whether or not a value is rendered in the field. This is because the ListView must be able to show activity for all types of accounts. But you'll recall, for checking and savings accounts the amount can be positive or negative, and based on that, the value should show up correctly in either the Deposit or Withdrawal column, but not both.

For other types of accounts, it's the new_balance field we're interested in. This value needs to go in the New Balance column, but then the Deposit and Withdrawal columns should be blank. So, we use the <tpl if> tag (which is one of the tags the XTemplate facility provides) to make the appropriate determination.

For the deposit field, we're checking to see if the amount field in the ActivityRecord is greater than or equal to 0, in which case the value goes there. The Withdrawal field checks to see if amount is less than 0, and if so it goes there instead. (Note that the conditions on those two fields exclude the possibility of the amount value showing up in both. Also note that if there is no value in the amount field, then neither column will be populated.)

Likewise, if the new_balance field has a value greater than 0, then the value is inserted into that column.

Using this tpl attribute and the XTemplate formatting functions means we don't have to write complex logic to do any of this work ourselves. We don't have to conditionally populate the ActivityRecords, for example; we instead let the ListView make the determinations for us and populate the data as needed.

The next bit of configuration defines the Window that will be used to add new activity. You can see this Window in all its majesty in Figure 9-21.

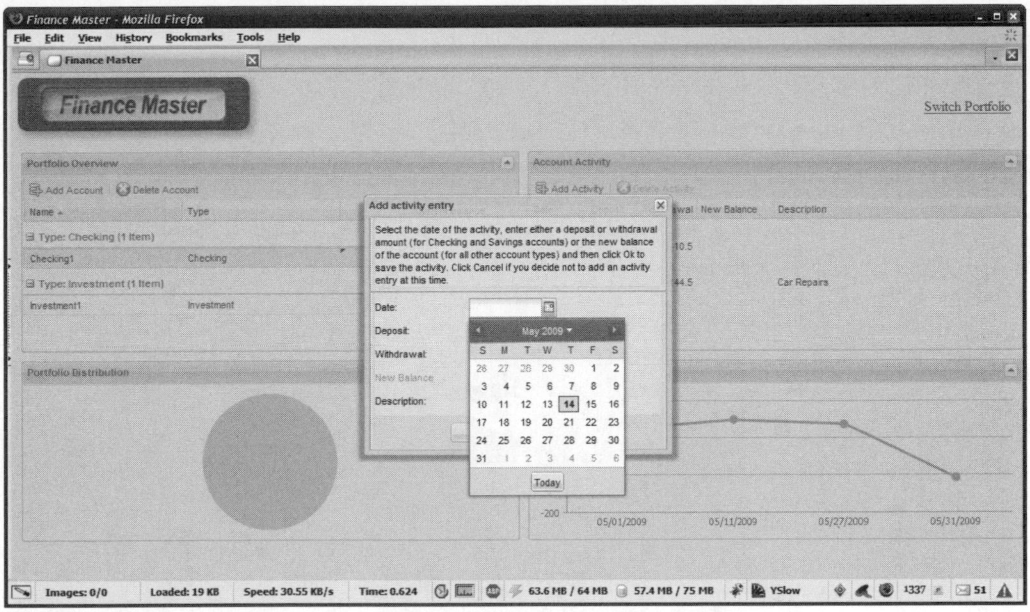

Figure 9-21. *Selecting a date for a new account activity record*

As you can see, there is a DateField involved here, along with some other stuff. That stuff is apparent in the configuration for the Window, which is inside the handler callback for the Add Activity Button:

```
tbar : [
  { text : "Add Activity", icon : "img/Add.gif", disabled : true,
    cls : "x-btn-text-icon",
    id : "FinanceMaster.Portlets.AccountActivity.btnAdd",
    handler : function() {
      new Ext.Window({
        closable : true, modal : true, width : 350, height : 290,
        minimizable : false, resizable : false, draggable : false,
        id : "FinanceMaster.Portlets.AccountActivity.winAddActivity",
        shadowOffset : 8, title : "Add activity entry",
        items : [
          { frame : true,
            html : "Select the date of the activity, enter either a " +
              "deposit or withdrawal amount (for Checking and Savings " +
              "accounts) or the new balance of the account (for all other " +
              "account types) and then click Ok to save the activity.  " +
              "Click Cancel if you decide not to add an activity entry at " +
              "this time."
          },
```

This first bit is where we find the `Window`'s configuration beginning. All of the attributes are the usual suspects, and the first item in the `items` array is simply some instructional text. What follows that is the definition of the `FormPanel` where users make their entries:

```
{ xtype : "form", frame : true, monitorValid : true,
  id : "FinanceMaster.Portlets.AccountActivity.frmAddActivity",
  items : [
    { xtype : "datefield", fieldLabel : "Date", name : "date",
      allowBlank : false,
      id : "FinanceMaster.Portlets.AccountActivity.addDate" },
    { xtype : "textfield", fieldLabel : "Deposit", name : "deposit",
      id : "FinanceMaster.Portlets.AccountActivity.addDeposit" },
    { xtype : "textfield", fieldLabel : "Withdrawal",
      name : "withdrawal",
      id : "FinanceMaster.Portlets.AccountActivity.addWithdrawal" },
    { xtype : "textfield", fieldLabel : "New Balance",
      name : "new_balance",
      id : "FinanceMaster.Portlets.AccountActivity.addNewBalance" },
    { xtype : "textfield", fieldLabel : "Description",
      name : "description" }
  ],
```

So, it's probably about what you'd expect, or so I'd hope at this point in the book! We have some `TextFields` for entering a deposit and withdrawal amount, one for entering a new balance, and one for entering a description of the activity. There is, of course, that `DateField` at the top for selecting the date the activity occurred.

One thing that should jump out at you here is that having the deposit, withdrawal, and new balance fields all available is not the best UI design because which of those fields the user enters date in is dependent on the type of the account. Rest assured, the correct field(s) will be enabled and disabled as required.

Also note that only the `DateField` has `allowBlank` set to `false`, so only that field *appears* to be required. In fact, some of the others are as well logically, but we'll have to deal with that when the user tried to save the activity, as we'll see shortly.

To finish up the definition of the Add Activity `Window` we find that there are two `Buttons`:

```
buttons : [
  { text : "Ok", formBind : true, icon : "img/Ok.gif",
    cls : "x-btn-text-icon",
    handler : function() {
      FinanceMaster.Portlets.AccountActivity.addActivity();
    }
  },
  { text : "Cancel", icon : "img/Cancel.gif",
    cls : "x-btn-text-icon",
    handler : function() {
      Ext.getCmp(
        "FinanceMaster.Portlets.AccountActivity.winAddActivity"
```

```
                    ).close();
                }
            }
        ]
    }
]
}).show("divSource");
```

The methods they call on will be explored shortly. However, there's still some work that needs to happen immediately after the Window is constructed—enabling and disabling form fields as required:

```
var accountType = FinanceMaster.currentAccount.get("type");
if (accountType == "Checking" || accountType == "Savings") {
  Ext.getCmp(
      "FinanceMaster.Portlets.AccountActivity.addDeposit").enable();
  Ext.getCmp(
      "FinanceMaster.Portlets.AccountActivity.addWithdrawal").enable();
  Ext.getCmp(
      "FinanceMaster.Portlets.AccountActivity.addNewBalance").disable();
} else {
  Ext.getCmp(
      "FinanceMaster.Portlets.AccountActivity.addDeposit").disable();
  Ext.getCmp(
      "FinanceMaster.Portlets.AccountActivity.addWithdrawal").disable();
  Ext.getCmp(
      "FinanceMaster.Portlets.AccountActivity.addNewBalance").enable();
  }
 }
},
```

The code is quite straightforward. Remember that override we saw in FinanceMaster.js that allows the labels of the form fields to be disabled along with the fields themselves? Notice that there's nothing special we need to do in the code here—the override takes care of it just fine.

With the Add Activity Window code taken care of, the only thing left is a final bit of UI configuration for the portlet's main Panel: the Delete Activity Button.

```
{ text : "Delete Activity", icon : "img/Delete.gif", disabled : true,
  cls : "x-btn-text-icon",
  id : "FinanceMaster.Portlets.AccountActivity.btnDelete",
  handler : function() {
    FinanceMaster.Portlets.AccountActivity.deleteActivity();
  }
 }
]

}; };
```

Keep in mind that all the code we saw for the Add Activity Window was within the handler for the Add Activity Button, but that was all part of the tbar of the portlet's main Panel, as is the Delete Activity Button. A simple callout to the deleteActivity() method is all it takes—and what a coincidence, that's the very next piece of code in this source file!

Deleting an Activity Record

The deleteActivity()method is the next thing we come across as we traverse this source file, and as we saw, it's called when the user clicks the Delete Activity Button:

```
FinanceMaster.Portlets.AccountActivity.deleteActivity = function() {

  Ext.MessageBox.confirm("Confirm Deletion",
    "Are you sure you want to delete the selected detail record?",
    function(inButtonClicked) {
      if (inButtonClicked == "yes") {
        var selectedRecord = Ext.getCmp(
          "FinanceMaster.Portlets.AccountActivity.grdActivity"
        ).getSelectedRecords()
        selectedRecord = selectedRecord[0];
        FinanceMaster.Portlets.AccountActivity.activityStore.remove(
          selectedRecord);
        Ext.getCmp(
          "FinanceMaster.Portlets.AccountActivity.btnDelete").disable();
        FinanceMaster.currentAccount.set("balance",
          FinanceMaster.Data.getAccountBalance(
            FinanceMaster.currentPortfolio.get("name"),
            FinanceMaster.currentAccount.get("name"),
            FinanceMaster.currentAccount.get("type")
          )
        );
        FinanceMaster.msgBus.publish("ActivityDeleted");
      }
    }
  );

};
```

The Ext.MessageBox.confirm()function is used to make sure the user really wants to delete this activity record. The confirmation pop-up is shown in Figure 9-22. If the user confirms the deletion, then the Grid is consulted to get a reference to the selected ActivityRecord. That gives us what we need to call the remove() method on the activityStore. This updates the UI and the database as a result of the remove event firing on the Store.

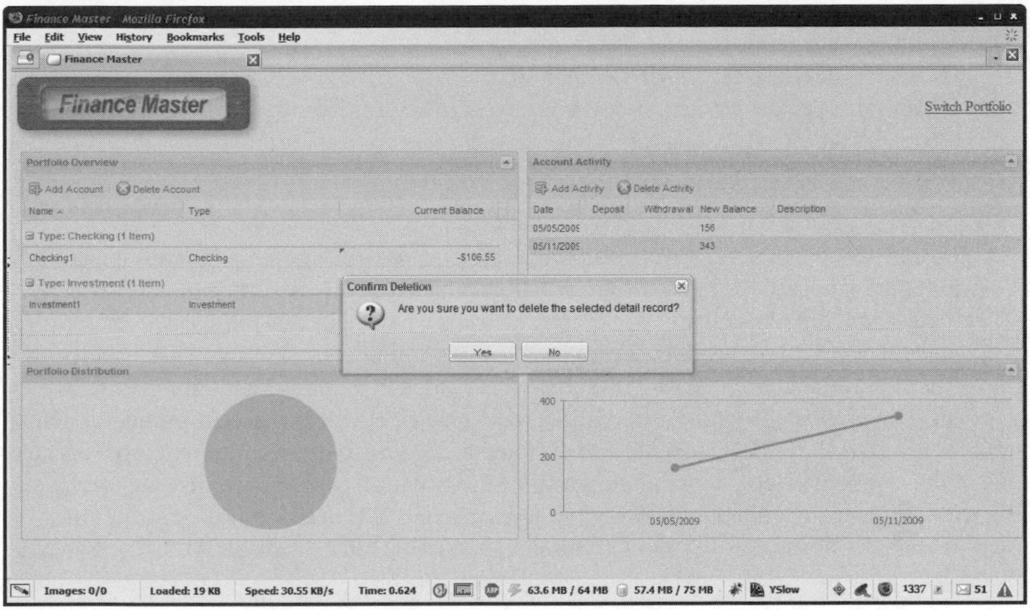

Figure 9-22. *Confirming activity record deletion*

There are just a couple of cleanup tasks to complete, which amounts to disabling the Delete Activity Button and getting the newly calculated balance of the account, which is set on the AccountRecord. Finally, the "ActivityDeleted" message is published so that the rest of the portlets can update themselves as necessary.

Adding an Activity Record

Adding an ActivityRecord is the next logical thing to look at; otherwise we'd have nothing for deleteActivity() to delete! Here's the code that accomplishes that task, or rather, the first part of it:

```
FinanceMaster.Portlets.AccountActivity.addActivity = function() {

  var vals = Ext.getCmp(
    "FinanceMaster.Portlets.AccountActivity.frmAddActivity"
  ).getForm().getValues();
  var addDate =
    Ext.getCmp("FinanceMaster.Portlets.AccountActivity.addDate").getValue();

  if (!Ext.isEmpty(vals.deposit) && !Ext.isEmpty(vals.withdrawal)) {
    Ext.MessageBox.alert("Cannot Add Activity",
      "Please enter an amount for either Deposit or Withdrawal, but not both");
    return;
  }
```

```
if (Ext.isEmpty(vals.deposit) && Ext.isEmpty(vals.withdrawal) &&
  Ext.isEmpty(vals.new_balance)) {
  Ext.MessageBox.alert("Cannot Add Activity",
    "Please enter an amount (Deposit or Withdrawal for Checking and " +
    "Savings account, New Balance for all other account types)");
  return;
}
```

The code begins by getting the values of the form in the Window opened for adding activity. Note that the DateField has to be gotten individually because the date attribute of the vals object is a string, not a JavaScript Date object, which is what we'll need here.

Once the values have been retrieved, some simple validations are done. First, we ensure that either the Deposit or the Withdrawal field has a value in it. If that validation passes, we then check to be sure that a Deposit, Withdrawal, or New Balance has been entered. Remember that the fields have been enabled and disabled according to the account type, so basically one of these tests will always be redundant since the situation could never arise anyway. But there's no harm in double-checking (other than a few CPU cycles, but these aren't the C64[5] days, so we have some to spare). If this later validation fails, the result is what you see in Figure 9-23.

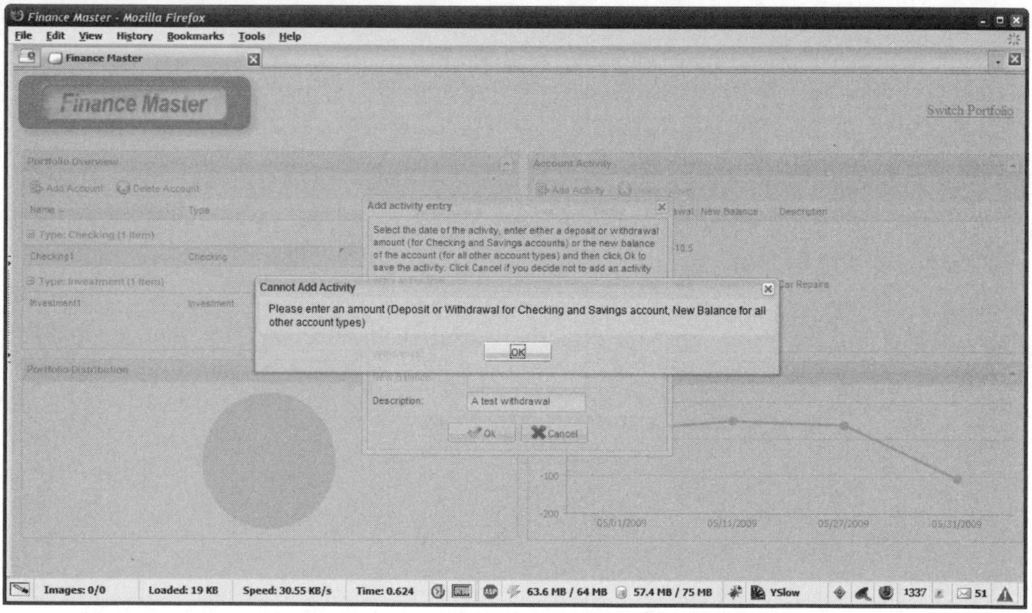

Figure 9-23. *The amount or new balance is required, depending on the account type.*

---

5 The C64, short for the Commodore 64, is the best-selling personal computer of all time. It was an 8-bit machine released in the mid-80s that had a blazing (ahem) 1MHz CPU and a spacious 64Kb of memory. Many of us really learned about computers with a C64, and while I've met lots of great coders who never owned a C64, I'd say that every good C64 programmer is now one of the best programmers around. And in proper C64 tradition, here's a greetings "scroller"… Infiltrator, FBR, RAD, Newage, NWA, LTL, and all the folks who frequented The Lost Caverns and The Cove BBSs.

Assuming the validations pass through, it's time to go about creating the ActivityRecord and associated database content:

```
var recID = new Date().getTime();
var amount = vals.deposit;
if (!amount && !vals.new_balance) {
  amount = vals.withdrawal * -1;
}
rec = new FinanceMaster.Data.ActivityRecord({
  id : recID, date : addDate,
  portfolio : FinanceMaster.currentPortfolio.get("name"),
  account : FinanceMaster.currentAccount.get("name"),
  amount : amount, new_balance : vals.new_balance,
  description : vals.description
}, recID);
FinanceMaster.Portlets.AccountActivity.activityStore.add(rec);
Ext.getCmp("FinanceMaster.Portlets.AccountActivity.winAddActivity").close();
```

Here we're getting the time off a new Date object and using it as the unique key of the record. Next, we get the value of the deposit attribute of vals. Now, if the result of that is the variable amount being null, and if the new_balance attribute of vals is also null, then we know it was a withdrawal amount that was entered. So we multiply amount by –1 to get ourselves a negative number. If it was a deposit, then the amount variable is already a positive value, so we're all set.

Next, a new ActivityRecord is constructed and populated with the entered data, and that record is added to the activityStore. The add event fires as a result and the data is written out to the database via a call to FinanceMaster.Data.addActivity(). Finally, the Window is closed.

A few more tasks are needed at this point:

```
FinanceMaster.currentAccount.set("balance",
  FinanceMaster.Data.getAccountBalance(
    FinanceMaster.currentPortfolio.get("name"),
    FinanceMaster.currentAccount.get("name"),
    FinanceMaster.currentAccount.get("type")
  )
);

FinanceMaster.msgBus.publish("ActivityAdded");

};
```

The balance of the current account is recalculated and the "ActivityAdded" message is published so that all interested subscribers can do their thing (such as the portfolio distribution portlet's chart being redrawn).

Reacting to Events

A couple of events need to be handled here as in the previous portlets, beginning with "InitComplete":

```
FinanceMaster.msgBus.subscribe("InitComplete", function() {

  Ext.getCmp("AccountActivity").collapse();

});
```

As before, we need to collapse the portlet since it is initially expanded, to avoid the rendering problems we previously talked about.

Following that is the "PortfolioOpened" message:

```
FinanceMaster.msgBus.subscribe("PortfolioOpened", function() {

  Ext.getCmp("AccountActivity").collapse();
  Ext.getCmp("FinanceMaster.Portlets.AccountActivity.btnAdd").disable();
  Ext.getCmp("FinanceMaster.Portlets.AccountActivity.btnDelete").disable();

});
```

Since no account will be current when a portfolio is first opened, we need to collapse this portlet in response to this message. We also need to ensure that the Add Activity and Delete Activity Buttons are disabled to begin with, so that is done as well.

After that comes the subscription to the "AccountOpened" message:

```
FinanceMaster.msgBus.subscribe("AccountOpened", function() {

  Ext.getCmp("AccountActivity").expand();
  Ext.getCmp("FinanceMaster.Portlets.AccountActivity.btnAdd").enable();
  Ext.getCmp("FinanceMaster.Portlets.AccountActivity.btnDelete").disable();

  var rec = arguments[0];

  var activity = FinanceMaster.Data.retrieveActivity(
    rec.get("portfolio"), rec.get("name"));

  FinanceMaster.processStoreEvents = false;
  FinanceMaster.Portlets.AccountActivity.activityStore.removeAll();
  for (var i = 0; i < activity.length; i++) {
    FinanceMaster.Portlets.AccountActivity.activityStore.add(activity[i]);
  }
  FinanceMaster.processStoreEvents = true;

});
```

First, the portlet is expanded and the Add Activity and Delete Activity Buttons are enabled. Next, we get the AccountRecord that was passed along as part of the message publication and retrieve the activity for it. We take the array returned by the call to FinanceMaster.Data. retrieveActivity() and add each ActivityRecord in it to the activityStore; we make sure we turn off Store event handling during the load.

To round out the message handling is the code that executes in response to the "AccountDelete" message being published:

```
FinanceMaster.msgBus.subscribe("AccountDeleted", function() {

  Ext.getCmp("AccountActivity").collapse();
  Ext.getCmp("FinanceMaster.Portlets.AccountActivity.btnAdd").disable();
  Ext.getCmp("FinanceMaster.Portlets.AccountActivity.btnDelete").disable();

});
```

All this handler has to do is collapse the portlet and disable the two buttons and its job is done.

AccountHistoryPortlet.js

The final portlet to examine is the account history portlet, and by and large, it's just like the portfolio distribution portlet. Figure 9-24 is the ubiquitous UML class diagram for the namespace associate with this portlet.

```
FinanceMaster.Portlets.AccountHistory
+accountHistoryStore : Ext.data.Store
+getConfig() : Object
+refreshChart()
```

Figure 9-24. *The FinanceMaster.Portlets.AccountHistory namespace*

Just like the portfolio distribution portlet, we'll be drawing a chart here, and the chart needs to be backed by a data Store:

```
FinanceMaster.Portlets.AccountHistory.accountHistoryStore =
  new Ext.data.Store({});
```

Defining the Portlet's UI

Also like that other portlet is the basic UI configuration, sans the chart:

```
FinanceMaster.Portlets.AccountHistory.getConfig = function() { return {

  title : "Account History", id : "AccountHistory", height : 200,
  layout : "fit"

}; };
```

As was the case with the portfolio distribution portlet, the UI configuration is extremely simple and Spartan—the good stuff is in the refreshChart() method.

Refreshing the Chart

We again have a refreshChart() method that takes care of getting the chart onto the screen. We'll break this up a bit since it's fairly lengthy:

```
FinanceMaster.Portlets.AccountHistory.refreshChart = function(inRec) {

  FinanceMaster.Portlets.AccountHistory.accountHistoryStore =
    new Ext.data.Store({});

  var activity = FinanceMaster.Data.retrieveActivity(
    inRec.get("portfolio"), inRec.get("name") );
```

We re-create the accountHistoryStore, in the same way and for the same reason as we did for the portfolio distribution portlet. Next, the FinanceMaster.Data.retrieveActivity() method is used to get an array of ActivityRecords for the account.

The goal of this chart is to show every ActivityRecord in chart form, so the next step is to take that array and populate the accountHistoryStore from it:

```
  var acctType = inRec.get("type");
  if (acctType == "Checking" || acctType == "Savings") {
    var balance = 0;
    for (var i = 0; i < activity.length; i++) {
      balance = balance + activity[i].get("amount");
      FinanceMaster.Portlets.AccountHistory.accountHistoryStore.add(
        new FinanceMaster.Data.ActivityRecord({
          pretty_date : activity[i].get("pretty_date"), new_balance : balance
        })
      );
    }
  }
```

Note the branching logic done based on the type of the account. For checking and savings accounts we need to calculate the balance of the account for each ActivityRecord. Remember that the amount field can have a negative or positive number, for withdrawals and deposits correspondingly. Since the chart is going to be a line graph—where each point on the line is the balance of the account after applying each ActivityRecord's amount in chronological order—this works out very well.

Notice that the pretty_date is coming into play here. This is again strictly for the purposes of the chart so that we're showing a formatted date rather than the default JavaScript toString() version of a Date object (which is very long and would make the chart look horribly cluttered).

For other types of accounts, the logic is a little different:

```
  } else {
    for (var j = 0; j < activity.length; j++) {
      FinanceMaster.Portlets.AccountHistory.accountHistoryStore.add(
        new FinanceMaster.Data.ActivityRecord({
          pretty_date : activity[j].get("pretty_date"),
          new_balance : activity[j].get("new_balance")
        })
      );
    }
  }
}
```

Here we are simply copying the new_balance field to the ActivityRecord that is added to the accountHistoryStore, since that field actually *is* the balance of the account after each activity record is applied.

The next step is to re-create the chart:

```
var p = Ext.getCmp("AccountHistory");
var c = Ext.getCmp("ahChart");
if (c) {
  p.remove(c, true);
}
p.add(new Ext.chart.LineChart(
  { xField : "pretty_date", yField : "new_balance", id : "ahChart",
    store : FinanceMaster.Portlets.AccountHistory.accountHistoryStore }
));
p.doLayout();
```

```
};
```

Once again, as with the portfolio distribution portlet, we remove the existing chart if it is present and then add a whole new chart, this time a LineChart. On the x-axis is the pretty_date field and on the y-axis is the new_balance field, so the line goes in chronological order left to right (because that's the order the SQL specifies the results should be sorted in).

Reacting to Events

After that are a couple of message subscriptions:

```
FinanceMaster.msgBus.subscribe("InitComplete", function() {

  Ext.getCmp("AccountHistory").collapse();

});
```

Again, the portlet needs to be collapsed once the application initializes. Also, when a portfolio is first opened we need to collapse the portlet as well since the account is initially selected. So we handle the "PortfolioOpened" message in the same way:

```
FinanceMaster.msgBus.subscribe("PortfolioOpened", function() {

  Ext.getCmp("AccountHistory").collapse();

});
```

When an account is selected, it's time to call on the refreshChart() method, as you can see here:

```
FinanceMaster.msgBus.subscribe("AccountOpened", function() {

  var p = Ext.getCmp("AccountHistory");
  p.expand();

  var rec = arguments[0];

  FinanceMaster.Portlets.AccountHistory.refreshChart(rec);

});
```

It's also necessary to expand the portlet in response to that message.

Another situation that impacts this portlet is when an account is deleted because it will necessarily be the account that is currently displayed in this portlet (because it's clicking an account in the portfolio overview portlet, and thereby making it current, that generates the "AccountOpened" message):

```
FinanceMaster.msgBus.subscribe("AccountDeleted", function() {

  Ext.getCmp("AccountHistory").collapse();

});
```

All that we need to do in this case is collapse the portlet, so it's a quick and easy message handler.

Similarly, adding activity to an account needs to result in the chart being updated, and the "ActivityAdded" message informs us of that situation:

```
FinanceMaster.msgBus.subscribe("ActivityAdded", function() {

  FinanceMaster.Portlets.AccountHistory.refreshChart(
    FinanceMaster.currentAccount);

});
```

A simple call to refreshChart() is all it takes.

Similarly, when an `ActivityRecord` is deleted from the account, the "ActivityDeleted" message is published and handled here:

```
FinanceMaster.msgBus.subscribe("ActivityDeleted", function() {

  FinanceMaster.Portlets.AccountHistory.refreshChart(
    FinanceMaster.currentAccount);

});
```

The chart needs to reflect this change as well, so `refreshChart()` is once again called and that's a wrap!

Suggested Exercises

So, if you want to compete with Quicken, there's certainly plenty of opportunity for extending Finance Master, all of which could be excellent learning opportunities. Here are just a few suggestions:

Add a new portlet and allow the ability to remove and add it, along with the portfolio distribution and account history portlets. You'll have to come up with a UI mechanism to list available portlets and allow the user to add them, as well as add some sort of close `Button` to those portlets (the portfolio overview and account activity portlets probably need to always be present).

Add the ability to delete portfolios. Admittedly, I just got lazy and didn't add that feature! Also, how about being able to change passwords on a portfolio?

Provide the capability to edit existing accounts and activity records. This is trickier than you think because the account name is the key of the accounts table, so you'll first have to modify the database structure to use a unique key for each, as in the activity table. But I know you're up to it!

Summary

And with this chapter, your journey through the world of Ext JS, courtesy of this book, is complete! I sure hope you've enjoyed the ride and learned a bunch in the process. I'd like to thank you for buying this book and more important, spending your time on it, and I hope you find it to have been a worthwhile experience.

I'll leave you with this thought: if you've enjoyed my book half as much as I enjoyed writing it, then you enjoyed reading it twice as much as I enjoyed writing it.

Hmm, wait, maybe that's not quite right. Eh, I'll go work on the Venn diagram to get this right—you go have a bunch of fun working with Ext JS!

Index

You Need the Companion eBook

Your purchase of this book entitles you to buy the companion PDF-version eBook for only $10. Take the weightless companion with you anywhere.

We believe this Apress title will prove so indispensable that you'll want to carry it with you everywhere, which is why we are offering the companion eBook (in PDF format) for $10 to customers who purchase this book now. Convenient and fully searchable, the PDF version of any content-rich, page-heavy Apress book makes a valuable addition to your programming library. You can easily find and copy code—or perform examples by quickly toggling between instructions and the application. Even simultaneously tackling a donut, diet soda, and complex code becomes simplified with hands-free eBooks!

Once you purchase your book, getting the $10 companion eBook is simple:

❶ Visit **www.apress.com/promo/tendollars/**.

❷ Complete a basic registration form to receive a randomly generated question about this title.

❸ Answer the question correctly in 60 seconds, and you will receive a promotional code to redeem for the $10.00 eBook.

THE EXPERT'S VOICE™

2855 TELEGRAPH AVENUE | SUITE 600 | BERKELEY, CA 94705

Offer valid through 01/2010.